AZURE THE ONE

PART 1
CLOUD FUNDAMENTALS & DATA MIGRATIONS

INTERVIEW Q&A MASTERPIECE FOR DATA PEOPLE

TEAM
THE ONE

INDIA • SINGAPORE • MALAYSIA

ISBN 979-8-89588-667-0

Disclaimer

The views, thoughts, and opinions expressed in this book are solely my own and do not reflect the views of any current or former employers, clients, or customers. No proprietary or confidential information from any organization has been used in this book. All information presented is derived from publicly available resources, including product documentation, data community members, and personal experimentation on cloud platforms using our personal devices and accounts. Any references to software, platforms, or tools are purely based on publicly available information and personal experience. Any references to products, services, or technologies are for informational purposes only and do not constitute an endorsement or recommendation. We have taken care to ensure the accuracy and reliability of the information presented. However, readers should verify any information before making decisions based on its content.

Dedicated

To My Source of Strength

Lakshmi Narayana Murthy

Parvathi Parameshwara

Jagadambika Devi

Special Thanks

Research and Review Crew

Vaishanavi Srinivasan

Chris Lott

Ayaka Shibata

Indrakshi Iyer

Crestina Smith

Isla Jack Wilson

Serge Marwick

Raghav Ram Mazumdar

Sudha Arumilli

Vindhya Alapati

Mohana Krishnan

Shrutakirti Devi

Devendranath Sharma

Shiva Priya Indukuri

Srinivas Arvind Gupta

Chaitra Patil

Achyuta Narayan Dwivedi

Pratishtha Jain

Contents

Introduction

We are excited to present our new book on the Azure Data Ecosystem. Mastering the Azure Data Ecosystem can be challenging. Even for experienced professionals, recalling all the elaborate details for customer meetings or interviews can be overwhelming.

Since early 2019, I've been gathering Azure interview questions from members of the Azure Data community, friends, colleagues and blog followers. I assist them in understanding the Azure concepts and questions correctly and providing detailed answers and solutions. Over time, I compiled these questions and answers into a self-reference material.

Content & Structure:

Drawing on the author's experience and insights from a dedicated community, the book offers a comprehensive collection of Azure Data Ecosystem interview questions. These questions, meticulously categorized, cover all essential topics, from basic concepts to advanced internals. Whether you're a recent graduate or a seasoned professional, you'll find valuable content to prepare for interviews or refresh your knowledge on Azure Data Ecosystem topics.

Target Audience & Applicability:

The book is designed for professionals across various roles, including Azure SQL DBAs, Azure Migration Engineers, Data Consultants, Data Engineers, Database Developers, Data Analysts, and Cloud Admins, working in both service-oriented and product-oriented organizations, from startups to industry giants.

Book Series:

Given the breadth and depth of the Azure Data Ecosystem, this book is designed as a three-part series:

- **Part 1:** Focuses on Azure Cloud Fundamentals, Data Fundamentals, and Azure Migrations.
- **Part 2:** Specially designed for Azure SQL Family.
- **Part 3:** Concentrates exclusively on Azure Data Analytics.

Question & Answer Format:

The Q&A format ensures clarity and conciseness. Questions and answers are carefully crafted, and nearly 90% of the questions provides answers in two flavours:

- **Straight to the point:** Short and concise answers.
- **Explore section:** In-depth explanations for deeper understanding.

Feedback:

As a reader of this book, you are our most valued critic and commentator. We appreciate your opinion and want to know what's working well, and where we can improve. Feel free to write directly to us (teamtheoneind@gmail.com) with your valuable feedback.

About the Author

Hailing from a remote village in India, the author holds a postgraduate degree in Computer Science. With extensive expertise in architecting, advocating, modeling, designing, developing, tuning, administering, migrating, supporting, and implementing secure and optimized modern enterprise data ecosystem solutions for world-class clients, the author is a recognized data expert.

In "**Azure The One**" series, the author leverages vast industry experience and practical insights to deliver a comprehensive Q&A guide that empowers Azure data professionals to excel in their careers and navigate the rapidly evolving world of cloud computing.

This work has been made possible by ***"Team The One"***. The crew is a collective of dedicated data professionals who participated in research, review, brainstorming sessions, and shared their experiences.

We extend our special gratitude to "Team The One" for their collaboration and commitment. Moving forward, all future technology books from our collective will be authored under the name "Team The One".

Connect with "**Team The One**" through personal email or social media.

- **Email** : teamtheoneind@gmail.com
- **LinkedIn** : linkedin.com/in/teamtheoneind
- **Facebook** : facebook.com/teamtheoneind
- **X** : x.com/teamtheoneind
- **Instagram** : instagram.com/teamtheoneind/

Acknowledgments

First and foremost, I would like to thank my parents for giving me the best foundation and support throughout my life. Your guidance, love, and the freedom to chase dreams have been invaluable.

Special thanks to "**The One Couple**", **Satheesh Duggina** and **Sudha Duggina** for their constant support and boundless encouragement. Your faith in me kept me going, and this series would not have been possible without you.

I extend my heartfelt gratitude to my close mates **Veeraju Chowdary Rayudu**, **Bhanu Prasad Kota**, **Sai Sri Harsha Yada**, **Ramarao Gampala**, **Venkatarao Tallapaneni, Kanaka Balaji Akula, Mandarapu Bala Balaji Shiva Kumar, Vaishanavi Srinivasan, Sreeja Madala,** and **Harika Parvathaneni** for their eternal support during the tough times. Your friendship and encouragement have meant the world to me.

I am grateful to my colleagues, blog followers, and the data community members for sharing their work experiences, interview experiences, and insights, which enriched the content of this book.

I would also like to express my gratitude to all those who provided support, discussed ideas, read drafts, offered comments, and gave feedback. Your contributions have been invaluable.

A big thank you to the **Notion Press team** for supporting us in bringing our "**THE ONE**" series to the world market. Your assistance and professionalism have been greatly appreciated.

I cannot forget to mention my heartfelt gratitude to **Swati**. You are "**The One**" who motivates me, encourages me, and reminds me to keep moving forward, no matter the challenges. Your support, love and unwavering belief in me have made this journey possible. This series is as much a reflection of your encouragement as it is of my efforts. Thank you for being **"The One"** in my life.

CHAPTER 01

Fundamentals of Azure Cloud Computing

1. What is Cloud-Computing?

Ans:

Cloud computing is the delivery of different services through the Internet, including servers, storage, databases, networking, and software applications. Instead of relying on local resources, businesses and individuals can access and utilize these services remotely via the internet.

Explore:

Consider the below example:

- Imagine you have a business that needs a lot of storage space and processing power.
- You don't have to buy and maintain your own hardware, networking components and servers anymore. Instead, you can use cloud computing services. **Ex:** You can store your company's data (files and documents) on a cloud storage service like Google Drive, Microsoft OneDrive, or Dropbox.
- These services provide a secure and easy way to store and access your data from anywhere with an internet connection.

2. What are the primary benefits of cloud computing?

Ans:

Cloud computing offers the below primary benefits:

- Provides automatic updates, security patches, and maintenance.
- Offers auto scaling (up/down) based on your business needs.
- You don't need to purchase the hardware and infrastructure, resulting in minimal upfront charges.
- Allows easy access through the internet worldwide.
- Contributes to faster development and innovation.
- Offers advanced security and built-in high availability (HA) and disaster recovery (DR) features.

Explore:

- **Updates and Maintenance:** Cloud providers automatically handle routine maintenance, backups, updates, and patches for the underlying infrastructure and software. It reduces our IT people time and ensures that we have access to the latest features and security enhancements without additional effort.

- **Ex:** Imagine we are running a customer relationship management (CRM) system. By utilizing a cloud-based CRM solution like Salesforce or HubSpot, the provider takes care of software updates, security patches, and infrastructure maintenance. We can focus on utilizing the latest features and functionalities without the need to allocate resources for manual updates and maintenance tasks.

- **Scalability:** Cloud computing is highly scalable, so businesses can easily add or remove resources as needed.
  - **Ex:** Let's say we run an e-commerce website, and during peak shopping seasons, our website experiences a surge in traffic. With cloud computing, we can easily scale up our computing and storage resources such as CPU, RAM, Storage, Network Bandwidth etc. Once the peak season is over, we can scale down the resources to avoid unnecessary costs.
- **Flexibility:** We can choose the services that we need and how we want to use them.
  - **Ex:** A business that needs to develop a new application can use cloud computing to quickly and easily spin up a virtual machine and a Database. This allows us to focus on developing the application, rather than worrying about managing the underlying infrastructure.
- **Cost-Efficiency:** It can help us save money on IT infrastructure costs, such as the cost of servers, storage, and networking.
  - **Ex:** Imagine we're a startup developing a new software application. Instead of investing in expensive servers and infrastructure upfront, we can use cloud computing services. We only pay for the computing resources we use. This allows us to start small and quick, validate our product, and gradually increase our usage as our business grows.
- **Mobility:** A business that has employees who work remotely can use cloud computing to give them access to their data and applications from anywhere with an internet connection.
  - **Ex:** Team members can access and edit the files stored in cloud from anywhere, using different devices like laptops, tablets, or smartphones, making it easy to work together regardless of physical location.
- **Innovation:** A cloud provider can offer access to the latest technologies.
  - **Ex:** We can leverage the latest artificial intelligence and machine learning technologies and develop new products and services without worrying about underlaying hardware deployments and maintenance.

- **Time to market:** Cloud computing can help us get our products and services to market faster. This is because businesses don't need to invest in and maintain their own IT infrastructure.
  - **Ex:** If we want to deploy a new web application, we can quickly provision the necessary infrastructure, such as servers and databases, with a few clicks or through automated scripts within minutes. It accelerates our time-to-market and enabling us to gather user feedback and iterate faster
- **Security:** A cloud provider can offer a variety of advanced security features to help protect our data.
  - **Ex:** Consider handling sensitive data. By leveraging a cloud service, we can benefit from advanced security features such as automatic Data Encryption at rest and transit, applying user and object level access control, multi-factor authentication, automatic threat detection and monitoring etc.
- **Reliability and Availability:** Cloud providers offer built-in High Availability, Disaster Recovery and Load Balancing features. This ensures that our applications and data are accessible and protected from hardware failures or natural disasters.
  - **Ex:** When we choose storing our data on Microsoft Azure, our data is stored across multiple data centers in different geographic locations. In the event of a hardware failure or natural disaster in one location, the cloud provider automatically redirects/failover traffic to the backup data center, ensuring uninterrupted access to our services.

3. What does it mean by CSP?

Ans:

CSP stands for Cloud Service Provider. A cloud service provider (CSP) is a company that provides cloud computing services to businesses and individuals. **Ex:** AWS, Azure etc.

Explore:

- **The Big Three CSP:** These are the leaders in the cloud computing market, holding the majority of the market share. They are:
  - **Amazon Web Services (AWS):** Offers wide range of services, and high-performance compute infrastructure.
  - **Microsoft Azure:** A strong choice for businesses already invested in the Microsoft ecosystem.
  - **Google Cloud Platform (GCP):** A leader in AI and ML technologies.
- **Other Major Players:** Alibaba Cloud, IBM Cloud, Oracle Cloud Infrastructure (OCI), etc.
- **Additional Players:** Salesforce Cloud, DigitalOcean, Tencent Cloud, Linode, Dell Technologies Cloud etc.

4. What are the different types of cloud deployment models?

Ans:

Cloud computing offers several deployment models that allow us to choose the most suitable approach based on our requirements. The common cloud deployment models are:

- **Public Cloud:** Infrastructure is handled by a CSP and it is shared between multiple organizations.
- **Private Cloud:** Dedicated to a single organization.
- **Community Cloud:** Dedicated to a group of organizations with the similar interests.
- **Hybrid Cloud:** Combination of public and private clouds.
- **Multi-Cloud:** Combination of multiple public cloud platforms.
- **Edge Cloud:** allows us to extend the capabilities of the cloud to our on-premise datacenter, enabling us to run cloud services in close proximity to our data origin or source.

Explore:

- **Public Cloud:** In this model, the cloud infrastructure is owned and operated by a third-party/ Cloud Service Provider (CSP). The resources, such as servers and storage, are shared among multiple organizations or individuals.
    - **Pros:** Cost-effectiveness, scalability, ease of use
    - **Cons:** Limited control on infrastructure, security and data, vendor lock-in
    - **Ex:** Azure, AWS, GCP, Oracle Cloud, IBM Cloud, etc.
- **Private Cloud:** A private cloud is dedicated to a single organization and can be located on-premises or hosted by a third-party provider in a dedicated datacenter.
    - **Pros:** High security, full control over the infrastructure, more customization options, compliance with specific regulations.
    - **Cons:** Higher upfront costs, not as scalable as public cloud, complex management and maintenance
    - **Ex:** VMware, HPE GreenLake, IBM Cloud Private, Cisco CloudCenter, Dell EMC Private Cloud, Microsoft Azure Stack, AWS Outposts Family, Oracle cloud at customer.
- **Community Cloud:** A community cloud is shared by a group of organizations with common interests or requirements, such as government agencies or research institutions.
    - **Pros:** Cost sharing among community members, high security, shared expertise, compliance with industry-specific regulations.
    - **Cons:** Scalability is limited when compared to public cloud, create some dependency on cloud provider service, expert skills are required for managing the cloud operations.
    - **Ex:** AWS GovCloud & Azure for US Government specially designed for US government agencies, GE Predix for IoT Apps, Airbus Skywise for aviation industry, Shell Cloud for

Oil and Gas Industry, Indian Government is also using community cloud for government agencies including Indian Railways, smart-city project, Document management system etc.

- **Hybrid Cloud:** A hybrid cloud is a combination of public, private, and community clouds. Hybrid clouds allow businesses to take advantage of the benefits of each cloud deployment model. For example, an organization can use Public Cloud for non-sensitive operations and Private Cloud for hosting sensitive data.
    - **Pros:** Offer best of both the worlds Private and Public Cloud, highly flexible as we can use both Public and Private clouds as per the business need, optimal resource allocation, offers ability to handle variable workloads.
    - **Cons:** More complex management, specialized skills are required, we may face some integration challenges between private and public cloud platforms.
    - **Ex:** Azure Stack, AWS Outposts, Google Anthos, IBM Cloud, Oracle Cloud Infrastructure (OCI) etc.
- **Multi-Cloud:** We deploy our workloads on multiple public clouds from different providers. This gives us more flexibility and choice, as we can choose the cloud provider that best meets our business needs for each application or workload.
    - **Pros:** More choices of specialized services are available from multiple public cloud providers, we can reduce the vendor lock-in, improved fault tolerance (Ex: if one cloud provider experiences downtime, we can seamlessly shift and utilize resources from another cloud provider.) etc.
    - **Cons:** More complex management, more skills are required, cost may increase due to diverse subscriptions with multiple clouds.
    - **Ex:** For a big enterprise, using AWS for operational applications, GCP for data science and machine learning apps, and Azure for data analytics and collaboration services.
- **Edge-Cloud:** Edge cloud computing or fog computing, involves the deployment of cloud resources and services closer to the devices or users generating data. It aims to minimize latency, improve response time, and save bandwidth by processing data closer to its source.
    - **Pros:** Reduced latency, improved response times, more security, reduced bandwidth utilization
    - **Cons:** More maintenance is required; computing power is limited and more expensive than other cloud models.
    - **Ex:** Azure IoT Edge, AWS Greengrass, Google Cloud IoT Edge.

5. Can you please explain how to choose the right deployment model for our business case?

Ans:

When it comes to selecting the appropriate deployment model for your business case, the decision relies on several factors. However, here are some relevant use cases to consider:

Public Cloud:

- **Suits:** Hosting Web Applications and Web Sites, Big Data Workloads, Data Storage and Backup, Startups who can't afford of buying infrastructure, Collaboration tools, DevOps, etc.
- **Use Case:**
    - A software-as-a-service (SaaS) provider leverages a public cloud infrastructure to host their application, allowing them to easily scale their services to meet customer demand and reduce infrastructure costs.
    - An Enterprise is hosting its Bigdata workloads on a Public Cloud platform and utilizing its services, such as data warehouses, data lakes, and analytics tools to efficiently process, store, and analyze their data at scale.

Private Cloud:

- **Suits:** Workloads with high security and compliance requirements, more control required on underlaying infrastructure, High-performance computing requirements etc.
- **Use Case:**
    - A Healthcare or financial institution builds a private cloud to host its core healthcare or financial systems, allowing for strict data security and maintaining regulatory compliance.
    - A hospital implements a private cloud infrastructure to store and manage electronic health records (EHR) securely, ensuring compliance with healthcare regulations and protecting patient privacy.
    - A research institution using a private cloud to run its High-Performance Computing workloads such as climate modelling simulations.

Hybrid Cloud:

- **Suits:** To host the mixed workloads, data backup, disaster recovery, and business continuity scenarios, to handle the temporary spikes in demand etc.
- **Use Case:**
    - An online media streaming service implements a hybrid cloud strategy, utilizing a public cloud for transcoding and content delivery while maintaining customer billing and user authentication in a private cloud for enhanced security.
    - An ecommerce or manufacturing business often use a hybrid cloud approach, with mission-critical workloads running on the private cloud and others running on a public cloud.

Community Cloud:

- **Suits:** Businesses with the similar interests or industry specific collaboration such as Government Agencies, R&D Labs, Universities,
- **Use Case:**
    - Multiple law firms form a community cloud to share legal research databases and case management systems, improving collaboration and reducing costs.
    - Multiple government agencies create a community cloud to host and exchange data related to public safety, emergency response, and disaster management, enabling effective coordination and information sharing.

Multi-Cloud:

- **Suits:** Business cases that need to get the best features and services from different providers, avoiding vender-lock-in, distributing workloads across multiple providers, Disaster Recovery and Risk Mitigation scenarios etc.
- **Use Case:**
    - A multinational corporation deploys its customer relationship management (CRM) system on one cloud provider, while leveraging another provider's machine learning capabilities for data analysis and insights, maximizing the benefits of both platforms.
    - Leading providers of OTT streaming services, professional networking platforms are the best examples of multi-Cloud workloads. They utilize AWS, Azure and GCP to host their workloads. It allows them to get the best features and services from each provider.
    - A financial institution replicates its critical systems and data across multiple cloud providers to ensure business continuity in the event of an outage.

Edge-Cloud:

- **Suits:** IoT applications where we have certain limitations on network bandwidth, IoT application with low-latency and fast response time requirements etc.
- **Sample Use Cases:**
    - A manufacturer implements edge cloud computing to process and analyze sensor data in real-time, enabling quick decision-making for safe navigation and efficient operations.
    - An airline company has implemented an edge computing infrastructure for real-time aircraft health monitoring. Each aircraft is equipped with dedicated edge computing devices or gateways capable of processing and analyzing critical data locally, directly onboard the aircraft itself. This setup ensures that the monitoring system remains operational and unaffected by any limitations or disruptions in internet connectivity or bandwidth.
    - Edge clouds are often used for Industrial automation, real-time video streaming, Self-driving cars etc.

6. What is the difference between Hybrid and Multi Cloud?

Ans:

Although Hybrid-Cloud and Multi-Cloud may appear similar, they are distinct cloud models created to serve different purposes.

- Hybrid cloud is a combination of a public cloud and a private cloud.
- Multi-cloud is a deployment model that uses multiple public clouds from different providers.

7. What is "Grid Computing", and is it considered a cloud deployment model?

Ans:

- **Grid Computing:** It involves pooling together computer resources from multiple locations to reach a common goal. It functions by aggregating processing power, storage capacity, and other resources from numerous computers (often belonging to different administrative domains) into a virtual supercomputer. **Ex:** It is used in fields such as scientific research, simulations, and large-scale data analysis.
- **Grid Computing vs. Cloud Deployment Model:** Grid computing is not considered a cloud deployment model. Instead, it is a distinct method of computing that focuses on distributed, high-performance tasks. While both cloud computing and grid computing involve distributed resources, they serve different purposes and are implemented in different ways.

8. What are the Cloud Computing Service Models?

Ans:

Cloud Service Providers (CSPs) provide a range of services. Based on its characteristics and capabilities these services can be classified into three distinct Cloud Service Models:

- **IaaS (Infrastructure as a Service):**
    - In IaaS, a cloud provider offers virtualized computing resources for rent, including servers, storage, and networking.
    - You can rent a virtual machine, install an operating system of your choice, and can deploy your own applications on it, without having to concern yourselves with the underlying hardware.
    - **Ex:** Azure Virtual Machines (VM), Azure Virtual Networks (VNet), Azure Storage Account etc.

- **PaaS (Platform as a Service):**
    - In PaaS, a cloud provider offers a pre-built platform for developing, testing, and deploying applications, eliminating the need to manage the underlying infrastructure.

  - You can rent a database and start creating tables, views, and stored procedures without the need for installing or maintaining the underlying hardware and software.
  - **Ex:** Azure SQL Database, Azure Cosmos DB, Azure App Service, Azure Functions etc.

- **SaaS (Software as a Service):**
  - SaaS involves a cloud provider offering a ready-to-use software application that is already hosted in the cloud and accessible over the internet.
  - Gmail is hosted and maintained by Google, allowing us to simply log in and use it through a browser or app. We don't need to worry about the underlying software, hardware, or application deployment and maintenance.
  - **Ex:** Power BI, Office 365, Dynamics 365, Microsoft Entra (Earlier Azure Active Directory), GitHub, Azure DevOps etc.

Explore:

For easy understanding, I am comparing it with transportation modes.

- **On-premise datacenter (Owning a Car):** Owning a car means we have complete control and responsibility for its maintenance, owning an on-premise datacenter means we have complete control and responsibility for the infrastructure, including hardware, networking, and software, required to run our applications.
- **IaaS (Renting a Car):** When we rent a car, we don't need to worry about the maintenance or ownership of the vehicle itself. Similarly, with IaaS, we don't need to worry about the physical infrastructure. Instead, we rent virtualized computing resources such as virtual machines, storage, and networks from a cloud provider. We have control over the operating systems, applications, and data we run on that infrastructure.
- **PaaS (Hiring a Taxi):** Hiring a taxi is similar to using PaaS. When we hire a taxi, we don't need to worry about the details of the car or its maintenance. We only need to focus on our specific destination and tasks. Similarly, with PaaS, we don't need to worry about the underlying infrastructure or the operating system. Instead, we focus on developing and deploying our applications or services using the platform provided by the cloud provider. The provider manages the underlying infrastructure, including hardware, networking, and runtime environment.
- **SaaS (Using Public Transportation):** When you use public transportation, such as buses or trains, we simply board the vehicle and reach our destination without any concern for the underlying infrastructure, pre-defined routes or how it operates. Similarly, with SaaS, we use software applications or services provided by a cloud provider without worrying about the infrastructure, platform, or underlying technology. The provider handles everything, from infrastructure to software, and we only need to access and use the software through a web browser or a client application.

9. If I choose a PaaS solution to host my SQL Database, who will be responsible for patching and updates to the database?

Ans:

In a PaaS (Platform as a Service) model:

- **CSP (Cloud Service Provider):** CSP is responsible for patching and updating the database. This is because the cloud provider owns and manages the underlying infrastructure that hosts the database.
    - **Ex:** If we host our database on Azure using the PaaS model (Azure SQL Database), the updates and patching will be automatically handled by the Azure Cloud Service team internally.
- **Customer (We/Customer):** We are responsible for configuring some of the database settings and managing the data and objects that are stored in the database.
    - **Ex:** If we host our database on Azure using the PaaS model (Azure SQL Database), we will be responsible for creating and managing database tables, views, functions, stored procedures, users, etc.

Explore:

The image provided illustrates the division of responsibilities between the Cloud Service Provider and the Customer in the IaaS, PaaS, and SaaS models, categorized by resources.

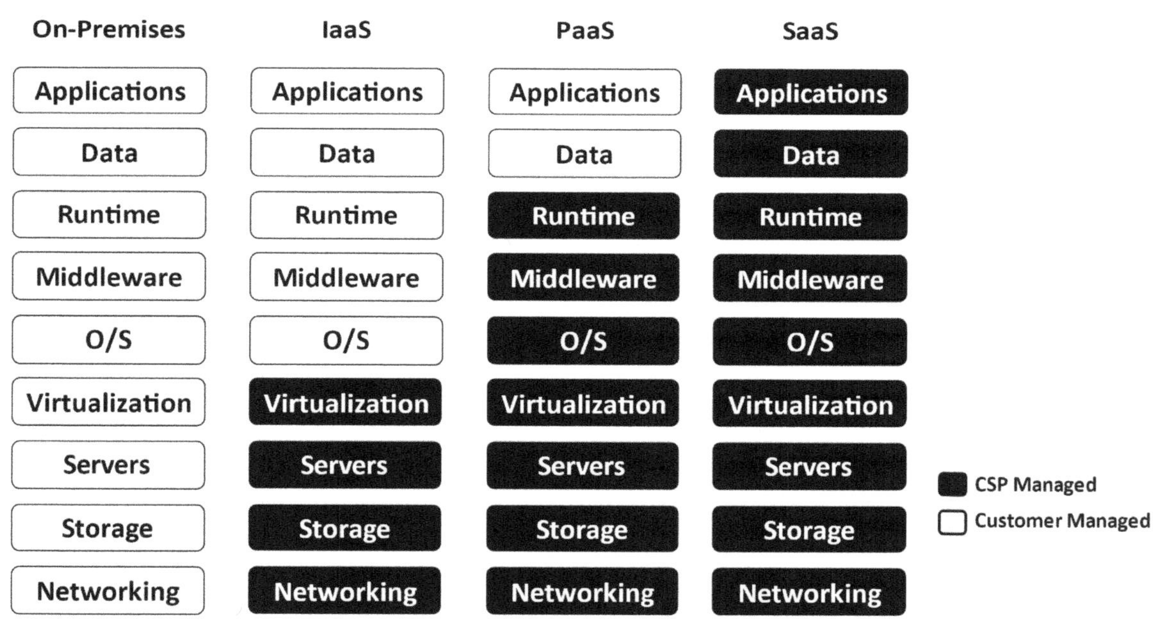

Image 1.1

10. Can I host SQL Server in Azure using IaaS and PaaS model? If yes, can you list out the responsibilities between CSP (Azure) and Customer?

Ans:

SQL Server on VM – IaaS:

- We rent an Azure Virtual Machine (VM) and install SQL Server on it.
- We have more control and responsibility for managing the VM, including tasks like choosing the operating system, configuring SQL Server, and handling backups, updates, and security.

Azure SQL Database / Azure SQL Managed Instance (MI) – PaaS:

- With Azure SQL Database or SQL MI, we don't have to worry about managing a VM. Instead, we simply rent a managed database service from Azure.
- We can create and manage our databases, tables, and queries without dealing with the underlying infrastructure. Azure takes care of tasks like backups, updates, networking, storage and security for us.
    - **Azure SQL Database:** Similar to renting a single database.
    - **Azure SQL Managed Instance:** Similar to renting a full SQL Server instance.

Explore:

Check this for more detailed understanding.

Feature	**IaaS**	**PaaS**
Underlaying Hardware	Azure	Azure
Virtual Machine	Azure	Azure
OS Selection	Customer	Azure
OS Installation	Azure	Azure
OS Patching	Customer	Azure
OS Backup	Customer	Azure
OS HA & DR	Customer	Azure
OS Licensing	Customer	Azure
SQL Server Installation	Customer	Azure
SQL Server Patching	Customer	Azure
SQL Server Backup	Customer	Azure
SQL Server HA & DR	Customer	Azure
SQL Server Licensing	Customer	Azure
Database Schema and Objects	Customer	Customer

Feature	IaaS	PaaS
Application to DB Connectivity	Customer	Customer
Storage	Azure	Azure
Networking	Azure	Azure
Security	Customer & Azure	Azure & Customer
Configurations	Customer & Azure	Azure & Customer

Table 1.1

***Key Notes:**

The mentions of "Azure" or "Customer" in the boxes indicate the primary responsible party or entity for that specific resource. For example:

- Azure provides and handles the OS installation, while allowing us to choose and customize the OS configurations.
- Azure offers automatic patching, but we have the option to disable it and customize the patching schedule according to our needs.
- Similarly, Azure provides numerous features and options for security, networking, storage, backup, HA&DR, and licensing. However, it is our responsibility to select the appropriate solution and configure it properly.

Certain responsibilities are **shared** between Azure and the customer, such as security:

- **Azure** is responsible for the security "**of the cloud**," which includes securing the underlying infrastructure, network, and physical data centers.
- The **customer** is responsible for the security "**in the cloud**," which involves configuring and securing the resources they deploy on the cloud platform, including the operating system, applications, data, and user access controls.
- In IaaS, the customer has more control and responsibility in the shared model, particularly in areas like security and configurations.
- In PaaS, the CSP has more control and responsibility in the shared model, especially regarding security and configurations.

SaaS Model: In a SaaS model, we simply connect to the service through a web browser, and all responsibilities for managing the software are transferred to the cloud service provider (CSP) or Azure.

Power BI Service in Azure – (Consider a SaaS Example):

- With Azure based Power BI service offering, we can access and utilize the Power BI service through a web browser or mobile application.

- Azure takes care of the underlying infrastructure, including servers, storage, and networking as well as the ongoing maintenance and updates to the Power BI service.
- We do not need to install or manage any software on our local machines.
- We can focus on creating, sharing, and consuming reports, dashboards, and data visualizations using the Power BI tools.

11. I'm considering using a public cloud to host my workloads. What factors should I consider when deciding between IaaS, PaaS, and SaaS service models?

Ans:

IaaS, PaaS, and SaaS, offer different levels of control and responsibility. The right model for us will depend on our specific business needs and requirements. Below matrix can help us understanding when to choose the right service model:

Feature	IaaS	PaaS	SaaS
Flexibility	High	Good	Medium
Scalability	High	Good	Medium
Level of Control	High	Medium	Low
Level of Customer Responsibility	High	Medium	Low
Cost	High	Medium	Low
Technical Expertise requirement	High	Good	Low
Compatibility of legacy applications	Medium	Low	Least compatible
Development & Deployment	We are accountable for Platform, App Development and deployment	PaaS provider offers a platform on which we can develop & deploy applications.	Fully managed by SaaS provider.
Security	CSP takes care of infrastructure and physical datacenter security while we need to handle App and Data security.	Shared responsibility	Fully managed by SaaS provider

Feature	IaaS	PaaS	SaaS
Best Suited for	> Developers > IT Administrators > DevOps Teams > Lift-and-Shift Migrations > Businesses with more custom application and infrastructure needs.	> Developers > Startups and small businesses > Businesses with standard application needs	> End Users > Businesses with limited IT resources or looking for ready-made solutions

Table 1.2

***Note:**

- The level of control/responsibility refers to the extent of control that customers can have over their cloud services.
- We usually assess each workload, product, or application individually, considering its priorities, immediate and long-term goals, compatibility, flexibility, and budget requirements. Based on this evaluation, we can then determine the most suitable service model.

12. Are you aware of what 'XaaS' refers to?

Ans:

XaaS stands for "Anything as a Service" or "Everything as a Service" in cloud computing. It refers to the extensive variety of services and applications that are delivered over the internet, rather than being provided locally or on-premises.

Explore:

Essentially, any IT resource or function can be offered as a service using the cloud computing model. Ex:

- **Software as a Service (SaaS):** Google Workspace, Microsoft Office 365, Salesforce, Dropbox.
- **Platform as a Service (PaaS):** Google App Engine, Microsoft Azure App Service, AWS Elastic Beanstalk.
- **Infrastructure as a Service (IaaS):** Google Compute Engine, AWS EC2, Azure VM.
- **Database as a Service (DBaaS):** Amazon RDS, Google Cloud SQL, Azure SQL Database.
- **Storage as a Service (STaaS):** Amazon S3, Google Cloud Storage, Azure Storage.
- **Network as a Service (NaaS):** Aryaka SmartServices, Cisco Plus NaaS, Akamai Aura Managed CDN.
- **Security as a Service (SECaaS):** Proofpoint, Symantec.cloud, Okta, UnderDefense, Expel.
- **Function as a Service (FaaS):** AWS Lambda, Google Cloud Functions, Azure Functions.
- **Communication as a Service (CaaS):** Twilio, Zoom, Microsoft Teams.

- **Desktop as a Service (DaaS):** Amazon WorkSpaces, Citrix DaaS, VMware Horizon Cloud.
- **Disaster Recovery as a Service (DRaaS):** AWS Elastic Disaster Recovery, Azure Site Recovery, Veeam DR etc.

13. Can you explain what does it mean by "Open-source Cloud Computing?

Ans:

- Open-source cloud refers to cloud computing solutions that are built using open-source software and technologies.
- The main advantages of open-source cloud platforms include cost-effectiveness, flexibility, and freedom to choose from a wide variety of frameworks, clouds, and services.
- **Ex:** OpenStack, Cloud Foundry, Open-Nebula, Cloud Stack, Eucalyptus, AppScale, Apache CloudStack etc.

14. What is the full form and the usage of 'Eucalyptus' in Cloud Computing?

Ans:

Eucalyptus stands for 'Elastic Utility Computing Architecture for Linking Your Programs to Useful Systems'. It's an open-source software platform that allows organizations to build their own private or hybrid cloud environments.

15. Could you provide a brief overview of the general architecture of cloud computing?

Ans:

Cloud computing architecture refers to the design and layout of the various components and technologies that make up a cloud computing environment. It's like a blueprint that outlines how different elements, like servers, clusters, nodes, storage, networking, and software, are arranged and interact to create a functional cloud environment. The cloud architecture typically consists of 4 essential components:

- **Front-end:** This is the user or client side of the cloud computing system. **Ex:** User interfaces, client-side applications, and the client device or network that enables users to interact with and access cloud computing services.
- **Back-end:** This refers to the cloud architecture components that make up the cloud itself. **Ex:** Computing resources, storage, security mechanisms, management, and more.
- **Cloud-based Delivery:** This is the model through which cloud services are delivered. **Ex:** SaaS, PaaS, IaaS etc.
- **Network:** It connects all the components together. **Ex:** Internet, Intranet, or Intercloud.

16. What is a Microservice and how do microservices benefit modern cloud development?

Ans:

A microservice is a small, independently deployable service that focuses on a specific business function within a larger application. Each microservice runs in its own process and communicates with other microservices through lightweight mechanisms, typically HTTP APIs.

- **Importance of Microservices:** Microservices are crucial for cloud environments because they offer scalability, flexibility, and resilience. They allow organizations to develop, deploy, and scale individual components independently, which leads to faster development cycles and more efficient resource utilization.
- **Ex:** In an e-commerce application, separate microservices might handle user authentication, product catalog, order processing, and payment processing. Each service can be developed, deployed, and scaled independently based on demand, improving overall system efficiency and reliability. For example, during a sale, the order processing microservice can be scaled up without affecting other services.

17. Can you describe what an API Gateway is?

Ans:

An API Gateway acts as a single-entry point for all API calls that come into an application. It's often referred to as the "front-door" for applications to access data and business logic from backend services.

Explore:

An API Gateway is a server that acts as an intermediary between clients (mobile app, web app) and a collection of backend services. It is a key component in microservices architecture, providing a unified entry point for external requests to interact with various microservices.

Ex: Imagine an online store with a microservices architecture. The store has separate services for user management, product catalog, order processing, and payment processing. Without an API Gateway, a client application would need to make individual requests to each of these services, which can be complex and inefficient.

API Gateway in Action:

- **Client Request:** A client application (like a web or mobile app) sends a request to view a product and its reviews.
- **Unified Entry Point:** The client sends the request to the API Gateway rather than directly to the product or review services.

- **Routing and Aggregation:** The API Gateway routes the request to the product service to fetch product details. It also routes a request to the review service to fetch reviews for the product. The API Gateway aggregates the responses from both services.
- **Response Transformation:** The API Gateway may transform the data format to a unified structure suitable for the client application.
- **Return to Client:** The API Gateway sends the aggregated and transformed response back to the client application.

18. What does it mean by Rate Limiting in Cloud computing?

Ans:

Rate limiting is a technique used to control the volume of requests sent to a service or resource within a specific timeframe. It's like a traffic light for API calls or data access, ensuring things don't get overloaded.

Explore:

Here's how Rate Limiting works:

- **Limits are set:** The cloud service provider or application defines a maximum number of requests allowed per user, application, or IP address within a certain time window (Ex: per second, minute, or hour).
- **Requests are monitored:** The system keeps track of incoming requests and compares them to the defined limits.
    - **Traffic is controlled:** If a request exceeds the limit, the system might:
    - **Throttle:** Slow down the request processing for that user/application.
    - **Queue:** Hold the request in a queue until resources become available.
    - **Reject:** Block the request entirely and return an error message.

19. Can you provide definitions for CapEx, OpEx, TCO, and ROI in the context of cloud computing?

Ans:

- **Capital expenditure (CapEx – Initial Cost):** It refers to the upfront costs of acquiring or building new assets that a company makes to support its operations.
    - **Ex:** Purchasing and deploying on-premises hardware, servers, networking equipment, storage disks, cooling systems etc. From the cloud context, Cloud Migration cost is a CapEx.
- **Operational Expenditure (OpEx – Recurring Costs):** It refers to the ongoing costs of running and maintaining business operations.
    - **Ex:** Software licenses, employee salaries, power bills etc. In Cloud context, subscription fees, services like computing, storage, bandwidth usage bills, cloud consultant salaries etc. are into OpEx.

- **Total cost of ownership (TCO):** The overall cost associated with owning, operating, and maintaining a technology infrastructure or solution over its entire lifecycle.
    - **Ex:** TCO = CapEx + OpEx + Hidden Costs (Like Training)
- **Return on investment (ROI)**: It refers to the profit generated by an investment over a period of time, expressed as a percentage of the initial investment. In cloud computing, ROI indicates the return or benefit gained from utilizing cloud services compared to the costs incurred.
    - **Ex**: ROI = (Net Profit / Cost of investment) x 100%

20. Can you explain the concept of elasticity in cloud computing.

Ans:

- Elasticity in cloud computing is the ability to automatically increase or decrease the resources (Virtual Machines, CPU, Memory, Storage, Network Bandwidth) allocated to an application or service in response to changes in demand.
- Elasticity helps our cloud infrastructure adapt to changing needs, providing a scalable and cost-effective solution.
- **Ex:** Let's say we have an e-commerce website that experiences a sudden spike in traffic during a festival sale.
    - **Automatic Scale-up:** We can automatically scale up our website's resources to handle the increased traffic. This will ensure that our website remains responsive and our customers can continue to shop without any problems.
    - **Automatic Scale-down:** Once the festival sale is over, we can then automatically scale down our website's resources to save money. This will prevent us from overpaying for resources that we're not using.

21. What does it mean by scalability in the context of Cloud Computing?

Ans:

Scalability: The ability of a system to adapt to changing computing requirements by either increasing or decreasing its resources, such as computing power, storage, or network capacity on demand.

- **Ex:** Let's imagine we have an ETL system that processes data feeds in the cloud. As our data grows, we want to make sure our system can handle the extra workload. Scalability allows us to easily add more computing power or expand our data processing capabilities, ensuring that the data is processed quickly and accurately.

22. What is the difference between Scale-up and Scale-Out?

Ans:

These are two types of scaling:

Scale-Up (Vertical Scaling): Adding more resources to the existing VM's or Servers. This is a good option for Memory or Storage-bound workloads.

- **Ex:** Increase Memory, CPU, Network Bandwidth, Storage of an existing servers or VM's.

Scale-Out (Horizontal Scaling): Adding more machines/nodes/Servers/VMs of same type to distribute the workload across multiple instances. This is a good option for CPU-bound workloads.

- **Ex:** Imagine we have a cluster for processing incoming ETL data. To horizontally scale, we can simply add more nodes or virtual machines to the cluster, which helps distribute the workload across a larger number of instances.

23. Can you explain the difference between Manual Scaling and Automatic Scaling?

Ans:

Cloud services offers both manual and auto scaling features.

Manual scaling: Manually adjusting the resources allocated to a system or application to meet the changing demands. It requires human intervention to monitor the workload and make the necessary adjustments to the infrastructure.

- **Ex:** if we notice that the ETL workload is causing resource conflicts or significantly slowing down the data processing, we can manually increase the processing power, such as CPU, memory, or virtual machines, to ensure that it meets the expected performance levels required by the business.

Auto-Scaling: It is a method of scaling a system automatically in response to changes in demand. This can be done by using a cloud-based service that monitors the system's resources and automatically adds or removes resources based on predefined rules or policies (Ex: If CPU > 90% add more CPU).

- **Ex:** With auto-scaling for an ETL data feed, we can set up rules to monitor the incoming data volume or processing time.
    - When workload increases: The system will automatically add more resources.
    - When the workload decreases: The system can scale down the resources to optimize costs.

***Note:** Sometimes, we can mix up the terms scaling and elasticity. Auto-scaling is used to achieve elasticity in cloud computing.

Explore:

Key difference:

- **Scalability** involves adding more resources (upgrading or adding more servers) to handle increased demand. It can be planned and is more static.
- **Elasticity** involves automatic adjustment of resources in real-time to match demand, ensuring optimal performance and cost-efficiency.

24. What are the different types of Automatic-Scaling strategies available?

Ans:

There are several types of auto-scaling strategies available. Here are the main-types:

- **Reactive / Dynamic auto-scaling:** It scales resources in response to real-time changes in demand. This is the most common type of auto-scaling.
- **Scheduled auto-scaling:** It scales resources at predetermined times. This can be useful for applications that experience predictable traffic patterns, such as a website that experiences more traffic during certain hours of the day.
- **Predictive auto-scaling**: It scales resources based on predicted demand. This type of auto-scaling uses machine learning to forecast future demand and scale resources accordingly.
- **Other types:** Container, Application-level, baseline-based, threshold-based auto-scaling etc.

Explore:

Consider the below examples:

- **Dynamic Scaling:** A company can use dynamic scaling to automatically add servers to an ETL environment if an ETL job takes longer than expected. This ensures the job completes on time, even with a sudden increase in data volume.
- **Scheduled Scaling:** A financial institution runs an ETL job to process financial data at the end of every week. However, they anticipate higher data volumes and processing requirements on the last Sunday of each month, which is when they reconcile and close their monthly accounts. To ensure that the job completes on time, the institution uses scheduled scaling to automatically add more servers to the ETL environment on the last Sunday of every month.
- **Predictive Scaling:** Using predictive auto-scaling, an e-commerce platform analyses past shopping trends to proactively increase server capacity before major sales events, ensuring seamless customer experiences during high-demand periods.

25. Can you define the term virtualization in Cloud Computing?

Ans:

Virtualization is the fundamental technology of cloud computing. It refers to the process of creating a virtual version of something, such as a server, a storage device, an operating system or network resources.

- **Ex:** Azure acquires a high-capacity physical server, and whenever a user requests a virtual machine (VM), Azure creates a specific number of isolated VMs on that single physical server based on its capacity.

Explore:

- Virtualization allows multiple VMs to run on a single physical server or across multiple servers, enabling efficient utilization of resources and scalability.
- The virtualization layer acts as an intermediary between the physical server and the virtual machines. It manages underlying hardware, allocation of resources, isolation between VMs, communication between the VMs
- **Ex:**
    - Let's suppose we may request two VMs in Azure.
    - Azure has a physical server with high computing power and ample storage capacity.
    - Using virtualization, Azure can create multiple VMs on this physical server.
    - Each VM is an isolated and independent software container that emulates a complete computing environment, including an operating system, applications, and data.
    - We can then install our preferred OS, deploy our applications, and configure the virtual machines as needed.

26. Can you define the term Hypervisor?

Ans:

A hypervisor is a piece of software, firmware, or hardware that creates and runs virtual machines. It is also known as a virtual machine monitor (VMM). The hypervisor sits between the hardware and the operating system, enabling multiple operating systems to share a single hardware host.

Explore:

There are two main types of hypervisors:

- **Type 1 Hypervisor (Bare-metal):** Installed directly on the server hardware. They provide high efficiency and performance because they interact directly with the physical resources. **Ex:** VMware ESXi, Microsoft Hyper-V, and Xen.

- **Type 2 Hypervisor (Hosted):** Runs on top of an existing operating system. They are generally easier to install and use but offer slightly lower performance compared to Type 1 due to the additional overhead of the host OS. **Ex:** VMware Workstation, Oracle VirtualBox, and Parallels Desktop.

27. What do you know about Serverless computing?

Ans:

- Serverless computing is a cloud computing execution model where the cloud provider dynamically manages the allocation and provisioning of servers.
- In serverless computing, we do not need to worry about provisioning or managing servers, databases, or storage. Instead, we can focus on writing code that executes when a specific event occurs, such as a database table row insert/update/delete, user request, a file upload, scheduled timer etc.
- With serverless, we never pay for unused capacity. This process, known as "scaling to zero," ensures that resources are only active during execution. Billing begins when execution starts and stops when execution ends. Pricing is determined based on the duration of execution and the resources utilized.

Explore:

Example Use Case:

- Let's say we have a website that allows users to upload images. With serverless, we can easily create a function that will process the images as they are uploaded.
    - **Cost Effective:** The function will only be triggered when an image is uploaded, so we will only be charged for the compute time that is used to process the image.
    - **Highly Scalable:** If we suddenly start receiving a lot of image uploads, our serverless function will automatically scale up to handle the increased load. This means that we will never have to worry about our website crashing due to a surge in traffic.

28. Does serverless computing mean that there are no servers at all?

Ans:

No!

- Although the term "serverless" can be confusing, it's important to know that servers are still involved in providing backend services. But, the entire infrastructure creation, configuration and management will be automatically taken care by the service provider.
- The term "serverless" mainly describes the developer's experience with those servers. For developers, the servers are like invisible helpers. They don't see or have to manage them directly. Developers can simply focus on their work without getting caught up in server details.

29. Does it mean that Serverless Computing and PaaS are the same thing? Is that correct?

Ans:

Not Exactly!

- Serverless computing is like a super upgraded version of PaaS.
- Serverless computing makes things even easier for us by handling more of the technical stuff, so we can concentrate on writing specific bits of code that do certain things when something happens or an event occurs.
- With PaaS, we can create and launch applications without having to worry about all the complicated stuff behind the scenes. But with serverless computing, we take it up a notch. Instead of building a whole application, we focus on writing small pieces of code that do specific tasks when they are triggered by events.

Explore:

Imagine we want to build a web application that allows us to upload images, apply filters to them, and store the processed images. Let's see how to do this using IaaS, PaaS, SaaS and Serverless:

- **IaaS:** We need to rent VMs, setup and configure OS, install the necessary software, manage networking, load-balancing and maintain the servers. We would need to do all the development and deployment work on these VMs, including building the web app and the database.
- **PaaS:** Instead of going through all the trouble of setting up and managing VMs, PaaS makes things easier. We would use a platform provided by the cloud provider to build and deploy our web application and databases. The cloud provider manages the underlying infrastructure, including the runtime environment, servers, and networking.
- **SaaS:** There's already a ready-to-use web app for image processing provided by a cloud service provider. We don't need to build anything from scratch. We simply sign up for the SaaS application and start using it through a web browser.
- **Serverless:**
    - We run our OLTP web application and databases using PaaS services like Azure App Service and Azure SQL Database. However, for the image processing part, we use serverless features so that we don't need to allocate a dedicated VM or compute resources and ensure they are up and running all the time for processing images.
    - With serverless computing, we would write functions or code snippets to handle specific tasks or events in our application. For image processing, we would write a function (Ex: Azure Functions or AWS Lambda) to apply filters to the uploaded images. Whenever a new image is uploaded, the function is triggered, processes the image, and stores the result.
    - That means, with serverless computing, when an image is uploaded, it triggers a function, and then only your billing starts.

30. Can you define an "Azure Resource"?

Ans:

An Azure resource is a manageable item or component that is available through Azure Cloud. It is a physical or virtual entity that is used to build and run applications and services in the cloud.

Ex: Virtual machines, Virtual networks, storage accounts, databases, Web apps etc.

31. Can you describe the resource hierarchy in Azure Cloud?

Ans:

In Azure, the resource hierarchy is a structure that helps organize and manage resources within the cloud environment. It consists of the 5 levels:

- **Tenant:** The tenant represents your organization in Microsoft Entra ID (Previously Azure Active Directory/Azure AD).
- **Management Group:** A logical container for subscriptions.
- **Subscription:** A logical container for Azure resource groups.
- **Resource Group:** A logical container for related Azure resources.
- **Resource:** An individual Azure service.

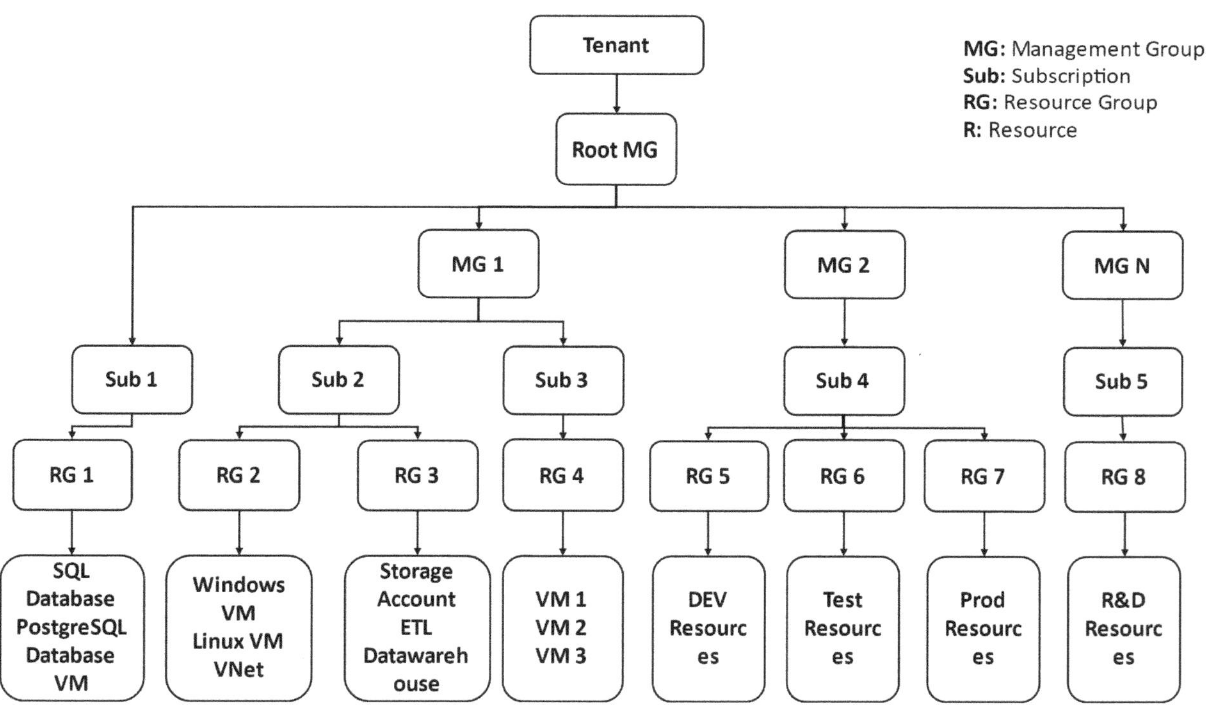

Image 1.2

***Note:** We can either create a Subscription or another Management Group under Root MG.

Explore:

Azure Account: An Azure Account is the first step to start working with Azure. If we want to use Azure services, we will need an Azure account. When we create an Azure Account it automatically creates a tenant for us. Each Azure account can only have one tenant hence not showing in image.

Tenant: It refers to an instance of Microsoft Entra ID (Azure AD) dedicated to a specific organization or a single account.

- The tenant serves as the security and administrative boundary within Azure.
- It provides identity and access management (IAM) services for users, groups, and applications.

Management Groups: Management groups are containers that help organize and manage resources at scale.

- **Root Management Group:** It is the top-level management group in a tenant. It is created automatically when we create our Tenant. Root MG can't be deleted. We can either create subscriptions or other management groups under the root.
- **User Created Management Group:** We can create as many as Management Groups under the Root. It can be deleted.
- **We can use management groups to:**
    - Apply standards, policies and governance controls across multiple subscriptions.
    - Organize your subscriptions by department, team, or project.
    - Delegate access to subscriptions to different groups of users.

Subscriptions: A subscription is a billing and management container within Azure. It represents an agreement with Microsoft to use Azure services and resources. Subscriptions are used to:

- Organize and manage Azure resources.
- Control access to the Azure resources. Subscriptions can be assigned to different users or groups, so that each user or group only has access to the resources that they need.
- Track costs, so that we can see how much we are spending on each subscription.

Resource Groups: It is a fundamental building block and a logical container for organizing and managing resources within a subscription. It is used to:

- Group related resources that belong to the same application, project, or organizational unit that share the same resource lifecycle.
- Deploy Azure resources together, so that we can easily manage, update or delete them as a group.
- It allows us manage resources collectively, including provisioning, monitoring, applying policies and access control.

Resource: A service or an entity managed by Azure. Resources are created and managed within resource groups. They can be deployed, configured, scaled, monitored, and deleted independently. Ex: Azure SQL Database, Azure Storage Account etc.

Example: We could create a tenant for each of our business units. Within each tenant, we could create management groups for different departments or teams. And within each management group, we could create resource groups for specific applications or services.

***Note:** Azure Active Directory (Azure AD) is renamed or rebranded as Microsoft Entra-ID in Jul,2023.

32. Let's suppose, we are a retail organization planning to move to Azure Cloud. Our organization has different businesses, departments, products, projects, teams, and environments. We operate in 30+ countries around the world. Can you help us design the resource hierarchy in Azure?

Ans:

Sure! Here's an example of how you can map your organization's structure to the Azure resource hierarchy.

- **Tenant:** Create your organization's Entra-ID tenant, which represents your company's identity and access management. **Ex:** ABCCorp
- **Management Groups:** Create management groups based on regions or continents where your organization operates. **Ex:** North America, South America, Europe, Asia-Pacific, Africa or create a Global Management Group to apply network and security policies on cloud resources across the organization.
- **Subscriptions:** You could create a subscription for each business unit, product, or project within each region. **Ex:** Create subscriptions for Retail, Ecommerce, and Marketing etc.
    - **Regional Subscriptions:** Create subscriptions within each regional management group to manage resources specific to that region. **Ex:** Create subscriptions for North America Retail, Europe Retail, etc.
    - **Project/Product Subscriptions:** Create subscriptions within each regional subscription to manage resources associated with specific projects or products. **Ex:** create subscriptions for E-commerce Platform, Inventory Management, Marketing Analytics, etc.
- **Resource Groups:** We could create resource groups based on:
    - **Application-Based:** Create resource groups for each application or service. **Ex:** E-commerce App, CRM System, Supply Chain Management, etc.
    - **Environment-Based:** Create resource groups to separate resources based on environments. **Ex:** Development, Testing, Staging, and Production.
- **Resources:** Deploy the specific resources required for each project or environment within the corresponding resource group. **Ex:** Azure SQL Database, Virtual Network, Virtual Machines, Azure Storage Account etc.

Explore:

A sample resource hierarchy may look like below:

- **Tenant** – ABCCorp
    - **MG** - USA_North
        - **Sub** - USA_North_Retail
            - **RG** - USA_North_Retail_Dev
                - **R:** Database, VM, Storage
            - **RG**- USA_North_Retail_Test
                - **R:** Database, VM, Storage
            - **RG** - USA_North_Retail_Prod
                - **R:** Database, VM, Storage
        - **Sub** - USA_North_eCommerce
            - **RG** - USA_North_eCommerce_Dev
                - **R:** Database, VM, Storage
            - **RG** - USA_North_eCommerce_Test
                - **R:** Database, VM, Storage
            - **RG** - USA_North_eCommerce_Prod
                - **R:** Database, VM, Storage
    - **MG** - USA_South
        - **Sub** - USA_South_Retail
            - **RG** - USA_South_Retail_Dev
                - **R**: Database, VM, Storage
            - **RG** - USA_South_Retail_Test
                - **R**: Database, VM, Storage
            - **RG** - USA_South_Retail_Prod
                - **R**: Database, VM, Storage
        - **Sub** - USA_South_eCommerce
            - **RG** - USA_South_eCommerce_Dev
                - **R**: Database, VM, Storage
            - **RG** - USA_South_eCommerce_Test
                - **R**: Database, VM, Storage
            - **RG** - USA_South_eCommerce_Prod
                - **R**: Database, VM, Storage

Note:

- **MG:** Management Group
- **Sub:** Subscription
- **RG:** Resource Group
- **R:** Resource

***Note:** Keep in mind that this is a general approach, and the actual hierarchy may vary depending on the size and complexity of your organization technology infrastructure, users and workloads.

33. Can you explain one or two benefits of designing and mapping our organization technology infrastructure to Azure Resource Hierarchy?

Ans:

Sure! Here are some real use cases where the Azure resource hierarchy is useful:

- Resource Isolation
- Managing access
- Deleting resources
- Applying policies
- Monitoring and Cost Management

For example, when you apply a security policy to a Management Group in Azure, all its associated subscriptions, resources groups and resources will automatically inherit that rule too. So, you don't have to apply it separately to each one, making it easier to manage and ensure consistent security throughout the hierarchy.

Explore:

Resource Isolation and Management: Resource hierarchy helps in maintaining clear separation between environments, minimizing risks of production outages. It also simplifies resource management, deployment, and tracking for complex applications or distributed teams.

- **Ex:** Separate DEV, Test and Prod resources using Resource Groups.

Managing access: Tenants and Management Groups allow centralization of RBAC (role-based access control) policies, ensuring consistent security across subscriptions.

- **Ex:** We want to ensure that no one can accidentally make changes to production resources from the development environment. We can use Azure resource hierarchy to block access to production resources from the development resource group.

Deleting a group of resources: If you need to delete a group of resources, you can simply delete the resource group that contains them. This will delete all of the resources in the resource group, so that you don't need to delete individual resources separately.

- **Ex:** A project-specific subscription can be deleted when the project is completed, ensuring resource cleanup.

Applying policies to multiple resources: You can use policies to manage access, security, and compliance for our Azure resources.

- **Ex:** By applying policy (Disable Public Internet Access to a VM) to a management group, you can ensure that all of the subscriptions and resource groups in the management group inherit the policy. This can save us time and effort, as we don't have to apply the policy to each resource individually.

Managing costs: We can use resource groups to track costs for our Azure resources.

- **Ex:** By creating a resource group for each project or department, we can easily see how much each project is costing. This can help us to identify areas where we can save money.

Tagging and Centralized Monitoring: Management Groups can be used to aggregate logs and monitoring data across subscriptions. This enables centralized monitoring, alerting, and auditing for compliance and troubleshooting purposes. Also, it helps us quickly tagging the relative resources.

- **Ex:** We could tag all of our production or a business unit resources with the tag "retail-production". This can be useful for auditing, billing, and troubleshooting.

34. Do you understand the concept of a Multi-Tenant Application? If so, could you elaborate on its appropriate use cases?

Ans:

A multi-tenant application is a software application that is designed to be used by multiple organizations or customers. Each tenant has its own data and configuration, but they all share the same underlying infrastructure.

- **Isolated/separated for each Tenant:** Database and Configurations.
- **Shared between Tenants:** Application (Code-base), Infrastructure (servers, storage, and networking components)

Use Case: Multi-tenancy is commonly used in Software-as-a-Service (SaaS) applications, where a provider hosts the application centrally and serves it to multiple customers over the internet. **Ex:** Salesforce, Databricks, Snowflake etc.

Explore:

Below are the most common business cases:

- **Customer relationship management (CRM) applications:** It allows multiple organizations to track their customers and sales data in a single system. **Ex:** Salesforce, Microsoft Dynamics 365, Oracle CRM etc.
- **Human resources (HR) applications:** It allows multiple organizations to manage their employees' data in a single system. **Ex:** Workday, Oracle HCM etc.

- **Enterprise resource planning (ERP) applications:** Multiple organizations can manage their financial, inventory, and manufacturing data in a single system. **Ex:** Microsoft Dynamics 365, SAP Business Suite, Oracle NetSuite etc.

35. What are the top benefits of a Multi-Tenant Application?

Ans:

Below are the major benefits:

- Cost efficiency
- Highly Scalable
- Ease of Maintenance
- Ease of Development, Maintenance and Onboarding
- Security

Explore:

- **Cost-Savings:** As it shares the same infrastructure and resources among multiple tenants, multi-tenancy applications can significantly reduce costs compared to deploying separate instances for each customer. **Ex:** Reduces development costs.
- **Scalability:** Multi-tenant applications can be easily scaled up or down to meet the needs of different tenants.
- **Easy-of-Maintenance:** Maintaining a single codebase and database schema simplifies updates and bug fixes, which can be applied centrally and automatically to all tenants/customers/organizations.
- **Ease-of-development:** It can be developed once and then reused by multiple tenants. This can save a significant amount of development time and resources.
- **Easy-of-Onboarding:** Onboarding new tenants/customers becomes much easier and quicker as they can be provisioned within the existing infrastructure.
- **Data Security:** It shares the infrastructure but data for each tenant is isolated from the data and configurations of other tenants.

36. Let's suppose there's an insurance company offering a SaaS application called the 'Insurance Policy Management System (IPMS).' This application is hosted on Azure and can handle policies for various brokers or agencies. Could you explain how the multi-tenancy works in this scenario?

Ans:

The IPMS is a multi-tenant SaaS application, which means that it is hosted on a single instance of the application but can be used by multiple tenants / brokers / agencies. Let's see how it works:

- **Multi-Tenant Architecture**: The application is built with a multi-tenant architecture. This allows multiple brokers or agencies (tenants) to access the same application while keeping their data and configurations separate from each other.

- **Single Application Instance**: This means there is only one codebase and one set of application files that serve all the brokers or agencies.
- **Shared Infrastructure**: All brokers or agencies access the IPMS through the same endpoint (Ex: a web portal or API gateway). They share the underlying infrastructure, including servers, storage, and networking components.
- **Tenant Identification**: When a broker or agency signs up for the application, they are assigned a unique tenant ID. This ID is used to identify their data and configuration within the application. When a broker or agency accesses the application, it uses an authentication method (Ex: username/password, API key) to identify which broker or agency is trying to access our application.
- **Database and Data Isolation**: Based on the business requirement we can choose the most appropriate database design pattern for a multi-Tenant application. Ex:
    - **Database-per-tenant:** We will create a separate database for each tenant.
    - **Database-sharded:** It involves partitioning or splitting the data for different tenants across multiple smaller databases, referred to as "shards." Each shard contains data for a specific subset of tenants.
    - **Single-Database:** This approach uses a single, sometimes large database containing data for all tenants. Each record in the database has an additional column for the tenant ID or key so that we can easily retrieve data relevant to a specific broker or agency based on their tenant identifier.
- **Separate Configuration and Policies**: While the application code is shared among all tenants, the configuration settings and policies can be tailored to each broker or agency. Ex: Branding, pricing rules, or security configurations may differ based on the tenant.
- **Upgrades and Maintenance:** System upgrades and maintenance can be performed centrally for all tenants, reducing administrative overhead.

In summary, the multi-tenancy architecture of the IPMS saves the insurance company money on hosting costs and makes it easier to manage the application.

37. What are the various subscription types offering by Microsoft Azure?

Ans:

Azure offers various types of subscriptions:

- Free Trial
- Pay-As-You-Go
- Enterprise Agreement
- Visual Studio Subscription
- Cloud Solution Provider (CSP) Subscription
- Azure Windows Virtual Machines Desktop Reserved Instances

- Azure in Open Licensing
- Azure Sponsorship Subscription
- Azure for Government Subscription
- Azure for Education Subscription
- Azure for Nonprofit Subscription

Explore:

Free Trial Subscription: This is a free subscription that allows us to try out Azure services for 12 months.

- **Use Case:** We can use this subscription to test out different Azure services and see if they are a good fit for our requirements. When we want to explore Azure and try out its services without incurring any costs.

Pay-As-You-Go Subscription: This type of subscription allows us to use Azure services without having to commit to a long-term contract. We only pay for the Azure services that we use.

- **Use Case:** This is a good option for businesses that need to be flexible with their IT spending. It's ideal for short-term projects, prototyping, or development and testing environments where resource usage may vary.

Enterprise Agreement Subscription: It is designed for large organizations. It includes volume discounts, as well as access to dedicated support resources. It provides cost predictability and the ability to negotiate custom terms with Microsoft.

- **Use Case:** Large organizations with predictable and steady cloud resource usage can benefit from an Enterprise Agreement.

Visual Studio Subscription (formerly MSDN Subscription): Designed for developers, this subscription provides access to software, services, and Azure credits for development and testing purposes.

- **Use Case:** A perfect choice for Developers who need access to software, services, and Azure credits for development and testing purposes.

Cloud Solution Provider (CSP) Subscription: The CSP program allows partners to offer Azure services to their customers and manage the billing and support. In this scenario, a CSP is a company that helps businesses to adopt and use cloud computing services. Ex: Consulting, deployment, management and support.

- **Use Case:** A small business wants to use Azure services, but they do not have the time or expertise to manage their own Azure subscriptions. They decide to work with a CSP to help them manage their Azure subscriptions. The CSP helps the business to provision resources, manage costs, and troubleshoot problems.

Azure Windows Virtual Machines Desktop Reserved Instances: For individual users and small to medium-sized businesses, there's a special subscription option that allows you to reserve Azure virtual machines for one or three years. You can choose to pay upfront or monthly, and by doing so, you'll get big discounts and priority access to computing power in Azure's data centers.

- **Use case:** It is suitable for individual users or businesses that require virtual desktops for a fixed term and want to take advantage of reserved instance pricing to save on costs.

Azure in Open Licensing: This subscription type allows customers to purchase Azure services through participating resellers.

- **Use Case:** Good option for businesses that have an existing Microsoft Open License agreement. It allows you to use Azure services with your existing licensing.

Azure Sponsorship Subscription: Sometimes, organizations or events receive Azure sponsorships, providing them with specific resources and services.

- **Use Case:** Organizations or events that receive Azure sponsorships can utilize this subscription to access specific resources and services as part of their sponsorship benefits.

Azure for Government Subscription: Offers specialized features and pricing for government organizations.

- **Use Case:** Government agencies and organizations in the public sector can use this subscription, which is designed to meet specific compliance and regulatory requirements.

Azure for Education Subscription: Offers discounted pricing and access to educational resources for students and educational institutions.

- **Use Case:** Designed for schools and universities to provide cloud resources for learning, research, and academic projects.

Azure for Nonprofit Subscription: Offers discounted pricing and access to support resources for nonprofit organizations.

- **Use Case:** Azure offers cloud services with discounted pricing for nonprofit organizations.

38. What are the different pricing models offered by Microsoft Azure Cloud?

Ans:

Azure offers several pricing models based on usage scenarios and customer needs.

Azure Main Pricing Models:

- **Pay-as-You-Go (PAYG):** Pay for the resources we use.
- **Enterprise Agreements (EAs):** For large organizations, Azure offers additional discounts when they enter into long-term agreements.

Azure Savings Options:

- **Reserved Instances (Discount up to 70%):** Reserve the capacity for the discounted price.
- **Spot Pricing (Unpredictable):** We can bid on Azure Spot Instances to access unused capacity (a VM) at a significant discount.
- **Azure Hybrid Benefit (Discount up to 72%):** We can bring our own Windows Server or SQL Server licenses to Azure and get a discount on your Azure compute costs.
- **Azure Dev/Test Pricing (Discount up to 50%):** Azure offers a special lower price for non-production workloads.
- **Azure Price Matching:** In certain cases, this option allows us to match the price of a competitor's cloud offering for Azure services.

Explore:

Let's see some practical examples:

- **Pay-as-you-go:** If we use a virtual machine for 1 hour, we'll be charged for 1 hour of usage.
- **Enterprise Agreement:** Pricing varies based on an enterprise's volume usage and the specific agreement with Microsoft.
- **Reserved Instances:** If you commit to using a virtual machine for 1 or 3 years, you'll get a discount of up to 70% off the pay-as-you-go price.
- **Spot Pricing:** Azure Spot VMs allow us to bid on unused Azure compute capacity, and if our bid is accepted, we can run our workloads at a significantly lower cost. However, there's a risk that Azure can reclaim the resources with little notice if the capacity is required elsewhere. Ex: It is the best option to run a non-critical batch job.
- **Azure Hybrid Benefit:** If you bring your own Windows Server or SQL Server license to Azure, you'll get a discount of up to 72% off the pay-as-you-go price.
- **Azure Dev/Test Pricing:** If your developers need to test a new feature on the database, you can take advantage of Azure SQL Database Dev/Test pricing, which allows you to save up to 50% off the pay-as-you-go price.
- **Azure Price Matching:** If you have a workload hosted on a different cloud platform (AWS or GCP) and wish to migrate it to Azure SQL Database, you can use Azure Price Matching to get competitive pricing on equivalent database services and save on your migration costs.

***Notes**

***Unused Capacity:** In any cloud environment, including Azure, there are instances when certain resources, such as virtual machines (VMs), are provisioned by the cloud provider but are not actively being utilized by any paying customer. This is known as "unused capacity." The cloud provider can make these unused resources available for temporary use by other customers at a reduced cost.

***Relation between Azure Subscriptions and Pricing:**

- Azure Subscription type and pricing models are related but are not the same thing. Azure Subscription is essentially an agreement with Microsoft that allows us to use Azure services and resources. It acts as a container for all the resources and services you use within Azure. Pricing models in Azure refer to the different ways Azure charges us for using its services and resources.
- We can choose a different pricing model for each subscription. **Ex:** We could have one subscription that uses the pay-as-you-go pricing model for development workloads, and another subscription that uses the reserved instances pricing model for production workloads.

39. What tools and services are there to help understand Azure pricing?

Ans:

There are a number of tools and services available to calculate, analyze, and understand the Azure pricing.

- **Azure Pricing Calculator:** An official native tool.
- **Azure TCO Calculator:** Useful for migration cost planning.
- **Azure Cost Management and Billing:** Helps in understanding and optimizing your Azure cloud workloads.
- **Azure Advisor:** Offers recommendations for cost optimization.
- **Azure Pricing API:** Enables building custom pricing calculators.
- **Third-party Cloud Cost Management Tools:** Offer more advanced features and customizations.

Explore:

- **Azure Pricing Calculator:** This is an official free tool provided by Microsoft Azure. It allows us to estimate the costs of using various Azure services based on your specific requirements. **Ex:** We can specify our workload requirements, such as the number of VMs, amount of storage, Databases, capacity requirements etc. The calculator will then provide us with an estimate of our monthly Azure costs.
- **Azure TCO Calculator:** This tool helps you estimate the total cost of ownership (TCO) of migrating your workloads to Azure. The TCO calculator considers factors such as hardware costs, software costs, operational costs, and migration costs. **Ex:** You can input the number of servers, storage, network, and their capacity, and then it will provide an assessment of potential savings.
- **Microsoft Cost Management (Azure Cost Management and Billing)**: This is an Azure service that provides in-depth cost management and billing analysis. It allows us to track and analyze our Azure spending, set up budgets and alerts, and view detailed billing reports. **Ex:** You can set up an alert that will notify you if the cost of the project exceeds a certain threshold. This will help you to keep track of the costs of your project and to take action if the costs start to get out of control.

- **Azure Advisor:** While not a direct pricing calculator, Azure Advisor provides cost optimization recommendations based on your current resource usage. **Ex:** Shutdown unused resources, right size underutilized resources, reserve instances for consistent workloads, use serverless options etc.
- **Azure Pricing API:** This API allows you to programmatically retrieve Azure pricing information. This can be useful for integrating Azure pricing into your own applications or tools. **Ex:** It is helpful for building custom pricing calculators in your applications.
- **Third-party Cost-Management Tools:** Some third-party vendors offer cost management and optimization tools with advanced analytics. **Ex:** CloudZero, CloudHealth, Apptio, Flexera etc.

***Note:** "Azure Cost Management and Billing" has been rebranded as "Microsoft Cost Management" in 2022.

40. What is Azure Portal?

Ans:

- Azure Portal is a web-based user interface provided by Microsoft for managing and interacting with all of your services and resources in the Microsoft Azure cloud platform.
- Azure Portal (https://portal.azure.com)acts as a central hub where we can create, configure, monitor and manage Azure services and resources effectively.

Explore:

To log into the Azure portal, first we need to register and signup for an Azure Account. Azure Portal offers a powerful user experience that includes:

- **Dashboard Overview:** It provides a customizable view of our resources and services. We can pin important resources, such as databases and VMs, for quick access.
- **Explore using Menus and Categories:** Services and resources are categorised into various sections such as Compute, Networking, Databases, AI + Machine Learning etc. You can explore these categories to find the services you want to use.
- **Explore using Global Search:** It is a powerful feature that allows us to quickly search for resources and services by using name, type, or tag.
- **Explore using Advanced Global Search Techniques:** Along with the simple keyword search, Global Search also supports advanced capabilities. Here are some examples:
    - Use "@" to search for a specific resource: @my-abcProd-azuresqldatabase
    - Use "*" to search for a pattern: *virtual machine*
    - Use ":" to search within a resource group: resource group:my-abcTest-resource-group
    - Use "type:" to search for a specific type of resources: type:virtualmachine
    - Use "tag:" to search for resources with specified tags: tag:environment=production
    - Use "where:" to filter the results: where:state=Running

- Logical Operators like AND, OR: tag:environment=development AND where:state=Stopped.

- **Create and Configure Resources:** Search for the required resources, select and configure the resources by providing all necessary parameters. **Ex:** VM, Database, Storage Account etc.
- **Resource Monitoring and Management:** Using Azure Portal, we can view resource metrics, set up alerts based on specific conditions, and access logs.
- **Cost Management:** Azure Portal offers cost management tools, including cost analysis, budgeting, and recommendations to optimize spending.
- **Documentation and Help:** Azure offers extensive documentation and tutorials to help us get started and troubleshoot any issues.

41. What are tags in Azure, and when should we use them?

Ans:

- Tags in Azure are metadata elements that we can apply to our Azure resources.
- They're key-value pairs that help us identify, categorize and organize resources.
- We can assign multiple tags to a resource and Tags are commonly used for
  - Resource tracking
  - Resource management
  - Cost Tracking
- **Ex:** Below are the sample tags that we can assign while creating an Azure Resource such as an Azure SQL Database, VM etc.:
  - **Environment:** Development, Staging, Production
  - **Application:** AbcSalesApp, AbcAnalyticsApp
  - **Cost Center:** K12345, T67890
  - **Owner:** dbaL2Team, appTeam9
  - **Data Sensitivity:** Low, Medium, High, PII
  - **Compliance:** GDPR, HIPAA, PCI-DSS
  - **Backup**: Daily, Weekly, Monthly
  - **SLA:** Gold, Silver, Bronze

Explore:

Let's see some practical use cases of resource tags:

- We could create a tag for the cost center that each resource belongs to. This would allow us to see how much each cost center is spending on Azure resources.
- We could easily track and filter resources in our Azure environment. **Ex:** Track all resources that are belongs to a specific application, region, owner, cost center etc.
- Tags can be used in automation scripts to identify resources and perform actions (backup, scale, apply a policy etc.) on them based on their assigned tags.

42. Is it really important to follow specific naming conventions for Azure resources? If yes, what are the standards or recommendations?

Ans:

Yes! Adopting a well-thought-out naming convention is a best practice for managing Azure resources effectively. While Azure doesn't enforce specific naming conventions, it is up to us (organization/ Customer) to define and follow naming standards that align with our needs and workflows.

Best Practices:

- Define a standard approach for naming conventions at the organizational level.
- Use meaningful names.
- Maintain uniqueness and consistency.
- Keep names short and simple.
- Avoid special characters.
- Use lowercase letters.
- **Consider the Scope:** A resource must have a unique name within its scope. **Ex:** There can be only one network named vnet-prod-eastus-001 in a resource group rg-test. A global scoped resource (Management Group) must have a name that's unique across the entire Azure platform.
- **Consider Naming Rules:** We must consider the resource scope, maximum allowed length, valid characters, case sensitivity. **Ex:** Resource Group name max length should be <=64.
- **Use Azure Recommended Abbreviations:** We must use abbreviations to shorten the resource name. **Ex:** Azure SQL Database – sqldb, MySQL Database – mysql, PostgreSQL database – psql, Azure Data Factory – adf, Azure Databricks Workspace – dbw, Azure Synapse Analytics Workspaces – synw, Virtual Machine – vm, Virtual Network - vnet etc.

Explore:

There are no restrictions on defining the resource naming and tagging strategy. However, for better resource organization and management, we should define a naming strategy. Below are some sample strategies:

We can consider below while defining a resource name hierarchy:

- **Region:** westus, eastus2, westeu, usva, ustx
- **Resource type:** sqldb, vm
- **Business Unit / Organization:** abcorg, it, fin, mktg, product
- **App or Service Name:** sharepoint, custtrack, warehouse
- **Environment:** dev, test, stag, prod, client, shared
- **Resource Instance:** 01, 02, 003 etc.

Sample Patterns and examples:

- {region}-{org}-{env}-{workload Instance}-{type}:
    - **Azure SQL Database:** uswest2-abcorg-dev-web01-sqldb
    - **VM:** uswest2-abcorg-dev-web01-vm
- {company}-{department}-{product Line}-{environment}-{Workload Instance}-{type}
    - **Azure SQL Database:** abcorg-sales-ecommerce-dev-web01-sqldb
    - **VM:** abcorg-sales-ecommerce-dev-web01-vm
- {type}-{org}-{workload}-{env}-{region}-{instance}
    - **Azure SQL Database:** sqldb-abcorg-web-dev-uswest2-01
    - **VM:** vm-abcorg-web-dev-uswest2-01

43. Could you explain what Azure Geographies are and why they are significant?

Ans:

- **Azure Geographies:** Represent specific countries or regions.
- **Azure Regions:** Refers to an area or part of a Geography/Country.
- **Azure Region Pairs:** Pairing two regions within the same Geography for Business Continuity and Disaster Recovery (BCDR).
- **Azure Availability Zones:** Connect two or more data centers within a region.
- **Azure Physical Data Center:** A unique physical location where actual Azure infrastructure is hosted.
- **Azure Resource:** Any resource (such as SQL Database, VM, Storage account, etc.) created on the Azure cloud and hosted in a physical data center.

Azure Geographies, Regions, and Availability Zones are designed for:

- **Data Residency**: Define Geographical boundaries for our data.
- **Data Sovereignty**: Refers to the legal concept that data is subject to the laws of the country or region where it is stored.
- **Compliance requirements**: Align with industry specific, country or region level regulatory compliance.
- **Fault Tolerance, High Availability, Disaster Recovery and Redundancy**: Protecting our data and applications from datacenter level, zone level and region level failures or natural disasters.

For Example:

- Some important data, like personal identifiable information, financial, healthcare, or credit information, must stay within the country where it belongs because of strict rules and compliance.

- Using Azure Geographies and regions when we pick a specific geography, like India, Microsoft ensures that our data remains stored only in India. Likewise, if we choose the United States, our data stays within the country.
- We have complete control over where our data and applications are kept.

Explore:

Azure Geographies:

- An Azure geography represents a large area on the world map containing one or more countries or regions where Microsoft's Azure services are available.
- **Ex:** Americas (United States, Canada, Brazil, Mexico, etc.), Asia Pacific (India, Australia, Japan, New Zealand, etc.), Europe (Germany, France, Italy, etc.), Middle East (UAE, Qatar, etc.), and Africa (South Africa).
- Azure allows customers to choose where data is stored, ensuring compliance with data residency and regulatory requirements.
- An Azure Geography contains one or more Regions.

Azure Regions: Area/Part of a Geography/Country

- An Azure Region consists of a group of datacenters deployed within a Geography and connected via a dedicated regional low-latency network.
- When deploying applications on Azure, selecting the closest Region to your users ensures low-latency and better network performance.
- **Ex:** In the geography of India, Azure Datacenters are established in regions such as Central India (Pune), South India (Chennai), South Central India (Hyderabad), and West India (Mumbai). Similarly, in the USA, regions include Central US (Iowa), East US (Virginia), North Central US (Illinois), South Central US (Texas), West Central US (Wyoming), West US (California), etc.

Azure Region Pairs (Paired Regions):

- A region is paired with another region in the same Geography for BCDR (Business Continuity and Disaster Recovery).
- There are three main benefits of Region Pairs:
    - If one region experiences a disaster or failure, services in that region will automatically failover to the secondary region in the pair.
    - If both regions in the pair are down due to a disaster, Azure prioritizes restoration in one of the regions to ensure quick service restoration.
    - Azure serializes platform updates so that only one region is updated at a time.
- Azure prefers at least 300 miles of distance between datacenters in a region pair to reduce the likelihood of simultaneous disasters affecting both regions.
- **Ex:** East US is paired with West US, and Central India is paired with South India.

Availability Zones:

- Azure Availability Zones are distinct physical locations within an Azure region, each containing one or more datacenters with independent power, cooling, and networking.
- Microsoft has established several data centers either in the same city or very close to each other, connected through a high-speed, low-latency network.
- The primary purpose of Azure Availability Zones is to safeguard applications and data from data center-level failures, such as hardware failures, network issues, or natural disasters.
- Not all regions support Availability Zones.
- **Ex:** Some regions that support availability zones include East US, Central US, East US 2, France Central, Qatar Central, Australia East, and Central India etc.

Physical Data Center:

- A unique physical location/building where the actual Azure physical infrastructure is hosted.

Azure Resource:

- Fundamental building blocks of Azure cloud solutions, including Virtual Machines, storage solutions like Azure Blob Storage, Azure SQL Database, or networking components like Virtual Networks.
- Each Azure Resource is provisioned and hosted within one of Azure's physical data centers strategically located across the globe.

44. What are the phases in an Azure Service Lifecycle?

Ans:

The Azure service lifecycle defines how every Azure service is released for public use. It mainly has three phases:

- **Private Preview:** Only limited number of customers are invited to explore the service features.
- **Public Preview:** Available to all customers for exploration and experiment purpose. We can explore the features and provide feedback to the Azure Development team.
- **Generally Available (GA):** Service is live for the production usage.

Explore:

Here is the more detailed info:

Development:

- Azure Development team internally works on the product or service development.
- It is not available to the public usage.

Private Preview:

- This is the first release of the product.
- Azure invites a limited number of customers to try the service.
- Customers are expected to spend time with the Azure Product Group providing their feedback of the product or service.
- SLA (Service Level Agreement) and Customer support is not covered in the phase.
- It is generally offered free of charge.
- Also, no guarantee that a preview feature will go into General Availability.

Public Preview:

- Product or service is available to all customers
- This is when everyone can try out the service to see how it works and give feedback.
- This helps the Azure team understand what customers want and make the product even better in the future.
- Basic customer service will be provided but no SLAs are applicable.
- It is generally offered free of charge.

Generally Available (GA):

- After the public preview is completed, the feature is open for any licensed customer to use and is supported via all Microsoft support channels.
- It comes with full support through SLAs and customer support (basic and premium), and it is a chargeable service as well.

Deprecated:

- Some services may become deprecated over time.
- Deprecated services are still supported for a limited time.
- Azure announces deprecation in advance, and customers are encouraged to migrate to newer alternatives.
- SLAs, customer support, and charges are applicable as-is during this phase.

End-of-life:

- The service is no longer supported by Microsoft.
- Customers must migrate to a new service in this phase.

45. What is Azure Customer Support, and what are the available support options?

Ans:

Microsoft Azure customer support is a service provided by Microsoft to assist customers with technical issues, inquiries, troubleshooting problems, security and compliance issues, billing & pricing inquires and challenges related to their use of the Azure cloud computing platform.

Microsoft Azure offers several customer support plans, each with different levels of benefits, response times, and service availability.

- **Basic:** Basic access to Azure documentation, whitepapers, and support forums. It doesn't provide direct technical support from Microsoft.
- **Developer:** Basic + Provides technical support for development and testing environments with standard response times.
- **Standard:** Developer + 24×7 access to support engineers via email and phone with faster response times.
- **Professional Direct (ProDirect):** Standard + High-priority technical support with faster response times
- **Premier:** ProDirect + It is part of Enterprise support offering and offers the highest level of support. It includes a dedicated support team, personalized hands-on assistance and trainings etc.

Explore:

Feature	**Basic**	**Developer**	**Standard**	**ProDirect**
Price per month	$0	$29	$100	$1000
Designed for	All Azure Customers	Dev and Test workloads	Production workloads	Business-critical workloads
Support Time	NA	Business Hours	24X7	24X7
Support Type	NA	Email	Email and Phone	Email and Phone
Third-Party Software Support	NA	Yes	Yes	Yes
Severity Types	NA	C	A, B, C	A+, A, B, C
Response Time	NA	C – 8 Hrs.	A (1 Hr.), B(4 Hrs.), C (8 Hrs.)	A+(15 Min), A(1 Hr.), B(4 Hrs.), C(8 Hrs.)
Architecture Support	NA	General guidance	General guidance	ProDirect Expert

Table 1.3

Premier Support: It has been designed to accelerate our cloud adoption journey through a complete coverage for cloud, hybrid, and on-premise solutions across all Microsoft products. With Premier Support, we get everything included in ProDirect. Additionally, we get personalized help, and a dedicated Technical Account Manager who offers proactive support for all our business solutions, even if they are not from Microsoft.

***Note-1:** All plans cover the below features:

- Unlimited support tickets.
- Billing & Subscription Support.
- 24/7 self-help recourses – Docs, Support Forums etc.
- Azure Advisor and health status notifications.

***Note-2:** Severity refers the business impact

- C – Minimal
- B – Moderate
- A – High
- A+ - Critical

46. What is Microsoft Azure Service Level Agreement (SLA)?

Ans:

The Azure SLA describe Microsoft's commitments for uptime and connectivity for Azure Services such as Virtual Machines, Network, Storage, Databases etc. An Azure SLA is a contract between Microsoft and its customers that defines the availability and performance guarantees for Azure services. The SLAs specify the following:

- The uptime for the service.
- The metrics that will be used to measure the uptime of the service.
- The process for reporting and resolving service outages.
- The compensation that Microsoft will provide if the service does not meet the uptime guarantee.

Ex: SLA Monthly guaranteed uptime samples for:

- **Azure SQL Database:** 99.995 %
- **Azure Virtual Machine:** 99.99 %
- **Azure Data Factory:** 99.9%
- **Azure Storage:** 99.99%

***Note:** Microsoft clearly defines SLA based on all relevant factors, including service tiers, HA & DR features, etc. The SLA uptime may vary depending on these factors.

Explore:

The SLAs are important for businesses that rely on Azure services to ensure that their applications and data are available when they need them. It's important to understand the uptime and downtime calculations outlined in the provided SLA to effectively design our HA&DR strategy.

For example, lets calculate the maximum downtime per day, week and month for the below given uptime SLAs:

Calculation Formula: Maximum downtime calculation

- **Per day:** (24 hours) x (1 - Service Uptime Percentage)
- **Per Week:** (7 days) x Maximum Downtime per Day
- **Per Month:** (30.44 days) x Maximum Downtime per Day

Consider the below examples:

- Azure SQL Database: 99.995 %
- Per Day = 24 x (1 - 0.99995) = 0.0012 hours X 60 X 60 = 4.32 Seconds
  - **Per Day:** 4.32 seconds
  - **Per Week:** 30.24 seconds
  - **Per Month:** 2.19168 minutes
- Azure Data Factory (ADF): 99.9%
  - **Per Day:** 1.44 minutes
  - **Per Week:** 10.08 minutes
  - **Per Month:** 43.834 minutes

***Note:** While a 99.9% uptime for ADF may sound impressive, it means there could be around 44 minutes of potential downtime per month. It's important to take this calculation into account when planning your HA & DR strategy to meet your business's required SLAs.

47. If an Azure Service fails to meet its specified SLA, what potential consequences might arise?

Ans:

If an Azure service is unable to meet the specified SLA uptime, we may be eligible for a service credit as compensation for the downtime. The amount of the service credit will depend on the specific SLA and the amount of time that the service was unavailable.

Ex: Suppose, Azure offers an Azure SQL Database with a promised uptime of 99.995%.

- If the uptime is below 99% but above 95%, they will give a service credit of 25% to compensate for the downtime.
- If the uptime drops below 95%, they will provide a 100% service credit as compensation.

Explore:

Service Credit: A service credit in Azure SLA is a percentage of the monthly service fees that is credited to our account following Microsoft's claim approval if an Azure service is unable to meet the specified SLA uptime.

Claim: A claim is a request for a service credit from Microsoft if an Azure service is unable to meet the specified SLA uptime. To be eligible for a service credit, we must submit a claim within two months of the end of the billing month in which the incident occurred. A claim must include:

- Subscription ID.
- Service details.
- The date, time and amount of time that the service was unavailable.
- Evidence that the service was unavailable, such as screenshots or logs etc.

Once you submit a claim, Microsoft will investigate the issue and determine if you are eligible for a service credit. If you are eligible, Microsoft will credit your account for the appropriate amount.

Other Consequences:

- Service credits are not a substitute or a solution for a well-designed and resilient application.
- A long period of service downtime can cause various problems like unhappy customers, financial losses, loss of trust, higher support costs, and compliance issues.
- To avoid this, we can use methods like load balancing, redundancy, and failover, which help keep our applications accessible even if some Azure services experience problems.

48. What is Azure Marketplace?

Ans:

- Azure Marketplace is an online store (similar to a play store, app store) provided by Microsoft as part of the Microsoft Azure cloud computing platform.
- It contains thousands of IT software applications and services built by industry-leading technology companies.
- It allows developers and businesses to find, purchase, and deploy various applications, services, and solutions that are specifically designed to integrate with Azure and enhance its functionalities.

Examples:

- Pre-configured virtual machine images with different operating systems and software configurations that you can quickly deploy to the Azure cloud. **Ex:** Windows VM with SQL installed.
- SaaS and third-party software offerings such as Datadog, Splunk, Tableau server, Jenkins, ServiceNow, Workday etc.
- Similarly, we can find a lot of products and services that includes security related, storage solutions, data and Analytics offerings etc.

Explore:

Let's say we want to set up a web application on Azure. Instead of building everything from scratch, we can go to the Azure Marketplace and find pre-configured virtual machine images that come with OS, web servers and databases installed. We can then choose the one that best fits our needs, deploy it to our Azure subscription, and start using the web application immediately without having to handle all the setup and installation tasks ourself.

49. What are the different ways to deploy and configure resources in the Azure Cloud?

Ans:

There are several ways to deploy or create and configure a resource in Azure:

Most Popular Azure Resource Management Tools and Services:

- **Azure portal:** A web-based GUI that we can use to manage our Azure resources.
- **Azure Resource Manager (ARM) templates:** JSON files that we can use to define the configuration of our Azure resources.
- **Bicep Files:** Bicep is a way more powerful and advanced tool than ARM Templates. It is a superset of ARM templates, and it offers a number of advantages over ARM templates.
- **Azure CLI:** A command-line tool that we can use to manage our Azure resources from a terminal window.
- **Azure PowerShell:** A set of PowerShell modules that we can use to manage our Azure resources from PowerShell.
- **Azure Cloud Shell:** A hosted shell environment that runs on an Ubuntu container. We can use Cloud Shell to manage our Azure resources from a web browser.

Explore:

Other Approaches to deploy and manage resources in Azure:

- **Azure DevOps:** We can build CI/CD (Continuous Integration/Continuous Deployment) pipelines to automate the deployment and configuration of Azure resources.
- **Azure SDKs:** We can use Microsoft Azure provides Software Development Kits (SDKs) to programmatically create, manage, and configure Azure resources using code. Ex: SDKs for .NET, Python, Java, Node.js, etc.
- **Azure Marketplace:** The Azure Marketplace is a collection of pre-configured applications, services, and solutions that we can deploy directly to our Azure subscription.
- **Azure Automation:** Azure Automation allows us to automate various tasks, including resource deployment and configuration. We can create runbooks that use PowerShell or Python scripts to manage resources.
- **Azure Service Fabric:** A platform that we can use to deploy and manage microservices applications.
- **Azure Templates in Visual Studio:** We can leverage Azure Resource Group projects and Azure templates to deploy and configure resources directly from within Visual Studio.

Third Party Tools and Services:

- **Terraform (Open-source):** A widely used open-source infrastructure as code (IaC) tool that can be used to automate the deployment of Azure resources. It makes easy to create and manage complex resource deployments.
- **Ansible (Open-source):** A popular configuration management and automation tool that can be used to deploy and manage Azure resources. It uses YAML-based playbooks. Which means it uses a simple, declarative syntax to define tasks, which makes it easy to write and maintain automation scripts.
- **Chef (Open-source):** Chef is a powerful automation platform that can be used to automate the deployment and management of Azure resources using recipes and cookbooks. It uses a more complex, imperative syntax than Ansible, but it offers more features and flexibility.
- **Puppet (Open-Source or Enterprise/Licensed):** Another automation tool and it uses a declarative syntax similar to Ansible. It has modules specifically designed for working with Azure resources.
- **Jenkins (Open-source):** An automation server that can be used to set up CI/CD pipelines for deploying applications and resources to Azure.

***Note: YAML -** Yet Another Markup Language, and it is a human-readable data serialization language.

50. What is Azure Cloud Shell, and what are its capabilities?

Ans:

Azure Cloud Shell is a web-based, interactive shell environment provided by Microsoft Azure. Which means it offers an interface to run Bash, PowerShell, or Azure CLI commands. It is a hosted shell environment that runs on an Ubuntu container.

Offers two shell environments: Bash (with Azure CLI preinstalled) and PowerShell (with Azure PowerShell preinstalled). A dropdown list at the top of the Cloud Shell window allows you to easily switch between the two environments.

It could be used to:

- **Resource Management:** Create, configure, delete, and manage Azure resources like databases, virtual machines, storage accounts, networks, monitoring and more.
- **Execute commands and scripts:** We can run Bash, PowerShell, Azure CLI commands/scripts. It also, supports executing Python and JavaScript.
- **Edit Files:** We can edit code and configuration files
- **Upload/Download files:** It also supports file operations on Azure Storage.

Explore:

We Data Engineers, DBA's or Developers work with many environments, platforms and cloud infrastructure such as Azure, AWS, GCP etc. We can either work on their web portal or use the command-line interface (CLI). The CLI commands are an easier way to manage cloud resources with a set of scripts and parameters. However, we need to install and configure the CLI tools on our local machines.

Accessing:

- Azure Cloud Shell allows us to access a CLI directly from web browsers, without the need to install any local tools.
- We can directly access the cloud shell from Azure Web Portal (A PowerShell like Icon >_AT TOP Top) or browse to URL https://shell.azure.com.

Commands and Scripts options:

- When we first open Azure Cloud Shell, we will be presented with a dropdown list of two options:
    - **Bash:** A shell that is used to run commands on a Unix-like operating system
    - **PowerShell:** A Microsoft-specific command-line tool that is used to automate tasks and run scripts.
- **Azure CLI:** A command-line interface that is specifically designed to create and manage Azure resources. Azure Cloud Shell gives us the option to run Bash or PowerShell commands, we can also run Azure CLI commands just by typing "az" at the prompt.
- **Additional Programming Languages:** Azure Cloud Shell also supports Python and JavaScript. This means that we can use Cloud Shell to run code that interacts with Azure resources. **Ex:** We could use Cloud Shell to run a Python script that queries an Azure database.

Edit Files: Azure Cloud Shell includes a built-in text editor that we can use to edit files. **Ex:** Text files, ARM templates, code files like Python, Bash or PowerShell scripts etc.

Pricing:

- Azure Cloud Shell is Free to use but we may need to pay for the Azure File Share attached to it.
    - Compute and Infrastructure - Free
    - Storage usage – Billing is calculated
- Only the Azure Files share used to store our data for Cloud Shell is considered for the billing. Storage transactions, outbound data transfers, and redundancy options will affect our total cost.
- By default, Azure Cloud Shell creates a storage account on our behalf with an Azure Files share. For Bash, this share will also contain a 5-GB disk image.

51. When I log into the Azure portal and open Azure Cloud Shell, and then start running my Bash or PowerShell scripts, what exactly happens behind the scenes? How does Azure manage everything?

Ans:

Azure Cloud Shell internally uses a combination of containers and VMs. Azure Cloud Shell is a lightweight, self-contained unit of software that can be run on any platform that supports Docker. Here is the internal workflow:

- **Request for an Azure Cloud Shell Session:** When we lunch it, a request is sent to cloud shell service.
- **Resource Provision:** Azure first checks to see if we have already created a Cloud Shell instance for our user account. If we have, Azure will reuse that instance. If not, Azure will create a new instance.
- **Instance Creation:** Azure Cloud Shell uses a container-based architecture to host the shell environment. It internally creates a Linux based Virtual Machine and hosts the Cloud Shell container on it.
- **Configuration:** The container is configured with all the necessary tools and utilities required for the shell environment. **Ex:** Azure CLI, AzCopy, PowerShell modules, development tools, commonly used packages, libraries, authentication and network access etc.
- **Attaching Storage:** Azure then attaches an Azure Files share to the VM. This share is used to store our Cloud Shell files and data.
- **Shell session initialization and interaction:** Azure then opens a browser-based terminal to the VM. This terminal is what you use to interact with Cloud Shell. We can then start running commands and scripts. It ensures that our data persists between sessions during the session lifetime.
- **Session Cleanup:** Once our session becomes inactive for a specific period (ex: 20 min), the Cloud Shell container is stopped, and the allocated resources (VM) are released. However, the Azure File Share is not deleted. We can reopen Cloud Shell at any time and resume working with our files and data.

52. What is Azure CLI, and how can you use it to control and manage Azure resources?

Ans:

The Azure Command-Line Interface (CLI) is a cross-platform command-line tool to connect to Azure and execute administrative commands on Azure resources.

- **Installation:** We can install the Azure CLI locally on Windows, Linux or Mac computers. It can also be used from a browser through the Azure Cloud Shell or run from inside a Docker container.
- **Usage:** For interactive use, we first launch a shell such as cmd.exe on Windows, or Bash on Linux or macOS, and then issue a command at the shell prompt.

Explore:

Azure CLI Extensions: An Azure extension is a small piece of software that can be installed on an Azure resource to add new functionality or capabilities. Extensions can be used to do things like install software, configure settings, or run scripts. These are nothing but Python wheels (a pre-compiled Python package) that aren't shipped as part of the CLI. We can simply install and start using it. Ex: Data Migration, IoT, DevOps, Firewall etc.

Here are the commonly used Azure CLI commands:

- Resource: az resource
- VM: az vm
- Storage: az storage
- Synapse: az synapse
- SQL Database: az sql

Example: Below are the common commands that we use it for creating and managing an Azure SQL Database.

- **az login:** To login to our Azure Account
- **az sql db create:** Creates a new Azure SQL Database.
- **az sql db list:** Lists all of the Azure SQL Databases in our subscription.
- **az sql db show:** Shows information about a specific Azure SQL Database.
- **az sql db delete:** Deletes an Azure SQL Database.
- **az sql db update:** Updates the properties of an Azure SQL Database.
- **az sql db grant-access:** Grants access to an Azure SQL Database to a user or group.
- **az sql db revoke-access:** Revokes access to an Azure SQL Database from a user or group.
- **az sql db backup:** Backs up an Azure SQL Database.
- **az sql db restore:** Restores an Azure SQL Database from a backup.
- **az sql db rename:** To rename a database
- **az sql db tde:** Manage a database's transparent data encryption.

Ex: Let's see how to rename a database using Azure CLI command

- az sql db rename --name MyCurrentAzureSQLDatabase
    - --new-name MyNew
    - --resource-group MyResourceGroup
    - --server myserver

***Note:** These are just a few examples. There is a large list of commands that can be used to manage any database-related operations using Azure CLI.

53. What is Azure PowerShell, and how can you use it to control and manage Azure resources?

Ans:

Azure PowerShell is a command-line interface (CLI) tool that allows us to manage Azure resources using PowerShell cmdlets. The Az PowerShell module is based on the .NET Standard.

- **Installation:** Install PowerShell locally on Windows, Linux, and macOS and also import the Az module (Install-Module -Name Az) which is specifically designed for Azure resource management. Once installation is done, we can connect to our Azure account using Connect-AzAccount command. We can also use PowerShell from a browser through Azure Cloud Shell or inside a Docker container.
- **Usage:** For interactive use, we first launch a PowerShell on Windows, or terminal window on Linux or macOS, and then issue PowerShell commands at the shell prompt.

Explore:

Custom PowerShell Modules: It is a way to extend the functionality of PowerShell by creating new functions or cmdlets. Once a module is created, it can be published to the PowerShell repository so that others can install and use it in their scripts. PowerShell modules are similar to Python wheels in that they both contain pre-compiled code that can be used to extend the functionality of a programming language.

Here are the commonly used Azure PowerShell commands: Azure PowerShell offers separate PowerShell module for each Azure Resource.

- **Resource group:** Az.Resources
- **Virtual Machines:** Az.Compute
- **Storage Accounts:** Az.Storage
- **Synapse:** Az.Synapse
- **SQL Database:** Az.Sql

Azure PowerShell cmdlets follow a standard naming convention for PowerShell, Verb-Noun or Action-ResourceType. **Ex:** {Action}-Az{ResourceName} – New-AzSqlDatabase.

Below are the sample PowerShell cmdlets:

- **Get-AzSqlDatabase:** Gets a SQL database by name or resource ID.
- **New-AzSqlDatabase:** Creates a new SQL database.
- **Update-AzSqlDatabase:** Updates an existing SQL database configuration.
- **Remove-AzSqlDatabase:** Deletes a SQL database.

Sample PowerShell command to upgrade an Azure SQL Database from Standard to Premium:

- Update-AzSqlDatabase -Name myAzureSQLDatabase

- ResourceGroupName myResourceGroup
- ServerName myServer
- Edition Premium

54. How can I pick the best one between Azure CLI and Azure PowerShell?

Ans:

Azure CLI and Azure PowerShell are both command-line tools provided by Microsoft to interact with Azure services, but they have different command syntax and scripting capabilities.

Choose Azure CLI if:

- You are more used to writing scripts in the Bash shell style.
- You are comfortable with traditional command line interfaces and you need a CLI to run the straightforward and simple tasks.

Choose Azure PowerShell if:

- You already using PowerShell for other tasks and feel comfortable with it.
- You have advanced automation scripts with complex logic, like using Object-Oriented Programming (OOP).

55. Do you have any idea what a JMESPath query means?

Ans:

Yes!

- When we use Azure CLI commands, they can sometimes give us big results in JSON format. JMESPath is a powerful query language that helps us filter and work with this JSON data.
- It allows us to extract specific information from the JSON responses without having to process the entire data structure manually.
- The Azure CLI uses the "—query" parameter to execute a JMESPath query on the results of commands.
- **Ex:** when retrieving resource data, instead of getting all unnecessary details, we can choose to retrieve only the specific resource properties we need. It's similar to SQL, where instead of using '*', we select the specific columns.

Explore:

Consider the below scenario:

When we want to get information about Azure SQL Databases, we use the command "az sql db list." This command gives us a lot of details about each database, like its name, resource group, server name, status, edition, collation, maximum size, and any associated tags. However, sometimes we only need specific information, such as the database names and the resource groups they are in. To get just that, we can use a JMESPath query.

- az sql db list --query "[].{DBName: name, RGroup: resourceGroup}"
- **az sql db list:** It lists all the Azure SQL Databases in our Azure account.
- **--query:** It allows us to apply the JMESPath query to the output of the command.
- **"[].{DBName: name, RGroup: resourceGroup}":**
- []: Indicate that we want to apply the query to the entire list of databases.
- {...}: An expression that selects and renames (like Select name as "DBName" in SQL) specified properties in JSON output. In the above statement we are renaming "name" property to DBName and resourceGroup property to RGroup.

56. What is Azure Resource Provider?

Ans:

Resource Provider is a fundamental component of the Azure Resource Manager (ARM) architecture. It is a service that supplies Azure resources. When we create a resource (Ex: A Database) in Azure, we are essentially making a request to the corresponding resource provider to create and manage that resource on our behalf. Resource providers ensure that the requested resources are properly provisioned, configured, and maintained according to your specifications.

Ex:

- **Microsoft.Compute**: It handles VM provisioning, configuration, scaling, and operations.
- **Microsoft.Storage**: It is responsible for creating and managing Azure Storage accounts.
- **Microsoft.SQL**: It is responsible for managing Azure SQL Database instances and related resources.
- **Microsoft.Network**: It handles virtual networks, public IP addresses, network security groups, and application gateways.
- **Other:** Microsoft.PowerBI, Microsoft.Databricks, Microsoft.DataFactory, Microsoft.DBforMySQL, Microsoft.DBforPostgreSQL, Microsoft.DocumentDB, etc.

Explore:

Below are the reasons why Azure utilizes the 'Resource Provider' approach:

- **Unified and consistent resource management experience:** Resource providers define a set of REST operations that can be used to create, update, delete, and manage Azure resources. This means that regardless of the underlying services, developers and admins can use a consistent set of APIs and tools to interact with resources across Azure.
- **Granular Access Control:** For example, I want to prevent a specific user group from creating HDInsight clusters in Azure. I need to block or restrict their access to the 'Microsoft.HDInsight' resource provider so that no one from that group can create these clusters.

- **Modularity and Extensibility:** Azure can easily design or introduce new services over time without affecting existing ones.

57. What is Azure Resource Manager (ARM)?

Ans:

- Azure Resource Manager (ARM) is a management framework provided by Microsoft Azure. In other words, ARM serves as the Azure-native platform for Infrastructure as Code (IaC), allowing us to manage Azure resources through code.
- It provides a management layer that enables us to create, update, and delete resources in our Azure account.
- When we send a request through any of the Azure APIs, tools, or SDKs, Azure Resource Manager receives the request, authenticates, and authorizes it before forwarding it to the relevant Azure service. As all requests are processed through the same API, we experience consistent results and capabilities across all the different tools.

Explore:

Below image illustrates the role of ARM in handling Azure requests.

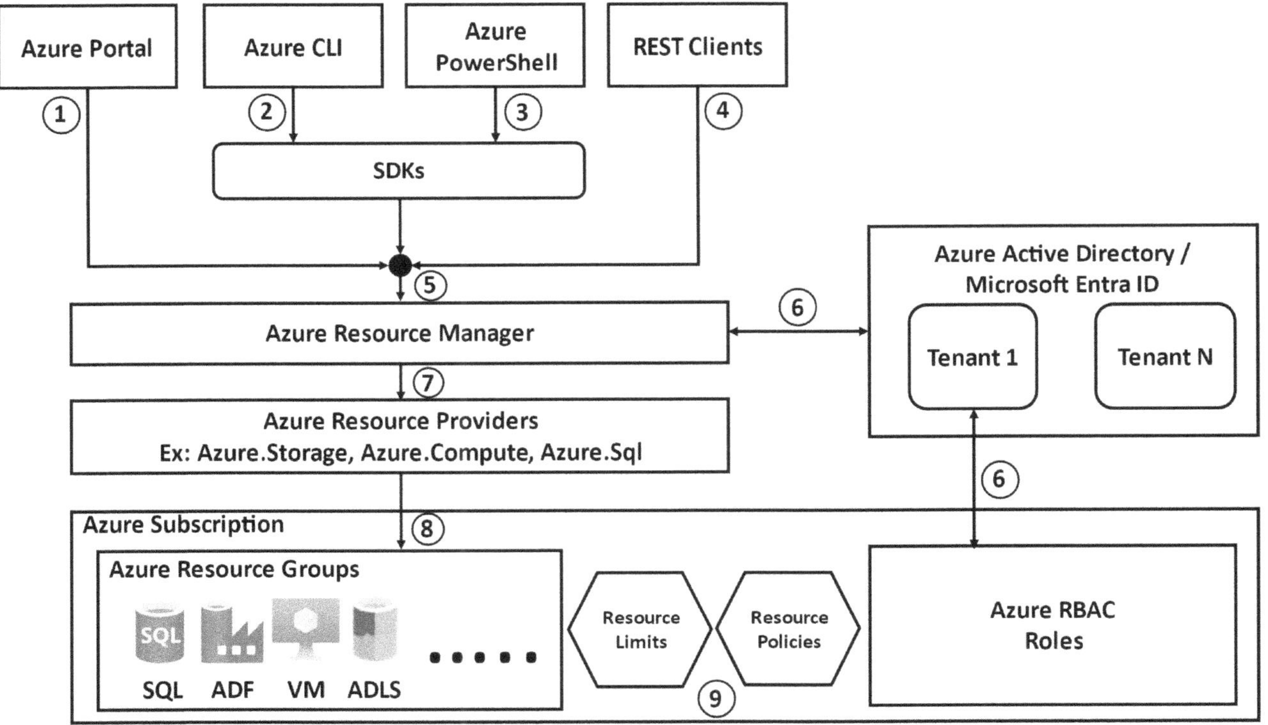

Image 1.3

ARM Workflow:

- **1, 2, 3, 4:** Requests are initiated from various APIs.
- **5:** All requests are directed to the Azure Resource Manager (ARM).
- **6:** ARM validates and authenticates the incoming requests.
- **7:** The ARM then redirects the requests to the appropriate resource provider.
- **8:** Based on the allowed permissions, the specified resource undergoes the requested action, such as Create, Delete, Update, etc.
- **9:** Before applying the operation, ARM validates the resource limitations and policies defined on the resource group.

***Note:**

- **SQL:** Azure SQL Database
- **ADF:** Azure Data Factory
- **VM:** Azure Virtual Machine
- **ADLS:** Azure Data Lake Storage
- **RBAC:** Role Based Access Control

Here are the key elements of ARM that we should understand:

- **Resource:** A manageable item that is available through Azure.
- **Resource Group:** A container that holds related resources for an Azure solution.
- **Resource Provider:** A service that supplies Azure resources.
- **Authentication:** When an API makes a request to Azure Resource Manager, it validates and authenticates with Entra ID.
- **Declarative Syntax:** Syntax that lets you state "Here's what I intend to create" without having to write the sequence of programming commands to create it. ARM templates and Bicep files are examples of declarative syntax. In those files, you define the properties for the infrastructure to deploy to Azure.
- **ARM Template:** A JavaScript Object Notation (JSON) file that defines one or more resources to deploy to a resource group, subscription, management group, or tenant.
- **Bicep file:** A file for declaratively deploying Azure resources. Bicep is a language that's been designed to provide the best authoring experience for infrastructure as code solutions in Azure.

58. What is Infrastructure as Code (IaC)?

Ans:

- IaC is the practice of creating, configuring and managing infrastructure through code.
- This code is generally written in a declarative language, such as JSON or YAML, and it describes the desired state of the infrastructure.
- When the code is executed, it creates or updates the infrastructure (VM, Network, Database, Storage Account etc.) to match the desired state.

- ARM Templates and Bicep files are the primary way of implementing IaC in Azure.
- By using IaC, we can easily manage our Azure infrastructure, share it with our team, and automate the provisioning and configuration of resources, reducing manual errors and promoting efficient collaboration.

Ex: We can simply create a JSON file to deploy and configure an Azure SQL Database including its name, region, size, collation, backup retention period, auditing settings, data encryption settings etc.

59. What is an ARM template, and how can we utilize it to deploy an Azure resource?

Ans:

- ARM Template is a JSON file that defines the infrastructure and resources to be deployed within Microsoft Azure.
- ARM Templates are used for automating and orchestrating the deployment and management of Azure resources.
- With ARM templates, we can specify various resource details, including names, locations, storage, security, network, and advanced settings, among others.
- Once a template is created, we can repeatedly use the same template to deploy identical resources, which is especially useful for distributed applications, testing, or development purposes.
- **Ex:** If you make an ARM template to create an Azure SQL Database, you can use that same template to create as many Azure SQL Databases as you want. Moreover, you can customize the template by sending different database properties and configurations from the script (PowerShell/Bash/Custom). This makes automation much easier and saves time.

Explore:

- **Deployment:** We can deploy Azure ARM templates using Azure Portal, Azure CLI, Azure PowerShell, Azure Cloud Shell, REST API, Azure DevOps, ARM Templates Visual Studio Code Extension.
- **Creating and Editing ARM Templates:** Azure Portal, Visual Studio Code (VS Code) with Azure Resource Manager Tools extension, Azure Cloud Shell etc.
- **Azure QuickStart Templates (Template Repository):** Azure QuickStart Templates is a community-contributed repository of sample ARM Templates covering a wide range of Azure services. We can use these templates as a starting point for our own projects.
- **ARM Template Test Toolkit:** It validates and checks whether our ARM template uses recommended practices, provides warnings, and makes recommendations. **Ex:** Validates the Schema, identifies and highlights hardcoded values, checks if outputs contain any secrets, and identifies blank spaces in a template etc.

60. Besides handling repetitive deployments, are there any additional benefits to using ARM templates?

Ans:

ARM templates provide several advantages beyond streamlining repetitive deployments:

- **Multiple Resource Deployment:** Deploy multiple resources together in a single unit. Resource Manager often deploys these resources in parallel, accelerating deployments compared to serial deployments.
- **Orchestration of Dependencies:** When resources have dependencies (one resource relies on another being created first), ARM templates eliminate the need to worry about complex deployment order. Resource Manager orchestrates the deployment of interdependent resources, ensuring they are created in the correct sequence.
- **Version Control Integration:** Since ARM templates are JSON files, they can be integrated with source control systems like Git, SVN, or TFS, allowing them to be managed just like any other application code file.
- **Extensibility with Scripts:** PowerShell or Bash scripts can be incorporated into your templates. These scripts can be included directly in the template or stored externally and referenced within it. Deployment scripts empower you to set up your entire environment in a single, unified ARM template.
- **Built-in Validation:** Resource Manager validates your ARM template before deployment, ensuring a higher chance of successful deployment.
- **Exporting Existing Templates:** There's no need to build a new ARM template from scratch by decoding JSON syntax. Once you have a well-tested and validated resource group, you can simply export the template from your existing environment. This exported template can then be used for subsequent deployments.

61. What is the difference between complete and incremental deployment modes in ARM?

Ans:

The deployment mode in an Azure Resource Manager (ARM) template determines how resources are deployed and managed within an Azure environment. There are two deployment modes:

- **Incremental Mode**: Only creates or updates the resources specified in the template, leaving all other resources untouched.
- **Complete Mode**: Creates or updates the resources specified in the template and deletes all other resources in the resource group.

Explore:

- **Incremental Deployment (Default):** In this mode, resources are deployed or updated incrementally without affecting existing resources that are not included in the template. If a resource already exists in the resource group but is not specified in the template, it remains untouched. This mode is typically used for production environments where you want to ensure that only the specified changes are applied without affecting other resources.

- **Complete Deployment:** In this mode, the entire resource group is deleted and then redeployed based on the contents of the template. This means that any resources not defined in the template are removed. It's like starting from scratch with only the resources specified in the template. This mode is useful for development or testing scenarios where you want to ensure a clean and consistent deployment environment.

Ex:

Let's assume:

- **Your resource group contains:** R1, R2, R3, R4
- **Your ARM template contains:** R1, R2, R5

After ARM template deployment, your resource group contains:

- **Incremental mode:** R1, R2, R3, R4, R5
- **Complete mode:** R1, R2, R5

***R:** Resource. Ex: Azure VM, Storage Account, SQL Database, VPN etc.

62. Do you have experience creating and deploying resources using ARM templates? Are you familiar with the different parts of an ARM template?

Ans:

Yes! Below are the main components of an ARM template:

- **Schema:** JSON file schema.
- **Content Version:** ARM template version.
- **Parameters:** Dynamic inputs that we can pass at the runtime.
- **Variables:** Helps us forming reusable expressions.
- **Functions:** We can create a function to handle more complex deployments.
- **Resources:** Type and properties of Azure resources that needs to be deployed or managed.
- **Output:** Resource deployment output.

Explore:

- **Schema**: The schema part tells Azure what version of the ARM template we're using. It's like a label that helps Azure understand the format we're using to describe our resources. Ex: "$schema": https://schema.management.azure.com/schemas/2023-08-01/sqlTemplate.json#.
- **Content Version**: The content version part is like a version number for the entire ARM template. It helps Azure keep track of changes and updates to the template itself. Ex: "contentVersion": "1.0.0.0".

- **Parameters:** Allows us to use the same template in different environments during deployment. **Ex:** Database Name, Server name, edition etc. In the below example, we are parameterizing the database edition. We can dynamically pass the edition while deploying the resource using Azure CLI, PowerShell code. By default, it takes "Standard" edition.
- "parameters": {

```
"databaseEdition": {
"type": "string",
"allowedValues": [
"Basic",
"Standard",
"Premium"
],
"defaultValue": "Standard",
"metadata": {
"description": "The edition of the Azure SQL Database."
}}}
```

- **Variables:** Variables can use values from parameters. **Ex:** In an ARM template, we may need to specify the location (Azure region) where the resources will be deployed. Since the same location is likely to be used for multiple resources, we can use a variable to store the location value and reference it across the resources. **"location": "[variables('location')]"**.
- **User-Defined Functions:** We can define customized elements to simplify templates. **Ex:** Functions can be used to generate resource names based on the naming convention rules. Or a UDF that can be used to generate a random password for the Azure SQL Database.
- **Resources:** Specifies Azure resources to be deployed. **Ex:**
    - **Azure SQL Database:** Microsoft.Sql/servers/databases;
    - **VM:** Microsoft.Compute/virtualMachines;
    - **Storage Account:** Microsoft.Storage/storageAccounts;
- **Outputs:** The return value of the deployed resource. Ex: serverName: The name of the Azure SQL Server that the database was created on; databaseName: The name of the Azure SQL Database that was created. Other: Number of resources created, status, resource ID & URL etc.

63. How to create and deploy an ARM Template?

Ans:

We can either create a new ARM file from scratch or find thousands of ARM templates from the Microsoft Azure Community repository. After importing the required ARM template, we can make the necessary changes and deploy it using one of the approaches, such as Azure Portal, Azure CLI, Azure PowerShell, Azure Cloud Shell, or VS Code, among others.

Azure Portal: Below are the steps to deploy a resource (Ex: Azure SQL Database) using an ARM template:

- Azure Portal > Create Resource > Template deployment > Load a template from file > Browse and upload the ARM template file > Specify all necessary parameters > Create

Azure PowerShell:

- New-AzResourceGroupDeployment -ResourceGroupName <resource-group-name>

  -TemplateFile <path_to_template_file>

Azure CLI:

- az deployment group create --resource-group <resource-group-name>

  --template-file <path-to-template>

Explore:

- **Azure QuickStart Template Gallery:** It is a collection of pre-built, reusable, and community-contributed templates provided by Microsoft. This gallery helps us quickly deploy and configure complex Azure solutions with just a few clicks.
- **Create an ARM Template from an existing resource:** We can make an ARM Template from a resource we already created. **Ex:** In the Azure Portal, if we have an Azure SQL Database that we want to use as a template, we can find an option called 'Export Template' which we can use it to download the ARM template into our local machine. With this template, we can easily deploy more Azure SQL Databases just like the one we exported.

***Note:** Don't worry too much about memorizing all these commands. In everyday work, the deployments are fully automated using CI/CD pipelines for different environments like Development, Testing, and Production. Just for your information, let's see the sample Azure PowerShell script to deploy an ARM template.

Azure Power Shell:

- **# Import the Azure PowerShell modules**
  - Import-Module Az
- **# Set the subscription ID and resource group**
  - $subscriptionId = "my-subscription-id"
  - $resourceGroupName = "abc-proj001-resource-group"
- **# Set the path to the ARM template file**
  - $templatePath = "D:\abcOrg\armRepo\azuresql-arm-template.json"
- **# Set the parameters for the ARM template**
  - $serverName = "MyServer"

    - $sqlDBName = "MyDatabase"
    - $location = "WestUS"
    - $databaseSize = "Standard_D1_v1"
- **# Deploy the ARM template by passing the parameters**
    - New-AzResourceGroupDeployment -ResourceGroupName $resourceGroupName
        - -TemplateFile $templatePath
        - -parameters
        - @{
            - serverName = $serverName
            - sqlDBName = $sqlDBName
            - location = $location
            - databaseSize = $databaseSize
    - }

64. Do you know what the 'ARM-Template What-If' operation is, and how it can be helpful?

Ans:

- A feature that allows testing and validation of the ARM template without applying it to the resources.
- It's an ARM feature that allows us to preview the outcome of an ARM template deployment without actually executing it.
- The what-if operation doesn't make any changes to existing resources. Instead, it predicts the changes if the specified template is deployed. Instead of executing the deployment directly, we run the "what-if" operation.
- It compares the current state of our resources with the target state described in the template.
- It creates a detailed output report showing what changes will happen if we use the template to deploy resources.
- The generated report includes information about resource creations, updates, deletions, ignored (no effect) and any potential conflicts or validation errors.

Explore:

- When we run a what-if operation, in outcome the operations are indicated with the symbols. Ex: Create (+), Delete (-) and Modify (~).
- We can execute ARM What-if operation using:
    - **Azure CLI:** az deployment group what-if
    - **Azure PowerShell:** New-AzResourceGroupDeployment -WhatIf
- **Ex:** Below is the sample outcome of an ARM What-if operation for deploying new Azure SQL Server and Database on it. Here + symbol indicates that we are adding new resource/property.

- + Microsoft.Sql/servers/myserver
  + Microsoft.Sql/databases/mydatabase
  + properties.edition: Standard
  + properties.service_objective: S1

- **Benefits of ARM What-if operation:**
  - **Validation and Testing:** We can run deployment tests without actually making any changes to the resources.
  - **Risk-Mitigation:** When dealing with complex production deployments, by previewing changes before actual deployment, we can identify and mitigate potential issues, conflicts, or unexpected changes.
  - **Compliance and Audit:** We can validate the proposed changes align with our compliance policies before applying them. Also, output generated by what-if operation can be useful for audits, reviews, or any future references.

65. What is YAML file?

Ans:

- YAML (Yet Another Markup Language or YAML Ain't Markup Language), is a human-readable data serialization language that is often used to define configuration files.
- YAML uses spacing and layout to show how different pieces of information are related to each other. This makes it simple for people to understand and write, and also makes it easy for computers to process and interpret the data.

Explore:

Use cases of YAML file in Azure:

- **CI/CD pipelines:** Azure DevOps or other CI/CD tools uses YAML files for storing pipeline configurations.
- **Infrastructure as Code (IaC):** YAML can be used to define Azure resources as code using tools like ARM templates or Azure Bicep.
- **Azure Data Factory:** YAML can be used to define the data pipelines and data transformation processes in Azure Data Factory.
- **Other:** For defining Azure Kubernetes Service manifests, Azure Functions etc.

66. Can we use YAML file instead of ARM templates for deploying Azure Resources?

Ans:

Yes, YAML files can be used instead of ARM templates, but it is not recommended!

- YAML is not a replacement for ARM templates and they serve different purposes.

- For general Infrastructure as Code (IaC) scenarios, ARM templates or Azure Bicep are the recommended approaches.
- YAML and ARM templates are very similar and the main difference is the syntax.
- YAML templates are easier to read and understand, while ARM templates are faster to deploy.

Explore:

Here is a sample that demonstrates the difference between YAML and JSON / ARM files:

YAML:

- resources:
    - name: SqlDb
    - type: Microsoft.Sql/databases
    - properties:
    - name: abcSqlDatabase
    - location: eastus
    - ....

JSON / ARM Template:

- {
    - “resources”: [
    - {
        - “name”: “SqlDb”,
        - “type”: “Microsoft.Sql/databases”,
        - “properties”:
            - {
                - “name”: “ abcSqlDatabase”,
                - “location”: “eastus”,
                - ....
            - }
    - }
    -]
- }

***Note:** We can observe the contrast in syntaxes. As our deployments become more detailed, the JSON format becomes more complicated. Hence, in certain cases, we can create a YAML file and then convert it into JSON or we can use Bicep files.

Convert YAML into JSON:

Some Azure resources need long and complex definitions, making it hard to understand with lots of nested brackets. In these scenarios we can write our templates in YAML and then convert them to JSON when we're ready to deploy. Here is the command to convert a .yaml file to .json file.

- yarm convert -i azureSqlDb.yaml -o azureSqlDb.json

***YARM:** A command-line tool to convert YAML templates to ARM templates and vice versa.

67. What are Bicep files? And when should we choose the right format between Bicep and ARM/ JSON?

Ans:

- Bicep is a Domain-Specific Language (DSL) developed by Microsoft for deploying Azure resources.
- Bicep files are designed to have a more user-friendly and readable syntax (similar to TypeScript) and to minimize the amount of code required.

Choose ARM Template:

- When you are already familiar with JSON and ARM templates and using it in your existing environment.
- If you are instantly looking for Infrastructure as Code (IaC) solution in Azure, then ARM templates are a good choice. They are easier to learn and understand.

Choose Bicep File:

- You should be aware that Azure is moving/promoting towards Bicep files.
- If you are looking for user-friendly language with more readable syntax then Bicep is the right choice.
- If you are planning to deploy your templates to multiple clouds, then Bicep files are a good choice. They are more portable than ARM templates.

Explore:

- Bicep files support all ARM template features such as parameters, variables, loops, functions etc.
- Similar to ARM templates, you can deploy a Bicep file using Azure CLI, Azure PowerShell, Azure Cloud Shell, or VS Code etc.
- Bicep files are inspired by YAML in terms of their readability and user-friendliness. While Bicep is not directly based on YAML syntax, it shares similar goals such as human-readable language.

JSON: We have already seen how it looks.

Bicep:

- resource sqlDatabase 'Microsoft.Sql/servers/databases@2024-01-01-preview' =
- {
    - name: abcSQLDatabase
    - parent: sqlServer
    - location: resourceGroup().location
    - properties: {
        - edition: 'Standard'
        - maxSizeBytes: 1073741824
        - ....
        - }
- }

68. Can you tell me what is Azure Resource Graph and how it can benefit my cloud management?

Ans:

Azure Resource Graph is a service that we can use to explore and analyze our entire Azure environment, providing deep insights into our resources and their configurations. Its capabilities include querying resources, resource change tracking, policy assessment, troubleshooting, cost optimization etc.

Explore:

- **Querying Resources:** We can query resources (using KQL) with complex filtering, grouping, aggregating, joining, and sorting by resource properties. This allows us to explore resources iteratively based on governance requirements.
- **Resource Inventory:** Explore and categorize resources based on specific criteria. **Ex:** Find all VMs running a specific OS version or all storage accounts with public access enabled.
- **Policy Assessment:** It helps assess the effect of applying policies in a vast cloud environment. We can understand how policies impact our resources.
- **Tracking Changes:** It allows us to query changes made to resource properties, helping us stay informed about modifications.
- **Troubleshooting:** Quickly identify misconfigured resources or diagnose performance issues. When issues arise, we can use Resource Graph to investigate resource properties, dependencies, and changes.
- **Security and Compliance:** Enforce security policies and ensure compliance with regulations.
- **Cost Optimization:** Analyze resource usage and identify opportunities for cost reduction.
- **Automation:** Automate resource management tasks based on specific criteria.
- **Reporting and Insights:** Gain valuable insights into your Azure environment for informed decision-making.

Note: KQL - Kusto Query Language.

69. If you are already using Azure Resource Graph, could you provide one or two use cases where Azure Resource Graph can be utilized?

Ans:

Here are the general Scenarios:

- Finding all virtual machines in a specific region that are not tagged for cost tracking.
- Grouping all storage accounts by their access tier and calculating total storage cost.
- Identifying all resources that haven't been accessed in the past 30 days.

Explore:

Additional scenarios from a database perspective where we can derive benefits from the Azure Resource Graph:

- Create an inventory of all our SQL databases across multiple subscriptions.
- Query for databases with public endpoints, weak authentication settings, or unencrypted connections.
- Query for databases with specific SKUs (Standard, Premium, etc.) to understand cost distribution.
- Optimize spending by identifying over-provisioned or underutilized resources.
- Check dependencies by querying firewall rules, or virtual network configurations. Understand how resources interact and troubleshoot connectivity issues.
- Query for modifications in database configurations, firewall rules, or access control.
- Identify databases or managed instances that are no longer in use.
- Query for resources with low activity or outdated versions.

70. Could you provide a sample KQL query in Azure Resource Graph that identifies the underutilized Azure SQL Databases specifically from the Business-Critical tier?

Ans:

Here is the sample KQL query:

- Resources
- | where type == 'microsoft.sql/servers/databases'
- | where properties.sku.tier == 'BusinessCritical'
- | extend avg_cpu_percent = todouble(properties.metrics.cpu_percent.Average)
- | extend avg_storage_percent = todouble(properties.metrics.storage_percent.Average)
- | where avg_cpu_percent < 20 and avg_storage_percent < 20
- | project databaseId = id, databaseName = name, avgCPU = avg_cpu_percent, avgStorage = avg_storage_percent

Explanation:

- Filter for databases of type microsoft.sql/servers/databases.
- Specifically target those in the BusinessCritical tier.
- Calculate the average CPU utilization and average storage utilization.
- The condition avg_cpu_percent < 20 and avg_storage_percent < 20 identifies databases with low utilization.
- It projects/displays databaseId, databaseName, avgCPU, and avgStorage

71. Could you provide a sample KQL query to pause Azure SQL Databases in the Development environment during off-business hours (between 8 PM and 6 AM) to effectively reduce costs?

Ans:

Here is the sample KQL query:

- resources
- | where type == ‘microsoft.sql/servers/databases’
- | where hour(currentTime()) > 20 or hour(currentTime()) < 6
- | where tags[‘Environment’] == ‘Development’
- | invoke(‘Microsoft.Sql/servers/databases/pause’, resourceId)

Explanation:

- Filter for databases of type microsoft.sql/servers/databases.
- Check if the current hour is greater than 20 (8:00 PM) or less than 6 (6:00 AM), which corresponds to off-hours.
- We further filter based on a tag named Environment with the value Development.
- Finally, we invoke the pause action on the identified databases.

***Note:** Don’t worry too much about memorizing these commands and scripts. Whether you’re a Cloud Admin, DBA, or Data Engineer, it’s essential to have a basic understanding of Azure Cloud Shell, Azure CLI, PowerShell, ARM, Bicep, YAML, KQL, Resource Graph etc. Just understand the concepts so you can discuss them confidently when asked in interviews.

72. What is the difference between Azure Resource Manager and Azure Resource Graph?

Ans:

- **Resource Manager:** It’s the hands-on tool for building and managing your Azure infrastructure. **Ex:** creating, deploying, deleting, and updating.
- **Resource Graph:** It’s the analytical tool for understanding and optimizing your existing Azure resources. **Ex:** Query and analyse resource configuration, utilization, and relationships.

Explore:

For example, we want to deploy a web app with related resources like a virtual machine, Database and storage account.

- **Resource Manager:** We use it to create and configure each resource individually, define their relationships, and set access control.
- **Resource Graph:** Later, we can use Resource Graph to find all resources belonging to this web app, analyze their performance metrics, and identify any underutilized resources for cost optimization.

73. As enterprise cloud customers, we use wide range of Azure services. We're aware that cloud services undergo maintenance. How Azure informs us about upcoming maintenance so we can plan our business accordingly?

Ans:

Azure provides several ways to inform customers about upcoming maintenance and planned service interruptions to help you plan your business accordingly. Here are the primary ways:

- **Azure Status Page:** Real-time health and status of Azure services worldwide.
- **Azure Service Health:** Health of the Azure services and regions we're using.
- **Azure Resource Health:** Health of our individual Azure resources.
- **Email Notifications:** Emails sent to subscribers about upcoming planned maintenance.

Explore:

- **Azure Status Page:** It is a public-facing website (https://azure.status.microsoft), so anyone can access it. The Status Page shows the status of all Azure services, as well as any known incidents or planned maintenance.
  - **To monitor:**
    - The status of all Azure services across the globe.
    - Known incidents or planned maintenance that may affect Azure services.
  - **Ex:** We can check for issues affecting Azure Virtual Machines, Azure Storage, Azure App Service, or other core services.
- **Azure Service Health:** It provides a more detailed view of the health of Azure services and regions you're using. The best way to use Service Health is to set up Service Health alerts to notify you via your preferred communication channels when service issues, planned maintenance, or other changes may affect the Azure services and regions you use.

- **To Monitor:**
    - The health of your specific Azure subscriptions and resources.
    - Incidents, planned maintenance, and service health advisories for Azure services that you subscribed to.
- **Ex:** You can receive alerts and updates regarding issues affecting your Azure SQL Database, Azure Virtual Network, or Azure App Service instances.

- **Azure Resource Health:** It provides information about the health of individual Azure resources. This can be useful for troubleshooting problems with specific resources. Resource Health along with Azure Monitor notifications will help you stay better informed about the availability of your resources.
    - **To monitor:**
        - The health history of Azure resources that are part of your applications.
        - The impact of incidents or planned maintenance on your Azure resources
    - **Ex:** You can check if a particular virtual machine is running smoothly, diagnose connectivity problems with a specific storage account, or determine whether a database is experiencing any performance issues.
- **Email notifications:** Azure will send email notifications (in general 72 hours' notice) to the subscription owners and admins about upcoming planned maintenance. These notifications will include information about the affected services, the start and end times of the maintenance, and any steps that we need to take to prepare.

74. What are Azure Advisor and Azure Monitor?

Ans:

- **Azure Advisor:** It is a service designed to provide best practices and recommendations for optimizing your Azure resources.
- **Azure Monitor:** Azure Monitor is an Azure native centralized monitoring solution for collecting, analyzing, and responding to monitoring data from your cloud and on-premises environments.

Explore:

Azure Advisor: It provides personalized recommendations to help us optimize your Azure resources. It uses machine learning to analyze your Azure environment and identify areas where you can improve.

- **Use Case:** It analyses your Azure environment and gives you the action recommendations to improve the efficiency, security posture, cost management, performance and high-availability of our Azure environment.

- **Ex:**
  - Downsizing an over-provisioned virtual machine or deleting unused resources.
  - Enabling multi-factor authentication for user accounts or applying network security group rules.
  - Scaling up a database to handle increased load.
  - Deploying resources across multiple Azure regions for redundancy.

Azure Monitor: It collects telemetry data from various sources, including Azure resources and custom applications. It offers advanced monitoring, alerting, and visualization capabilities. It provides a wide range of features including metrics, logs, alerts, dashboards, notebooks etc.

- **Use Case:** It can be used by organizations of all sizes to monitor their Azure resources. It helps us in real-time monitoring, performance optimization, diagnosing & troubleshooting issues, security monitoring etc.
- **Ex:**
  - Azure Monitor provides insights into database query performance, helping us optimize SQL queries for better application performance.
  - We can use it to analyze application logs to identify the root cause of performance problems.
  - It can trigger alerts when CPU usage on a virtual machine exceeds a certain threshold.
  - It can detect abnormal login activities and alert you to potential security threats.

75. As a large organization, we extensively utilize various Azure services. Given Azure's continuous innovation and development, new features are introduced, and older ones may be deprecated or retired. How can we identify the deprecated services or features in our Azure subscription?

Ans:

- Normally, notifications regarding the retirement of services or features are conveyed to customers through **email**, the **Azure update site**, or via **Azure Service Health**.
- Azure has recently introduced a new feature known as the '**Service Retirement Workbook**' within Azure Advisor. This feature offers a centralized resource-level view of service retirements and assists us in evaluating the impact, exploring migration options, and planning for the transition.
- To prevent service disruptions, it is essential to review and migrate any affected resources before the retirement date.

76. What is "Azure Updates" page?

Ans:

We can use it to get the latest updates on Azure products and features to meet our cloud investment needs. It provides information about:

- Latest announcements about Azure products, features, APIs, and tools.
- New Azure technologies that can be useful for our immediate and future business needs.
- Changes and enhancements to the Azure offerings that we are currently using

77. What do you know about Azure Blueprints?

Ans:

- Azure Blueprints are a governance tool that allows you to define and enforce standards for Azure resources. They provide a way to create and manage consistent environments across multiple subscriptions and resource groups.
- Azure Blueprints are a powerful feature in Microsoft Azure that allow cloud architects and central IT groups to define a repeatable set of Azure resources following to an organization's standards, patterns, and requirements.
- Blueprints essentially allows you to package up a set of pre-configured resources & resource groups, security policies, and access controls into a single blueprint definition. This blueprint can then be reused to quickly and consistently deploy new Azure environments that meet your organization's specific requirements.

Explore:

Key Features of Azure Blueprints

- **Environment Setup:** Azure Blueprints help with environment setup, which typically includes resource groups, ARM templates, policies, and role assignments. A blueprint is a package that brings together these different artifact types, allowing you to compose and version the package.
    - **Resource Groups**: Create a new resource group for use by other artifacts within the blueprint. These placeholder resource groups enable you to organize resources exactly the way you want them. **Ex:** based on the business requirement, resource group is designed by combining VMs, storage accounts, Azure SQL Databases, etc.
    - **ARM Templates**: Define and describe infrastructure and policies using ARM templates.
    - **Policy Assignments**: Allows assignment of a policy or initiative to the subscription the blueprint is assigned to. **Ex:** Assigning security policies requiring VMs to be encrypted at rest or enforcing strong password policies. Blueprints can define network security group (NSG) rules that block inbound traffic to specific ports or protocols etc.
    - **Role Assignments**: Add an existing user or group to a built-in role to make sure the right people always have the right access to your resources. Role assignments can be defined for the entire subscription or nested to a specific resource group included in the blueprint.
- **CI/CD:** You can use continuous integration and continuous delivery (CI/CD) pipelines to manage blueprints.

- **Versioning:** Keep track of different versions of a blueprint, allowing for easier updates and rollbacks. The relationship between the blueprint definition (what should be deployed) and the blueprint assignment (what was deployed) is preserved, enabling better tracking and auditing of deployments.
- **Subscription Management**: Apply blueprints to multiple subscriptions for standardized deployments across the organization.

78. Can you share one or two scenarios where using Azure Blueprints can be beneficial?

Ans:

Here are some practical examples of how Azure Blueprints can be used:

- **Standardized Environments:** A software development company can use blueprints to provide developers with pre-configured development environments that include necessary tools, libraries, and permissions.
- **Streamlined Global Deployments:** A multinational company can apply blueprints to new regional data centers to ensure they follow the same infrastructure standards and policies as existing locations, ensuring a seamless global operation.
- **Regulatory Compliance:** A financial or a healthcare institution can use Azure Blueprints to ensure all deployed environments comply with GDPR, HPAA and PCI-DSS standards by enforcing specific security policies and role assignments.

79. In cloud computing, are you familiar with the terms "vendor-agnostic" and "platform-agnostic"?

Ans:

Certainly!

- **Vendor-agnostic:** Compatible with multiple cloud providers.
- **Platform-agnostic:** Compatible with various operating systems and hardware.

Explore:

Vendor-agnostic hosting means that an application or service can run on various cloud service providers without being tied to any single one. This allows organizations to switch between cloud providers or use multiple providers simultaneously, depending on their needs.

- **Ex:** Company ABC offers a cloud-based file storage service. They have built their platform to be compatible with the APIs and services of multiple cloud providers (Ex: Azure, AWS, GCP etc.). This allows them to offer their file storage solution to customers who use any major cloud platform, without requiring the customer to switch providers.
- Examples of vendor-agnostic tools and services include Snowflake, Databricks, Apache Spark, and NetApp Storage etc.

Platform-agnostic hosting refers to the capability of an application or service to run on various operating systems, runtime environments, or hardware platforms. This means the application is designed to work across different platforms without requiring significant modifications.

- **Ex:** A company develops a Java or .Net based application that can run on any OS with a Java Virtual Machine (JVM). Whether the underlying OS is Windows, Linux, or macOS, the application will function correctly.

80. Is the public cloud really reliable? Although cloud service providers offer SLAs on service uptime, we still see global impacts when services go down. Is it really safe to trust the reliability of a cloud provider? What's your opinion on this?

Ans:

Public cloud platforms offer a very high degree of reliability when compared to traditional on-premise infrastructure. However, it's not about blind trust but about understanding the shared responsibility model and implementing best practices to build secure and resilient cloud solutions. By choosing a reputable provider and taking proactive measures, you can significantly enhance the reliability of your cloud environment.

Explore:

Public cloud providers like Azure, AWS, and Google Cloud have indeed established high levels of reliability and service availability, but it is true that no system can be completely immune to outages or disruptions.

Outages:

There have been instances of global service outages, but they are relatively rare and are usually addressed promptly by the cloud providers. For example:

- **2017 - Mistyped Command:** A human error during a routine debugging exercise on a public cloud service led to a major outage lasting several hours. This incident impacted major business customers and resulted in millions of dollars in losses.
- **2020 - Authentication Outage:** A critical authentication service failure in a public cloud platform prevented users from accessing any of their cloud resources for an extended period.
- **2023 - Power Surge:** A utility power surge caused a partial cooling system failure in a public cloud data center located in Southeast Asia. This resulted in a major regional outage that lasted several hours, impacting businesses critical operations relying on that provider.
- **2023 - Routing Change Error:** A public cloud provider deployed a faulty routing change within their Wide Area Network (WAN). This error triggered a global outage affecting email and storage services for 5-6 hours. Businesses worldwide were unable to send/receive emails and access cloud storage content, causing significant disruption.

- **2024 - Security update on Windows**: It caused a significant global impact on IT systems and businesses, including those relying on cloud services. While the cloud services themselves weren't the root cause, the update affected their functionality.
- **Reasons:** While some outages are caused by events like hardware failures, power grid issues, and weather conditions, many stem from human error.

However, public cloud providers have invested heavily in creating highly reliable and resilient infrastructures. They employ multiple strategies to ensure high availability, including redundancy, failover mechanisms, robust disaster recovery plans and regular maintenance and updates.

Traditional Infrastructure vs. Public Cloud:

- When compared to traditional on-premises infrastructure, public cloud services often provide better reliability. On-premises solutions require significant investment in redundancy, failover systems, and maintenance, which can be cost-prohibitive for many organizations. Public cloud providers offer these capabilities at a scale and cost that individual organizations usually cannot match.

Shared Responsibility:

- Reliability also involves a shared responsibility model. While cloud providers are responsible for the underlying infrastructure, it's crucial for customers to architect their applications and services for resilience. This includes using multiple regions, implementing backup and disaster recovery strategies, and regularly testing failover procedures.

My opinion:

- In my opinion, while no system is infallible, the reliability offered by public cloud providers is generally superior to most on-premises setups. Trusting a cloud provider for reliability is reasonable, but it's also important to design your systems to handle potential disruptions gracefully.
- For large enterprises, we always recommend architecting systems using a hybrid cloud architecture. This approach allows for critical workloads to be distributed across both public and private clouds, mitigating risks and ensuring that essential services remain operational even if there is a disruption in the public cloud.

CHAPTER 02

Fundamentals of Azure Networking

1. Explain how network devices identify each other and communicate using concepts like MAC address, IP address, ARP, DHCP, DNS, broadcasts, and unicasts?

Ans:

- **MAC Address:** Unique hardware identifier (physical address) for a network interface card.
- **IP Address:** An assigned logical address for a device on a network.
- **ARP:** Maps IP addresses to MAC addresses within a local network.
- **Gratuitous ARP:** Special ARP broadcast to announce or update information about a device's IP and MAC addresses.
- **DHCP:** Automatically assigns IP addresses and network settings to devices.
- **DNS:** Translates domain names to IP addresses.
- **Broadcast:** Sends network traffic to all devices in a local network segment.
- **Unicast:** Sends network traffic directly between a specific sender and receiver.

Explore:

MAC (Media Access Control) Address:

- Every device that connects to a local network has a unique MAC address also known as physical machine address.
- Think of it as a permanent identification number assigned to the network interface card (NIC) of your device (laptop, phone, etc.).
- It's a 12-digit alphanumeric code (like 00:1A:2B:3C:4D:5E) burned into the hardware and unique to each device.

IP Address (Internet Protocol Address): This is another identifier assigned to your device on a network, but unlike the MAC address, it can be temporary.

ARP (Address Resolution Protocol):

- ARP is a protocol used to map an IP address to a device MAC address.
- Devices use IP addresses to talk to each other, but they also need MAC addresses to send data directly.
- Here's how ARP works:
    - A device wants to send data to another device on the network using its IP address.

  - The device broadcasts an ARP request on the network asking "Who has this IP address (Ex: 192.168.X.XXX)?".
  - The device with the matching IP address (Ex: your laptop or a Server) hears the request and responds with its MAC address.
  - Now, the first device has the MAC address it needs and can send the data directly to the intended recipient.

Gratuitous ARP:

- This is a special type of ARP message sent by a device to announce its presence or update its IP-to-MAC address mapping on the network.
- A device might send a gratuitous ARP:
  - After its IP address has changed (Ex: Renewing a lease with DHCP).
  - When it joins a new network.
  - To periodically remind other devices of its presence.

DHCP (Dynamic Host Configuration Protocol):

- DHCP is a network protocol that automates the assignment of IP addresses and other configuration parameters to devices on a network.
- It operates on a client-server model where devices requesting an IP address (DHCP clients) contact a DHCP server to obtain lease agreements for IP addresses and additional network settings like subnet mask and default gateway.
- DHCP helps manage IP address allocation efficiently and simplifies network administration by automating this process.

DNS (Domain Name System):

- DNS is a hierarchical and distributed naming system for computers, services, or any resource connected to the internet.
- It translates human-readable domain names (like www.abc.com) into machine-readable IP addresses (like 192.168.1.1).
- DNS servers act as a directory, resolving domain names to IP addresses and vice versa, enabling users to access resources on the internet using memorable names instead of complex numerical addresses.

Broadcast (One-to-All):

- A broadcast is a network transmission technique where a data packet is sent to all devices on a network segment.
- All devices on the segment receive the broadcast message, regardless of whether it's intended for them.

- Broadcasts are typically used for network discovery protocols like ARP (Address Resolution Protocol) or sending network alerts to all devices.
- Due to potential inefficiency caused by sending data to all devices, broadcasts are generally not preferred for regular communication.

Unicast (One-to-One):

- Unicast is a network transmission technique where a data packet is sent from a single source device to a single destination device identified by its unique MAC address.
- This is the most common method for communication on a network as it delivers data efficiently and directly to the intended recipient.
- Unicast communication requires knowing the recipient's MAC address, which is typically obtained through ARP prior to data transmission.

To make things clear, let's use a college campus analogy:

- **MAC Address:** Your student ID (unique and unchanging).
- **IP Address:** Your hostel room number (assigned, can change if you move).
- **ARP:** Like a campus directory that helps find people by ID (MAC) based on hostel room (IP).
- **Gratuitous ARP:** You moving in and letting everyone know your new room number (like a device announcing its new IP).
- **DHCP:** The hostel admin office (assigns rooms/IP addresses).
- **DNS:** The department directory (maps department names to building codes/IP addresses).
- **Broadcast:** A campus-wide announcement like a fire alarm (all staff/students/devices hear it).
- **Unicast:** A professor calling a specific student to their office (direct message to one device).

2. Do you know the difference between a Public IP and Private IP?

Ans:

- **IP Address:** An IP (Internet Protocol) address is a unique address that identifies a device on the internet or a local network.
- **Public IP (Globally Unique):** They are routable on the internet. Which means that they can be used to access devices from anywhere on the internet. **Ex:** Web server, Email server, IoT device etc.
- **Private IP (Unique to the local network):** They are not routable on the internet. Which means that they can only be used to access devices within a private network. Since it is unique within each private network, the same private IP can be used in multiple private networks. **Ex:** Local Area Network, Virtual Machines in a Private Network, Nodes in a cluster, Database servers etc. are the typical examples where we use Private IP addresses.

3. Do you have any idea about Network Address Translation (NAT)? If yes, could you please explain what it is?

Ans:

Network Address Translation (NAT):

- NAT is a technique used to map multiple private addresses inside a local network to a single public IP address for communication with the internet.
- NAT allows multiple devices within a private network to share a single public IP address when communicating with devices outside the private network, such as the internet.
- **SNAT (Source NAT):** It maps a private IP to a public IP when traffic is going from the private network to the internet.
- **DNAT (Destination NAT):** It maps a public IP to a private IP when traffic is coming from the internet to a private network.

Explore:

Consider the below example:

On our home network, we have several devices like computers, smartphones, and other smart devices, all connected to a single Wi-Fi router. Each device on our home network is assigned a private IP address, which is unique within our local network but not globally unique on the internet. When a device wants to communicate with the internet, it needs to have a public IP address. However, our home network has only one public IP address assigned to our router. Let's see how NAT works here:

- **Outgoing Traffic – SNAT:** When we try to access a website from our mobile through a home Wi-Fi router, the router uses NAT to replace our mobile's private IP with the public IP of the router. This way, the web server sees the data packets are coming from our router's public IP address, and when it sends a response, it sends it back to our router's public IP.
- **Incoming Traffic - DNAT:** When the web server sends back the response to our router's public IP address, the router uses NAT again to replace the public IP address of the router with the private IP address of our mobile, which originally requested the web page. This way, the response reaches the correct device on our home network.

4. What is the difference between IPv4 and IPv6 IP addresses?

Ans:

IPv4 and IPv6 are two types of Internet Protocol. IPv4 (32-bit) is the older one, used a lot, while IPv6 (128-bit) is newer, fixing IPv4's limitations and giving more unique addresses for the growing internet.

Explore:

IPv4:

- IPv4 is the older and most widely used version of the Internet Protocol.
- IPv4 address is written as four sets of decimal numbers separated by periods / dots. Ex: 192.168.1.1.
- It uses 32-bit addresses. Each of the four decimal numbers in an IPv4 address represents 8 bits of data. **Ex:** 4 Decimal Numbers X 8 Bits = 32 Bits
- 192.168.1.1 >> Binary Numbers >> 11000000.10101000.00000001.00000001
- IPv4 can accommodate approximately 4.3 billion unique IP addresses.
- IPv4 addresses are running out because of the internet's fast growth and the many devices joining it, so IPv6 was created to solve this problem.

IPv6:

- IPv6 is the newer version designed to replace IPv4.
- IPv6 addresses are written in 8 sets of hexadecimal notations separated by colons. Ex: 2001:0db8:85a3:0000:0000:8a2e:0370:7334. Also, we can use "::" to represent the series of consecutive zeros - 2001:0db8:85a3::8a2e:0370:7334.
- It uses 128-bit addresses. Each of the eight hexadecimal numbers in an IPv6 address represents 16 bits of data. Ex: 8 Hexadecimal Numbers X 16 Bits = 128 Bits
- IPv6 can accommodate approximately 340,000 billion (340 undecillion) unique IP addresses.
- IPv6 is better than IPv4 because it has lots of unique addresses, works faster, and is more secure.

5. Are you familiar with the concepts of Classful IP Addresses and CIDR in networking?

Ans:

Traditional class-based addressing:

- IP addresses were divided into classes **Ex:** Class A, B, C, D and E.
- The number of hosts that could be assigned to each class is determined by the class of the address.
- Class A addresses could support up to 16 million hosts, Class B supports up to 65 thousand hosts while Class C addresses could only support up to 254 hosts.
- This system worked well for a while, but as the internet grew, it became clear that it was not sustainable. There were simply not enough IP addresses to go around.
- CIDR was introduced in 1993 to address this problem.

CIDR (Classless Inter-Domain Routing):

- It uses a different method of assigning IP addresses. Instead of dividing addresses into classes, CIDR uses a variable-length subnet mask (VLSM).

- This allows network administrators to create subnetworks of different sizes, which can be more efficient in terms of address utilization.

Explore:

Note:

- **Network Portion:** This part of the IP address identifies the specific network to which the device belongs. **Ex:** Office network, home network.
- **Host Portion:** This part of the IP address identifies the specific device (or host) within that network. **Ex:** Mobile, laptop, TV, VM, Server etc.
- **/n Notation**: The "/n" indicates that the first n bits are used for the network portion.

Old / Traditional Class-Based IP Addresses:

IP addresses are divided into five main classes: A, B, C, D, and E. Each class has a different range of addresses and is used for different purposes.

Class A:

- **IP Range:** 0.0.0.0 to 127.255.255.255
- **Representation:**
  - **Network Portion:** First 8 bits (the first octet)
  - **Host Addresses:** 24 bits (255.255.255).
  - **Ex:** 1.0.0.1/8, 10.0.0.5/8, 25.15.100.200/8, 50.100.150.200/8, 127.255.255.254/8 (these are sample addresses to help you understand).
- **Total Supported Hosts:** 2^24 - 2 = 16,777,214 hosts (subtracting 2 for network and broadcast addresses).
- **Use Case:** Multinational corporations

Class B:

- **IP Range:** 128.0.0.0 to 191.255.255.255.
- **Representation:**
  - **Network Portion:** First 16 bits (the first two octets).
  - **Host Addresses:** 16 bits (255.255).
  - **Ex:** 128.0.0.1/16, 128.0.10.2/16, 150.150.0.1/16, 150.150.0.10/16, 191.255.255.254/16.
- **Total Supported Hosts:** 2^16 - 2 = 65,534 hosts (subtracting 2 for network and broadcast addresses).
- **Use Case:** Medium-sized organizations.

Class C:

- **IP Range:** 192.0.0.0 to 223.255.255.255.
- **Representation:**
  - **Network Portion:** First 24 bits (the first three octets)
  - **Host Addresses:** 8 bits (255).
  - **Ex:** 192.0.0.1/24, 192.0.0.2/24, 200.100.100.1/24, 200.100.100.2/24, 223.255.255.254/24
- **Total Supported Hosts:** 2^8 - 2 = 254 hosts (subtracting 2 for network and broadcast addresses)
- **Use Case:** Smaller organizations and home networks.

Class D:

- **IP Range:** 224.0.0.0 to 239.255.255.255.
- **Use Case:** Reserved for multicast like Live streaming video casting.

Class E:

- **IP Range:** 240.0.0.0 to 255.255.255.255.
- **Use Case:** Reserved for experimental and research purposes.

***Note:** Class D and E are not used for general networking scenarios.

CIDR:

- It is a modern networking technique that allows for more flexible allocation and routing of IP addresses compared to the traditional class-based IP addressing system.
- In the traditional class-based system, IP addresses were divided into fixed classes, each with a predefined range of addresses. This led to inefficient use of IP address space and challenges in routing.
- CIDR allows for variable-length subnet masks, which means that IP address blocks can be divided into smaller, more manageable subnets, regardless of the original class boundaries.
- This allows network administrators to allocate IP addresses more efficiently based on their actual needs and improve routing efficiency.
- CIDR notation represents IP addresses with a combination of the IP address itself and a prefix length.
- **Ex:** A "Class C" address with a subnet mask of 255.255.255.0/24 can support up to 254 hosts. However, if a network administrator only needs to support 100 hosts, they can use a subnet mask of /25. Here are the details.
  - **Network Address Example:** 192.168.1.0/25.
  - **Network Portion:** 192.168.1 (first three octets + first bit of the last octet). Total 25 Bits.
  - **Host Portion:** Remaining 7 bits of the last octet.
  - **Total IP Addresses:** 2^7 = 128.
  - **Usable IP Addresses:** 128 - 2 = 126 (subtracting 2 for network and broadcast addresses).

  - **Supports:** Up to 126 hosts.
  - **Usable Host Range:** 192.168.1.1 to 192.168.1.126.

- This subnet mask allows for up to 126 hosts, which comfortably supports the requirement of 100 hosts while providing room for growth and additional devices.
- In the classful model, network administrators were forced to allocate the entire block of 254 IP addresses, even if they only needed a fraction for their network (Ex: 100 hosts). CIDR addressed this inefficiency by allowing the creation of smaller, more flexible subnets.

Real world analogy:

- **Classic Approach:** We reserved a vast park for our party. However, this space is so extensive that certain areas might remain unused, while others could become excessively crowded.
- **Utilizing CIDR:** We efficiently organized the expansive area by separating distinct sections such as the "Salad Corner," "Dessert Spot," "Drinks Corner," "Games Zone," "Veg," "Non-Veg," and more. Each section is carefully sized according to its intended purpose and expectations, allowing for precise planning and coordination.

6. What is a CIDR notation?

Ans:

CIDR notation represents an IP address and a suffix that indicates network identifier bits in a specified format. CIDR notation consists of an IP address followed by a forward slash ("/") and a number, which represents the number of significant bits in the routing prefix. These significant bits indicate the network portion of the address, while the remaining bits represent the host portion.

Ex: CIDR notation 192.168.1.0/24 means that the first 24 bits of the address (192.168.1) are used for the network portion, and the remaining 8 bits (.0) are used for the host portion.

Explore:

For DBAs, SQL developers, or Data Engineers who are new to networking, it is highly recommended to grasp the CIDR notation, as we frequently utilize it when working with Cloud resources.

Let's say we have a range of IP addresses from 192.168.10.0 to 192.168.10.255. To represent this range in CIDR notation, we need to find the common bits in the addresses:

- IP Address 1: 192.168.10.0 (11000000.10101000.00001010.00000000)
- IP Address 2: 192.168.10.255 (11000000.10101000.00001010.11111111)

In binary form, the common bits are "11000000.10101000.00001010", which corresponds to 24 bits. This means the first 24 bits are used to define the network, and the remaining 8 bits can be used for individual host addresses within that network. Hence, the CIDR notation for this range of IP addresses would be: 192.168.10.0/24.

Imagine we have an organization with a building using the IP address range of 192.168.10.0/24.

- **Network Address:** It represents the beginning of the subnet or network segment. It is used to identify the network itself. In this case, 192.168.10.0 is the network address for the entire building.
- **Usable Host Addresses:** These are the individual addresses that can be assigned to devices within the organization's building. **Ex:** Computers, printers, phones, etc. These addresses are considered the "hosts" within the network. In this case 192.168.10.1 to 192.168.10.254 are the usable host addresses.

Below are the more examples:

- **CIDR Notation:** 192.168.10.0/24
  - Network Address: 192.168.10.0
  - Usable Host Addresses: 192.168.10.1 to 192.168.10.254
  - Total Hosts: 254
  - Broadcast Address: 192.168.10.255
- **CIDR Notation:** 10.0.0.0/8
  - Network Address: 10.0.0.0
  - Usable Host Addresses: 10.0.0.1 to 10.255.255.254
  - Total Hosts: 16 million
  - Broadcast Address: 10.255.255.255
- **CIDR Notation:** 172.16.0.0/16
  - Network Address: 172.16.0.0
  - Usable Host Addresses: 172.16.0.1 to 172.16.255.254
  - Total Hosts: 65,534
  - Broadcast Address: 172.16.255.255
- **CIDR Notation:** 192.168.100.0/28
  - Network Address: 192.168.100.0
  - Usable Host Addresses: 192.168.100.1 to 192.168.100.14
  - Total Hosts: 14
  - Broadcast Address: 192.168.100.15
- **CIDR Notation:** 172.31.0.0/20
  - Network Address: 172.31.0.0
  - Usable Host Addresses: 172.31.0.1 to 172.31.15.254
  - Total Hosts: 4,094
  - Broadcast Address: 172.31.15.255

7. Do you aware of subnet, subnet mask, supernet, routing, routing table, routing protocols, static and dynamic routing, default gateway in networking?

Ans:

- **Subnet:** A network within the network. Or a logical division within a larger network into smaller networks.
- **Subnet mask:** A 32-bit number to identify network and host IP addresses.
- **Supernet:** A larger network that is formed by combining two or more smaller networks or subnets.
- **Routers:** Devices that connect different networks together and route data packets between them.
- **Routing protocols:** Protocols that routers use to exchange routing information.
- **Routing tables:** Tables that store information about the routes to different networks.
- **Static or dynamic routing:** Methods of routing data packets between networks. Static routing is manually configured, while dynamic routing is automatically configured.
- **User defined Routes:** Custom routes that we can create to overwrite the Azure default routing
- **Default gateway:** The router that is used to route packets to destinations outside of the local network.

Explore:

- **IP Range:** A set of IP addresses that are allocated to a particular network or subnet.
- **Subnet:** The practice of dividing a larger network into smaller, more manageable segments called subnets. It is used to improve network efficiency, security, and organization. Subnetting allows us to logically group devices based on their geographical location, department, function, or any other criteria.
- **Subnet Mask:** A subnet mask is a 32-bit value and it is applied to an IP address to determine which part of the address represents the network and which part represents the host. It is represented in dotted decimal notation, such as 255.255.255.0. Each "255" represents 8 bits that are used for the network portion, and each "0" represents 8 bits that are used for the host portion. **Ex:** In the IP address 192.168.1.10 with a subnet mask of 255.255.255.0, the first 24 bits (3 octets) represent the network, and the last 8 bits (1 octet) represent the host.
- **Supernet:** It is the opposite of subnetting. It is the process of combining two or more subnets into a single larger subnet. This can be useful if you have a network that is not very large, but you need to conserve IP addresses.
- **Routing:** It is the process of sending data packets from one network to another.
- **Routers:** These are devices that connect different networks together and route data packets between them. Routers use the IP addresses of the hosts and the subnet masks to determine which network a data packet should be sent to. The router then forwards the data packet to the next router on the path to the destination host.

- **Routing Protocols:** Routing protocols are algorithms that are used by routers to communicate with each other and exchange routing information. **Ex:** RIP (Routing Information Protocol), OSPF (Open Shortest Path First), and BGP (Border Gateway Protocol).
- **Routing Table / Routing Information Base (RIB):** A routing table in networking is a data structure stored within a router or networking device. It serves as a crucial component for routing decisions, which determine the best path for data packets to travel from one network to another. When a router receives a data packet, it consults its routing table to determine the most appropriate route based on the destination IP address of the packet. A RIB or routing table may contain list of available routes, next-hop router (immediate next router), metrics (quality, cost, distance of the route) etc.
- **Static and Dynamic Routing:** Static routing involves manually configuring routing tables on routers, while dynamic routing protocols allow routers to automatically learn and update routes based on network changes.
- **User Defined Routes (UDR):**
    - When we deploy resources within an Azure VNet, the routing table is automatically managed by Azure, and traffic is routed according to default routes.
    - However, we can overwrite the Azure default routing with the UDR feature. It allows us to define and control the flow of network traffic between resources within our VNet or between our VNet and external destinations.
    - **Ex:** Redirect traffic through an advanced security firewall, support hybrid connectivity such as redirecting traffic from Azure VNet to on-premises network, route through Network Virtual Appliances such as load balancers etc.
- **Default gateway:** It is a router or other networking device that acts as a gateway between a local network and a larger network, such as the internet. When a computer on a local network wants to send a packet to a destination outside of the local network, it sends the packet to the default gateway. The default gateway then forwards the packet to the destination network.
- **Firewalls:** Devices that filter network traffic and prevent unauthorized access to a network.
- **Network Security Groups (NSGs):** Sets of security rules that control network traffic within a virtual network.

Sample Network Workflow:

Imagine I'm at work, using my laptop connected to the office network. When I send a web form to the end customer, let's find out how it goes through the network.

- I submit an online form using a web application from my laptop in the office network.
- My laptop is assigned an IP address and subnet mask by my office network. The subnet mask helps to determine which devices are on the same subnet as my laptop.
- The form data is broken into smaller data packets for transmission.
- The packets are encapsulated with source and destination IP addresses.

- Network Address Translation (NAT) might modify the source IP address to my office's public IP address.
- The packets pass through firewalls and Network Security Groups (NSGs), which enforce security policies.
- The packets reach our office's router.
- The router consults its routing table to determine the best path for the packets.
- If necessary, the router communicates with other routers using routing protocols to determine the optimal route.
- The packets traverse the internet, passing through various routers and networks.
- The router then sends the data packets to the next router in the path to the end customer. This process continues until the data packets reach the router that is closest to the end customer.
- The packets arrive at the end customer's network.
- The end customer's router directs the packets to the appropriate destination within their network.
- The destination server reassembles the packets and processes the form submission.

8. Suppose we have a company with a network utilizing the IP address range 192.168.1.0/24. Our task is to establish distinct subnets within this range. One subnet should have a minimum of 60 host IPs, while the other should accommodate only 10 IP addresses. Could you clarify the process of subnet creation?

Ans:

We have a company with a network that uses the IP address range 192.168.1.0/24. This means we have 256 IP addresses available (from 192.168.1.0 to 192.168.1.255), and the subnet mask is 255.255.255.0.

Let's see how we calculated the Subnet mask as 255.255.255.0:

- **IPv4 Address:** 32 bits (4 X 8 Bits)
- **IP Range:** 192.168.1.0/24
- **/24:** 24 Bits to identify the network and remaining 8 bits to identify the host
- **Subnet Mask:** We can create the Subnet Mask based on "/24". Which means the first 24 bits are set to 1 and the remaining 8 bits set to 0. Ex: 11111111.11111111.11111111.00000000. If we convert it into number, it will be 255.255.255.0

Two Subnets:

In this scenario, we want to divide our network into smaller logical segments. Let's say we have two departments: Sales and Marketing. To keep our network traffic separate, we decide to create two subnets:

- Subnet 1 (Sales): 192.168.1.0/26

- Subnet 2 (Marketing): 192.168.1.64/28

Each of these subnets will have its own set of IP addresses for devices within that department.

Subnet Mask:

Now, let's see how subnet mask looks like for the subnets defined:

- **Subnet 1:** 192.168.1.0/26
  - **Logic:** The first 26 bits are set to one, and the remaining 6 bits are set to zero.
  - **Binary:** 11111111.11111111.11111111.11000000
  - **Subnet Mask – Convert binary to number:** 255.255.255.192
  - **Formula to calculate the number of usable hosts:** In this subnet (.11000000), the first 2 bits of the last octet are used for subnetting, leaving 6 bits for host addressing. Formula = 2^6 – 2 = 64-2 = **62** IP Addresses
  - **Network Portion:** 192.168.1.0
  - **Usable Host Range:** 192.168.1.1 to 192.168.1.62
  - **Broadcast Address:** 192.168.1.63

- **Subnet 2:** 192.168.1.64/28
  - **Logic:** The first 28 bits are set to one, and the remaining 4 bits are set to zero.
  - **Binary:** 11111111.11111111.11111111.11110000
  - **Subnet Mask - Convert binary to number:** 255.255.255.240
  - **Formula to calculate the number of usable hosts:** In this subnet (.11110000), the first 4 bits of the last octet are used for subnetting, leaving 4 bits for host addressing. Formula = 2^4 – 2 = 16-2 = **14** IP Addresses
  - **Network Portion:** 192.168.1.64
  - **Usable Host Range:** 192.168.1.65 to 192.168.1.78
  - **Broadcast Address:** 192.168.1.79

Note: It's evident that we are allocating 62 addresses in the Sales subnet and 14 addresses in the Marketing subnet

9. Could you explain what ingress and egress traffic mean in the context of Azure Networking?

Ans:

These terms describe the traffic or data flow direction.

- **Ingress:** Traffic coming into our resource or network.
- **Egress:** Traffic going out from the resource or network.

Explore:

These terms are used to describe the direction of data flow or networking traffic between our Azure resources and the external world, including the internet and other Azure resources.

Ingress: It refers to incoming data or communication that enters your Azure resources (**Ex:** VNet or a VM) from external sources.

- **Ex:** Loading data from an on-premises database into Azure SQL Database. As data traffic flows into the Azure network from outside the environment, it is classified as ingress.

Egress: It refers to outgoing data or communication that leaves your Azure resources and is sent to external destinations.

- **Ex:** Exporting files from Azure Storage to an Amazon Web Services (AWS) S3 bucket. Since data is moving from the Azure network to another cloud service provider, it falls under the category of egress.

10. Could you explain the difference between the Azure Backbone Network and the Azure Global Network? Do these terms convey the same concept?

Ans:

Yes, the Azure backbone network and the Azure global network refer to the same thing.

The Azure backbone/global network is the network of physical and virtual resources that connect Microsoft's Azure data centers around the world. It is a high-speed, low-latency and highly available network that is designed to provide reliable and secure connectivity for Azure services.

- **Azure Backbone Network:** More commonly used to refer to the physical network infrastructure.
- **Azure Global Network:** More commonly used to refer to the entire network (physical + virtual).

Explore:

Microsoft has built a global network of data centers located around the world. These data centers are interconnected by the Azure backbone, allowing data to traverse efficiently across geographical distances. Azure Backbone/Global Network consists of:

- **Physical Network Infrastructure:** Optic cables, routers, switches, load balancers, firewalls etc.
- **Virtual Networking:** Virtual networks, subnets, Setwork Security Groups, Azure ExpressRoute and Virtual WAN etc.
- **Routing protocols:** Routing Information Protocol (RIP), Border Gateway Protocol (BGP), Open Shortest Path First (OSPF), Intermediate System to Intermediate System (IS-IS) etc.

11. What is Azure Virtual Network (VNet)?

Ans:

- Azure VNet is similar to a traditional network that we would operate in our own data center. Azure VNet enables us to create a private, isolated network in the cloud.
- A VNet is made up of subnets, which are smaller logical networks within the VNet. Subnets can be used to group resources together and to control how they can communicate with each other.
- We can connect VMs, Databases, services, and other Azure resources to the VNet for secure communication.

Explore:

Suppose we are working on a web application that needs to be hosted in the Azure cloud. We want to ensure that our web application's components, such as the web servers, application servers, and databases, can communicate with each other securely while being isolated from other Azure resources. Here is the workflow:

- Create a VNet.
- Define separate subnets for Web Servers, Application Servers and Databases.
- Deploy web servers in the "WebServers" subnet, and a database server in the "Database" subnet etc.
- Configure Network security to control the traffic flow between the subnets.

12. What is a VPN Gateway in Azure Networking?

Ans:

- A Virtual Private Network (VPN) Gateway is a networking service that provides a secure and encrypted connection between two virtual networks.
- **Ex:** it can establish a connection between our on-premises network and an Azure VNet, or between two Azure VNets.
- It enables us to establish a private and secure communication channel over the public internet or dedicated connections.

Explore:

Azure VPN Gateway supports multiple VPN protocols. Here are the protocols along with example scenarios:

- **Site-to-Site (S2S) VPN:** This VPN connects our on-premises network to an Azure VNet. It's useful for:
    - Meeting connection requirements for a branch office to access central office resources.

    - Enabling on-premise to Azure connectivity, making Azure resources appear as if they're part of the same network as on-premise.
- **Point-to-Site (P2S) VPN:** With this VPN, individual client devices can connect to an Azure VNet. It's beneficial for:
    - Allowing remote workers to securely access Azure resources from their homes.
    - Enabling training teams or customer support teams to access Azure resources from their personal mobile devices through a P2S VPN Gateway.
- **VNet-to-VNet VPN:** This type of VPN connects two or more Azure VNets securely.
    - Connect the QA and DEV VNets to facilitate data transformation and application deployments.
    - Establish cross-region VNet connections to provide a global Disaster Recovery solution.

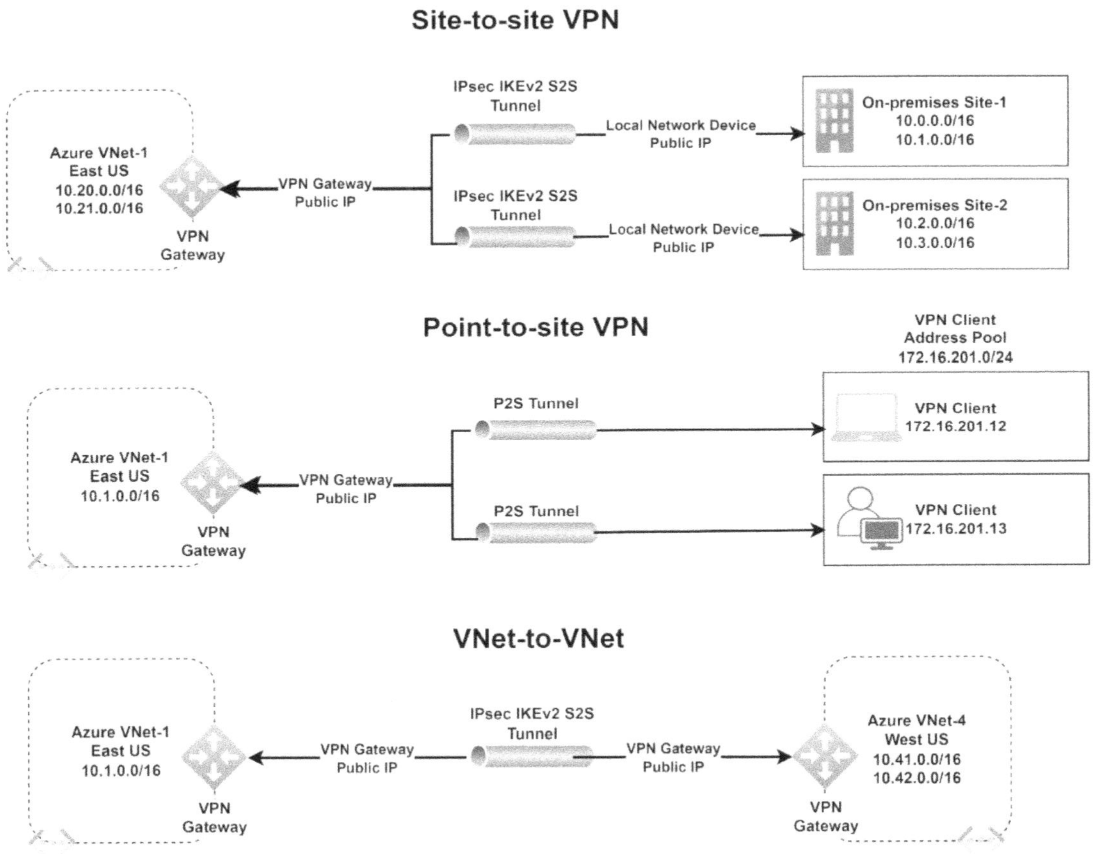

Image 2.1

13. What are the available network connectivity features in Azure for connecting two networks, whether within the Azure backbone or between Azure and on-premises?

Ans:

Azure offers various network connectivity options, and we need to select the appropriate one based on its features and our business use case. Below are the options:

- **VNet-to-VNet:** Creates a secure connection between Azure virtual networks (VNets).
- **VNet peering:** Creates a secure connection between Azure VNets that are in the same region.
- **Global VNet Peering:** Creates a secure connection between Azure VNets that are in different regions.
- **Site-to-Site (IPsec):** Creates a secure connection between our on-premises network and Azure using IPsec.
- **ExpressRoute:** Creates a dedicated private connection between our on-premises network and Azure.
- **ExpressRoute Global Reach:** Extend private connectivity across regions for communication between datacentres through a single ExpressRoute circuit.
- **Azure Virtual WAN:** Provides a global network for connecting our VNets, on-premises networks, and remote users.
- **Azure Private Link:** Securely access Azure services privately from our virtual network.

Explore:

VNet-to-VNet:

- A type of VPN connection that allows us to connect two virtual networks (VNets) in Azure. This enables resources in different virtual networks to communicate with each other as if they were part of the same network.
- **Choose it when:** We need to connect two VNets that are in the same Azure region. It also supports connecting Cross-Region VNets; however, it can't deliver the high-performance as other options.
- **Use case:** We can use it to securely connect our Dev, Test and Production VNets, allowing developers to access resources in the testing or production network without exposing them directly to the development network.
- **Bandwidth** – Up to 10 GBPS |**Scope:** Single Region| **Traffic** – Azure Backbone | **Cost**- Free.

VNet peering:

- A type of connection that allows us to connect two VNets in Azure that are in the same region.
- **Choose it when:** We want to enable seamless and efficient communication between resources in different virtual networks within the same region.
- **Use case:** We have separate virtual networks for our front-end web application and back-end database. VNet peering can be used to connect these VNets, allowing the web servers to communicate directly with the database servers without exposing them to the public internet.
- **Bandwidth** – Up to 100 GBPS | **Scope:** Single Region| **Traffic** – Azure Backbone | **Cost**- Free.

Global VNet Peering:

- A type of connection that allows us to connect two VNets in Azure that are in different regions. This provides a global network connectivity solution for multi-region architectures.

- **Choose it when:** We need to connect two VNets that are in different regions and we need the same level of security as a VPN connection.
- **Use case:** In a multinational corporation, we can use Global VNet Peering to connect networks form regional offices. **Ex:** Connecting a VNet that hosts your European datacentre to a VNet that hosts your Asian datacentre.
- **Bandwidth** – Up to 100 GBPS | **Scope:** Multi-Region| **Traffic** – Azure Backbone | **Cost**- Free.

Site-to-Site (IPsec):

- A type of VPN connection that allows us to connect our on-premises network to Azure. It enables communication between resources in the on-premises network and Azure as if they were part of the same network.
- **Choose it when:** We need to connect our on-premises network to Azure for hybrid cloud deployments, disaster recovery, or to connect to Azure services that are not available on-premises.
- **Use case:** Connecting our corporate headquarters to our Azure datacentre.
- **Bandwidth** – Up to 10 GBPS | **Scope:** Single Region| **Traffic** – Over VPN Tunnel (Internet) | **Cost**- Depends on the bandwidth and location.

ExpressRoute:

- A dedicated private connection between our on-premises network and Azure Datacentre. This connection is established over a high-speed, low-latency link.
- **Choose it when:** We need a high-bandwidth, high-security and low-latency connection to Azure.
- **Use case:** A financial institution handling sensitive customer data might use ExpressRoute to establish a dedicated and secure connection to Azure.
- **Bandwidth** – Up to 100 GBPS | **Scope:** Single Region| **Traffic** – Dedicated private link | **Cost**- Depends on the bandwidth and location.

ExpressRoute Global Reach:

- A feature of ExpressRoute that allows us to connect to multiple Azure regions through a single ExpressRoute circuit.
- **Choose it when:** We need to establish private and high-speed communication between multiple on-premises datacentres in different regions with Azure Datacentres located in different regions.
- **Use case:** A manufacturing company with production facilities in different countries might use ExpressRoute Global Reach to connect its regional datacentres. This enables real-time data synchronization, central monitoring, and coordination of manufacturing processes across multiple locations.
- **Bandwidth** – Up to 100 GBPS |**Scope:** Multi-Region| **Traffic** – Dedicated private link |**Cost**- Depends on the bandwidth and location.

Azure Virtual WAN:

- A managed service that provides a global network for connecting our VNets, on-premises networks, and remote users. It simplifies networking connectivity and provides optimized, automated, and secure routing between Azure VNets and on-premises networks. We can think of virtual WAN like an umbrella which includes lots of services including connections to Azure ExpressRoute and VPN.
- **Choose it when:** We need to connect a large number of VNets and on-premises networks in a global scale.
- **Use case:** Connecting all of our company's VNets and on-premises networks in a single global network. **Ex:** A retail chain with multiple stores might use Azure Virtual WAN to connect its store locations to a centralized datacentre.
- **Bandwidth** – Up to 100 GBPS | **Scope:** Global (Multi-Region) | **Traffic** – Azure Backbone | **Cost**- Depends on the number of VNets, bandwidth and location.

Azure Private Link:

- A feature that allows us to create private endpoints for Azure services. It enables us to connect to Azure services over a private endpoint, reducing exposure to the public internet.
- **Choose it when:** We need to connect to Azure services in a secure way without exposing them to the public internet.
- **Use case:** A healthcare organization using Azure for its electronic health record (EHR) system. The application is installed on an Azure Virtual Machine, and it could utilize Azure Private Link to establish a secure connection to the Azure SQL Database where patient data is stored.
- **Bandwidth** – Up to 1 GBPS | **Scope:** Single Region | **Traffic** – Azure Backbone (Traffic is encrypted using Azure Native technology) | **Cost**- Depends on the Azure service.

***Note:** All of the Azure networking models support data or traffic encryption. The encryption technique used is IPsec, which is a secure and widely-used encryption protocol.

14. Could you provide an explanation of the Azure ExpressRoute architecture?

Ans:

Azure ExpressRoute provides a private, secure, and high-speed connection between your on-premises network and Azure. Your data flows through firewalls, partner edges, dedicated ExpressRoute connections, and Microsoft Edges to reach Azure services or VMs.

At On-premises / Customer Network:

- **Devices (VMs, Databases, and other services):** These are the various services and resources in your on-premises datacenter that you want to connect with Azure.
- **Firewalls (Primary and Secondary):** These are security devices that manage and control incoming and outgoing traffic between your on-premises network and Azure.

- **Partner Edge:** This represents the edge devices responsible for connecting our on-premises network to Azure ExpressRoute. These devices are owned and operated by Microsoft's ExpressRoute partners. **Ex:** Network Routers with 100 Gbps such as Juniper MX Series etc.
  - **Primary Partner Edge:** This device connects to the primary Azure ExpressRoute circuit.
  - **Secondary Partner Edge:** This device connects to the secondary Azure ExpressRoute circuit.

At Azure ExpressRoute:

- **Azure ExpressRoute Circuit:** This is a logical connection between your on-premises network and Microsoft's ExpressRoute network. It consists of one or more physical connections between your on-premises network and Microsoft's ExpressRoute partners.
  - **Primary Connection:** A physical connection between the primary Partner Edge and the primary Microsoft Edge.
  - **Secondary Connection:** A physical connection between the secondary Partner Edge and the secondary Microsoft Edge.

At Azure Cloud:

- **Microsoft Edge:** This device is located in Microsoft's data center. It acts as the entry point into Microsoft's network from your on-premises network. It's responsible for routing your data traffic between your organization's environment and various Azure services and resources. **Ex:** 100 Gbps routers such as Microsoft DE Series or PE Series.
  - **Primary Microsoft Edge:** It connects to the primary Azure ExpressRoute circuit and to both Azure Public Services and Azure Private Virtual Networks.
  - **Secondary Microsoft Edge:** It connects to the secondary Azure ExpressRoute circuit and to both Azure Public Services and Azure Private Virtual Networks.
- **Azure Public Services:** These are Microsoft-managed cloud services that are available to all Azure customers. **Ex:** Office 365, Azure SQL Database, Azure Storage, Synapse Analytics, Cosmos DB etc.
- **Azure Private Virtual Network:** This is a virtual network that is created in your Azure subscription. It can be used to connect Azure resources together and to connect Azure resources to your on-premises network. **Ex:** Applications hosted in Azure VM.

Primary and Secondary paths: Designing primary and secondary ExpressRoute connections when connecting from on-premises to Azure offers several advantages in terms of redundancy, high availability, disaster recovery, reliability, scalability, high performance and business continuity. **Ex:**

- If one of the connections fails, we can failover to the other connection and that can be used to ensure that traffic continues to flow.

- You can balance the load using two connections which can improve performance. This can help to reduce latency and improve throughput.
- You can make it easier to scale your connectivity as your needs grow. You can simply add more bandwidth to both connections as needed.

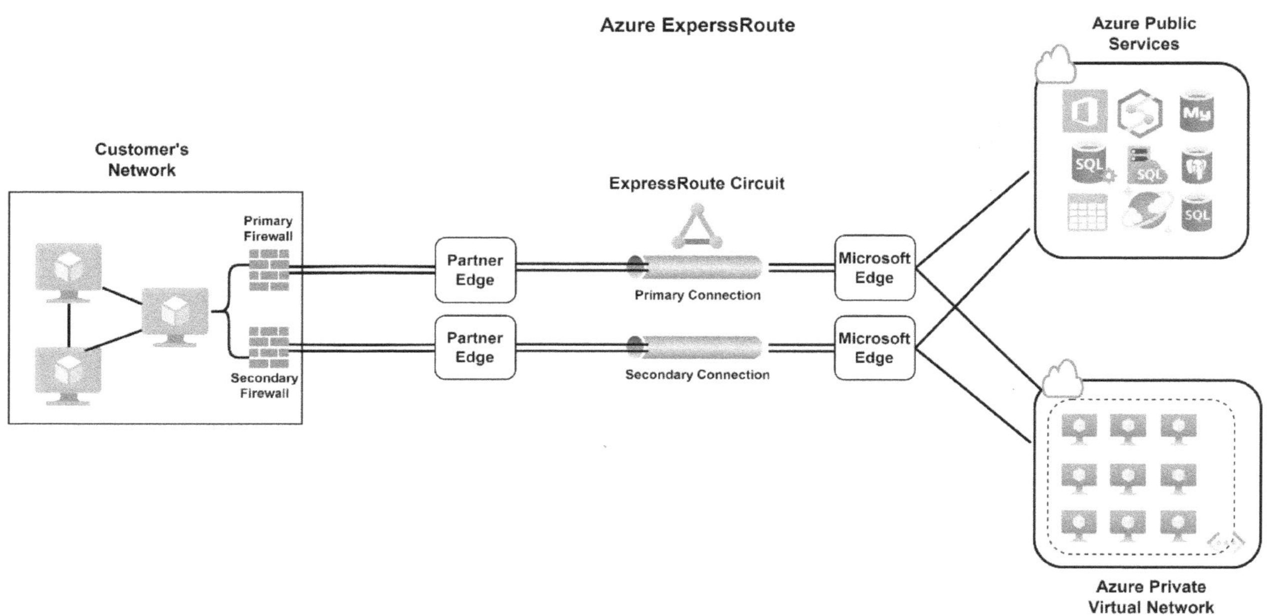

Image 2.2

15. Do you know what does it mean by "Microsoft ExpressRoute peering location"?

Ans:

- A Microsoft ExpressRoute peering location is a physical location where Microsoft's network meets the network of a third-party telecommunications carrier.
- We can connect our on-premises network to a Microsoft ExpressRoute peering location using a dedicated connection, such as a Fiber-optic cable or a dedicated Ethernet line.
- We cannot connect our on-premises network directly to a Microsoft datacenter. Instead, we need to connect through a Microsoft ExpressRoute peering location.
- Microsoft datacenters and Microsoft ExpressRoute peering locations are not the same. To connect our on-premises network to a Microsoft datacenter, we need to establish a connection with a Microsoft ExpressRoute peering location first. This connection will link our networks.

Explore:

Let's explore the high-level process of connecting our on-premises datacenter to an Azure datacenter using a Microsoft ExpressRoute peering location.

- Choose a telecommunication carrier that has a Microsoft ExpressRoute peering location in a required region. **Ex:** AT&T, CenturyLink, Comcast, TATA Communications etc.

- Contact the chosen Tele Communication carrier and order a Microsoft ExpressRoute circuit. They will provide you with the necessary hardware and software to connect our datacenter to their network.
- Configure the network. **Ex:** Configure Routers and switches to use the Microsoft ExpressRoute protocol.
- Establish, test and start utilizing the connection.

16. What are the different types of connectivity models provided by Azure ExpressRoute for establishing secure connections between our on-premises network and Azure Cloud?

Ans:

Azure ExpressRoute provides four connectivity models to connect our on-premises network to Azure:

- **CloudExchange Co-location:** Our network equipment is physically located in the same datacenter as Azure's infrastructure.
- **Point-to-point Ethernet:** We can connect our on-premises datacenters or offices to the Microsoft cloud through point-to-point Ethernet links.
- **Any-to-Any (IPVPN):** We can integrate our WAN with the Microsoft cloud.
- **ExpressRoute Direct:** High-speed, dedicated direct connection (reliable, cost-effective).

Explore:

CloudExchange Co-location: This model uses a direct connection between our on-premises network and a Microsoft ExpressRoute peering location in a colocation facility. Our network equipment is physically located in the same datacenter as Azure's infrastructure. This is the most reliable and highest-performance connectivity model, but it is also the most expensive.

- **Ex:** let's say that our on-premises data center is located in a colocation facility that has a Microsoft ExpressRoute peering location. We could connect our on-premises network to the peering location using a dedicated Fiber-optic cable.

Point-to-point Ethernet: It uses a dedicated Ethernet connection between our on-premises network and a Microsoft ExpressRoute peering location. This is a reliable and high-performance connectivity model, and it is less expensive than CloudExchange Co-location.

- **Ex:** let's say that our on-premises data center is located in a different city from the Microsoft ExpressRoute peering location that we want to connect to. We could rent a dedicated Ethernet line from a telecommunications carrier to connect our on-premises network to the peering location.

Any-to-any (IPVPN): It uses a virtual private network (VPN) connection between our on-premises network and a Microsoft ExpressRoute peering location. This is a less reliable and lower-performance connectivity model, but it is the most cost-effective.

- **Ex:** Let's say that we have multiple on-premises locations that we want to connect to Azure Cloud. We could establish a VPN connection between each of our on-premises locations and a Microsoft ExpressRoute peering location.

ExpressRoute Direct: It uses a direct connection between our on-premises network and a Microsoft ExpressRoute peering location over the public Internet. This is a reliable and high-performance connectivity model, and it is less expensive than CloudExchange Co-location.

- **Example:** let's say that we have an on-premises data center that is located in a remote area and there is no Microsoft ExpressRoute peering location nearby. We could use ExpressRoute Direct to establish a dedicated direct connection between our on-premises network and a Microsoft ExpressRoute peering location. This would provide us with a reliable and high-performance connection to Azure Cloud, even though there is no peering location nearby.

17. Can you provide a list of Azure's networking options for connecting networks within the same region, across regions, and for connecting from on-premises to Azure?

Ans:

- **Connect two Azure VNets:**
  - **Single region:** VNet Peering, VPN Gateway.
  - **Cross region:** Global VNet Peering, ExpressRoute Global Reach.
- **Connect On-premises to Azure:** VPN Gateway, ExpressRoute, ExpressRoute Global Reach.
- **Connect AWS, GCP with Azure VNets:** VPN Gateway, ExpressRoute Global Reach.

Explore:

Within the Azure Cloud:

- **Connecting two different VNets in the same region:**
  - **VNet Peering:** A low-cost, secure, and easy-to-set-up option.
  - **VPN gateway (Site-to-site):** More secure option than virtual network peering, but it is also more complex to set up and manage.
- **Connecting two different VNets in the cross region:**
  - **Global VNet Peering:** Latency between the two VNets will be higher than if they were in the same region.
  - **ExpressRoute Global Reach:** The most secure and reliable option for connecting VNets in different regions.

Connecting on-premises workloads with Azure VNet:

- **Azure VPN Gateway (Site-to-Site VPN):** This is a less expensive option than ExpressRoute, but it is also less reliable and has a higher latency.
- **Azure VPN Gateway (Point-to-site VPN)**: To connect a single device to an Azure VNet over the public internet.
- **ExpressRoute / ExpressRoute Global Reach:** Most reliable and secure option

Connect virtual networks from other cloud providers (AWS and GCP) with Azure:

- **Azure ExpressRoute Global Reach:** We can establish connections from AWS Direct Connect and GCP Dedicated Interconnect to Azure ExpressRoute circuits.
- **Azure Virtual Network Peering with AWS VPCs and GCP VPCs:** This allows us to connect Azure VNets with AWS Virtual Private Clouds (VPCs) and GCP Virtual Private Clouds (VPCs) directly using Azure's VNet peering capability. This works for VNets in the same region.
- **VPN Gateway (Site-to-Site):** Azure VPN Gateway can be used to establish Site-to-Site VPN connections between Azure VNets and AWS VPCs or GCP VPCs. This allows communication over encrypted tunnels via the public internet.
- **Third-party solutions:** Megaport, CloudConnect etc.

Azure Global Networking Solutions:

- "ExpressRoute Global Reach" and "Azure Virtual WAN" are Azure's global networking solutions that offer optimal and reliable network connectivity across Azure's worldwide data centers.

Azure Network communication happens through:

- **Azure Backbone:** VNet peering, Global VNet Peering.
- **Public Internet:** Azure VPN Gateway (Point-to-Site, Site-to-Site), Public IP.
- **Dedicated channel / line:** ExpressRoute, ExpressRoute Global Reach.
- **Azure Virtual WAN:** It uses a combination of the Azure backbone, public internet, and dedicated connections to connect our offices with the Azure global network.

18. Have you ever heard the term "OSI Layers" or "TCP/IP Layers"? If yes, could you explain them?

Ans:

OSI Layers:

- The OSI (Open Systems Interconnection) model and the TCP/IP (Transmission Control Protocol/ Internet Protocol) model are both reference models for computer networking.
- Therse models define how data travels across a network, from one device to another.
- The OSI model is a theoretical framework and it consists of 7 layers.

TCP/IP Layers:

- The TCP/IP model is a more practical and widely adopted framework and it consists of 4 layers.
- The first layer that receives traffic or data is the Physical layer and the last layer that receives traffic or data is the Application layer.

The OSI and TCP/IP models are not used directly by applications. Instead, they are used by protocols, which are sets of rules that govern how data is exchanged between different devices on a network. Ex: Ethernet, IP, TCP, UDP etc.

Explore:

OSI Layers:

- **Physical (L-1):** Responsible for the physical transmission of raw bit stream data over the network.
- **Data Link (L-2):** Responsible for defining the format of the data on the network. It offers error detection, flow control, and framing. Divided into two sub-layers: LLC (Logical Link Control) and MAC (Media Access Control).
- **Network (L-3):** Responsible for logical addressing, routing, and forwarding of data packets. It decides which physical path that data will take.
- **Transport (L-4):** Responsible for providing reliable end-to-end delivery and error recovery through protocols like TCP and UDP.
- **Session (L-5):** Manages communication sessions, including establishment, maintenance, and termination. It controls and manages ports, connections, re-connections and sessions.
- **Presentation (L-6)**: Responsible for formatting data so that it can be understood by the application layer. It handles data translation, encoding, encryption, and compression to ensure compatibility between different systems.
- **Application (L-7):** Human-computer interaction layer and it is responsible for providing services to the user such as file transfer, email, and web browsing. Deals with user interface, application functionality, and high-level protocols like HTTP, FTP, SMTP.

TCP/IP layers:

- **Network Access Layer / Link (L-1):** It maps to the first two layers (**Physical** and **Data Link**) of OSI model.
- **Internet (L-2):** It maps directly to the **Network layer** of the OSI model.
- **Transport (L-3):** It maps directly to the **Transport layer** of the OSI model.
- **Application (L-4):** The application layer of the TCP/IP model maps to the last three layers, i.e., **session**, **presentation** and **application** layer of the OSI model.

Note:

- **(L-N):** Layer-Number
- The TCP/IP model has 4 layers, which match up with the 7 layers of the OSI model. This makes the TCP/IP model a simpler way of organizing networks.
- In the world of cloud computing, when discussing networking frameworks and the services that belong to specific layers, we refer to them using the framework's name and layer number. Ex: OSI Layer-7, TCP/IP Layer-1, etc.
- **Azure Service Mapping:** Azure Web Apps and Azure Functions, which fall under OSI Layer-7 (Application Layer). Azure Key Vault aligns with OSI Layer-6 (Presentation Layer). Azure Load Balancer is situated in OSI Layer-3 (Network Layer) and corresponds to TCP/IP Layer-2 (Internet Layer). Etc.

19. Could you explain what is the difference between "Azure VNet Service Endpoint", "Azure Private Link Service" and "Private Endpoint"?

Ans:

Azure VNet Service Endpoint:

- **Purpose:** Service Endpoints allow you to restrict access to your PaaS resources (like Azure SQL Database or Azure Storage) to traffic coming from your Azure Virtual Network (VNet). **Ex:** Imagine a tunnel connecting your VNet to a specific Azure service (PaaS).
- **Traffic Flow:** Traffic to the PaaS service still leaves your VNet and uses the public endpoint but remains within the Azure backbone network.
- **Compatibility:** Only supports traffic originating from within the Azure Virtual Network, not from on-premises networks.
- **Use VNet Service Endpoint:** For a simpler approach to securing traffic between your VNet and specific Azure services.

Azure Private Link Service (Highest security):

- **Purpose:** To provide secure, private connectivity to Azure services by enabling access through private endpoints within your virtual network. **Ex:** Imagine directly attaching the Azure service to your VNet, assigning it a private IP address from your VNets address space. The service essentially becomes part of your VNet.
- **Traffic Flow:** Traffic to the PaaS service uses a private IP address within the VNet, completely bypassing the public internet. Your network traffic stays within your VNet.
- **Compatibility:** Supports access from both within the Azure Virtual Network and from on-premises networks via VPN or ExpressRoute.
- **Azure Private Endpoint (Part of Private Link Service):** A network interface that connects us privately and securely to a service powered by Azure Private Link.

- **Use Private Link Service / Endpoints**: for the highest level of isolation and potential access from on-premises environments, but be prepared for a slightly more complex setup.

Explore:

Both Azure VNet Service Endpoints and Private Endpoints help secure your resources within a Virtual Network (VNet), but they achieve this in different ways

Azure VNet Service Endpoint:

- A Service Endpoint is a configuration setting that allows us to privately connect a virtual network to a specific Azure PaaS service (**Ex:** Azure SQL Database, Storage, Cosmos DB etc.) without exposing the service to the public internet.
- When we create a service endpoint, Azure creates a private IP address for the service in our VNet. This private IP address is only accessible from our VNet; hence our traffic is not exposed to the public internet.
- **How it works:** Service Endpoints work by enabling specific subnets on your virtual network to support these endpoints. Once enabled, you can configure your PaaS resources to only accept traffic from these designated subnets. There's no need for IP filtering or NAT translation; you simply specify which VNET and subnet the PaaS resource should allow traffic from. With Service Endpoints enabled, the PaaS resource sees traffic coming from the private IP address of your VNET, rather than its public IP address.
- However, with Service Endpoints, the PaaS service is still separate to your VNet. That means the traffic is still leaving your virtual network to access the PaaS service. However, the PaaS service is configured to be able to identify traffic coming from your virtual network and allow that, without the need to configure public IPs on your VNet to allow filtering.
- **Limitations of Service Endpoints**
    - Traffic to a Service Endpoint still leaves your virtual network, and the Azure PaaS resource is still accessed on its public address.
    - Service Endpoints cannot be used by traffic originating on-premises, through VPN, or Express Route; they are only for traffic coming from your Azure Virtual Network.
    - If you want to allow your on-premises resources access, you would need to whitelist their public IPs as well.

- **Sample Use Case:** Suppose we have a virtual network hosting our application resources and an Azure Storage account where we store sensitive data. By configuring a Service Endpoint for Azure Storage, we establish a private connection between our virtual network and the Storage service. This means that our application can access the storage account without data traversing the public internet. Technically, traffic still leaves our VNet to reach the Azure Storage account.

Azure Private Link Service:

- Private Link is a newer and secure solution than Service Endpoints.
- **The key difference** between Private Link and Service Endpoints is that with Service Endpoints, traffic still left you VNET and hit the public endpoint of the PaaS resource, with Private Link the PaaS resource sits within your VNET and gets a private IP on your VNET. When you send traffic to the PaaS resource, it does not leave the virtual network.
- We can create a service in our network and configure it to be accessible via Private Endpoints from different VNets.
- The Private Link Service pairs your internal service or application with a Standard Load Balancer that allows access from parties outside your network. Access is restricted via RBAC (within the same tenant).
- **Sample Use-case:** We have an Azure Cosmos DB used by multiple applications across different virtual networks. By creating a Private Link Service for our Cosmos DB, we enable other virtual networks to connect to it privately using Private Endpoints. This ensures that data traffic between the applications and the Cosmos DB remains within the Azure backbone, maintaining security and low-latency communication.

Azure Private Endpoint:

- Azure Private Endpoint is a component of Azure Private Link.
- When we create a Private Link Service, Azure creates a private endpoint for our service in the customer's VNet.
- It serves as the entry point for accessing the Private Link Service you've set up.
- Private endpoints are more secure than service endpoints because they provide an additional layer of network isolation.

Difference between Azure VNet Service Endpoint and Private Link Service / Endpoint:

Imagine you are a kid and you have a special area in your room called the "Special Toys Space." This is where you keep your favourite toys.

- **Azure VNet Service Endpoint**:
  - It's like having a small secret door from your room to the "Special Toys Space." Only you can open this door, and nobody else from the outside can sneak in and play with your toys. This is great when you want to keep your toys just for yourself.
  - In the same way, when we set up an Azure Service Endpoint for our Azure SQL Database, we're creating a special connection from our Virtual Network to the database. Only applications from our VNet can use this connection to talk to the database.
  - But remember, traffic is still leaving our VNet and hitting the public endpoint of Azure SQL Database.

- **Azure Private Link Service and Private Endpoint**:
  - Imagine you created a magical doorway that connects not only your room but also your best friend's room to the "Special Toys Space." This way, both you and your best friend can go through the magical door and play with your special toys. But other kids from outside can't use this magical door, so your toys stay safe and sound. It's like sharing your favourite toys with your best friend while making sure nobody else can join the fun.
  - In the same way, we and our trusted friend (another Azure service or a virtual network) get to use this private endpoint to connect to our Azure SQL Database. This way, only we and our trusted friend can access and use the database.
  - Traffic to Azure SQL Database remains within your VNet and doesn't leave the virtual network.

Note: A deep understanding of private endpoint is essential.

20. What is Azure Traffic Manager?

Ans:

Azure Traffic Manager is a **DNS-based traffic load balancer** offered by Microsoft Azure. It enables us to control the distribution of user traffic to our public-facing applications that are hosted across multiple Azure regions or datacenters.

Explore:

Traffic Manager uses DNS to direct client requests to the appropriate service endpoint based on a traffic-routing method. Traffic Manager can also be used to route traffic to different endpoints based on the health of those endpoints. This means that if one endpoint becomes unavailable, Traffic Manager will automatically route traffic to the next healthiest endpoint.

Scenarios:

- **DNS-Based Load Balancing:** Traffic Manager uses DNS to direct client requests to the appropriate endpoint based on configured routing methods (Ex: priority, weighted, performance, geographic).
- **Global Distribution:** Distributing user traffic across multiple Azure regions to reduce latency for global users.
- **Failover scenario:** Redirecting traffic to a backup datacenter if the primary datacenter experiences an outage.

Sample Use Case:

Imagine an e-commerce website that has customers all over the world. They have data centers in North America, Europe, and Asia. They use Azure Traffic Manager to route users to the nearest data center based on their geographical location. This makes the website load faster and gives users a better experience. If one data center goes down, Azure Traffic Manager can automatically redirect traffic to the next available data center. This keeps the website up and running so that customers can keep shopping.

21. What is Azure Front door?

Ans:

Azure Front Door is a cloud-based content delivery network (CDN) and web application firewall (WAF) service that helps us deliver our web content and applications to users around the world with high availability, performance, security, and scalability.

Ex: Azure Front Door can be used to deliver live streams to users around the world with low latency. This is important for live streaming services because users want to be able to watch the stream without any buffering or lag.

Explore:

Consider the following use case for a more detailed understanding.

A global e-commerce company that sells products online have multiple data centers located in different regions to serve their customers. The company wants to ensure a seamless and fast shopping experience for users across the world while maintaining high availability and security. In this scenario, the company can use Azure Front Door to achieve these goals:

- **Global Load Balancing:** Azure Front Door can distribute incoming customer requests to the nearest data center, reducing latency and providing a consistent experience to users.
- **Delivering static content / Application Acceleration:** The platform can cache static content such as CSS, JavaScript files, product images, descriptions etc. at various edge locations, improving content delivery speed for shoppers.
- **SSL Offloading:** Azure Front Door can handle SSL/TLS encryption and decryption, freeing up backend resources to process more business logic and transactions.
- **Protecting web applications from cyberattacks:** Azure Front Door's Web Application Firewall (WAF) can protect our web applications from common attacks such as cross-site scripting (XSS), SQL injection, and denial-of-service (DoS).
- **Scaling web applications:** Azure Front Door can scale to meet the needs of our growing traffic. This can be helpful if we experience sudden spikes in traffic, such as during a marketing campaign or product launch.
- **High Availability:** If a data center experiences an outage, Azure Front Door can automatically route traffic to healthy data centers, minimizing downtime and ensuring uninterrupted shopping.

By leveraging Azure Front Door, the e-commerce company can create a fast, secure, and highly available online shopping platform, enhancing customer satisfaction and driving business growth.

22. Azure Traffic Manager and Azure Front Door seem similar to me. Is that right? Can you explain how they differ and when I should use each one?

Ans:

Azure Traffic Manager and Azure Front Door are both application delivery networks (ADNs) that can be used to distribute traffic to your applications across multiple regions and zones. However, they serve different purposes and have distinct features.

Choosing:

- Choose Traffic Manager for simple and cost-effective load balancing scenarios.
- Choose Azure Front Door for large workloads with advanced load balancing feature requirements.

Explore:

Purpose:

- **Azure Traffic Manager:** A DNS-based global traffic routing service which allows us to distribute incoming traffic across multiple endpoints.
- **Azure Front Door**: A content delivery and application acceleration platform. It acts as a secure entry point for your web applications, APIs, and backend services.

Workflow:

- Traffic Manager is a DNS-based load balancer, while Front Door is a reverse proxy.
- This means that Traffic Manager uses DNS to route traffic to your applications, while Front Door terminates connections at its edge points of presence (PoPs) and then proxies the traffic to your applications.

Suitable scenarios:

- Traffic Manager is a good choice for simple load balancing scenarios, such as distributing traffic across two or three servers.
- Front Door is a good choice for more complex load balancing scenarios, such as delivering content to users around the world or protecting your applications from attacks.

23. What is Azure Load Balancer?

Ans:

Azure Load Balancer distributes incoming network traffic (TCP or UDP) across multiple virtual machines (VMs) or containers within an Azure virtual network. It ensures high availability and scale by evenly distributing traffic.

Use Load Balancer for distributing traffic to backend VMs or services within the same virtual network, such as a web application running on multiple VMs.

Explore:

Consider the below examples:

- If you have a web application deployed on several VMs and need to evenly distribute user requests, Azure Load Balancer can help achieve that.
- In SQL Server Always-On Availability Group deployment, you can use Azure Load Balancer to distribute incoming database connection requests among the replicas in the availability group.
- Similarly, you can use Load Balancer for scenarios like database failover, disaster recovery, redirecting read-only workloads to reporting servers, handling redirections in hybrid cloud environments etc.

24. When choosing a load balancer in Azure, what factors differentiate internal vs. external options?

Ans:

Internal Load Balancers: These are used to load balance traffic within a virtual network. They use a private IP address for the listener. It's invisible to the internet and cannot be accessed directly from the outside world.

- **Use Case:** Used for balancing traffic between resources within a multi-tier application or for load balancing traffic to internal web applications or services.

External Load Balancers: These are used to load balance external traffic to an internet-connected endpoint. It acts as a single-entry point for external traffic, providing a public IP address that users can access to reach your resources.

- **Use Case:** Used for highly available web applications or services that need to be accessible from the public internet.

25. What is Azure Application Gateway?

Ans:

Application Gateway is a web traffic load balancer that allows us to manage and route incoming HTTP/HTTPS traffic to backend servers based on URL path or host headers.

Choose Application Gateway when we need to manage and optimize web application traffic, perform SSL termination, URL-based routing, and application-layer load balancing.

Explore:

Here are the example scenarios:

- If you have a complex web application with multiple URLs and need to route traffic to different backend services based on URL paths, Application Gateway is a suitable choice.
- An ecommerce website can use Azure Application Gateway to improve the performance and security of its website. Application Gateway can cache static content, such as product images, to improve performance. It can also protect the website from attacks, such as XSS and SQL injection.
- We are managing multiple versions of an API and need to route requests to the appropriate version based on the API version specified in the request. We can use Application Gateway with URL-based routing to direct requests to the correct version of the API based on the URL path or query parameter.

26. What is the difference between Azure Load Balancer and Application Gateway?

Ans:

Azure Load Balancer and Azure Application Gateway are both services provide load balancing capabilities, but they operate at different layers of the network stack and are designed for different use cases.

Load Balancer:

- Operates at the transport layer (Layer 4) of the OSI model, distributing incoming network traffic (TCP/UDP) across multiple backend resources (VMs or instances) based on IP and port.
- Typically used for distributing traffic to VMs within a virtual network for load balancing and high availability scenarios.
- **Features:** Traffic distribution, health checks, failover, automatic scaling, cost-effective solution

Application Gateway:

- Operates at the application layer (Layer 7) of the OSI model, making routing decisions based on content of the HTTP requests.
- Best suited for scenarios where we need to manage and optimize traffic for web applications or APIs.
- **Features:** Content caching, WAF, URL rewriting, SSL offloading, manual scaling, expensive when compared to the load balancer.

27. Azure offers a range of traffic distribution and load balancing solutions. I am currently confused about selecting the appropriate one for my diverse business cases. Could you kindly guide me on how to choose the right solution from the following options for my business use cases?

- **Azure Traffic Manager**
- **Azure Front Door**
- **Azure Application Gateway**
- **Azure Load Balancer.**

Ans:

Each of these services serves a distinct purpose and is suited for different scenarios. They all have different features and capabilities, so it's important to understand the differences between them in order to choose the right one for our needs.

- **Azure Load Balancer:** Distributes network traffic across multiple backend resources within a virtual network.
- **Azure Application Gateway:** Offers advanced load balancing and application delivery features such as caching, WAF (Web Application Firewall) etc.
- **Azure Traffic Manager:** A DNS-based load balancer that distributes traffic to services across global Azure regions.
- **Azure Front Door:** A content delivery network (CDN) and application delivery service that optimizes content delivery, accelerates application responsiveness, and enhances security.

Choosing the right solution:

- **Load Balancer:** Choose it for distributing the load at the network layer. **Ex:** Traffic distribution, health checks, failover.
- **Application Gateway:** Choose it if you want to distribute the load among your servers within a specific region using the application layer or optimizing or securing your web applications. **Ex:** Content caching, WAF, URL rewriting, SSL offloading.
- **Azure Traffic Manager:** Choose it if you're interested in routing traffic globally using DNS and you don't need features like SSL termination, handling per-HTTP/HTTPS requests, or application-layer processing. **Ex:** Traffic distribution, failover, geo-routing.
- **Azure Front Door:** Choose it if your goal is to improve the way your web traffic is routed around the world and ensure better end-user performance and reliability, especially during quick global changes. **Ex:** Content caching, WAF, URL rewriting, SSL offloading, global load balancing

Explore:

Let's understand this with a practical example. Imagine we have an insurance client named "ABC" operating globally with a range of applications, APIs, backend services, and databases distributed across different Azure regions. Now, let's explore the appropriate load balancing and distribution service choices based on the business use case.

Use Case-1: Global Traffic Distribution

- **Requirement:** Distribute user traffic among multiple Azure regions to provide low-latency access and optimal performance. Provide international customers with responsive access to the insurance portal. Users across different regions should experience minimal latency.
- **Solution**: Azure Traffic Manager using performance-based routing to direct users to the closest region based on latency.

Use Case-2: Service High Availability

- **Requirement:** Ensure continuous availability for policyholders' claims submission system. The application must remain functional even if a data center becomes unavailable.
- **Solution:** Azure Traffic Manager with failover routing can direct users to healthy endpoints in different regions, ensuring continuous availability.

Use Case-3: Web Application Optimization & Security

- **Requirement:** Securely handle policyholder data in the online claims management system. Protect against potential cyber threats while ensuring smooth user experience.
- **Solution:** Azure Front Door with static content caching, SSL termination, URL-based routing, and Web Application Firewall (WAF) to enhance performance and protect against threats.

Use Case-4: Global Content Delivery and Caching:

- **Requirement:** Deliver policy-related documents and marketing collateral to agents and policyholders worldwide efficiently.
- **Solution:** Azure Front Door's CDN capabilities can cache and deliver static content from edge locations for improved performance.

Use Case-5: API Management and Versioning:

- **Requirement:** Manage APIs with different versions and route requests accordingly. Ex: Vendors may request insurance premium quotes based on various factors. As a result, we need to serve their requests using different versions of the API. It's essential to identify and route their requests to the appropriate API version.
- **Solution:** Azure Application Gateway with URL-based routing can direct requests to different API versions based on the URL path.

Use Case-6: Microservices Load Balancing

- **Requirement:** Balance traffic between microservices handling claims processing, policy management, and customer support across various global locations.

- **Solution:** Azure Application Gateway's Layer 7 routing ensures requests are directed to the appropriate microservices based on URL paths.

Use Case-7: Database Backend Load Balancing

- **Requirement:** Process incoming insurance claim data submitted by agents across different regions. Ensure balanced distribution to regional claim processing databases.
- **Solution:** Azure Load Balancer evenly distributes incoming database connection requests to backend processing databases for consistent load distribution.

Use Case-8: Internal Application Load Balancing:

- **Requirement:** Balance traffic between backend services within a virtual network, such as policyholder authentication and authorization services.
- **Solution:** Azure Load Balancer distributes traffic within the virtual network, ensuring efficient communication between internal services.

28. Can you explain the various traffic routing methods offered by Azure Traffic Manager?

Ans:

Traffic Manager supports four traffic-routing methods:

- **Performance routing:** Routes users to the endpoint with the lowest latency.
- **Priority routing:** Routes users to the endpoint with the highest priority. We can define the priority of each endpoint in our Traffic Manager profile.
- **Weighted round robin:** Routes users to endpoints in a round-robin fashion, but with weights assigned to each endpoint. This allows you to distribute traffic unevenly across your endpoints.
- **Geographic routing:** Routes users to the endpoint that is closest to their geographic location.

Traffic Manager also supports health monitoring for all of its endpoints. If an endpoint becomes unhealthy, Traffic Manager will automatically route traffic to the next healthy endpoint. This ensures that our users are always able to access our applications, even if one or more of our endpoints are unavailable.

29. Can you explain how Azure Traffic Manager (ATM) distributes the traffic across multiple endpoints?

Ans:

Azure Traffic Manager distributes incoming traffic across multiple endpoints and Azure regions using a DNS-based routing method. Here is the step-by-step process:

- Prepare end-points (Ex: Multiple instances of a website or a service).
- Create Traffic Manager Profile.

- Configure ATM by mapping the created end-points, traffic routing methods etc.
- Configure health monitoring for endpoints.
- Update the DNS records.
- When a user sends a DNS query for your domain name, ATM responds with the IP address of the closest healthy endpoint. The endpoint can be any Internet-facing service hosted inside or outside of Azure.

Explore:

Let's consider the below example and see how ATM works in this scenario.

- **Business Case:** A global insurance company has a website that is hosted in Azure. The website is used by customers all over the world to purchase insurance policies, file claims, and get customer support. The company wants to ensure that the website is always available and performs well for all of its customers, regardless of their geographic location.
- **Solution:** The company can use Azure Traffic Manager to distribute incoming traffic across multiple Azure regions. This will ensure that users are always routed to the closest healthy endpoint, which will improve performance and reduce latency. Additionally, Traffic Manager can be configured to use health monitoring to automatically route traffic away from unhealthy endpoints, which will further improve availability.

ATM Workflow:

Step 1: Creating and configuring Azure Traffic Manager:

- **Prepare Endpoints:** Before setting up ATM, we need to have multiple instances of our insurance website deployed in different Azure regions (endpoints). These instances should host the same content and services.
- **Create a Traffic Manager Profile:** In Azure portal, create a new Traffic Manager profile and specify the required parameters such as name, subscription, resource group, routing method (**Ex:** priority, weighted, performance), etc.
- **Configure Endpoints:** In your Traffic Manager profile, add each of your website's instances deployed in different Azure regions as endpoints.
    - Specify a DNS name for each endpoint **Ex:** endpoint-eastus, endpoint-westus, endpoint-eu etc.
    - Choose the appropriate type of endpoint. **Ex:** Azure endpoint, External endpoint, etc.
    - Configure the priority or weight for each endpoint based on your routing method.
- **Configure DNS Settings**: In your domain's DNS settings (where your domain is registered), add a CNAME record pointing to the Traffic Manager DNS name. This enables the Traffic Manager to direct users to the appropriate endpoint.

- **Test the solution**: Test the setup to ensure that DNS resolution is directing users to the right endpoints.

Step 2: Actual ATM workflow:

- **DNS Query:** When a user (insurer, member, TPA, hospital admin, etc.) types your insurance website's URL in their browser, a DNS query is sent to resolve the domain name.
- **DNS Resolution:** ATM DNS servers receive the query and based on the routing method (Ex: performance), select the best endpoint (instance of your insurance app) for the user's location.
- **Traffic Routing:** Based on the chosen traffic routing method (priority, performance etc.), ATM determines which endpoint to return in the DNS response.
- **DNS Cache:** ATM will first check its DNS Cache to see if it has a record for the requested domain name. If it does, it will return the IP address from the cache to the user. If it does not have a record for that domain name, it will query its own DNS servers for the IP address.
- **TTL (Time-To-Live)**: It is a property of DNS records that specifies how long a record can be cached. **Ex:** TTL of 300 seconds means that the record can be cached for 5 minutes. After the TTL expires, the DNS resolver will discard the record and query a DNS server for the IP address again.
- **DNS Response:** The client's device receives the DNS response, which contains the IP address(es) of the selected endpoint(s).
- **Connecting to Endpoint:** The user's device connects to the specified endpoint's IP address, which corresponds to the closest or best-performing instance of your website.
- **End-point monitoring:** ATM constantly monitors the health of endpoints. If an endpoint becomes unavailable, Traffic Manager automatically routes traffic to other healthy endpoints. Once the unavailable endpoint becomes healthy again, Traffic Manager resumes directing traffic to it.

30. We've implemented Azure Traffic Manager (ATM) to handle traffic distribution for our website. We're encountering a 500 internal server error. Could you please suggest the possible reasons behind this issue?

Ans:

There are a number of possible root causes. Here are a few of the most common:

- An unhealthy endpoint.
- Configuration issues with ATM profile.
- DNS cache on your computer or network device may be stale.
- Application itself may be experiencing a problem.

Possible Solutions:

- Clear the DNS Cache.

- Check and fix the endpoint health. We can check the status/health of the Endpoint from the Traffic Manager profile > Endpoints Tab.
- Change the traffic routing method.
- Increase the Traffic Manager Timeout value.
- When all else fails, get in touch with the Microsoft Azure support team.

31. How does Azure Traffic Manager know which region or location a user is querying from?

Ans:

ATM determines where a user is querying from by looking at the source (device) IP address of the DNS query. Traffic Manager uses a variety of methods to determine the geographic location of the source IP address, including:

- **Geolocation databases:** These databases are updated on a regular basis to ensure that they are accurate.
- **Internet Latency Tables:** ATM maintains a table of internet latency data for different regions of the world. This data is used to determine the best route for a DNS query to take, based on the geographic location of the source IP address.
- **User Queries:** ATM can also use user queries to determine the geographic location of users. This is done by asking users to provide their geographic location when they make a DNS query.

32. Could you provide an explanation of the following Azure services:

- **Azure Firewall**
- **Network Security Groups (NSG)**
- **Application Security Groups (ASGs)**
- **Azure Web Application Firewall (WAF)**

Ans:

- **Azure Firewall:** Centrally filters traffic between Azure VNets, offering granular control and threat intelligence.
- **NSG:** Lightweight firewalls filtering traffic at the subnet or VM level based on IP addresses and ports.
- **ASG:** Group VMs for easier security rule application at scale within NSGs.
- **WAF:** Protects web applications from common attacks like SQL injection and cross-site scripting.

Explore:

Azure Firewall:

- Azure Firewall is a fully managed, cloud-native firewall service that protects our Azure virtual networks. It acts as a barrier between our Azure resources and potential threats from the internet or other networks. It centrally filters traffic between virtual networks (VNets) deployed in a hub-spoke architecture, even across subscriptions.

- **It is used:** To protect Azure virtual networks from a variety of threats, including:
  - Unauthorized access
  - Data exfiltration
  - Denial-of-service (DoS) attacks
  - Malware infections
- **Use case:** A company that hosts its web applications in Azure can use Azure Firewall to protect its web traffic from malicious attacks. Azure Firewall is implemented to set up rules that allow traffic from specific IP ranges and block traffic from suspicious sources. Azure Firewall can block common attack vectors such as SQL injection and cross-site scripting, and it can also be used to implement custom security policies.
- **Ex:** In a complex retail company cloud environment, it has a hub-spoke VNet architecture. The hub VNet contains critical resources like a customer database and marketing automation platform. Spoke VNets house various departments like the online store (e-commerce platform) and internal applications for logistics and inventory management.
- Azure Firewall acts as a central security gateway. It enforces granular traffic control between the hub and spoke VNets. This simplifies security management, improves threat protection, and reduces overhead compared to managing individual NSG rules for each application across spoke VNets.

Network Security Groups (NSGs):

- An NSG functions as a lightweight or basic firewall, filtering traffic at the network layer. It covers security rules based on 5-tuple information: Protocol (TCP, UDP, ICMP), Source IP address, Source port, Destination (IP Address or Service Tag) or Destination port. NSGs can be associated with a subnet or the network interface of an Azure VM, and the same NSG can be applied to multiple subnets.
- **Firewall vs. NSG:** In enterprise network configurations, both NSG and Firewall are commonly used. NSG is typically employed for subnet-level traffic filtering, while Firewall is utilized for VNet-level traffic filtering.
- **It is used:** To control network traffic within an Azure virtual network for a variety of reasons.
  - To restrict access to specific resources.
  - To prevent unauthorized access to the virtual network.
  - To protect against DoS attacks.
- **Example-1:** A company has a multi-tier application deployed in Azure, consisting of web servers, application servers, and a database. NSGs are implemented to restrict direct traffic from the internet to the database servers, allowing only the application servers to access the database. This isolates and secures sensitive data from potential external threats.

- **Example-2:** To enable RDP access to a VM from a JumpBox, a rule can be created in the Network Security Group for the target VM over TCP port 3389 (RDP Access).

Application Security Groups (ASGs – Part of NSG):

- In environments with numerous subnets and virtual machines, managing traffic using individual IP addresses becomes complex. ASG offers a solution by allowing the logical grouping of VMs to apply security rules at scale.
- **It is used:** To group Azure VMs together based on specific application requirements, and then security rules can be applied to these groups collectively. ASGs simplify network security management by allowing us to define and manage security rules for groups of VMs rather than individual VMs. It is used to:
    - Enhance security
    - Reduces administrative complexity.
    - Protect applications from unauthorized access
    - Prevent DoS attacks
    - Improve application performance
- **Example:** For a group of VMs serving a web application, without ASG, controlling traffic would require adding individual IP addresses to security rules. With ASG, the VMs can be placed in a group called "webappvm," simplifying traffic control using a single rule within an NSG.

Azure Web Application Firewall (WAF):

- Azure WAF is a cloud-based web application firewall that protects our web applications from common web-based attacks. It offers a pre-configured set of rules that can be used to block common attack vectors, and it can also be used to implement custom security policies.
- **It is used:** To protect web applications from a variety of threats, including:
    - Cross-site scripting (XSS)
    - SQL injection
    - Session hijacking
    - DoS attacks
- **Example:** An e-commerce website is hosted on Azure and processes sensitive customer information. To prevent potential data breaches and maintain the trust of their customers, the organization deploys Azure WAF. This helps detect and block malicious traffic attempting to exploit vulnerabilities in their web application, ensuring that customer data remains secure.

33. What are route tables and user-defined routes in Azure networking?

Ans:

Route Table:

- A route table is a collection of routes that Azure uses to determine how network traffic is routed within a virtual network.
- Route table dictates how network traffic should be directed within a virtual network (VNet) or between VNets and on-premises networks.
- Each route in a route table specifies a destination CIDR (Classless Inter-Domain Routing) block and a next hop, which can be either a virtual appliance (like a firewall or a virtual network gateway) or a network interface.

Custom Route Table: A custom route table is a type of route table that you can create to override Azure's default routes.

User-Defined Routes: User-defined routes are the specific routes that you define within a custom route table. These routes allow you to control the flow of traffic between subnets, VNets, and on-premises networks. You can specify routes for traffic intended for certain IP ranges to be directed to specific next hops.

Explore:

For example, we have configured two different subnets within a VNet. One for databases and another for web applications.

Here's a step-by-step explanation of how a route table works when a request is initiated from a web application in an Azure VM to a database located in a different subnet within the same VNet:

- **Request Initiation:** The web application running on an Azure VM in Subnet A of VNet sends a request to access the database located in Subnet B of the same VNet.
- **Route Lookup in Source Subnet's Route Table:** The route table associated with Subnet A is consulted to find a matching route for the destination IP address of the database server (located in Subnet B).
- **Next Hop Determination:** The route table identifies a route entry that matches the destination IP address of the database server (located in Subnet B) and it specifies the next hop for the traffic destination. The next hop could be a virtual network appliance, a firewall, or a load balancer, depending on the route configuration.
- **Forwarding the Packet**: The network packet is forwarded to the determined next hop based on the matched route information.
- **Route Lookup in Database Subnet's Route Table**: In Subnet B of VNet (where the database resides), the received packet undergoes another route lookup in the route table associated with that subnet B. It determines the next hop for sending the packet to the database server.

- **Forwarding to Database Server**: The packet is forwarded to the determined next hop within Subnet B, which could be the database server's network interface.
- **Processing and Response Generation:** The database server processes the request, generates a response, and sends it back to the requesting VM (Web App) in Subnet A.
- **Route Lookup in Database Subnet's Route Table for Response:** The response packet generated by the database server goes through another route lookup in Subnet B's route table to determine the appropriate next hop for returning the response.
- **Forwarding Response to Web Application VM**: The response packet is forwarded to the determined next hop based on the route table in Subnet B, ultimately reaching the network interface of the web application VM in Subnet A.
- **Delivery of Response to Web Application:** The web application VM receives the response from the database server, completing the communication process.

Let's see how a custom route table can help us controlling the network traffic:

- **A company has a VNet with two subnets:** a web subnet and a database subnet.
    - **Web subnet:** It has a load balancer that distributes traffic to two web servers.
    - **Database subnet:** It has a firewall that protects the database servers.
- The company wants to route all web traffic to the load balancer, but it wants to route all database traffic to the firewall.
- The company can create a custom route table and add two routes:
    - **Route 1:** It routes all traffic with a destination IP address in the web subnet to the load balancer.
    - **Route 2:** It routes all traffic with a destination IP address in the database subnet to the firewall.
- The company then associates the custom route table with the two subnets.
- Now, all web traffic will be routed to the load balancer, and all database traffic will be routed to the firewall.

34. What is Azure DNS Service?

Ans:

Azure DNS is a fully managed, authoritative domain name system (DNS) service provided by Microsoft Azure. DNS translates human-readable domain names (**Ex:** www.mysite.com) into IP addresses that computers use to identify each other on the network. Azure DNS allows us to host our DNS domains and manage DNS records within the Azure cloud infrastructure.

Explore:

Azure DNS can be used to:

- **Hosting our own domain names:** Azure DNS can be used to host our own domain names. This means that we can register a domain name with a domain registrar and then use Azure DNS to manage the DNS records for that domain name.
  - **Ex:** Imagine a company called "ABCCorp" that wants to host their own domain names (www.abccorp.com) using Azure DNS. They have a website, an email server, and various services they want to manage under their domain. This would give them more control over their DNS records and allow them to customize their DNS settings.
  - They use Azure DNS to host DNS records for "abccorp.com". They configure DNS records like "A records" for their website's IP address, "MX records" for their email server, and "TXT records" for verification and security purposes.
- **Delegating your domain names:** Azure DNS can also be used to delegate your domain names to other DNS providers. This can be useful if you want to use a different DNS provider for your domain names, or if you want to use a DNS provider that offers additional features, such as load balancing or content delivery network (CDN) services.
  - **Ex:** A company that uses a third-party DNS provider, such as GoDaddy or Cloudflare, could delegate their domain names to Azure DNS. This would allow them to take advantage of Azure DNS's high availability, scalability, and security features.

35. Based on the needs of my business, I have to set up an application on an Azure Virtual Machine. I also want to establish a custom domain (www.abcmyapp.com) for this application. Could you please guide me through the process of configuring a custom domain using the Azure DNS service?

Ans:

Here are the steps:

- Register the custom domain name with a domain registrar.
- Create a DNS zone for your custom domain name in Azure DNS.
- Create a CNAME record in your Azure DNS zone that points to the public IP address of your Azure Web App.
- Configure your Azure Web App to use your custom domain name.

Explore:

- **Domain registration:** Register a custom domain name (www.abcmyapp.com) with a domain registrar. **Ex:** GoDaddy, Namecheap etc.

- **Create a DNS zone:** We can create a DNS Zone for our custom domain name in Azure DNS. A DNS zone is a collection of DNS records that are associated with a particular domain name. When we create a DNS zone for our custom domain name in Azure DNS, we are creating a container for the DNS records that will be used to resolve our domain name.
- **CNAME record creation:** We need to create a CNAME record in our Azure DNS zone that points to the public IP address of our Azure Web App. A CNAME record is a type of DNS record that maps a domain name to another domain name or an IP address. In this case, we will be mapping our custom domain name to the public IP address of our Azure Web App or Azure Virtual Machine.
- **Configure our Azure Web App:** We need to configure our web application to use our custom domain name. To do this, go to the Azure portal > Web Apps blade > Name of our Azure Web App > Configuration tab > Custom domains section > Enter our custom domain name > Save.

Note: Understand DNS Zone

- **DNS Zone:** Think of a DNS zone like your phone contacts list. It's a special place where you keep all the phone numbers you need. Each contact has a name (like "Maa", "Helpdesk", "Boss" etc.) and a phone number. Just like that, a DNS zone has a name (like "abcmyapp.com") and important information such as domain name, name servers, zone type, resource group, location etc.
- **DNS Records:** Inside this DNS zone, we add special notes called "DNS records." These records are like the phone numbers in our contacts. Each DNS record has a job. For example, we might have a record that says, "When someone asks for www.abcmyapp.com, show them this IP address."
- **Resolving the Domain Name:** When someone wants to visit our website, their computer asks the DNS zone where our website is. The DNS zone tells the computer the right address to find our website. This helps people reach our website on the internet.

36. What are the different network monitoring solutions offered by Microsoft Azure?

Ans:

Azure provides the following network monitoring options. These could be like a package of tools, features, and services for monitoring.

- **Azure Network Watcher:** A suite of tools that helps us monitor, diagnose, and troubleshoot our Azure network resources.
- **Azure Monitor:** A cloud-based monitoring service that collects telemetry data from our Azure resources and provides insights into their health, performance, and security.
- **Azure Monitor - Network Insights:** A service that provides a comprehensive view of our network topology, health, and metrics.

- **Azure Monitor - DNS Metrics and Alerts:** A feature of Azure Monitor that helps us track the performance of our DNS servers and generate alerts when problems are detected.

***Note:** When Azure Monitor teams up with Azure Network Watcher, it improves network monitoring by giving a complete look at Azure network health. Azure Monitor's analysis, alerts, visuals, and reports work well with Network Watcher's diagnostics, giving admins what they need for a smooth Azure network.

Explore:

Azure Network Watcher:

- It is a comprehensive network monitoring solution that provides insights into the health, performance, and security of our Azure network. It is a regional service, so we need to enable it in each region where we have Azure resources.
- **Functionality:** It uses a variety of methods to monitor our Azure network:
    - **Flow logs:** Tracks network traffic between VMs and other network resources.
    - **Connectivity tests:** It verifies that our VMs and other network resources can communicate with each other.
    - **Topology discovery:** It maps out our Azure network and identifies potential security vulnerabilities.
    - **Features:** Network Watcher is a suite of tools and it offers features/tools/services for monitoring, diagnostics and logging.
- **Use Cases:** It can be used to troubleshoot network issues, identify security threats, optimize network performance, and to meet compliance requirements.
- **Monitoring Scope:** It provides a suite of tools to monitor, diagnose, view metrics, and enable or disable logs for IaaS (Infrastructure-as-a-Service) resources. It isn't a solution for monitoring PaaS (Platform-as-a-Service) infrastructure or getting web/mobile analytics. It can be used to monitor the following aspects of our Azure network:
    - Virtual machines
    - Virtual Networks
    - Load balancers
    - VNet peering
    - Network security groups (NSGs)
    - Azure Firewall
    - Application gateways
    - ExpressRoute connections
    - Connectivity between on-premises and Azure networks
    - Traffic patterns in your virtual network

Azure Monitor Network Insights:

- It is a newer (out-of-the box monitoring solution) service that provides a more visual and interactive way to monitor our Azure network without requiring any configuration. It includes features such as network topology visualization, Network health and metrics, traffic analytics, and Diagnostic Toolkit.
- **Functionality:** It uses a variety of data sources to monitor our Azure network, including Azure Monitor metrics, Flow logs, Connectivity tests, Topology discovery etc.
- **Use case:** It is a good choice if you are looking for a more visual and interactive view of your Azure network.
- **Monitoring Scope:** It can be used to monitor, Network topology, Health metrics, Traffic analytics. This network monitoring service is already enabled for various Azure services including Application Gateway, Azure Bastion, Azure Firewall, Azure Front Door, Azure NAT Gateway, VPN Gateway, ExpressRoute, Load Balancer, Local Network Gateway, Network Interface, Network Security Group, Private Link, Public IP address, Route table / UDR, Traffic Manager, Virtual Network, Virtual WAN etc.

DNS Analytics (Metrics and Alerts):

- DNS Metrics and Alerts is a service that helps us monitor our DNS traffic and identify potential security threats. It can be used to track DNS queries, Record Set Count metrics, Record Set Capacity Utilization metric to identify malicious domains, and investigate DNS-based attacks.
- **Functionality:** It internally utilizes Azure Monitor Service for capturing data and displaying metrics. **Ex:** It uses DNS logs to track DNS queries that are sent to our DNS servers. With the metrics in Azure DNS, we can configure alerting based on conditions that are met.
- **Use case:**
  - Monitoring the health of your Azure DNS servers.
  - Optimizing the performance of your Azure DNS servers.
  - Identifying potential security threats.
- **Monitoring Scope:** It can used to monitor DNS queries, DNS traffic, DNS latency, DNS errors, DNS cache hits etc.

37. What are the different set of tools or features offered by Azure Network Watcher?

Ans:

Network Watcher provides three major sets of capabilities:

- **Monitoring:** It focuses on providing insights into the health and performance of your network resources. It helps you keep a close watch on how your network is functioning and identify any potential issues or areas for improvement. It includes the features like Topology View, Connection Monitor.

- **Diagnostics:** It focuses on finding and solving network problems. It provides tools to analyze network traffic, detect issues, and verify the correctness of your network configuration. Key features under this capability includes IP flow verify, NSG Diagnostics, Next hop, Connection Troubleshoot etc.
- **Logging:** It involves the capture and analysis of network-related data for the purpose of security analysis, compliance auditing, and understanding network traffic patterns. This capability includes NSG Flow Logs and Traffic Analytics.

Explore:

Here are the Azure Network Watcher features grouped by categories, along with their specific use cases:

Monitoring:

- **Topology view:** Provides a graphical representation of your virtual network and the resources in it, including virtual machines, subnets, and network interfaces.
  - **Use Case:** This can be helpful for understanding how your network is connected and for troubleshooting problems. **Ex:** We can use it to see if there are any misconfigurations in our network, such as misconnected subnets or missing network interfaces.
- **Connection monitor:** It allows us to monitor the connectivity and latency between endpoints inside and outside Azure.
  - **Use Case:** This can be helpful for ensuring that your applications are able to communicate with each other and with the internet.

Diagnostics:

- **IP flow verify:** It allows us to detect traffic filtering issues at a virtual machine level.
  - **Use Case:** It helps us identifying and troubleshooting issues that might be affecting communication to or from a specific VM. Also, it can be helpful for troubleshooting problems with NSG rules. **Ex:** We can use it to verify that a rule is allowing the traffic that we expect it to allow.
- **NSG diagnostics:** It allows us to detect traffic filtering issues at a virtual machine, virtual machine scale set, or application gateway level. This can be helpful for troubleshooting problems with NSG rules.
  - **Use Case:** Helps pinpoint and address network security group (NSG) rule conflicts affecting traffic flow.
- **Next hop:** Verifies traffic routes and identifies routing issues. This can be helpful for troubleshooting problems with network connectivity.

  - **Use Case:** Assists in diagnosing and correcting routing problems that could impact communication between network elements. **Ex:** We can use it to verify that a packet is taking the expected route to its destination.

- **Connection troubleshooting:** It enables a one-time connectivity and latency check between a virtual machine and Bastion host, application gateway, or another virtual machine.

  - **Use Case:** It helps in diagnosing connectivity issues between specific virtual machines or network hosts. **Ex:** We can use it to verify that a VM is able to communicate with another VM.

- **Packet capture:** It allows us to capture our virtual machine traffic. This can be helpful for troubleshooting problems with network applications.

  - **Use Case:** Facilitates the analysis of network behavior and troubleshooting of communication problems. **Ex:** We can use it to capture traffic from a web server hosted on a VM to see if there are any errors in the requests or responses.

- **VPN troubleshoot:** Runs multiple diagnostics checks on our VPN gateways and connections to help debug issues.

  - **Use Case:** Assists in identifying and resolving problems affecting virtual private network (VPN) connectivity. **Ex:** We can use it to verify that a VPN gateway is connected to the internet.

Logging:

- **NSG flow logs:** It allows us to log network traffic passing through our network security groups (NSGs).

  - **Use Case:** Provides visibility into network traffic patterns for security analysis and compliance auditing. **Ex:** We can use them to see if a NSG rule is allowing more traffic than we expected.

- **Traffic analytics:** It processes our NSG flow log data enabling us to visualize, query, analyze, and understand our network traffic.

  - **Use Case:** Helps us gain insights into network usage, patterns, and potential anomalies for better network management. **Ex:** We can use it to see which applications are using the most bandwidth.

38. Drawing from your experience as a cloud admin, could you highlight the common networking challenges you've encountered while working with Azure Networking?

Ans:

Here are the top five common Azure Networking issues that are frequently encountered:

- **Connectivity:** Challenges related to establishing and maintaining communication between network components and resources.
- **Performance:** Issues affecting the speed, efficiency, and responsiveness of data transfer and network operations.
- **Security:** Concerns involving the protection of network resources, data, and communications from unauthorized access and threats.
- **Cost:** Problems associated with managing and optimizing network-related expenses and resource utilization.
- **Scalability:** Matters pertaining to the ability of the network to handle increasing demands and accommodate growing workloads effectively.

Explore:

- **PS:** Problem Statement
- **RC:** (Possible) Root Causes
- **PSO:** Possible Solutions

Network connectivity issues:

- **PS:** Azure VMs cannot connect to each other, to the internet, or to on-premises networks.
- **RC:**
    - Incorrect network configuration. **Ex:** Misconfigurations of routing table entries, firewall, NSG, load balancer, DNS, network gateways, network service endpoints etc.
    - Private IP addresses conflicts.
    - Faulty network hardware.
    - Network congestion.
    - DDoS attack.
- **PSO:**
    - Check the network configuration of the Azure VMs.
    - Verify NSG rules, troubleshoot route tables.
    - Ensure VM health and connectivity settings.
    - Use a load balancer to distribute traffic and prevent congestion.
    - Implement DDoS protection.

Network performance issues:

- **PS:** Azure VMs experience slow network performance.
- **RC:**
    - Overloaded network resources.
    - Insufficient bandwidth.
    - Bottlenecks in the network infrastructure.
    - Excessive data transfer volume.
    - External factors **Ex:** Network congestion or geographical location.
- **PSO:**
    - Optimize the network resources. **Ex:** Bandwidth upgrade, resource scaling, load balancer optimization, etc.
    - Identify and remove bottlenecks.
    - Distribute workloads efficiently.
    - Implement data compression, caching, or CDN usage to reduce data transfer volume.

Network security issues:

- **PS:** Azure VMs are vulnerable to security attacks.
- **RC:**
    - Improper network security configuration.
    - Vulnerabilities in the network infrastructure.
    - Malicious traffic.
    - Misconfigured or unnecessary public endpoints.
    - Unpatched network components.
    - Lack of robust logging and monitoring practices.
- **PSO:**
    - Implement proper network security measures, such as firewalls, break-in detection systems, and encryption.
    - Keep the network infrastructure up to date with the latest security patches.
    - Apply least privilege principle to NSG rules.
    - Use Azure Application Gateway or Web Application Firewall (WAF).
    - Carefully configure and monitor public endpoints, disabling unnecessary ones.
    - Monitor the network for malicious traffic.
    - Enable logging and monitoring practices to detect and respond to security events.

Excessive network expenditure:

- **PS:** Azure Networking costs are more than expected.
- **RC:**
    - Overprovisioned network resources.
    - Excessive usage of network bandwidth.
    - Unnecessary network services.
    - Lack of Monitoring.
    - Uncontrolled Data Egress.
    - Misconfigured Load Balancers.
    - Replicating data across multiple regions.
- **PSO:**
    - Optimize the network resources.
    - Monitor the network usage and adjust the bandwidth accordingly.
    - Regularly review and terminate unnecessary network services.
    - Implement egress traffic controls and review egress-heavy applications.
    - Review and optimize load balancer configurations.
    - Carefully plan data redundancy and replication across regions based on cost considerations.

Network scalability issues:

- **PS:** Azure Networking cannot scale to meet the changing demands of the business.
- **RC:**
    - Insufficient resource allocation.
    - Poorly designed network architecture.
    - Lack of auto-scaling.
    - High utilization of gateways or load balancers.
    - Misconfigured subnet sizes.
    - Manual network management.
    - Limited bandwidth, inefficient routing etc.
- **PSO:**
    - Enable auto-scaling features.
    - Assess, predict, plan and implement the network architecture by considering the future growth.
    - Optimize load balancers, gateways and routing configurations.
    - Ensure subnets are appropriately sized to accommodate growth and new resources.
    - Regularly assess bandwidth needs and upgrade as necessary.
    - Use IaC (Infrastructure-as-Code) tools to automate and streamline network management.

39. How can we achieve high availability and disaster recovery for Azure Networking Solutions?

Ans:

Providing HA and DR for network solutions in Azure involves a combination of architectural design, redundancy, failover mechanisms, and automated recovery processes. Here are the HA and DR features for Azure Networking Solutions:

- **Availability Zones** – Deploy resources in different datacenters with in the same region.
- **Multi-region deployments** – Leverage cross region deployment features.
- **Load balancing features** – Distribute load across multiple resources.
- **Traffic Manager** - Global Traffic Management.
- **Redundant Virtual Network Peering** – Offers failover capabilities.
- **Azure Site Recovery** – Replicate resources to secondary location etc.

Explore:

HA & DR Azure Networking:

- **Utilize Availability Zones:** Azure Availability zones are separate physical locations within an Azure region. By deploying our resources across multiple availability zones, we can ensure that our services are running in physically isolated datacenters, reducing the risk of single point of failure (power outage or hardware failure).
- **Multi-Region Deployment:** If our HA requirements extend beyond a single region, deploy resources in multiple Azure regions. This way, we can ensure that our services remain available even if an entire region experiences an outage.
- **Load Balancing Features:** Use Azure Load Balancers or Application Gateways to distribute incoming traffic across multiple instances or services, preventing overloading of a single resource.
- **Azure Traffic Manager:** It helps us to distribute traffic across different regions or datacenters, ensuring seamless user experience even during regional outages.
- **Redundant Virtual Network Peering**: Establish peering connections between VNets across different regions or Availability Zones. This allows for cross-region communication and failover capabilities.
- **Azure Site Recovery (ASR):** It can be used to replicate our network resources to a secondary location. This can help us to recover our network in the event of a disaster. ASR provides automated failover and failback, enabling us to maintain business continuity during outages.
- **Azure Virtual WAN:** It can be used to create a hub-and-spoke network architecture. This can help to improve the resiliency of your network. Azure Virtual WAN supports a variety of features, including traffic routing, security, and policy management.
- **Other features:** Azure VPN Gateway Redundancy, ExpressRoute Redundancy, Azure Firewall High Availability etc.

- **Monitoring & Alerting:** Azure Monitor and Azure Network Watcher can be used to monitor our network for potential problems. This can help us to identify and address problems before they cause a failure.

40. Are you familiar with Azure Bastion? If yes, could you explain what it is and when it should be used?

Ans:

Azure Bastion is a fully managed PaaS (Platform-as-a-Service) that provides a secure way to access our Azure VMs without exposing them to the public internet. It is a good solution to use in the following cases:

- We need secure, easy, and centralized access to Azure VMs without exposing them to the public internet.
- We need to provide secure remote access to Azure VMs for administrators or developers, enabling them to easily access Azure VMs from anywhere in the world.
- Eliminate the need to manage and maintain public IP addresses for our Azure VMs.

Explore:

Azure Bastion Workflow:

- Azure Bastion is a fully managed PaaS that provides secure, seamless RDP (Remote Desktop Protocol) and SSH (Secure Shell Protocol) access to our Azure VMs directly from the Azure portal over TLS.
- Azure Bastion uses a bastion host, which is a virtual machine that is deployed in our Azure virtual network. The bastion host has a public IP address and is configured with RDP and SSH access.
- When we connect to a VM via Azure Bastion, our VMs don't need a public IP address, agent, or special client software.
- This secure connection is established over HTTPS and authenticated through Microsoft Entra (Azure AD).
- Azure Bastion acts as an intermediary layer between the end client and the Azure VM, with traffic passing through the Bastion host VM.
- By avoiding direct exposure of our VM to the public network, suspicious traffic can be filtered or addressed within the Bastion host itself.
- This approach effectively prevents potential attacks and safeguards our VM from threats.

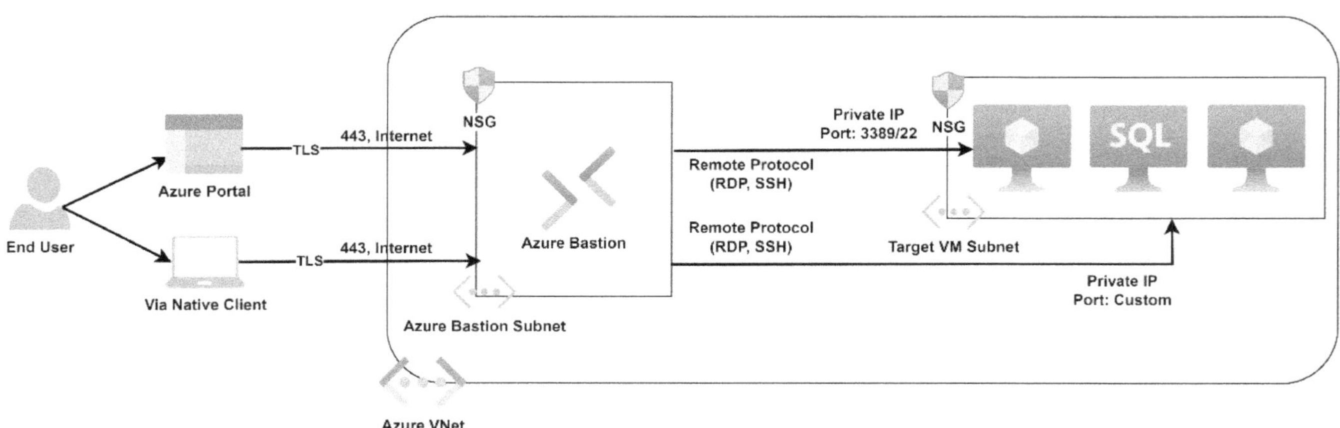

Image 2.3

Use Case:

- **Problem Statement:** Consider a software development company that runs multiple development and testing environments on Azure VMs. The company's development team often needs to remotely access these VMs for coding, debugging, and testing purposes. However, they are concerned about the security risks associated with exposing RDP ports to the internet.
- **Solution:** The company can deploy Azure Bastion within the same VNet as the VMs. Developers can then use the Azure portal to securely connect to the VMs through Azure Bastion. This eliminates the need for public IP addresses and direct RDP access, enhancing the security posture of the VMs and simplifying remote access management. Developers can securely access their development environments from anywhere, knowing that their connections are protected within the Azure network.

41. What are inbound and outbound connections in Azure?

Ans:

- **Inbound Connections:** These are network requests that come into your Azure resource (such as a VM, Database) from external sources. Ex:
    - A user accessing an Azure SQL Database.
    - A remote administrator using SSH or RDP to manage a VM.
- **Outbound Connections:** These are network requests that originate from your Azure resource and are sent to external destinations. Ex:
    - An Azure VM accessing an external database or API.
    - An application sending data to a cloud storage service.

42. What is an augmented security rule in Azure Network Security Group?

Ans:

An augmented security rule in an Azure NSG is a powerful feature that simplifies managing complex security policies. It allows you to combine multiple elements into a single rule, reducing the number of rules needed and improving readability.

- You can include multiple ports, IP addresses (individual or ranges), service tags, and application security groups within a single rule.
- Having fewer, more comprehensive rules makes it easier to understand and maintain your NSG configuration.

43. What happens to an existing connection if I update a security rule from allow to deny or remove the rule entirely?

Ans:

The behavior depends on the action you take:

- **Removing the Rule:** Existing connections won't be immediately interrupted. However, they may be terminated once there's no active traffic flow in either direction for a few minutes.
- **Updating the Rule from Allow to Deny:** If you change a rule to block previously allowed traffic, all active connections relevant to that rule will be dropped immediately.

44. We have a user who needs access to a SQL Server instance on an Azure VM. We created an inbound security rule on port 1433 for their IP address. Since the user will receive results (Ex: rows) from the database, do we also need an outbound rule?

Ans:

Not required! Azure NSG is a stateful service. That means if you allow a port for inbound traffic to receive a request, you don't need to open the same port in outbound traffic to send the response back.

Explore:

The essential rule for creating a security rule is "from where the request is getting initiated." If the request is initiated from outside, we create an INBOUND rule. If the request is initiated from our SQL Instance in the VM, then we need to create an OUTBOUND rule.

In the given scenario, as the request originates from outside and the response goes back to the same IP, the existing inbound rule allows both directions of communication.

45. Is there a timeout setting for TCP connections at Azure Firewall?

Ans:

Yes, Azure Firewall has a default idle timeout of 4 minutes for TCP connections. This means if there's no activity on a connection for more than 4 minutes, the connection may be dropped. To maintain the connection, applications or devices can enable TCP keep-alive functionality.

Explore:

- **East-west traffic (traffic coming within a specific network scope):** Azure Firewall has a default idle timeout of 4 minutes. This setting is not configurable. Ex: Traffic between VMs within the same region.
- **North-south traffic (traffic coming into and out of network scope)**: The default idle timeout is also 4 minutes. However, you can contact Azure Support to request an extension of this timeout up to 15 minutes for specific scenarios. **Ex:** Traffic coming from IoT devices via internet to your VMs.

46. Do you have any idea about the default rule "AllowVnetInBound" in Azure Network Security Group?

Ans:

The "AllowVnetInBound" default rule permits all the hosts inside the virtual network (including subnets) to communicate with each other without any blocks.

Ex: Let's suppose, you have a web server VMs and Database VMs located on different subnets within the same VNet. The "AllowVnetInBound" rule acts like a green light, allowing the communication to flow freely within the same virtual network. This ensures your web server can access the database without needing any additional firewall configurations as long as both VMs reside within the same VNet.

Explore:

By default, every Azure VM comes with a pre-configured Network Security Group (NSG). This NSG acts as a virtual firewall, protecting your VM from unauthorized and malicious access. To balance security and accessibility within the VNet, Azure configures each NSG with default rules:

- **AllowVnetInBound:** This rule permits all hosts within the virtual network (including subnets) to communicate with each other freely.
- **AllowAzureLoadBalancerInBound:** This rule allows an Azure load balancer to communicate with your VM for health checks and management purposes.
- **DenyAllInBound:** This is a "deny-all" rule that blocks any inbound traffic to the VM from outside the Azure VNet.

- **Outbound rules:** Similar to InBound, there are default Outbound rules will be added.
    - **AllowVnetOutBound** allows communication within the VNet.
    - **AllowInternetOutBound** allows communication from the VNet to the Internet.
    - **DenyAllOutBound** blocks any outbound traffic that is not explicitly allowed by other rules.

47. How does 'priority' work in Azure Network Security Groups (NSGs), and why is it important?

Ans:

In Azure Network Security Groups (NSGs), "priority" is a crucial attribute that determines the order in which rules are applied to network traffic. Each rule within an NSG is assigned a unique priority number ranging from 100 (Highest priority) to 4096 (Least Priority). The lower the number, the higher the priority of the rule. Azure processes rules in order of their priority, from the lowest number to the highest.

Significance of Priority:

- **Order of Evaluation (First Match Wins):** Rules are evaluated in ascending order of priority. The first rule that matches the traffic (based on source, destination, port, and protocol) is applied, and no subsequent rules are evaluated.
- **Conflict Resolution:** In cases where multiple rules could apply to the same traffic, the rule with the lowest priority number takes precedence.

Explore:

Let's consider an example:

- **NSG Rules:** Imagine you have an NSG with two inbound rules for a web server VM:
    - **Rule 1 (Priority 100):** Allow inbound traffic on port 80 (HTTP) from any source (0.0.0.0/0). This grants broad access for anyone to access the web server.
    - **Rule 2 (Priority 200):** Deny all inbound traffic. This acts as a safety net rule with lower priority.
- **Rule Evaluation:** A user tries to access the web server on port 80.
    - Rule 1 (Priority 100): This rule matches because the user is accessing port 80. Since it has a higher priority (100), the evaluation stops. The user is granted access to the web server because of Rule 1, even though Rule 2 denies all traffic.

48. Let's consider a scenario where you have web applications, web services, and databases hosted on separate VMs in different subnets within the same VNet. Here's the network setup:

- **App VMs Subnet: 10.0.1.0/24**
- **Database VMs Subnet: 10.0.2.0/24**
- **Web Services VMs Subnet: 10.0.3.0/24**

The requirement is to control traffic between these subnets as follows:

- **Enable inbound access to the App Subnet for HTTP (port 80) and HTTPS (port 443).**
- **Enable access to the Database Subnet from the App Subnet on port 1433 (SQL Server).**
- **Restrict access from the Web Services Subnet to the Database Subnet.**

By utilizing NSG rules, can you achieve this granular control over traffic flow within your VNet?

Ans:

Yes. You can manage and control network traffic effectively using NSG. Here are the sample rule definitions.

Define NSG Rules:

- **Rule 1 - Allow HTTP and HTTPS Traffic to Web Servers**
  - Rule Name: Allow-HTTP-HTTPS
  - Priority: 100
  - Source: Any
  - Source Port Ranges: *
  - Destination: App subnet
  - Destination Port Ranges: 80, 443
  - Protocol: TCP
  - Action: Allow
- **Rule 2 - Allow Database Traffic from App Subnet to DB Subnet**
  - Rule Name: Allow-DB-Traffic
  - Priority: 200
  - Source: App subnet
  - Source Port Ranges: *
  - Destination: DB subnet
  - Destination Port Ranges: 1433
  - Protocol: TCP
  - Action: Allow
- **Rule 3 - Deny All Traffic from WebService Subnet to DB Subnet**
  - Rule Name: Deny-WebService-To-DB
  - Priority: 300
  - Source: WebService subnet
  - Source Port Ranges: *
  - Destination: DB subnet

- Destination Port Ranges: *
- Protocol: Any
- Action: Deny

Rule Evaluation:

- When a request for HTTP/HTTPS (port 80/443) traffic comes in, the rule-1 with priority 100 is evaluated and matches, allowing the traffic.
- If the traffic is from the App subnet to the DB subnet for SQL Server (port 1433), the rule-2 with priority 200 allows this traffic.
- If the traffic is from the WebService subnet to the DB subnet, the rule with priority 300 denies it, regardless of the port or protocol.

Note to Data People: This information is provided for your general understanding. In large enterprises, network administration is typically handled by cloud or network admins. However, understanding these networking concepts can still be valuable for designing and troubleshooting your data workloads.

CHAPTER 03

Fundamentals of Microsoft Entra

1. What are the key elements of Windows Active Directory?

Ans:

Here are the key elements of AD:

- **Domain:** Group of objects (users, computers etc.)
- **Tree:** Collection of one or more domains.
- **Forest:** Collection of one or more trees.
- **Other Elements:** Objects, attributes, security principals, roles and permissions etc.
- **Services:** AD DS and AD FS.

Explore:

- **Domains:** A domain is a logical grouping of objects that share a common schema, configuration, and policy.
    - **Ex:** "myorgabc.com" is a domain where all user accounts, computers, and resources are managed. Users within this domain can communicate and share resources without having to reauthenticate.
- **Trees:** A tree is a collection of one or more domains that share a common root domain.
    - **Ex:** In the "myorgabc.com" domain, a new division called "sales.myorgabc.com" is created as a child domain. Both of these domains are part of the same tree. Objects in a tree can communicate with each other even if they are in different domains because they share a common root domain / Tree.
- **Forests:** A forest is a collection of one or more trees that are not in any way related to each other.
    - **Ex:** We have two separate domains, "myorgabc.com" and "myorgxyz.com" each with its own tree structure. They are part of the same forest because they are managed by the same instance of Active Directory. Objects in a forest can communicate with each other, but they cannot communicate with objects in other forests.
- **Objects:** Basic unit of information in Active Directory.
    - **Ex:** Users, computers, printers, files, and other resources.

- **Attributes:** Attributes are the properties of an object.
  - **Ex:** User's name, password, and email address etc.
- **Security principals:** Security principals are objects that can be authenticated and authorized to access resources in Active Directory.
  - **Ex:** Users, computers, groups, and other objects.
- **Roles and permissions:** Roles and permissions are used to control access to resources in Active Directory. They can be assigned to users, groups, and other security principals.
  - **Ex:** Active Directory Administrator.
- **AD DS (Active Directory Domain Services):** AD DS is the core service of Active Directory that stores and manages information about users, computers, and other resources in a hierarchical structure. AD DS enables authentication, authorization, and access control for these resources.
  - **Ex:** In an organization, using AD DS we can register and manage employees, computers, printers etc.
- **AD FS (Active Directory Federation Services):** It allows users from one organization (or domain) to securely access resources and applications in another organization without needing to create separate user accounts. It enables Single Sign-On (SSO) and facilitates trust between organizations' authentication systems.
  - **Ex:** With AD FS, users from Company A can use their own company credentials to access resources in Company B's domain. This is useful when we are working with partner companies on common projects.

***Note:** Knowing the basics of Windows AD will help you understand Azure Active Directory better.

2. Can you provide a definition for "Azure Active Directory"?

Ans:

- Azure AD is a cloud-based identity and access management (IAM) service.
- It is designed to help organizations manage user identities and access to applications and resources.
- Azure AD is a fundamental component of Microsoft's cloud ecosystem, providing a secure and scalable way to manage identities and access for users and applications across various cloud and hybrid environments.

3. Have there been any recent changes to the name of Azure Active Directory by Microsoft?

Ans:

- Yes! Microsoft has changed (in July 2023) the name of "Azure Active Directory (Azure AD)" to "**Microsoft Entra ID**".
- Customers who have access to Azure AD will continue to have access to Microsoft Entra ID without any planned disruptions. Which means all existing Azure AD deployments, configurations, and integrations will continue to function as they do today without any action from us.
- Prices, terms and service level agreements (SLAs) remain the same.

Note: In this document, the terms Azure AD, Azure Active Directory, ME-ID and Entra all refer to Microsoft Entra ID.

Explore:

- Acronym usage is not encouraged. However, if you are already using AAD, you need to replace it with ME-ID.
- Capabilities or services formerly known as "Azure Active Directory <feature name>" or "Azure AD <feature name>" will be rebranded as Microsoft Entra product family features. Ex:
    - "Azure AD Conditional Access" is now "Microsoft Entra Conditional Access"
    - "Azure AD single sign-on" is now "Microsoft Entra single sign-on"

4. Describe some of key features of Azure AD / Microsoft Entra-ID (ME-ID)?

Ans:

Key features of Microsoft Entra-ID:

- Centralized identity management
- Single sign-on (SSO)
- Multi-factor authentication (MFA)
- Conditional access policies
- Role-Based Access Control (RBAC)
- Application Management
- Microsoft Entra Connect
- B2B and B2C Collaboration
- Identity Federation
- Device Management
- Advanced Security Features

Explore:

Centralized Identity Management: Provides a single place to manage user identities and access rights across all of your applications and resources. This can help to simplify your IT administration and improve security.

- **Use Case:** A company uses Entra to create and manage user accounts for their employees. When a new employee joins the company, the HR department adds their details to Entra, granting them access to necessary resources like email, cloud storage, and internal applications.

Single Sign-On (SSO): Entra can be used to implement SSO for your applications, which means that users only need to sign in once to access all of their authorized applications. This can help to improve the user experience and reduce the need to remember and enter multiple usernames and passwords.

- **Use Case:** An employee in an organization uses Entra SSO to seamlessly access their email, project management tool, and document collaboration platform without needing to sign in separately for each application.

Application Management: Entra provides a number of features for managing applications, such as application provisioning, application lifecycle management, and application auditing. This can help us to simplify the management of our applications and improve security.

- **Use Case:** An organization uses Entra to integrate Office 365, Salesforce, and Slack. Users can access these applications using their Entra credentials, and the IT team can manage access to all three apps from a single dashboard.

Microsoft Entra Connect (Azure AD Connect): It is a tool that helps organizations synchronize their on-premises Active Directory (AD) with Microsoft Entra.

- **Use case:** Entra Connect can be used to synchronize user accounts and group memberships from on-premises Active Directory (AD) to Entra. This allows users to sign in to both on-premises and cloud-based applications using their existing AD credentials.

B2B and B2C Collaboration: Entra supports business-to-business (B2B) collaboration for sharing resources with external partners and business-to-consumer (B2C) identity management for customer-facing applications.

- **Use Case 1:** An insurance company can use Entra B2B to collaborate with external partners, such as insurance brokers, claims adjusters, and reinsurers. This can help to improve efficiency and productivity by allowing these partners to access the company's applications and data without having to be on-boarded to the company's internal IT systems.
- **Use Case 2:** An insurance company can use Azure AD B2C to provide self-service access to its customers for tasks such as making claims, viewing policy information, and updating contact information. This can help to improve customer satisfaction by making it easier for customers to manage their accounts.

Identity Federation: Entra can integrate with on-premises Active Directory and other identity providers, allowing users to use their existing credentials to access cloud resources.

- **Use Case:** An organization integrates their on-premises Active Directory with Entra. This enables employees to use their corporate credentials to access both on-premises and cloud resources.

Device Management: Entra supports device registration, management, and conditional access policies, ensuring that only trusted and compliant devices can access organizational resources.

- **Use Case:** An organization enforces a policy that only devices with up-to-date security patches and antivirus software can access their Azure resources, increasing the overall security posture.

Advanced Security Features: Entra supports a lot of advanced security features to protect our organization identity that suits for the modern technology world. **Ex:** Role based access control, Multi Factor Authentication, Conditional Access, Identity protection, Privileged identity management (PIM), Data loss prevention (DLP), Threat protection etc.

- **Use Case:** These capabilities are valuable tools for improving security posture and ensuring that access to sensitive resources is granted only when necessary and under controlled circumstances.

5. How Microsoft Entra is different from Windows Active Directory?

Ans:

Microsoft Entra ID and Windows AD are both identity and access management (IAM) solutions from Microsoft, but they serve different purposes and are designed for different environments.

- **Windows AD:** It is an on-premises IAM solution that is tightly integrated with the Windows OS. It is a good choice for organizations that are not ready to move to the cloud or that need to support a purely on-premises environment.
- **Microsoft Entra ID:** It is a cloud-based IAM solution that can be used to manage users and devices across on-premises and cloud resources. It is a good choice for organizations that want to move to the cloud or that need to support a hybrid environment.

Explore:

Here are the more feature differences:

- Both supports user and group management, directory synchronization, SSO, Role Based Access Control (RBAC), etc.
- Entra supports advanced Multi-Factor-Authentication (MFA). Windows AD also supports MFA, but it is not as widely supported as MFA in Entra.
- Additionally, Entra supports more advanced features such as conditional access, identity protection, Privileged Identity Management (PIM) etc.
- Both supports passwords, certificates, and smart cards authentication methods.

- **Geographical Flexibility and Scalability:**
    - **Entra:** Built to handle large-scale cloud-based scenarios and supports elasticity for growing organizations.
    - **Windows AD:** Scaling and remote access can be more challenging and might require additional domain controllers as the network grows.
- **Communication protocol support:**
    - **Entra:** OpenID Connect, OAuth 2.0, and SAML 2.0.
    - **Windows AD:** Kerberos, NTLM, and LDAP.
- **Licensing:**
    - **Entra:** Included with Microsoft cloud subscription models. **Ex:** Pay-as-you-go or per-user/per-device.
    - **Windows AD:** Licensing is often associated with Windows Server licenses. **Ex:** Per-user/per-device.

6. What are the licensing models in Microsoft Entra ID?

Ans:

Microsoft Entra ID offers following licensing models:

- **Free:** Basic active directory features.
- **Paid:**
    - **Premium P1:** Free + Additional features like MFA (Multi-Factor Authentication) etc.
    - **Premium P2:** Supports all Entra features. **Ex:** Free + P1 + More advanced features.
    - **Microsoft Entra ID Governance:** This is an advanced set of identity governance capabilities available for Microsoft Entra ID P1 and P2 customers.
    - **Pay-as-you-go:** We can purchase an individual Entra feature.
    - **Microsoft 365 and Office 365 Plans:** Certain Microsoft 365 and Office 365 subscriptions include Microsoft Entra ID features as part of their offerings.

Explore:

Azure AD Free: It includes basic features such as user and group management, directory synchronization, and single sign-on.

- **Use Case:** Suits for small organizations with a limited number of users.

Azure AD Premium P1: It allows your hybrid users to access both on-premises and cloud resources. It includes additional features such as multi-factor authentication, conditional access, self-service password reset for your on-premises users, and reporting.

- **Use Case:** Suits for organizations that need to improve the security and compliance of their identities.

Azure AD Premium P2: It includes all of the features of Premium P1, plus additional features such as identity protection, privileged identity management (PIM) etc.

  - **Use Case:** It's suitable for businesses with strict security requirements and regulatory compliance needs. **Ex:** Required comprehensive identity governance, advanced security, and privileged access management.

Microsoft Entra ID Governance: This is an advanced set of identity governance capabilities available for Microsoft Entra ID P1 and P2 customers. It includes features like entitlement management, access reviews, and lifecycle workflows, Identity governance dashboard, etc.

- **Use Case:** Suitable for large scale enterprises with compliance requirements.

Pay-as-you-go feature licenses: Microsoft Entra ID supports a pay-as-you-go model for certain services, particularly for its External Identities and Workload Identities.

- **External Identities:** Microsoft Entra External Identities enables organizations to collaborate with external partners, customers, and users. The pay-as-you-go model for External Identities is based on Monthly Active Users (**MAUs**). This means you are billed only for the unique external users who authenticate in a given month.
- **Workload Identities:** Microsoft Entra Workload Identities manage identities (Service Principals and Managed Identities) for applications, services, and automation tools. The pricing model can be based on the number of identities and their activity.

7. What factors determine the pricing of Microsoft Entra?

Ans:

Entra pricing depends on the following factors:

- Edition like Free, Premium 1, Premium 2, etc.
- Number of Entra users.
- The region where your Entra tenant is located.
- The amount of data stored in Entra.
- The number of authentication requests made to Entra.
- The number of users who use self-service password reset.

However, we can use the Azure pricing calculator to estimate the cost of Entra as per the latest rate card.

8. What are the actions that Microsoft Entra-ID can perform? Or what is the core functionality of Entra?

Ans:

Below is the core functionality of Microsoft Entra / Azure AD:

- **Identity Management:** This involves central user identity management.
- **Identity Federation:** It enables us to federate our identities with other organizations.
- **User Provisioning and Deprovisioning:** This functionality automates the provisioning and deprovisioning of user accounts.
- **Access Control:** Ensures that users only have access to the resources they need to perform their tasks.
- **User Authentication:** It helps identify who is accessing our resources.
- **User Authorization:** This aspect validates and permits user actions on resources based on their permissions.
- **Reports and Monitoring:** This functionality allows us to track user activity and identify security threats.

Explore:

Identity Management: It involves creating, storing, and managing user identities and attributes. Entra provides a central repository for user information and attributes.

- **Ex:** We can create user accounts in Entra for employees in our organization. Each user account includes attributes such as name, email address, location, job title and contact info.

Identity Federation: It allows us to use their existing identities from one system to access resources in another system. Entra supports federation with other identity providers using protocols like SAML (Security Assertion Markup Language) and OAuth.

- **Ex:** We can set up federation between Entra and an external identity provider, such as Google or Facebook, allowing users to sign in to Entra applications using their Google or Facebook credentials.

User Provisioning and Deprovisioning: User provisioning involves creating and configuring user accounts automatically based on predefined rules. Deprovisioning refers to the process of disabling or deleting user accounts when they are no longer needed.

- **Ex:** When a new employee joins our organization, Entra can automatically create a user account for them and assign them to relevant groups and applications based on their role.

Access Control: Entra allows us to control user access to applications and resources based on their roles and permissions. This helps to ensure that users only have access to the resources they need to do their jobs.

- **Ex:** We might create a "VM Operator" role that allows users to start and stop virtual machines but not delete them.

User Authentication: It verifies the identity of users trying to access resources. It supports various authentication methods, including username and password, multi-factor authentication (MFA) etc.

- **Ex:** Users accessing a company's SharePoint site might need to provide their username and password along with a verification code sent to their mobile device via MFA.

User Authorization: It controls what resources a user can access after they have been authenticated. Entra allows us to define access policies and permissions for users and groups.

- **Ex:** A user in the "Marketing" group might have read-only access to certain files in a storage account, while a user in the "Finance" group might have read and write access to financial reports.

Reports and Monitoring: Entra provides reporting and monitoring capabilities to track user activities, sign-in events, and access patterns.

- **Ex:** Entra's reporting features can provide insights into failed sign-in attempts, successful sign-ins from new locations, and application usage patterns, allowing administrators to track and identify the potential security threats and take action if necessary.

9. What are the various types of user access controls that Microsoft Entra ID offers?

Ans:

Entra access control functionality offers various options.

- **RBAC:** Assign permissions to users based on user roles.
- **Conditional Access:** Based on certain conditions.
- **JIT:** Need basis or temporary or time bound.
- **Resource Group Access Policies:** Resource group level access control.
- **App Access Permissions:** Application user level access control

Explore:

- **Role-based access control (RBAC):** It allows organizations to assign permissions to users based on their roles. **Ex:** We assign the "Reader" role to a contractor. This role allows them to view resources like Azure VM and storage but prevents them from making any changes or deletions.
- **Conditional access:** We can create policies that define conditions under which users are granted access. **Ex:** We can enforce multi-factor authentication (MFA) for users accessing sensitive applications.

- **Just-in-time (JIT) access:** It allows us to grant users access to resources on an as-needed basis. **Ex:** With JIT access, an IT administrator can request temporary access to a critical database server during maintenance. Entra grants access for a specific duration.
- **Resource Groups and Access Policies:** We can organize our resources into resource groups and set access policies for those groups. **Ex:** We can grant the marketing team read-only access to the marketing-related resource group, ensuring they can view but not modify or delete resources.
- **App Access Permissions:** We can control which application users have access to and the level of access they have. **Ex:** We can grant the sales team access to the CRM application but restrict their access to certain modules within the app.

10. What are the Authentication and authorization standards supported by Microsoft Entra?

Ans:

These are some of the most well-known and commonly used authentication and authorization standards:

- **OAuth 2.0:** Framework for authorization that allows third-party apps to access resources on behalf of a user.
- **OpenID Connect (OIDC):** Authentication protocol that builds on OAuth 2.0 and adds identity claims to the access token.
- **JSON web tokens (JWTs):** Compact and self-contained way to securely transmit information between parties.
- **SAML:** XML-based standard for exchanging authentication and authorization information between security domains.
- **SCIM:** Open standard for provisioning and managing user identities and attributes across systems.
- **Web Services Federation (WS-Fed):** XML-based standard for exchanging authentication and authorization information between web services.

Explore:

Let's see the suitable use cases:

OAuth 2.0: Suits for single sign-on (SSO) and API access.

- **Ex-1:** Imagine a mobile application that needs to access a user's calendar and contacts stored in their Office 365 account without directly handling the user's password. OAuth 2.0 is used here to enable the application to request and obtain access tokens to access the user's data.
- **Ex-2:** We could use OAuth 2.0 to allow users to sign in to our web application using their Google or Facebook accounts.

OpenID Connect (OIDC): Suits for SSO and identity federation.

- **Ex:** Consider a scenario where a user wants to log in to a third-party application using their Microsoft account. OpenID Connect is used to authenticate the user, provide their identity information (like name and email), and enable single sign-on (SSO) between the application and Entra.

JSON Web Tokens (JWTs): Used to represent claims about a user, such as their identity, email address, or role.

- **Ex:** In a microservices architecture, services need to communicate and trust each other's identity. JWTs can be used as secure tokens to pass user identity information between services without repeatedly querying the identity provider.

Security Assertion Markup Language (SAML): Suits for SSO and identity federation.

- **Ex:** In an enterprise setting, an employee wants to access a partner company's application without creating a new account. SAML is used to achieve SSO between the two organizations' systems, allowing the employee to authenticate once and access both systems.

System for Cross-Domain Identity Management (SCIM): Used for provisioning users to cloud applications.

- **Ex:** A company uses multiple cloud applications and wants to streamline user provisioning and deprovisioning across these apps. SCIM is used to automate user lifecycle management, ensuring consistency in access across different platforms.

Web Services Federation (WS-Fed): Used for SSO and identity federation.

- **Ex:** In a hybrid environment, where on-premises applications and cloud applications need to coexist, WS-Fed can be used for SSO between them. For example, a user accessing an on-premises SharePoint site could be authenticated through Entra using WS-Fed.

11. What is RBAC in Azure, and what is its purpose?

Ans:

Role-based access control (RBAC) is a security model that allows us to control who has access to Azure resources and what they can do with those resources. RBAC is used to:

- **Separate duties:** Assign different roles to different users, groups, or service principals.
- **Grant least privilege:** Grant only the permissions that users need to perform their jobs.
- **Audit access:** Track who has accessed resources and what they have done with those resources.

Explore:

Here are some use case examples:

- **IT Operations:** Instead of giving broad permissions, RBAC allows us to grant different roles to IT staff based on their responsibilities. **Ex:** A user can be assigned the "Virtual Machine Contributor" role for managing VMs and the "Storage Blob Data Reader" role for accessing storage data.
- **Compliance Auditing:** Rather than giving auditors full access, we can assign them the "Reader" role for specific resource groups. This allows them to view configurations and activity logs without making any changes.
- **Software Development Teams:** In Azure environment, we might have multiple development teams working on different applications. We can use RBAC to grant the "Contributor" role to each development team for their specific resource group. This allows each team to manage their resources without interfering with other teams' resources.

12. What is a security principal in Azure RBAC?

Ans:

In Azure RBAC, a security principal is an object that is requesting access to Azure resources. Here are the different types of security principals:

- **User:** Individual user.
- **Group:** Group of users.
- **Service principal:** An identity that can be used by apps or services.
- **Managed Identity:** An identity that is assigned to an Azure resource and that is automatically managed by Azure.

Explore:

Here are the different types of security principals in Azure RBAC:

User: An individual who has a profile in Microsoft Entra. We can assign roles to users directly, or we can assign roles to groups that contain users.

- **Use Case:** Grant access to a resource to a specific person.
- **Ex:** We could create a user called "Claims Administrator" and assign it the "Contributor role" to the Azure SQL Database. This would give the Claims Administrator the permissions to create, update, and delete insurance claims data.

Group: A collection of users that have been grouped together for administrative purposes. We can assign roles to groups directly.

- **Use Case:** Grant access to a resource to a group of people.
- **Ex:** A development team needs access to Azure VM for testing. Instead of assigning permissions individually, create a group for the team and assign the necessary roles to the group.

Service principal: A security identity that can be used by applications or services to access Azure resources. You can create service principals for your own applications, or you can use pre-provisioned service principals for Azure services.

- **Use Case:** Grant access to a resource to an application or service.
- **Ex:** A monitoring application requires read-only access to Azure resources to collect metrics and monitor performance. A service principal is created for the application, and the appropriate RBAC role is assigned to it.

Managed identity: An identity that is automatically managed by Azure. We can use managed identities when developing cloud applications to manage the credentials for authenticating to Azure services.

- **Use Case:** Grant access to a resource to an Azure resource.
- **Ex:** In an Azure VM, we are running an insurance web application. This application is using an Azure SQL Database. Managed Identity allows the app to securely access the database without storing sensitive credentials. The VM's Managed Identity is granted access to the database, simplifying authentication and enhancing security. We're setting up a way for different services/ resources of Azure to talk to each other. Ex: We're giving a 'read-only' or 'contributor' role to a virtual machine on a database. This means, whenever our app connects to the database, it will automatically get the required permissions, without needing username and password.

13. What is the difference between Azure Roles and Microsoft Entra-ID Roles in Azure Role-Based Access Control (RBAC)?

Ans:

Azure Roles:

- Controls access to **Azure resources** like Virtual Machines, Storage, Databases etc. Azure RBAC includes over 100+ built-in Azure roles.
- **Scope:** Management group, subscription, resource group, resource.
- **Fundamental Azure roles:** Owner, Contributor, Reader, User Access Administrator.
- **Ex:** Assigning the "Virtual Machine Contributor" role to a user allows them to create and manage virtual machines in a specific Azure resource group.

Azure AD/Entra Roles:

- Controls access to Azure AD resources like **users, groups and applications**. There are 80+ built-in Azure AD Roles available.

- **Scope:** Tenant, directory, user, group, application.
- **Fundamental Azure AD/Entra Roles:** Global Administrator, User Administrator, Billing Administrator.
- **Ex:** Assigning the "User Administrator" role in Entra to a user grants them the authority to manage user accounts and their access within Entra.

Note: Both supports custom roles.

Explore:

Azure Roles:

- **Owner:** The owner role has full control over the resource. They can create, modify, and delete the resource. They can also grant access to other users.
- **Contributor:** The contributor role can create, modify, and delete the resource. They cannot grant access to other users.
- **Reader:** The reader role can view the resource, but they cannot modify it.
- **User Access Administrator:** It can manage user access to the resource. They can create, modify, and delete user access assignments. They can assign themselves or others the Owner role.
- **Other Built-in Roles:** Virtual Machine Contributor, Disk Backup Reader, Disk Restore Operator, SQL DB Contributor, SQL Managed Instance Contributor, SQL Server Contributor etc. All these roles are categorised based on the types of service Ex: Compute, Storage, Networking, Databases, AI and ML, Security, DevOps etc.

Entra roles:

- **Global administrator:** It has full control over Microsoft Entra ID. They can create, modify, and delete users, groups, and domains. Also, they can assign administrator roles to others and reset passwords and manage permissions.
- **User administrator**: They can create, modify, and delete users and groups. They can also manage support tickets, monitor service health, manage permissions, reset passwords for users, Helpdesk administrators, and other User Administrators.
- **Billing administrator**: They can perform common billing related tasks like updating payment information. They can view billing information, create and manage billing profiles, and view and manage billing alerts. They can also make purchases, manage subscriptions, manage support tickets, and monitor service health.
- **Other Built-in Roles:** Application Admin, Authentication Admin, Azure DevOps Admin, Compliance Admin, Security Admin, Password Admin etc.

14. What are the key components of Azure Role-Based Access Control (RBAC) and how do they work together to manage access to Azure resources?

Ans:

Below are the key elements of Azure RBAC:

- **Security Principal:** Determines who can access our Azure resources.
- **Role:** Specifies the actions a security principal can perform.
    - **Role Definition:** Outlines the permissions included in the role.
- **Scope:** Defines the boundaries within which a security principal can access resources and carry out actions.
- **Role assignment:** A link between a security principal and a role at a specific scope.

Explore:

- **Security principal:** An entity that can be granted access to Azure resources. It includes users, groups, and service principals (represents applications).
- **Role:** A collection of permissions that define what actions a security principal can take on Azure resources. **Ex:** A "Virtual Machine Contributor" role is an instance of the role definition. When we assign this role to a user or group, it grants them the specific permissions defined in the role definition.
    - **Built-in roles:** Predefined roles that come with Azure.
    - **Custom roles:** We can create to meet the specific needs of our organization.
- **Role definition:** A role definition is a blueprint for a role. It defines the permissions that are included in the role. Role definitions are used to create roles. Ex: A "Virtual Machine Contributor" role definition specifies that the assigned user can start, stop, and restart virtual machines.
- **Scope:** A scope is a container for Azure resources. The scope defines the level at which a role assignment applies. Scopes can be management group, subscription, resource group, or individual resource.
- **Role assignment:** A role assignment is a link between a "security principal" and a "role" at a specific "scope". Role assignments are used to grant access to Azure resources to security principals. This determines what actions the security principal can perform on resources within that scope.
    - **Multiple Role Assignments:** A security principal can be assigned multiple roles at the same scope.
        - **Ex:** Let's say we can assign both contributor and reader roles to the same user "MrU" at the subscription scope. This means that MrU can create, update, and delete

resources in the subscription, and he/she can also read the details of any resource in the subscription.

- **Deny Assignments:** It allows us to explicitly prevent a security principal from performing specific actions. Deny assignments can be used to enforce stricter security policies. Deny assignments take precedence over allow assignments, so if a security principal has both an allow assignment and a deny assignment for the same action, the deny assignment will take precedence.
  - **Ex:** Let's say a user named 'MrU' who has been assigned the 'Contributor' role at the subscription scope. Additionally, there is a deny assignment for the 'Delete' permission for the user MrU within the subscription. In this case, MrU will have the ability to create or update resources but will not have the capability to delete any resources within the subscription, even though he has the "Contributor" role.

15. Can you share a simple business case and walk through how to create an RBAC strategy for the described business situation?

Ans:

Business Case:

Let's say we have a health insurance customer and imagine we are architecting an Azure cloud infrastructure to host the technological backbone of our product, ABC. Here are the requirements for the cloud resources:

- **Subscription:** We have established a subscription specifically for our insurance product, ABC.
- **Resource Groups:** Within this subscription, we have set up three resource groups—DEV, QA, and PROD.
- **Resources:** Within each of these resource groups, we have deployed various resources, categorized as follows:
  - **Databases:** Azure SQL Databases, responsible for storing the transactional data of our product.
  - **Storage:** Azure Blob Storage, utilized for hosting documents and images.
  - **Virtual Machines:** Azure VMs employed to host our web applications and services.

Sample RBAC Strategy:

Let's design the RBAC strategy for the given business use case:

Step 1: Create Entra (Azure AD) Groups and Add Users

Begin by creating the following Entra Groups and adding the appropriate users to each group:

- **Cloud Administrators:** These users should have full access to all Azure resources within the subscription. Their permissions should include resource creation, management, deletion, as well as the ability to grant and revoke access for other users.

- **Database Administrators:** Users in this group require full access to all Azure SQL Databases within the subscription. They should be able to create, manage, and delete databases, in addition to managing access for other users.
- **Developers:** Users in this group should be granted read-write access exclusively within the DEV resource groups. Their permissions should include resource creation, viewing, and modification exclusively within the DEV resource group.
- **Testers:** Members of this group should be provided with read-only access specifically to the required resources within the TEST resource group.
- **Production Support Team:** Users in this group should have read-write access to the essential Azure resources within the PROD resource group.
- **Additional Groups:** Depending on requirements, other groups such as Security Admins, Compliance Admins, and Storage Admins can also be established.

Step 2: Create Service Principals

Proceed to create service principals for the following purposes:

- **Web Applications:** Develop a service principal to facilitate the interaction of our web application, hosted on a VM, with resources like Azure SQL Database or Blob Storage.
- **CI/CD Pipelines:** Create a dedicated service principal intended for CI/CD integration.

Step 3 - Role Assignments

Assign appropriate roles to each Entra Group and Service Principal:

- **Cloud Administrators (Scope – Subscription):** Grant the Owner role or specific roles like SQL DB Contributor, Virtual Machine Contributor, and Blob Storage Contributor.
- **Database Administrators (Scope – Subscription):** Assign the SQL DB Contributor role.
- **Developers (Scope – DEV Resource Group):** Provide roles such as Virtual Machine Contributor and SQL DB Contributor. Alternatively, access can be granted at the OS level or via SQL Logins.
- **Testers (Scope – TEST Resource Group):** Provide read-only access at both the application and database levels.
- **Production Support Team (Scope – PROD Resource Group):** Assign the Contributor role, tailored to the specific requirements.
- **Service Principals:**
  - **Web Application:** Depending on needs, assign SQL DB Contributor and Blob Storage Contributor roles.
  - **CI/CD Pipeline:** Grant the Contributor role for streamlined resource deployment.

16. What are the security features of Microsoft Entra ID?

Ans:

Entra offers a wide range of security features.

Core Access Security Features:

- Microsoft Entra Private Access
- Microsoft Entra Internet Access
- Microsoft Entra ID Governance
- Microsoft Entra ID Protection
- Microsoft Entra Verified ID

Core Identity and Access Management Features:

- Role Based Access Control (RBAC)
- Multi-Factor Authentication (MFA)
- Conditional access
- Privileged Identity Management (PIM)

Advanced Security and Compliance Features:

- Password protection
- Device Management
- Auditing
- Compliance
- Application Proxy
- Machine Learning (ML) based reports
- Integrated Security and Data Protection Features

Explore:

Core Access Security Features:

- **Entra Private Access:** Securely connects users to private applications and resources using Zero Trust principles, replacing traditional VPNs.
- **Entra Internet Access:** Provides secure, managed access to internet resources and SaaS applications, helping protect against online threats.
- **Entra ID Governance:** Automates identity and access management to ensure the right people have the right access to the right resources at the right time.
- **Entra ID Protection:** A feature that helps detect, investigate, and respond to identity-related risks, such as compromised accounts, using AI and machine learning.

- **Entra Verified ID:** Digitally verifies identity information for trustworthy self-service enrolment and faster onboarding.

Core IAM Features:

- **RBAC:** It allows you to granularly control the level of access that users have. Ex: We can limit a user to only manage virtual networks and another user to manage all resources in a resource group.
- **Multi-factor authentication (MFA):** MFA requires users to provide two or more additional pieces of evidence to authenticate themselves, such as a password and a code from their phone.
- **Conditional access:** It allows us to control access to resources based on factors such as the user's location, device, or time of day. This helps to prevent unauthorized access to resources, even if users have valid credentials.
- **Identity protection:** Helps to identify and mitigate risks to our identities, such as compromised credentials and suspicious activity.
- **Privileged identity management (PIM):** PIM helps us to manage privileged accounts in a secure and compliant way.

Advanced Features:

- **Password protection:** Entra offers a variety of features to help us protect passwords, such as password complexity requirements, password expiration, and password history.
- **Device management:** Helps us managing devices, such as mobile device management (MDM) and conditional access.
- **Auditing:** Helps us to track all activity in Entra, such as sign-ins, password changes, and access to resources.
- **Compliance:** Entra is compliant with a variety of industry standards, such as the General Data Protection Regulation (GDPR).
- **Application Proxy:** Entra Application Proxy is a cloud-based service that makes on-premises applications (Ex: SharePoint sites, Outlook Webapp etc.) accessible to users anywhere, on any device. Application proxy uses a reverse proxy architecture to expose on-premises applications to the internet, while maintaining the security and compliance of those applications. It allows us to access on-premises applications by signing in with their Entra account.
- **ML Based Reports:** We can use these reports to gain visibility into the integrity and security of our organization's directory. These reports are categorised into anomaly reports (sign-in events), integrated application reports, error reports, user-specific and activity logs (password reset, group changes etc.)
- **Integrated Security and Data Protection Features:** Microsoft Entra integrates seamlessly with "Microsoft Defender Threat Intelligence" and "Azure Purview's Data Loss Prevention" features to provide comprehensive enterprise security, combining identity protection, threat detection, and data governance.

17. Can you please explain the below concepts with an example business use case?

- **Role-Based Access Control (RBAC)**
- **Multi-Factor Authentication (MFA)**
- **Conditional Access Policies**
- **Microsoft Entra ID Protection**
- **Privileged Identity Management (PIM)**

Ans:

RBAC: It is an authorization system built on Azure Resource Manager that provides fine-grained access management of resources in Azure. It allows us to assign specific roles and permissions to users and groups. This helps control what actions users can perform within Azure resources.

- **Use Case:** A senior developer is granted the "Contributor" role for an Azure subscription. This allows them to create and manage resources within that subscription, while a business analyst might only have "Reader" access to view resources.

MFA: Entra supports MFA, which can help to protect our applications and resources from unauthorized access. MFA requires users to provide two or more pieces of evidence to authenticate themselves, such as a password and a code from their phone.

- **Use Case:** A user logs into a sensitive financial application using Entra MFA. After entering their password, they also receive a verification code on their mobile phone that they must enter before gaining access.

Conditional Access Policies: It allows us to define specific conditions that must be met for a user to access resources. This ensures that access is granted based on certain requirements, such as location, device health, time of the day or risk level.

- **Use Case:** An organization sets up a conditional access policy that requires users to perform MFA if they are accessing company resources from outside the corporate network or from an unrecognized device. In other scenario, we can create a policy that requires users to be in the office network to access sensitive data.

Entra ID Protection: It helps us to protect our identities from unauthorized access and misuse.

- **Risk-based authentication:** It uses machine learning to assess the risk of each sign-in attempt and prompts users for additional authentication factors if the risk is high.
- **Suspicious activity detection:** Identifies and alerts us to suspicious activity, such as unusual sign-in attempts or failed authentication attempts.
- **Identity assurance:** It helps us to verify the identity of users, such as by requiring users to provide additional information, such as their date of birth or mother's maiden name.

  - **Use Case:** Imagine a scenario where a developer typically logs in from a specific location during business hours. However, on a certain day, this user attempts to log in from an entirely different location in the middle of the night. This feature assists us in identifying this unusual sign-in pattern and raises a red flag alert, indicating a potential security breach or a compromised account.

Privileged Identity Management (PIM): It helps us to manage privileged accounts in a secure and compliant way. Privileged accounts are accounts that have elevated permissions, such as the ability to access sensitive data or make system changes.

- **Just-in-time access:** It allows us to grant access to privileged accounts only when they are needed.
- **Role separation:** It allows us to separate the privileges of different roles, so that no single user has too much power.
- **Auditing:** It allows us to track all access to privileged accounts, so that they can investigate any suspicious activity.

  - **Use Case:** Imagine a big financial company using Entra to control their cloud systems. Some jobs there have a lot of power, which could be risky if abused. Roles like Global Admins or Security Admins give wide access. PIM helps limit access to these roles, reducing risks.

18. What are the different types of identities in Microsoft Entra?

Ans:

Microsoft Entra supports various identity types, each influencing the authentication process.

- **Entra Cloud-Only Identities:** These user accounts are created and managed entirely within the Azure cloud.
- **Entra Hybrid Identities:** These identities represent users originally stored in an on-premises Active Directory that are synchronized with Microsoft Entra. This enables Single Sign-On (SSO) with two options:

  - **Azure AD Password Hash Synchronization:** User credentials (username and password) are synced to the cloud for authentication.
  - **Azure AD Pass-through Authentication:** User accounts are synced to the cloud, but password validation remains on-premises.

- **Federated Identities:** These identities are mapped or imported from on-premises Active Directory Federation Services (AD FS) to Microsoft Entra.
- **Microsoft Entra External ID (B2B, Azure AD B2C etc.)** refers to all the ways you can securely interact with users outside of your organization. If you want to collaborate with partners, distributors, suppliers, or vendors, you can share your resources and define how your internal users can access external organizations.

Once an identity is established in Microsoft Entra, you can grant access to various cloud resources like Azure SQL Database, SQL Managed Instance, Synapse Analytics, and more.

19. What's the difference between Cloud-Only and Hybrid Identities in Microsoft Entra?

Ans:

Cloud-Only Identities:

- User accounts created and managed entirely within the Azure cloud.
- These users can only authenticate with cloud resources like Azure SQL Database, SQL Managed Instance, Office 365 etc.
- Authentication happens entirely in the cloud, allowing access to all advanced Entra features.

Hybrid Identities represent on-premises Active Directory users synchronized with Microsoft Entra. This enables Single Sign-On (SSO) for both cloud and on-premises resources. There are two main approaches for synchronization and authentication:

- **Entra ID Password Hash Synchronization:**
    - Synchronizes user identities and password hashes from on-premises AD to Entra.
    - User authentication happens in the Azure cloud.
    - Users maintain their existing on-premises credentials for seamless access.
    - Requires Microsoft Entra Connect for synchronization (runs every two minutes).
    - Offers high availability through cloud scaling.
    - Ideal for minimal infrastructure changes and leveraging Entra security features.
    - Bonus: Provides leaked credential reports.
- **Entra ID Pass-Through Authentication:**
    - Synchronizes user identities to Entra, but password validation remains on-premises.
    - Authentication involves both Azure cloud and on-premises infrastructure.
    - Users log in through the cloud, with password verification happening on-premises agents.
    - Requires Entra Connect and additional lightweight agents on-premises servers.
    - These agents need access to on-premises AD and internet connectivity.
    - High availability requires deploying additional pass-through agents.
    - Preferred for maintaining on-premises password policy control.

Federated Identities (Entra ID Federated Domain) involve integrating trusted external identities, such as users from another organization's Active Directory Federation Services (AD FS).

- Authentication happens entirely on-premises.
- Entra hands off authentication to a trusted system like AD FS.
- Requires managing and maintaining a separate federated system outside Entra control.

- Suitable for organizations with existing federation services, smartcard/certificate authentication, or third-party authentication solutions.

20. Do you have any insights into what a Microsoft Entra External ID is?

Ans:

Microsoft Entra External ID is a broader solution for managing various external identities and their integration with internal resources. It is a new converged platform which is future proof and developer friendly to meet all your identity needs for below scenarios:

- B2B (Business to Business) Collections.
- B2B Direct Connect.
- Azure AD B2C (Business to Customer).
- Microsoft Entra multi-tenant organization.

Explore:

- **B2B collaboration** - Collaborate with external users by letting them use their preferred identity to sign in to your Microsoft applications or other enterprise applications (SaaS apps, custom-developed apps, etc.). B2B collaboration users are represented in your directory, typically as guest users.
    - **Ex**: Company A invites the financial advisor (user from Company B) as a guest user to their secure document sharing platform within Microsoft Entra. The advisor can access relevant tax documents using their existing Company B credentials, enabling secure collaboration without creating a new account in Company A's system.
- **B2B Direct Connect**: B2B direct connect is a feature that establishes a mutual trust relationship between two Entra organizations. This allows users from both organizations to collaborate seamlessly using their home credentials within specific Microsoft Teams features.
    - **Ex**: As of now, B2B direct connect primarily works with Microsoft Teams shared channels. This enables users from different organizations to collaborate on projects, share files, and communicate within a designated channel.
- **Azure AD B2C**: Providing secure and engaging experiences for customers. It offers Customer Identity and Access Management (CIAM) solution. For now, Azure AD B2C is a separate product offering, but Microsoft is planning to integrate it as solution in Microsoft Entra External ID.
    - **Ex**: We can leverage Microsoft Entra External ID to allow customers to register on an e-commerce website using their existing social logins (Facebook, Google, Microsoft, Twitter, LinkedIn etc.) for a faster and more convenient signup experience.

- **Microsoft Entra multi-tenant organization**: Collaborate with multiple tenants in a single Microsoft Entra organization via cross-tenant synchronization.
    - **Ex**: When organizations merge or acquire other companies, they often end up with multiple instances of Microsoft Entra. Each acquired company might retain its existing tenant, and the parent organization would manage these separate tenants. This allows for smooth collaboration while maintaining distinct identities and access controls.

21. Can you give me an example business case where Microsoft Entra B2B or Azure AD B2C services could be leveraged?

Ans:

B2B: It is suitable for scenarios involving collaboration and resource sharing with external partners or organizations.

- **Business case:** Imagine a manufacturing company collaborating with multiple suppliers. Instead of creating separate internal accounts, they use Entra B2B to invite supplier employees to access specific resources like inventory management and project collaboration tools etc. Azure B2B enables controlled access and authentication, ensuring that only authorized individuals from partner organizations can access the shared resources.

B2C: It is ideal for scenarios where businesses interact directly with consumers or customers, offering a flexible and user-friendly authentication and profile management experience.

- **Business Case:** Consider an e-commerce platform. Azure B2C can be used to enable customers to create accounts, log in, and make purchases securely. Customers can choose to log in using their social media accounts or create a new username and password.

22. Who are referred to as guest users in Entra?

Ans:

In Microsoft Entra, guest users are typically external users who are invited to access your organization's resources. They are not employees or members of your organization, but they need access to certain resources in your organization's directory. These users can come from any domain, and they use their own credentials to sign in. Entra supports guest user access to applications and resources through its B2B collaboration feature.

- **Ex:** You need to share a SharePoint document with a contractor who isn't part of your organization. You can invite them as a guest user in Entra, granting them access to the specific document without needing a full account in your directory.

23. I'm building a web app hosted in Azure. Users need to log in with their Gmail or Facebook account. How can I achieve this login functionality?

Ans:

To allow users to log in with their Gmail or Facebook accounts in an Azure web app, you can use Azure Active Directory B2C (Azure AD B2C). Azure AD B2C is a service that enables you to integrate social identity providers, such as Google and Facebook, into your application for user authentication.

Note: Microsoft Entra currently doesn't include Azure AD B2C, but plans are underway to integrate it as a service. Until then, Azure AD B2C remains a separate service.

Explore:

Enable social login (Gmail & Facebook) for your Azure web app:

- **Set up Azure AD B2C:**
    - Create an Azure AD B2C tenant and link it to your Azure subscription.
    - Register your web application within this tenant and also register your application with Google and Facebook to obtain the necessary client IDs and secrets.
    - In Azure AD B2C, configure these identity providers by entering the client IDs and secrets.
- **Design user flows:** Configure sign-up/sign-in policies using Google and Facebook for authentication.
- **Integrate to your app:** Integrate these user flows into your web application, allowing users to authenticate using their social accounts. This setup provides a seamless login experience for users with Gmail or Facebook accounts.

24. What are the various options available to connect an on-premises Windows Active Directory to Microsoft Entra-ID?

Ans:

Below are the possible options:

Option 1 - Integrate on-premises domains with Entra using Microsoft Entra Connect:

- It allows us to synchronize our entire on-premises AD with Entra. This is the most common and widely used option.

Option 2 – AD DS in Azure joined to an on-premises forest:

- We create AD DS servers in Azure and join it with on-premises forest. Using this option, we are extending our on-premises Active Directory infrastructure to the cloud. We need to handle the infra maintenance.

Option 3 - AD DS in Azure with a separate forest

- This is similar to option 2 but we need to choose this to create a completely separate Active Directory environment in Azure.

Option 4 - Extend AD FS to Azure

- We create AD DS and AD FS servers in Azure and join it with on-premises AD FS domains. It allows us to extend our on-premises AD FS infrastructure to Azure.

***Note:** Infrastructure deployment and maintenance will be taken care by:

- **Option 1:** Azure
- **Option 2,3 and 4:** Customer (VM Maintenance, load balancing, patching backup etc.)

Explore:

Integrate on-premises domains with Azure AD:

- It creates a trust between our on-premises Active Directory domain and Entra.
- **Workflow:** Entra AD Connect is used to synchronize user accounts, passwords, and groups from your on-premises AD to Entra. User authentication and authorization are handled through Entra, allowing users to access both on-premises and cloud resources with the same credentials.
    - All objects are synchronized from on-premises AD to Entra directory.
    - Changes made to these items on-premises are copied to Entra, but changes made in Entra are not replicated back to the on-premises domain.
- **When to choose:**
    - We want to leverage cloud services while keeping our on-premises infrastructure intact.
    - To provide a unified login experience for users across both on-premises and cloud resources. Which means, allow users in our on-premises domain to sign in to Entra-enabled applications and services using their on-premises Active Directory credentials.
- **Use case:** A company wants to move some of its applications to the cloud while keeping user management centralized in its on-premises AD. By integrating on-premises domains with Azure AD, employees can access both local and cloud-based resources using a single set of credentials.

AD DS in Azure joined to an on-premises forest:

- This option deploys new AD DS servers in Azure and joins it to our existing on-premises Active Directory Forest. This allows us to create new user and group accounts in Azure that are part of our existing on-premises Active Directory domain.

- **Workflow:** We deploy two or more AD DS servers (Azure VMs) in Azure and join it to our existing on-premises Active Directory Forest. We then create user and group accounts in the new AD DS server. We can authenticate user, service, and computer accounts on-premises and in Azure. We need to manage the AD DS servers in Azure VMs. This includes tasks such as deploying updates, applying security patches, and backing up the data.
- **When to choose:** Use Entra features that are not available on-premises, such as password writeback.
- **Use case**: A company that wants to create new user and group accounts in Azure for a new cloud-based application, but they also want to keep those accounts synchronized with their on-premises Active Directory domain.

AD DS in Azure with a separate forest:

- This option deploys a new AD DS forest in Azure. This allows us to create a new set of user and group accounts in Azure that are separate from our on-premises Active Directory domain.
- **Workflow:** We deploy two or more AD DS servers (Azure VMs) in Azure and join it to a new forest. We then create user and group accounts in the new forest. We need to manage the AD DS servers in Azure VMs. This includes tasks such as deploying updates, applying security patches, and backing up the data.
- **When to choose:** Select this option when we need to maintain a clear separation between our on-premises and cloud environments. Also, we need to leverage Entra features.
- **Use case:** A company sets up a separate forest in Azure to manage user accounts and resources for its cloud-based applications. This ensures that cloud resources are managed separately from on-premises resources, providing a clear boundary between the two environments.

Extend AD FS to Azure:

- This option extends our on-premises AD FS deployment to Azure. This allows users to sign in to Entra-enabled applications and services using their on-premises Active Directory credentials.
- **Workflow:** We must deploy our AD DS, AD FS, and AD FS Web Application Proxy servers (Azure VMs) in Azure and join it to our on-premises AD FS farm. We then configure the AD FS server in Azure to trust our on-premises AD FS farm. When users attempt to access a cloud resource, AD FS verifies their identity against the on-premises AD and issues a security token that Azure AD trusts.
- **When to choose:**
  - Authenticate and authorize users from partner organizations.
  - Allow users to authenticate from web browsers running outside of the organizational firewall.
  - Allow users to connect from authorized external devices such as mobile devices.
  - When we have a complex on-premises AD environment and want to leverage AD FS for federated authentication with Microsoft Entra.

- **Use case:** ABC Corp partners with XYZ Inc to share app access. ABC Corp has been using an on-premises AD FS setup to provide secure and seamless access to their shared applications for both internal users and XYZ Inc employees. ABC Corp is migrating some of the shared application to Azure. To keep login smooth, ABC extends AD FS to Azure. Now, ABC Corp and XYZ Inc staff can access Azure apps using their AD FS with the same credentials.

***Note:**

- **AD DS:** Active Directory Domain Services
- **AD FS:** Active Directory Federation Services

25. What is Microsoft Entra Connect?

Ans:

Entra Connect is a Microsoft tool that helps organizations to automatically synchronize their on-premises Active Directory identities with Entra. That way, users can use the same credentials to access both on-premises applications and cloud services.

26. What are the features of Entra Connect?

Ans:

Features of Entra Connect:

- Identity synchronization
- Password Hash Synchronization (PHS)
- Pass-Through Authentication (PTA)
- Federation
- Password writeback
- Conditional access
- Health Monitoring

Entra Connect Services:

- Entra Connect sync
- Entra Connect Health

Explore:

Features:

- **Identity synchronization:** It can synchronize user accounts, group memberships, and other identity information from on-premises Active Directory to Entra.
- **Password hash synchronization (PHS):** Without any additional infrastructure or complex configuration, it synchronizes a hash of the user's on-premises AD password with Entra, so that the user can sign in to both environments with the same credentials.

- **Pass-through authentication (PTA):** It allows the user to use the same password on-premises and in the cloud, but instead of storing the password hash in Entra, it validates the password against the on-premises AD. This feature requires a lightweight agent to be installed on one or more on-premises servers.
- **Federation**: Azure AD Connect supports federation scenarios, such as AD FS, which allow users to access both on-premises and cloud resources without the need for separate authentication.
- **Password writeback:** Entra Connect can write passwords from Entra back to on-premises Active Directory. This can help us improve security by ensuring that passwords are synchronized between the on-premises and cloud environments.
- **Conditional access:** It can be used to configure conditional access policies for Entra. This allows us to control who can access cloud applications, and from where.
- **Health monitoring:** It provides health monitoring capabilities that can help us identify and troubleshoot problems with our identity synchronization configuration.

Services:

- **Entra Connect sync:** It is responsible for synchronizing identity information between on-premises Active Directory and Azure AD.
- **Entra Connect Health:** It provides health monitoring capabilities for Entra Connect.

27. Imagine we're a large organization with computers, users, and groups in our on-premises Active Directory. We want to connect our on-premises AD with Entra using Entra Connect. Can you explain the step-by-step solution?

Ans:

Here are the high-level steps involved:

- Install Entra Connect on a physical server or a virtual machine in your on-premises environment.
- Configure Entra Connect with the required parameters. **Ex:** Source and target directories, sync type, sync frequency, user credentials etc.
- Start synchronizing on-premises AD with Entra.
- Once the synchronization is complete, we can use Entra for single sign-on (SSO) to cloud applications, and manage our users and groups in the cloud.

Explore:

Here is the detailed explanation:

Prerequisites:

- **On-Premises:** Set up a dedicated Windows Server for installing Entra Connect.
- **Azure:** Ensure we have an Azure subscription and an Entra tenant.

Step 1: Install and Configure Entra Connect

- Download the Entra Connect from official Microsoft Azure Website.
- Install Entra Connect on Windows Server at on-premises.
- Specify the Configurations:
  - **Directories:** Source and Target Directories from On-premise AD and Entra. We may need to specify Entra Tenant ID, On-premises AD Domain name, and admin credentials for both On-premises AD and Entra.
  - **Objects:** Entities that needs to be synchronized. **Ex:** user accounts, group memberships, etc.
  - **Attributes:** Entities that needs to be synchronized. **Ex:** User name, email address, etc.
  - **Synchronization Type:** Select it based on your requirements **Ex:** PHS, PTA, Federation (AD FS).
  - **Synchronization schedule:** Determines how often synchronization needs to be happened. It is controlled by a scheduler component. By default, a sync task runs every 30 minutes.
  - **Filtering and Scoping:** Using this option we can exclude specific objects from synchronization if required.
  - **Password Writeback**: Enable it to sync password changes from Entra to on-premises AD.

Step 2: Start Synchronization

- **Initial Sync:** The initial synchronization process can take several hours to complete, depending on the size of your on-premises environment.
- **Delta Sync:** As per the sync schedule, only changes made since the last sync are replicated, reducing network and resource impact. Microsoft recommends that a delta sync must happen within 7 days from the last delta or full sync.
- **Metaverse Management:** The Entra Connect Metaverse (storage area) holds central repository or combined data from on-premises AD and Azure AD.
  - Metaverse is managed by the Entra Connect sync engine. The sync engine uses the Metaverse to keep track of which identities have been synchronized, and to ensure that only the latest changes are synchronized. Also, Metaverse can be used to troubleshoot synchronization problems.

Step 3: Test the synchronization by logging in to a cloud application using Active Directory credentials.

Step 4: Monitoring Solutions:

- **Entra Connect Health:** Install Entra Connect Health agents to monitor the synchronization process and server health.
- **Monitor and Troubleshoot:** Monitor synchronization logs and reports for any issues. Use Entra Connect Health for insights into synchronization performance.

- **Manage Password Synchronization/Validation:**
  - For PHS, securely synchronize password hashes to Entra for user authentication.
  - For PTA, validate passwords against on-premises AD for single sign-on.

Step 5: Continuous Monitoring, Administration and Tuning:

- **Review and Update Configurations as Needed:** Regularly review and update synchronization rules, filtering, and attribute mappings to reflect organizational changes.
- **Scale and Optimize:** Adjust synchronization intervals and configuration settings based on organization growth and resource availability.
- **Security and Compliance:** Ensure that security policies and compliance requirements are met throughout the synchronization process.

***Note:**

- **PHS:** Password Hash Synchronization
- **PTA:** Pass-Through Authentication

28. What is Entra Cloud Sync how it is different from Entra Connect?

Ans:

Entra Cloud Sync is a cloud native solution alternative to Entra Connect software. It is a lightweight tool and a new offering from Microsoft Azure.

Difference:

Both Entra Connect and Entra Cloud Sync can be used to synchronize data from on-premises AD to Entra. However, each has its own purpose.

- With Entra Connect, most of the configuration is performed on the dedicated on-premises server. However, with Cloud Sync, the intention is to transfer these configurations to the cloud, requiring only a small and easy-to-install program on the on-premises side.

Explore:

Let's explore more differences:

- Currently, Entra Cloud Sync does not support all of the features that are supported by Entra Connect.
- Features supported by Entra Cloud Sync which are not available in Entra Connect:
  - Synchronizing from a multi-forest disconnected AD environment (useful in business merger & acquisition scenarios).
  - Using multiple provisioning agents which helps us simplifying high availability environments.

- Features supported by Entra Connect which are not available in Entra Cloud Sync:
  - Support for Pass-Through Authentication.
  - Filter on objects' attribute values.
  - Microsoft Entra Domain Services support.
  - Unlimited number of objects per AD domain.

When to choose:

- **Entra Connect:**
  - Advanced authentication requirements.
  - Complex identity management architectures.
  - Extensive Customization Needs.
  - Very Large Organizations.
- **Entra Cloud Sync:**
  - Cloud centric configurations.
  - Quick and simplified AD Sync deployments.
  - Simplified High-Availability management.
  - Smaller organization.

29. What is SSPR in Entra?

Ans:

SSPR stands for Self-Service Password Reset. It is an Entra feature that allows users to reset their passwords without having to contact the IT helpdesk. This can help to reduce the number of helpdesks calls and improve productivity.

Explore:

SSPR allows users to:

- Change their password.
- Reset their password in case of a forgotten password.
- Unlock their account when it is locked out.
- Write back the password to an on-premises directory.

30. We're generating and syncing a significant amount of identity-related data into Microsoft Entra. Could you please explain where Azure stores this data?

Ans:

- Entra is a fully managed service. That means, data storage, HA&DR, security, data and service availability, scalability and underlaying infrastructure maintenance will be automatically taken care by Azure team.

- However, Entra uses a variety of databases, object storage to store identity data. Ex: SQL Database, Cosmos DB etc.

Explore:

The storage and management of Entra data is abstracted from users and administrators, meaning we interact with Entra through its APIs and interfaces without needing to be concerned about the underlying storage mechanism. Some of the data stores include:

- **Azure SQL Database (RDBMS):** Stores user profile, group membership information etc.
- **Azure Cosmos DB (NoSQL):** Stores dynamic membership rule definitions.
- **Azure Table Storage:** Stores audit logs.
- **Azure Blob Storage:** Stores backups.

***Note:**

- The data is stored in multiple locations/regions to ensure availability and redundancy.
- It's important to trust Entra's infrastructure for data storage, as Microsoft invests heavily in security and compliance measures to protect our data.

31. What is Microsoft Entra Joined devices?

Ans:

Entra Join is a feature for joining a device (mobile, laptop etc.) to Entra ID. When a device is Entra joined, it is managed by Azure and can access cloud-based resources such as Microsoft 365 apps and services. It offers simplified device management, advanced resource security, and Single Sign-on (SSO).

32. What is the key difference between Entra joined devices, Entra Hybrid joined devices and Microsoft Entra registered devices?

Ans:

It offers three different join types:

- **Entra Joined:** Devices will be managed by Entra. **Ex:** Office provided laptop.
- **Hybrid Entra joined:** Devices will be managed by both Entra and On-premise AD Domain. **Ex:** Office laptop that needs to access both on-prem and cloud.
- **Entra registered:** Devices will not be managed by Entra. **Ex:** Personal phone, Buy Your Own Device (BYOD) scenarios.

Explore:

Entra Joined:

- Windows 10/11 devices that are directly integrated with Entra for user authentication and management. They are typically corporate-owned devices.
- **Suits:** Startups or modern enterprises with a fully cloud-based infrastructure, using devices primarily connected to cloud resources.
- **Use Case:** Company laptops used by employees who sign in with their work email accounts (Entra credentials) to access company resources, such as files and applications, while ensuring centralized device management and security policies.

Hybrid Entra Joined:

- Windows devices (Win 10+, Win Server 2016 +) that are connected to both an on-premises Active Directory and Entra. This allows for a seamless experience when transitioning from on-premises to cloud services.
- **Suits:** Large enterprises with significant on-premises infrastructure migrating to the cloud while maintaining access to local resources.
- **Use Case:** A scenario where an organization has an existing on-premises Active Directory but is gradually migrating to Azure. Hybrid Entra Joined ensures that devices can access both on-premises and cloud resources (Apps, Storage etc.) during the transition.

Entra Registered:

- Typically, personal devices, including Windows, iOS, and Android, that are registered with Entra for access to company apps and resources. This registration is often user-driven and provides limited management control.
- **Suits:** Bring Your Own Device scenarios.
- **Use Case:** An employee uses their personal iPhone / Android phone to access company email and apps. They register the device with Entra to enable single sign-on (SSO) for easier access to company resources on their mobile device.

33. Can you describe Microsoft Intune and explain how it differs from Microsoft Entra Joined Devices?

Ans:

Microsoft Intune is a cloud-based service that focuses on mobile device management (MDM) and mobile application management (MAM).

While both Intune and Entra Joined Devices are part of the device management strategy in an organization, they serve different purposes. Intune is about managing the device and its applications, while Entra ID join is about giving the device an identity in Entra.

Explore:

Microsoft Intune: It is a cloud-based MDM and MAM service. It is a part of the Microsoft 365 suite of products and services.

- It helps organizations manage and secure corporate-owned and personal devices.
- **Microsoft Intune can be used to:**
  - Configure (Password policies, screen lock etc.), secure (PIN, encryption etc.) and track devices.
  - Deploy and manage Apps on devices.
  - It allows you to control how your organization's devices are used, including mobile phones, tablets, and laptops. It can provide you with configuration management, software updates, remote wipe capabilities, and more.
- **Supported devices:** Windows 10/11, Mac OS X, iOS, Android and Chromebooks devices.

Microsoft Entra Joined Devices vs. Microsoft Intune:

- **Entra Joined Devices:** Entra-ID is a cloud-based identity and access management (IAM) service that primarily focused on managing user identities. Entra joined devices often use Intune for deeper device management capabilities.
  - **Use Case:** Best for organizations leveraging Entra (Azure AD) for IAM, looking for seamless authentication and SSO capabilities, and intending to use cloud-first management without relying on traditional Active Directory.
- **Microsoft Intune**: It is a cloud-based MDM & MAM that primarily focused on managing devices.
  - **Use Case:** Ideal for organizations needing detailed control over device settings, security, and application management across various device types and platforms.

34. Are you familiar with Universal Print?

Ans:

Yes! While I haven't had hands-on experience with it personally, I have observed a customer conducting a Proof of Concept (POC) on the Azure Universal Print Service.

- Universal Print is a cloud-based print management service that allows organizations to manage printers from anywhere.
- Universal Print works by connecting printers to Azure and then allowing users to print to those printers from any device, regardless of where they are located. Users can print to printers using their Entra credentials.

Explore:

Use Cases:

- A large enterprise with multiple offices can use Universal Print to centralize the management of printers and make it easier for employees to print to the printers they need.
- A marketing team can use Universal Print to print marketing materials from their laptops.
- A law firm can use Universal Print to allow lawyers to print documents from their tablets while they are in court.
- A hospital can use Universal Print to allow patients to print medical records from their phones while they are waiting to see a doctor.

35. What is MFA in Microsoft Entra and how it works?

Ans:

- Multi-Factor Authentication (MFA) in Entra is a security feature that adds an extra layer of protection to user accounts. MFA can be configured for users, groups, and applications.
- It requires users to provide multiple forms of verification before they can access their Entra accounts.
- When we enable MFA in Entra, users will be prompted to provide two or more factors (Password + Code received on user mobile etc.) when they sign in.
- This makes it more difficult for attackers to gain unauthorized access to our resources.

Explore:

MFA Supports below verification methods:

- **Text message (SMS):** We receive a one-time code (OTP) message on our registered mobile.
- **Phone call:** We receive a one-time code (OTP) call on our mobile.
- **Push notification:** We receives a push notification on our registered mobile app (Ex: Microsoft Authenticator, Authenticator Lite) and must approve the login request.
- **Security key:** We insert a security key (Ex: FIDO2) into our computer or mobile device.
- **OATH Tokens:** We can use OATH software or hardware tokens to generate authentication codes.

36. What is a passwordless authentication method? Does Microsoft Entra ID support passwordless authentication?

Ans:

Passwordless authentication is a method of verifying a user's identity without requiring them to enter a traditional password. Instead, it relies on more secure and user-friendly alternatives, such as biometrics, hardware tokens, or mobile apps.

Microsoft Entra ID does support Passwordless authentication using Microsoft Authenticator, Windows Hello for Business etc.

Explore:

Here are the Entra Passwordless options:

- **Windows Hello for Business:** Ideal for users with their own designated Windows PC. The biometric and PIN credentials are directly tied to the user's PC, which prevents access from anyone other than the owner.
- **Platform Credential for macOS:** A new capability on macOS that is enabled using the Microsoft Enterprise single sign-on extension (SSOe).
- **Platform Single Sign-On (PSSO) for macOS with Smart Card Authentication:** A new capability on macOS for smart card-based authentication that is enabled using the Microsoft Enterprise single sign-on extension (SSOe).
- **Microsoft Authenticator App:** Users can sign in using the Microsoft Authenticator app on their mobile devices (iOS or Android). The app provides two passwordless options:
    - **Push Notifications:** Users receive a push notification to approve or deny the sign-in attempt.
    - **Time-based One-Time Passcodes (TOTPs):** Users enter a TOTP generated by the app.
- **Passkeys (FIDO2):** Useful for users who sign in to shared machines like kiosks, in situations where the use of phones is restricted, and for highly privileged identities.
- **Certificate-Based Authentication:** This method uses digital certificates to authenticate the user.

37. What is Conditional Access in Entra, and what are some use cases for it? How does it work?

Ans:

Conditional Access in Entra is a security feature that allows us to define conditions that must be met before a user is granted access to a resource.

Workflow:

- **User Initiates access request:** User raises a request to access an Azure Resource or Data.
- **Condition Evaluation:** Entra evaluates the conditions defined in the Conditional Access policies. **Ex:** User location, Device Compliance etc.
- **Policy enforcement and Access Decision:** If it passes condition evaluation phase, the policy is enforced. **Ex:** taking through multi-factor authentication (MFA), granting access, blocking access, etc.
- **Audit and reporting**: Conditional Access policies generate audit logs and reports so that admins can track, review the access events and policy enforcement.

Use Cases:

- Protecting sensitive data.
- Data leakage prevention.
- Managing privileged access.
- Enforcing BYOD (Bring Your Own Device) policies.

Ex: We can use this feature to enforce MFA for work from home users, ensuring that only authorized individuals can access corporate resources from outside the corporate network.

Explore:

Various types of conditions that we can define:

- **User location:** We can require users to sign in from specific locations. **Ex:** Corporate network or a trusted IP address range.
- **Device:** We can require users to sign in from specific devices. **Ex:** Company-owned or registered devices.
- **User's risk profile:** We can require users to sign in using MFA if their risk profile is high. **Ex:** When signing in from an unknown location or using a compromised device.
- **Application or resource specific:** Customize access controls for individual applications or services, ensuring that sensitive data is protected appropriately based on the application's importance.

38. What is the Microsoft Entra Application Proxy?

Ans:

- It is a feature of Entra that enables users to access on-premises web applications from a remote client.
- This allows users to access internal applications from outside the corporate network without the need for traditional VPN solutions.
- Application Proxy serves as a bridge between your internal network and external users or devices, enabling remote access without the need for complex network configurations or VPNs.

Explore:

Workflow:

- Application Proxy includes both the Application Proxy service which runs in the cloud, and the Application Proxy connector which runs on an on-premises server.
- Both these components work together to securely pass the user sign-on token from Entra to the web application.

- When a user attempts to access an on-premises application, their request is routed to the proxy service in Azure. The proxy service then authenticates the user and redirects their request to the on-premises application.

Sample Use Case:

- A multinational corporation uses Entra Application Proxy to securely provide remote access to its on-premises SharePoint server for employees working from home, ensuring data security and compliance while simplifying access.

39. What are the various ways to monitor Microsoft Entra-ID?

Ans:

Here are some of the most common methods:

- **Entra Built-in monitoring solutions:** Entra reporting and Usage Insights, Entra Logs, Entra Connect Health etc.
- **Other Azure Services:** Azure Monitor, Azure Sentinel and Azure Security Center.
- **Third party tools and services:** Serverless360, Dynatrace, Datadog etc.

Explore:

- **Entra Reporting and Usage Insights**: With this feature, we can get an application-centric view of our sign-in data. Usage & insights includes a report on authentication methods, service principal sign-ins, and application credential activity. We can access these reports in the Azure portal to understand user behavior and application adoption. **Ex:** We can find answers for "Top used applications", "Apps with most failed sign-ins", "App wise top sign-in errors", etc.
- **Entra Logs:** Entra offers various types of logs and we can access these logs from Azure Portal.
  - **Audit Logs:** Entra generates audit logs that record various activities. **Ex:** role assignments, password resets, configuration changes etc.
  - **Sing-in Logs:** Activity related to sign-ins. **Ex:** User sign-in patterns, number of sign-ins, successful and failed sing-ins etc.
  - **Provisioning Logs:** It provides information around users provisioned in your tenant through a third-party service. **Ex:** You can use the provisioning logs to find answers to questions like "What groups were successfully created in ServiceNow?", "What users from Workday were successfully created in Active Directory?" etc.
- **Entra Connect Health**: If we have an on-premises AD and are using Entra Connect to synchronize identities, this feature can monitor the health and performance of our synchronization infrastructure.
- **Azure Monitor:** A centralized platform for monitoring Azure services, including Entra. Using this we can also setup custom monitoring, and alerting rules. **Ex:** Monitor Entra events and send an email when sign-in activity fails for the same user three consecutive times.

- **Azure Sentinel:** Azure Sentinel is a cloud-native SIEM (Security Information and Event Management) and SOAR (Security Orchestration, Automation, and Response) solution that can be used to monitor Entra and other Microsoft cloud services. Azure Sentinel can be used to detect and investigate threats, and to respond to incidents.
- **Azure Security Center**: It offers security monitoring and threat detection capabilities for Azure services, including Entra. It provides insights into identity-related security issues and offers recommendations to improve security.
- **Third-party monitoring tools:** We can choose third party solutions that can provide additional features and functionality beyond what is available in Azure native features.

40. What is Azure Policy?

Ans:

- Azure Policy service allows us to create, assign, and manage policies to enforce organizational standards, best practices and compliance for our Azure resources.
- Policies can be assigned to resources at the subscription, resource group, or resource level.

Explore:

Consider the sample scenarios below where defining Azure Policies can help us enforce organizational standards:

- We could create a policy to ensure that all Azure SQL Databases are encrypted using Transparent Data Encryption (TDE) for security compliance. This policy would deny the creation of databases without encryption.
- Create a policy that denies the creation of Azure VMs with passwords that are less than 12 characters long.
- We can create a policy to limit the number of Azure Storage accounts that can be created in a subscription.
- Define a policy that requires all Azure VMs to be tagged with the department that owns them.
- Enforce a policy that mandates geo-replication for critical databases to ensure high availability and disaster recovery.
- Define policies to restrict the use of specific VM sizes to control costs or ensure performance.
- Create a policy to ensure that VMs are configured with regular backups to protect against data loss.
- Create a policy that requires all Azure Storage accounts to be encrypted with a specific encryption algorithm.

41. Can you explain the components of Azure Policy and provide an example illustrating how Azure Policy works?

Ans:

Here are the main elements of an Azure Policy:

- **Policy Definition:** It defines the desired state of the resource and the effect that should be taken if the resource is not in the desired state. A Policy Definition (JSON Format) is a set of rules that specify what is allowed or not allowed in our Azure environment.
    - **Ex:** We create a policy definition named "SQL Security Policy TDE " with a rule that says, "All Azure SQL Databases must have Transparent Data Encryption (TDE) enabled."
- **Policy Assignment:** This assigns the policy definition to a scope such as a subscription, resource group, or resource.
    - **Ex:** We assign the "SQL Security Policy TDE" policy to the entire Azure subscription.
- **Initiatives (Optional):** It allows us grouping multiple policies as a single unit.
    - **Ex:** We create an initiative called "Data Security Standard" that includes the "SQL Security Policy TDE" policy along with other data security policies.
- **Compliance Evaluation:** Azure Policy continually evaluates resources within the assigned scope to check for compliance with policy definitions.
    - **Ex:** Azure Policy regularly evaluates all SQL Databases in the subscription to ensure they have TDE enabled as required by the policy.
- **Policy effect:** This specifies what action should be taken if the policy is violated. The possible effects are Deny (deny the action), Audit (log the event), Warn (log a warning message), Do nothing.
    - **Ex:** If we try to create a new Azure SQL Database without TDE enabled, Azure Policy can prevent its creation (deny), trigger an audit, or notify administrators.
- **Auditing and Reporting:** Azure Policy provides auditing and reporting capabilities, allowing you to view compliance data and reports.
    - **Ex:** We can generate a compliance report that shows the status of TDE compliance across all SQL Databases in the subscription, helping us identify any non-compliant databases.

42. It seems like both Entra Conditional Access and Azure Policies have similar functions. Is there a difference between these two services?

Ans:

- Both are part of cloud security services; however, they serve different purposes and are used in different contexts.
- **The main difference:** Entra Conditional Access is focused on **controlling access** to resources, while Azure Policies is focused on **enforcing policies** on resources.

Explore:

- **Entra Conditional Access**: It can be used to control access to resources based on a variety of factors, such as the user's identity, the device they are using, and the location they are accessing the resource from. **Ex:** We could use it to enforce MFA for users who access resources from untrusted networks.
- **Azure Policies (Broader solution):** It can be used to enforce policies on resources, such as encryption requirements or tag policies. **Ex:** We could use Azure Policies to enforce encryption requirements for all Azure SQL Databases.
- **Combination:** In the real world, we use both Azure Policy and Entra Conditional Access together to establish a more comprehensive security posture. **Ex:** Through Entra Conditional Access, we can enforce MFA, and using Azure Policy, we can ensure that storage containers access must be set to private (disable public access).

43. Explain the concept of Microsoft Entra ID Governance and its role in access management?

Ans:

Microsoft Entra ID Governance is a suite of tools and services within the Microsoft Entra family designed to help organizations manage and control access to their resources in a secure and compliant manner. It provides a comprehensive framework for ensuring that the right individuals have the right access to the right resources at the right times, and that this access is managed and monitored efficiently.

Explore:

Key components of Entra ID Governance Framework:

- **Access Reviews:** Regularly review and recertify access to ensure that users only have the necessary permissions.
- **Privileged Identity Management (PIM):** Manage, control, and monitor access within Entra, Azure, and other Microsoft Online Services. It includes just-in-time privileged access, approval workflows, and access reviews.

- **Entitlement Management:** Automate the provisioning of access packages to external and internal users based on predefined policies. This includes lifecycle management for access, ensuring that access rights are granted and revoked as needed.
- **Terms of Use:** Ensure that users agree to specific terms of use before accessing resources, providing a way to inform users about policies and collect their acceptance.

Example:

Consider a large enterprise that collaborates with numerous external partners and contractors. Managing access for these external users can be challenging, especially when ensuring that access is granted appropriately and revoked when no longer needed. With Microsoft Entra ID Governance, the enterprise can:

- Use Entitlement Management to create access packages that include all the necessary permissions for external users.
- Automate the access request and approval process, ensuring that external users get the access they need without unnecessary delays.
- Conduct regular Access Reviews to verify that external users still need the permissions they were granted and revoke access when it is no longer required.
- Utilize Privileged Identity Management (PIM) to manage and monitor any elevated access required by external users, ensuring that such access is granted only when necessary and for the minimum duration required.

44. As a cloud administrator, you're tasked with adding over 1,000+ users to Microsoft Entra ID. You also need to set a default password and enable Multi-Factor Authentication (MFA) for these users. How can you accomplish this efficiently for bulk user creation?

Ans:

If we need to create a small number of users, we can use the Azure Portal UI. However, in enterprise environments, it's often more efficient and scalable to create users using scripts and automation. Here is the high-level process to add bulk users to Microsoft Entra:

- **CSV Preparation:** Create a CSV file with user details including passwords.
- **User Import:** Use Azure AD PowerShell module to bulk import users from the CSV into Entra Admin Center.
- **Enable MFA (Multi Factor Authentication):** Use MSOnline PowerShell module to enable MFA for each user.

Explore:

- **Prepare a CSV File:** Create a CSV file with the necessary user details. The CSV file should include columns like

  - **UserPrincipalName:** The unique identifier for the user in the format of an email address. **Ex:** user1@abc.com.
  - **DisplayName:** The full name of the user. **Ex:** User One
  - **MailNickname:** The mail alias for the user. **Ex:** user1
  - **PasswordProfile.ForceChangePasswordNextSignIn:** A Boolean value indicating whether the user is required to change their password upon their next sign-in. **Ex:** true/false
  - **PasswordProfile.Password:** The initial/default password assigned to the user.

- **Import Users using PowerShell:** Use a foreach loop to iterate through each individual row in the CSV file and add the user to Entra (Azure AD) using "New-AzureADUser".
- **Enable MFA for Users:** Use PowerShell to enable MFA for the newly created users. This can be done by updating the user settings in the Azure portal or using the MSOnline (Set-MsolUser) PowerShell module.

45. What are the common issues users encounter with Microsoft Entra authentication and access, and how can these issues be efficiently troubleshooted?

Ans:

Here's a breakdown of common problems and troubleshooting steps:

- **Incorrect Credentials:** Users are unable to sign in due to incorrect username or password.
  - **Solution:** Verify that the user is entering the correct username and password. Reset the user's password if necessary. Check if the account is locked or disabled and unlock/enable it if needed.
- **Insufficient Permissions:** Users might lack the necessary permissions to access specific resources.
  - **Solution:** Ensure users have the appropriate permissions to access the desired resources. Cloud admins can manage permissions in the Entra admin center.
- **Multi-Factor Authentication (MFA) Problems:** Users cannot complete the MFA process.
  - **Solution:** Ensure the user has registered the correct MFA methods. Verify the user's device settings (**Ex:** push notifications for the Microsoft Authenticator app). Check the MFA service health status in the Azure portal. Reset MFA settings for the user and guide them to re-register their MFA device.
- **Conditional Access Policy Issues:** Users are blocked from accessing resources due to conditional access policies.
  - **Solution:** Review the applied conditional access policies in the Azure portal. Check if the user's location, device, or application falls under any restrictive policies. Modify the policies as needed to allow legitimate access while maintaining security.

- **Account Lockout:** Users are locked out of their accounts due to multiple failed sign-in attempts.
  - **Solution:** Verify the account lockout policy settings. Investigate the reason for failed sign-ins (**Ex:** password issues, malicious attempts). Manually unlock the user's account from the Entra admin portal.
- **Application Access Issues:** Users cannot access specific applications integrated with Azure AD.
  - **Solution:** Verify that the user has been assigned the appropriate roles and permissions for the application. Check the application's single sign-on (SSO) configuration and ensure it is working correctly.
- **Synchronization Issues:** Problems with directory synchronization between Microsoft Entra and on-premises Active Directory.
  - **Solution:** Verify that Microsoft Entra Connect is running and properly configured. Check the synchronization status and logs in Entra Connect. Manually trigger a synchronization cycle if necessary.
- **Network Issues:** Users experience connectivity issues when accessing Entra services.
  - **Solution:** Ensure that the network settings allow access to Entra endpoints. Check if there are any firewall or proxy settings that might be blocking access. Verify the health status of Entra services in the Azure portal.

Explore:

Additional Entra Troubleshooting Tips:

- **Enable Entra Sign-in Logs:** Check sign-in logs, audit logs and custom logs and reports in the Azure portal to gather information about failed authentication attempts and access issues.
- **Health Status:** Always check the Azure service health status to identify if there are any ongoing issues or outages affecting Entra.
- **Error Codes:** If you encounter specific error codes during authentication or authorization, refer to the Microsoft Entra error codes documentation. This can provide you with descriptions of the errors, potential fixes, and suggested workarounds. Ex: AADSTS50000 (TokenIssuanceError), AADSTS50001 (InvalidResource), AADSTS50005(DevicePolicyError), AADSTS50012 (AuthenticationFailed), AADSTS50034(UserAccountNotFound), AADSTS50053 (IdsLocked) etc.
- **Microsoft Support:** If the problem persists, consider reaching out to Microsoft support for further assistance.

CHAPTER 04

Fundamentals of Data Engineering & Analytics

1. What is "Data Analytics"?

Ans:

Data Analytics is the process of examining, cleaning, transforming, and modelling data to discover useful information, draw conclusions, and support decision-making. It involves using statistical techniques and software tools to analyze data sets and uncover patterns, trends, and relationships that can inform business strategies and improve outcomes.

2. What are the different types of data analytics?

Ans:

There are four main types of data analytics:

- **Descriptive Analytics** (What happened).
- **Diagnostic Analytics** (Why something happened).
- **Predictive Analytics** (What might happen in future).
- **Prescriptive Analytics** (What to do).

Explore:

- **Descriptive Analytics:** This type focuses on summarizing historical data to understand what has happened in the past. It uses data aggregation and data mining techniques to provide insights into past performance. **Ex:** Generating reports on e-commerce sales trends over the last quarter.
- **Diagnostic Analytics:** This type aims to determine why something happened. It digs deeper into data to identify patterns and relationships, often using techniques such as drill-down, data discovery, data mining, and correlations. **Ex:** Investigating why sales traffic dropped after a recent product catalog redesign.
- **Predictive Analytics:** This type uses statistical models and machine learning techniques to predict future outcomes based on historical data. It helps forecast trends and behaviours, aiding in proactive decision-making. **Ex:** Analyze purchase history to predict customer churn (customers stop making purchases). This can help you identify customers at risk of leaving.
- **Prescriptive Analytics:** This type goes a step further by recommending actions to achieve desired outcomes. It uses algorithms, simulations, and optimization techniques to suggest the best course of action for future scenarios. **Ex:** Recommending personalized product offers based on browsing behavior or optimizing supply chain logistics etc.

3. Can you describe the end-to-end steps involved in the Data Analytics Life Cycle?

Ans:

The data analytics cycle involves several key steps:

- Problem Definition and Goal Setting
- Data Collection
- Data Preprocessing/Cleaning
- Data Exploration
- Feature Engineering
- Data Modelling & Analysis
- Business Insights and Decision-Making
- Common factors like Data quality, security, governance etc.

Remember, this cycle is iterative, and you may revisit steps as needed to refine your analysis.

Explore:

Here are the detailed steps:

- **Define Objectives:** Clearly define the problem or question your business wants to answer. Identify the goals and objectives of the data analysis.
    - **Ex:** In a Healthcare Entity, determine the factors affecting patient readmission rates within 30 days of discharge.
- **Data Collection:** Gather relevant data from various sources such as databases, files, APIs, surveys, or external datasets. Ensure the data is reliable and suitable for analysis.
    - **Ex:** Gather patient records, including demographics, medical history, treatment details, and readmission data from hospital databases.
- **Data Cleaning:** Inspect the collected data for errors, missing values, and inconsistencies. Clean the data by handling missing values, duplicates, correcting errors, and standardizing formats.
    - **Ex:** Identify and correct errors in patient records, handle missing values in medical history, and standardize date formats.
- **Data Exploration:** Conduct exploratory data analysis (EDA) to understand the data's structure, patterns, and relationships. Use visualization tools and summary statistics to gain insights into the data.
    - **Ex:** Use summary statistics and visualizations to understand the distribution of patient ages, readmission rates, and treatment types.

- **Data Transformation / Feature Engineering:**
    - Transform the data into a suitable format for analysis. This may involve normalization, aggregation, encoding categorical variables, or creating new features.
    - Create new features or modify existing ones to improve model performance. **Ex:** Combining date and time fields to create a single timestamp.
    - **Ex:** Normalize patient age, encode categorical variables like treatment type, and create a feature for the number of previous hospital visits.
- **Data Modelling:**
    - **Model building:** Select appropriate statistical or machine learning models based on the analysis objectives. **Ex:** Choose appropriate algorithms (regression, classification, clustering, etc.) to predict the likelihood of patient readmission based on the prepared data.
    - **Model Evaluation:** Assess the model's performance using metrics (accuracy, precision, recall, etc.). Fine-tune the model if necessary.
    - **Model Deployment:** Deploy the model, monitor its performance and update as needed.
- **Data Analysis:** Apply the selected models to analyze the data. Interpret the results to derive insights, trends, and patterns.
    - **Ex:** Train and apply the logistic regression model on historical patient data to identify patterns and factors contributing to readmissions.
- **Data Visualization & Story telling:** Create visualizations such as charts, graphs, and dashboards to represent the analysis results. Use visualization to communicate findings effectively to stakeholders.
    - **Ex:** Create visualizations such as bar charts and heatmaps to show the relationship between patient demographics and readmission rates.
- **Interpretation and Insights:** Interpret the analysis results in the context of the defined objectives. Draw actionable insights and conclusions from the data.
    - **Ex:** Interpret the model results to identify key factors like age, extra health conditions, and length of stay that influence readmission rates.
- **Reporting and Communication:** Compile the findings, insights, and visualizations into a comprehensive report. Present the results to stakeholders, ensuring clarity and relevance.
    - **Ex:** Compile a report summarizing the findings, including visualizations and key insights, to present to hospital administrators.
- **Decision Making:** Use the insights derived from the analysis to inform business decisions and strategies. Implement actions based on the data-driven recommendations.

- **Ex:** Based on the insights, recommend changes to discharge procedures and follow-up care to reduce readmission rates.

- **Monitoring and Evaluation:** Continuously monitor the outcomes of the implemented decisions. Evaluate the impact and effectiveness of the actions taken, and refine the process as needed.
  - **Ex:** Implement the recommended changes and continuously monitor readmission rates to evaluate the effectiveness of the new procedures.

- **Common Factors:** Here are some common factors that apply across all phases of the data analytics lifecycle:
  - **Domain Knowledge:** Understanding the context and domain-specific requirements.
  - **Flexible and Scalable Solutions:** Adapting to changes in data, business needs, and technology advancements. Ensuring that the data infrastructure can grow with increasing data volumes and complexity.
  - **Data Quality:** Ensuring data accuracy, completeness, and consistency throughout the process.
  - **Data Security:** Implementing measures to protect data from unauthorized access, breaches, and other security threats.
  - **Privacy Protection:** Ensuring that personal and sensitive data is anonymized and protected according to privacy laws and best practices.
  - **Data Governance:** Implementing policies and procedures to manage data quality, privacy, and security.
  - **Regulatory Compliance:** Ensuring that data practices comply with relevant laws and regulations, such as GDPR, HIPAA, etc.
  - **Ethical Considerations:** Ensuring that data usage aligns with ethical standards and does not cause harm or bias.
  - **Documentation:** Properly documenting requirements, processes, assumptions, decisions and results.
  - **Optimization:** Continuously monitoring and improving processes, models, and tools for better performance and efficiency.
  - **Iterative Approach:** Iterating and refining steps based on feedback and insights.
  - **Repeatability & Automation:** Aim for repeatable and automated processes where possible. Utilize scripting or tools to automate repetitive tasks, improving efficiency and reducing human error.
  - **Stakeholder Involvement:** Regularly involve stakeholders (**Ex:** subject matter experts, business users, data scientists) throughout the process. This allows for gathering feedback, addressing concerns, and ensuring the final analysis aligns with their needs.
  - **Documentation & Version Control:** Maintain proper documentation of the methods, tools, and decisions made at each stage. This facilitates reproducibility, collaboration, and future

reference. Version control systems help track changes and revert to previous versions if needed.

4. What are some real-world examples of how data analytics is used in different businesses?

Ans:

Here are some practical use cases of data analytics across different industries:

- **Healthcare:** Analyzing patient data to predict and prevent illnesses.
- **Retail:** Recommending products customer might like based on their purchase history.
- **Finance:** Identifying patterns to prevent fraudulent credit card transactions.
- **Manufacturing:** Monitoring sensors to predict equipment failure and prevent downtime.
- **Transportation:** Optimizing delivery routes for faster and cheaper deliveries.
- **Media & Entertainment:** Suggesting shows or movies customer might enjoy based on what they watched before.
- **Telecommunications:** Analyzing network usage patterns to optimize performance and reduce outages.
- **Energy:** Predicting energy demand to optimize production and reduce costs.
- **Hospitality:** Using historical data to customize services and enhance guest satisfaction.
- **Sports:** Analyzing player data to improve training and game strategies.
- **Education:** Analyzing feedback and performance data to improve educational programs.

Explore:

Real-world use cases:

- A famous **OTT platform** performs big data analytics to make on-the-fly decisions about what customers want to watch next, based on what's most popular right now.
- A top **social media platform** uses Big Data and Real-time Analytics to identify and remove fake news and abusive posts. Remember, it needs to analyze an average of 4.75 billion posts per day.
- One of the top **oil and gas** companies implemented a system where machine vision-equipped cameras can be used to sound alarms when suspicious activity is detected. For example, they can spot and warn customers when smoking on their forecourts.
- **Stock markets** are extensively using Big Data and Advanced Analytics to identify trends of market manipulation, especially insider trading and price manipulation, which are done to gain profit in real time. They collect data from social media streams, newsfeeds, company public announcements, and other external data streams to identify potential attempts to manipulate the market.
- A top **cab service provider** makes extensive use of Big Data. To provide optimized routes and services to customers, it must maintain a large database of drivers, customers, rate cards, etc., and continuously collect weather and traffic data.

- In **manufacturing**, real-time analytics can help continuously track, control, and fine-tune manufacturing processes, such as managing inventory, plant maintenance, predicting failures, and identifying process bottlenecks.

5. What are the most popular tools, services, and programming languages used in the data analytics life cycle?

Ans:

- **Data Integration Tools:** These tools automate the process of moving data from various sources (databases, applications, files) into a central location (Data Warehouse, Data Lake) for analysis. They can handle tasks like extracting, transforming, and loading (ETL) data.
  - **Generic:** Talend Open Studio, Informatica PowerCenter, IBM DataStage, Oracle Data Integrator (ODI), SQL Server Integration Services (SSIS), Apache Nifi, Pentaho, FiveTran etc.
  - **Azure/AWS/GCP-Native:** Azure Data Factory, Azure Logic Apps, AWS Glue, AWS Data Pipeline, Google Cloud Dataflow, Google Cloud Data Fusion.
- **Data Wrangling:** This refers to the process of cleaning, manipulating, and transforming raw data into a usable format for analysis. Data wrangling tools can help identify missing values, fix inconsistencies, and format data for specific needs.
  - **Generic:** Microsoft Power Query, Alteryx, Alteryx Designer Cloud (Earlier Trifacta), OpenRefine etc.
  - **Azure/AWS/GCP-Native:** Azure Data Factory Wrangling Data Flow, AWS Glue DataBrew, Amazon SageMaker Data Wrangler, Google Cloud DataPrep (by Trifacta).
- **Visualization & Reporting Tools (BI):** These tools help turn data into insights through interactive visualizations (charts, graphs) and reports. Business intelligence (BI) tools allow users to explore data, identify trends, and communicate findings effectively.
  - **Generic:** Tableau, Power BI, Qlik Sense, Looker, Zoho Analytics, SAS (Statistical Analysis System), ThoughtSpot etc.
  - **Azure/AWS/GCP Native:** Azure Power BI, Amazon QuickSight, GCP Looker etc.
- **Programming Languages:** These are essential tools for data analysts. They provide functionalities for data manipulation, analysis, and visualization.
  - **Python:** Data analysis, machine learning, and data wrangling.
  - **R:** Statistical analysis.
  - **SQL:** Querying relational/tabular datasets.
  - **Scala:** Big data processing using Apache Spark.
  - **Java:** Enterprise-level data processing.
  - **Julia:** Scientific computing and data analysis.

- **Data Warehouses:** These are specialized databases designed for storing large amounts of historical data for analysis. Data warehouses are optimized for querying and reporting, allowing users to analyze trends and patterns over time.
  - **Generic:** Teradata, Teradata Vantage Cloud, IBM db2 Warehouse, Snowflake etc.
  - **Azure/AWS/GCP-Native:** Azure Synapse Analytics (Dedicated SQL Pool), Microsoft Fabric (Synapse Data Warehouse), Amazon Redshift, GCP BigQuery.
- **Data Lakes:** In contrast to data warehouses, data lakes store all data in its native format, regardless of structure. This allows for flexibility in storing and analyzing various data types, including raw, semi-structured, and structured data.
  - **Generic:** Hadoop Distributed File System (HDFS).
  - **Azure/AWS/GCP-Native:** Azure Data Lake Storage (ADLS) Gen 2, Amazon S3, AWS Lake Formation, Google Cloud Storage etc.
- **Lakehouse:** This combines the strengths of data lakes and data warehouses. A Lakehouse stores data in its native format within a data lake, but also allows for data transformation and querying capabilities like a data warehouse. This provides flexibility and scalability for data storage while enabling efficient data analysis.
  - **Generic:** Databricks Lakehouse Platform, Snowflake, Apache Hudi, Cloudera Data Platform (CDP), Dremio, Starburst, IBM Cloud Pak for Data etc.
  - **Azure/AWS/GCP-Native:** Microsoft Fabric, Azure Synapse Analytics, Amazon Redshift Spectrum, Google BigLake.
- **Machine Learning for Data Analysis:** Machine learning has revolutionized data analysis by automating the process of extracting meaningful patterns and insights from complex datasets. By employing sophisticated algorithms, these models can make predictions, classifications, and uncover hidden relationships within data. Some of the most commonly used machine learning algorithms include Decision Trees, Random Forests, Support Vector Machines, and Neural Networks.

Note: In the modern data world, many popular data analytics products are offered as Software-as-a-Service (SaaS) solutions. This means you can simply host them on your preferred cloud platform. Examples include Databricks and Snowflake, which support Azure, AWS, and GCP. This approach offers flexibility: you can choose the service on your desired cloud platform and run your data analytics workloads there. Additionally, if you ever need to switch cloud providers in the future, SaaS solutions often allow for easier migration between cloud platforms with minimal or no changes required.

6. What are the key machine learning algorithms commonly used in data analysis?

Ans:

Popular machine learning algorithms widely used for data analysis include:

- **Supervised Learning:** Learns from labelled data, improves through correction. **Ex:** Imagine a student learning with a teacher.
- **Unsupervised Learning:** Finds patterns in unlabelled data. **Ex:** Imagine a child exploring the world without a teacher.
- **Semi-Supervised Learning:** Uses both labelled and unlabelled data. **Ex:** Sits between supervised and unsupervised learning.
- **Reinforcement Learning:** Learns by interacting with an environment and receiving rewards. **Ex:** Similar to training a dog.
- **Deep Learning:** Uses deep neural networks to learn from large, complex datasets. **Ex:** Inspired by the structure and function of the human brain. It involves artificial neural networks with multiple layers to learn complex patterns from large amounts of data.

Explore:

Supervised Learning Algorithms: It learns from labelled training data. The algorithm makes predictions or decisions based on this training, and it gets corrected when it makes mistakes. Over time, it improves its accuracy. **Ex:** A spam email classifier that learns from examples of spam and non-spam emails.

- **Linear Regression:** Used for predicting continuous values. **Ex:** Predicting house prices.
- **Logistic Regression:** Used for binary classification problems. **Ex:** Spam detection.
- **Decision Trees:** Used for both classification and regression tasks. **Ex:** Customer segmentation.
- **Random Forest:** An ensemble method using multiple decision trees for better accuracy. **Ex:** Predicting credit risk.
- **Support Vector Machines (SVM):** Used for classification and regression tasks. **Ex:** Image classification.
- **k-Nearest Neighbors (k-NN):** A simple, instance-based learning algorithm used for classification. **Ex:** Recommendation systems.
- **Naive Bayes:** A probabilistic classifier based on Bayes' theorem. **Ex:** Text classification.
- **Gradient Boosting Machines (GBM):** Includes algorithms like XGBoost, LightGBM, and CatBoost, used for classification and regression. **Ex:** Fraud detection.

Unsupervised Learning Algorithms: It analyzes and group unlabelled data based on inherent patterns or similarities. They don't require labelled data for training. **Ex:** A clustering algorithm that groups customers into different segments based on their purchasing behavior.

- **K-Means Clustering:** Used for partitioning data into k clusters. **Ex:** Customer segmentation.

- **Hierarchical Clustering:** Builds a hierarchy of clusters. **Ex:** Gene sequence analysis.
- **Principal Component Analysis (PCA):** A dimensionality reduction technique. **Ex:** Reducing the number of features in a dataset.
- **t-Distributed Stochastic Neighbour Embedding (t-SNE):** A technique for dimensionality reduction, particularly useful for visualization. **Ex:** Visualizing high-dimensional data by giving each datapoint a location in a two or three-dimensional map.

Semi-Supervised Learning Algorithms: It uses a small amount of labelled data and a large amount of unlabelled data for training. They are useful when labelling data is expensive or time-consuming. **Ex:** Improving the accuracy of a speech recognition system using a small dataset of transcribed audio and a large dataset of un-transcribed audio.

- **Self-Training:** Uses a small amount of labelled data to iteratively label and train on larger unlabelled datasets. **Ex:** Improving speech recognition models.

Reinforcement Learning Algorithms: It involves an agent learning to make decisions by interacting with an environment. The agent receives rewards or penalties based on its actions, and it learns through trial and error to maximize rewards over time. **Ex:** A game-playing AI that learns to win by playing thousands of games and receiving rewards for winning moves.

- **Q-Learning:** A value-based reinforcement learning algorithm. **Ex:** Game playing AI.
- **Deep Q-Network (DQN):** Combines Q-Learning with deep learning. **Ex:** Robotics.

Deep Learning Algorithms: Deep learning algorithms are a subset of ML that use neural networks with many layers (deep networks) to learn from large amounts of data. They are especially powerful for tasks involving unstructured data like images, audio, and text. **Ex:** A deep learning model that can recognize objects in images, such as identifying fruits and animals in photos.

- **Convolutional Neural Networks (CNNs):** Used for image and video recognition. **Ex:** Facial recognition.
- **Recurrent Neural Networks (RNNs):** Used for sequential data analysis. **Ex:** Language modelling.
- **Long Short-Term Memory Networks (LSTMs):** A type of RNN used for time-series prediction. Ex: Stock price prediction.
- **Generative Adversarial Networks (GANs):** Used for generating new data samples. **Ex:** Creating realistic images.
- **Autoencoders:** Used for unsupervised learning of efficient coding. Its purpose is to learn efficient data encodings by training the network to capture the most important features of input data. **Ex:** Anomaly detection, Noise reduction etc.

Note: Don't worry too much about ML as we won't be digging deep into the data science world. This is just to ensure you're familiar with the fundamentals of data analytics.

7. As an expert in the industry, what do you see for the future of data analytics?

Ans:

In the future, data analytics will focus on gaining more value from data and making it easier for businesses to use. Here are the key trends:

- **AI-powered Analytics:** Artificial intelligence (AI) and machine learning (ML) are becoming increasingly integrated into data analytics tools. This allows for automated data preparation, faster analysis, and even the generation of insights and recommendations.
- **More focus on Real-time Analytics:** The emphasis is shifting towards analyzing data as it's generated. It allows businesses to respond instantly to market changes, customer behavior, and operational issues. This is particularly relevant for sectors like finance or manufacturing where quick responses are crucial.
- **Synthetic Data:** Synthetic data is artificially generated rather than collected from real-world events. It is used to train machine learning models, test systems, and protect privacy. This trend is gaining traction as it allows for the creation of vast datasets without compromising sensitive information.
- **Edge Analytics & Advanced IoT:** Analytics performed at the edge of networks, closer to data sources, will grow in importance, particularly for IoT devices and applications requiring low-latency processing.
- **Natural Language Processing (NLP):** NLP will play a larger role in data analytics, making it easier for non-technical users to interact with data through natural language queries and receive insights in a more understandable format. Expect more applications of NLP in sentiment analysis, chatbots, and text-based data analysis.
- **Augmented Analytics**: It leverages AI, ML and NLP to automate data preparation, insight generation, and explanation, making it easier for users to understand and act on data-driven insights without needing deep technical expertise.
- **Data Democratization:** Tools and platforms that make data accessible to a broader range of users within organizations will continue to develop, empowering more employees to make data-driven decisions.
- **Data Mesh Architecture:** Data Mesh is an emerging architecture that decentralizes data ownership and governance to domain-specific teams. This approach treats data as a product and promotes greater scalability, agility, and data democratization within organizations.
- **Enhanced Business Intelligence (BI):** Data visualization tools will become more sophisticated, enabling richer, more interactive, and more intuitive representations of data. Businesses will demand real-time dashboards and actionable recommendations. Context-driven analytics will empower decision-makers with relevant information
- **Quantum Computing for Analytics:** As quantum computing technology matures, it will revolutionize data analytics by enabling the processing of complex datasets and performing computations at unprecedented speeds. Quantum computers excel at solving complex

problems that take traditional computers years, even centuries, to crack. This could enable data analysis of massive datasets or highly intricate simulations that are currently infeasible. **Ex:** Analyzing customer behavior across millions of users in real-time.

- **Integration of Multimodal Data:** The ability to integrate and analyze data from various sources and formats, including text, images, video, and sensor data, will provide a more comprehensive understanding of complex phenomena.
- **Ethical and Responsible AI & Analytics:** To build trust with consumers, there will be a growing focus on ensuring that AI and analytics are used ethically and responsibly, with frameworks and guidelines developed to address bias, fairness, and transparency.
- **Data Privacy, Security, Regulation and Compliance:** As data analytics grows, so does the importance of data privacy and security. Enhanced techniques for anonymizing data and ensuring compliance with regulations like GDPR will be crucial. Businesses must stay informed and adapt to changing compliance requirements.

8. What is the difference between ETL and ELT in the context of data analytics?

Ans:

ETL and ELT are distinct approaches to data integration:

- **ETL:** Extract, transform, and load data into a target system.
- **ELT:** Extract data and load it into a target system, then transform it within the target system.

Explore:

ETL (Extract, Transform, Load): ETL is a traditional data integration process where data is extracted from various sources, transformed into a desired format, and then loaded into a data warehouse, data mart or data lake.

- **Use Case:** Suitable for environments where data transformation needs to happen before data can be used (Traditional data warehouses).
- **Ex:** A retail company extracts sales data from multiple stores (databases, APIs, flat files), cleanses it (handling missing data, removing duplicates, correcting inaccuracies etc.), aggregates it (time based, product based, customer based, geographic aggregations etc.), and loads it into a data warehouse for analysis.

ELT (Extract, Load, Transform): It is similar to ETL but with a different sequence of steps. In ELT, data is first extracted from the source systems, then loaded into the target system (typically a data warehouse or data lake), and finally transformed within the target system.

- **Use Case:** Suitable for environments with powerful data processing capabilities (Modern cloud-based data warehouses and data lakes).
- **Ex:** An e-commerce company might use ELT to load raw clickstream data into a data lake and then transform it to analyse customer behaviour and generate personalized recommendations.

Key difference between ETL and ELT:

- **Timing of Transformation:** ETL transforms data before loading, while ELT transforms after loading.
- **Data Volume:** ETL is often used for smaller, structured datasets, while ELT is better suited for large, complex, and unstructured data.
- **Flexibility:** ELT offers more flexibility due to delayed transformation.
- **Cost:** ELT can be more cost-effective due to reduced infrastructure requirements.

9. What is a data processing model? What are the different data processing models available?

Ans:

A data processing model is a framework or methodology used to handle, manipulate, and analyze data. These models define how data is collected, processed, stored, and analysed to transform raw data into meaningful information and insights. The choice of a data processing model depends on the nature of the data, the required processing speed, the volume of data, and the specific use case or business requirement.

- **Types of Data Processing Models:** OLTP (Online Transaction Processing), OLAP (Online Analytical Processing), Batch processing, Stream processing etc.

Explore:

Here are the different data processing models:

Transactional Processing (OLTP - Online Transaction Processing):

- Manages transaction-oriented applications, typically for data entry and retrieval transaction processing.
- **Use Cases:** Banking systems, e-commerce, order management.
- **Technology:** Relational databases like SQL Server, MySQL, PostgreSQL, Oracle DB, etc.
- **Ex:** A system handling ATM transaction in a bank.

Analytical Processing (OLAP - Online Analytical Processing):

- Enables complex queries and analysis of multidimensional data.
- **Use Cases:** Business reporting, data mining, financial analysis.
- **Technology:** OLAP cubes, SQL Server Analysis Services (SSAS), data warehouses like Amazon Redshift, Google BigQuery, Azure Synapse Analytics etc.
- **Ex:** Generating a sales report that shows trends over time.

Batch Processing:

- Processing large volumes of data at once at scheduled intervals.

- **Use Cases:** End-of-day reports, data warehousing updates, ETL processes.
- **Technology:** SQL Server Integration Services, Azure Data Factory, Azure Batch, AWS Glue, AWS Batch, Google Cloud Dataflow (in batch mode), Apache NiFi, etc.
- **Ex:** Running payroll processing at the end of each month.

Real-time Processing (Stream Processing):

- Processing data continuously as it arrives, often with low latency.
- **Use Cases:** Fraud detection, real-time analytics, monitoring systems.
- **Technology:** Apache Kafka, Apache Flink, Apache Storm, AWS Kinesis, Azure Stream Analytics, Google Cloud Dataflow (in streaming mode).
- **Ex:** Analyzing live social media feeds to detect trending topics.

Micro-batch Processing:

- A hybrid approach that processes data in small, frequent batches, almost in real-time.
- **Use Cases:** Near real-time data analysis, log processing, IoT data analysis etc.
- **Technology:** Apache Spark Streaming, Apache Kafka etc.
- **Ex:** Processing and analyzing web server log every few minutes.

Distributed Processing:

- Divides a large problem into smaller ones, processes them across multiple clusters/machines, and aggregates the results.
- **Use Cases:** Large-scale data analysis, distributed computing tasks.
- **Technology:** Apache Hadoop, Apache Spark, Amazon EMR, Azure HDInsight, Google Cloud Dataproc, SingleStore, Azure Synapse Analytics, Amazon Redshift, Google BigQuery, etc.
- **Ex:** Distributed data processing in insurance can be used to analyze vast claims data across multiple data centers to detect fraudulent activities in real-time.

Interactive Processing:

- Allows users to interact with data and perform ad-hoc queries in real-time.
- **Use Cases:** Data exploration, business intelligence.
- **Technology:** Azure Synapse Analytics, Amazon Redshift, Google BigQuery, Power BI, Tableau, Looker etc.
- **Ex:** A business analyst uses an interactive dashboard to explore sales data.

Edge Processing:

- Data processing performed at or near the data source, often in IoT scenarios.
- **Use Cases:** IoT data processing, real-time analytics on devices.

- **Technology:** AWS IoT Greengrass, Azure IoT Edge, Google Cloud IoT Edge etc.
- **Ex:** Capturing and analyzing sensor data on a factory floor to detect equipment failures.

In-Memory Processing:

- Data processing performed in RAM, allowing for high-speed data access and computation.
- **Use Cases:** Real-time analytics, high-performance computing.
- **Technology:** Apache Spark, Redis, Apache Ignite, SingleStore (MemSQL), SAP HANA.
- **Ex:** Running real-time financial analytics using in-memory databases like SAP HANA.

Hybrid Processing:

- Combines multiple processing models to leverage the advantages of each.
- **Use Cases:** Scenarios requiring both real-time and batch processing capabilities.
- **Technology:** Most modern data analytics suites/services/tools support multiple data processing models. Ex: Apache Spark, Azure Synapse Analytics, Azure Databricks, Snowflake, AWS Redshift, Google Cloud Dataflow, etc.

10. What is a data pipeline?

Ans:

A "Data Pipeline" is a series of processes and tools used to automate the movement and transformation of data from various sources to a destination, such as a data warehouse, data lake, or another database system. The pipeline ensures data is collected, processed, and delivered in an organized and efficient manner.

Explore:

Imagine a retail company that wants to analyze its sales data to understand customer behavior and optimize inventory.

- **Data Source:** The company's sales data originates from its online store, physical store point-of-sale systems, and customer service databases.
- **Ingestion:** A data integration/ETL tool (**Ex:** SSIS, Azure Data Factory) can be used to create pipelines that extract data from various sources and load it into a central location such as Blob storage or a Data Lake.
- **Processing:** Once data from different sources is ingested into a staging area, we can use a pipeline to clean it (removing duplicates, correcting errors) and transform it (aggregating sales data by day, calculating total sales per product).
- **Storage:** The processed data is then loaded into cloud data warehouses (Azure Synapse, Amazon Redshift or Google BigQuery).
- **Analysis and Reporting:** Data analysts use Power BI/Tableau to connect to Synapse Analytics and create dashboards that show daily sales trends, top-selling products, and inventory levels, which help the company make informed decisions.

In this example, the data pipeline ensures that data flows smoothly from various sources to actionable insights, enabling the company to improve its operations and strategy.

11. What is the difference between batch processing and real-time data processing?

Ans:

Batch Processing involves collecting and processing data in large volumes at scheduled intervals. Data is gathered, stored, and processed in batches, often during off-peak hours.

- **Suits:** For periodic, large-scale data analysis.

Real-Time Data Processing handles data immediately as it arrives, allowing for continuous input, processing, and output of data with minimal latency.

- **Suits:** It is essential for immediate, actionable insights and responses.

Explore:

Here is an example:

Batch Processing:

- **Use Case**: Generating daily sales reports for a retail e-store.
- **Ex**: All sales data from the day is collected and processed overnight. Reports are generated and available the next morning.

Real-Time Data Processing:

- **Use Case**: Detecting and preventing fraud during online transactions.
- **Ex**: A customer makes an online purchase, and the system immediately checks the transaction against fraud detection rules. If the transaction is deemed suspicious, it is flagged or declined instantly, preventing potential fraud.

12. What are the main data processing architectures? Or, what are Lambda and Kappa architectures?

Ans:

- **Lambda architecture**: A two-layer architecture that separates real-time processing from batch processing.
- **Kappa architecture**: A single-layer architecture that combines both real-time processing and batch processing.

Explore:

Lambda architecture: It uses separate pipeline to process data:

- **Batch Layer / Cold Path:** Processes data in large, scheduled batches to provide comprehensive views and historical data analysis.
- **Stream Processing / Speed Layer / Hot Path:** Processes data in real-time to provide low-latency updates and immediate insights.
- **Serving Layer:** Merges results from both batch and speed layers to provide a unified view.
- **Suits:** When both historical batch processing and real-time insights are required. Ideal for complex analytics that benefit from comprehensive historical context.

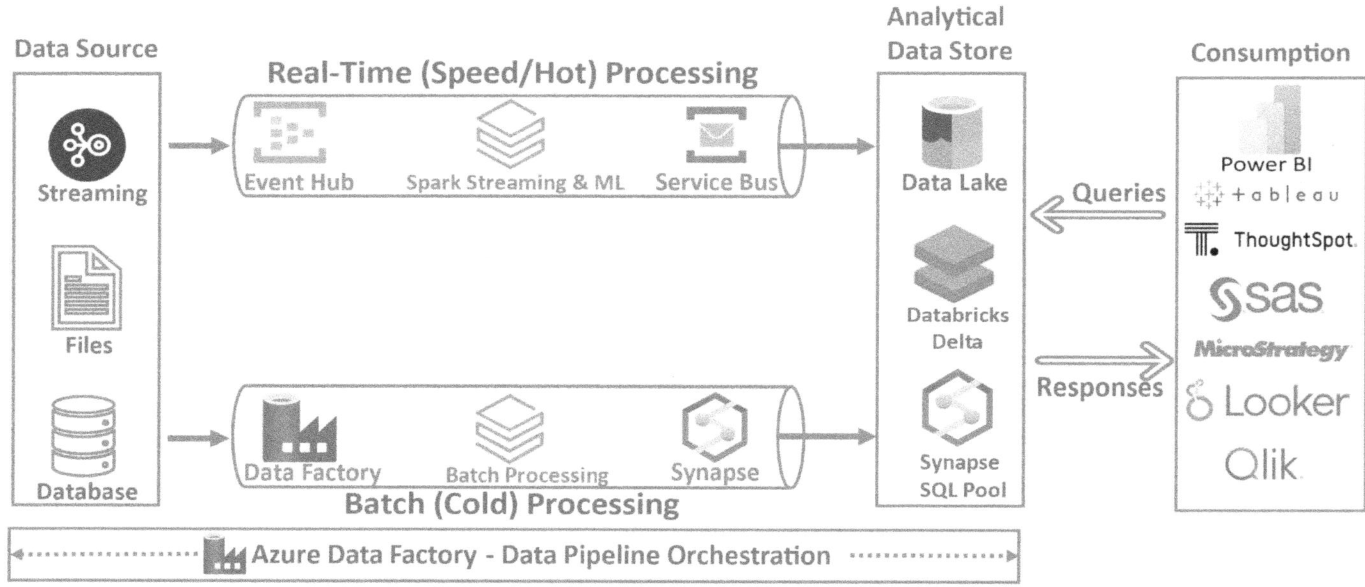

Image 4.1

Kappa Architecture: It was developed as an alternative to Lambda architecture. Kappa simplifies the architecture by focusing only on-stream processing. It uses a single data pipeline to handle both batch processing and stream processing workloads, as it treats everything as streams.

- **Stream Processing**: All data is processed as a continuous stream. There is no separate batch layer; instead, historical data is reprocessed through the same stream processing pipeline if needed.
- **Simplification**: Easier maintenance and scalability, as there is only one processing path.

- **Suits:** When the primary requirement is real-time processing with simpler data reprocessing needs. Ideal for applications requiring immediate insights and low latency.

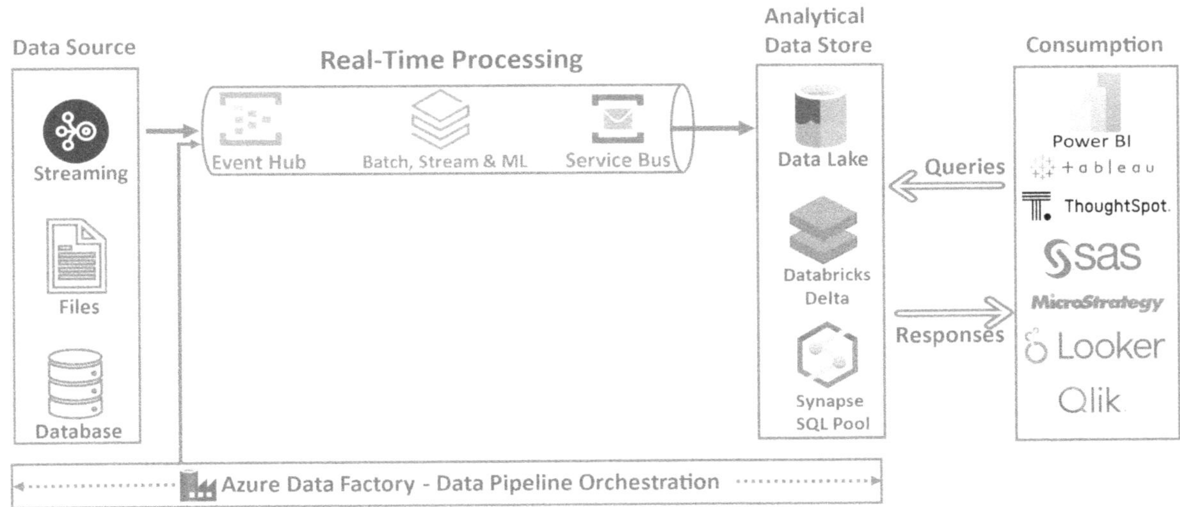

Image 4.2

Choosing the right option:

- **Data Volume:** For large and complex datasets requiring both immediate insights and comprehensive historical analysis, Lambda architecture is a suitable choice.
- **Real-time needs:** If low latency and immediate insights are crucial, Kappa is suitable.
- **Data accuracy:** If historical data accuracy is priority, Lambda is preferred.
- **Complexity:** Kappa is simpler to implement, while Lambda requires managing both batch and stream processing systems.
- **Cost:** Kappa generally has lower operational costs, while Lambda might incur higher infrastructure costs.

Note: Do not worry about the analytical data products and services shown in the diagrams. You will learn about all of them in "Azure The One – Part 3".

13. What is Data virtualization?

Ans:

Data virtualization is a data management technique that provides a unified view of data from multiple sources without physically moving or copying the data. It creates a virtual layer on top of existing data sources, allowing users to access and analyse data as if it were stored in a single location.

Ex: In SQL Server, by leveraging External Data Sources, Bulk Insert, and OPENROWSET, we can connect to various other database systems like Oracle and Azure Data Lake Storage, and query data directly from a single database. This allows us to create queries joining datasets from multiple sources and then build a view on top. By providing this view to business analysts or report developers, they can access data from different sources without understanding its underlying location or format, eliminating the need for an ETL process.

Explore:

Data virtualization allows you to create a virtual data layer that provides a unified view of data from multiple sources. This virtual layer acts as an abstraction layer, enabling users to query and retrieve data in real-time from diverse sources such as databases, cloud storage, big data environments, and even APIs.

Example Scenario:

A large Retail enterprise has data stored in multiple systems, including SQL Server, Oracle, Teradata, MongoDB, Cosmos DB, and Data Lake Storage. The company needs to generate reports that require data from all these sources.

Traditional Approach:

- Data from each system would need to be extracted, transformed, and loaded (ETL) into a centralized data warehouse.
- This process can be time-consuming, require significant storage and computing resources, and lead to delays in accessing the most up-to-date information.

Using Data Virtualization:

- The company implements a data virtualization platform that connects to the SQL Server, Oracle and other data sources.
- The data virtualization layer provides a unified view of all relevant data across these systems.
- Analysts can run queries against this virtual data layer to generate reports without worrying about where the data resides or how it is formatted.
- Data from the SQL Server, Oracle, MongoDB, Teradata, Cosmos DB, and Data Lake Storage are accessed in real-time, allowing the company to produce up-to-date reports quickly and efficiently.

Benefits:

- **Speed**: Reports and analytics are generated faster since data doesn't need to be moved or duplicated.
- **Cost Efficiency**: Reduces the need for extensive ETL processes and large data warehouses.
- **Agility**: Easily integrates new data sources without re-engineering the entire data infrastructure.

Tools for Data Virtualization: Top enterprise grade tools and services for data virtualization includes Denodo Platform, Starburst, TIBCO Data Virtualization, IBM Cloud Pak for Data, Microsoft Azure Data Share, Oracle Data Virtualization, etc.

14. Have you ever heard the term "Data Blending"?

Ans:

Yes! Data blending is the process of combining data from multiple sources to create a unified dataset for analysis. Unlike traditional data integration, where data is combined at the database level, data blending typically occurs at the analysis level, allowing you to integrate and analyze data from different sources without physically merging them into a single database.

- **Use Case:** Useful for reporting and analysis when data comes from diverse sources and doesn't need to be fully integrated into the warehouse.
- **Ex:** Blending data from an Oracle table, a SQL Server table, and a data lake dataset into a single visualization chart/graph/dashboard.

Explore:

Consider the following example.

- **Business case:** Imagine an insurance company wants to analyze customer satisfaction along with their policy details.
- **Data Sources:**
  - **CRM System:** Contains customer feedback and satisfaction survey results.
  - **Policy Management System:** Contains details about each customer's insurance policies, including policy type, premium, and coverage.
- **Data Blending Process:**
  - The data analyst blends the customer satisfaction data from the CRM system with policy details from the Policy Management System to correlate satisfaction levels with different types of insurance policies.
  - This process is primarily used in data analytics by data analysts where data is blended using visualization or self-service analytics tools like Tableau and Power BI.
- **Outcome:** The company can identify which types of policies have the highest satisfaction rates and make informed decisions about product improvements or customer outreach.

Note: Data blending involves physically combining data, while data virtualization provides a virtual view of the data without moving it.

15. What is data sparsity in the context of data and analytics, and how can it be effectively handled?

Ans:

Data sparsity refers to the occurrence of many null, empty or zero values in a dataset. In other words, a dataset is considered sparse when the majority of its elements are zeros or missing values. Data sparsity is a common issue in large datasets, particularly those involving high-dimensional data like user-item interactions or text data.

In a database, columns that tend to have more NULL or empty values are typically those that capture optional, rarely applicable, or infrequently updated information. Ex: Secondary Email, Secondary Phone Number, Middle Name, etc.

Impact of Data Sparsity:

- Sparsity can make it difficult to perform certain types of data analysis or machine learning, as many algorithms are less effective when working with sparse data.
- Processing and storing sparse data can be inefficient due to the increased computational costs.

Handling Data Sparsity:

- **RDBMS:**
    - **NULL Values:** Data is stored row by row. Even if a column value is null or empty for most rows, space is allocated for it in every row. This can lead to storage inefficiency.
    - **Leverage the SPARSE capabilities:** For example, SQL Server offers built-in support for sparse columns, which optimize storage for columns with predominantly null values.
    - **Create separate tables:** For infrequently used sparse columns, consider storing them in separate tables to minimize storage overhead.
    - **Common Techniques:** Relational databases often use techniques like compression or null value optimization to mitigate the impact of sparse columns, but they are generally less efficient than columnar databases in handling such data.
- **Columnar Databases:**
    - **Efficient Storage:** Data is stored column by column. Only non-null values are stored, significantly reducing storage space.
    - **Compression Techniques:** Columnar databases apply compression techniques like run-length encoding (RLE) and dictionary encoding, which are highly effective when dealing with sparse columns, as they can significantly reduce the storage required for sparse data.
- **Handling Data Sparsity for Big Data:**
    - **Imputation:** Filling in missing values with estimated values.
    - **Dimensionality reduction:** Reducing the number of features.

  - **Sparse data structures:** Efficiently storing and processing sparse data.
  - **Specialized algorithms:** Using algorithms designed for sparse data.

16. Any idea about "Data Fabric" and "Data Mesh" data management architectures?

Ans:

Data Fabric and Data Mesh are two modern data architecture concepts that address the challenges of data management within an organization. Although they share the goal of improving data accessibility, governance, and usage across organizations, they differ significantly in their philosophies and implementations.

- **Data Fabric:** It focuses on a centralized view of data, providing a unified access point to diverse data sources.
- **Data Mesh**: It is a decentralized data architecture that focuses on treating data as a product, with each domain (**Ex:** business unit, department) owning and managing its own data.

Note: Remember that Data Fabric and Data Mesh are enterprise-level data management architectures. The optimal choice between the two depends on factors such as the geographic distribution of data sources, operational requirements, business unit needs, data usage patterns, and specific business objectives.

17. Can you explain the differences between Data Fabric and Data Mesh architectures?

Ans:

Data Fabric might be better for organizations seeking a unified approach to data management, while Data Mesh could be more suitable for those looking to decentralize data ownership and empower individual teams.

Data Fabric

- **Centralized approach:** Data Fabric focuses on a centralized view of data, providing a unified access point to diverse data sources.
- **Automation:** It leverages automation to discover, connect, and integrate data from various systems.
- **Metadata-driven:** A robust metadata layer is crucial for understanding and managing data effectively.
- **Data virtualization:** Often employs data virtualization techniques to provide a unified view without moving the underlying data.
- **Data Governance**: Data Fabric tends to have a more centralized governance model,
- **Goal:** To create a seamless and efficient data landscape for analytics and applications.
- **Suits:** Suitable for organizations with complex data landscapes, requiring a unified view and centralized control over data quality and governance.

Data Mesh:

- **Decentralized approach:** Data Mesh distributes data ownership and management across domain-specific teams.
- **Data as a product:** Treats data as a product with clear owners, consumers, and lifecycle management.
- **Self-service platform:** Provides a self-service platform for data consumers to access and utilize data.
- **Federated governance:** Enforces data governance through a federated model, with shared responsibilities.
- **Goal:** To empower domain teams to own and manage their data, fostering agility and innovation.
- **Suits:** Ideal for organizations with diverse business domains, seeking agility, and wanting to empower domain teams with data ownership.

18. How can Data Fabric and Data Mesh be applied to a large enterprise? Can you explain using real-world business use case?

Ans:

Data Fabric Use Case: Global Healthcare Organization

A global healthcare organization operates hospitals, research centers, and clinics across different countries. They face challenges integrating patient data, research data, and operational data from various locations and systems, making it difficult to provide consistent care, conduct research, and comply with health regulations.

Data Fabric Implementation Steps:

- **Unified Data Layer:** Create a unified data management layer that integrates data from various sources like EHRs (Electronic Health Records), clinical trials, and lab systems across different locations.
    - **Technology:** Use Azure Data Factory for data integration, data movement and orchestration. Azure Data Lake Storage can be used as a centralized repository for storing raw and processed data. Azure Synapse Analytics can serve as a robust data warehouse for storing and querying consumption-ready, aggregated datasets.
- **Advanced Data Governance:** Implement consistent data governance policies, including data lineage, auditing, and security controls to comply with healthcare regulations like GDPR and HIPAA.
    - **Technology:** Use Microsoft Purview for data cataloging, lineage tracking, and governance. Azure Policy and Azure Security Center can enforce security and compliance across the data landscape.

- **Patient 360-Degree View:** Develop a comprehensive patient view by combining data from EHRs, diagnostics, and treatment histories.
    - **Technology:** Leverage Azure Data Factory and Azure Synapse Analytics to integrate and model data from various sources. Azure SQL Database or Azure Cosmos DB can be used to store and manage structured and semi-structured data for real-time querying and reporting.
- **Real-Time Data Integration:** Enable real-time data integration and analytics to monitor patient vitals, disease tracking, and resource management.
    - **Technology:** Use Azure Stream Analytics for real-time data processing and Azure Event Hubs for data streaming from IoT devices like patient monitors. Azure Time Series Insights and Eventhouse in Microsoft Fabric can be used for analyzing time-series data in real time.
- **Research and Innovation:** Facilitate medical research by integrating clinical trial data, genomics, and epidemiology studies.
    - **Technology:** Azure Synapse Analytics and Azure Databricks can be used for large-scale data processing and analysis, while Azure Machine Learning and Databricks can facilitate advanced analytics and predictive modelling for research purposes.
- **AI and Machine Learning:** Integrate AI and machine learning to automate data processing tasks like anomaly detection in patient data and predictive analytics.
    - **Azure Technology:** Use Azure Machine Learning for building, training, and deploying ML models. Azure AI Services can add intelligence to applications, such as natural language processing for analyzing unstructured clinical notes.

Outcome:

- The organization achieves a unified, governed, and real-time data environment, enabling consistent patient care, accelerated research, and compliance with health regulations across all locations.

Data Mesh Use Case: Global E-Commerce Enterprise

A global e-commerce company operates multiple business lines across various regions. They face challenges integrating and scaling data across decentralized business units, making it difficult to manage data ownership, analytics, and cross-functional collaboration.

Data Mesh Implementation Steps:

- **Decentralized Data Ownership:** Reorganize the data architecture around domain-oriented teams (**Ex:** marketplace, logistics, payments, customer support etc.), where each team owns and manages its data as a product.

  - **Technology:** Each domain can use Azure SQL Database or Azure Cosmos DB for their specific data storage needs. Azure Data Factory can be used for domain-specific ETL processes.

- **Data-as-a-Product:** Establish the concept of "**Data Products**" within each domain, ensuring data is well-documented, discoverable, and easily consumable by other domains. A data product is a group of data assets (tables, files, BI reports, etc.), a packaged offering to an enterprise that provides assets with a use case to be shared to data consumers. Here are the domain wise sample Data Products:

  - **Market Place Domain:** Product Catalog, Customer Behavior.
  - **Logistics Domain:** Shipping, Warehouse Inventory.
  - **Payments Domain:** Transactions, Refunds and Returns.
  - **Customer Support Domain:** Support Ticket, Customer Feedback.
  - **Technology:** Implement Azure Synapse Analytics and Azure Data Share to share data products across domains. Azure API Management can be used to expose data products as APIs for consumption by other teams.

- **Self-Service Data Infrastructure:** Provide a self-service infrastructure that allows domain teams to independently manage their data products without relying on a central data team.

  - **Technology:** Use Azure Synapse Analytics for self-service data analytics and Microsoft Purview for data discovery and documentation. Azure Kubernetes Service (AKS) can be used for deploying domain-specific data processing applications.

- **Federated Governance:** Implement federated governance to ensure consistency in data management across domains while allowing domains to retain control over their specific data products.

  - **Technology:** Use Microsoft Purview to establish federated governance policies across domains. Microsoft Entra can be used for managing access controls and identity management across different domains.

- **Collaboration and Data Sharing:** Enable collaboration and data sharing between domains by making data products easily accessible through a centralized catalog or marketplace.

  - **Technology:** Data Products in Microsoft Purview feature can be used to create a centralized data catalog where all domains can publish and discover data products. Microsoft Purview Data Product access policies and Azure Data Share allows secure sharing of data across different domains and teams.

Outcome:

- The organization enables decentralized data management, empowering domains to manage their data products independently while ensuring consistency, collaboration, and scalability across the enterprise. This leads to faster innovation, better data-driven decision-making, and enhanced cross-functional collaboration.

Note: Kappa, Lambda, Data Fabric, and Data Mesh are fundamental architectures and processes that you must understand to grasp the relevance of individual analytical tools and services.

19. What is data governance and why is it essential for organizations?

Ans:

Data governance is the framework of processes, policies, roles, and standards that ensure the proper management and utilization of an organization's data.

It involves defining Data Ownership / Data Stewardship, ensuring data quality, protecting sensitive information, and complying with relevant regulations. Essentially, Data Governance is about making sure that data is accurate, accessible, and secure throughout its lifecycle.

Explore:

Data governance is crucial for several reasons:

- **Improved Data Accessibility and Usability:** By establishing clear guidelines for data access and usage, data governance ensures that the right people have access to the right data when they need it.
- **Improved Data Quality:** Ensures data accuracy, consistency, and completeness, leading to better decision-making.
- **Enhanced Data Security:** Protects sensitive information from unauthorized access, breaches, and loss.
- **Increased Compliance:** Helps organizations adhere to industry regulations and legal requirements.
- **Better Decision Making:** High-quality data enables informed and strategic decisions.
- **Cost Reduction:** Streamlines data processes, reduces errors, and minimizes the risk of costly data breaches.
- **Enhanced Trust:** Builds trust among stakeholders by demonstrating a commitment to data integrity and security.
- **Aligns Data with Business Goals:** Data governance helps align data management practices with the organization's strategic goals, ensuring that data is used effectively to support business objectives and deliver value.

By implementing effective data governance practices, organizations can leverage their data as a valuable asset to drive business growth and success.

20. Can you describe what Data Lineage is?

Ans:

Data lineage is the process of tracking and visualizing the flow of data from its origin to its final destination. It helps understand how data is transformed and used over time.

Ex: In an insurance company, data lineage could trace a customer's claim data from the moment it's collected through various systems (Ex: claim processing application, data entry, etc.), processed and stored in the operational database, transformed to a data warehouse for analysis, and finally used in a report/visualization/dashboard analysing claims trends. This helps ensure data accuracy, compliance, and transparency in understanding how the data was used to make decisions.

21. Can you describe the difference between Data Engineering and Data Science?

Ans:

- **Data Engineering:** Building and maintaining the infrastructure for data processing and storage.
- **Data Science:** Extracting knowledge and business insights from data.

Explore:

Data Engineers: Data Engineering is about creating the infrastructure and processes that allow data to flow efficiently, ensuring it is available, accurate, and accessible for analysis.

- **Skillset:** Software engineering, data architecture, and systems optimization.
- **Key Responsibilities:**
  - **Building Data Pipelines:** Develop and maintain data pipelines that extract, transform, and load (ETL) data from various sources into a centralized data lake or data warehouse.
  - **Data Storage Solutions:** Design and manage databases, data lakes, data warehouses, and lake houses.
  - **Data Quality Management:** They implement processes and tools to ensure the accuracy, completeness, and integrity of data.
  - **Optimization and Performance:** Data engineers focus on optimizing data processes and infrastructure for speed and efficiency, especially for handling Big Data workloads.
  - **Developing Tools:** Developing tools and frameworks for data access and manipulation.
- **Key Technology:**
  - **Programming:** SQL, Python, Java, Scala etc.
  - **ETL and Orchestration tools:** Azure Data Factory, Apache Airflow, Talend, AWS Glue etc.
  - **Databases and storage:** Relational, NoSQL, Timeseries databases, Data Warehouses, Data Lakes, Object Storage etc.

  - **Big Data tools:** Apache Hadoop, Apache Spark, Cloudera, Azure Synapse analytics, Databricks, Snowflake etc.

Data Scientists: Data Science is about analyzing that data, extracting insights, building models, and providing actionable business intelligence.

- **Skillset:** Statistics, machine learning, and data-driven hypothesis testing.
- **Key Responsibilities:**
  - **Data Analysis:** Data scientists analyze structured and unstructured data to uncover trends, patterns, and correlations. They develop data products and solutions.
  - **Statistical Modelling:** They apply statistical techniques to model and predict future trends based on historical data.
  - **Machine Learning:** Data scientists develop and train machine learning models to solve problems such as classification, regression, clustering, and recommendation.
  - **Data Visualization:** They create visualizations and dashboards to communicate findings and insights to stakeholders.
  - **Experimentation:** Data scientists design and run experiments (Ex: A/B testing) to validate hypotheses and measure the impact of changes.
- **Technology:**
  - **Programming:** Python, R, SQL etc.
  - **Machine learning frameworks:** TensorFlow, PyTorch, Scikit-learn etc.
  - **Data visualization tools:** Matplotlib, Seaborn, Tableau, Power BI etc.
  - **Statistical tools:** R, SAS, SPSS.
  - **Big data tools:** Data Lakes, Apache Hadoop, Apache Spark, Cloudera, Databricks, Azure Machine Learning, Azure AI Services, AWS SageMaker, AWS AI Services, GCP Vertex AI, etc.

Collaboration:

- In Enterprise environments, Data Engineers and Data Scientists work closely together. Data engineers ensure that data is accessible, reliable, and efficient, while data scientists focus on turning that data into actionable insights.

22. What is Data Democratization?

Ans:

Data democratization is the process of making data accessible and understandable to everyone within an organization, regardless of their technical expertise. It enables non-technical users to work with data and make data-driven decisions without needing specialized skills in data science or engineering.

Explore:

Imagine a retail company with large amounts of data on sales, customer behavior, inventory, and marketing campaigns. Traditionally, only data analysts or data scientists could access and interpret this data. With data democratization, the company can:

- **Empower sales teams:** Provide sales representatives with access to customer purchase history, preferences, and inventory levels, allowing them to personalize interactions and increase sales.
- **Enable marketing teams:** Grant marketing teams' access to customer segmentation data to create targeted campaigns and measure their effectiveness.
- **Support operational teams:** Equip store managers with data on sales trends, inventory levels, and customer foot traffic to optimize staffing and inventory management.

23. Can you describe the high-level steps to implement data democratization in an enterprise?

Ans:

Here are the high-level steps to implement it.

- Define Data Governance Strategy
- Build Data Infrastructure
- Define Data Security Framework
- Promote Data Driven Culture and provide necessary training
- Monitor and improve the framework

Explore:

By democratizing data, organizations can improve decision-making, increase efficiency, and drive innovation across all levels of the business.

- **Define Data Governance Strategy:**
    - **Establish Data Ownership:** Clearly define who is responsible for different data assets.
    - **Set Data Quality Standards:** Ensure data is accurate, consistent, and reliable.
    - **Create Data Catalog:** Develop a centralized repository of metadata to describe data assets. A data catalog is introduced to help employees discover and understand available data assets. The catalog provides metadata, data lineage, and usage guidelines, making it easier for users to find the data they need and understand how to use it correctly. Top data cataloging, metadata management and data lineage tools include Azure Purview, Atlan, Collibra, Apache Atlas, Octopai, Solidatus etc.
- **Build Data Infrastructure:**
    - **Data Warehouse or Data Lake:** Create a centralized repository for storing and managing data.

- **Data Integration Tools:** Implement tools to extract, transform, and load data from various sources.
- **Data Visualization Tools:** Provide user-friendly interfaces for exploring and analyzing data.
- **Self-Service Analytics Tools:** Providing user-friendly (low-code/no-code) tools for data exploration and analysis. It allows employees from various departments (marketing, operations, sales, etc.) to access, explore, and visualize data without needing to write complex code or queries. **Ex:** Power BI, Tableau, Qlik Sense, Sisense, Alteryx, Looker, Domo, MicroStrategy etc.

- **Establish a strong Data Security Framework:** To ensure data security and privacy, implement robust access controls, adhere to relevant regulations like GDPR and CCPA, and use data masking or anonymization techniques to protect sensitive information.
- **Provide Training and Education:**
  - **Data Literacy Programs:** Offer training to employees on basic data concepts, data analysis techniques, and how to use data tools.
  - **Data Storytelling Workshops:** Teach employees how to communicate data insights effectively.
- **Promote Data-Driven Culture:**
  - **Top-Down Support:** Demonstrate leadership commitment to data-driven decision-making.
  - **Reward Data-Driven Initiatives:** Recognize and reward employees who use data to improve their work.
  - **Create Data Communities:** Foster collaboration and knowledge sharing among data enthusiasts.
- **Improvement:** Continuously monitor data usage patterns, gather user feedback, and iterate on data democratization efforts to address evolving needs and challenges.

24. What does it mean by "Data Harmonization"?

Ans:

Data Harmonization is the process of aligning and standardizing data from different sources so that it can be compared, analysed, and used together. This involves resolving differences in formats, units, or structures, ensuring consistency across datasets. Data harmonization increases the value and utilization of data.

Explore:

Here are the examples:

- Imagine, in an e-commerce company, you're analyzing sales data from two different stores. One store measures sale in dollars, while the other uses euros. To compare sales figures accurately, you would need to harmonize the currency by converting all values to a single unit, such as US dollars.

- An insurance company collects customer data from multiple branches, each using different formats for dates (**Ex:** MM/DD/YYYY, DD/MM/YYYY). During data harmonization, they standardize all date formats to MM/DD/YYYY so that data can be easily aggregated and analysed across the company.

25. What is Master Data Management (MDM) and why is it crucial for businesses?

Ans:

Master Data Management (MDM) is the discipline/method of creating and maintaining a single, consistent view of critical data entities such as customers, products, locations, and employees across an organization. It ensures data accuracy, consistency, and completeness, which is essential for effective decision-making, operational efficiency, and customer satisfaction.

Explore:

Components of MDM:

- **Data Integration:** Combining data from various sources to create a unified view of master data.
- **Data Synchronization:** Ensuring that master data is consistently updated and synchronized across all systems and applications.
- **Data Quality Management:** Ensuring the accuracy, completeness, and consistency of master data.
- **Data Stewardship:** Assigning roles and responsibilities for maintaining and managing master data.
- **Data Governance:** Establishing rules, policies, and procedures for managing master data.

26. Suppose I am a customer from the manufacturing industry, and you are assisting me in designing and improving my data ecosystem. Could you describe some enterprise-level challenges we might face without a Master Data Management (MDM) solution? Additionally, could you suggest how to implement MDM in my enterprise?

Ans:

Let's suppose you are a global automotive manufacturer with multiple plants, suppliers, and a complex supply chain.

Challenges: Without MDM, the company might face challenges like:

- **Customer Data Silos:** Customer data is stored in separate systems used by sales, customer service, and logistics, leading to difficulties in providing consistent customer service and managing customer relationships.

- **Product Data Inconsistencies:** Different product descriptions, specifications, or part numbers across different departments or systems.
- **Supplier Data Issues:** Inaccurate or duplicate supplier information leading to delays in procurement and quality issues.
- **Material Shortages:** Inconsistent data on material availability and usage resulting in production stoppages.

Implementation of MDM:

- Define business objectives and scope for MDM.
- Define data governance policies and establish data stewardship.
- Conduct a data assessment on source datasets.
- Select the right MDM solution.
- Create data models and standards.
- Develop data integration processes.
- Provide training and support to end users.
- Monitor master data quality and performance, and expand MDM to new data domains.

Outcome of MDM Solution:

By implementing MDM, your manufacturing company achieves a single, accurate view of its customer, product, material, and supplier data, leading to improved production efficiency, better supplier management, and enhanced customer satisfaction. The MDM solution also reduces data-related errors and redundancies, resulting in cost savings and more streamlined operations.

- **Customer Master Data:** Customer data from different departments is consolidated into a single customer profile. This unified view of customer data enables better customer service, more accurate sales forecasting, and improved order fulfilment. **Ex:** sales teams can access the same customer information as customer service and logistics teams, ensuring consistent communication and service.
- **Product Master Data:** A centralized repository of product information, including specifications, components, and manufacturing processes, ensures consistency across the entire value chain.
- **Material Master Data:** Accurate and up-to-date information about raw materials, work-in-progress, and finished goods helps optimize inventory levels and production planning.
- **Supplier Master Data:** A single view of supplier information, including contact details, performance metrics, and certifications, facilitates efficient supplier management and collaboration.

Explore:

Below are the detailed steps involved in successfully implementing an MDM solution in a large manufacturing company:

Define Business Objectives and Scope:

- **Identify Business Goals:** Determine the specific business objectives you want to achieve with the MDM implementation. **Ex:** Improving product data accuracy, enhancing supplier relationships, or ensuring regulatory compliance.
- **Scope Definition:** Define the scope of the MDM project, including which master data domains (**Ex:** customer, product, supplier) will be managed, and which departments or systems will be included.

Establish a Data Governance Framework:

- **Build a Data Governance Team:** Assemble a team of stakeholders from various departments (**Ex:** IT, production, procurement, sales, compliance) to oversee the MDM project. Assign roles such as Data Stewards, Data Owners, and Data Custodians.
- **Create Data Governance Policies:** Develop policies, standards, and procedures for data management, including data entry, validation, quality checks, and access controls.
- **Define Data Ownership:** Clearly define who owns and is responsible for different data domains, ensuring accountability for data accuracy and consistency.

Conduct Data Assessment:

- **Data Inventory:** Conduct an inventory of existing data sources and systems (**Ex:** ERP-Enterprise Resource Planning, CRM-Customer Relationship Management, PLM-Product Lifecycle Management, MES-Manufacturing Execution System) to understand where master data currently resides.
- **Data Quality Assessment:** Evaluate the quality of the existing data, identifying issues such as duplicates, inconsistencies, and inaccuracies. Use data profiling tools to analyze data quality.
- **Gap Analysis:** Identify gaps between the current state and the desired state of data management, focusing on data integration, quality, and governance.

Choose the Right MDM Solution:

- **Evaluate MDM Tools:** Based on your business needs, evaluate MDM solutions (**Ex:** SAP Master Data Governance, Informatica MDM, IBM InfoSphere MDM, Oracle MDM, Tibco EBX, Dell Boomi, Profisee, SQL Server Master Data Services (MDS) etc.) that best align with your organization's requirements.

Design and Architect the MDM Solution:

- **Data Model Design:** Develop a comprehensive data model that defines the structure, relationships, and attributes of master data entities (Ex: Customer, product, supplier, etc.).
- **Data Integration Strategy:** Design the integration architecture to connect various data sources and ensure seamless data flow into the MDM system. Use tools like Azure Data Factory for data integration.

- **Data Quality Management:** Implement data quality rules and validation processes within the MDM system to ensure data accuracy and consistency. Incorporate data cleansing and enrichment tools as needed.
- **Data Synchronization:** Establish data synchronization mechanisms to keep master data consistent across all systems in real-time or near-real-time.

Pilot the MDM Solution:

- **Select a Pilot Domain:** Choose a specific data domain (Ex: product data) or a specific business unit to pilot the MDM solution. This allows you to test the system on a smaller scale before a full rollout.
- **Data Migration:** Migrate existing data to the MDM system, ensuring it is cleansed, standardized, and enriched before loading. Use ETL (Extract, Transform, Load) tools like Azure Data Factory.
- **User Training:** Train the pilot group on the MDM system, data governance policies, and procedures. Ensure they understand how to use the system effectively.
- **Monitor and Refine:** Monitor the pilot implementation, gather feedback from users, and make necessary adjustments to the MDM solution, data processes, or governance framework.

Full-Scale Implementation:

- **Expand Scope:** Based on the success of the pilot, roll out the MDM solution to other data domains and departments across the organization.

Continuous Monitoring and Improvement:

- **Data Quality Monitoring:** Continuously monitor data quality within the MDM system, using automated tools to detect and correct any issues.
- **Feedback Loop:** Establish a feedback loop with users to gather insights on system performance and usability. Use this feedback to make ongoing improvements.
- **Governance Audits:** Regularly audit data governance processes to ensure compliance with policies and standards. Update governance policies as needed to reflect changes in business operations or regulations.
- **Scalability Planning:** Plan for future scalability, including the addition of new data domains, integration with new systems, or expansion to new business units or geographies.

Success Measurement:

- **Key Performance Indicators (KPIs):** Define and track KPIs to measure the success of the MDM implementation. **Ex:** Improvements in data quality, reduction in data-related errors etc.
- **ROI Analysis:** Conduct a return on investment (ROI) analysis to assess the financial benefits of the MDM implementation. **Ex:** Cost savings from reduced data duplication or efficiency gains in operations.

27. Can you describe what Data Profiling is?

Ans:

Data Profiling is the process of analyzing and reviewing data from an existing dataset to understand its structure, content, and quality. It involves examining metadata (**Ex:** table structure, column types) and actual data values to identify patterns, inconsistencies, errors, and potential issues. The goal is to ensure the data is accurate, complete, and ready for further use.

- **Ex:** An insurance company is preparing to launch a new claims processing system. Before migrating data from their old system, they use a data profiling tool to analyze customer records. The profiling reveals that 10% of the records have missing policy numbers, and several others contain inconsistent date formats. Also, data profiling reveals that 15% of addresses are incomplete or have inconsistent formatting, such as missing ZIP codes or incorrect state abbreviations. By identifying these issues early, the company can clean the data before migration, ensuring accurate and efficient claims processing in the new system.

Explore:

Data profiling involves:

- **Data Structure Discovery**: Identifying the structure of the data (schemas, tables, columns, etc.).
- **Data Quality Assessment**: Checking for data accuracy, completeness, consistency, and validity.
- **Anomaly Detection**: Identifying missing values, outliers, duplicates, or incorrect data types.
- **Metadata Generation**: Producing insights about data patterns, distributions, and statistical measures (mean, median, frequency distributions).

Here are some of the top data profiling tools:

- **Informatica Data Quality**: A market-leading tool for profiling, cleansing, and managing data quality across enterprise datasets.
- **Talend Data Quality**: Helps assess the quality of data through a variety of metrics like duplicates, completeness, and consistency.
- **Trifacta/Alteryx Designer Cloud**: A user-friendly tool that focuses on data wrangling and profiling. Provides data profiling insights during the data preparation process, allowing users to quickly discover data issues.
- **Microsoft SQL Server**: Offers data profiling features via SQL Server Integration Services (SSIS – Data Profiling Task) and Data Quality Services (DQS). Helps in detecting and resolving data quality issues.
- **Oracle:** Offers built-in Data Profiling functionality via Oracle Enterprise Data Quality (EDQ) and Oracle Data Integrator (ODI).

- **IBM InfoSphere Information Analyzer**: Offers in-depth data profiling and metadata analysis with support for large-scale datasets.
- **Ataccama ONE**: An AI-powered data quality and data governance platform. Provides real-time data profiling and integrates with big data environments.
- **DataRobot Paxata**: A cloud-based self-service data preparation tool with built-in data profiling capabilities. Allows users to profile data visually and interactively while preparing it for analysis.
- **SAP Data Services**: Provides robust data profiling and cleansing functionalities. Used in enterprise-level environments for managing and improving data quality in complex data landscapes.

28. What is Big Data?

Ans:

Big Data refers to extremely large and complex datasets that cannot be easily managed, processed, or analysed using traditional data processing tools and techniques. It's characterized by the five Vs:

- **Volume:** Refers to the sheer size of data generated from various sources, such as social media, sensors, transactions, and more.
- **Velocity:** The speed at which data is generated and needs to be processed. In the Big Data world, data often arrives in real-time or near-real-time.
- **Variety:** The different types of data, including structured, unstructured, and semi-structured data, coming from various sources like text, images, videos, and logs.
- **Veracity:** The quality or trustworthiness of the data, which can vary greatly and may need to be validated.
- **Value:** The potential insights and business value that can be derived from analyzing Big Data.

Explore:

Big Data - Challenges and Opportunities:

- **Data Storage:** Big Data often requires distributed storage systems that can handle vast amounts of data across multiple servers.
- **Data Processing:** Traditional processing methods like relational databases may struggle with Big Data. Instead, technologies like Apache Hadoop, Apache Spark, and NoSQL databases, are used to process and analyze Big Data.
- **Analytics:** Big Data analytics involves advanced techniques like machine learning, predictive analytics, data mining, and artificial intelligence to extract valuable insights from the data.

Big Data Technology Stack:

- **Distributed Storage:** Hadoop Distributed File System (HDFS), Cloud Storage, Data Lakes, Data Lakehouse, etc.

- **Distributed Processing:** Apache Hadoop, Apache Spark, Azure Synapse Analytics, Google BigQuery, etc.
- **Stream Processing:** Apache Kafka, Apache Flink, Amazon Kinesis, Azure Event Hubs, etc.
- **NoSQL Databases:** MongoDB, Apache Cassandra, Couchbase, Azure Cosmos DB, Amazon DynamoDB, etc.
- **Data Integration:** Azure Data Factory, Apache Nifi, Talend etc.
- **Machine Learning and Advanced Analytics:** Databricks, TensorFlow, Apache Mahout, H2O.ai, Azure ML, AWS SageMaker, Google Cloud AI. etc.
- **Big Data analytics:** Apache Hive, Starburst, Azure Synapse Analytics, Azure HDInsight, Amazon EMR (Elastic MapReduce), Google Cloud Dataproc, Databricks, Cloudera Data Platform etc.

29. What is data mining in the context of data analytics?

Ans:

Data mining is the process of discovering patterns, correlations, trends, and useful information from large datasets using techniques such as machine learning, statistics, and database systems. The goal of data mining is to extract valuable insights that can support decision-making, identify hidden patterns, and predict future trends.

- **Data Source for Data Mining:** While a Data Warehouse is traditionally the primary data source for data mining due to its structured and organized nature, a Data Lake and Data Lakehouse are also a viable source, particularly when dealing with diverse and large datasets that include unstructured and semi-structured data.

30. What are the various "Data Mining" techniques?

Ans:

Data mining employs a variety of techniques to uncover patterns and insights from data. Most common techniques include classification, regression, clustering, time series analysis, anomaly detection etc.

Explore:

Predictive Modelling Techniques:

- **Classification:** Assigns data into predefined categories or classes.
  - **Ex:** Email filtering, where emails are classified as "spam" or "not spam" to manage inboxes efficiently.
- **Regression:** Predicts a continuous outcome based on input variables.
  - **Ex:** Predicting sales revenue for a retail store based on factors like advertising spend and seasonal trends.

- **Time Series Analysis:** Analyzes time-ordered data to forecast future trends.
    - **Ex:** Forecasting monthly demand for a product based on historical sales data, to optimize inventory management in retail.

Descriptive Modelling Techniques:

- **Clustering:** Groups similar data points into clusters without predefined labels.
    - **Ex:** A marketing team uses clustering to segment customers based on purchasing behavior, demographics, and preferences to target marketing campaigns effectively.
- **Association Rule Mining:** Discovers relationships between variables in large datasets.
    - **Ex:** Market basket analysis in retail. A grocery store uses association rule mining to identify products frequently purchased together (Ex: bread and butter) to optimize product placement and promotions.
- **Anomaly Detection:** Identifies data points that deviate significantly from the norm.
    - **Ex:** Detecting fraudulent transactions in a financial organization by flagging unusual spending patterns.

Other Techniques:

- **Neural Networks:** Mimics the human brain to recognize patterns and relationships in data.
    - **Ex:** An insurance company uses neural networks to assess risk and determine premium rates based on various factors like age, health, and driving history.
- **Decision Trees:** Uses a tree-like model of decisions and their possible consequences.
    - **Ex:** Loan approval process, where the tree helps decide if an applicant qualifies based on factors like credit score.
- **Ensemble Methods:** Combines multiple models to improve prediction accuracy.
    - **Ex:** A telecommunications company uses a combination of decision trees, neural networks, and regression models to predict whether a customer will churn or continue their subscription based on factors like usage patterns, contract terms, and customer support interactions.
- **Text Mining:** Extracts useful information from text data.
    - **Ex:** Analyzing customer reviews on e-commerce sites or social media to determine overall sentiment about a product.
- **Dimensionality Reduction:** Reduces the number of variables in a dataset while retaining essential information.

- **Ex:** Simplifying data for faster processing in image compression used in digital media companies.

31. Describe the key differences of operational databases, data marts, data warehouses, data lakes, delta lakes, and data Lakehouses?

Ans:

- **Operational Database**: Support daily business operations.
- **Data Mart:** Support data analytics for specific business units.
- **Data Warehouse**: Enterprise level data analytics.
- **Data Lake:** Store raw data in its native format.
- **Delta Lake/Hudi/Iceberg:** Provides ACID transactional capabilities to Data Lakes.
- **Data Lakehouse:** Combine the advantages of data lakes and data warehouses.

Explore:

Operational Database: A database used for managing and storing real-time transactional data in day-to-day operations.

- **Use Case:** Operational databases handle online transactional processing (OLTP) and record transactions as they occur.
- **Ex:** An insurance company's policy issuance system maintains an operational database to store policy details, premium payments, and claims.
- **Tech:** SQL Server, Oracle, MySQL, PostgreSQL, MongoDB, Cassandra etc.

Data Warehouse: The core analytics system of an organization, a data warehouse integrates data from various databases. It stores historical, cleaned, and transformed data (structured) for analysis.

- **Use Case:** Aggregating data from different branches of an insurance company to generate comprehensive reports on customer demographics, policy sales, and claims.
- **Ex:** A data warehouse that combines data from multiple operational databases to provide a unified view of all customer policies, used for strategic decision-making by management.
- **Tech:** Teradata, Azure Synapse SQL Pool, Amazon Redshift, Google BigQuery, Snowflake etc.

Data Mart: A subset of a data warehouse focused on a specific department or function, providing targeted insights.

- **Use Case:** Analyzing claims data for a specific type of insurance, such as auto or health insurance.
- **Ex:** A data mart that consolidates and stores data related to auto insurance claims, used by the claims department to analyze trends and assess risk.
- **Tech:** Similar to Data Warehouse.

Data Lake: A storage system that holds vast amounts of raw data in its native format, both structured and unstructured, for future analysis.

- **Use Case:** Storing diverse data types, such as call center logs, social media mentions, and customer feedback, to perform advanced analytics and machine learning.
- **Ex:** An insurance company's data lake that stores raw data from IoT devices in insured vehicles, used to analyze driving patterns and calculate personalized premiums.
- **Tech:** Hadoop Distributed File System (HDFS), Azure Data Lake Storage (ADLS) Gen 2, Amazon S3, Google Cloud Storage, Teradata VantageCloud Lake etc.

Delta Lake/Hudi/Iceberg: A storage layer that brings ACID (Atomicity, Consistency, Isolation, Durability) transactions, scalable metadata handling, and unified streaming and batch data processing to data lakes. It is essentially a layer on top of data lakes that provides structure, reliability, and consistency in big data environments.

- **Use Case:** Delta Lake is used to build reliable data pipelines, ensuring data consistency and quality when ingesting and processing large volumes of data into Data Lakes. It supports use cases like real-time analytics, machine learning, and data warehousing on top of data lakes.
- **Ex:** By using Delta Lake, an insurance company can ensure data consistency for all ingested data, including policies, claims, and IoT information. Without Delta Lake, a traditional approach would involve storing raw data in a data lake and aggregated data in a data warehouse. However, Delta Lake allows for both unstructured and structured data to reside in a single location, providing a unified data platform. Combining the capabilities of a data lake and Delta Lake forms the foundation of a Lakehouse architecture.
- **Tech:** Similar to Data Lakehouse such as Apache Spark with Delta Lake, Azure Databricks with Delta Lake, Synapse with Delta Lake, Apache Hudi, Iceberg etc.

Data Lakehouse (Data Lake + Data Warehouse): A modern data architecture that combines the capabilities of data lakes and data warehouses, enabling both structured and unstructured data storage and analysis.

- **Use Case:** Performing real-time analytics on large volumes of data, like processing claims data and generating predictive models to detect potential fraud.
- **Ex:** Imagine an insurance company merging data from its data lake (raw claims data, customer feedback, IoT data) with structured data from its data warehouse (policy details, financials). This unified view enables insurance company's data science team to build and deploy fraud detection models.
- **Tech:** Azure Synapse Analytics, Microsoft Fabric, Google BigLake, AWS Redshift Spectrum, Data Lakehouse with Snowflake, Data Lakehouse with Databricks, Cloudera Data Platform (CDP) – Open Data Lakehouse, Teradata VantageCloud Lake etc.

CHAPTER 05

Fundamentals of Data Modelling

1. What is the difference between a data mart and a data warehouse?

Ans:

- **Data Warehouse:** A data warehouse is a centralized repository of integrated data from various sources within an organization. It stores historical data and is designed for analysis rather than operational processing. It is designed to support complex queries and analytics, facilitating enterprise level reporting and business intelligence.
- **Data Mart:** A data mart is a smaller, more focused subset of a data warehouse, tailored for specific business units, departments, or functions. It contains data relevant to a particular group of users, providing quicker access to the information they need for specific analysis or reporting tasks.
- **Difference:** A data warehouse covers the entire organization, integrating data from all business areas, while a data mart focuses on a specific subject area or business function.

Explore:

Consider the following example:

Data Warehouse:

- An insurance company has a data warehouse that stores comprehensive data from all areas of the business. **Ex:** Customer information, policy details, claims history, financial transactions, and regulatory compliance data.
- This data warehouse supports enterprise-wide analytics, enabling the company to perform in-depth analyses. **Ex:** Risk assessment, customer segmentation, and overall financial performance.

Data Mart:

- The claims department within the insurance company needs to analyze claims data. **Ex:** To identify patterns of fraudulent claims, process efficiency, and claims settlement trends etc.
- To meet this specific need, a claims data mart is created. This data mart extracts relevant data from the larger data warehouse (**Ex:** Claims history, policyholder information, and claim processing times etc.) and organizes it in a way that is optimized for the claims department's analysis.

2. What are the primary approaches to Data Warehouse design?

Ans:

Designing a data warehouse involves selecting the right approach or methodology based on the organization's needs, data sources, and analysis requirements. Here are the different ways:

- **Top-Down:** Builds a centralized data warehouse first, followed by data marts.
- **Bottom-Up:** Creates data marts independently and integrates them later into a data warehouse.
- **Hybrid:** Combines elements of both top-down and bottom-up approaches.
- **Federated:** Integrates data from multiple sources without moving it to a central location.
- **Data Vault:** A data modelling technique focused on immutability and auditability.
- **Data Lakehouse:** Combines the strengths of data lakes and data warehouses for unified data analytics.

Explore:

Top-Down Approach (Inmon Approach):

- Proposed by Bill Inmon, this approach starts with creating an enterprise-wide data warehouse that integrates data from multiple sources into a centralized repository. Once the enterprise data warehouse is built, data marts are created to serve specific business units or departments.
- **Use Case:** Suitable for large organizations that need a comprehensive, integrated view of enterprise data.

Bottom-Up Approach (Kimball Approach):

- Proposed by Ralph Kimball, this approach starts by building data marts for specific business processes or departments. These data marts are later integrated into a data warehouse, creating a unified view of data.
- **Use Case:** Suitable for organizations that want to deliver value quickly by focusing on specific business areas first.

Hybrid Approach:

- It combines elements of both the top-down and bottom-up approaches. It begins with creating a high-level data warehouse design and then incrementally develops data marts. The data warehouse and data marts are built concurrently, ensuring both enterprise-wide integration and quick wins for specific business units.
- **Use Case:** Ideal for organizations that need to deliver immediate business value while also working towards a comprehensive data warehouse.

Federated Approach:

- In this approach, multiple, independent data warehouses or data marts are linked together through a common metadata layer. Data remains distributed, and the integration happens virtually at the time of querying.
- **Use Case:** Suitable for organizations with existing, distributed data systems that need to be linked without full integration.

Data Vault Approach:

- A more recent methodology focused on creating a flexible, scalable, and auditable data warehouse. The Data Vault model separates data into three categories: hubs (unique business keys), links (relationships), and satellites (descriptive data). This approach is highly scalable and suitable for handling large volumes of data and complex, evolving business rules.
- **Use Case:** Suitable for large organizations with complex, evolving data environments that need to track changes over time and support large-scale data integration.

Data Lakehouse Approach:

- This modern approach combines the features of data lakes and data warehouses into a single platform, enabling both large-scale data storage and high-performance analytics. It supports structured, semi-structured, and unstructured data and allows for both batch and real-time processing.
- **Use Case:** Ideal for organizations that need to manage large volumes of diverse data and require a unified platform for analytics and machine learning.

Key factors influencing the choice of approach:

- Organizational structure and decision-making processes.
- Data volume, complexity and data processing requirements.
- Time-to-market requirements.
- Budget constraints
- Technical expertise

3. What are the different approaches for loading data into a data warehouse?

Ans:

There are several patterns and approaches for loading data into a data warehouse, including full loads, bulk loads, incremental loads, ETL/ELT, data replication, change data capture, and data virtualization.

Explore:

Populating or loading data into a data warehouse involves extracting data from various sources, transforming it to meet business and technical requirements, and loading it into the data warehouse. Here are the different ways to do this:

- **Full Load:** The process of completely loading or reloading all data from source systems into the data warehouse.
    - **Use Case:** Suitable for initial data loading, when there's a significant change in the data structure or when there's a need to refresh the entire dataset due to the data quality issues.
- **Incremental Load:** The process of loading only new or changed data since the last data load, rather than reloading the entire dataset. This method is more efficient and reduces the load on the data warehouse.
    - **Use Case:** Ideal for daily, hourly, or real-time updates where loading the entire dataset would be inefficient.
- **Bulk Loading:** Large volumes of data are loaded into the data warehouse in bulk, usually during initial data loading or batch processing. Data is collected over a period and then loaded in large chunks (batches) into the data warehouse.
    - **Use Case:** Suitable for loading historical data or when dealing with very large datasets.
- **ETL (Extract, Transform, Load) Process:** The traditional approach where data is first extracted from source systems, transformed in a staging area, and then loaded into the data warehouse.
    - **Use Case:** Suitable for complex transformations and large data sets where data needs to be pre-processed before loading.
- **ELT (Extract, Load, Transform) Process:** A modern approach where data is extracted and loaded directly into the data warehouse, and transformations are performed within the warehouse.
    - **Use Case:** Useful for large-scale data processing, cloud-based data warehouses, and scenarios where transformation logic can be implemented using the data warehouse's processing capabilities.
- **Data Replication:** This method involves replicating data from the source systems to the data warehouse without significant transformation. It is often done in real-time or near real-time.
    - **Use Case:** Suitable for scenarios where near real-time data is needed, such as operational reporting or when minimal transformation is required.
- **Streaming Data Ingestion:** Data is ingested in real-time from streaming data sources into the data warehouse using streaming data platforms (Ex: Kafka, Azure Event Hubs, AWS Kinesis).
    - **Use Case:** Ideal for real-time analytics, IoT data, or scenarios where time-sensitive data needs to be analysed immediately.
- **Change Data Capture (CDC):** CDC tracks changes in source systems (inserts, updates, deletes) and applies these changes to the data warehouse.

- **Use Case:** Useful for keeping the data warehouse up-to-date with minimal latency, particularly in scenarios where the source data changes frequently.

- **Data Virtualization:** Instead of physically loading data into the data warehouse, data virtualization allows real-time access to source data as if it were stored in the data warehouse.
    - **Use Case:** Suitable for scenarios where real-time data access is needed without the overhead of data replication, or when data from multiple sources needs to be integrated on-the-fly.

Each of these methods can be used depending on the specific requirements of the data warehouse, such as the volume of data, data velocity, the complexity of transformations, data quality requirements, and the need for real-time data availability.

4. What is data modelling and its purpose in database design?

Ans:

Data modelling is a process of creating a visual representation or blueprint of how data is organized and structured within an information system or database. It involves defining how data is stored, organized, and related to other data entities.

Explore:

Goals of Data Modelling:

The primary goal of data modelling is to design a blueprint for a database or data system that accurately reflects the business requirements and ensures data consistency, integrity, and efficiency.

- **Understanding data:** Clearly defining what data is needed and how it's used.
- **Defining relationships:** Identifying connections between different data elements.
- **Organizing data:** Structuring data efficiently for storage and retrieval.
- **Communicating data:** Creating a shared understanding of data among stakeholders.

5. What are the essential components or elements of a data model?

Ans:

Key Components of Data Modelling:

- **Entities:** Represent real-world objects or concepts. **Ex:** Customers, products, orders, or employees. Each entity typically becomes a table in a database.
- **Attributes:** Properties or characteristics of an entity. **Ex:** Customer's name, address, or phone number. These attributes become the columns or fields in a database table.

- **Relationships:** Defines how entities are connected to each other. **Ex:** A relationship might describe how customers are related to orders or how products are related to suppliers. These relationships often translate into foreign key constraints in a relational database.
- **Data integrity**: It ensures that data is accurate, consistent, and reliable throughout its lifecycle. It's a critical aspect of data modelling as it guarantees the quality and trustworthiness of information. These data integrity rules often translate into integrity constraints (CHECK, NOT NULL, UNIQUE etc.) in a database.

6. Can you outline the typical stages or phases involved in the data modelling process?

Ans:

Data Modelling process typically involves several stages:

- **Requirement Gathering:** Understanding the business needs and data requirements.
- **Conceptual/Semantic Modelling:** Creating a high-level overview of the data without considering specific database systems.
- **Logical Modelling:** Defining data structures and relationships in more detail.
- **Physical Modelling:** Translating the logical model into a specific database structure.
- **Implementation:** Creating the actual database based on the physical model.

7. What are the different types of data models?

Ans:

Data models can be categorized based on level of abstraction and data structure.

Based on Level of Abstraction:

- Conceptual Model
- Logical Model
- Physical Model

Based on Structure:

- Relational Model
- Dimensional Model
- Hierarchical Model
- Network Model
- Object-Oriented Model
- Document Model
- Graph Model

Explore:

Abstraction based data models:

- **Semantic / Conceptual Model:** A high-level representation of the data, focusing on entities and their relationships.
- **Logical Model:** A more detailed representation of the data, defining data structures and relationships without considering physical implementation.
- **Physical Model:** A low-level representation of the data, specifying how data is stored in a database.

Structure based data models:

- **Relational Model:** This is the most widely used model, organizing data into tables with rows and columns. Relationships between tables are defined using primary and foreign keys. Used for designing Online Transaction Processing (OLTP) databases. **Ex:** CRM, Inventory management systems, reservation system, patient management system etc.
- **Dimensional Model:** Specifically designed for data warehousing and online analytical processing (OLAP), focusing on measures and dimensions. **Ex:** Retail sales analysis, healthcare analytics, E-commerce customer behavior analysis, telecommunications usage analysis etc.
- **Hierarchical Model:** Data is structured in a tree-like hierarchy, with a parent-child relationship between records. **Ex:** File systems, organizational charts, biological classification etc.
- **Network Model:** Similar to hierarchical but allows for more complex relationships, with a record potentially having multiple parents. **Ex:** Telecommunication network topology.
- **Object-Oriented Model:** Data is represented as objects with properties and methods, reflecting real-world entities. **Ex:** Geographic Information Systems (GIS), Computer-aided design (CAD) software, Image and video databases etc.
- **Document Model:** Stores data in flexible, semi-structured documents, often used in NoSQL databases. **Ex:** Content management systems (CMS), e-commerce platforms, managing JSON/XML data etc.
- **Graph Model:** Represents data as nodes (entities) and edges (relationships), suitable for complex networks and social data. **Ex:** Social networks, product recommendation systems etc.

8. How do the conceptual, logical, and physical data models flow together in the design of a database? Can you walk through a complete database design cycle to illustrate this?

Ans:

Let me walk you through the design of a database system for an online retail business:

Requirement Specification and Analysis:

- In this phase, a detailed analysis of the requirements is conducted. The objective is to gain a clear understanding of the business needs.

- The database designer's first step is to create a data requirements document. This document provides a concise, non-technical summary of the data items to be stored in the database and their relationships.
- **Input:** User needs, existing systems, business rules.
- **Output:** Data requirements document, preliminary specifications document.
    - **Activities:** Gather information through various methods, remove redundant or unimportant details, distinguish data and operations, identify data items, define high level attributes, and constraints.

Conceptual Data Model: The conceptual data model provides a high-level overview of the data structure, focusing on the main entities and relationships. It is used to communicate with business stakeholders to ensure the model aligns with the business requirements.

- **Characteristics:**
    - No technical details like data types or storage methods.
    - Emphasizes understanding the business domain and its data needs.
    - Typically represented using entity-relationship diagrams (ERD).
    - **Input:** Data requirements document, preliminary specifications document.
    - **Output:** Entity-Relationship (ER) diagram.

Activities: Create entities, define attributes, establish relationships, determine cardinality and relationships etc.

- **Components:**
    - **Entities:**
        - **Customer:** Represents individuals who shop on the website.
        - **Product:** Represents items available for purchase.
        - **Order:** Represents purchases made by customers.
    - **Relationships:**
        - **Customer places Order:** A one-to-many relationship where a single customer can place multiple orders.
        - **Order contains Product:** A many-to-many relationship where each order can contain multiple products, and each product can be part of multiple orders.

Logical Data Model: The logical data model translates the conceptual model into a more detailed structure, including specific entities, attributes, relationships and constraints. It is used by data architects and analysts to define the logical structure of data.

- **Characteristics:**
  - Includes attributes (fields) for each entity.
  - Defines primary keys and foreign keys.
  - Focuses on the logical structure, independent of the DBMS.
  - **Input:** ER model.
  - **Output:** Normalized relations, data dictionary.
  - **Activities:** Map ER components to database tables, apply normalization, apply integrity constraints etc.
- **Components:**
  - **Entities & Attributes:**
    - **Customer:** CustomerID (Primary Key), CustName, Email, Phone, Address.
    - **Product:** ProductID (Primary Key), ProductName, Category, Price, StockQuantity.
    - **Order:** OrderID (Primary Key), OrderDate, CustomerID (Foreign Key), TotalAmount.
    - **OrderLine:** OrderLineID (Primary Key), OrderID (Foreign Key), ProductID (Foreign Key), Quantity, LineTotal.
  - **Relationships:**
    - **Customer (1) — places —> Order (M):** A single customer can place multiple orders.
    - **Order (1) — contains —> OrderLine (M)**: An order can contain multiple order lines (representing different products).
    - **Product (1) — appears in —> OrderLine (M)**: A product can appear in multiple order lines.

Physical Data Model: The physical data model provides a detailed description of how data will be physically stored, including table structures, column types, indexes, and storage details. It is used by DBAs and developers to implement the actual database.

- **Characteristics:**
  - Includes technical details such as data types, indexes, constraints, and table structures.
  - Optimized for performance, storage efficiency, and data retrieval.
  - Dependent on the specific database product (SQL Server, MySQL, PostgreSQL, Teradata etc.) being used.
  - **Input:** Normalized relations, data dictionary, system constraints (hardware, software, performance requirements).
  - **Output:** Physical database design, data dictionary.
  - **Activities:** Select data types, indexing, storage structures, security measures, backup and recovery plans etc.

- **Components:**
  - **Tables:**
    - **Customer:** Columns includes CustomerID (INT, Primary Key, Auto Increment), CustName (VARCHAR(100)), Email (VARCHAR(100), UNIQUE), Phone (VARCHAR(15)), Address (TEXT).
    - **Product:** Columns includes, ProductID (INT, Primary Key, IDENTITY), ProductName (VARCHAR(100)), Category (VARCHAR(50)), Price (DECIMAL(10, 2)), StockQuantity (INT).
    - **Order:** Columns includes, OrderID (INT, Primary Key, Auto Increment), OrderDate (DATETIME), CustomerID (INT, Foreign Key referencing Customer), TotalAmount (DECIMAL(10, 2)).
    - **OrderLine:** Columns includes, OrderLineID (INT, Primary Key, Auto Increment), OrderID (INT, Foreign Key referencing Order), ProductID (INT, Foreign Key referencing Product), Quantity (INT), LineTotal (DECIMAL(10, 2)).
  - **Indexes:**
    - Use clustered indexes on primary keys and non-clustered indexes on foreign keys to optimize data retrieval.
    - Index on CustomerID in the Order table for fast lookup.
    - Index on ProductID in the OrderLine table to optimize queries involving products.
  - **Storage Details:**
    - Place data and log files on separate physical disks to optimize performance. Utilize disks with characteristics suited for random access (data files) and sequential access (log files) respectively.
    - Tables could be partitioned by date (**Ex:** by month or year) for the Order table to optimize storage and query performance.

Optimization and Administration:

- **Input:** Physical database design, system performance metrics.
- **Output:** Optimized database, performance reports.
- **Activities:** Monitor performance, tune database, manage user access, perform backups, implement security measures.

Note: Please note that this example provides a high-level overview for quick understanding and it does not include complete normalization principles.

9. What are the primary visual data modelling techniques?

Ans:

Visual data modelling techniques help in representing the structure, relationships, and constraints of data in a visual format. Most common techniques include:

- **ER-Diagrams:** Visualize entities and their relationships.
- **Data Flow Diagrams:** Show data movement through a system.
- **UML Diagrams:** Useful for various system aspects, including structure, behavior, and interactions.
- **Dimensional Modelling Diagrams:** Visualize Star and Snowflake schemas.

Explore:

Visual Data Modelling techniques are often used to design and communicate the architecture of databases, data warehouses, and data flows.

- **Entity-Relationship Diagrams (ERD):** ERDs are used to model the relationships between entities (tables) in a database. They visually represent entities, their attributes, and the relationships between them.
    - **Use Case:** ERDs are widely used in relational database design to define how data will be structured, including primary keys, foreign keys, and cardinality of relationships.
    - **Tools:** Microsoft Visio, Lucidchart, ER/Studio, etc.
- **Unified Modelling Language (UML) Class Diagrams:** UML Class Diagrams are used to model the structure of a system by showing its classes, attributes, operations, and the relationships between the classes. It includes class diagrams (similar to ER diagrams), use case diagrams, sequence diagrams, and more.
    - **Use Case:** Commonly used in object-oriented design, UML class diagrams help in visualizing the data structure for systems that require complex relationships and inheritance.
    - **Tools:** Enterprise Architect, StarUML etc.
- **Data Flow Diagrams (DFD):** DFDs represent the flow of data within a system, highlighting how data moves between processes, data stores, and external entities.
    - **Use Case:** DFDs are useful for understanding and documenting the data flow in a system, especially in the context of system analysis and design.
    - **Tools:** Lucidchart, Draw.io, etc.
- **Dimensional Models (Star & Snowflake Schemas):** Visual representation of a data warehouse schema, where the central fact table is linked to surrounding dimension tables.
    - **Use Case:** Used for designing data warehouses and OLAP systems, where the focus is on the dimensions of analysis.

  - **Tools:** Erwin Data Modeler, Microsoft Visio, Lucidchart, Toad Data Modeler etc.

- **Other Techniques:**
  - **Object-Oriented Data Modelling (OODM):** It is used to represent data in an object-oriented way. OODM diagrams consist of objects, classes, attributes, and methods, and are commonly used in software design.
  - **Business Process Modelling Notation (BPMN):** It is used to model business processes. BPMN diagrams consist of activities, gateways, events, and flows, and are commonly used in business process management.

10. What is reverse engineering in data modelling, and when is it typically used?

Ans:

Reverse engineering in data modelling refers to the process of analyzing an existing database or data system to create a visual representation (data model) of its structure. This involves generating diagrams, schemas, and documentation that describe the database's tables, columns, relationships, keys, and other constraints.

- **Purpose:** Reverse engineering is often used for creating database documentation, or when modifications to a database are needed. It helps data architects, developers, and business analysts understand the existing data structure, improve it, or integrate it with new systems.
- **Tools:** We can use a data modelling tool that supports reverse engineering. **Ex:** Erwin Data Modeler, Toad Data Modeler, IBM InfoSphere Data Architect, Microsoft Visio, SQL Server Management Studio – Database Diagrams, SAP PowerDesigner, Oracle SQL Developer etc.

11. In the context of data modelling, what is a relationship, and what are the different types of relationships?

Ans:

A relationship in data modelling defines how two or more entities are connected or associated with each other. It represents the interaction between data elements and provides a structure for understanding how data is related within a database.

Types of Relationships: There are three primary types of relationships:

- **One-to-One (1:1):**
  - Occurs when one instance of an entity is associated with at most one instance of another entity.
  - **Ex:** A person can have only one social security number, and a social security number belongs to only one person.

- **One-to-Many (1:N):**
    - Occurs when one instance of an entity can be associated with multiple instances of another entity, but each instance of the second entity is associated with only one instance of the first entity.
    - **Ex:** A customer can place multiple orders, but an order belongs to only one customer.
- **Many-to-Many (M:N):**
    - Occurs when multiple instances of one entity can be associated with multiple instances of another entity.
    - **Ex:** A student can take multiple courses, and a course can be taken by multiple students.

12. Why is data integrity crucial in data modelling?

Ans:

Data integrity ensures that data is accurate, consistent, and reliable throughout its lifecycle. It's a critical aspect of data modelling as it guarantees the quality and trustworthiness of information. There are primarily four types of data integrity:

- Entity Integrity
- Domain Integrity
- Referential Integrity
- User-defined Integrity

Explore:

Entity Integrity:

- Ensures that each entity (or table row) is uniquely identifiable.
- **Implementation:** Typically enforced through the use of primary keys. Each table must have a primary key, and no part of this key can be null.
- **Ex:** In a customer table, the CustomerID is the primary key, guaranteeing that each customer record is distinct.

Domain Integrity:

- Ensures that all entries in a column adhere to the defined data type, format, or range.
- **Implementation:** Implemented through data types, constraints (Ex: CHECK, UNIQUE, NOT NULL etc.), and default values, ensuring that data entered into a column is valid and within the expected range.
- **Ex:** If a Price column in a Product table is defined as a decimal, the database ensures that only decimal values (within a specified range) are entered. Other examples include, Social Security Number is a mandatory and unique column, employee age must be greater than 18 years etc.

Referential Integrity:

- Ensures that relationships between entities (or tables) are maintained correctly.
- **Implementation:** Enforced through foreign keys. A foreign key in one table must correspond to a primary key in another table, ensuring that relationships between tables remain consistent.
- **Ex:** If an Order table references a CustomerID from the Customer table, it ensures that every Order has a valid CustomerID that exists in the Customer table.

User-Defined Integrity:

- Custom business rules that ensure data meets specific criteria beyond entity, referential, and domain integrity.
- **Implementation:** Implemented through triggers, stored procedures, or application logic to enforce complex business rules (Ex: ensuring an order total is never negative).
- **Ex:** A rule that ensures the total quantity of an order cannot exceed the product's available stock. Passport number is not a mandatory field, but if entered, it must be unique.

13. What is the difference between natural keys and surrogate keys?

Ans:

Natural Key: A natural key is a column or set of columns that already exist in the data and uniquely identify a record based on their business meaning.

- **Ex:** In a customer database, the Social Security Number (SSN) or Email Address can be a natural key, as these are unique identifiers that exist within the data and have real-world significance. Similarly, in an insurance database, a Policy Number can be a natural key, as it uniquely identifies each insurance policy.

Surrogate Key:

- An artificially generated key that has no business meaning. It is usually an auto-incrementing integer or a universally/Globally unique identifier (UUID/GUID) used to uniquely identify a record in a table.
- **Ex:** A Customer ID that is auto-generated by the database system (1001, 1002, etc.) is a surrogate key. It is used purely for internal purposes to uniquely identify each customer record. Similarly in an insurance database, the Customer ID assigned to each policyholder is a surrogate key. This ID does not have any real-world meaning outside the database but ensures each customer is uniquely identified.

When to Use:

- **Natural Keys:** Use when the natural key is stable, unique, and meaningful (Ex: ISBN, SSN, Employee ID, Policy No etc.).

- **Surrogate Keys:** Use when the natural key is prone to change, is complex, or when there isn't a single natural key (Ex: GUID, Auto-incrementing integer etc.).

14. Can you explain the concept of normalization in database design?

Ans:

Normalization is a process in database design that organizes data to reduce redundancy and improve data integrity. It involves dividing a database into smaller tables and defining relationships between them to minimize data duplication and ensure that data dependencies are logical.

Normalization is done in stages, referred to as "normal forms." Each normal form addresses specific issues of redundancy and dependency in database tables. There are 6 normal forms available such as First Normal Form (1NF), 2NF, 3NF, Boyce-Codd Normal Form (BCNF), 4NF and 5NF.

Explore:

First Normal Form (1NF):

- **Definition:**
    - Each column contains only atomic (indivisible) values.
    - Each column contains values of a single data type.
- **Action:** Remove repeating groups by moving those groups into new columns or tables.
- **Ex:** Divide Name column into "First_Name", "Middle_Name", and "Last_Name".
- Create one field named 'Month' instead of 12 separate columns for 'Jan', 'Feb', etc.

Second Normal Form (2NF):

- **Definition:** A table is in 2NF if it is in 1NF and all non-key attributes are fully dependent on the primary key.
- **Action:** Remove Partial Dependencies (A column in a table is partially dependent on a primary key).
- **Ex:** Consider a table with columns: StudentID, CourseID, StudentName, Grade.
- Here, "StudentID" and "CourseID" together form a composite key uniquely identifying each row in the table.
- Notice that "StudentName" is partially dependent on the primary key. This means that "StudentID" alone is sufficient to uniquely identify the "StudentName," and "CourseID" is unnecessary in this context.
- Since there's a partial dependency, this table is not in 2NF.
- To achieve 2NF, we can divide this table into two tables:
- **Students:** StudentID, StudentName
- **Grades:** CourseID, StudentID, Grade

Third Normal Form (3NF):

- **Definition:** A table is in 3NF if it is in 2NF and every non-key attribute is dependent only on the primary key and not on any other non-key attribute.
- **Action:** Remove transitive dependencies. That means, if column C is dependent on B and B is dependent on A, that means C is indirectly dependent on A. This is called transitive dependency. We should remove it to ensure that a table is in 3NF.
- **Ex:** Consider a table with columns: OrderID, ProductName, ProductModel, Qty, SupplierName, SupplierCity. Here, OrderID is the primary key.
- However, ProductModel is dependent on ProductName, and SupplierCity is dependent on SupplierName. Since these columns (ProductModel and SupplierCity) are dependent on non-key attributes, this table is not in 3NF.
- To achieve 3NF, we can divide this table into:
    - **Product:** ProductID, ProductName, ProductModel
    - **Supplier:** SupplierID, SupplierName, SupplierCity
    - **Orders:** OrderID, ProductID, SupplierID, Qty

Higher normal forms: Next level normal forms such as Boyce-Codd Normal Form (BCNF), 4NF, 5NF, etc. exist but are less commonly used in practical database design.

15. What is denormalization and when should it be used?

Ans:

Denormalization is the process of intentionally introducing redundancy into a database by combining tables or reducing the level of normalization. This is done to improve query performance by reducing the number of joins required to retrieve related data.

Explore:

When to use denormalization:

- **High query volume:** When your system needs to handle a large number of complex queries quickly.
- **Reporting and analytics:** For generating reports and performing data analysis that requires combining data from multiple sources.
- **Read-heavy workloads:** When the database is primarily used for reading data rather than writing or updating it.
- **Data Integrity is Less of a Concern:** When slight data redundancy is acceptable and the risk of data inconsistency is low or manageable.

16. What is a bridge table in data modelling? When to use it?

Ans:

A bridge table in data modelling is used to manage many-to-many relationships between two tables.

Example:

Imagine a university database system where:

- Students can be enrolled in multiple courses.
- Courses can have many students enrolled.

Without a Bridge Table:

If we try to record this without a bridge table, we might create a table like this:

Student_ID	Student_Name	Course_Name
1001	Alison	Mathematics
1001	Alison	Computers
1001	Alison	Physics
1002	Indrakshi	Mathematics
1002	Indrakshi	Computers
1002	Indrakshi	Physics

Table 5.1

Problems:

- **Data Duplication**: Student 1001, 1002 appears thrice because they enrolled in 3 courses.
- **Maintenance**: If a student name changes, we have to update it in multiple places.

Solution:

- **Student Table:** Contains one row per student. Ex: Student_ID and Student_Name.
- **Course Table:** Contains one row per course. Ex: Course_ID and Course_Name.
- **Student_Course (Bridge Table):** Links students to courses, handling the many-to-many relationship. Ex: Student_ID, Course_ID.

Benefits of Using a Bridge Table:

- **No Duplication**: Each student and each course are listed only once in their respective tables.
- **Easy Maintenance**: If a student information changes, we update it just once in the Student table.
- **Clear Relationships**: The bridge table clearly shows which students are enrolled in which courses without duplicating data.

This way, the bridge table efficiently manages the many-to-many relationship between students and courses.

17. What is Dimensional data modelling and when to use it?

Ans:

Dimensional Data Modelling is a design technique used in data warehousing to structure data for efficient querying and reporting. This is often used for analytical purposes like data warehousing, Online Analytical Processing (OLAP), ad-hoc analysis and reporting etc.

18. What are the core elements of Dimensional Data Modelling?

Ans:

Fact and Dimension are the key elements of Dimensional Modelling.

- **Fact:** A FACT is something (numerical value) which is measurable. **Ex:** sales, profit, quantity etc.
- **Dimension:** A dimension is something that qualifies a measure. In other words, a dimension is something that gives meaning to a measure. They describe "who, what, where, when, why, and how" related to the facts. **Ex:** Time, location, product, customer etc.

For Example: If I simply say "5 items" as a measure or fact, it's meaningless. However, when I say "Customer 'ABC' has purchased 5 EOS-Cameras on 15th Oct 2024 at 15:00 Hrs. from the Australia e-store," this information provides context. Customer, product, country, store, date and time are dimensions that give meaning to the measure or fact "5 items."

19. Can you describe a few scenarios where dimensional modelling is a best fit?

Ans:

Dimensional data modelling is:

Ideal for:

- **Data Warehousing:** It is commonly used in data warehouses, where data from various sources is integrated, stored, and then used for reporting purposes.
- **Reporting and Analytics:** Ideal for business intelligence systems where the primary goal is to enable fast, efficient querying and reporting.
- **OLAP Systems:** When building OLAP cubes for multi-dimensional analysis, dimensional models allow users to slice and dice data along various dimensions.
- **Performance Optimization:** When high performance for aggregate queries is required, such as summing, counting, or averaging large datasets, a dimensional model is often more efficient than a normalized model.

Not ideal for:

- **Transactional Systems:** It is not suitable for systems that require heavy transactional operations (**Ex:** update, delete) as it is optimized for reading large volumes of data rather than transactional integrity.
- **Highly Normalized Systems:** If the primary goal is data consistency and elimination of redundancy, a more normalized, entity-relationship model (ERD) is preferred.

20. What are the two popular Dimensional Data Models?

Ans:

- **Star Schema:** This is the simplest and most common model. It consists of a central fact table surrounded by dimension tables.
- **Snowflake Schema:** This is an extension of the star schema where dimension tables can be further normalized into smaller tables.

21. Can you explain the difference between a Star Schema and a Snowflake Schema?

Ans:

Star schema:

- A star schema is the simplest form of a dimensional model.
- **Fact and Dimensions:** It consists of a central fact table surrounded by dimension tables. The fact table contains numerical data (measures) and foreign keys referencing the dimension tables.
- **Denormalized:** The dimension tables in a star schema are denormalized, meaning they contain redundant data to minimize joins and simplify queries.
- **Advantage:** Queries are straightforward as the structure is flat, with fewer joins required.
- **Ex:**
    - **Fact table:** Sales (SaleID, ProductID, CustomerID, StoreID, DateID, Quantity, Price, Total)
    - **Dimension tables:** Product, Customer, Store, Date

Snowflake Schema:

- A snowflake schema is a normalized version of a star schema.
- **Fact and Dimensions:** Like star schema, it also consists of a central fact table surrounded by dimension tables. But dimension tables are further divided into smaller tables based on dependencies. This reduces data redundancy but increases query complexity.
- **Normalized Dimension Tables:** Dimension tables are further divided into sub-dimension tables that capture hierarchical relationships, leading to a more complex schema.
- **Advantage:** Normalization reduces data redundancy and the chance of inconsistency. Also, it requires less storage as repeated data is minimized.

- **Ex:**
    - **Fact table:** Sales (SaleID, ProductID, CustomerID, StoreID, DateID, Quantity, Price, Total)
    - **Dimension tables:**
        - Product (ProductID, ProductName, CategoryID)
        - Category (CategoryID, CategoryName)
        - Customer (CustomerID, CustomerName, CityID)
        - City (CityID, CityName, StateID)
        - State (StateID, StateName, CountryID)
        - Country (CountryID, CountryName)
        - Store (StoreID, StoreName, CityID)
        - Date (DateID, Date, Month, Year)
        - Similarly, we can divide Date dimension into sub-dimensions like Date, Month, Quarter and Year dimensions.

Choosing the right option:

- **Star schema** is ideal for simple data models with high query performance requirements especially in environments where read operations dominate. This is the most common dimension model used in data warehouse design because of its simplicity and performance.
- **Snowflake schema** is ideal for complex data models where data integrity, storage efficiency, and data updates are critical.

22. In dimensional modelling, what are the different types of dimensions?

Ans:

Dimensions provide context to the measures in a fact table. There are several types of dimensions such as Conformed Dimensions, Role-Playing Dimensions, Degenerate Dimensions, Slowly Changing Dimensions (SCD), Rapidly Changing Dimensions, Static Dimensions, Junk Dimensions etc.

Explore:

In dimensional data modelling, dimensions are the descriptive attributes that provide context to the facts in a fact table. There are 12 types of dimensions which are categorized based on their structure, behavior, and purpose in the data model.

Structural Dimensions: These dimensions are categorized based on their structure and relationship to other dimensions or fact tables.

- **Conformed Dimensions:**
    - Dimensions that are shared across multiple fact tables or data marts in a data warehouse. They have the same meaning and structure, allowing them to be reused in different contexts.

- **Ex:** A Date dimension used in both Sales and Inventory fact tables. The structure and meaning of dates remain consistent across both areas. Similarly, a customer dimension used in both sales and marketing fact tables.

- **Role-Playing Dimensions:**
  - A single physical dimension used in different roles within the same fact table or across different fact tables.
  - **Ex:** A Date dimension might play the role of Order Date, Ship Date, and Delivery Date in an Orders fact table.

- **Degenerate Dimensions:**
  - Dimensions that do not have a corresponding dimension table but exist as keys in the fact table. These are often transactional identifiers.
  - **Ex:** Invoice Number, Order Number, or Transaction ID in a Sales fact table, where the key itself is meaningful without additional descriptive attributes.

- **Outrigger Dimensions:**
  - A dimension that is related to another dimension rather than being directly related to the fact table. It acts as a secondary dimension that provides additional detail or context to the primary dimension.
  - **Ex:** The Employee dimension contains basic employee details and a reference (Department_ID) to the Department dimension.
  - The Department dimension provides additional context, like department name and location.
  - The Department dimension is an outrigger because it's connected to the Employee dimension, not directly to the fact table (Payroll_Fact).

- **Mini-Dimensions:**
  - Smaller, highly volatile dimensions separated from the main dimension to reduce the overhead of managing changes. It is a small dimension tables with a limited number of attributes.
  - **Ex:** A Customer Preferences mini-dimension extracted from a larger Customer dimension, where preferences change frequently. Similarly creating a mini dimension for product sizes extracted from Product dimension.

Behavioural Dimensions: These dimensions are categorized based on how they change or behave over time.

- **Slowly Changing Dimensions (SCD):**
  - Dimensions that change over time, and the changes need to be tracked. There are different types of SCDs based on how the changes are managed:

  - **Type 1:** Overwrites the old data with new data without maintaining history.
  - **Type 2:** Tracks historical data by creating a new record for each change, with start and end dates.
  - **Type 3:** Tracks limited history by adding new columns to store previous values.
- **Ex:** A Customer dimension where customer address or phone number might change over time.

- **Rapidly Changing Dimensions:**
  - Dimensions where the attributes change frequently, making it impractical to track historical data.
  - **Ex:** A Product dimension where product attributes like Price, Discount or Specifications change frequently.

- **Static Dimensions:**
  - Dimensions that do not change over time or change very infrequently.
  - **Ex:** A Country dimension where the list of countries remains stable over long periods.

- **Inferred Dimensions:**
  - Temporary placeholder dimensions created when a fact record arrives before the corresponding dimension record is available. These are later updated when the actual dimension data becomes available.
  - **Ex:** When performing ETL to load data into a data warehouse, sales fact data arrived first, before the product dimension data. An inferred Product dimension was created and later updated with the correct data.

Purpose-Based Dimensions: These dimensions are categorized based on their specific purpose or function in the data model.

- **Junk Dimensions:**
  - A single dimension that groups together low-cardinality attributes (attributes with very few unique values) that don't naturally belong in other dimensions.
  - **Ex:** A Junk Dimension might include attributes like flags and indicators. **Ex:** Yes/No, True/False etc.

- **Shrunken Dimensions:**
  - A subset of a dimension containing only the necessary attributes for a specific analysis.
  - **Ex:** A customer dimension containing only high-value customers for a targeted marketing campaign. Similarly, a Month_Dates dimension derived from a more detailed Date dimension that includes daily granularity.

- **Hierarchical Dimensions:**
  - Dimensions that naturally form a hierarchy, where attributes can be organized in levels of granularity.
  - **Ex:** A Geography dimension with hierarchy levels like Country -> State -> City.

23. What is a junk dimension? Provide an example to illustrate your explanation.

Ans:

A junk dimension is a special type of dimension table in a data warehouse that is used to combine multiple low-cardinality attributes (attributes with a small number of distinct values) into a single dimension. This is done to improve query performance and simplify the data model.

Real-World Fact Tables & Junk Dimensions:

- Fact tables typically store large datasets. For example, a sales fact might contain product sales data spanning several years.
- During fact table design, we often encounter numerous low-cardinality fields (Yes/No, True/False, Male/Female, etc.) in the source system.
- To optimize performance and simplify the data model, these fields can be consolidated into a junk dimension. This approach reduces the number of dimensional tables and significantly decreases the size and complexity of the fact table.
- The junk dimension itself contains all possible combinations of the original indicator field values.

Example:

Let's consider a retail sales data warehouse.

Here is a sample fact table:

- **Sales_Fact:** Transaction_Id, Product_Id, Customer_Id, Order_Id, Payment_Method_ID, Location_ID, IsCouponUsed, etc.

In this Sales_Fact, we have several low-cardinality attributes like:

- **Payment Method:** Cash, Card.
- **Location:** Instore, online.
- **Is Coupon Used:** Yes, No.

Challenge:

- Since we are dealing with large fact tables (with billions of rows), it is necessary to create separate dimensions (Dim_Payment_Method, Dim_Purchase_Location, etc.) and use their IDs in the fact table. But, these attributes each have only a few possible values and don't naturally belong in larger dimensions like Product, Customer, or Date.

Junk Dimension Structure:

- Instead of creating separate dimensions for each of these low-cardinality attributes, you can combine them into a single junk dimension. Here is the structure of junk dimension for the given scenario:

Junk_ID	Payment_Method	Purchase_Location	Is_Coupon_Used
1	Cash	Instore	Yes
2	Cash	Instore	No
3	Cash	Online	Yes
4	Cash	Online	No
5	Card	Instore	Yes
6	Card	Instore	No
7	Card	Online	Yes
8	Card	Online	No

Table 5.2

Here is the simplified Fact table with Junk Dimension reference:

- **Sales_Fact:** Transaction_Id, Product_Id, Customer_Id, Order_Id, Junk_ID etc.

As you can see, the fact table now references only one dimension (junk dimension) instead of multiple small dimensions. This simplifies the data model and improves query performance.

Cartesian product:

A junk dimension is essentially a Cartesian product of its low-cardinality attributes. This means that every possible combination of values from these attributes is represented in the dimension table. Here is the formula to calculate the total possible number of rows in a Junk Dimension table:

- **Number of combinations** = (Distinct values in attribute 1) * (Distinct values in attribute 2) * ... * (Distinct values in attribute n).
- **Ex:**
  - Attribute 1: Gender (Male, Female)
  - Attribute 2: Marital Status (Single, Married, Divorced)
  - Number of combinations = 2 * 3 = 6
- Similarly in the above given table, 2 * 2 * 2 = 8 possible combinations.

Use a Junk Dimension When:

- You have multiple low-cardinality attributes.
- The combination of these attributes is frequently used in queries.
- Creating separate dimensions for each attribute would lead to a complex data model.
- You need to improve the query performance by reducing the number of joins.

24. What is a Slowly Changing Dimension? What are its types, and how do you choose the right SCD type?

Ans:

A Slowly Changing Dimension (SCD) is a technique used in data warehousing to handle changes in dimension attributes over time. Since these changes happen gradually (Ex: a customer moving to a new address or an employee getting promoted), an SCD allows you to track and manage this historical data in different ways, depending on the business requirements. There are primarily three types of SCDs:

- **SCD Type 1:** Overwrites data—use when only current data matters.
- **SCD Type 2:** Adds new rows—use when tracking history over time is essential.
- **SCD Type 3:** Adds new columns—use when tracking limited history (just previous and current state) is sufficient.
- **Other SCD Types:**
    - **Type 0:** Data remains unchanged (static).
    - **Type 4:** Use a separate historical table.
    - **Type 6:** Hybrid of Types 1, 2, and 3.

Note: Depending on the business requirements, we select the appropriate SCD type, and based on the chosen SCD type, we implement the corresponding logic in the ETL/data pipeline that loads data into our data warehouse dimension tables.

Explore:

SCD Type 1: Overwrite

- In this type, when an attribute in a dimension changes, the old value is simply overwritten with the new value, and no history is kept.
- **Use Case:** Use Type 1 When historical data is not required, and the current value is sufficient.
- **Ex:** A Product dimension where you correct a typo in the product name. You overwrite the old name with the correct one.

Type 2: Add New Row

- Type 2 involves adding a new row with a new surrogate key whenever an attribute value changes, while retaining the old record with its original values. This method keeps a complete history of changes.

- **Use Case:** Use Type 2 when it's important to keep track of historical data and changes over time.
- **Ex:** A Customer dimension where a customer moves to a new address. The old address is retained with an end date, and a new row is added with the new address and start date.

Type 3: Add New Column

- In Type 3, a new column is added to the dimension to store the previous value of the changing attribute. This allows you to keep a limited history by storing only one previous value.
- **Use Case:** Use Type 3 when you need to track just the previous value, not the entire history.
- **Ex:** An employee dimension where you track an employee's current and previous job titles. The dimension table has both Current_Job_Title and Previous_Job_Title columns.

Other SCD Types: These are less commonly used SCD types:

- **SCD Type 0**: It is typically not implemented explicitly but rather represents a decision to ignore changes or handle them outside the dimension.
- **SCD Type 4:** The dimension table has the latest value while its history is maintained in a separate table.
- **SCD Type 6:** A combination of Type 1, 2 & 3 are used to track changes in dimension.

25. What are the different types of fact tables in dimensional data modelling?

Ans:

According to Ralph Kimball's dimensional modelling, depending on the nature of the business process and the type of analysis required, there are four primary types of fact tables:

- **Transaction Fact Table:** Captures individual transactions.
- **Snapshot Fact Table:** Captures data at regular intervals.
- **Accumulating Snapshot Fact Table:** Tracks the progress of a process over time.
- **Factless Fact Table:** Tracks events or conditions without measures.

Explore:

Transaction Fact Table:

- Contains a record for each transaction, capturing detailed information about the event.
- **Use Case:** Use when you need to track detailed, granular events. Best suited for analyzing detailed transaction-level data, such as sales trends, product performance, and customer behavior.
- **Ex:** A Sales Fact Table recording each individual sale with measures like Quantity Sold, Total Sales Amount, and Discount.

Periodic Snapshot Fact Table:

- Captures data at specific intervals (Ex: daily, monthly, yearly etc.) to provide a snapshot of the data at that point in time.
- **Use Case:** Use when you need to track the status or performance of a process over time. Best suited for analyzing trends and patterns over time.
- **Ex:** A "Monthly Inventory Fact Table" that records the inventory levels at the end of each month.

Accumulating Snapshot Fact Table:

- Stores the cumulative value of a metric over time. It tracks the lifecycle of a process by storing multiple dates and measures that get updated as the process progresses.
- **Use Case:** Use when you need to monitor the progress of a process from start to finish such as tracking account balances, inventory levels, and project progress.
- **Ex:** An "Order Processing Fact Table" that tracks an order from initiation through delivery, updating fields like Order Date, Shipment Date, and Delivery Date as the process unfolds.

Factless Fact Table:

- Contains only keys to the dimensions, without any quantitative measures or numeric values, used to record the occurrence of events.
- **Use Case:** Use when you need to track events or conditions without associated numeric values.
- **Ex:** A Factless Fact table might record "customer visits to a website", without any associated numeric values. Similarly, an "Attendance Fact Table" that tracks student attendance in classes, where the fact table records only the presence or absence without any measures.

Choosing the right type of fact table depends on the specific business requirements and the desired level of detail in the analysis.

26. Can you explain the differences between additive, semi-additive, and non-additive measures in a dimensional model?

Ans:

Additive Measures:

- Can be summed up across all dimensions in a fact table.
- **Ex:** Sales amount, quantity sold. You can add sales for different products, regions, and time periods to get total sales.

Semi-Additive Measures:

- Can be summed up across some dimensions but not others.
- **Ex:** Inventory levels. You can add inventory for different products or warehouses, but adding inventory across time periods (adding up inventories for January and February) doesn't make sense.

Non-Additive Measures:

- **Definition:** Cannot be summed up across any dimension.
- **Ex:** Unit price, exchange rate, profit margin percentage. Adding unit prices of different products doesn't provide meaningful information.

Understanding these measure types helps in designing efficient data warehouse queries and reports.

27. What is a date/time dimension in dimensional modelling, and how is it constructed?

Ans:

A time dimension is a crucial component of a dimensional model. It provides a structured way to analyze data across different time periods. Based on the business requirements, identify the necessary columns and date range. Create the dimensional table and populate it with data using an SQL script.

Explore:

Date/Time dimension allows users to analyze trends over time, perform time-based aggregations, and compare metrics across different time periods. It typically includes attributes such as date, day, month, quarter, and year, etc.

Preparing a Date/Time Dimension:

- **Define the granularity:** Determine the level of detail needed for analysis. For most business scenarios, year, quarter, month, date, day, and possibly hour granularity is sufficient.
- **Identify attributes:** Include attributes like date, month, quarter, year, etc. Based on the business requirement we may need to consider additional attributes like day of the week, week of year, month name, quarter name, fiscal year, fiscal month etc. and any other relevant time-related information.
- **Include flags:** Add flags for specific time periods (Ex: is_weekend, is_holiday) for easy filtering and analysis.
- **Create the Date Range:** Define the range of dates you need in your Time Dimension, typically covering several years, from the earliest date in your data to some point in the future. Ex: From January 1, 2010, to December 31, 2030.
- **Create a dimension table:** Design a table with a unique time key as the primary key and include all identified attributes.
- **Populate the dimension table:** Generate data for all possible time values within the desired range. Each row represents a unique date and includes all the attributes identified earlier. This can be done using SQL Script.
- **Consider time zones:** If applicable, include time zone information to accommodate different geographical locations.

Why Time/Date Dimension is crucial:

- Typically, when calculating aggregated sales reports for a specific time zone, incorporating time logic directly into the query or stored procedure suffices. However, at the enterprise level, considering factors like region, time zone, start day of the week, and holidays becomes complex. To maintain consistency and avoid data redundancy, a dedicated time or date dimension is beneficial. By mapping the appropriate time dimension row ID to the fact table, date and time can be represented uniformly throughout the data warehouse.

28. What is a cube in dimensional modelling?

Ans;

In dimensional modelling, a cube (OLAP cube) is a multi-dimensional data structure that allows for efficient querying and analysis of data. It organizes data into dimensions and measures, enabling users to perform complex queries, aggregations, and analyses quickly.

- Think of a cube as a multi-dimensional spreadsheet. Its sides represent dimensions (**Ex:** time, product, customer, geography), and the inside of the cube contains measures (**Ex:** sales, profit, quantity).
- A cube is essentially a pre-aggregated table with multiple dimensions (grouping criteria) and measures (precalculated numerical values). Although it's technically a table, its structure and purpose are optimized for analytical queries.

Key Components of a Cube:

- **Dimensions:** Represents the different perspectives or categories by which data can be analysed. Each dimension contains attributes that describe the data. Ex: Customer, Product, Location, Time.
- **Measures/Facts:** Measures are the numeric data or metrics that you want to analyze, such as Sales Revenue, Quantity Sold, or Profit. **Ex:** Total Sales, Number of Policies Sold.
- **Cells:** Each cell in the cube represents a specific intersection of the dimensions, containing a measure or set of measures. **Ex:** The cell at the intersection of August 2024 (Time dimension), Auto Insurance (Product dimension), and California (Location dimension) might contain the measure Total Sales for that particular combination.

Explore:

An insurance company wants to analyze sales data across different dimensions like time, product type, and region.

Dimensions:

- **Time:** Year, Quarter, Month

- **Product:** Auto Insurance, Home Insurance and, Life Insurance
- **Region:** State, City

Measures:

- Total Premium Collected
- Number of Policies Sold

Cube Structure: Imagine a cube where each axis represents one of the dimensions:

- The **X-axis** could represent Time (**Ex:** January 2024, February 2024).
- The **Y-axis** could represent Product (**Ex:** Auto Insurance, Home Insurance).
- The **Z-axis** could represent Region (**Ex:** California, Texas).
- Each cell in the cube would then contain values for **Total Premium Collected** and **Number of Policies Sold** for a specific combination of **time, product,** and **region**.

Example Queries:

The insurance company might want to know:

- **Total Premium Collected** for **Home Insurance** in **Texas** for the Entire Year **2024**:
  - This query aggregates the total premium collected for Home Insurance across all months in Texas for 2024.
- **Number of Policies Sold** for **Life Insurance** in **New York City** for **November 2024**:
  - This query retrieves the number of Life Insurance policies sold in New York City during November 2024.
- **Number of Auto Insurance Policies Sold in Texas for Each Month in 2023:**
  - This query retrieves the number of Auto Insurance policies sold in Texas for each individual month throughout 2023, allowing for month-by-month comparison.
- **Comparison of Total Premium Collected for Auto Insurance Between California and Texas for Q4 2024:**
  - This query compares the total premium collected from Auto Insurance sales in California against that in Texas during the fourth quarter of 2024.

Using the cube structure, these queries would be executed quickly, as the cube pre-aggregates and organizes data, making it efficient to retrieve this information.

29. Is an OLAP cube like a normal table designed for analytics purposes? Are enterprises still using cubes for all their analytics needs? What are the alternatives to cubes in the modern data analytics world?

Ans:

An OLAP cube is a conceptual representation of data, not a physical structure like a table. it's a special object designed for multi-dimensional data analysis. While a table typically organizes data in rows and columns, a cube organizes data in a way that allows for efficient querying across multiple dimensions simultaneously.

Modern Alternatives to Cubes:

- Cloud-Native Data Warehouses
- Direct Query & Live Connection
- In-Memory Analytics Engines
- Data Lakehouse Architecture

Explore:

Technology for CUBE design and management:

- To design and use a cube, you typically need an OLAP tool or service like SQL Server Analysis Services (SSAS), Azure Analysis Services (AAS), or third-party tools that can integrate with data warehouses.
- These tools enable you to build, query, and analyze cubes from your data stored in platforms like SQL Server, Snowflake, or Synapse SQL Pool etc.

Evolution and Alternatives to CUBEs:

While OLAP cubes are still used in some scenarios, especially in enterprise environments with legacy systems, many modern data analytics solutions offer alternatives that better align with today's demands for agility and cloud-native architectures.

- **Tabular Models:** Tabular models are a modern alternative to traditional multi-dimensional OLAP cubes. They use an in-memory columnar storage engine, which can process data more efficiently and allow for faster query responses. Ex: Power BI, Azure Analysis Services etc.
- **Cloud-Native Data Warehouses:** Cloud-native data warehouses are designed to handle complex queries and large datasets without the need for cubes. They often offer features like distributed processing, automatic scaling, machine learning integration, and real-time analytics. **Ex:** Snowflake, Azure Synapse, Google BigQuery, Amazon Redshift.
- **Direct Query & Live Connection:** Instead of pre-aggregating data in a cube, modern tools allow for direct querying of underlying databases and data warehouses. This provides real-time or near-real-time access to data without the need to build and manage cubes. **Ex:** Power BI, Tableau, Looker, etc.

- **In-Memory Analytics Engines:** In-memory analytics engines process data in memory, offering extremely fast query responses. They often replace the need for cubes by allowing interactive analysis of large datasets without pre-aggregation. **Ex:** Spark (with Databricks), Apache Kylin, Azure Synapse Analytics.
- **Data Lakehouse Architecture:** Data Lakehouse architecture combines the best of data lakes and data warehouses, allowing for both structured and unstructured data to be stored and queried. This can eliminate the need for traditional cubes by leveraging distributed processing and query engines. **Ex:** Databricks, Azure Synapse Analytics, Google BigQuery etc.

30. A retail company's data warehouse has ETL pipelines that loads product (Dimension) and sales (Fact) data nightly. If the company launches a new product like the 'Z Phone' and starts selling it online. The "product" data load pipeline failed due to some error. How can you still load the sales data without errors, even if the product information is missing from the dimension table? Specifically, how do you handle the scenario where we need to insert the 'Product_Id' column into the fact table, even though it's currently missing due to the failed dimension load pipeline?

Ans:

Inferred dimensions provide a practical solution to this problem where fact records arrive before the corresponding dimension data is available, ensuring that your ETL processes remain robust and your data warehouse stays consistent.

Inferred Dimension:

- An inferred dimension is a technique used in data warehousing to handle situations where a fact record arrives before the corresponding dimension record is available. It creates a placeholder (temporary record) in the dimension table with minimal or default information, allowing the fact record to be loaded without violating referential integrity.

Implementation: In our case, since the product dimension data was missing when the fact table (product sales) was loaded, an inferred dimension approach could have been beneficial. Here's how it could work:

- **Fact Load:**
  - When the ETL process for the fact table encounters a product ID that does not exist in the product dimension, it automatically inserts a placeholder record in the product dimension table.
  - This additional logic should be incorporated in the ETL process.
  - This placeholder record includes the product ID and minimal information (Ex: "Unknown Product Name" or default values for other attributes).
  - The fact table can then reference this placeholder record, maintaining data consistency.

- **Dimension Load:**
  - Once the ETL process for the product dimension is successfully rerun and the actual product data is available, the placeholder record is updated with the correct information.
  - The product name, description, and other attributes are filled in, replacing the default values.

Explore:

Benefits of Inferred Dimensions

- **Avoids Fact Load Failures:** Prevents fact load failures due to missing dimension data.
- **Preserves Data Integrity:** Ensures that all fact data is captured, even if dimension data is delayed.
- **Improved Data Quality:** Allows for correction of dimension data without affecting existing fact data.

Considerations:

- **Complexity:** Implementing inferred dimensions can add complexity to the ETL process.
- **Performance Impact:** Frequent updates to inferred dimension records might impact performance.

31. Describe an end-to-end data modelling project you significantly contributed to. What were the primary challenges encountered, and how did you design and implement a successful solution?

Ans:

I worked on a project to create a “Customer 360 View” for a global retail company. The goal was to consolidate customer data from multiple sources, including online purchases, in-store transactions, loyalty programs, and social media interactions, into a single, unified view.

Key challenges included:

- **Data Integration:** The company had customer data scattered across various systems, each with different formats, structures, and quality. Integrating these diverse data sources into a consistent model was complex.
- **Data Quality:** The customer data had inconsistencies, such as duplicate records, missing information, and conflicting data (Ex: different addresses for the same customer). This posed a significant challenge to creating an accurate and reliable Customer 360 View.
- **Data Warehouse and Scalability:** The data model needed to handle large volumes of data and support real-time updates as new customer interactions occurred. Ensuring that the model could scale to accommodate growing data and user demands was a critical requirement.

- **Data Privacy:** With regulations like GDPR (General Data Protection Regulation) in place, ensuring that the solution complied with privacy regulations and protected sensitive customer information was essential.

Solution Design:

- **Data Integration:**
    - I used a Data Lake (Azure Data Lake Storage) to ingest and store data from all sources in their raw format. This allowed for flexible data processing and transformation.
    - I implemented data pipelines using tools/services/capabilities like Azure Data Factory, Apache Spark, SQL, PolyBase, Azure Functions, and Azure Databricks to clean, normalize, and integrate data from different sources into a unified data model.
- **Data Quality:**
    - I used data profiling techniques to identify data quality issues such as duplicates and missing fields. Ex: Azure Data Factory Mapping Data Flow.
    - To resolve these issues, I developed a master data management (MDM) strategy that included deduplication algorithms and data cleansing rules. I leveraged Azure Purview for Data Lineage and Data Governance.
    - I also implemented fuzzy matching techniques to merge records that were likely to be the same customer but had slight variations. **Ex:** Azure Data Factory Mapping Data Flow fuzzyLookup and fuzzyMatch built-in capabilities, Azure Databricks notebooks (using Python, Scala, Spark), Custom Scripts (using fuzzy matching functions like SOUNDEX, DIFFERENCE, and Levenshtein distance etc.), Azure AI services.
- **Data Model Scalability:**
    - The dimensional data model was implemented in Azure Synapse Analytics using a combination of star and snowflake schema techniques for optimized query performance and storage efficiency.
    - I implemented partitioning and indexing strategies to ensure that the data warehouse could handle large volumes of data and deliver fast query responses.
    - Azure Synapse also provided the necessary scalability through its dedicated SQL pool, serverless SQL pool and Spark Pool options, ensuring that performance could scale as data volumes increased.
- **Data Privacy:**
    - I incorporated data masking and encryption techniques to protect sensitive customer information in the data model.
    - Access controls were put in place to ensure that only authorized users could view or modify sensitive data.

- I ensured that the data model was compliant with GDPR and other data privacy regulations by including features like data anonymization and the ability to delete customer data upon request.
- I leveraged features like Microsoft Entra, built-in data encryption and data masking features, Azure Key vault, Role-Based Access Control and Azure Purview etc.

Outcome:

- The data model was scalable, reliable, and compliant with data privacy regulations. The project successfully delivered a unified Customer 360 View that allowed the company to gain deeper insights into customer behavior, preferences, and trends. This led to more personalized marketing campaigns, improved customer satisfaction, and increased sales.

32. Can you share an experience where you needed to restructure a data model to enhance its performance? Detail the modifications you implemented and their impact.

Ans:

Business case:

- At an insurance company, I was involved in a project where the existing data model was leading to performance issues during the generation of policy and claims reports. The system managed millions of insurance policies and claims, and as the volume of data increased, generating reports became progressively slower, especially during quarterly audits.

Problem:

- The data model was initially designed with a highly normalized structure, separating policyholder information, policy details, and claims data into different tables. This design led to complex joins across multiple tables, which became inefficient as the data volume grew, causing significant delays in generating the necessary reports.

Changes Made:

- **Denormalization**: I refactored the data model by de-normalizing certain tables. **Ex:** I combined policy details and policyholder information into a single table for frequently accessed data (columns). This reduced the number of joins required to generate reports.
- **Partitioning**: The claims table, which had grown significantly, was partitioned based on the claim date. This allowed the system to query only the relevant partitions, rather than scanning the entire table, when processing date-specific reports.
- **Index Optimization**: I identified the columns frequently used in WHERE, JOIN, Aggregations, particularly those related to policy status and claim dates, and created composite indexes. This optimization sped up query execution by allowing the database to quickly locate relevant records.

- **Materialized Views**: I introduced materialized views for complex and frequently accessed queries, such as those that aggregated policy data by region or by insurance type. This precomputed and stored the results of these queries, drastically reducing the time taken to retrieve data for reporting.

Outcome:

- The performance improvements were significant, with report generation times reduced by over 60%. This enabled the company to complete quarterly audits more efficiently and provided underwriters and claims adjusters with faster access to the information they needed. The refactored model also better supported the growing data volumes, ensuring the system remained scalable and capable of handling future growth in policy and claims data.

33. How do you model hierarchical data structures in relational databases?

Ans:

While relational databases are fundamentally flat, we can effectively represent hierarchical structures through careful normalization and the use of foreign keys.

Modelling Techniques:

- Adjacency List.
- Nested Sets.
- Closure Table.

Explore:

- **Adjacency List Model (Most commonly used):** Each record includes a reference to its parent record. This is the simplest method for representing hierarchical relationships.
    - **Ex:** In a company's employee table, each employee record contains a ManagerID that refers to the EmployeeID of their manager.
- **Nested Sets Model:** Each record has a Left and Right value that defines its position within the hierarchy. This method is efficient for read operations but complex for updates.
    - **Ex:** In a content management system, categories are nested with Left and Right values to quickly retrieve hierarchical structures.
- **Closure Table Model:** Use a separate table to store all ancestor-descendant pairs. This approach facilitates querying and updating hierarchical data.
    - **Ex:** In a corporate organizational hierarchy, Category Closure table tracks every managerial relationship at various levels of depth starting from an associate to CEO.

34. What are the key considerations when designing data models for IoT data?

Ans:

Modelling IoT Data:

- A common approach is to adopt a time-series database or a data lake for storing IoT data in its raw format. However, for analytical purposes, a relational database or a data warehouse can be used for storing aggregated and structured data.

Core Entities of IoT Dataset:

- **Device:** Contains device metadata (**Ex:** ID, type, location, installation date, etc.).
- **Measurement:** Represents a specific measurement (**Ex:** temperature, humidity, pressure, etc.).
- **Data Point:** Records the actual measurement value with a timestamp.

Key Considerations and Challenges in IoT Data Modelling:

- **Data Volume and Velocity:** IoT devices often generate a massive volume of data at high speed. The data model must be designed to handle high ingestion rates and large datasets.
    - **Approach:** Use a time-series database or a Data Lake to store IoT data in raw format. Consider using distributed databases or cloud-based storage solutions to scale horizontally. **Ex:** InfluexDB, Graphite, Azure Cosmos DB, Azure Timeseries Insights, Azure Data Lake Storage Gen 2 etc.
- **Time-Series Data:** IoT data is typically time-series data, with each data point associated with a specific timestamp.
    - **Approach:** Structure the model to efficiently store and query time-series data. Use appropriate indexing strategies, such as indexing and partitioning on time columns, and consider retention policies for managing old data.
- **Data Variety:** IoT devices may produce diverse types of data, including sensor readings, status updates, and metadata.
    - **Approach:** Device capabilities and data formats may change over time. Hence, design a flexible schema that can accommodate different data types. Use a combination of structured (relational) and semi-structured (JSON) storage to handle diverse data formats.
- **Data Integrity and Reliability:** IoT data can be prone to gaps, duplicates, or errors due to network issues or device malfunctions.
    - **Approach:** Implement data validation and cleansing processes in the model to ensure data quality. Consider adding metadata fields to track data source, reliability, and integrity checks.

- **Real-Time Processing:** Most of the use cases may require real-time or near-real-time processing of IoT data, such as alerts or monitoring.
    - **Approach:** Integrate the data model with streaming data platforms (Ex: Azure Stream Analytics, Azure IoT Hub, Kafka Streams, Spark Structured Streaming) to process and store data in real-time. Ensure that the model can support both real-time and historical queries.
- **Scalability:** As the number of IoT devices increases, the data model must scale to handle growing data volumes and maintain performance.
    - **Approach:** Use a cloud-native approach with scalable storage and compute services, such as Azure Data Lake Storage or Azure Cosmos DB, to handle the growing data load.

CHAPTER 6

Azure Storage - Part 1

1. I noticed that cloud providers like Azure, AWS, and GCP use data size notations like MiB, GiB, TiB. Are these the same as MB, GB, TB, or do they represent something different based on a different unit base?

Ans:

They represent different values based on different unit bases. MiB, GiB, and TiB use binary (1024) prefixes and are based on a binary system, while MB, GB, and TB use decimal (1000) prefixes and are based on a decimal system.

Explore:

- Both MB and MiB are units for information or computer storage, but they differ in their basis.
- MB is based on the decimal system, while MiB is based on the binary system.
- In current digital systems, there's ambiguity in how 'MB' is used. It can represent either 1024 KB or 1000 KB, which can lead to confusion.
- To address this, the International Electrotechnical Commission (IEC) established standard names and symbols:
    - Decimal prefixes (KB, MB, GB, TB, PB, EB, ZB, YB) use powers of 1000.
    - Binary prefixes (KiB, MiB, GiB, TiB, PiB, EiB, ZiB, YiB) use powers of 1024.
- Here is the mapping between Decimal and Binary units:
    - Kilobyte (KB) = Kibibyte (KiB)
    - Megabyte (MB) = Mebibyte (MiB)
    - Gigabyte (GB) = Gibibyte (GiB)
    - Terabyte (TB) = Tebibyte (TiB)
    - Petabyte (PB) = Pebibyte (PiB)
    - Exabyte (EB) = Exbibyte (EiB)
    - Zettabyte (ZB) = Zebibyte (ZiB)
    - Yottabyte (YB) = Yobibyte (YiB)
- **Ex:**
    - 1 GB = 1000 MB
    - 1 GiB = 1024 MiB

Since most data storage and transmission systems consider 1024 format, we generally use the binary prefixes (KiB, MiB, GiB, TiB, PiB etc.) to avoid ambiguity.

2. What is Azure Storage, and could you explain the range of services it offers?

Ans:

Azure Storage is Microsoft's cloud storage solution offering highly available, secure, scalable, and durable storage for a variety of data objects. It serves various purposes, from hosting websites and applications to storing backups and large datasets.

Think of it as a massive storage in the cloud where we can store all sorts of digital stuff, from tiny files to massive amounts of data. We can access it from anywhere in the world, making it ideal for modern cloud-based solutions.

Azure Storage Services:

- **Azure Blob Storage:** Designed for storing unstructured data.
- **Azure File Storage:** Unstructured data and replacement for on-prem file and network shares.
- **Azure Disk Storage / Managed Disks:** Virtual Hard Disks which can be attached to Azure VMs.
- **Azure Data Lake Storage:** Designed for storing and processing large amounts of unstructured data.
- **Azure Queue Storage:** Store messages for asynchronous process.
- **Azure Table Storage:** Low-cost option to store structured NoSQL data.

3. Can you please provide a detailed explanation of Azure Storage Services, including Blob, File, Disk, Queue, Table and Data Lake storage? I am looking for three key aspects:

- **What is the functionality of each specific service?**
- **How can I access and utilize each service?**
- **What are the ideal use cases for each service?**

Ans:

Azure Blob Storage:

- Azure Blobs are content libraries of unstructured data that are randomly accessed from anywhere across the globe.
- There are three types of Blobs includes Block, Append and Page Blobs.
- Ideal for storing unstructured data like images, videos, logs, and archives.
- Highly scalable and cost-effective for storing massive amounts of data.
- Offers various access tiers to optimize performance and cost.
- **Use Case:** Storing log files, backups, disaster recovery files, and media content (audio, video, photos, documents etc.). Serving images or documents directly to a browser, streaming video, and audio, etc.

- **Ex:** An e-commerce application stores product images, user-generated content, and backups in Azure Blob Storage.
- **Access method:** Web Browser, Azure Storage Explorer, or programmatic (Azure Storage REST API over HTTP/HTTPS, Azure PowerShell, Azure CLI, or Azure Storage client library for .NET, Java, Node.js, Python, PHP, and Ruby).

Azure File Storage:

- Azure Files are fully managed file shares that we can access from anywhere. via the industry standard Server Message Block (SMB) protocol.
- We can mount Azure file share as a local drive from cloud or on-premises deployments of Windows, Linux, and macOS. This means it acts like a local file share.
- Similar to traditional file servers but with the benefits of cloud storage.
- **Use Case:** Azure File Share is a great lift-and-shift solution for migrating applications relying on local file shares, file servers, or NAS devices to Azure. It allows us to:
    - Store development and debugging tools, configuration files accessible from multiple VMs.
    - Centralize resource logs, metrics, and crash dumps from various VMs for efficient processing and analysis.
- **Ex:** A company uses Azure File Storage to share configuration files across multiple virtual machines (VMs) in a web application.
- **Access Methods:** Azure Storage Explorer, or programmatic (Azure Storage REST API over HTTP/ HTTPS, Azure PowerShell, Azure CLI, or Azure Storage client library for .NET, Java, Node.js, Python, PHP, and Ruby).

Azure Disk Storage / Managed Disks:

- Azure Disks are managed virtual hard disks (VHDs) that offer durable, high-performance block storage for Azure Virtual Machines.
- They are similar to on-premises virtual disks but are virtualized and managed by Azure, simplifying storage administration.
- Azure Disks offer a variety of disk types to suit different workloads include Ultra Disks, Premium SSDs, Standard SSDs and Standard HDDs.
- Azure Disks are available in two deployment models Managed (fully managed by Azure), Unmanaged (High availability and security is our responsibility).
- **Use case:**
    - Persistent storage for Azure Virtual Machines, ensuring consistent performance and direct disk access.
    - Lift-and-shift of applications that use native file system APIs to read and write data to persistent disks.
    - Database workloads that demand high IOPS and throughput.

- **Ex:** An organization runs its SAP environment on Azure VMs, using Azure Disk Storage for reliable and low-latency storage.
- **Access Methods:** Managed disks can be accessed by attaching them to an Azure Virtual Machine.

Azure Data Lake Storage:

- Scalable and secure data lake for big data analytics.
- Designed for storing and processing large amounts of unstructured data.
- **Use case:** Analyzing massive amounts of structured and unstructured data with various analytics services. Building data lakes for big data analytics. Running analytics workloads with Azure Databricks and HDInsight and Synapse Analytics.
- **Ex:** A data-driven organization uses Azure Data Lake Storage to store raw data from IoT devices for subsequent analysis.
- **Access method:** Web Browser, Azure Storage Explorer, or programmatic (Azure Storage REST API over HTTP/HTTPS, Azure PowerShell, Azure CLI, or Azure Storage client library for .NET, Java, Node.js, Python, PHP, and Ruby).

Azure Queue Storage:

- Azure Queues are used to store messages using HTTP or HTTPs. We typically use these to queue up work and process it asynchronously like a Service Broker.
- It enables asynchronous messaging between applications.
- Useful for decoupling application components and handling background tasks.
- Highly scalable and reliable for mission-critical applications.
- **Use Case:** Decoupling application components, handling background tasks and workflows and, building scalable distributed systems etc.
- **Ex:** A web application uses queues to handle image thumbnail generation, allowing users to upload pictures without waiting for immediate processing.
- **Access Methods:** Programmatic (Azure Storage REST API over HTTP/HTTPS, Azure PowerShell, Azure CLI, or Azure Storage client library for .NET, Java, Node.js, Python, PHP, and Ruby).

Azure Table Storage:

- It is a low-cost option for storing structured schema-less NoSQL data.
- Storing semi-structured NoSQL data requiring a key/attribute store for fast access.
- Simple and scalable for storing and querying large datasets.
- **Use Case:** Often used for building scalable web applications, building low-cost NoSQL databases, and mobile backends.
- **Ex:** An online gaming company uses Azure Table Storage to store player profiles, scores, and game progress information.

- **Access Methods:** Azure Storage Explorer, Programmatic (Azure Storage REST API over HTTP/HTTPS, Azure PowerShell, Azure CLI, or Azure Storage client library for C++, .NET, Java, Node.js, Python, PHP, and Ruby).

4. What are the key factors that we need to consider before finalizing the suitable Azure Storage Service for a given business case?

Ans:

As a public cloud provider, Microsoft Azure offers a Platform as a Service (PaaS) solution for data storage through its feature called "Azure Storage." Before selecting the right storage feature, it is essential to delve into specific considerations:

- **What type of data needs storage?** Ex: Structured, semi-structured, or unstructured data, transactional records, compliance data, infrastructure performance metrics, logs, backups, database files, media, etc.
- **Where is your on-premises data currently stored?** Is it in RDBMS, NoSQL databases, Network File System (NFS) or Server Message Block (SMB) file shares, hard disks, etc.?
- **How frequently is data accessed?** Is it frequently and continuously accessed, infrequently accessed on a monthly basis, or rarely accessed for long-term storage?
- **Considering the criticality of data, what storage redundancy, backup, and protection strategies are required or currently implemented on-premises?** Ex: File backups, snapshots, disk backups, off-site backup storage, storage replication, third-party backup tools or services, etc.

By addressing these questions, we aim to align our business's storage needs with the features and services offered by Azure Storage.

5. Could you explain the concept of storage redundancy and outline the redundancy options provided by Azure Storage?

Ans:

Azure Storage redundancy (also known as storage replication) refers to the methods and strategies used by Azure Storage to ensure data resilience, durability, and availability in the event of hardware failures, data center outages, or other potential disruptions. Azure Storage provides several redundancy options to meet different performance, availability, and cost requirements. These options include:

- LRS – Locally Redundant Storage
- ZRS – Zone Redundant Storage
- GRS – Geo Redundant Storage
- RA-GRS - Read Access-Geo Redundant Storage

- GZRS - Geo Zone Redundant Storage
- RA-GZRS – Read Access-Geo Zone Redundant Storage

Explore:

Azure Storage always stores multiple copies of our data so that it is protected from planned and unplanned events, including transient hardware failures, network or power outages, and massive natural disasters. Choosing the right redundancy option involves understanding our data's criticality, our tolerance for downtime and data loss, and our budget constraints.

LRS – Locally Redundant Storage:

- **Replication:** Maintains 3 synchronous copies within a single data center in a primary region. 3 copies are maintained in 3 different server racks within the same Data Center/Building.
- **Data Protection:** It can protect from node or hardware failures within a data center. It can't handle the entire data center level failures. It's the most affordable option.

ZRS – Zone Redundant Storage:

- **Replication:** Maintains 3 synchronous copies across different Availability Zones within the same region. Which means 3 copies are placed in 3 different physical locations/data centers in the primary region.
- **Data Protection:** This provides higher availability compared to LRS and protects against zone-level failures. However, it may not cover region level failures (if entire region is failed). It comes at a slightly higher cost than LRS.

GRS – Geo Redundant Storage: Data is asynchronously replicated to a secondary region located hundreds of miles away.

- **Replication:** 3 synchronous copies in the primary region and 3 asynchronous copies in a secondary region.
    - **Primary Region:** It maintains 3 synchronous copies in a single data center.
    - **Secondary Region:** Replicates 3 asynchronous copies in a single data center.
- **Data Protection:** This offers strong protection against major disasters like regional outages and ensures data accessibility even if the primary region becomes unavailable. If entire region fails, we can failover and start using data from secondary region. However, there is a possibility of read latency due to the geographical distance.

RA-GRS - Read Access Geo-Redundant Storage: Similar to GRS, data is replicated to a secondary region but with the added benefit of read access from the secondary location. This allows our applications to continue functioning in case of a primary region outage with minimal downtime. However, the cost is higher than GRS due to the additional read replicas.

- **Replication:** Same as GRS
- **Data Protection:** Same as GRS.

GZRS - Geo Zone Redundant Storage: It combines the benefits of ZRS and GRS.

- **Replication:** Replicates 3 synchronous copies across different Availability Zones in the primary region and 3 asynchronous copies in a secondary region.
    - **Primary Region:** It maintains 3 synchronous copies across 3 different Availability Zones/ Data Centers.
    - **Secondary Region:** Replicates 3 asynchronous copies within a single data center.
- The primary difference between GRS and GZRS replication lies in how the data is replicated in the primary region. In both cases (GRS & GZRS), data in the secondary Azure region is always replicated three times within a single datacenter.
- **Data Protection:** This option offers the highest level of availability and durability among all the choices but comes at the highest cost. In the event of a data center failure, we can utilize the secondary data center/availability zone within the primary region. Moreover, if a regional outage occurs due to a natural disaster, we can perform a failover to the secondary region.

RA-GZRS: Similar to GZRS but with read access enabled from the secondary region. This provides the ultimate combination of availability, durability, and read performance, but at the highest cost.

- **Replication:** Same as GZRS
- **Data Protection:** Same as GZRS.

6. Could you outline the key differences among the various Azure Storage redundancy models, including LRS, ZRS, GRS etc.?

Ans:

Feature	**LRS**	**ZRS**	**GRS/RA-GRS**	**GZRS/RA-GZRS**
Data Copies	3 within a same datacenter	3 across different availability zones within a single region	6 copies (3 within a primary region + 3 asynchronously in a secondary region. RA-GRS enables read-access in secondary)	6 copies (3 across different availability zones in the primary region and 3 locally redundant copies in the secondary region. RA-GZRS enables read-access in secondary)
Protect from	Single Datacenter level failures	Zone-level failures	Region level failures	Region and Zone level failures

Feature	LRS	ZRS	GRS/RA-GRS	GZRS/RA-GZRS
Read access to the secondary region	NA	NA	YES (RA-GRS)	YES (RA-GZRS)
Availability	Low	High – Automatic Failover between Zones	Very High – Automatic Failover and Regional redundancy plus read access to secondary copies in RA-GRS	Highest - Automatic failover between zones and regional redundancy, plus read access to secondary copies in RA-GZRS.
Cost	Lower	Moderate	Higher	Higher
Latency	Low	Moderate	Higher	Higher

Table 6.1

7. What factors should we consider when selecting the appropriate redundancy model for our Azure Storage Account?

Ans:

Storage redundancy is crucial for ensuring high availability and durability. Its primary purpose is to mitigate single points of failure in our business workloads, where a single malfunction, fault, or failure can lead to the entire system stopping to function. Azure addresses this by creating multiple copies of storage, protecting data from both planned and unplanned events such as transient hardware failures, network or power outages, and large-scale natural disasters.

The choice of the right redundancy model for your Azure Storage depends on several key considerations, including data availability, durability, cost, compliance, and performance.

Explore:

We cannot simply choose a redundancy option; instead, we carefully consider key factors when selecting the right redundancy for our storage:

- **Business SLA:** It is essential to consider business expectations and Service Level Agreements on Data Availability, Durability, Consistency, etc. **Ex:** Recovery Time Objective (RTO), Recovery Point Objective (RPO), Maximum Tolerable Downtime (MTD), Data Loss Objective (DLO), etc.
- **Compliance & Regulatory Requirements:** We must verify that our chosen redundancy model complies with industry or organizational standards. **Ex:** Dealing with government-sensitive data may require adherence to regulations specifying that data cannot be moved beyond the primary region boundary.

- **Performance:** Evaluate the potential impact of different redundancy options on the performance of storage operations. **Ex:** LRS and ZRS offer lower latency as data resides within the same region, while geo-redundant models can introduce additional latency when accessing data from the secondary region.
- **Future Scalability and Growth:** Consider how easily our storage can scale and accommodate future growth with the chosen redundancy model. **Ex:** When our application grows, serving a global user base becomes a priority. However, with LRS, scaling to multiple regions for better performance and disaster recovery might be challenging. Hence, GRS becomes a more suitable choice.
- **Commercial/Cost:** Redundancy levels come with varying costs. Higher redundancy models often provide better resilience but may incur higher expenses. **Ex:** LRS is the most cost-effective option, whereas geo-redundant models are typically more expensive. Assess the trade-offs between cost and redundancy requirements, and consider optimizing storage costs using features such as blob tiers or archive storage for less frequently accessed data.
- **Change Management and Complexity:** Assess the impact of implementing and managing different redundancy models on operational processes. **Ex:** Unmanaged disks may require more manual configuration and management.

8. What recommendations do you have for selecting the appropriate redundancy level for my Azure Storage services?

Ans:

- Choose LRS for cost-effective storage when regional protection isn't crucial.
- Go for ZRS for high availability within a region.
- Select GRS or RA-GRS for disaster recovery and compliance needs.
- Consider GZRS or RA-GZRS for the highest levels of protection and availability.
- Balance cost, availability, and durability requirements when selecting a redundancy option.

Explore:

LRS – Locally Redundant Storage:

- **Use Case:**
  - Development and testing environments.
  - Data with low criticality and easy replaceability.
  - Cost-sensitive workloads.
- **Ex:** A small business uses LRS to store employee training materials and non-sensitive documents, ensuring local redundancy in case of hardware failures within the data center.

ZRS – Zone Redundant Storage:

- **Use Case:**
  - Production workloads requiring high availability within a region.
  - Protecting against zonal failures.
  - Applications with strict uptime requirements.
- **Ex:** An e-commerce platform uses ZRS to store transaction logs and critical customer data, ensuring data availability even if one Availability Zone experiences an outage.

GRS – Geo Redundant Storage:

- **Use Case:**
  - Disaster recovery and business continuity.
  - Protecting against regional outages.
  - Compliance requirements for offsite data backup.
- **Ex:** A financial institution utilizes GRS to store sensitive financial records and customer information, providing failover capabilities between primary and secondary regions during regional outages.

RA-GRS – Read Access Geo Redundant Storage:

- **Use Case:**
  - Global applications requiring low-latency reads from multiple regions.
  - Fast failover to the secondary region for read-only operations.
- **Ex:** A content delivery network uses RA-GRS to replicate and serve multimedia content across regions, allowing read access to cached content in the secondary region for faster media streaming or downloads.

GZRS – Geo Zone Redundant Storage:

- **Use Case:**
  - Mission-critical applications demanding the highest levels of availability and durability.
  - Protecting against both zonal and regional failures.
- **Ex:** A healthcare organization uses GZRS to store patient records and medical imaging data, ensuring both zone-level and regional redundancy for critical healthcare information.

RA-GZRS – Read Access Geo Zone Redundant Storage

- **Use Case:**
  - Global applications requiring high availability, durability, and low-latency reads from multiple regions.
  - Fast failover with read/write capabilities in the secondary region.
- **Ex:** An IoT platform utilizes RA-GZRS to collect and process sensor data from devices, allowing read access to replicated data in the secondary region for real-time analytics and decision-making.

9. What is an Azure Storage Account?

Ans:

An Azure Storage Account is your gateway to all the various storage services offered by Microsoft Azure. It acts as a central container for all your data objects, regardless of type, within a specific Azure region. Essentially, it provides a unique namespace for your data and manages access control, security, and billing for all the storage services you utilize within that account.

Ex: You can create a storage account for your project and then utilize Blob, File, Queue, or Table storage services within that account. This approach allows for centralized control and management of access control, security, and billing.

10. What are the different types of Azure Storage Accounts?

Ans:

There are several types of storage accounts offered by Azure Storage, each with its own pricing model and feature set. Here is a brief overview:

- **Standard general-purpose v2:** Supports all types of storage services including Blob, Data Lake, File, Table and Queue.
- **Premium block blobs:** Optimized for Blob Storage.
- **Premium file shares:** Optimized for file shares.
- **Premium page blobs:** Optimized for Page Blobs.

Explore:

Standard general-purpose v2: The most versatile and recommended type for most general-purpose storage needs. It supports all Azure storage services (Blob, File, Disk, Queue, Table), offers multiple access tiers for cost optimization, and provides flexible management options.

- **Redundancy:** It supports all redundancy options LRS, ZRS, GRS, RA-GRS, GZRS, RA-GZRS.
- **Choose it when:**
    - We need support for a variety of storage services within a single account.
    - We want flexibility in access tiers and management options.
    - We are unsure of specific performance requirements or anticipate diverse workloads.

Premium block blobs: A performance-optimized tier for Blob Storage designed for low-latency and high-throughput scenarios. It delivers consistent sub-millisecond latency for read and write operations, and offers high IOPS and throughput.

- **Redundancy:** It supports LRS and ZRS.
- **Choose it when:**
    - We need to store large amounts of unstructured data such as text or binary data and require high performance and low latency.
    - Low-latency reads and writes are essential for our application's performance.

Premium file shares: This account type is optimized for storing and sharing files in the cloud or on-premises applications. It provides low-latency file operations, supports SMB 3.1.1 protocol for modern features, and offers high IOPS and throughput for file-based workloads.

- **Redundancy:** It supports LRS and ZRS.
- **Choose it when:**
    - We are hosting high-performance file shares for applications like HPC, media editing, or databases that require low latency and high throughput for file operations.

Premium page blobs: It is optimized for storing virtual machine (VM) disks (VHD and VHDX files). It delivers consistent, low-latency performance for random I/O operations, ideal for running I/O-intensive workloads on virtual machines.

- **Redundancy:** It supports LRS and ZRS.
- **Choose it when:**
    - We are using Page Blobs to host virtual machine disks that demand high performance, especially for workloads with frequent random I/O patterns.

Legacy Storage Accounts: It is not recommended to use these legacy account types.

- **Standard General-purpose v1:** Legacy version of v2. It does not support data access tiers.
- **Standard Blob storage:** Legacy version of Premium Block Blob.

Note:

- Premium performance storage accounts use solid-state drives (SSDs) for low latency and high throughput.

- Premium performance tiers are more expensive than standard tiers, so consider and balance between cost and performance.

11. Can you define an Azure Storage Endpoint?

Ans:

An Azure storage endpoint is the address used to access your data stored in an Azure Storage Account. In Azure, a storage endpoint refers to the unique URL that is used to access a specific Azure Storage service or resource within a storage account. Each Azure Storage service has its own endpoint.

- **Blob Storage:** https://<storage-account-name>.blob.core.windows.net
- **Data Lake Storage Gen2:** https://<storage-account>.dfs.core.windows.net
- **Azure Files:** https://<storage-account-name>.file.core.windows.net
- **Queue Storage:** https://<storage-account-name>.queue.core.windows.net
- **Table Storage:** https://<storage-account-name>.table.core.windows.net

Here, <storage-account-name> is replaced with the actual name of your Azure Storage account. These endpoints are used in applications, scripts, or tools to access and interact with specific Azure Storage services over the internet.

Ex: The invoice PDF file located in Blob storage can be accessed using its URL:

- https://abcorgstorage.blob.core.windows.net/projectOne/Invoice.pdf

12. What are the different types of Azure Storage Endpoints?

Ans:

We can create different types of Azure Storage Account Endpoints:

- **Standard Endpoint:** The default, publicly accessible endpoints for Azure storage.
- **DNS Zone Endpoint:** DNS Zone endpoints allow us to use custom domain names to access our Azure Storage accounts instead of the default endpoint format.
- **Private Endpoint (No Public Internet):** Secure endpoints accessible only from within a specific virtual network (VNet).

Explore:

Standard Endpoints:

- These are the default public endpoints provided by Azure Storage to access various services like Blob, File, Queue, and Table storage. They are accessible over the internet and use a standard naming convention.
- **Ex:** https://<storage-account-name>.blob.core.windows.net/projectOne/invoice.pdf.
- **Choose it:** For general-purpose storage access without specific branding or security isolation needs.

DNS Zone Endpoint:

- It is a feature that allows us to access our Azure Storage resources using a custom domain name. It provides a way to map our storage account endpoints to a custom domain, making it easier to access your storage resources with a user-friendly URL.
- **Ex:**
    - https://<storage-account-name>.z[00-50].blob.storage.azure.net/projectOne/invoice.pdf
    - z[00-50] indicates the specific DNS zone associated with our endpoint.
    - We can also customize our storage account like below:
    - https://www.abcorg.com/projectOne/invoice.pdf
- **Choose it:** For custom branding, friendly URLs, or to align with company domain policies.

Private Endpoint:

- It enables private access to Azure services from within a Virtual Network (VNet) without traversing the public internet. They provide a private IP address within the VNet and allow secure connectivity to specific Azure services. A private endpoint URL for the Azure Blob storage account will look different from the standard public endpoint URL and will be associated with a private IP address within your Virtual Network (VNet).
- **Ex:**
- https://<storage-account-name>.privatelink.blob.core.windows.net/projectOne/invoice.pdf
- **Choose it:** For sensitive data requiring high security, network isolation, and protection from public internet access.

Note:

- We can create multiple endpoints of different types for the same storage account.
- Creation, deletion, and modification of endpoints are done through the Azure portal, Azure CLI, or PowerShell.
- Choose endpoint types carefully based on your security and access control requirements.

13. I have a requirement to establish a custom domain for my Azure Storage account, intending to offer a personalized storage URL for our customers. I'm currently using the URL "abcazurestorage.blob.core.windows.net" to access my storage account. I'd like to customize it to something like "files.abccompany.com". Can you tell me the steps involved?

Ans:

We can implement it using below steps:

- Get ready with the Azure Storage endpoint and custom domain details.
- Configure the custom domain on your registered website to redirect requests to Azure Storage.

- Register the custom domain with Azure.
- Test and validate that the custom domain is functioning correctly.

Explore:

Here's how it works:

Get the Host Name of your Azure Storage Endpoint:

- In the Azure Portal > Our Storage Account > Settings > Endpoints > Blob Service Endpoint. Ex: abcazurestorage.blob.core.windows.net.

Get the Custom Domain Name:

- We purchased a custom domain at a third-party domain register. We want to use it to access our Azure Storage resources. Ex: abccompany.com

Domain Register (Where you registered abccompany.com):

- **Update NS records:**
    - You need to visit your domain name registrar (Ex: GoDaddy, Namecheap, HostGator etc.) and replace the name server records with the Azure DNS name servers. Ex: ns1-04.azure-dns.com.
- **Create a Canonical Name (CNAME) Record:**
    - Login to your domain registrar's website, under manage DNS settings, create a CNAME record that points to your Azure Storage Account. We may need to specify domain (abccompany.com) and subdomain (www or files or photos etc.)
    - **Ex:** files.abccompany.com CNAME abcazurestorage.blob.core.windows.net
    - When someone accesses a resource using your custom domain (Ex: https://files.abccompany.com), the DNS resolution is redirected to the Azure-provided DNS name (Ex: https://abcazurestorage.blob.core.windows.net).

Register the Custom Domain with Azure:

- In your Azure storage account > Networking > Custom domain tab > Domain Name > Enter the name of our Custom Domain Ex: files.abccompany.com.

Verify and Test:

- After configuring the DNS Zone and storage account settings, verify the setup.
- Test the custom domain by accessing our storage resources using the custom domain name (Ex: https://files.abccompany.com/projectOne/Invoice.pdf).

Check Existing Applications:

- Existing applications configured with Azure storage standard endpoints will continue to function as usual.
- The new custom domain setup won't impact existing applications. Ex: We still can access your files using standard endpoint:
- Ex: https://abcazurestorage.blob.core.windows.net/projectOne/Invoice.pdf.

***Note:**

If you want to manage your custom domain's DNS records within Azure, you can do it by creating **Azure DNS Zone** and **DNS Records**. So that you can keep your DNS management centralized and integrated with other Azure services.

14. What is Azure Blob Storage, and what are the different types of Blobs available?

Ans:

Azure Blob (Binary Large Object) Storage is Microsoft's object storage solution for the cloud. It is designed to store massive amounts of unstructured data accessible from anywhere globally via HTTP or HTTPS. This can include text files, images, videos, audio, logs, backups, machine learning models, and more. The stored data can either be exposed to the public or kept private.

Types of Blobs:

- **Block Blobs:** Ideal for storing large text and binary files, optimized for efficient upload and download of blocks in any order.
- **Append Blobs:** Designed for log files and similar data, allowing only appending data to the end for tamper-proofing.
- **Page Blobs:** Optimized for random read/write operations, enabling updates to specific ranges within the blob for efficient data manipulation.

Explore:

Components of Blob Storage:

The Azure Blob Service contains three main components:

Storage Account > Container > Blob

- **Storage Account:** This can be a General Storage Account or Blob Storage Account registered in Microsoft Azure. **Ex:** Standard General-purpose v2, legacy v1, premium Block Blobs, etc.
- **Container:** Containers organize a set of blobs, similar to directories in a file system. Typically, a storage account can hold an unlimited number of containers, and each container can store an unlimited number of blobs within the specified size limits. Container names should start with

lowercase letters. **Ex:** We can create separate containers for better organization, such as one for pictures, another for documents, and another for videos.

- **Blob:** A blob is like a file or document of any type and size. Azure supports three types of Blobs:
  - **Block blobs:** Ideal for storing text and binary files. Large files can be divided into blocks for parallel uploading, downloading, and reassembly in any order. Each block within a blob has a unique Block ID.
    - **Ex:** Storing documents, pictures, movies, and TV shows for live broadcast streaming etc.
  - **Append blobs:** Append blobs are similar to block blobs but optimized for append operations, allowing efficient append-only operations to the data. When modifying an append blob, blocks are added only to the end of the blob.
    - **Ex:** Logs, Sensor Data etc.
  - **Page blobs:** These are optimized for frequent read/write operations, enabling the writing of a range of pages to an existing page blob. Page blobs do not create a new blob but write to an existing one. They are ideal for storing index-based and sparse data structures like OS and data disks for Virtual Machines and Databases.
    - **Ex:** Azure SQL Database utilizes Page Blobs as underlying persistent storage for storing Data and Log files, Page Blobs are used to store VHD (Virtual Hard Disk) files associated with Azure Virtual Machines.

15. I am confused about the difference between Block and Blob. Could you explain it?

Ans:

The terms "blob" and "block" in Azure Blob Storage can indeed be confusing,

- **Blob:** The complete file or data object. Azure offers three different types of Blobs. Ex: A movie file stored as a blob. A digital book is stored as a blob.
- **Block:** A smaller piece of data that makes up a blob. A Block Blob is a specific type of Blob. Ex: The movie Blob is split into 10 smaller video blocks for efficient upload and streaming. A digital book is splint into separate chapters and uploaded it into Blob storage. This enables efficient upload, download, and replacement of individual blocks within a blob as needed.

16. What are the data access tiers available in Azure Blob Storage?

Ans:

Azure Blob Storage offers four data access tiers, categorized based on the frequency of data access. These tiers are designed to optimize storage costs, particularly for archival data that experiences minimal usage.

- **Hot:** Frequently used data – Daily or continues with no latency.
- **Cool:** Infrequent access – Minimum 30 days.
- **Cold:** Rarely accessed – Minimum 90 days.
- **Archive:** Storing for long term purpose – Minimum 180 days.

Explore:

Data Access Tiers for Azure Blob Storage:

- **Hot (Online):** This tier is suitable for data frequently accessed by applications with low-latency requirements, accessed or modified regularly.
  - **Cost:** Storage costs are higher while access charges are lower.
  - **Ex:** An operational application allowing frequent upload/download of documents stores them in Blob storage's Hot tier to facilitate quick and frequent access.
- **Cool (Online):** Optimized for storing infrequently accessed data. Data must remain in this tier for a minimum of 30 days.
  - **Cost:** Compared to the Hot tier, storage costs are slightly lower, but access charges are slightly higher.
  - **Ex:** It's suitable for short-term storage needs like backups, telemetry data, or media files.
- **Cold (Online):** Optimized for storing data that is rarely accessed or modified, but still requires fast retrieval. Data in the cold tier should be stored for a minimum of 90 days.
  - **Cost:** Compared to the Cool tier, storage costs are slightly lower, but access charges are slightly higher.
  - **Ex:** A pharmaceutical company that conducts extensive research and clinical trials. Once a study is completed, the raw data and results need to be archived for future reference, quarterly regulatory review, or potential re-analysis. This data is rarely accessed after the study's conclusion but must be retained and quickly retrievable for at least a few years to comply with regulatory standards or to validate future findings.
- **Archive (Offline):** This tier is designed for storing rarely accessed data. Data must stay in this tier for a minimum of 180 days.
  - **Cost:** It offers the lowest storage costs but with the highest access charges.
  - **Ex:** Ideal for storing large volumes of inactive data, such as compliance-required data, long-term backups, or archived datasets.

17. If we have created an Azure storage account of the Premium Block Blob type, is it possible to change it to the Premium File Shares storage type?

Ans:

No, we cannot directly change the type of an Azure storage account after it's created. However, we can move our data to a storage account of a different type:

- Create a New Storage Account with the Desired Type.
- Migrate data to the newly created Storage Account. Use tools like AzCopy, Azure Storage Explorer, Azure Data Factory, or PowerShell for efficient migration

Explore:

Here are the more scenarios:

Changing a storage account type:

- Not directly possible.
- We can create a new storage account of the desired type and then transfer the data from the existing storage account to the new one.

Move a storage account to a different subscription:

- It is possible.
- Go to the storage account and select "Move resource" under "Settings." Then, choose the target subscription and resource group.

Move a storage account to a different resource group:

- It is possible.
- Same process as moving to different subscription.

Move a storage account to a different region:

- Not directly possible.
- To move a storage account to a different region, we need to follow a similar process as changing the storage account type. Create a new storage account in the desired region, then migrate or transfer the data from the existing storage account to the new one.

Upgrade legacy storage accounts to a Standard general-purpose v2 storage account:

- It is possible.
- Navigate to Azure Portal > Existing legacy storage account > Settings > Configuration > Account kind > Upgrade > Confirm upgrade.
- Note that this action can't be undone.

***Note:** Always remember to back up critical data and review any potential impacts or dependencies before performing any migrations or upgrades.

18. I have created a Block Blob. Can I change it to a Page Blob or Append Blob in Azure Blob Storage?

Ans:

No, the type of a blob cannot be changed once it has been created. Each blob type has a distinct structure and optimization for specific use cases, and modifying it would disrupt the underlying data organization.

- **Reason:** The type of a blob is determined at the time of creation and is stored as metadata along with the blob data. Changing the type of a blob would require modifying the metadata, which is not possible without creating a new blob.

Explore:

Here are the possible solutions for the given requirement:

- **Carefully choose the right blob:** When uploading a new blob, carefully choose the appropriate type based on our usage needs.
- **Copy data to a new blob:** If we need to switch a blob's type, create a new blob with the desired type and copy the data from the original blob using tools like AzCopy or Azure Storage Explorer. Once the copy operation is complete, we can delete the original Block Blob.

19. Can we change the storage tier (Hot, Cool, Cold, Archive) of a blob after its creation?

Ans:

Yes, we have the flexibility to switch storage tiers for both individual blobs and entire storage accounts in Azure Blob Storage. This allows us to fine-tune costs and access times based on our specific data needs.

Explore:

Key Points:

- **Flexibility:** We can switch between the storage tiers Hot, Cool, Cold and Archive.
- **Scope:**
  - Hot and Cool tiers can be enabled at the storage account level or at the blob level.
  - However, the Cold and Archive tiers can only be enabled at the blob level.
- **Coexistence:** All storage access tiers can exist in the same storage account. **Ex:** The default tier for the Storage Account is Hot; however, some blobs are in the Archive tier, and some are in the Cool or Cold tier.
- **Default Behaviour:** The default tier for a blob is inherited from the account-level setting.
- **Rehydration:** The process of switching from the Offline tier (Archive) to Online tier (Hot, Cool or Cold) is known as rehydration. It typically takes several hours or days, depending on the blob size, so plan accordingly.

- **Typical transition times:**
    - **Hot to Cool/Cold:** Immediate.
    - **Cool/Cold to Hot:** A few hours.
    - **Hot/Cool/Cold to Archive:** Several hours or days.
    - **Archive to Hot/Cool/Cold:** Several hours or days (rehydration).

Process:

- **Switching storage tier at the account level:** Azure Portal > Storage Account > Settings > Configuration > Access Tier (Default) > Change between Hot and Cool > Save.
- **Switching storage tier at the Blob level:** Azure Portal > Storage Account > Blob Service > Blobs > Container > Blob -> Blob Properties > Change Tier > Choose from Hot, Cool, and Archive.

Note:

- We can also use Azure CLI or PowerShell for tier management.
- The default access tier setting of the account can't be set to cold tier.

20. Can you please describe the basic size limitations of Blob storage?

Ans:

Block Blob:

- Maximum number of blocks: 50,000 Blocks
- Maximum size of a block: 4000 MiB / 3.9 GiB Approx.
- Maximum size of a block blob: (50,000 X 4000 MiB) / (1024 X 1024) = 190 TiB Approx.
- **Ex:** Imagine storing a large 4K video file in Azure Blob Storage as a Block Blob. Each block can represent a segment of the video, with a maximum size of 3.9 GiB, and the complete blob can reach up to approximately 190 TiB when assembled from 50,000 blocks.

Append Blob:

- Maximum number of blocks: 50,000 Blocks
- Maximum size of a block: 4 MiB
- Maximum size of an append blob: (50,000 X 4 MiB) / (1024) = 195.3 GiB Approx
- **Ex:** Consider using Append Blobs for continuously updating log files. Each block can have a maximum size of 4 MiB, allowing the append blob to reach a total size of around 195.3 GiB when fully populated with 50,000 blocks.

Page Blob:

- Maximum Page size: 512 Byte
- Maximum size of a page blob: 8 TiB

- **Ex:** Storing a virtual hard disk (VHD) for a virtual machine with a maximum size of 8 TiB, where random access to specific data blocks is crucial for performance.

***Note:** The limits for premium accounts vary based on specific use case requirements, so it's advisable to engage with the Microsoft Azure support team for more precise information.

21. What is the maximum storage capacity of an Azure Storage account?

Ans:

The maximum capacity of an Azure Storage Account varies depending on the type of account and the specific storage services within it. Here are some general guidelines:

- **Standard storage accounts:** These accounts have a maximum capacity of 5 PiB (Pebibytes).
- **Premium storage accounts:** The maximum capacity varies based on the specific premium storage offering. We can communicate with the Microsoft team to increase the quota limits based on our needs.

Explore:

More details:

- **Storage Account Level:**
    - Number of storage accounts per region: 250
    - Maximum size of a storage account: 5 PiB
    - Maximum request rate: 20,000 requests per second
    - Maximum ingress (Incoming data):
        - US and Europe: 10 GiB per second
        - Other Regions: 5 GiB per second
    - Maximum egress (Outgoing data):
        - US: 50 GiB per second
        - Other Regions: 10 GiB per second
- **Blob Storage:**
    - Maximum size of a Block Blob: 190 TiB
    - Maximum size of a Append Blob: 195 GiB
    - Maximum size of a Page Blob: 8 TiB
- **File Share:**
    - Maximum size of a File Share: 100 TiB
    - Maximum File Size: 4 TiB

    - Maximum throughput (ingress, egress) for a file: 60 MiB per second

- **Queue Storage:**
    - Maximum size of a single queue: 500 TiB
    - Maximum size of a message in a queue: 64 KiB
    - Maximum throughput for a single queue: 2,000 messages per second (1 KiB messages)

- **Table Storage:**
    - Maximum size of a single table: 500 TiB
    - Maximum throughput for a single table partition: 2,000 entities per second (1 KiB-entities)

Note:

- These limits are applicable to general-purpose v2. The limits for premium accounts vary based on specific use case requirements.
- There are no limits for the number of blob containers, blobs, entities, queues, tables, or file shares.
- These limits apply to a single storage account, and we can create multiple storage accounts (250 per region) in our Azure subscription to increase our storage capacity and performance.

22. What are the 3 key differences between Azure Block Blob, Append Blob, and Page Blob?

Ans:

Below are the essential differences:

Feature	**Block Blob**	**Append Blob**	**Page Blob**
Basic element	Block	Block	Page
Primary Use	Storing text and binary data.	Continuous append-only operations.	Frequent read/write operations.
Optimized for	Handling large files with parallel operations.	Log files and similar sequential data.	Random read and write operations.
Use Case	Images, videos, documents, backups, archives etc.	Logs, transaction data, event streams etc.	VHDs for Azure VMs, database files, IaaS disks etc.
Write Operations	Overwrite blocks, upload entire blob at once.	Append blocks only to the end.	Write to specific ranges within the blob.
Single Block/Page max size	Block: 4000 MiB	Block: 4 MiB	Page: 512 Bytes

Feature	Block Blob	Append Blob	Page Blob
Max number of Blocks / Pages	Blocks: 50000	Blocks: 50000	Pages: No limit
Maximum Blob Size	190.7 TiB	195 GiB	8 TiB
Update Delete or Overwrite existing Blocks or Pages in the Blob.	Update – Yes Overwrite – Yes Delete - Yes	Updating, deleting, or overwriting existing blocks in a blob is not possible.	Update – Yes Overwrite – Yes Delete- No
Update/Overwrite Process	Upload and commit the block at the end of the process.	NA	It supports in-place updates, enabling modifications to individual pages or ranges of pages within the blob. Write operations are done and get committed immediately.
***Concurrency**	Not possible.	Possible.	Not Possible.
Cost (In General)	Lower for storage, higher for access.	Higher for storage, lower for access.	Higher for both storage and access

Table 6.2

***Concurrency:** Multiple clients writing to the same block/page at the same time.

23. What are Azure Managed Disks, and what are the various types of managed disks available to suit different workload needs?

Ans:

Azure Managed disks are like a physical disk in an on-premises server but, virtualized. With managed disks, all we have to do is specify the disk size, the disk type, provision the disk, and use it with Azure Virtual Machines. Once we provision the disk, Azure handles the rest.

Azure managed disks currently offer five disk types:

- **Ultra disks:** Extreme IO-intensive workloads.
- **Premium SSD v2:** Production and performance-sensitive workloads that consistently require low latency and high throughput.
- **Premium SSDs:** Production and performance-sensitive workloads.
- **Standard SSDs:** Less I/O-intensive applications
- **Standard HDDs:** Most cost-effective option that can tolerate lower performance.

***SSD:** Solid-State Drives

***HDD:** Hard Disk Drives

Explore:

Capabilities and suitable use cases:

Ultra Disks:

- **Max Capacity:** Size: 64 TiB | IOPS: 160,000 | Throughput: 4,000 MB/s
- **Use cases:**
  - Mission-critical applications.
  - High-performance databases (Ex: SAP HANA, SQL Server, Oracle).
  - Transaction-heavy workloads.
  - Large-scale virtual desktop infrastructure (VDI).
  - Data warehousing and analytics.

Premium SSD v2:

- **Max Capacity:** Size: 64 TiB | IOPS: 80,000 | Throughput: 1200 MB/s
- **Use cases:**
  - Business-critical applications.
  - Production databases.
  - Virtual machines running I/O-intensive workloads.
  - Online transaction processing (OLTP) systems.
  - Enterprise file servers.

Premium SSDs:

- **Max Capacity:** Size: 32 TiB | IOPS: 20,000 | Throughput: 900 MB/s
- **Use cases:**
  - General-purpose applications requiring good performance.
  - Medium-to-large non-critical databases.
  - Development and testing environments.
  - Web servers.
  - Application servers.

Standard SSDs:

- **Max Capacity:** Size: 32 TiB | IOPS: 6,000 | Throughput: 750 MB/s
- **Use cases:**
  - Boot volumes for virtual machines.

- Less I/O-intensive applications.
- Low-traffic websites.
- File storage.
- Development and testing environments.

Standard HDDs:

- **Max Capacity:** Size: 32 TiB | IOPS: 2,000 | Throughput: 500 MB/s
- **Use cases:**
  - Archival data.
  - Backups.
  - Infrequently accessed data.
  - Non-critical applications.

Note:

*Please note that the availability and support of specific disk types may vary based on region, VM type (Ex: memory optimized, storage optimized, compute optimized etc.), and other factors. Thoroughly verify compatibility before making your selection.

30. Azure Managed Disks come in various types/flavours, such as Ultra, Premium etc. Does each of these types offer different performance levels or tiers within it?

Ans:

Yes, similar to Azure SQL Database, Azure Managed Disks offer various performance tiers to accommodate diverse workload demands. Choosing the appropriate tier depends on your specific needs, including disk size, IOPS, throughput, and latency. Here is a breakdown of the available tiers:

- **Ultra Disks:** Offer in several fixed sizes, ranging from 4 GiB up to 64 TiB. Ultra disks feature a flexible performance configuration model that allows us to independently configure IOPS and throughput both before and after we provision the disk.
- **Premium SSD v2:** Its disk size ranges from 1 GiB to 64 TiBs. IOPS ranges from 3,000 to 80,000, throughput ranges from 125 to 1,200.
- **Premium SSD Sizes:** It comes in various fixed sizes, designated by a simple naming system using **P1, P2, P3,** and so on, up to **P80**. Disk size: 4 GiB to 32 TiB. IOPS: 120 to 20,000. Throughput: 25 to 900 MB/s.
- **Standard SSD Sizes:** It comes in various fixed sizes, designated by a simple naming system using **E1, E2, E3,** and so on, up to **E80**. Disk size: 4 GiB to 32 TiB. IOPS: 500 to 6,000. Throughput: 60 to 750 MB/s.

- **Standard HDD Sizes:** It comes in various fixed sizes, designated by a simple naming system using **S4, S6, S15,** and so on, up to **S80**. Disk size: 32 GiB to 32 TiB. IOPS: 500 to 2,000. Throughput: 60 to 500 MB/s.

***Note:** We can change the performance tier of our Azure Managed Disk at any time, without downtime, by using the Azure portal, Azure CLI, or Azure PowerShell.

25. What storage options are available for Azure SQL workloads?

Ans:

- PaaS offerings (Azure SQL Database & SQL MI) provide managed storage options that automatically adjust based on your service tier.
- IaaS deployments (SQL Server on Azure VM) require you to select and manage the storage disks for your VMs.

Explore:

The storage options for your Azure SQL workload depend on two factors: the deployment type (PaaS vs. IaaS) and the chosen service tier.

- **Azure SQL Single Database:**
    - **DTU:**
        - Basic Tier: Blob storage
        - Standard Tier: Blob storage
        - Premium Tier: Locally attached SSD
    - **vCore:**
        - General Purpose Tier: Premium Blob Storage
        - Business Critical Tier: Locally attached SSD
        - Hyperscale Tier: Standard Blob Storage + Data is fully cached on local SSD storage
- **Azure SQL Managed Instance:**
    - General Purpose: Premium Blob Storage
    - Business Critical: Locally attached SSD
- **SQL Server running in Azure VM:**
    - **Storage Selection based on Workload:** Azure recommends suitable disks based on your workload type (OLTP or data warehousing), storage size requirements, IOPS (Input/Output Operations Per Second), and desired disk throughput.
    - **Managed Disk Options:** You can choose from Standard HDD, Standard SSD, Premium SSD V2, and Ultra SSD managed disks to meet your performance and cost needs.

  - **Unmanaged Disks:** We must explicitly create Virtual Hard Disks and the disk management is our /customer responsibility.

Note: Learn more about the Azure SQL Family in the volume "Azure The One – Part 2 Azure SQL Family".

26. What are the disk roles in Azure Managed Disks?

Ans:

In Azure, there are three main disk roles for managed disks:

- **OS disk (Persistent):** OS files.
- **Data disk (Persistent):** Application, Database files.
- **Temporary disk (Non-Persistent):** Short-term storage

Explore:

Operating System (OS) Disk: Every Azure VM has one attached OS disk. That OS disk has a pre-installed OS, which was selected when the VM was created.

- **Ex:** OS installation, system files, and boot files necessary for the VM to run.
- *Only Premium SSD, Standard SSD, and Standard HDD disks can be used as the OS disk. Ultra and Premium SSD v2 disk types are not compatible with the OS disk role.

Data Disk: Data disks are managed disks attached to Azure VMs, separate from the OS disk, used for storing data, applications, databases, or any additional files required by the applications running on the VM.

- **Ex:** SQL Server data, log, and tempdb files.

Temporary disk: Most VMs contain a temporary disk, which is not a managed disk. The temporary disk provides short-term storage for applications and processes running on VM. It provides high-speed local disk performance but is volatile and not intended for permanent data storage. Data on the temporary disk may be lost during a maintenance event, when we redeploy a VM, or when we stop the VM. On Azure Linux VMs, the temporary disk is typically "/dev/sdb" and on Windows VMs the temporary disk is "D:" by default.

- **Ex:** Page files, swap files, caching or SQL Server tempdb.

27. We are hosting our SQL Server workloads on Azure VM. When it comes to hosting TempDB, should I choose a managed disk or a temporary disk?

Ans:

Here is the recommendation:

- For production environments where data durability and consistent performance are paramount, **Managed Disks** are strongly recommended.
- For development, testing, or non-critical workloads where data persistence is less crucial and cost optimization is a priority, **Temporary Disks** can be considered.

Explore:

Several key factors must be considered when selecting the appropriate disk type, including database size, performance requirements, environment (development, testing, or production), database availability requirements (LRS, ZRS, GRS, etc.), and budget constraints. Here are the general recommendations for hosting Data, Log and TempDB files:

Data (MDF) files:

- **Ideal:** Premium SSD v2 or Ultra Disks
- **Alternative:** Premium SSDs
- **Caching:** Enable Read-Only cache
- **Reason:** High IOPS and throughput for data access, write operations, and query execution.

Log (LDF) files:

- **Ideal:** Premium SSD v2 or Ultra Disks
- **Alternative:** Premium SSDs
- **Caching:** Do not enable caching
- **Reason:** High IOPS and throughput for transaction logging, ensuring database consistency and fast recovery.

TempDB files:

- **Ideal:** Ultra Disks
- **Alternative:** Premium SSD v2 or Premium SSDs or Temporary Disk
- **Caching:** Enable Read-Only cache
- **Reason:** Extremely fast, low-latency storage for temporary data, enhancing sorting, joining, and other database operations.
- **Scenarios:**
    - **Case 1:** For mission-critical SQL Server workloads, place TempDB on the local SSD (D:\ drive).
    - **Case 2:** If the capacity of the local drive is insufficient for your TempDB size, then place TempDB on a storage pool striped across premium SSD disks with read-only caching.

Special Cases: While technically possible, storing TempDB files on Temporary Disks (D: drive) when configuring Failover Cluster Instances (FCIs) is strongly discouraged. Managed Disks are the recommended option in this scenario.

28. At on-premises, we separated our SQL Server data and log files onto different drives. During migration to an Azure VM, do we still need to follow this practice, or can we keep both files on the same disk?

Ans:

Despite the SQL Server's location, separating data and log files onto different drives is always a good practice. This principle applies to Azure VMs as well.

- **Reason:** Data and log files have different access methods (MDF for random IO, LDF for sequential) and caching requirements (MDF with read-only cache, LDF with no cache).
- **Ex:** During a medium-scale test workload, we observed up to a 25% performance gain when MDF and LDF were placed on separate drives.

29. While creating an Azure VM with a SQL Server image, what are the storage configuration options available?

Ans:

Azure VMs with SQL Server images offer three storage configuration options based on your workload type:

- **General (Default):** This option configures a single data disk with a maximum of 5000 Input/ Output Operations Per Second (IOPS). The same disk is used to store MDF, LDF, and Tempdb files. It's suitable for less demanding workloads.
- **Transactional Processing:**
    - This option creates two separate disks: one for data and another for logs. Ideally, tempdb resides on the local SSD (temporary drive "D").
    - Storage is optimized for Online Transaction Processing (OLTP) workloads with a stripe size of 64 KB and trace flags 1117 & 1118 enabled (these flags can improve performance in specific scenarios).
    - If you choose premium storage disks, you can enable read-only cache for the drives containing MDF and tempdb files.

- **Data Warehousing:**
    - Similar to transactional processing, this option creates two disks for data and logs. Tempdb is ideally placed on the local SSD.
    - Storage is optimized for Online Analytical Processing (OLAP) workloads with a stripe size of 256 KB and trace flags 1117 & 610 enabled (these flags can improve query performance for data warehousing).
    - As with transactional processing, read-only cache can be enabled for premium storage disks containing MDF and tempdb files.

- **Important Note:** These are general guidelines. The exact configuration may vary depending on the VM size and your specific workload requirements.

Explore:

Customizing Storage with Premium Disks:

If you choose to customize storage configurations with premium disks during VM creation, here's what happens:

- Azure creates and attaches Premium SSDs to your VM.
- It configures the data disks for SQL Server access.
- The new drive is optimized based on your chosen workload type (data warehousing, transactional processing, or general).

Trace Flags:

- **Trace Flag 1117:** This tells SQL Server to grow all files within a Filegroup equally. When a data file in a filegroup grows, it forces other files in that group to grow as well. This can be beneficial for tempdb, which often uses multiple data files, but applies to all databases on the instance.
- **Trace Flag 1118:** This instructs SQL Server to avoid "mixed extents" and use "full extents." Each newly allocated object in every database on the instance gets its own dedicated 64KB of data, reducing tempdb allocation contention.
- **Trace Flag 610:** This controls minimally logged inserts into indexed tables. For instance, during a bulk load operation that allocates a new page, all rows sequentially filling that page are minimally logged.

30. Are Page Blobs and Managed Disks the same?

Ans:

No! Azure Managed Disks and Azure Page Blobs serve different purposes, but they are related in functionality.

Azure Managed Disks are backed by Azure Page Blobs. That means, when we provision a managed disk and attach it to an Azure VM, Azure internally utilizes Page Blob to store the virtual hard disks (VHDs) of managed disks.

Explore:

You might grasp the difference better if I explain the use cases:

Azure Managed Disks:

- **Azure VM Storage:** Azure Managed Disks are commonly used as OS disks and data disks for Azure VMs.

- **High-Performance Computing (HPC):** Workloads requiring high I/O performance, such as scientific simulations, financial modelling, or rendering applications, can benefit from high-performance managed disks like Ultra Disks for their storage needs.
- **Enterprise Applications:** Enterprise applications with critical performance requirements, such as ERP systems, CRM databases, or transactional systems, often utilize Premium SSD or Ultra Disk managed disks to ensure optimal performance and reliability.

Azure Page Blob:

- **To store Managed Disks:** Azure Managed Disks, utilize Azure Page Blobs as the underlying storage mechanism. They are used to store VHD (Virtual Hard Disk) files, which are utilized as disks for Azure Virtual Machines.
- **Database Storage:** In PaaS mode, Azure SQL Database uses page blobs as the underlying persistent storage for its databases, enabling fast random read-write operations for the database.
- **Big Data and Analytics:** In big data and analytics scenarios, Page Blobs can be used to store large datasets, data lakes, or data warehouse files, allowing for efficient data access and management for analytics platforms like Azure HDInsight or Azure Databricks.
- **Hosting files for video editing software:** Employing Page Blobs to store large video files and enable fast, random access to specific frames for editing and manipulation tasks.

31. Does Azure support attach a Managed Disk to multiple Virtual Machines simultaneously?

Ans:

Yes! **Azure Shared Disks** is a feature for Azure managed disks that allows us to attach a managed disk to multiple VMs simultaneously. This feature is useful when we want to deploy new or migrate existing clustered applications to Azure. Shared disks require a cluster manager, like Windows Server Failover Cluster (WSFC), or Pacemaker, that handles cluster node communication and write locking.

Explore:

Use cases for Azure Shared Disks:

- **Running clustered databases:** For applications like SQL Server failover cluster instances, high availability databases, and distributed databases.
- **Deploying scale-out file servers:** Enabling collaborative file access and high performance for workloads like media editing and scientific computing.
- **Hosting persistent containers:** For containerized applications requiring shared data storage and high availability.
- **Running distributed applications:** Supporting applications utilizing distributed file systems and cluster-aware deployments.

32. Have you heard anything about Azure Elastic SAN?

Ans:

Azure Elastic SAN is a cloud-native Storage Area Network (SAN) service built on Azure that provides a scalable, cost-effective, high-performance, and comprehensive storage solution. Think of it as an on-premises SAN experience brought to the cloud, but with greater scalability and flexibility.

Explore:

Primary features of Elastic SAN:

- **Workload optimization:** It provides millions of IOPS, double-digit GiBps throughput, and single-digit millisecond latency to our mission-critical applications.
- **Integration:** Connects seamlessly with various Azure compute services like Azure VMs, Azure Kubernetes Service (AKS), and Azure App Service.
- **Data migration:** We can migrate our data to Elastic SAN to achieve the performance of most on-premises SAN environments with the advantages of an efficient cloud-native solution.
- **Business continuity:** It provides ZRS and LRS to protect business-critical data and applications that require high availability.
- **Storage consolidation:** Azure Elastic SAN lets us share the provisioned performance across volumes, so you can easily achieve high performance at an efficient rate.
- **Cost-effectiveness:** Pay only for the storage we use, with granular sizing options.

33. What is the difference between Elastic SAN and Managed Disks, and how can one choose the right option for a specific business case?

Ans:

Basic difference:

- **Managed Disks:** For individual VM storage with a wider range of disk types and cost-effective options.
- **Elastic SAN:** For shared storage across multiple compute resources with high performance and scalability.

Choosing between Elastic SAN and Managed Disks:

- For individual VM storage with diverse disk types and cost-effectiveness, Managed Disks remain a valid option.
- For shared storage with high performance and scalability for demanding applications, consider Elastic SAN.

34. Are you familiar with the terms Bursting, Disk Stripping, Disk Caching, and Write Accelerator? If yes, could you provide a brief explanation of each?"

Ans:

These are advanced performance improvement techniques for Azure Managed Disks suitable for demanding workloads.

- **Disk-level bursting:** Temporarily increase the performance of your managed disk.
- **VM-level bursting:** Temporarily increase the performance of your VM.
- **Disk-Stripping:** Data is distributed across multiple disks simultaneously for a faster performance.
- **Disk-Caching:** Stores frequently accessed data in memory.
- **Write Accelerator:** Increases the write performance of our disk by caching writes in buffer.

Explore:

Bursting:

- **Disk-level bursting:** It allows a managed disk to briefly exceed its provisioned performance limits for short intervals to handle sudden spikes in workload demands.
  - **How it works:** When a workload temporarily requires more performance than the provisioned limit, Azure allows the disk to burst beyond the baseline performance level for a limited duration. There are two models of bursting for disks:
  - **An on-demand bursting model**, where the disk bursts whenever its needs exceed its current capacity. This model incurs additional charges anytime the disk bursts.
  - **A credit-based model**, where the disk will burst only if it has burst credits accumulated in its credit bucket. It leverages a credit-based system, accumulating credits during idle periods and using them during bursts. This model does not incur additional charges when the disk bursts.

- **VM Level Bursting:** A feature that allows Azure VMs to temporarily exceed their provisioned performance limits for a short duration. VM-level bursting only uses the credit-based model for bursting.
  - **How it works:** Each VM has a "burst bucket" that stores credits for bursting. These credits accumulate automatically when the VM is running below its provisioned performance level. When a sudden workload spike occurs, the VM can tap into these credits to burst above its usual performance limits for a limited time.
  - **When to use:** When our workload has occasional spikes in I/O and CPU demands, but we don't need consistently high performance all the time. We can use it to improve startup times, handle batch jobs, and traffic spikes.
  - **Ex:** A web application that handles bursts of traffic during sales events or marketing campaigns. If we have a VM with a P4 disk, which has a provisioned performance of up to

120 IOPS and 25 MB/s, you can use disk-level bursting to increase the performance of the disk up to 3500 IOPS and 170 MB/s, allowing for faster startup times.

Disk Striping: Disk striping is a technique that combines multiple disks (stripes) into a single logical volume, improving performance and increasing capacity.

- **How it works:** Data is divided into chunks and distributed across multiple disks simultaneously, allowing read/write operations to occur in parallel. Striping enhances performance by spreading the workload across multiple disks and can be configured using software or hardware RAID (Redundant Array of Independent Disks).
- **When to use:** When we need to boost overall I/O performance by combining multiple disks into a single, faster logical volume.
- **Ex:** A database server handling large data sets and complex queries, where faster performance is crucial. If we have four disks, when we stripe data across multiple disks, the data will be divided into stripes and spread across those disks. When a read or write request is made, it's distributed among the disks where the data is striped. This means that multiple disk heads (read/write mechanisms) can access different parts of the data concurrently, significantly enhancing performance compared to a single disk's capabilities.

Disk Caching: It involves temporarily storing frequently accessed data closer to the application, improving read performance by reducing latency.

- **How it works:** you have the ability to set the caching for the disks. Azure VMs have a multi-tier caching technology called Blob Cache when used with Premium Disks. Blob Cache uses a combination of the Virtual Machine RAM and local SSD for caching. This cache sits between the disk and the VM, allowing quicker access to frequently used data. It can be configured as ReadOnly (for read caching) or ReadWrite (for both read and write caching) or None.
- **When to use:** When we want to reduce read latency for frequently accessed data.
- **Ex:** A file server hosting frequently accessed documents or a web server caching static content.

Write Accelerator: It optimizes write operations, aggregating small writes into larger, more efficient writes to improve overall disk write performance.

- **How it works:** Instead of immediately writing small chunks of data to disk, the system buffers these writes and combines them into larger, sequential writes, reducing the number of disk operations and enhancing write performance.
- **When to use:** It should be used for the volumes that contain the transaction log or redo logs of a DBMS. It is ideally suited where log file updates are required to persist to disk in a highly performant manner for modern databases.
- **Ex:** A database server (SQL Server, Oracle, and SAP HANA) with frequent data updates or an application performing large file uploads.

***Please note** that, not all VM types and Managed Disk types support all these techniques. Always consult Microsoft's official documentation when considering these features. For example:

- Write Accelerator is available for M-series VMs only.
- Azure Premium SSD managed disks can use either bursting model (on-demand or credit-based), while standard SSDs currently only offer credit-based bursting.

35. What is Disk Caching in Azure VMs and how does it benefit database workloads?

Ans:

When using premium managed disks for your VM, Azure offers host caching, which utilizes a combination of the VM's local RAM and locally attached SSDs to cache frequently accessed data blocks. Here's how it benefits database workloads running on Azure VMs:

- **Reduced Read Latency:** Frequently accessed database tables stored on the premium managed disk can benefit from faster read speeds due to the cached data readily available on the VM's local resources.
- **Improved IOPS and Throughput:** Importantly, premium storage doesn't count reads served from the cache towards your provisioned IOPS (Input/Output Operations Per Second) or throughput limits. This effectively allows you to experience higher performance than the chosen limits for these metrics.

Explore:

Disk caching for Premium SSD comes with three different modes ReadOnly, ReadWrite or None.

- **ReadOnly:** Read-Only is highly beneficial for Database (SQL Server) data files (.mdf) that are stored on Premium Storage.
- **None:** This configuration should be used for the disks hosting Database Log file as the log file is written sequentially and does not benefit from ReadOnly caching.
- **ReadWrite:** We can't use disks with ReadWrite caching to host the SQL Server Data or Log files. Because SQL Server is a RDBMS and ReadWrite cache doesn't support the transaction consistency between cache and the disk.

36. Have you ever experimented with disk caching on Azure VMs to see how it benefits your database workloads?

Ans:

Absolutely! Here are some average statistics we measured on the same database workload to quantify the impact of disk caching:

- **Without disk caching (Un-cached reads):**
  - Average Latency: 4 Milliseconds.

    - IOPS per VM: 80,000
- **With disk caching enabled (Cached reads):**
    - Average Latency: < 1 Millisecond.
    - IOPS per VM: 160,000 (Reads from cache don't count towards the provisioned IOPS limit).

Overall Throughput Increase:

The benefit extends beyond just latency. We observed significant throughput improvements based on the SQL workload profile:

- **Case 1: Workload Profile**: 50% reads, 50% writes, light TempDB activity.
    - **Observation:** Up to 25% more throughput with cached reads.
- **Case 2: Workload Profile:** 80% reads, 20% writes, light TempDB activity.
    - **Observation:** Up to 40% more throughput with cached reads.

Conclusion: Disk caching on Azure VMs significantly improves database performance, especially for read-heavy workloads.

37. What are the differences between managed and unmanaged disks in Azure?

Ans:

Managed disks and unmanaged disks are two types of storage options available in Azure. The basic difference between them is that managed disks are managed by Azure, while unmanaged disks are managed by users.

Recommendation:

- **Managed Disks:** They are the recommended choice in most scenarios due to their ease of use, built-in redundancy, better security, and simpler management. We typically choose managed disks for most production workloads or when simplicity and high availability are priorities.
- **Unmanaged Disks:** Consider unmanaged disks when we require specific customization or management of storage accounts for specialized scenarios.

Explore:

Here are more differences:

Managed Disks:

- **Disk Management:** Azure handles everything including storage account creation, disk provisioning, performance monitoring, security, replication, patching and maintenance.
- **Pricing:** Managed disk price = Fixed Cost (Per disk size) + Operations cost.

- **Upgrading Tiers:** Upgrading tiers is simple and can be done with just a few clicks.
- **Benefits:** Simplified maintenance, scalability, built-in High availability and Disaster Recovery options, supporting Advanced features like bursting, shared disks, built-in encryption etc.

Unmanaged Disks:

- **Disk Management:** We manually need to create and manage a storage account, then configure disks (VHD files) within it.
- **Pricing:** Unmanaged disk price = (Storage_Usage_In_GB * Cost_per_GB) + Operations cost.
- **Upgrading Tiers:** Shifting between Standard and Premium tiers is a complex process that involves multiple steps.
- **Benefits:** Full control (managing access control, custom encryption, and custom replication strategies etc.). Lower cost (cheaper than managed disks).

38. A large enterprise initiating their cloud migration journey to Azure. We recognize the diverse storage needs across our numerous verticals and their individual projects. Each project possesses unique business case considerations and wide-ranging data requirements. In the context of this strategic move, I am interested in understanding the array of Azure Storage features in the following key areas:

- **Data Backup**
- **High Availability and Disaster Recovery**
- **Data Security and Protection**
- **Auditing and Monitoring**

Could you please describe one or two primary features within each of these categories?

Ans:

Within Azure Storage, here are some key features that address Backup, HA & DR, Security, and Monitoring:

***Note:** Please don’t feel overwhelmed by the extensive list of Azure Storage features and services provided. Instead, take a moment to review and grasp the various ways these offerings can provide to diverse business requirements. The goal is not to memorize each feature but to understand their essence and how they can address real-time, varied business needs we might encounter across our projects.

Backup:

- Operational Backup for Azure Blobs
- Vault Backups for Azure Blobs
- Point-in-time restore for Block-blob
- Azure File Share Backup

- Azure Backup
- Azure Backup for Managed Disks
- Backup vault/Recovery Service Vault
- Backup center
- Custom Backup solutions using Azure Native Services
- Third-party Backup solutions

HA & DR:

- Azure Storage Redundancy / Storage Replication
- Read-Access Azure Storage Redundancy
- Object replication for Block Blob
- Azure File Sync
- Azure Archive Blob Storage
- Azure Site Recovery
- Azure Site Recovery for Managed Disks
- Customized Cross-region Copy Jobs using Azure Native Services
- Third-party HA&DR solutions for Azure Storage

Storage Security & Data Protection Solutions:

- Soft Delete
- Delete Lock (Azure Resource Locks)
- Blob Snapshot
- Azure File Share Snapshot
- Blob Versioning
- Immutable Storage
- Microsoft Entra ID integration
- Authentication Mechanisms (Shared Key, Shared Access Signature etc.)
- Authorization Mechanisms:
- Azure RBAC (Role-Based Access Control)
- Azure ABAC (Attribute-Based-Access-Control)
- Access control lists (ACLs)
- Private Endpoints
- Azure Security Center
- Threat Detection and Response
- Azure Storage Encryption
- Azure Storage Lifecycle Management Policies

Auditing & Monitoring:

- Blob Change Feed
- Azure Monitor logs

- Azure Monitor Activity logs
- Log Analytics Workspace

Explore:

Backup:

- **Operational & Vault Backup for Azure Blobs:**
    - **Operational Backup:** Managed local data protection solution (Max retention 360 Days). A service providing operational backups for Azure Blobs and stores it in the same storage account locally.
    - **Vault Backup:** Managed offsite data protection solution (Max retention 10 Years). Provides off-site, isolated protection in a dedicated vault, separate from our storage account.
    - Captures incremental changes in blob data to create efficient backups, allowing for quick recovery in case of data loss.
    - **Ex:** An application accidentally deletes critical blob data; backup ensures a swift recovery to the latest consistent state.
- **Point-in-time restore for Block-blob:**
    - Feature enabling the restoration of Block Blob data to a specific point in time.
    - Maintains a historical record of changes, allowing users to select a precise timestamp for recovery, ensuring data consistency.
    - **Ex:** Accidental blob deletion; point-in-time restore enables recovery to the state just before the deletion occurred.
- **Azure File Share Backup:**
    - Backup solution designed for Azure File Shares.
    - Integrates with Azure Backup to create scheduled backups of file shares and store them in a Recovery Services vault.
    - **Ex:** Scheduling daily backups of a file share containing critical documents. If File share content accidentally modified; it allows restoration to a point before the unwanted changes.
- **Azure Backup:**
    - A centralized backup service in Azure that protects a variety of workloads, including virtual machines, databases, file shares, and blobs.
    - Uses Recovery Services vaults to store backups, provides scheduling and retention policies, and enables restores to original or alternate locations.
    - **Ex:** System-wide data loss; Azure Backup facilitates the recovery of affected storage resources through unified policies.

- **Azure Backup for Managed Disks:**
  - A feature within Azure Backup that protects Azure managed disks, which store virtual machine data.
  - Creates point-in-time snapshots of managed disks and stores them in a Recovery Services vault, enabling disk restores.
  - **Ex:** Corruption in a managed disk in a VM; It allows restoring a managed disk to a previous state to recover a virtual machine after a failure.
- **Backup vault/Recovery Service Vault:**
  - A logical container in Azure that stores backups and recovery points for various workloads protected by Azure Backup.
  - Acts as a central management point for backups, providing restore capabilities and access to backup data.
  - **Ex:** Creating a Recovery Services vault to store backups of virtual machines and file shares.
- **Backup center:**
  - A unified management portal in the Azure portal that provides a centralized view of all backups across multiple vaults and subscriptions.
  - Offers a unified interface for configuring, monitoring, reporting, alerting, and policy management capabilities for Azure Backup.
  - **Ex:** Using Backup center to view the status of all backups and configure alert rules for backup failures.
- **Custom Backup solutions using Azure Native Services:**
  - Tailored backup strategies designed using Azure's native services like Azure Data Factory, Azure Functions, Azure Logic Apps etc.
  - Allows for flexibility and control over backup processes, but requires more manual configuration and maintenance.
  - **Ex:** Developing a customized backup solution with Azure Data Factory to selectively copy data from an Azure Blob Storage to another storage account, exclusively for designated containers and blobs.
- **Third-party Backup solutions:**
  - Backup solutions provided by external vendors.
  - Utilizes third-party tools and services to offer diverse and specialized backup capabilities beyond native Azure offerings.
  - **Ex:** Commercial tools (Veeam Backup for Microsoft Azure, Commvault, Rubrik etc.) may offer additional features or specialized capabilities, such as backup for specific applications or file types.

HA & DR

- **Azure Storage Redundancy:**
    - It is a storage replication feature that ensures that our data is safe and available in the event of hardware failures, network failures, or natural disasters.
    - It works by synchronously or asynchronously replicating our data to multiple storage nodes within a single data center or across multiple data centers. This ensures that your data is always available, even if one or more storage nodes fail.
    - **Ex:** If a storage node fails, a redundant copy of the data is available, preventing data loss or service interruption. Redundancy options include LRS, ZRS, GRS, RA-GRS, GZRS, RA-GZRS.
- **Read-Access Azure Storage Redundancy:**
    - Extends Azure Storage Redundancy by allowing read access to data even in the event of a regional outage.
    - By replicating data to a secondary region, users can still read from the secondary location even if the primary region is inaccessible.
    - **Ex:** During a regional outage, applications can redirect read requests to the secondary region (in RA-GRS and RA-GZRS), ensuring continuous data access for users.
- **Object Replication for Block Blob:**
    - It is a feature that allows us to replicate our data to another storage account or another region.
    - We can configure replication rules to specify which blobs to replicate, to which destination and synchronously or asynchronously etc. Replication occurs according to the rules, ensuring data protection.
    - **Ex:** Replicating critical block blobs such as VM images or database backup to a secondary region for disaster recovery.
- **Azure File Sync:**
    - It enables synchronization of on-premises file servers with Azure Files, providing a centralized and distributed file-sharing and DR solution.
    - It works by creating a sync relationship between your on-premises file server and an Azure file share. Changes made to files on the on-premises file server are automatically synchronized with the Azure file share. It maintains a local cache for performance and accessibility.
    - **Ex:** A company with multiple branch offices syncs their file servers to Azure, allowing employees to access and share files across locations.

- **Azure Archive Blob Storage:**
  - It provides a cost-effective solution for storing rarely accessed data with high durability.
  - Data is stored offline and requires a retrieval request for access. Retrievals typically take hours for cost optimization.
  - **Ex:** Azure Archive Blob Storage itself is not typically considered a HA and DR feature. However, in a disaster recovery context, we might use Archive Blob Storage to store critical backup data or historical records that need to be preserved for compliance reasons. It ensures that our data is durable and available for retrieval when needed, which aligns with our DR plan.
- **Azure Site Recovery:**
  - Disaster recovery service for replicating and recovering virtual machines, physical servers, and applications. Supports recovery to Azure or on-premises. It supports recovery to Azure or on-premises.
  - Replicates workloads to a target site for failover. Orchestrates failover and recovery processes.
  - **Ex:** A business-critical application is replicated to a secondary region, ensuring minimal downtime and data loss in the event of a disaster.
- **Azure Site Recovery for Managed Disks:**
  - Extends Azure Site Recovery to include replication and recovery of Azure Managed Disks for virtual machines. It eliminates the need for a separate storage account for replication.
  - Managed Disks associated with virtual machines are automatically replicated to a secondary region for comprehensive disaster recovery.
  - **Ex:** Virtual machines with Managed Disks are protected by replicating the entire disk state to a secondary region, ensuring application consistency.
- **Customized Cross-region Copy Jobs using Azure Native Services:**
  - Allows custom configuration of cross-region data copy jobs using Azure native services such as Azure Data Factory, Azure Functions, Logic Apps, AzCopy etc.
  - Create data pipelines or scripts to copy data between storage accounts in different regions. Manage replication schedules and processes manually or automate it using Azure native services.
  - **Ex:** A company with specific compliance requirements sets up custom copy jobs to move sensitive data between regions securely.
- **Third-party HA&DR Solutions for Azure Storage:**
  - Third-party solutions provide additional options for high availability and disaster recovery in Azure Storage. Additional capabilities may include customized replication options, backup and restore capabilities, and more.

- These solutions integrate with Azure Storage to offer specialized features and capabilities for data protection.
- **Ex:** Utilizing a third-party solution for specific encryption or compliance requirements. Some of the commercial tools includes Zerto Virtual Replication, Veeam Backup for Microsoft Azure, Commvault, Druva, Rubrik etc.

Data Security and Protection:

- **Soft Delete:**
  - It is a feature that allows us to recover data that has been deleted or overwritten in our storage account.
  - When Soft Delete is enabled, when an object is deleted, it is not immediately removed; instead, it is marked as deleted and retained for the specified duration. During this period, the data can be recovered. After the retention period expires, the data is permanently deleted.
  - **Ex:** Suppose we accidentally delete a blob or container that contains important data. With Soft Delete enabled, we can recover the deleted data within the retention period.
- **Delete Lock (Azure Resource Locks):**
  - A safeguard feature that prevents accidental or malicious deletions of Azure Storage account or its content.
  - When Delete Lock (CanNotDelete and ReadOnly) is enabled, it prevents users from deleting or modifying configuration of a storage account.
  - **Ex:** Suppose we have a storage account that contains sensitive data. We can enable Delete Lock which provides an additional layer of protection by preventing the accidental deletion of the storage account.
- **Blob Snapshot:**
  - It allows the creation of read-only copies, or snapshots, of a blob's state at a specific point in time.
  - When we take a snapshot of a blob, a read-only copy of the blob is created. The snapshot is stored separately from the original blob and can be accessed using a unique URL. Snapshots are incremental, storing only changes from the previous version, and can be created manually or automatically.
  - **Ex:** Storing different versions of a document, where each snapshot represents a specific version, facilitating easy retrieval or rollback if needed.
- **Azure File Share Snapshot:**
  - Similar to Blob Snapshot, File Share Snapshot allows us to take a point-in-time snapshot of a file share.

    - When we take a snapshot, a read-only copy of the file share is created. The snapshot is stored separately from the original file share and can be accessed using a unique URL.
    - **Ex:** Suppose we have a file share that contains important data. We can take a snapshot of the file share before making any changes to it. If we need to revert to the original data, we can use the snapshot to restore the file share to its previous state.

- **Blob Versioning:**
    - A feature that automatically keeps previous versions of a blob, enabling rollback and recovery.
    - Each time a blob is modified, a new version is created, and older versions are retained for a specified period.
    - **Ex:** Tracking changes to a legal document and reverting to a previous version if needed. This is beneficial for compliance, auditing, and data recovery purposes.

- **Immutable Storage:**
    - A feature that makes blobs or containers write-once, read-many (WORM), protecting them from modification or deletion.
    - When Immutable Storage is enabled, data is stored in a WORM state it locks data from changes. This means that the data can be accessed for read purpose only and it cannot be modified or deleted for a specified period of time. After the retention period expires, the data can be deleted or modified.
    - **Ex:** Storing financial records that must remain tamper-proof for compliance purposes.

- **Azure AD / Microsoft Entra ID integration:**
    - It allows us to use Azure AD to authenticate and authorize access to our storage account.
    - When Azure AD integration is enabled, users and applications can authenticate and access Azure Storage resources using Azure AD credentials, enabling centralized identity management.
    - **Ex:** Controlling access to sensitive data in your storage account based on employee roles and departments.

- **Access Authentication Mechanisms**:
    - Azure Storage supports various access authentication mechanisms, including Shared Access Signatures (SAS), Shared Access Keys, Managed Identity and Service Principal Key etc.
    - SAS tokens grant limited access with specific permissions and time frames, while Shared Access Keys provide more extensive access. These mechanisms enhance security and control access.
    - **Ex:** Suppose we have an application that needs to access our storage account for a specified period of time. We can create a SAS with the required permissions and duration and provide

it to the application. This way, we can control the access of the application to our storage account.

- **Azure RBAC (Role-Based Access Control):**
  - Azure RBAC provides fine-grained access control by assigning specific roles to users or groups, limiting access to Azure Storage resources based on their responsibilities.
  - Simplifies access control by assigning roles like "Storage Account Contributor" or "Blob Data Reader" instead of managing individual permissions.
  - **Ex:** Granting developers access to upload data to a specific storage container while restricting their ability to manage the account itself. It helps us in enforcing the principle of "least privilege", where users only have access to the resources needed for their tasks.
- **Azure ABAC (Attribute-Based Access Control):**
  - Azure ABAC builds on Azure role-based access control (Azure RBAC) by adding conditions to Azure role assignments.
  - A security model that grants access to resources based on attributes of the user, resource, and environment, rather than fixed roles.
  - **Ex:** A company applies a condition (ABAC) to an RBAC assignment that only allows users with the "Finance" tag to access blobs tagged as "Financial Data".
- **Azure ACL (Access Control Lists):**
  - A legacy authorization mechanism to manage access permissions at the individual object or container level within Blob and Data Lake Storage.
  - ACLs are not recommended for new applications and should be replaced with Azure RBAC or Azure ABAC.
  - **Ex:** Let's say we have a storage account with a container named "abcSales". We want to grant read access to the container to a security principal named "salesAppReader". We can create an ACL entry that associates "salesAppReader" with the "read" permission.
- **Private Endpoints:**
  - Enables secure private network access to our Azure Storage account without going through the public internet.
  - It enables a secure connection to Azure Storage by assigning private IP addresses within a virtual network. Private endpoints connect our virtual network directly to our storage account using Azure Private Link, eliminating the need for public endpoints.
  - **Ex:** Connecting an on-premises application to your storage account without exposing data to the public internet.

- **Azure Security Center:**
    - A unified security management service that provides threat protection for Azure resources, including storage accounts.
    - Security Center analyzes telemetry data, identifies potential security vulnerabilities or threats, and provides recommendations for improving the security posture of Azure Storage resources.
    - **Ex:** Detecting unauthorized access attempts, malware infections, or data exfiltration attempts in storage accounts.
- **Threat Detection and Response:**
    - It is a feature of Azure Security Center and provides real-time monitoring and alerts for suspicious activities or security threats within Azure Storage.
    - When Threat Detection and Response is enabled, it monitors our storage account for suspicious activity and alerts us when it detects a threat. We can then investigate the threat and take appropriate action to mitigate it.
    - **Ex:** Identifying and stopping unauthorized access attempts or malware scans targeting your storage account.
- **Azure Storage Encryption:**
    - Azure Storage Encryption ensures data confidentiality by encrypting data at rest and in transit.
    - When it is enabled, our data is encrypted using industry-standard encryption algorithms. We can choose to use Microsoft-managed keys or customer-managed keys to encrypt our data. It also encrypts data in transit using SSL/TLS.
    - **Ex:** Protecting sensitive data stored in Azure Storage from unauthorized access, ensuring confidentiality and compliance with data protection regulations.
- **Azure Storage Lifecycle Management Policies:**
    - It is used to automate the management of data throughout its lifecycle by defining rules for data retention, deletion, and tiering.
    - Policies define actions based on criteria such as age or access tier, automating tasks like moving data to a different storage tier or deleting outdated data.
    - **Ex:** It can help us reduce storage costs and meet compliance requirements. Suppose we can create a Lifecycle Management Policy to transition the data to a lower-cost storage tier (Archive) after a specified period of time.

Monitoring and Auditing:

- **Blob Change Feed:**
  - Enables tracking and monitoring of changes to blobs within Azure Storage.
  - Captures events like blob creation, modification, deletion, and metadata changes. Can be accessed through Azure Event Grid or directly using REST API calls and react to changes in real-time.
  - **Ex:** Monitoring changes to critical data for analytics, auditing, or triggering downstream processes when new data is added or existing data is modified. Suppose, triggering actions based on blob changes, such as updating a search index or notifying applications of new data.

- **Azure Monitor logs:**
  - Azure Monitor logs provide centralized logging and analysis of data from various Azure resources, including Azure Storage.
  - It collects and stores logs, metrics, and performance data from Azure Storage, allowing users to gain insights into resource utilization, errors, and overall system health.
  - **Ex:** Monitoring and analyzing storage performance, identifying bottlenecks, and proactively addressing issues to ensure optimal operation.

- **Azure Monitor Activity logs:**
  - It captures a record of operations performed on resources, offering an audit trail for monitoring and compliance purposes.
  - Although there may be some overlap in the information, Activity logs and Blob Change Feed capture different kinds of data from our Azure Storage account.
    - **Activity Logs:** Focus on control plane operations that means they record actions performed on the storage account itself, such as creating, deleting, or modifying the account, changing access permissions, or enabling features.
    - **Blob Change Feed:** Focus on data plane operations. They capture changes made to the blobs within the storage account, such as creation, deletion, modification, or metadata updates.
  - **Ex:** Using Activity Logs, we can track who created or deleted a storage account, modified access permissions, or enabled a feature etc.

- **Log Analytics workspace:**
  - A tool within Azure Monitor that facilitates advanced querying and analysis of logs and telemetry data, including those from Azure Storage.

- It provides a centralized repository for log data, offering powerful querying capabilities and visualization tools to gain deep insights into the performance and behavior of Azure Storage resources.
- **Ex:** Creating a dashboard to visualize storage usage trends, disk latency, and capacity planning.

39. There are numerous features and services offered by Azure Storage for backup and HA-DR. What service do you recommend for my business case?

Ans:

Choosing the optimal solution depends entirely on our unique business needs. We must carefully analyze our requirements and map them to relevant Azure Storage options, considering factors like feasibility, support, data tier, storage account type, data size, budget, integration needs, and desired level of customization. Based on common scenarios, here are some potential recommendations:

- **Simple and straightforward:** Consider Azure Standard Backup and HA-DR solutions or leveraging native services like Azure Functions, Logic Apps, AzCopy, or Azure Data Factory (ADF) for cost-effective, basic backups.
- **Complex and large-scale data backup:** Utilize Azure Storage built-in features like Operational Backup for Azure Blobs, storage redundancy options (LRS, GRS, ZRS), Geo-Replication, Azure File Share Backup, Azure Backup Service, or Azure Site Recovery for robust protection at scale.
- **Highly customized solutions:** Explore leveraging Azure native options like ADF, Functions, or Logic Apps to tailor backup processes and integrations to our specific needs.
- **Cloud-agnostic approach (consistent backup across multiple clouds):** Consider dedicated third-party backup tools or solutions if we require cloud-agnostic functionality for consistent backup practices across different cloud providers.

40. How do Blob snapshots work?

Ans:

Azure Blob snapshots provide read-only point-in-time copies of blobs. We can create snapshots, each with a unique URL, to capture and preserve blob states. Snapshots are independent, remain unmodified, and can be used for data recovery or to revert to specific points in time.

Explore:

- Just like SQL Server Database snapshots, we can create a snapshot of a specific blob at a particular point in time.
- **Read-Only:** We can read, copy/restore, and delete the snapshot, but we can't modify it.
- **URI Structure:** A snapshot of a blob has the same name as the base blob, with the snapshot date and time appended at the end of the blob URI. For example:

- **Base Blob:** https://mystorageaccount.core.blob.windows.net/container/myblob
- **Snapshot:** https://mystorageaccount.core.blob.windows.net/container/myblob/snapshot=2024-01-21T15:00:00.1730000Z.

- **Persistence and Blob Type Support:** A blob may have any number of snapshots. Snapshots persist until they are explicitly deleted. Blob snapshots work for all Blob types.
- **Tier Support:** We can create a snapshot of a blob in the hot or cool tier. Snapshots on blobs in the archive tier aren't supported.
- **Metadata and Permissions:** The snapshot inherits the same metadata and access permissions as the original blob.
- **Management:** Snapshot creation and management can be done using Azure Storage Explorer, Storage SDKs, or the REST API.
- **Restoring:** If we want to revert the blob to a previous state captured by a snapshot, we can copy (restore) the snapshot back to the original blob or a new blob.
- **Container Level Support:** It's not possible to snapshot an entire Blob storage container in one go. Instead, we must take snapshots at the blob level. However, we can use PowerShell to create a script that creates snapshots of all the blobs in a container.
- **Sample Use Case:**
  - **VM disk snapshots:** Detach a VM disk or shut down the VM, take a snapshot of its VHD file, and later use it to recreate the VM at that point in time.
- **Price:** Blob snapshots are billed at the same rate as an active blob. However, understanding the snapshot pricing involves some complexity due to factors like Update Blob, Overwrite Blob, Base Blob, and Snapshot Data Access Tier, which need to be considered while calculating the pricing. There are no charges for snapshots associated with a base blob until we update the base blob. For example:
  - **Case 1:** No modification for Blocks 1, 2, 3 --> No charges for snapshots.
  - **Case 2:** Modified Block 2 --> Starts charging for Snapshot 2.
  - **Case 3:** Modified Blocks 2 & 3 --> Starts charging for Snapshot 2 and Snapshot 3.

41. Do you know how Blob Versioning works in Azure Blob Storage?

Ans:

Blob Versioning maintains previous versions of blobs, allowing data recovery by restoring to earlier states if modified or deleted.

Explore:

- Blob Versioning is a superior feature of Blob Snapshot
- When blob versioning is enabled, it maintains previous versions of the blob. So that we can restore an earlier version of a blob to recover our data if it is erroneously modified or deleted.

- Azure Storage automatically creates a new version with a unique Version ID when a blob is first created and each time that the blob is subsequently modified.
- We can restore any previous version to revert to a previous state.
- Deleted versions are retained based on our retention policy.
- **Storage Considerations:**
    - Be mindful of storage costs associated with maintaining multiple versions.
    - Optimize storage and performance by retaining less than 1000 versions per blob.
    - Utilize lifecycle management to automate the deletion of older versions.
- **Price:** Smiler to Blob Snapshot, we need to pay for the additional storage used by the Blob Versions.

42. Is there a difference between Blob versioning and Blob Snapshots, and if so, is it necessary to enable both features?

Ans:

- While they both offer ways to preserve previous states of your blobs, they work differently.
- A snapshot is created manually by us or our application, whereas a blob version is created automatically during a write or delete operation when blob versioning is enabled.
- If Blob versioning is enabled, we can stop taking snapshots as it doesn't add any additional protection. This is because all block blob updates and deletions are captured and preserved by versions. Hence, having both features leads to more costs and complexity.

Explore:

Consider the example below for a better understanding:

Action	**Blob State**	**Version**		**Snapshot**
		Current	**Previous**	
Create Blob	abc_Blob (v1)	abc_Blob (v1)	None	None
Create Snapshot 1	abc_Blob (v1)	abc_Blob (v1)	None	abc_Blob (s1)
Modify Blob	abc_Blob (v2)	abc_Blob (v2)	abc_Blob (v1)	abc_Blob (s1)
Modify Blob	abc_Blob (v3)	abc_Blob (v3)	abc_Blob (v1, v2)	abc_Blob (s1)
Create Snapshot 2	abc_Blob (v3)	abc_Blob (v3)	abc_Blob (v1, v2)	abc_Blob (s1, s2)
Delete Blob	None	None	abc_Blob (v1, v2, v3)	abc_Blob (s1, s2)

Table 6.3

Note:

- v*: Versions
- s*: Snapshots
- When versioning is enabled, the moment we create a new blob, it automatically creates the first version.
- Blob_State and Current Version both represent the current state of the blob.
- It's important to note that even when we delete a blob, its previous versions and snapshots persist until we manually delete them or until a specified time duration elapses.
- We can manage these older versions and snapshots through either manual deletion or by creating a Blob Lifecycle Policy to automate their removal.

Recommendation:

- **Use Blob Snapshots if:**
    - We need point-in-time references for backups or sharing data at a specific version.
    - We prefer manual control over version history.
- **Use Blob Versioning if:**
    - We want automatic protection against accidental modifications or deletions.
    - We need a complete audit trail of changes over time.
    - We rely on easy rollback options to previous states.

43. What is the difference between Soft Delete and Delete Lock in Azure Storage?

Ans:

Soft delete and delete lock are two distinct features in Azure Storage that help protect our data from accidental deletion or modification. Here is the difference:

- **Soft Delete** is designed to prevent accidental or malicious deletions of data (containers or blobs) in an Azure Storage Account.
- **Delete Lock (CanNotDelete and ReadOnly Locks)** can protect an Azure storage account from accidental deletion. Delete lock doesn't concern itself with the underlying data; it only protects the storage account resource.
    - CanNotDelete – Prevents Delete Operations.
    - ReadOnly – Prevents Delete and Modify Operations.

Therefore, with both of these features, we can achieve better protection against accidental deletion for our Azure storage account and the data stored inside the account.

Explore:

Soft Delete:

- **Purpose:** Soft Delete is a feature designed to prevent accidental or malicious deletions of data in Azure Storage.
- **Behavior:** When Soft Delete is enabled, deleted blobs and blob snapshots are not immediately removed. Instead, they are marked as "deleted" and retained for a specified retention period.
- **Retention Period:** The retention period specifies how long deleted data is retained before being permanently removed.
- **Recovery:** During the retention period, deleted blobs can be recovered, allowing for data restoration if needed.
    - We can find an option to recover deleted blobs in the Azure portal by navigating to Blob Storage Container > Show deleted blobs. If Soft-Delete is enabled, deleted blobs are visible with the status marked as "deleted." Simply select the desired blobs and choose "undelete" from the Blob level options menu.
- **Enabling/Disabling:** Soft Delete must be explicitly enabled on a storage account. Ex: Storage Account > Settings > Data Protection >
    - **Turn on soft delete for Blobs:** To recover deleted blobs.
    - **Turn on soft delete for Containers:** To recover entire container that is marked as deleted.
- **Price:** Soft deleted data is billed at the same rate as active data.

Delete Lock:

The most important thing to remember is that "CanNotDelete" and "Read-Only" locks are Azure Resource Manager Locks. This means that they are not exclusive to Azure Storage accounts; instead, they are applicable to other Azure resources, such as Azure SQL Database, Virtual Machine, Network Security Group, Azure Kubernetes Service (AKS), Azure Backup Service, Log Analytics Service, etc. There are two types of Azure Resource Manager resource locks:

- **CannotDelete Lock:** A CannotDelete lock prevents users from deleting a storage account but permits reading and modifying its configuration. It prevents delete and movement operations, such as:
    - Deletion of the storage account.
    - Removal of a resource group containing the storage account.
    - Moving the storage account between resource groups or subscriptions, etc.
- **ReadOnly Lock:** A ReadOnly lock prevents users from deleting a storage account or modifying its configuration but permits reading the configuration. It prevents any delete or modification actions, such as:

- Modification of account properties, like attempts to change account settings such as access tier, replication, encryption, or network configuration, would be blocked.

Price: No charge is applicable.

Note: A read-only lock or cannot-delete lock on a storage account doesn't prevent its data from deletion or modification. It also doesn't protect the data in a blob, queue, table, or file. This is a resource protection feature the protects a resource from an accidental deletion or modification.

44. What is the difference between backup and snapshot?

Ans:

Both protect our data, but backups go further when things go really wrong. Snapshots are helpful for quick comparisons or temporary backups within the same location.

- **Backup:** Offsite copy for disaster recovery (like having a spare key at home).
- **Snapshot:** Time capsule within your data storage (like revisiting an old photo album).

45. From an Azure Virtual Machine (VM) perspective, what's the difference between a snapshot and an image of a managed disk?

Ans:

- **Snapshot:** A snapshot or a Disk Snapshot is a copy of a disk at the point in time the snapshot is taken. It applies only to one disk. It's like taking a point-in-time backup for the managed disk. Using a snapshot, we can create a new managed disk with the point-in-time data.
- **Image:** An image is a copy of all disks attached to a VM. It captures the state of an entire VM, including the operating system, configuration, and data disks (all disks attached to the VM). It is useful for deploying multiple VMs with the same configuration.

46. Can you tell me about immutable storage in Azure and how it works?

Ans:

Immutable storage (policy) is a feature of Azure Blob Storage that allows users to store business-critical data in a WORM (Write Once, Read Many) state. While in a WORM state, data cannot be modified or deleted for a user-specified interval. By configuring immutability policies for blob data, you can protect your data from overwrites and deletes.

Explore:

Immutable storage, also known as an immutability policy on a container, enables us to store business-critical data objects in a WORM (Write Once, Read Many) state. This state renders the data non-erasable and non-modifiable for a user-specified period.

Key features:

- **Immutability:** Once a policy is set, objects can only be created and read, not modified or deleted.
- **Policy scope:** Protection applies at the container level. Once a blob is uploaded, it inherits the immutability policy of the container. If a blob is protected using an immutable policy, we cannot delete its container or the storage account.
- **High security:** Even administrators cannot modify or delete protected data, guaranteeing data integrity and auditability.

Types of immutability policies:

- **Time-based retention:** Retains data for a specified interval. After expiration, objects can be deleted but not overwritten.
- **Legal hold:** Stores immutable data until the hold is explicitly cleared, ideal for unknown retention periods or compliance needs.

Use cases:

- Secure storage of sensitive data, such as:
    - Healthcare records
    - Intellectual property (medicine/vaccine formulas, manufacturing designs)
    - Financial reports
    - Personal identification information
- Any scenario requiring creation and reading but prohibiting modification or deletion.

Pricing:

- No additional charge for using immutable storage. Data is priced the same as mutable data.

Caution:

- Policies are irreversible during the specified retention period. This means the immutability setting is a one-way operation, making data within the container non-erasable and non-modifiable for the duration of the retention period. Once a policy is in place, we can extend its duration, but we cannot shorten it.
- Immutable storage supports all types of Blobs (Block, Append, and Page) in data tiers (Hot, Cool, Cold, Archive). However, for active VMs, it's recommended to use immutable storage only for block and append blobs, as placing a page blob/VHD on immutable storage might lock the VM disk.

47. Can you explain the Blob Change Feed feature in Azure Blob Storage?

Ans:

Azure Blob Change Feed is a feature that provides a transactional log of changes that occur to blobs in a storage account. It allows us to track and analyze changes to blobs, making it easier to identify and respond to updates in your storage data. Primary use cases include auditing, monitoring, and syncing data.

Explore:

Blob Change Feed is a powerful tool for building responsive and scalable applications that react to changes in your Azure Blob Storage data.

- **Every change triggers a log entry:** Whether it's creating a new blob, modifying an existing one, changing metadata, or even deleting a blob, the change feed captures it all.
- **Durable and ordered:** Entries are recorded in a specific order and permanently stored, guaranteeing reliability and data integrity.
- **Storage and Format:** The change feed records are stored (appended to the change feed) as blobs in a special container in your storage account at standard blob pricing cost. Change events are appended to the change feed as records in the Apache Avro format specification.
- **Retention Period:** The Change Feed retains events for a specified period, and we can configure the retention duration based on our requirements.
- **Scalable and efficient:** We can read the change feed at our own pace, either in real-time or batch mode, even with millions of changes happening.
- **Multiple consumers:** We can process these logs asynchronously, incrementally or in-full. Multiple applications (Ex: Apache Drill, Apache Spark etc.) or services can access and process the change feed simultaneously, enabling various real-time or near-real-time data processing scenarios.
- **Enablement:** We need to enable it on our storage account (Data Management > Data Protection > Enable Blob Change Feed). This can be done through the Azure Portal, Azure CLI, or programmatically using Azure SDKs.
- **Sample Use Cases:**
    - Whenever a new blob is uploaded, update secondary indexes, synchronize with caches, search engines, or other content management systems.
    - Automatically trigger analytics pipelines for each new uploaded financial transaction record, enabling instant fraud detection and market response.
- **Price:** No charge for feature, but we need to pay for the additional storage for the retention period at the standard blob price.

48. Can you describe your understanding about the feature "Operational backup for Azure Blobs"?

Ans:

Operational backup for Azure Blobs is an Azure Block Blob built-in managed data protection solution that helps us safeguard our block blob data against various data loss scenarios. The data is stored locally within the source storage account and not transferred to the backup vault. You don't need to define any schedule for backups. All changes are retained, and you can restore them from the state at a selected point in time.

Explore:

- **Local backup:** The backup is stored locally within the source storage account and not transferred to the backup vault. This makes restore fast and cost-effective.
- **Continuous protection:** We don't need to define any schedule for backups. Our blobs are automatically and continuously backed up, keeping track of changes and deletions.
- **Point-in-time restore:** Need to recover data from a specific point in time? Operational backup lets us rewind to that state with granularity, within the retention period.
- **Granular restore options:** We can choose to restore all blobs, individual Blob, all Blobs in a single container, or all blobs in all containers in our storage account.
- **Enablement:**
    - **Enabling operational backup:** It is straightforward through the Azure Backup Center or directly from our storage account settings.
    - **Backup instance creation in Backup Vault:** Once Operational backup is enabled for a storage account, a corresponding backup instance is created within the Backup Vault. This instance allows you to perform backup-related operations for the storage account, such as initiating restores, monitoring backup status, stopping protection, and more.
    - **Backup Center integration:** Operational backup seamlessly integrates with Backup Center, providing centralized management of protected storage accounts. Through Backup Center, you can monitor backup jobs, view backup and restore states, track backup usage, and perform other essential tasks.
- **Capabilities:** Internally this feature uses blob platform capabilities that includes Blob change feed, Blob versioning, delete lock, soft delete and point-in-time restore.
- **Pricing:**
    - **No management or instance fees:** As a feature it doesn't incur any additional management charges or instance fees.
    - **Point-in-time restore charges:** We'll be charged based on the amount of data processed during point-in-time restores.
    - **Increased storage costs for data retention:** Due to features like Soft Delete for blobs, Change Feed support, and Blob versioning, we might need to allocate more storage space for data retention, which can increase storage costs.

Limitations:

- **Local backup:** Data remains within your storage account, making it vulnerable to regional disasters. Consider combining it with geo-redundant storage or Vaulted Backup for enhanced protection.
- **Retention period:** We can retain backups for up to 360 days. Vaulted Backup allows us to retain our data for up to 10 years.
- **Only standard block blobs supported:** Currently works only with Standard Block Blobs. Append blobs, Page blobs, and Premium Block Blobs are not supported.
- **Restore Support:** Operational backup supports operations on block blobs only and operations on containers can't be restored. Ex: If we delete a container from the storage account by calling the Delete Container operation, that container can't be restored with a restore operation. It's suggested we enable soft delete to enhance data protection and recovery.

49. What is the difference between operational backup and vault backup in Azure Blob Storage?

Ans:

- **Operational backup** is a managed local data protection solution that protects our block blobs from accidental deletion or corruption. The data is stored locally within the source storage account and not transferred to the backup vault. We don't need to define any schedule for backups. It allows us to retain our data for restore for up to 360 days.
- **Vaulted backup** is a managed offsite data protection solution that provides protection against any accidental or malicious deletion of blobs or storage account. The backup data using vaulted backups is copied and stored in the Backup vault. This ensures that even if our primary storage account is compromised or down, our backed-up data remains safe and accessible. We can define a backup schedule and specify retention settings via backup policy. We can choose to configure vaulted backups, operational backups, or both on our storage accounts using a single backup policy. It allows you to retain our data for up to 10 years.

CHAPTER 07

Azure Storage – Part 2

1. How to enable point-in-time restore (PITR) in an Azure Storage Account?

Ans:

- In Azure Portal, navigate to > Your Azure Storage Account > Settings > Data Protection > Turn on point-in-time restore.
- When we select this option, soft delete for blobs, versioning, and change feed are also automatically enabled. (Prerequisites for PITR)
- **Restore Point:** Set the maximum restore point for point-in-time restore, in days. It refers to the maximum number of days that we want to retain point-in-time recovery points for our blob data. Ex: If we specify 7 Days Azure will keep snapshots for the past 7 days.
- Save the changes.

2. Can you quickly explain how to perform a Point-in-time-restore (PITR) operation?

Ans:

- **Identify the Restore Point:** Determine the exact point in time (date and hour) when we want to revert the changes. This should be within the past 7 days since we enabled PITR with a 7-day restore point.
- **Initiate the PITR:** Navigate to Azure Portal > Storage Account > Blob Service > Affected Container > Restore container > Point-in-time restore option > Give the Restore Point (Date and Time that we identified in step 1) > Review and confirm.
- **Monitor** the restoration process through the progress bar displayed in the “Restore container” window. Once complete, we can verify the container reflects the data state at the chosen restore point.
- **We can restore:**
    - A single container (All blobs in a container)
    - All containers in the storage account, or
    - A range of blobs in one or more containers. Ex: Blob1 to Blob5 in container1 and Blob4 in container 2 etc.

Note: The restore operation is atomic, so it either succeeds completely in restoring all changes, or it fails. If there are any blobs that can’t be restored, then the entire operation fails, and read and write operations to the affected containers resume.

3. Are you familiar with what Object Replication for block blobs is in Azure Storage?

Ans:

Object replication is like a copy-paste for block blobs across Azure storage accounts. It lets you duplicate your data asynchronously, optimizing access, archiving to cheaper tiers, or syncing data for various needs.

When we configure object replication, we create a replication policy that specifies the source storage account and the destination account.

This flexible feature copies blobs in the background, giving us control over where and when our data lives.

Explore:

- Object replication for block blobs asynchronously copies block blobs between a source storage account and a destination account, either within the same or across different Azure regions.
- **Prerequisites:** Blob Change Feed and Blob Versioning must be enabled before configuring object replication.
- **Configuration:** Create a replication policy specifying the source and destination accounts. The policy defines:
    - Containers and blobs to replicate
    - Destination account
    - Optional filters for specific blob prefixes
    - Whether to replicate new blobs only or existing ones as well
- **Key Points:**
    - **Asynchronous Process:** The source and destination accounts are not immediately in sync due to the asynchronous nature of replication.
    - **Block Blobs Only:** Object replication supports block blobs exclusively; append blobs and page blobs are not supported.
- **Use Cases:**
    - **Low-Latency Read Workloads:** Enable clients to consume data from the nearest region for globally distributed applications.
    - **Data Distribution and Performance Optimization:** Process or analyze data in a single location and replicate only the results to additional regions for optimized access.
- **Pricing:** Object replication itself has no direct associated cost. However, charges apply for:
    - Read and write transactions against source and destination accounts

- Egress charges (data transfer) when replicating across different regions
- Additional storage costs for Change Feed and Blob Versioning

4. Are Object Replication for block blobs and Storage Replication/Redundancy the same concept? If not, what are the key differences between them?"

Ans:

No, object replication for block blobs and storage replication/redundancy are distinct features in Azure Storage, each designed for specific purposes. Object replication for block blobs is a replication feature that is designed for Block Blobs. Storage replication/redundancy refers to the redundancy options available for Azure Storage accounts.

Explore:

Object Replication for Block Blobs:

- **Optimized for** replicating block blobs between storage accounts within the same or different Azure regions.
- **Ideal for** Data distribution, archiving, synchronization.
- **Scope:** Specifically designed for Block Blobs only.
- **Configuration:** Customizable policies control which blobs are replicated, target destinations, and replication schedule.

Storage Redundancy:

- Storage replication/redundancy, refers to the redundancy options (LRS, ZRS, GRS etc.) available for Azure Storage accounts.
- **Essential for** high availability and data resilience.
- **Scope:** Replicates all data within the storage account (blobs (all types), queues, tables, files).
- **Configuration:** Built-in setting at the storage account level, not requiring custom policies.

5. How can I take a backup for Azure File Shares?

Ans:

Azure offers a native backup solution known as "**Azure File Share Backup**." This solution utilizes the Recovery Services Vault and Azure Backup service to manage the entire backup and restore cycle for Azure file shares. Here are the steps:

- **Create a Recovery Services Vault:** This serves as the storage location for the backups.
- **Establish and configure an Azure Backup Policy:** This controls the backup process, defining parameters such as frequency and retention.
- **Manage:** Review, initiate the backup job, monitor progress, and verify the backup's success.

Explore:

Azure File Share Backup is a native, cloud-based, fully managed backup solution that safeguards data in Azure File Shares. We have complete control over the backup cycle, which includes retention periods, backup schedules, instant restore, etc. Here are the detailed steps involved:

- **Create a Recovery Services Vault:** Navigate to the Azure Portal > Create a resource > Search for "Recovery Services Vault" > Provide the necessary details like subscription, resource group, and a unique vault name, then create it.
- **Configure Azure Backup:** Inside the Recovery Services Vault, go to Backup > Configure a new backup > Choose Azure Files as the workload type > Set up the backup.
- **Create a Backup Policy:** Define a backup policy specifying the frequency and retention of backups. Set the backup schedule, retention range, and other options based on our requirements.
- **Select File Share to Backup:** Choose the subscription and storage account containing the file shares. Select the specific file shares we want to back up.
- **Review and Enable Backup:** Verify the backup policy and selected file shares, then click "Enable Backup" to initiate the backup job.
- **Monitor Backup Jobs:** After enabling backup, monitor the status of backup jobs in the Azure Portal. We can view backup reports and logs to ensure the successful execution of our backups.
- **Restore from Backup:** In case we need to restore files, navigate to the Recovery Services Vault > Backup Items > Choose the file share and initiate the restore process > Configure restore options (restore point, destination, etc.) > Start the restore job.
- **Testing Backups:** Regularly test our backups to ensure they can be successfully restored when needed.

Cost: Azure File Share Backup incurs costs based on storage usage and data transfer.

6. Suppose we have a business case where we don't have any complex requirements for backing up Azure Blob Storage. It just involves a few containers and blobs that need to be copied once on a daily basis. Can you suggest a simple solution?

Ans:

Based on the given case, AzCopy is likely the best option. It's free, straightforward to use, and offers enough flexibility for scheduling. Here are the steps:

- **Install AzCopy:** Download and install AzCopy on our local machine or VM.
- **Create a Script:** Write a script using AzCopy commands to copy our desired containers and blobs.
- **Schedule Script:** Use Azure Automation Runbooks or Azure Functions with a Timer Trigger to run the script daily.
- **Monitor Jobs:** Check logs to ensure the successful execution of the backup.

7. When copying data from an Azure Storage Account using AzCopy, does it allow applying a filter to copy only the specified blobs and containers based on a condition?

Ans:

Yes, when copying data from an Azure Storage Account using AzCopy, you can apply filters to copy only the specified blobs and containers based on certain conditions. AzCopy provides options like --include and --exclude that allow us to filter files based on specific patterns or conditions during the copy operation.

Explore:

AzCopy supports a wide range of filters and conditions. For example:

- **Include/Exclude:** Use the --include and --exclude parameters to include or exclude specific files or blobs based on their name, extension, or other attributes. **Ex**: --include=".*jpg;*.png" --exclude="*.tmp".
- **Last Modified Time:** Utilize the --if-modified-since and --if-unmodified-since parameters to copy only the files or blobs that were modified before or after a specific date and time.
- **Size:** Use the --min-size and --max-size parameters to copy only the files or blobs that are larger or smaller than a specific size.
- **Content Type:** Use the --content-type parameter to copy only the files or blobs that have a specific content type. **Ex**: --content-type="application/json".
- **Recursive Copy:** Use the --recursive parameter to copy all the files or blobs in a container or directory, including all subdirectories.
- **Resume Copy:** Apply the --resume-from parameter to resume a failed or interrupted copy operation from a specific point.
- **SAS Token:** Use the --sas-token parameter to specify a shared access signature (SAS) token for the source or destination storage account.
- **Logging:** Utilize the --log-level parameter to specify the level of logging that you want to enable.
- **Overwrite:** Use the --overwrite parameter to overwrite the destination files or blobs if they already exist.
- **Delete Source:** Apply the --delete-source parameter to delete the source files or blobs after they have been successfully copied to the destination.
- **Tag-based filters:** Use tags to filter the data that we want to copy using AzCopy. **Ex:** --blob-tags ="key1=process&key2=claims". Based on this filter, files tagged to a process called claims are copied to the destination.

Here's a sample AzCopy command:

azcopy copy

"https://sourceaccount.blob.core.windows.net/container1/*" "https://destinationaccount.blob.core.windows.net/container2"

--include-pattern .jpg;.pdf

--exclude-pattern *.temp

--lastModifiedAfter 2024-01-01T00:00:00Z

--lastModifiedBefore 2024-01-31T23:59:59Z

--recursive

This command achieves the following:

- Copies blobs from source to destination storage accounts:
  - Source: https://sourceaccount.blob.core.windows.net/container1
  - Destination: https://destinationaccount.blob.core.windows.net/container2
- Includes only blobs with the extensions .jpg or .pdf.
- Excludes blobs with the ".temp" extension.
- Copies blobs modified after January 01, 2024, and before January 31, 2024.
- With the --recursive option, this command now:
  - Copies all blobs within source account, including any files within subdirectories.
  - Maintains the same filtering criteria for file extensions, modification dates.

8. Can the delete lock on an Azure Storage account resource protect containers and blobs from accidental deletion?

Ans:

No, the delete lock (CanNotDelete and ReadOnly) on an Azure Storage Account resource can only protect the account itself and not the underlying containers and blobs. To protect containers and blobs, enable Soft Delete for both the container and blob.

Explore:

Review the data protection matrix below for a better and quicker understanding.

Data protection option	Protects a storage account from deletion	Protects a container from deletion	Protects a blob from deletion	Protects a blob from overwrites	Protect from disasters	Data Lake Storage Support
Delete lock	Yes	No	No	No	No	Yes
Immutability policy	No	No	Yes	Yes	No	Yes

Data protection option	Protects a storage account from deletion	Protects a container from deletion	Protects a blob from deletion	Protects a blob from overwrites	Protect from disasters	Data Lake Storage Support
Container Soft Delete	No	Yes	No	No	No	Yes
Blob Soft Delete	No	No	Yes	Yes	No	Yes
Blob Versioning	No	No	Yes	Yes	No	No
Blob Snapshot	No	No	Yes	Yes	No	Yes
Operational Backup for Azure Blobs	No	No	Yes	Yes	Yes	No
Point-in-time Restore	No	No	Yes	Yes	No	No
Data Redundancy (LRS, ZRS GRS etc.)	No	No	No	No	Yes	Yes
Object Replication for block blobs	No	No	No	No	Yes	No
Custom backup Solution using Azure Services.	No	Yes	Yes	Yes	Yes	Yes

Table 7.1

- **Object Replication for Block Blobs:** Supports protection for blob deletes and overwrites because enabling Blob Versioning is mandatory for blob replication.
- **Immutability Policy:** It may not directly protect a storage account or a container, but if a blob is protected using an immutable policy, we cannot delete its container or the storage account.

- **Blob Soft Delete:** Please note that Blob Soft Delete doesn't afford overwrite protection for blobs in the archive tier. If a blob in the archive tier is overwritten with a new blob in any tier, then the overwritten blob is permanently deleted.
- **Blob Versioning:** Storage accounts with a hierarchical namespace enabled for use with Azure Data Lake Storage Gen2 are not currently supported.
- **Operational Backup for Azure Blobs:** It protects from disasters when we choose Backup Vault as a destination.
- **Custom Backup Solution:** We can use Azure services like AzCopy, Azure Data Factory, Azure Automation, Azure Functions, and Azure Logic Apps to provide custom backup functionality.

Note: You may wonder why features like 'Data Redundancy' or 'Object Replication for Block Blobs' cannot directly protect a blob or a container from deletion. The data protection matrix is designed based on the primary responsibilities of these features. To illustrate, consider the analogy of border security force and state police – both fall under the protection category but with distinct scopes and responsibilities.

9. Can you explain what you know about Azure File Sync and its features?

Ans:

Azure File Sync is a cloud service that enables organizations to synchronize their on-premises file servers with Azure Files. This synchronization allows for seamless access to files across different locations, providing a hybrid cloud storage solution.

Key features include centralized cloud-based file storage and DR solution, local caching and file storage optimization using cloud tiering policies, multi-site synchronization, automatic conflict resolutions etc.

Sample Use Case: Azure File Sync is ideal for distributed access scenarios. **Ex:** For each of our office branches, we can provision a local Windows Server as part of our Azure File Sync deployment. Changes made to a server in one office automatically sync to the servers in all other offices.

Explore:

Azure File Sync is a hybrid cloud feature that enables us to centralize our file shares in Azure Files while retaining local access and performance benefits. It essentially creates a seamless bridge between our on-premises file servers and Azure storage, offering several advantages:

Key Features:

- **Centralized file storage in Azure:** Store our files in Azure Files, ensuring cloud-based accessibility, scalability, and security. The the same file share can be accessible from both Azure and on-premises. For the end-user it is a transparent process and no additional tools or modifications required at application level.

- **Cloud tiering:** It helps optimize storage usage on our on-premises servers. With cloud tiering, frequently accessed files are kept on-premises (Local caching for performance), while less frequently accessed files are tiered to Azure Files. This helps in reducing on-premises storage costs.
- **Multi-site synchronization:** Maintain consistency across multiple file servers in different locations.
- **Cloud-based disaster recovery:** Simplify recovery from local server failures by leveraging Azure Files as a centralized backup. Azure File Sync is backed by Azure Files, which offers several redundancy options for highly available storage.
- **Integration with Windows Server features:** Supports NTFS permissions, Active Directory, and familiar file access protocols (SMB, NFS, FTPS).
- **Change detection and conflict resolution:** It automatically detects file changes and handles conflicts intelligently. Azure File Sync automatically detects file changes and handles conflicts that may arise if changes are made to the same file on both the on-premises server and in Azure Files. We can configure conflict resolution policies based on our requirements.

10. Can you briefly describe how to deploy the Azure File Sync service?

Ans:

- Create a storage sync service in Azure to manage synchronization.
- Register Windows Servers as sync agents.
- Create cloud endpoints and server endpoints.
- Link server and cloud endpoints to establish synchronization relationships.
- It starts syncing files between on-premise to Azure.

Explore:

There are three major components involved in Azure File Sync:

- **Source and Destination file servers/shares:** Source is the Windows Server on-premises or cloud and destination is an Azure File Share created on an Azure storage account.
- **End points:** There are two end points
    - **Cloud end point:** Represents the Azure File Share
    - **Server end point:** Represents a path on a Windows Server.
- **Sync Group:** The object that defines the sync relationship between a cloud endpoint, and a server endpoint.

Deployment & Configuration:

- Perform all required prerequisites. Ex: create a storage account, configure firewall and virtual network settings, etc.

- Create an Azure File Sync resource and deploy Storage Sync Service.
- Install the Azure File Sync agent on the on-premises Windows server.
- Register the Windows Server with Storage Sync Service.
- Create a sync group and a cloud endpoint (Azure File Share).
- Create a server endpoint on the share. A server endpoint is a folder path on the Windows server.
- Link server and cloud endpoints to establish synchronization relationships.
- Let the synchronization complete the full upload to the Azure file share (cloud endpoint).
- After the initial upload is complete, install the Azure File Sync agent on each of the remaining servers (if any). Register and repeat the same process for the remaining servers.
- Ensure synchronization completes and test your topology as desired.
- Redirect users and applications to this new share.

Synchronization Process:

- Initially, after File Sync Configuration, a full upload from the on-premise server to Azure File Share will occur.
- The sync agent on each server continuously monitors file changes.
- Changes are uploaded to Azure Files and propagated to other connected servers.
- Files are downloaded from Azure Files as needed based on caching and tiering policies.
- Conflicts are resolved using configurable rules (e.g., last writer wins).

11. What is Azure Blob Leasing, and how does it work?

Ans:

A lease on a blob provides exclusive write and delete access (lock) to the blob. We can either acquire a temporary or infinite lease based on the requirement.

How it works:

- **Acquire a lease:** We initiate the lease operation, specifying the desired duration (short-term or infinite). A unique lease ID is returned.
- **Exclusive access:** As long as the lease is active, only the client holding the lease ID can write to or delete the blob. Any other attempt by unauthorized users will be denied.
- **Renewing or releasing:** We can extend the lease duration before it expires by renewing it with the active lease ID. Alternatively, releasing the lease unlocks the blob and makes it accessible for others.

Explore:

Azure Blob Storage provides a feature called Lease Blob that creates and manages a lock on a blob for write and delete operations. Here are the lease blob concepts:

Lease ID: When a client acquires a lease, a lease ID is returned. The Blob service will generate a lease ID if one is not specified in the acquire request. The client may use this lease ID to renew the lease, change its lease ID, or release the lease.

Lease Type:

- **Temporary (15 to 60 seconds):** Ideal for short-term tasks like updating a specific block within a large blob. Ex:
  - An application is processing and updating a critical configuration file in Azure Blob Storage. During the update, it acquires a temporary lease to ensure exclusive write access, preventing other processes from modifying the file.
  - Two users simultaneously try to edit a shared document stored as a blob. A temporary lease ensures only one user's changes are saved at a time, preventing conflicting edits.
- **Infinite:** Perfect for scenarios where continuous exclusive access is needed. Ex:
  - Azure VMs are backed by Azure Page Blobs. So, when a VM is created, an infinite lease is acquired on the blob holding the VHD for that Azure VM so that no other process can modify or delete that blob.
  - A content management system stores user-uploaded files in Azure Blob Storage. The system acquires an infinite lease on each user's profile picture, ensuring that only one process can update the picture at a time, maintaining consistency across the platform.

Lease Modes: Here are the different modes in which you can call the Lease Blob operation:

- **Acquire:** to request a new lease.
- **Renew:** to renew an existing lease.
- **Change:** to change the ID of an existing lease.
- **Release:** to free the lease if it's no longer needed.
- **Break:** to end the lease, but ensure that another client can't acquire a new lease until the current lease period has expired.

12. How does Azure Blob Storage support lifecycle management for managing data?

Ans:

A lifecycle management policy is composed of one or more rules that define a set of actions to take based on a condition being met. **Ex:** We can create a rule to move data to a cooler storage tier after a certain number of days, or delete data that is no longer needed.

- **Benefits:** Reduced manual effort (automation), Cost optimization (reducing unnecessary hot tier charges), Enhanced data governance (automatically remove outdated or irrelevant data, promoting compliance and reducing security risks).

Explore:

We can use the Azure portal, PowerShell, Azure CLI, or an Azure Resource Manager template to add, edit, or remove a lifecycle management policy.

Capabilities:

- **Transition data between access tiers:** Move less-accessed data to cooler tiers (Cool or Archive) for reduced storage costs, and hot data back to the Hot tier for faster access when needed.
- **Expire data:** Automatically delete data after a specified time, eliminating stale or unnecessary information.
- **Manage snapshots:** Set retention periods for blob snapshots, ensuring point-in-time backups are retained or deleted automatically.

Example Use Cases:

- In an e-commerce application, product images used in campaigns become outdated after a season. Move images older than 6 months to the Cool tier, saving storage costs.
- In a health care application, patient medical records need long-term retention with secure access controls. Archive records after 7 years.
- In a research app, large research datasets are regularly updated with new versions. Delete older versions of datasets when a new version is uploaded.

13. Can you explain how to create a Lifecycle Management Policy in Azure Storage for the scenario "Move logs older than 45 days to the Cool tier"?

Ans:

We can create and manage life cycle policies using Azure Portal, Azure CLI etc. Navigate to Storage Account > Management > Lifecycle management > Add Rule > Create the actions, filters etc using GUI:

- **Create a policy rule:** First, we need to create a policy rule that defines the conditions and actions for the policy. We can define multiple rules with different actions.
- **Apply the policy rule:** Once you have created the policy rule, you need to apply it to a container or a blob. We can use filters and prefixes to target specific blobs or containers.

Here is the sample Rule created using Azure CLI for the scenario "Moves logs older than 45 days to the Cool tier":

Create a JSON file for the policy: Policy.json

- {"rules": [{
    - "enabled": true,
    - "name": "MoveLogsToCoolTier",
    - "type": "Lifecycle",
    - "definition": {
        - "actions": {
            - "baseBlob": {

        - "tierToCool": {
        - "daysAfterModificationGreaterThan": 45
    - }}},
    - "filters": {
        - "blobTypes": ["blockBlob"],
        - "prefixMatch": ["logs/"]
    - }
  - }}]
- }

Apply the policy:

- az storage account management-policy create --account-name <storage-account-name> --resource-group <resource-group-name> --policy @<path-to-json-file>

14. What authentication methods are available for accessing Azure Storage?

Ans:

Azure Storage offers several authentication options:

- **Shared Key (Not safe):** Like a master password, we can use it directly in our app to access storage.
- **Shared Access Signature (SAS):** Like a temporary key to share specific data without full account access.
- **Microsoft Entra Integration (Recommended):** Use your company's Entra identities for secure access control. We can leverage Managed Identity or Service Principle depends on the requirement.
- **Microsoft Entra/Active Directory Domain Services:** Use your existing on-premises AD credentials for seamless access.
- **Anonymous Public Read Access:** No authentication needed and anyone can view the data.

Recommendation:

- For production environments, consider using Managed Identity for the best security and ease of management.
- Use Service Principal if you require more control over the application identity or need to integrate with external systems.
- Shared Key and SAS tokens are better suited for temporary or less sensitive scenarios.

Explore:

Shared Key (Storage Account Key): Access is granted using the storage account name and key, similar to sharing a master key with the client application. Use it with caution.

- **Use Cases:**
    - Simple development and testing scenarios where ease of use is prioritized over robust security.
    - Legacy applications not yet integrated with Entra.
    - Internal tools within a trusted environment where key management is carefully handled.
- **Ex:** A developer uses the account access key in their legacy application code to upload and download files to Blob Storage.

Shared Access Signature (SAS): The SAS key is a token that can be used by a third party to access a specific resource for a specified time interval. This eliminates the need to provide full permissions for the entire storage account.

- **Use Cases:**
    - Sharing data with external users or services without disclosing account keys.
    - Providing limited access to specific resources with fine-grained control over permissions and expiration.
    - Creating temporary URLs for accessing data without requiring full account credentials.
- **Ex:** A company generates a SAS token to grant a third-party vendor temporary access to specific blobs for data analysis.

Microsoft Entra – Managed Identity: Managed Identity is a feature in Azure that provides an automatically managed identity for Azure resources. This identity can be used to authenticate to any service that supports Microsoft Entra ID authentication.

- **Use Case:** Managed Identities are primarily used to avoid hard-coding credentials in applications. They are ideal for scenarios where Azure services need to communicate with each other securely, such as Azure VMs accessing Azure Storage, or Azure Functions querying Azure SQL Database. Managed Identities simplify identity management by eliminating the need for developers to manually manage credentials.
- **Ex:** Imagine you have an Azure Data Factory pipeline that needs to read and write data to Azure Data Lake Storage Gen2. By enabling a system-assigned managed identity on the Azure Data Factory at Entra ID, you can grant this identity the necessary permissions to access the storage account. When the pipeline runs, Azure Data Factory will automatically use this identity to obtain an access token and securely access the storage without any hard-coded credentials.

Service Principal: A Service Principal is an identity created for use by applications, hosted services, or automated tools to access Azure resources. It acts as a way for applications to authenticate themselves in Microsoft Entra ID, and it can be assigned roles and permissions to control access to resources. Service Principals require manual management of credentials (client ID and secret or certificate).

- **Use Case:** Service Principals are useful in scenarios where applications or services, including those running outside of Azure, need to authenticate and access Azure resources. They are commonly used for automation tasks, CI/CD pipelines, and any scenario where an application needs to securely authenticate to access Azure resources.
- **Ex:** Suppose you have a web application hosted outside Azure, such as on-premises or in another cloud provider, and it needs to upload and retrieve files from Azure Blob Storage. You can create a Service Principal in Azure and grant it appropriate permissions on the Blob Storage account. The application will use the Service Principal's client ID and secret to authenticate with Microsoft Entra ID and obtain an access token to interact with Azure Blob Storage securely.

OAuth 2.0: Authentication with Managed Identity and Service Principal

OAuth is an authentication framework. Both Managed Identity and Service Principal utilize OAuth 2.0 with Microsoft Entra ID for authentication and authorization. Here's how the process works:

- **Token Request:** When a request is made to access an Azure resource using Managed Identity or Service Principal, it first requests a token from Microsoft Entra ID.
    - **Managed Identity:** Requests an access token using its managed identity.
    - **Service Principal:** Requests an access token by presenting its client ID and secret or certificate.
- **Token Issuance:** Microsoft Entra ID authenticates the request and issues an OAuth 2.0 access token.
- **Resource Access:** The resource uses this access token to authenticate and interact with the target service. The service validates the token to ensure it has the necessary permissions.

Microsoft Entra/Active Directory Domain Services: When using Azure Files via the SMB protocol, this is the preferred method of authorization. It can be configured through either Entra Domain Services or on-premises AD-DS. This functions similarly to traditional AD authentication and authorization for on-premise SMB storage (NAS).

- **Use Cases:**
    - Azure Files Access via SMB Protocol.
    - Extending on-premises authentication to Azure Storage for a unified experience.
    - Simplifying authentication for users and applications already integrated with AD DS.
- **Ex:** A company with on-premises AD DS enables seamless authentication for Azure Files via Server Message Block (SMB) protocol using their existing domain credentials.

Anonymous Public Read Access: Containers or Blobs can be set to be public, allowing anyone to read the data without authentication or authorization.

- **Use Cases:**
  - Sharing data with a wide audience without requiring authentication.
  - Creating public websites or web applications directly from Blob Storage.
- **Ex:** A company hosts publicly accessible content such as product images, marketing materials, or open-source software in Blob Storage, allowing anyone to view them without authentication.

15. Does Shared Key and Shared Access Signature support all types of Azure Storage (Blob, Queue, File, Table)?

Ans:

- **Shared Key:** Supports all types of storage.
- **Shared Access Signature:** Supports all types except the Azure File Share access over SMB.

Explore:

It's worthwhile to learn the security support matrix.

Azure Storage	Shared Key	SAS	Entra ID	AD DS	Public read access
Blobs	Yes	Yes	Yes	No	Yes
File Share (SMB)	Yes	No	Yes	Yes	No
File Share (REST)	Yes	Yes	Yes	No	No
Queues	Yes	Yes	Yes	No	No
Tables	Yes	Yes	Yes	No	No
ADLS Gen 2	Yes	Yes	Yes	No	No

Table 7.2

***File Share (SMB) - Entra AD**: YES (with on-premises AD DS integration).

***SAS -** Shared Access Signature.

***AD DS -** Azure AD DS or On-premises AD DS – Active directory Domain Services.

***ADLS Gen 2 -** Azure Data Lake Storage Generation 2.

16. What is the difference between a Shared Key and a Shared Access Signature (SAS)? Which is the more secure approach, and why?

Ans:

Shared Key: A Shared Key is essentially a master key for your Azure Storage account. It grants unrestricted access to everything within the account, including all resources stored there.

Shared Access Signature (SAS): It operates as a token with specific security constraints, such as controlling who can access it (based on IP addresses or ranges), specifying the duration of access (start time to expiry time), and defining the actions permitted (granted permissions). Additionally, SAS enables granting access to a specific resource, be it a single blob or a file, rather than providing access to the entire account.

Recommendation:

- By offering this granular control and limited access capabilities, SAS emerges as the more secure option. Sharing the account key carries significant risks, whereas SAS mitigates these by providing temporary, restricted access tokens.
- Microsoft strongly recommends using Microsoft Entra credentials (Azure AD) for authorization whenever feasible, even when creating SAS tokens.

Explore:

Shared Key:

- When creating a storage account, Azure generates two 512-bit storage account access keys.
- These keys are used to authorize access to data in the storage account through Shared Key authorization. Storage account access keys function like a root password for the storage account, and sharing them equates to providing unlimited access to the account.
- It is our responsibility to safeguard these storage keys, and we recommend using Azure Key Vault to securely manage and rotate our keys.
- Distributing access keys to other users, hard-coding them, or storing them in plain text accessible to others should be avoided.
- Using storage account keys in client applications poses a security risk, as it could lead to unauthorized access, compromising the security of the storage account.
- Therefore, it is strongly discouraged to share or use the account shared key for accessing data in Azure Storage.

Shared Access Signature (SAS):

- A shared access signature is a signed URI (Uniform Resource Identifier) pointing to one or more storage resources.

- Users or applications request a shared access signature from Azure Storage, specifying permissions, start time, expiry time, and other parameters for the SAS.
    - **Resources:** Specific containers, blobs, or files to grant access to.
    - **Permissions:** Allowed operations (read, write, delete, list, etc.).
    - **Start Time:** The point in time when the SAS token becomes valid. Access is not allowed before this time.
    - **Expiry Time:** The point when the SAS token becomes invalid.
    - **Signature:** A cryptographic hash generated using either the storage account key, Microsoft Entra Credentials, and the specified parameters, ensuring authenticity and integrity.
- Azure Storage generates a unique SAS token based on the provided parameters.
- The user or application receives the SAS token, which can be included in a URI to access the specified resources.

17. What are the different types of Shared Access Signatures (SAS)?

Ans:

There are three types of SAS:

- User Delegation SAS
- Service SAS
- Account SAS

Explore:

User Delegation SAS (Recommended):

- Secured with Microsoft Entra credentials and permissions specified in the SAS token.
- Provides granular control over access and permissions.
- It applies to Blob storage only.

Service SAS (Object Specific Access):

- Secured with the storage account key.
- Grants access to a specific **resource in only one of the Azure Storage Services** (Blob, Queue, Table, or Files) within the account.

Account SAS (Account Specific Access):

- Secured with the storage account key.
- Grants access to **resources in one or more Azure Storage Services** within the account.
- All of the operations available via a service or user delegation SAS are also available via an account SAS.

18. Any idea about "Ad hoc SAS" and "Service SAS with SAP (Stored Access Policy)"?

Ans:

Both "Ad Hoc SAS" and "Service SAS with SAP **(Stored Access Policy)"** are ways to create Shared Access Signature tokens for our Azure Storage resources, but they offer different levels of flexibility and control.

- **Ad hoc SAS:** Assign permissions directly to an individual SAS.
- **Service SAS with SAP (Stored Access Policy):** Assign all permissions to a single policy and map all similar SAS instances to that policy. This enables easy control of access from a single point.

Explore:

Ad Hoc SAS:

- **Quick and simple:** Assign permissions directly to a single SAS token within the URL.
    - Create SAS > Assign Permissions and other parameters to SAS > Share SAS with the client
- **Limited control:** Once created, the settings cannot be easily modified.
- **Scope:** It supports any type of (User delegation, service, account) SAS.
- **Ideal for**: Short-term access.
- **Ex:** A marketing team needs to share a confidential sales report with a freelance writer for a limited time.

Service SAS with SAP:

- **Reusable and flexible:** Define access rules in a centralized Shared Access Policy and apply them to multiple SAS tokens.
    - Create Stored Access Policy > Assign Permissions to SAP > Map all similar SAS to SAP
    - SAP > SAS 1 > Share it with Client 1
    - SAP > SAS 2 > Share it with Client 2
    - SAP > SAS 3 > Share it with Client N
- **Granular control** and Easier management: Update the policy once to modify access rules for all associated SAS tokens.
- **Scope:** It only supports Service SAS.
- **Ideal for:** Repeated access with more control requirements.
- **Ex:** A healthcare organization needs to grant different levels of access to patient records for various stakeholders.

Creating a SAS:

Navigate to Azure Portal > Storage account > Select the desired resource (Container or Blob) > Generate SAS

- Configure parameters like permissions, expiry time, and access policy.
- Download the generated SAS URI.

We can use Azure CLI, PowerShell, or Azure SDKs for programmatic control.

19. Is it true that using SAS (Shared Access Signature) with SAP (Stored Access Policy) is a better security practice than using Ad hoc SAS for accessing Azure Storage? If yes, can you justify your answer?

Ans:

Yes, the statement above is indeed true. To realize this, it is essential to understand the difference between Ad hoc SAS and SAS with SAP (Stored Access Policy).

Problem with Ad hoc SAS: Let's consider a scenario where we need to grant access to a Blob and create an Ad hoc SAS URI with parameters such as start time, expiration time, permissions, etc. To revoke this access:

- Either wait until the SAS URI reaches its expiry time.
- Alternatively, we need to change the storage account key.
- If we change the storage account key, it might have a severe impact depending on how many applications are using that storage account.

SAS URI with SAP: On the other hand, we can create a Stored Access Policy (SAP) and map all similar SAS URIs with the policy. When a client requests access, authorization information is retrieved from the Stored Access Policy. To revoke access:

- Either wait until the SAS URI reaches its expiry time.
- Alternatively, we can simply change the stored access policy. Consequently, permissions, timelines, and all other constraints for all SAS URIs associated/mapped with that SAP will be immediately modified.
- Similarly, we can simply delete the stored access policy, and all SAS tokens bound by the policy will be invalidated.
- Hence, there are no side effects as we are not altering the storage account key.

20. I noticed you mentioned SAS URI frequently. Could you clarify what "URI" stands for? Is it the same as a URL?

Ans:

Absolutely! URI stands for "Uniform Resource Identifier" and, yes, it's very similar to a URL (Uniform Resource Locator). Both identify and locate resources on the internet. However, there are some subtle differences:

URI (Uniform Resource Identifier):

- URIs are often used as a generic term to refer to any string of characters that identifies a resource.
- It identifies a resource on the web either by using location, name or both.
- Ex: HTTP, FTP, email addresses, etc.

Uniform Resource Locator (URL):

- A URL is a specific type of URI that identifies the location of a resource on the internet.
- It typically includes information such as the protocol, domain or IP address, and the path to the resource.
- Ex: Specifically refers to web resources accessible through HTTP or HTTPS protocols.

SAS URI:

- It identifies the specific Azure Storage resource (container, blob, etc.) and includes all the necessary information for authorized access, including permissions and expiry time. So, while a SAS URI shares similarities with a URL, it carries additional information beyond just the resource location.

Explore:

Imagine this SAS URI grants read-only permission to the blob sales_2024_Jan.pdf for 48 hours, effective from 22-Jan-2024 10:00 AM to 24-Jan-2024 10:00 AM. Here's an example of such a SAS URI:

- https://abcstorage.blob.core.windows.net/abcSlaes/sales_2024_Jan.pdf?sv=2022-08-01&st=2024-01-22T10%3A00%3A00Z&se=2024-01-24T10%3A00%3A00Z&sr=b&sp=r

Parameters:

- abcstorage: Storage Account Name
- abcSlaes: Container
- sales_2024_Jan.pdf: Blob
- sv: Version of the storage service used to create the SAS.
- st: Start time of the SAS
- se: Expiry time of the SAS
- sr: Resource type, which is set to b for blob in this case.
- sp: Permissions granted to the SAS, which is set to r for read-only access in this case.

21. What Azure built-in roles are available for Azure Storage? If my access requirements for Azure Storage don't match any built-in roles, is it possible to create custom roles?

Ans:

Azure role-based access control (RBAC) has several Azure built-in roles that we can assign to users, groups, service principals, and managed identities. Role assignments are the way we control access to Azure resources. If the built-in roles don't meet the specific needs of our organization, we can create our own Azure custom roles. Here are some of the built-in roles available for Azure Storage:

- Storage Blob Data Reader
- Storage Blob Data Contributor
- Storage Blob Data Owner etc.

Explore:

Here's a breakdown of some key roles:

Storage Account Roles:

- **Storage Account Contributor:** Allows management of storage accounts and access to data within them.
- **Storage Account Backup Contributor:** Allows management of backup operations for storage accounts, but cannot modify the account itself.
- **Storage Account Key Operator Service Role:** A specialized role intended for service principals to manage storage account keys without granting full account access.

Blob Data Roles:

- **Storage Blob Data Reader:** Read blob data within containers.
- **Storage Blob Data Contributor:** Read and write blob data within containers.
- **Storage Blob Data Owner:** Full control over blob data including reading, writing, deleting, and managing container permissions.
- **Storage Blob Delegator:** Can grant delegation tokens to others, allowing them to access blobs without knowing the account key.

File Data Roles:

- **Storage File Data Privileged Contributor:** Full control over all file shares and files within them, including managing access control lists (ACLs) and file system quotas.
- **Storage File Data Privileged Reader:** Read all file shares and files within them, but cannot modify them.
- **Storage File Data SMB Share Reader:** Read files within SMB shares, but cannot manage the shares themselves.
- **Storage File Data SMB Share Contributor:** Manage SMB shares and grant access to them, but cannot access files within the shares.

Queue Data Roles:

- **Storage Queue Data Reader:** Read messages from queues.
- **Storage Queue Data Contributor:** Read and write messages to queues.

- **Storage Queue Data Message Processor:** Dequeue and process messages from queues.
- **Storage Queue Data Message Sender:** Send messages to queues.

Table Data Roles:

- **Storage Table Data Reader:** Read table data.
- **Storage Table Data Contributor:** Read and write table data.

22. In Azure Blob Storage, how can I grant access to:

- **The entire storage account?**
- **A specific container?**
- **Multiple containers?**
- **A single blob/file within a container?**
- **Multiple blobs/files within a container?**
- **Containers/Blobs following a specific pattern (Ex: starting with "Sales_")?**

Ans:

Granting access to:

- **Storage Account:** Storage Account Key, SAS, or Azure RBAC.
- **Specific Container:** Azure RBAC or SAS.
- **Multiple Containers:** Azure RBAC.
- **Specific or multiple Blobs/Files within a container:** SAS.
- **Multiple Containers or Files Based on Pattern:** Generate SAS tokens programmatically.

Note: Granting access to an entire storage account is generally not recommended due to potential security risks.

Explore:

Using Azure RBAC to assign roles at the storage account or container level:

- Navigate to the Azure storage account > "Access Control (IAM)" > "Add role assignment" >
- Select a role (Ex: Storage Blob Data Contributor).
- Assign the role to the user or group.
- Specify the scope (storage account or specific containers).
- Repeat the steps for each of the containers.

Using Shared Access Signature (SAS): Generate a SAS token for the specific container.

- Navigate to the container in the Azure portal.
- Click on "Shared access signature".
- Configure the permissions (read, write etc.), start, and expiry time.

- Generate the SAS token and URL.
- Provide the SAS URL to the user.

Programmatically generating SAS Tokens:

- SAS tokens can be created programmatically using Azure Storage SDKs for .NET, Java, or Python. This approach is especially beneficial for complex scenarios like granting access based on file name patterns.

Access Control Lists (ACLs) in ADLS Gen2:

- ACLs in Azure Data Lake Storage (ADLS) Gen2 provide fine-grained access control to files and directories within a storage account, allowing you to define permissions at both directory and file levels. Useful for granular access control, hierarchical permissions, and multi-user collaboration. **Ex:** Leverage ADLS Gen2's ACL to manage permissions at the container, directory, and file levels.

23. Have you ever heard about NetApp? Can you explain what you know about it?

Ans:

NetApp is a company that specializes in data storage and management solutions. They offer a variety of hardware and software products that help businesses of all sizes to store, protect, and manage their data efficiently.

Explore:

Key Features of NetApp:

- **Unified data storage:** NetApp can store all types of data, from files and applications to databases and virtual machines, in a single place. This makes it easier for businesses to manage their data and keep it organized.
- **Data Storage Solutions:** NetApp offers storage solutions that include hardware and software components. Ex: SAN (Storage Area Network) and NAS (Network Attached Storage).
- **Data Management Software:** NetApp offers software solutions for data management, helping organizations organize, protect, and optimize their data. Ex: Data backup, recovery, and data deduplication.
- **Flash Storage:** NetApp provides flash storage solutions, which use solid-state drives (SSDs) to deliver high-performance storage for demanding workloads, applications, and databases.
- **Data Protection and Security:** NetApp focuses on ensuring data protection and security through features such as encryption, access controls, and backup solutions to safeguard data.
- **Other Services:** Analytics and Insights, cloud-based solutions, supporting hybrid-cloud infrastructures etc.

24. What is "Azure NetApp Files"?

Ans:

Azure NetApp Files is a cloud-based, enterprise-grade high performance file storage service provided by Microsoft Azure in collaboration with NetApp. It is designed to deliver high-performance, enterprise-grade file shares with the scalability and flexibility of the Azure cloud.

Explore:

Key Features of Azure NetApp Files:

- **Performance Tiers:** Choose from Standard, Premium, and Ultra options to match our workload needs.
- **Cost-Effective:** Pay only for the storage you use, with flexible pricing models.
- **Effortless Scaling:** Easily adjust your file share size up or down as your demands evolve.
- **Simple Management:** Manage everything through the Azure portal, CLI, or REST API.
- **HA & DR:** Built-in high availability and disaster recovery ensure peace of mind. We can leverage SnapMirror, a NetApp data replication technology, to replicate data between Azure NetApp Files and on-premises NetApp storage systems.
- **Robust Data Management:** Leverage features like snapshots, replication, and encryption for superior data protection and compliance.
- **Seamless Integration:** Works flawlessly with other Azure services and on-premises environments.
- **Protocol Support:** It supports NFS (Network File System), SMB (Server Message Block), and dual protocols volumes.

25. What are the use cases of Azure NetApp Files?

Ans:

Here are the common use cases:

- High Performance Computing (HPC) Workloads.
- Migrating POSIX-compliant workloads to Azure.
- Mission critical enterprise applications and databases.
- Big Data Analytics.

Sample Business Cases:

- High-performance editing of large video files.
- Real-time content delivery for live events.
- High-throughput data acquisition from IoT for a manufacturing factory automation.
- Refactoring and migrating Mainframe workloads to Azure.

- Hosting SAP HANA applications on Azure VM and Databases on NetApp Files.
- Hosting SQL Server service on Azure VM with VLDB Database Files on Azure NetApp Files.
- Deploying SQL Server Always-On Failover Cluster over SMB with Azure NetApp Files.

Explore:

- **High-Performance workloads:** Azure NetApp Files service is specifically designed for demanding workloads like high-performance computing (HPC) and analytics. This makes it ideal for tasks like scientific simulations, data processing, and machine learning.
- **Lift-and-Shift existing applications:** If we have POSIX-compliant Linux and Windows applications running on-premises, Azure NetApp Files allows us to migrate them to the cloud without needing to change any code. This can be a quick and cost-effective way to modernize your IT infrastructure.
- **Databases with High throughput requirements:** Azure NetApp Files can store database files for SAP HANA, SQL Server, Oracle, and other databases. This can improve performance and scalability, especially for mission-critical databases with high-throughput requirements.
- **Data lakes and Bigdata Analytics:** Create high performance data lakes in the cloud with Azure NetApp Files for Data Analytics needs. Ex: To process large amounts of data using various big data analytics tools, including Azure Databricks, Azure Synapse Analytics, and Azure HDInsight.
- **File sharing and home directories:** Azure NetApp Files can function as a high-performance shared file system for your organization.
- **Virtual Desktop Infrastructure (VDI):** Azure NetApp Files provides storage for VDI deployments, such as Azure Virtual Desktop and Citrix. This allows users to access their virtual desktops with high performance and responsiveness.

26. Does Azure NetApp Files are similar to Azure Files Shares? what is the difference and how to choose the right solution?

Ans:

Azure NetApp Files and Azure Files Shares are both cloud-based file storage services offered by Microsoft Azure. However, they have different strengths and use cases.

- **Azure Files Shares** is a general-purpose file storage service that is suitable for most workloads that require cloud file storage.
  - **Choose it:** For basic use cases and cost-effective cloud-based file share workloads.
- **Azure NetApp Files** is a specialized service that is designed for high-performance, low-latency workloads that require advanced data management capabilities.
  - **Choose it:** For high-performance needs and advanced feature requirements.

***Note:** Azure File Shares and NetApp Files share several similarities, including fully managed services, highly scalable, and seamless integration with Azure services.

Explore:

Here is the more detailed comparison:

Azure File Shares:

- **Performance:** Optimized for random access workloads with in-place data updates, ideal for general-purpose file storage like document sharing and web applications.
- **Data Management:** Offers basic features like snapshots, replication and tiering.
- **Cost:** Generally, more cost-effective for less demanding workloads due to its tiered storage options.
- **Use Cases:**
    - Document sharing and collaboration.
    - Web applications and content management systems.
    - Low-latency file access for small to medium workloads.

Azure NetApp Files:

- **Performance:** Delivers high performance and low latency for demanding workloads like media & entertainment, HPC, and databases, thanks to its NetApp ONTAP operating system and dedicated hardware.
- **Data Management:** Provides advanced data management capabilities like snapshots, cloning, replication, tiering, and deduplication for efficient data protection and optimization.
- **Cost:** Can be more expensive due to its high-performance hardware and advanced features, but cost-effective for workloads requiring high throughput and low latency.
- **Use Cases:**
    - High-performance computing (HPC) and analytics.
    - Media and entertainment content storage and editing.
    - Databases and enterprise applications.
    - Large-scale file sharing with demanding performance requirements.

27. Does Azure Storage support the Secure Shell File Transfer Protocol (SFTP)?

Ans:

Yes, Azure Storage supports SFTP. We can securely connect to the Blob Storage endpoint of an Azure Storage account by using an SFTP client, and then upload and download files.

Explore:

Here is the background:

- Azure allows secure data transfer to Blob Storage accounts using Azure Blob service REST API, Azure SDKs, and tools such as AzCopy. However, legacy workloads often use traditional file transfer protocols such as SFTP. We could update custom applications to use the REST API and Azure SDKs, but only by making significant code changes.

- Prior to the release of SFTP feature, if we wanted to use SFTP to transfer data to Azure Blob Storage we would have to either purchase a third-party product or orchestrate our own solution.
- Now, with SFTP support for Azure Blob Storage, we can enable an SFTP endpoint for Blob Storage accounts with a single click. Then you can set up local user identities for authentication to connect to our storage account with SFTP via port 22.

28. In what scenarios or applications are SFTP and Azure Storage commonly used together?

Ans:

Here are some of the top use cases of SFTP in the context of Azure Storage:

- **Integration with legacy systems:** SFTP can be used to integrate with legacy systems that only support SFTP for file transfer. By using SFTP, we can ensure that our data is compatible with these legacy systems.
- **Leveraging existing tools and skills:** Use familiar SFTP clients and tools with Azure Storage, minimizing retraining and onboarding efforts for IT teams.
- **Collecting data from edge devices:** Leverage SFTP on edge devices to securely upload sensor data or application logs to Azure Blob Storage for processing and analysis.
- **Automating file transfers:** Integrate SFTP with Azure Functions or Logic Apps to trigger automated file transfers based on events or schedules.
- **Compliance:** SFTP can be used to meet compliance requirements for data transfer. By using SFTP, we can ensure that our data is encrypted and secure during transfer, which can help us meet compliance requirements.

29. Could you provide a brief explanation of the steps involved in configuring SFTP for Azure Blob Storage?

Ans:

Here are the high-level steps to configure SFTP for Azure Blob Storage:

- Enable SFTP feature for your Azure Storage Account.
- Create local users.
- Set Permissions for Containers.
- Connect with SFTP Client and start transferring files.

Explore:

We can enable an SFTP endpoint for our Blob Storage accounts and connect to them with SFTP clients via port 22. Here are the detailed steps:

Prerequisites:

- SFTP supports standard general-purpose v2 or premium block blob storage account.
- The hierarchical namespace feature of the account must be enabled.
- Make sure that our client allows outgoing communication through port 22 used by SFTP.

Enable SFTP for our Azure Storage Account:

Navigate to Azure Portal > Our Storage Account > Settings > SFTP > Enable SFTP.

Create Local Users:

- Azure Storage doesn't support shared access signature (SAS), or Microsoft Entra authentication for accessing the SFTP endpoint. Instead, we must use an identity called local user that can be secured with an Azure generated password or a secure shell (SSH) key pair.
- Go to "SFTP" again and click "Add local user."
- Enter a username and choose our preferred authentication method (password or SSH key).
- We can add up to 1000 local users per storage account.

Set Permissions for Containers:

- Define the access level (read, write, list) for each local user on each container.
- This determines which files and folders users can access within the container.

Connect with an SFTP client and start transferring files:

- We can connect to Blob Storage using SFTP from an SFTP client on Azure or from our on-premises server. To do so, we'll need to ensure that our client allows outgoing communication through port 22 used by SFTP.
- Open our SFTP client (Ex: FileZilla, WinSCP, Cyberduck, PuTTY)
- Enter the required parameters:
  - Hostname provided when we enabled SFTP for our Azure Storage account (Ex: abcstorage.sftp.blob.core.windows.net).
  - Enter username and chosen authentication method (Ex: password or SSH key).
- Connect! We should now see our Azure Blob Storage containers (based on the permissions granted) like folders.
- We can now securely connect to the Blob Storage endpoint by using an SFTP client, and then upload and download files.

30. What is the hierarchical namespace in Azure Storage?

Ans:

The hierarchical namespace in Azure Storage is a feature in Azure Data Lake Storage Gen2 that enables the organization of data in a filesystem-like hierarchy (directory structure) for improved data management and access control.

Explore:

In ADLS Gen 2, a hierarchical namespace essentially refers to a way of organizing objects (files and blobs) within our storage account into a folder-like structure, similar to what we'd see on our computer's hard drive.

Traditional Azure Storage (Flat Namespace):

- Objects are organized within containers.
- No nested folders or directories exist.

Azure Storage with Hierarchical Namespace:

- Objects are organized into containers and then further into subdirectories and nested subdirectories.
- Mimics the familiar file system structure with folders and files.
- Simplifies navigation and access, especially for big data analytics tools.

Enable Hierarchical Namespace for ADLS Gen 2:

- Navigate to Azure Portal > Our Storage Account Settings
    - > Account Kind Section > Select Data Lake Storage Gen2
    - > Advanced Section > Select Hierarchical namespace > Save

Overall:

- Hierarchical namespace feature is currently available for Azure Data Lake Storage Gen2 (ADLS Gen2) accounts only.
- The hierarchical namespace is compatible with the Hadoop Distributed File System (HDFS) and supports Hadoop Distributed File System operations.
- The hierarchical namespace in Azure Storage enhances the capabilities of ADLS Gen2, making it well-suited for scenarios that require advanced analytics, big data processing, and flexible data organization.

31. Can Azure Blob Storage be cached, and what are the cache implementation options? What's your recommended approach?

Ans:

Implementing caching for Azure Blob Storage depends on your specific needs and application architecture. Here are three common approaches:

- Azure Content Delivery Network (CDN)
- Azure Cache for Redis
- Client-side caching

Recommendation:

- For most scenarios, Azure CDN is the most cost-effective and easiest way to implement caching for static content.
- Use Azure Cache for Redis when extremely low latency is crucial and justifies the additional complexity.
- Client-side caching can be beneficial for specific use cases but requires development effort.

Cost Analysis: Analyze, compare, and select the optimal caching option. Evaluate caching benefits for our business application against the development and maintenance costs of the caching solution.

Explore:

Azure Content Delivery Network (CDN):

- Azure CDN caches static content at geographically distributed edge locations, closer to users, significantly reducing download latency and cost.
- Ideal for frequently accessed content like website images, videos, and static files.
- Not ideal for frequently changing data or real-time applications.
- Easy to set up with just a few configuration steps in the Azure portal.
- **Ex:** A global e-commerce website stores product images and videos in Azure Blob Storage. Using Azure CDN caches those assets at edge locations worldwide, delivering them to users with lower latency and reduced bandwidth costs. This enhances user experience and saves on egress charges.

Azure Cache for Redis:

- Azure Cache for Redis is an implementation of the open-source Redis cache that runs as a managed in-memory cache service in an Azure data center.
- Stores frequently accessed blob data in memory for even faster retrieval than Azure CDN.
- Ideal for scenarios requiring very low latency, such as real-time applications or frequently refreshed data.
- Requires more complex integration with our application code and more expensive compared to Azure CDN.
- **Ex:** An analytical pipeline processes datasets stored in Azure Blob Storage. Caching intermediate results in Azure Cache for Redis eliminates redundant calculations and significantly speeds up subsequent iterations, reducing overall processing time and resource consumption.

Client-side caching:

- Implement caching directly within our application using libraries or frameworks.
- Stores downloaded blob data locally on the user's device or server.
- Offers the lowest latency for subsequent access, reduces reliance on network and storage.
- Requires additional development effort and may not be suitable for all scenarios.

- **Ex:** A travel app stores map data and offline content in Azure Blob Storage. Client-side caching enables users to navigate and access downloaded content smoothly even while offline, enhancing user experience and reducing reliance on network connectivity.

32. What are the essential steps for setting up Azure CDN and Azure Cache for Redis with Azure Blob Storage?

Ans:

Here are the high-level steps:

Create an Azure Storage Account: Create an Azure Storage account, create containers and upload blobs to our containers.

Azure CDN:

- **Create an Azure CDN profile:** Choose a pricing tier (Standard or Premium) and configure settings like origin (your Azure Blob Storage account), caching rules, security options, and edge locations (specific locations or leave it as "Worldwide").
- **Configure your blob storage account:** Enable CDN endpoint and associate it with the CDN profile. Ex: Navigate to our Blob Storage Account > Settings > Enable CDN End Point > Select the CDN Profile we just created.
- **Update content references:** Replace any direct blob storage URLs used in our application or website with the CDN endpoint URL provided by Azure.

Azure Cache for Redis:

- **Create an Azure Cache for Redis instance:** Choose a pricing tier (Basic, Standard, Premium, Enterprise, Enterprise Flash), cache size, and region.
- **Connect your application:** Use the provided connection string from Azure Cache for Redis to establish a connection from your application code.
- **Implement caching logic:** Use appropriate commands in our code to store frequently accessed blob data in Azure Cache for Redis. Retrieve data from the cache before checking the blob storage to improve performance.

Note: These are high-level steps, and the specific implementation will vary depending on our application architecture and needs.

Explore:

Additional considerations:

- **Cache invalidation:** Ensure our caching mechanism invalidates outdated cached data when the underlying blob is updated. Azure CDN offers automatic cache invalidation based on blob modification timestamps.

- **Cache duration:** Set appropriate cache expiration times based on data freshness and update frequency.
- **Utilize Azure tools:** Leverage tools like Azure Monitor and Application Insights to track caching performance and identify optimization opportunities.

33. Do all Azure Storage services support data partitioning?

Ans:

- **Blob Storage:** Uses range-based partitioning (internally managed, not user-configurable).
- **File Storage:** Create a proper folder structure and naming conventions for achieving a logical partitioning.
- **Queue Storage:** Partitions queues based on name (internal process, not user-controlled).
- **Table Storage:** Supports built-in partitioning features.
- **Data Lake Storage (ADLS Gen 2):** Achieves partitioning through hierarchical namespaces.

Explore:

Supports Partitioning:

- **Azure Table Storage:**
    - Azure Table Storage supports partitioning as a fundamental concept.
    - Each table is divided into partitions, and all entities within a partition have the same partition key.
    - This allows for efficient querying within a partition. The choice of a good partition key is crucial for optimal performance.
- **Azure Data Lake Storage Gen2 (ADLS Gen2):**
    - It supports hierarchical namespaces and directories, providing a built-in partitioning mechanism.
    - The directory structure can be leveraged to organize and partition data logically, improving data organization and query performance.
    - We can structure our data using paths within containers, similar to folders and subfolders. Each path level can act as a partition key, enabling efficient filtering and querying based on specific prefixes or combinations of elements in the path.
- **Azure Queue Storage:**
    - Azure Queue Storage automatically partitions data to distribute load. Azure partitions queues based on the name.
    - All messages for the same queue are stored in the same partition, which is controlled by a single server.

  - Different queues can be managed by different servers to help balance the load. The partitioning is handled by the service, and we don't have direct control over it. It's designed to handle high-throughput scenarios with automatic load balancing.

Limited Partitioning:

- **Azure Blob Storage:**
  - While Azure Blob Storage itself doesn't have built-in partitioning, it utilizes a concept called range-based partitioning behind the scenes for efficient data handling and load balancing.
  - Range-based partitioning takes this analogy further. It divides the entire blob storage into smaller, virtual sections based on the full blob name (account name +"/"+ container name + "/" + blob name).
  - These sections are called partitions. Each partition holds blobs whose entire names fall within a specific range, like "A-C", "D-F", "G-J", and so on.
  - This range is determined by lexicographical (dictionary) order of the full blob names.
  - This process is internal to Azure Blob Storage and does not require any external implementation.
  - **Ex:** Blobs can be distributed across many servers. All blobs within a container can be served by a single server until the load on these blobs requires further rebalancing of the partition ranges.
- **Azure Files:** Azure Files does not provide native partitioning mechanisms. Similar to Blob Storage, we can organize files using directories or naming conventions to achieve logical separation and load balancing.

Note: Naming conventions in Azure Blob Storage are crucial for effective data management, searchability, access optimization, and maintaining a well-organized and scalable storage system.

34. Does Azure Blob Storage provide any automatic data compression services?

Ans:

For now, Azure Blob Storage itself does not offer native auto data compression or decompression services while writing or reading data. However, we have below options to achieve compression in Azure Blob Storage / ADLS Gen 2:

- Client-side compression.
- ADLS Gen 2 native compression support for certain file formats.
- Azure Storage Transfer Service.
- Azure CDN.

Explore:

- **Client-side compression:** Compress data before uploading it to Blob Storage using tools like gzip, bzip2, or proprietary compression algorithms. Download the compressed data from Blob Storage and decompress it on your client side using the same tools.

- **Azure Data Lake Storage (ADLS) Gen2:** ADLS Gen2 enables native compression for certain file formats like Parquet, Avro etc.
- **Azure Storage Transfer Service:** This managed service can automatically compress data during upload (requires specific configurations).
- **Azure (CDN) Content Delivery Network Enabled Blob Storage:**
    - Similar to website content, Azure CDN can also compress data downloaded from our Blob Storage when served through the CDN edge servers.
    - This shrinks the file size before sending it to users, leading to even faster download times and reduced bandwidth consumption for both we and our customers.
    - We can easily enable compression and select the necessary file types within the CDN endpoint configuration settings.

Note: Major benefits of data compression include reduced storage costs, lower network bandwidth fees, and faster downloads, etc

35. Assuming our data is stored in Azure Blob Storage with diverse file formats, we aim to implement a search capability over the Azure Blob Storage. This requires searching for content across multiple files such as PDFs, CSVs, XML, JSON, and Excel. Are there any Azure services specifically designed to facilitate this type of search functionality?

Ans:

- Yes, Azure offers an excellent service called Azure AI Search (Formerly known as Azure Cognitive Search) for building search capabilities on top of various data sources including Azure Blob Storage with diverse file formats.
- Azure AI Search provides deep integration at the content layer, extracting and inferring textual information, which can then be queried in a search index.
- We can connect our Blob Storage to Azure AI Search, which automatically creates indexes for both data and metadata. We can then perform search operations on that index.

Explore:

Azure AI Search is an Azure managed search service that lets us index and search across various data sources, including unstructured content like PDFs, Word documents, text files etc. Here's how it works in the given scenario:

- **Indexing (Create an Indexer):** We configure an Azure AI Search service and connect it to our Azure Blob Storage container(s). The Blob Indexer component within Azure AI Search automatically extracts text and metadata from your files (CSV, EML, EPUB, GZ, HTML, JSON, KML, Microsoft Office formats, Open Document formats, PDF, plain text files, RTF, XML, and ZIP etc.) and builds a searchable index.

- **Searching:** Once indexed, we can use the Azure AI Search API or user interface to perform full-text searches across our blobs based on keywords, filters, and other criteria. It's incredibly powerful and supports advanced capabilities like fuzzy matching, faceting, and query spelling correction.

Sample Use Cases of Azure AI Search:

- **Product-search:** Customers instantly find relevant products across descriptions, specifications, reviews, and images stored in blob storage.
- **Music discovery:** Search for songs based on mood, genre, lyrics, or artist information extracted from audio files and metadata in blobs.
- **Patient information:** Medical professionals instantly retrieve relevant patient information (Ex: medical reports, imaging data etc.) stored in various formats within blob storage.

***Note:** Azure AI Search can index data stored in Blobs, Files, Tables, and ADLS Gen 2 storage.

36. What are the key differences between SMB and NFS file shares in Azure Files?

Ans:

Azure Files supports two main protocols for accessing file shares:

- **SMB (Server Message Block):** Familiar Windows file sharing with tight Active Directory integration, ideal for smaller files and frequent read/write operations.
- **NFS (Network File System):** Open-standard protocol for Linux and macOS environments, excels at handling large files and high concurrent access, perfect for cloud-native deployments.

Explore:

Here are the differences between SMB and NFS file shares in Azure Files:

SMB:

- **Protocol:** It is a protocol mainly used by Windows OS for sharing files, printers, and other resources on a network.
- **OS Support:** SMB is primarily used in Windows-based systems, but it is also supported on other platforms.
- **Performance:** More suitable for high-latency or high-bandwidth scenarios. Offers higher performance for small files and frequent read/write operations.
- **Authentication and Access Control:** Supports integration with Microsoft Entra ID, On-premises Active Directory etc. for user-based authentication. It also supports granular access control.
- **Version Support:** Azure Files supports SMB 3.1.1, SMB 3.0, and SMB 2.1.
- **Use Cases:**
    - To build centralized file storage for Windows desktops where users need shared access to documents, spreadsheets, and other business files.

  - Enable users to work on files offline and automatically sync changes when back online.
  - Applications that are tightly integrated with the Microsoft ecosystem, such as Microsoft Office Suite, often work seamlessly with SMB.

NFS:

- **Protocol:** It is a protocol commonly used by Unix and Linux systems for sharing files and directories over a network.
- **OS Support:** NFS is primarily used in Unix and Linux environments.
- **Performance:** Known for its simplicity and efficiency, making it suitable for certain high-performance computing environments. Scalable and efficient for large file sizes and high concurrent access.
- **Authentication and Access Control:** Typically relies on network-level authentication (Ex: Kerberos, or AUTH_SYS with client IP addresses). Granular access control requires additional configuration, often using Kerberos or NFSv4 ACLs.
- **Version Support:** Azure Files supports NFS version 4.1.
- **Use Cases:**
  - Ideal for building and deploying containerized applications and microservices in the cloud.
  - High-performance media streaming include video, audio, or other multimedia content from Azure Files shares.
  - NFS facilitates automated deployment and testing processes within DevOps pipelines, enabling continuous integration and continuous delivery (CI/CD) practices.
  - NFS is often chosen in high-performance computing environments for sharing data between nodes in a cluster.

37. Can you provide a quick recommendation for choosing between the SMB and NFS protocols in Azure Files Shares?

Ans:

- If your primary clients are Windows-based and you need tight integration with Entra/AD, SMB is the better choice.
- If you have a Linux/macOS environment, require high scalability and concurrency, or prefer cloud-native deployments, NFS is the better option. Also, NFS is the best option for the Workloads that require POSIX-compliant file shares, case sensitivity, or Unix style permissions (UID/GID).
- We can also consider hybrid deployments with both SMB and NFS shares within the same storage account to handle the diverse client needs.

38. Can NFS or SMB file shares be seamlessly mounted to Azure or on-premises VMs, similar to the way network drives are mounted?

Ans:

Yes, you can absolutely mount Azure file shares (SMB and NFS) to our VMs (Windows or Linux) in Azure or on-premises, just like mounting a network drive! This provides seamless access to your cloud storage as if it were locally available.

Explore:

Mounting process is almost similar for both:

- **Create an Azure File Share:** Select either SMB or NFS based on our client platform and specific needs.
- **Obtain Connection Details:** Navigate to Azure portal > File Share > Connect.
- **For SMB:**
    - Specify the desired drive letter (**Ex:** Z).
    - Choose the authentication method (Entra or storage account key).
    - The Azure portal provides a PowerShell script (**Ex:** New-PSDrive) to mount an SMB File Share on a Windows VM.
- **For NFS:**
    - Indicate your Linux distribution (**Ex:** Debian/Ubuntu).
    - Provide the intended mount path.
    - The Azure portal will then provide us with the Linux script (**Ex:** sudo mount) that we can run on our Linux VM to mount the NFS File Share.
- **Execute Mount Scripts:** Run the respective scripts on the appropriate VMs (Windows or Linux) to successfully mount the SMB or NFS file shares.

39. Any idea about SMB Multichannel and SMB Direct in Azure Files?

Ans:

SMB Multichannel and SMB Direct are two powerful features that can help improve the performance of Azure File Shares.

- **SMB Multichannel:** It enables an SMB client to establish multiple network connections to an SMB file share.
- **SMB Direct:** It allows SMB clients to use Remote Direct Memory Access (RDMA) network adapters for increased throughput and lower latency.

Explore:

SMB Multichannel:

- It allows an SMB client to establish multiple network connections to the same Azure file share, distributing I/O traffic across them.
- This leads to increased throughput and enhanced fault tolerance.
- It is enabled by default for premium file shares with no additional cost.
- **Ideal for:** Scenarios where you want to improve performance and fault tolerance, especially for applications with moderate I/O demands.

SMB Direct:

- It leverages RDMA (Remote Direct Memory Access) technology to bypass the traditional TCP/IP stack and send data directly between the client and server memory.
- This eliminates CPU overhead and network protocol processing, leading to Ultra-low latency and reduced CPU utilization.
- It may require specific hardware and software prerequisites on both client and server sides.
- **Ideal for:** High-performance workloads involving large files or intensive data transfer

40. What are the top 5 best practices for optimizing performance in Azure Storage?

Ans:

- **Choose the right:**
    - **Storage account type** (Standard, Premium)
    - **Data Access tier** (Hot, Cool, Archive)
    - **Blob Type** (Block, Append, Page)
    - **Configurations** (IOPS, SMB Multichannel and SMB Direct, Visibility Timeout Appropriately etc.)
- **File format:** Based on the data processing patterns (sequential, random, read/write optimized, etc.) Ex: csv, JSON, Parquet, Avro, ORC, etc.
- **File size:** Blob, File, Queue Message size etc.
- **Processing Approach:** Batch, item-level, Record-at-a-time, Message-at-a-time etc.
- **Data Compression:** Compress data on ingestion for reduced storage costs and network transfer bandwidth. **Ex:** Apply gzip compression to JSON files stored in Azure Blob Storage to reduce storage space and accelerate data transfer.
- **Data Caching:** Implement caching mechanisms to enhance data access performance. Ex: Azure CDN, Azure Cache for Redis, Azure File-Sync Caching feature, Managed Disk Caching feature etc.
- **Data Partitioning:** Organize data logically for efficient listing, filtering, & parallel processing. Ex: Hierarchical Namespace, choose a partition key in Azure Table Storage etc.

- **Always use the latest client libraries:** Update Azure Storage SDKs in our application to the latest version
- **Leverage Advanced features:** NetApp Files, Hierarchical Namespace, Premium Storage features, Disk bursting, stripping etc.
- **Data Indexing:** Enable Azure Blob Indexer (Applicable for Blobs, File Share, Tables and ADLS Gen 2). It helps us building a search capability using Azure AI Search.

Explore:

Azure Blob Storage:

- **Use Proper Storage Classes:** Choose the appropriate storage class and tier (Standard, Premium, or Hot/Cool/Archive) based on our access patterns and performance requirements.
- **Optimize object sizes:** Transfer larger objects (256 KiB+) for better throughput. Consider Azure Data Lake Storage gen2 for large datasets requiring high throughput.
- **Partition data strategically:** Partitioning improves query performance and distributes load across storage servers.
- **Parallelize Blob Operations:** Parallelize access to blobs by using multiple threads or processes, especially when dealing with a large number of small blobs.
- **Leverage caching:** Use Azure CDN for static content and Azure Cache for frequently accessed blob data.
- **Optimize client libraries:** Use the latest Azure Storage client libraries for optimized performance.
- **Azure Blob Storage lifecycle management policies:** Use it to automatically transition blobs to cooler or Archive storage tiers or delete them when they are no longer needed.

Azure File Share:

- **Choose the right storage account type:** Standard (HDD) for cost-sensitive scenarios, Premium (SSD) for high IOPS and low latency workloads.
- **Optimize file sizes:** Avoid small files (less than 64 KiB) for better performance.
- **Optimize Configurations:** Tune SMB/NFS settings like lease duration and directory caching based on our workload.
- **Leverage SMB Multichannel and SMB Direct:** Enable SMB Multichannel and SMB Direct for improved file access performance, especially in scenarios with high throughput requirements.
- **Use Azure File Sync – Caching feature:** We can use Azure File Sync (Cloud tiering feature) to cache and synchronize Azure Files shares on Windows Servers for local access.

Azure Queue Storage:

- **Optimize Message Size:** Choose the appropriate queue size based on expected message volume and processing time. The maximum size of a message is 64 KB, but it's recommended to keep messages smaller than 32 KB.

- **Use batching for efficiency:** Send and receive messages in batches for improved throughput and reduced overhead.
- **Optimize peek/dequeue operations:** Minimize the use of peek operations and prioritize dequeue for faster processing.
- **Leverage auto-scaling:** Enable queue metrics-driven autoscaling to handle variable workloads efficiently.
- **Utilize Azure Functions triggers:** Consider Azure Functions triggers for cost-effective queue message processing.
- **Set Visibility Timeout Appropriately:** It makes the message to become invisible after read for a specified period of time. Adjust the visibility timeout based on the time it takes to process messages to avoid unnecessary reprocessing.

Azure Table Storage:

- **Choose the Right Partition Key:** Choose partition and row keys that optimize query performance and data distribution.
- **Optimize Entity Design:** Design your entities efficiently, and avoid unnecessary properties to reduce storage and improve query performance.
- **Use Batch operations:** Perform batch inserts, updates, and deletes for better throughput and reduced latency.
- **Optimize filtering conditions:** Use efficient filters in queries to minimize data retrieval and improve query speed.
- **Leverage pre-filtering with Azure Functions:** Consider pre-filtering table data using Azure Functions for efficient downstream processing.
- **Utilize Azure Cosmos DB for scalability:** Migrate high-volume, globally distributed tables to Azure Cosmos DB for enhanced scalability.

Azure Managed Disks:

- **Choose the right disk type:** Standard HDD for cost-sensitive workloads, Premium SSD for high IOPS and low latency, Ultra SSD for extreme performance.
- **Optimize Disk Size and IOPS:** Choose an appropriate disk size and IOPS to avoid underutilization or overprovisioning, considering your application's storage needs.
- **Utilize caching mechanisms:** Enable Azure Cache for frequently accessed disk data for improved performance.
- **Monitor disk performance metrics:** Track metrics like IOPS, throughput, and latency to identify bottlenecks and optimize resource allocation.
- **Leverage advanced features:** Utilize Azure Disk bursting, stripping, caching, and Write Accelerator features to optimize the managed disk performance.

41. What are the various factors that may impact the cost of Azure Storage?

Ans:

All objects in a storage account are billed together as a group. Factors such as region, account type, storage type, tier, redundancy, transactions, and data transfers are the primary considerations that influence the overall cost of an Azure storage account.

Explore:

Below are the detailed factors that impact the cost:

- **Region:** Refers to the geographical region in which our storage account is created. **Ex:** East US, West US, etc.
- **Account Type:** Type of storage account. **Ex:** General-purpose v2, premium block blobs, etc.
- **Storage Type:** Type of storage we are using. **Ex:** Blob, File, Disk, Queue, Table, Data Lake.
- **Access Tier:** Hot, cool, or archive.
- **Capacity:** Storage account allotment or size we're using to store data. **Ex:** Volume of data stored per month.
- **Data Redundancy:** Determines how many copies of our data are maintained at one time and in what locations. **Ex:** LRS, ZRS, GRS, etc.
- **Transactions:** High transaction volumes can add up. **Ex:** Read and write operations, list requests, and other storage transactions.
- **Premium Features:** Certain features like geo-redundancy, advanced access control, managing shared access signatures (SAS), and advanced analytics incur additional costs.
- **Data Transfer**
    - **Ingress (Uploading):** Free for certain scenarios and limits, but otherwise charged based on GB transferred.
    - **Egress (Downloading):** Refers to any data transferred out of an Azure region. When the data in our storage account is accessed by an application that isn't running in the same region, we're charged for data egress. Always charged based on GB transferred, depending on the destination and data retrieval tier.
- **Monitoring and Logging:** Enabling Azure Storage Analytics for monitoring, logging, and metrics may involve additional costs.

42. What are the 5 most impactful cost-saving features in Azure Storage?

Ans:

- Organize data into access tiers.
- Regularly review and delete outdated data.
- Right-size the storage account for average workloads, not for the peak.
- Optimize data transfer costs.
- Utilize advanced cost-saving features, including auto-scaling.

Explore:

Storage Tier Optimization: Utilize the appropriate storage tier (Hot, Cool, or Archive) based on the frequency of data access to optimize costs.

- **Ex:** Move infrequently accessed data to the "Cool" or "Archive" storage tiers to benefit from lower storage costs.

Analyze and eliminate unused data: Regularly review and delete redundant or outdated data. Leverage tools like Azure Storage Lifecycle Management Policies for automated tiering and deletion based on access patterns.

- **Ex:** Set up a policy to automatically move blobs to a lower-cost storage tier or delete outdated data after a specified retention period.

Right-size our storage account and disks: Choose the appropriate storage account type and size.

- **Ex:** Choose Standard for general purpose needs and Premium and high throughput requirements and disk size based on our actual performance needs. Don't overprovision for peak scenarios, optimize for average usage.

Blob Size Optimization: Optimize blob sizes to reduce the number of transactions and storage costs.

- **Ex:** Consolidate small blobs into larger ones or use Azure Blob Storage's block blob append feature to efficiently append data to existing blobs.

Optimize data transfer costs: Utilize Azure Data Transfer options for cheaper inter-region data movement compared to standard egress charges.

- **Ex:** Choose the right option between Offline transfer using shippable devices (Azure Data Box, Data Disk etc.) or Network transfer (Data Pipeline, REST API etc.) based on the data volume, transfer frequency and the network bandwidth.

Leverage cost-saving features: Explore Azure Reservations, Compression, Caching features.

- **Ex:** We can save money by reserving capacity for Blob Storage, ADLS Gen 2 and Azure Files when we commit to one- or three-years reservation. Consider compressed formats to minimize transfer volume. Use Azure CDN or Azure caching to cache frequently accessed static content for reduced storage egress and improved user experience.

Monitoring and Auto-Scaling: Set up monitoring and auto-scaling to dynamically adjust resources based on demand, optimizing costs during periods of lower activity.

- **Ex:** Use Azure Monitor to track storage usage patterns, and configure auto-scaling policies to dynamically scale storage resources up or down as needed.

43. In your experience, what are the top challenges/problems encountered when working with Azure Blob Storage?

Ans:

In my experience, some top challenges when working with Azure Blob Storage include performance bottlenecks during data operations, occasional authentication and authorization issues, and the need to address data integrity concerns. Additionally, optimizing storage costs and efficiently managing large volumes of data have been common considerations.

Explore:

- **Authentication and Authorization Issues:** Check the access policies, shared access signatures (SAS), and ensure that the authentication credentials are valid. Use Azure Storage Explorer or Azure Portal to verify permissions.
- **Performance Bottlenecks:** Monitor Azure Storage Analytics metrics, use Azure Monitor, and analyze the storage account's performance metrics. Optimize the use of parallelism for multiple blob operations.
- **Data Corruption or Inconsistency:** Implement checksums or hashes when uploading data to Blob Storage. Regularly validate data integrity using these checksums. If the issue persists, contact Azure support.
- **Blob Not Found or Access Denied:** Verify the blob path, container name, and access permissions. Ensure that the blob is uploaded correctly, accidental deletion scenarios and that the container has the necessary permissions.
- **Network Connectivity Problems:** Use tools like Azure Storage Explorer or command-line tools to test connectivity. Check firewall settings and ensure that there are no issues with the network configuration.
- **Concurrency and Locking Issues:** Concurrent access or locking issues when multiple applications or users interact with blobs simultaneously. Implement proper synchronization mechanisms in our application. Use leases or optimistic concurrency control to manage concurrent access.
- **Storage Account Quotas Exceeded:** Review the storage account quotas and limits in the Azure Portal. Consider upgrading to a higher-tier storage account or optimizing storage usage.
- **Azure Service Outages:** Check the Azure status page for any ongoing issues. Subscribe to Azure Service Health alerts for proactive notifications about service incidents. If we have enabled the proper redundant feature, try to failover the storage account and operate it from the secondary region."
- **Insufficient Logging and Monitoring:** Enable Azure Storage Analytics and use Azure Monitor to collect and analyze logs and metrics. Implement logging in our application to capture relevant information during blob operations.
- **Engage Azure Support:** If issues persist, as a final step, engage Azure Support for assistance. Provide detailed information about the problem, including logs, metrics, and steps to reproduce.

44. As an Azure Data Engineer / DBA / Cloud Engineer, you likely encountered various challenges with Azure Blob Storage in your daily role. Could you please share insights into common issues, patterns in root cause analysis, and potential solutions based on your experience? Feel free to include an example if relevant.

Ans:

Heads up, while this answer may seem lengthy, understanding these scenarios provides valuable insights from real-life experiences.

Challenge 1 - Performance Issue:

Problem:

- Large volumes of policy documents causing slow upload/download times.
- Insurance claim processing delayed due to slow blob downloads during peak claim influx.

Root Cause Identification:

- **Monitor metrics:** Use Azure Monitor to analyze storage account metrics for high latency, throttling events. Here are the key metrics:
    - **Latency:**
        - **SuccessE2ELatency:** Measures the average time it takes to process a request, including network transit and server processing (Required processing time + Sending the response + Receiving acknowledgment.). High values indicate slow performance.
        - **Success Server Latency:** Focuses only on server processing time, excluding network latency. Spikes here point to server-side bottlenecks.
    - **Throughput:**
        - **Blob Read/Write Throughput:** Tracks the rate of data transferred during reads and writes, respectively. Lower values indicate potential throttling or limitations.
        - **Number of Requests:** Monitors the overall request volume to our storage account. Sudden spikes might overwhelm resources and contribute to slowdowns.
        - **Throttling Events:** Tracks instances where requests are throttled due to exceeding resource limits. Frequent throttling indicates under provisioning or unexpected demand.
- **Analyze logs:** Check for errors related to network bottlenecks, insufficient IOPS.
- **Profile client application:** Identify inefficient code causing slow downloads.

Possible Solutions:

- **Upgrade Storage Account:** Switch from Standard to Premium for higher IOPS.
- **Optimize Partitioning:** Spread download requests across multiple partitions.

- **Optimize Client Code:** Utilize asynchronous downloads, batch requests, efficient network libraries.
- **Use Azure CDN:** Use it for frequently accessed blobs.
- **Client-side Logging:** Implement application-level logging during blob operations.
- **Monitoring Alerts:** Add alert rules in the Azure portal that notify when any of the performance metrics fall below or exceed a threshold.

Ex: An insurance client experienced delays in processing claims due to slow access times for policy documents stored in Azure Blob Storage. After monitoring performance metrics, we identified that the high volume of concurrent access during peak hours is causing the slowdown. To address this, we implemented parallel processing for document retrieval and upgraded to a premium storage account tier, resulting in improved performance. As a long-term solution, we optimized the client-side code using asynchronous downloads and also added monitoring alerts.

Challenge 2 - Authentication and Authorization issues:

Problem:

- Incorrectly configured access policies leading to unauthorized access.
- Expired shared access signatures causing authentication failures.

Root Cause Identification:

- **Review SAS policies:** Check for overly permissive SAS tokens or expired ones granting access.
- **Monitor metrics and Audit access logs:** Check Active Directory (AD) logs and application logs for authentication failures. Monitor for suspicious access attempts targeting sensitive data. Herer are the key metrics and logs:
  - **Storage Account Requests:** Overall number of requests made to our storage account. Significant spikes or sudden drops could indicate suspicious activity or access attempts.
  - **Successful/Failed Requests:** A rise in failed requests, especially for authorization failures, suggests potential access control issues.
  - **API Operations:** Drill down into specific API operations like Put Blob, Get Blob, List Containers, etc. Analyze trends and identify unusual patterns in usage that might hint at unauthorized access attempts.
  - **Throttling Events:** Requests are throttled due to exceeding access limits could indicate misconfigured permissions or excessive legitimate activity requiring adjustment.
  - **Azure Monitor Logs:**
    - **Storage Insights Logs:** It provides detailed information about access attempts, including user agent, IP address, operation performed, and authorization outcome. Monitor for unauthorized attempts, failed logins, or unexpected access patterns from specific locations or users.

  - **Azure Activity Log:** Analyze events related to container or blob access attempts, particularly successful/failed attempts and changes to access control configurations. This helps identify who accessed what and any suspicious modifications to permissions.

- **Verify user roles and ACLs:** Ensure users have appropriate permissions for accessed containers/ blobs.

Possible Solutions:

- **Revoke over-privileged SAS tokens:** Generate new tokens with limited permissions and expiry.
- **Implement Microsoft Entra ID (Azure AD) authentication:** Enforce role-based access control for granular permissions and enable MFA (Multi-Factor Authentication).
- **Enable logging and alerts:** Set up alerts for suspicious access attempts and monitor access logs regularly.

Ex: An insurance company's claims processing application experienced intermittent failures when trying to access customer documents in Azure Blob Storage. After reviewing access policies, we discovered that an employee with outdated permissions is causing the issue. The solution involves updating access policies and ensuring proper role-based access control (RBAC) using Microsoft Entra for secure access.

Challenge 3 - Data Integrity or Inconsistency or Corruption issues:

Problem:

- Policy document corruption during upload, leading to inaccurate premium calculations.
- Inconsistent data due to concurrent writes without proper synchronization.
- Data corruption due to hardware failure, Data inconsistency due to network issues, and Data integrity issues due to software bugs.

Root Cause Identification:

- Monitor Metrics and logs for upload errors: Check for network glitches, storage service issues during upload. Use Azure Monitor and KQL queries to identify the issues. Here are the sample metrics and Logs:

  - **Blob Capacity:** Sudden drop in the capacity (size) could indicate that some data has been deleted or corrupted.
  - **Blob Count:** Unexpected sudden decreases, might indicate missing, deleted or corrupted data.
  - **Blob Download Latency**: Spikes could suggest network issues or potential data corruption causing slower reads.
  - **Blob Download Throttling:** Frequently throttled may indicate high demand or underlying issues impacting data access, potentially affecting data integrity.

- **Blob Download Success Rate:** A drop in this rate could suggest corrupted blobs causing download failures.
- **Blob Storage Errors:** Errors like “Blob data corrupted” or “CRC mismatch” are direct indicators of corruption.
- **Azure Monitor - Storage Insights Logs:** Analyze these logs for events related to blob deletions, overwrites, or unsuccessful operations. Unexpected deletions or corrupted blob edits might warrant further investigation.

- Compare downloaded data with source: Validate data consistency with the original policy documents.

Possible Solutions:

- Enable blob checksums (MD5/SHA256): Verify checksum mismatch between uploaded and downloaded data.
- Retry upload with checksum verification: Re-upload the policy document with proper checksum validation at both ends.
- Utilize blob versions: If enabled, roll back to a previous, known-good version of the document.
- Implement redundancy and backups: Ensure data backups are available for recovery in case of corruption.
- Other:
    - Implement proper synchronization mechanisms for concurrent writes.
    - Regularly validate data integrity through automated scripts.
    - Use client-side logging to capture errors during upload/download.

Ex: An insurance client stores customer contracts in Azure Blob Storage. They noticed discrepancies in the contract data during periodic integrity checks. Upon investigation, it is revealed that a bug in the application is causing partial data uploads. The solution involves fixing the bug, implementing checksum validation during uploads, and using versioning to revert to the last consistent state.

45. Do you have an understanding of what Control Plane and Data Plane operations are in Azure Storage?

Ans:

Control Plane Operations: It involves managing and configuring the Azure Blob Storage service itself. They define how we store and access our data but don’t involve the actual data transfer. Control plane operation requests are sent to the Azure Resource Manager URL.

- **Ex:** Creating or deleting storage accounts (Blob, File, Queue, Table, Data Lake), configuring access policies, and setting up Azure AD authentication etc.

Data Plane Operations: Data plane operations involve interacting with the actual data stored in Azure Storage. Data plane operation requests are sent to an endpoint that's specific to our storage account.

- **Ex:** Uploading and downloading files, reading and writing data to blobs, copying blobs between containers, enqueuing/dequeuing queue messages, Inserting/updating/deleting entities (rows) in Tables, etc.

46. Can you define what Blob Checksum is used for?

Ans:

Blob checksums in Azure Blob Storage act as digital fingerprints to verify data integrity during upload and download. Blob checksums refer to hash values generated from the content of a blob. These checksums are used to verify the integrity of the data during both storage and retrieval processes.

Benefits of Using Blob Checksums:

- **Early detection of data corruption:** Mismatched checksums instantly flag corrupted data for quick action.
- **Increased data reliability:** Add an extra layer of security for critical information especially during network transfers or long-term storage.

Explore:

Functionality: Blob Checksums are essentially cryptographic hash values calculated from the uploaded blob content. When we download the blob, its checksum is recalculated and compared to the stored one. If they match, we're assured the data hasn't been corrupted during transfer or storage.

Types of Blob Checksums: Azure Blob Storage supports two main checksum algorithms:

- **MD5 (Message Digest 5):** A widely used algorithm.
- **SHA256 (Secure Hash Algorithm 256):** A more secure algorithm for higher data integrity needs.

Enabling Blob Checksums: There are two ways to enable checksums for your blobs:

- **Client-side:**
  - Most Azure SDKs and tools allow setting the ContentMD5 header before uploading a blob. The SDK calculates the checksum and sends it with the upload request.
  - When downloading, the SDK recalculates the checksum and compares it to the stored one in the response headers.
- **Azure Blob Storage Service-side:**
  - Azure Blob Storage automatically calculates and stores the MD5 checksum for all blobs under 50 MB uploaded without a ContentMD5 header.

- We can access the stored checksum through the blob properties (x-ms-content-md5 header).

47. What are the different factors that may impact the price of a managed disk?

Ans:

The cost of Azure Managed Disks depends on several factors disk type, size, number of transactions, data redundancy option, snapshots, IOPS, throughput etc.

Explore:

- **Disk Type:** The type of disk you choose (Standard HDD, Standard SSD, Premium SSD, Ultra SSD) significantly impacts the price.
- **Disk Size:** You are charged for the entire capacity of the disk, regardless of actual storage usage.
- **Data Transactions:** A per-transaction fee applies for standard HDDs and standard SSDs (charged per 10,000 transactions). Premium SSDs do not incur this fee.
- **Data Redundancy:** The chosen redundancy option (Locally Redundant Storage (LRS), Zone Redundant Storage (ZRS), Geo-Redundant Storage (GRS), Read-Access Geographically Redundant Storage (RA-GRS), Geo-Zone Redundant Storage (GZRS), or Read-Access Geo-Zone Redundant Storage (RA-GZRS)) affects the price.
- **Other Options:** Additional features like IOPS (Input/Output Operations Per Second), throughput, snapshots, backup storage, saving options (Pay-As-You-Go or Reserved Instances), disk bursting, and shared disks can also influence the cost.

Ex: Here's a quick cost comparison for managed disks in the "East US 2" region using the LRS redundancy model, 1 TB size, and the Pay-As-You-Go billing option:

- Standard HDD: ~$41/month
- Standard SSD: ~$77/month
- Premium SSD: ~$135/month

Note: Ultra SSD pricing is based on per-hour, per-gigabyte charges for provisioned IOPS (like 5000 IOPS) and throughput (like 125 MB/s).

48. Is data encryption at rest and in transit enabled by default in Azure Storage?

Ans:

Absolutely! Azure Storage provides robust encryption for both data at rest and in transit by default. We can choose the level of encryption and key management (Microsoft managed or Customer managed) that best suits our needs.

Explore:

Encryption at rest:

- **Service-side encryption (SSE):**
- This is the default and recommended option.
- It automatically encrypts our data using 256-bit AES encryption, as soon as data is uploaded to Azure Blob storage or Azure File shares.
- Decryption happens automatically when we retrieve the data. This is transparent to our applications and requires no code changes.
- SSE supports encryption with Microsoft-managed keys (SSE with Microsoft-managed keys) or customer-managed keys (SSE with customer-managed keys using Azure Key Vault).

Encryption in transit:

- **HTTPS:** All communication between our application and Azure Storage endpoints occurs over HTTPS using TLS 1.2 or later, ensuring data confidentiality and integrity during transfer.
- **Azure Private Link:** For even stricter security, we can leverage Azure Private Link to establish a private connection between our on-premises network or Azure virtual network and Azure Storage. This bypasses the public internet altogether, minimizing the attack surface.

49. Is Azure Storage scalable? If so, what are its scalability features?

Ans:

Azure Storage is massively scalable, meaning it can effortlessly grow alongside our data needs, from gigabytes to petabytes and beyond!

Scalability features:

- **Petabyte-Scale Capacity:** Handle massive data lakes and demanding workloads with ease.
- **Elastic scaling:** Scale up or down instantly, no downtime needed.
- **Automatic load balancing:** Data flows smoothly even during peak loads.
- **Global reach:** Access our data from anywhere in the world. We can leverage storage redundancy, content delivery network etc.
- **Granular control:** Fine-tune storage for individual accounts, containers, and blobs.

50. What are the different methods for transferring data to and from Azure Storage?

Ans:

Transferring data to and from Azure Storage can be accomplished using various methods and tools including Azure Portal, Storage Explorer, CLI, PowerShell, REST API, AzCopy etc.

Explore:

- **Azure Portal:** We can use the Azure Portal to manually upload and download files to and from Azure Storage.
- **Azure Storage Explorer:** It is a graphical tool that allows us to manage our Azure Storage accounts.
- **Azure CLI (Command-Line Interface):** The Azure CLI provides commands for interacting with Azure services, including Storage. We can use commands like **az storage blob upload** and **az storage blob download** to transfer data from the command line.
- **Azure PowerShell:** Similar to Azure CLI, Azure PowerShell allows us to manage Azure resources through a scriptable command-line interface. We can use PowerShell cmdlets such as **New-AzStorageBlob** and **Get-AzStorageBlobContent** for data transfer.
- **AzCopy:** AzCopy is a command-line utility designed for high-performance data transfer to and from Azure Storage. It supports parallel transfers and can be useful for large-scale data migrations.
- **Azure Data Factory:** It is a cloud-based data integration service that allows us to create, schedule, and manage data pipelines. We can use it to automate the movement of data between on-premises and Azure Storage.
- **Azure Data Box / Azure Import/Export service:** For large-scale data transfer, Azure Data Box is a physical device that we can use to ship our data to Azure for initial seeding. We load our data onto the device and then ship it to Microsoft, where the data is uploaded to our Azure Blob Storage account.
- **Azure File Sync:** For seamless file synchronization between on-premises Windows Servers and Azure File Shares, utilize Azure File Sync. This keeps our local and cloud files in sync automatically.
- **BlobFuse2 (Opensource library / Program):** Using this we can mount an Azure Storage container to a Linux VM.
- **Mount Storage using NFS:** By enabling NFS 3.0 we can mount Azure Blob Storage container to a Linux VM.
- **Azure Storage SDKs (Software Development Kits):** Azure provides SDKs for various programming languages (Ex: .NET, Java, Python) that allows us to integrate Blob Storage operations directly into our applications.
- **Azure Storage Client Library for .NET:** A set of libraries provided by Microsoft that allows developers to interact with Azure Storage services using the .NET platform.
- **Azure Storage Data Movement Library:** A cross-platform (Windows, Linux, MacOS) open-source library that is designed for high performance uploading, downloading, and copying of blobs and files. Along with the basic upload/download operations, it provides additional and advanced features such as control the number of parallel operations, track transfer progress, easily resume a cancelled transfer, copy file from URL to Blob Storage and copy from Blob Storage to Blob Storage etc.

- **REST API:** Azure Blob Storage exposes a RESTful API that allows us to programmatically perform CRUD (Create, Read, Update, Delete) operations on our blobs. This can be useful if you are developing custom solutions or need to integrate with other systems.
- **SFTP (Secure File Transfer Protocol):** Securely transfer files from SFTP client to Azure Storage.
- **DistCp (Utility / Program):** Migrate data from Hadoop cluster to Azure Storage.

51. How does Azure Blob Storage handle concurrency (conflicting updates to blobs when multiple users access them simultaneously)?

Ans:

Imagine two users editing the same document at the same time. Concurrency models determine how Azure Storage handles such scenarios for our data, ensuring consistency and avoiding conflicts. Azure Storage supports three concurrency models:

- **Optimistic (Trusting Edits):** Ensures data consistency using ETags for version checks during updates.
- **Pessimistic (Acquires Lock):** Locks an object to prevent other users from updating the data.
- **Last Write Wins (Default):** Most recent update is accepted.

Explore:

Optimistic Concurrency:

- In optimistic concurrency, an application checks whether the data has changed since it was last read before performing an update.
- When reading data, the application retrieves an entity (such as a blob) along with an associated ETag (entity tag). The ETag represents the current version of the data.
- When updating the data, the application includes the ETag in the request.
- The storage service compares the provided ETag with the current ETag. If it matches, the update succeeds; otherwise, User is notified of the conflict.
- **Ex:**
    - Initial State: A blob contains a document with a ETag of version ID v1.
    - User U1 reads the blob and gets ETag with version v1.
    - User U2 reads the blob and gets ETag with version v1.
    - U1 updates the blob and sets the version to v2.
    - U2 attempts to update the blob. Before accepting the upload, Blob Storage checks the ETag version provided by U2 (ETag_v1) against the current version of the blob (v2). It sees that the version ID has changed to v2 and realizes that an update has occurred since they last read it. U2 must read the blob again and retry and merge their changes.

Pessimistic Concurrency:

- In pessimistic concurrency, an application explicitly locks an object (Ex: a blob) to prevent other users from updating it concurrently.
- Only one user can edit at a time, ensuring no conflicts but reducing concurrency.
- **Ex:** U2 will not be able to open the blob until U1 has finished making required changes and released the lock.

Last Writer Wins (Default):

- This method means the last update to the blob overwrites any previous updates, regardless of when they were initiated.
- It's typically used when data is partitioned (so multiple users don't access the same data simultaneously) or for short-lived data streams.
- **Ex:**
    - User U1 and User U2 both read the blob at the same time.
    - U1 updates the blob and saves changes.
    - U2 also updates the blob and saves changes after U1.
    - U2's changes overwrite U1's changes since U2 saved last.

52. Can you provide a comparison and differentiation between Azure Storage and alternative cloud storage solutions such as AWS S3 and Google Cloud Storage?

Ans:

Azure Storage, AWS S3, and Google Cloud Storage are all cloud storage solutions that offer similar functionalities (object storage, storage classes, durability, scalability, security, API and SDK supports etc.) but differ in pricing, features, performance, and integration.

- **Pricing:** The pricing structure of each service is different. Azure Storage offers a pay-as-you-go model, while AWS S3 and Google Cloud Storage offer tiered pricing models.
- **Features:** Each storage service has its own unique features. **Ex:** Azure Storage offers Blob storage, Table storage, Queue storage, File storage, Managed Disk, and Data Lake Storage. AWS offers Simple Storage Service (S3), Elastic Block Storage (EBS), and Elastic File System (EFS) etc. GCP offers Google Cloud Storage (GCS), Persistent Disk, File Store, etc.
- **Performance:** The performance of each service varies. **Ex:** Azure Storage offers high scalability and availability, while AWS S3 offers high durability and availability. Google Cloud Storage offers low latency and high throughput.
- **Integrations:** Azure Storage integrates well with other Azure services, tools and Microsoft products. AWS S3 has a large ecosystem and integrates well with wide range of third-party tools and services. Google Cloud Storage Integrates seamlessly with other Google Cloud services and AI and ML ecosystem.

CHAPTER 08

Azure Data Lake Storage

1. Can you define a Data Lake?

Ans:

- A data lake is a centralized repository for storing vast amounts of data in its raw, native format at any scale.
- It's designed to hold both structured and unstructured data, including tables, CSV, JSON, Parquet, log files, backups, social media data, and sensor data. This enables organizations to collect, store, and process large volumes of data from diverse sources in real time.
- Data lakes offer the flexibility to perform analytics and complex queries on data without prior structuring, simplifying access and usage for data scientists, analysts, and business users.

Explore:

Data Lake Background: The term "Data Lake" was first named in 2010 by James Dixon, the founder and CTO of Pentaho. Organizations are generating vast amounts of data from various sources. Structuring and organizing Big Data in a traditional Data Warehouse is practically impossible, especially from management and scaling perspectives. Rather than attempting to structure and organize all this data upfront, a data lake allows organizations to store raw data in its native format without the need for a predefined schema or data model.

2. What are the top benefits of a Data Lake?

Ans:

Below are the top benefits of a Data Lake:

- Scalability
- Flexibility
- Cost-effectiveness
- Faster data processing
- Centralized Data Governance
- Advanced Analytics

Explore:

Scalability:

- Decoupled storage and compute.
- Support for distributed storage and computing techniques.
- Cloud-based architecture, enabling easy capacity and storage expansion.
- **Ex:** A retail company can continuously add terabytes of sales data to their Data Lake without worrying about storage limits.

Flexibility:

- They require no pre-processing.
- A schema or pre-structure is not mandatory.
- Transformations can be applied on a usage or business-case basis.
- They support a variety of data formats, data types, and different data sources.
- They support a vast set of data processing (open-source and licensed) compute and language options for processing and analysing data.
- **Ex:** A healthcare provider can store patient records, medical images, and sensor data in various formats (Ex: CSV, JSON, Parquet, Image and video files) all in one place.

Cost-effectiveness:

- It doesn't require specialized hardware like high-end servers or premium storage arrays.
- Cloud-based options offer cost control through features like object storage, storage tiers (Hot, Cool, and Archive), and the pay-as-you-go model.
- There are no upfront schema design costs.
- **Ex:** A startup can store massive amounts of raw data in a Data Lake on cloud storage, paying only for what they use, rather than investing in expensive hardware or databases.

Faster Data Processing:

- It utilizes parallel processing and distributed computing across multiple nodes in a cluster.
- The schema-on-read approach eliminates the need for data transformations and schema modifications, reducing processing time.
- It offers flexibility and agility to easily add new data sources, types, and structures without extensive planning.
- **Ex:** A financial institution can quickly process and analyse streaming data from trading platforms in real-time using their Data Lake.

Centralized Data Governance:

- A data lake provides a central location for data management and governance. It allows organizations to manage data access, monitor data quality, and ensure compliance with regulatory requirements.

- **Ex:** An enterprise can enforce consistent data policies and security across all data types stored in their Data Lake, ensuring compliance with regulations.

Advanced Analytics:

- A data lake enables advanced analytics such as machine learning, Natural Language Processing (NLP), data mining, etc.
- **Ex:** A manufacturing company can apply machine learning algorithms directly on sensor data stored in the Data Lake to predict equipment failures.

3. What are the cloud-native data lake storage solutions offered by public cloud providers Azure, AWS, and GCP?

Ans:

- **Azure**: **ADLS (Azure Data Lake Storage) Gen 2** offers strong integration with Azure analytics services, hierarchical namespace, and fine-grained access control.
- **AWS**: **Amazon S3 (Simple Storage Service) with Lake Formation** provides scalable object storage, data cataloging, and extensive security features, making it ideal for setting up data lakes.
- **GCP**: **Google Cloud Storage** is a unified object storage service that supports data lakes. It offers high availability, durability, and security.

4. What is the difference between a Data Warehouse and Data Lake?

Ans:

Feature	**Data Warehouse**	**Data Lake**
Data Sources	Traditional sources (Databases, CRM, ERP systems)	Diverse Sources (Databases, IoT devices, weblogs, social media etc.)
Type of Data	Primarily Structured	Structured, Semi/Quasi, Unstructured
Schema	Predefined and enforced	Flexible, Schema-on-Read
Data Processing and Analysis	Batch processing, structured analysis	Batch, real-time, Machine Learning and Advanced analytics
Cost	Typically, higher	Lower, especially in cloud environment
Data Governance and Security	Offers more features and flexibility	More complex due to data variety

Feature	Data Warehouse	Data Lake
Flexibility	Limited by vendor specific tools	Supports a wide range of open-source and enterprise tools
Scalability	Scalable up to terabytes but costly	Highly scalable to Petabytes with lower costs

Table 8.1

5. Can you describe the architecture of Azure Data Lake Storage?

Ans:

Let's describe the architecture in a simple way, breaking it down into four parts:

- Designing a Data Lake Storage
- Data Ingestion
- Data Processing and Analytics
- Data Consumption

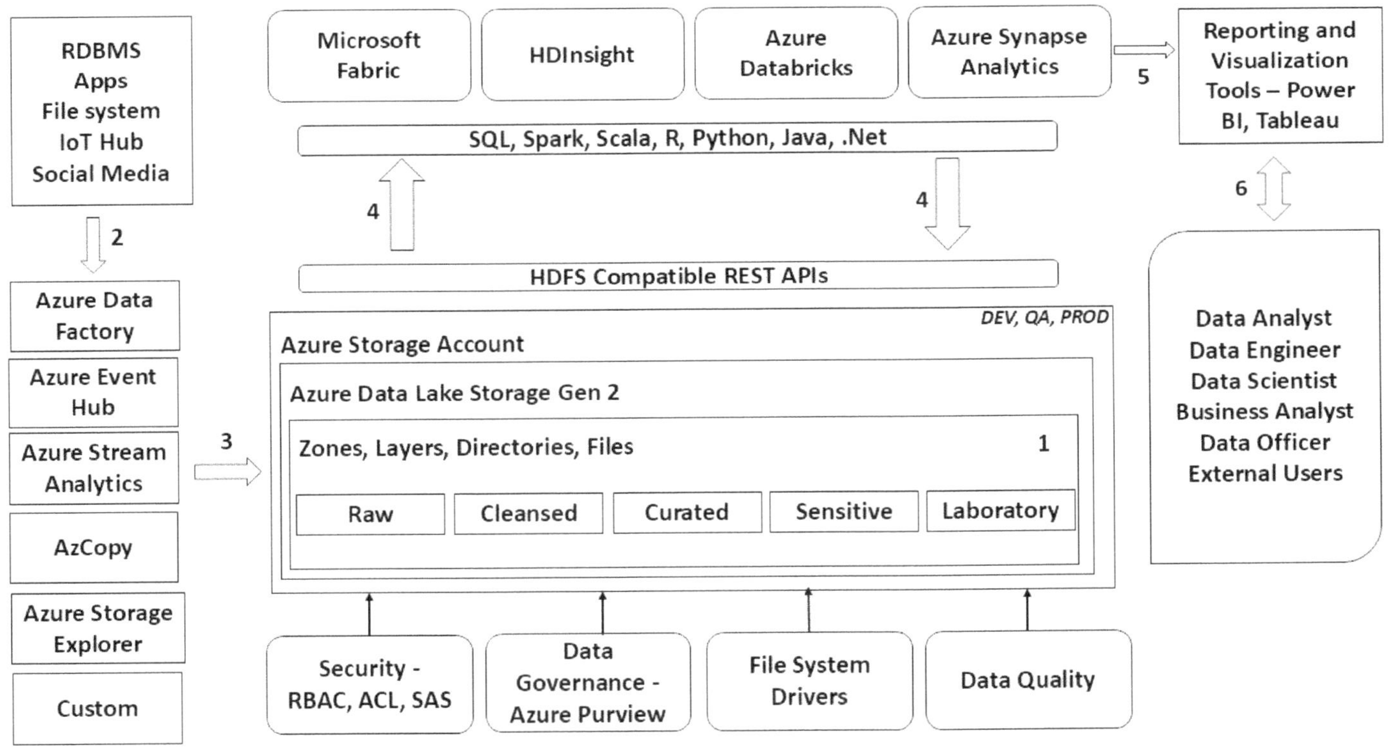

Image 8.1

Step 1: Designing the Data Lake Storage

- **Unlimited Storage:** ADLS is built on Azure Blob Storage, offering unlimited storage for various data formats and sizes.

- **HDFS-Inspired:** It adopts the Hadoop Distributed File System (HDFS) model for cloud-based storage.
- **Effective data lake design** is crucial for successful big data projects.
- **ADLS Gen2 supports hierarchical namespaces**, enabling folder-based organization similar to local file systems.
- **Folder Organization:** Folder structures can be organized based on data type (semi-structured, unstructured), data quality (Raw, Cleansed, aggregated, sensitive information, laboratory – exploration purpose, etc.), format (csv, JSON, Parquet, etc.), date (Year/Month/Date), or other relevant criteria.
- **Separate Environments:** Separate data lakes for development, testing, and production environments are recommended for security, disaster recovery, and scalability.
- **Implement robust authentication** and authorization using Role-Based Access Control (RBAC), Access Control Lists (ACLs), Microsoft Entra, and Shared Access Signatures (SAS).

Step 2 & 3: Data Ingestion

- **Data sources**:
  - **Source Types**: Applications, sensors, devices, etc.
  - **RDBMS**: SQL Server, MySQL, Oracle, PostgreSQL, etc.
  - **NoSQL**: MongoDB, Cosmos DB, Cassandra, Couchbase, Redis, HBase, etc.
  - **Streaming**: Kafka, Azure Stream Analytics, Azure Event Hub, etc.
  - **Location**: Azure, multi-cloud, on-premises, hybrid, etc.
- **Collect and Store Data in ADLS Gen 2:**
  - ADLS Gen 2 supports batch and real-time data ingestion from various sources using tools like Azure Data Factory, Azure Stream Analytics, and Azure Event Hubs.

Step 4: Data Processing and Analytics

- Process and analyze stored data to extract valuable insights.
- Utilize Azure services like Synapse Analytics, Databricks, HDInsight, and Microsoft Fabric Suit for data processing and advanced analytics.
- These tools support various processing frameworks (Hadoop, Spark, SQL, T-SQL) and analytics capabilities (machine learning, AI, predictive analytics).

Step 5 & 6: Data Consumption

- **Business Intelligence Tools:**
  - Processed data (ready for consumption) is typically stored in a **Gold/Curated Layer**.
  - The storage options include Azure Synapse Dedicated SQL Pool or Microsoft Fabric Synapse Data Warehouse, Azure Databricks Delta Lake, Azure Blob Storage/Data Lake Storage, or Cosmos DB based on data format, volume, and access patterns.

- Enable data virtualization using external tables for on-demand query access.
- You can integrate the Gold Layer with reporting tools like Power BI or Tableau.

- **Stakeholders:**
  - **Data Analysts and Data Scientists:** Use the service to run complex queries and gain insights.
  - **Application and Product Developers:** Build and maintain systems that use the processed data.
  - **Business and IT Leaders:** Utilize insights for strategic decisions and performance tracking.
  - **IT Administrators:** Manage access control, security, and resource monitoring.
  - **Partners and Third-Party Vendors:** May use Azure Data Lake as a data source for their tools.

Explore:

Additional Key points:

- **Azure ADLS Versions:** ADLS Gen2 is the current offering for data lake storage in Azure. The previous version, ADLS Gen1, was retired in February 2024.
- **Built on Azure Blob Storage:** ADLS Gen2 leverages the capabilities of Azure Blob Storage. This means you get features like diagnostic logging, access tiers, lifecycle management policies, data redundancy options, soft delete, and Azure monitor metrics.
- **Data Access:** Frameworks utilizing Apache HDFS can directly access ADLS Gen2 data through the ABFS (Azure Blob File System) driver. REST APIs are available through the dfs.core.windows.net endpoint.
- **Scalability:** ADLS Gen2 offers massive storage capacity. There are no limitations on account size, file size, or the total amount of data stored. Individual files can range from kilobytes (KBs) to petabytes (PBs).

6. What are the various security features offering by Azure Data Lake Gen 2?

Ans:

Azure is providing wide range of security features at various layers:

- **Authentication:** Entra ID, Managed Identity, Service Principle, SAS, Shared Access Key.
- **Authorization:** RBAC, ABAC, ACLs.
- **Network Security:** Firewalls, Private end point.
- **Data Protection:** Encrypt data at rest and transit.
- **Auditing and Monitoring:** Integration with Azure Security Centre and Azure Monitor.
- **Advanced Security:** Data Classification and ATP (Advanced Threat Protection).

Explore:

- **Authentication:** ADLS Gen2 supports following options:

- **Microsoft Entra ID - Managed Identity**: Provides a more secure and efficient way to grant access. Entra acts as the authorization server that issues access tokens using OAuth 2.0. It manages identities and enforces access policies.
- **Microsoft Entra ID - Service Principle:** Can be used if managed identities are not feasible. It is used for broader scenarios, including programmatical access, hybrid environments and external applications. scenario.
- **Shared Access Signature**: SAS – Give access only on specific data with specific operations and expiry date.
- **Shared Access Keys**: Super (Full control) user access.
- **Recommendation:**
    - **Managed Identity:** Ideal for production workloads.
    - **Service Principal:** Consider for programmatic access or external integrations when Managed Identity is not feasible.
    - **SAS:** Temporary and less sensitive access.
    - **Shared Key:** Avoid. High security risk.

- **Authorization:**
    - **Role-Based Access Control (RBAC):** It allows us to assign roles to users or groups to control access at the data lake level.
    - **Attribute-Based Access Control (ABAC):** Azure ABAC builds on Azure RBAC by adding role assignment conditions based on attributes in the context of specific actions. A role assignment condition is an additional check that you can optionally add to your role assignment.
    - **POSIX-like Access Control Lists (ACLs):** ACLs allow us to set permissions at the file and folder level.
- **Network Security:** We can configure network security using firewall, and private endpoints. Using these we can allow/deny access from a specific IP address or VNets.
    - **Firewall:** Firewall rules allow us to specify IP address ranges that are allowed or denied access to our data lake.
    - **Private endpoints for Azure Storage:** Network traffic between the clients on the VNet and the storage account traverses over the VNet and a private link on the Microsoft backbone network, eliminating exposure from the public internet.
- **Data Protection:** Azure Data Lake Storage Gen2 supports encryption at rest and in transit.
    - **Encryption at Transit:** Using HTTPS
    - **Encryption at rest:** Data is automatically encrypted by default. It supports Microsoft-managed keys or customer-managed keys.

- **Auditing and Monitoring:** ADLS Gen2 provides auditing and monitoring capabilities through Azure Monitor logs, which allow us to track activities such as data access and modifications, failed attempts to access resources, and changes to resource configurations.
- **Advanced Security:**
    - **Data Classification:** We can integrate ADLS Gen2 with Azure Purview to implement data classification. This allows us to label and classify data based on sensitivity and compliance requirements. This helps us track and manage data more effectively and ensures that sensitive data is properly protected.
    - **Advanced Threat Protection:** Microsoft provides an Azure-native service that utilizes advanced AI capabilities to monitor our Storage Account. Azure Defender for Storage, powered by Microsoft Threat Intelligence, alerts us on suspicious access patterns, suspicious activities (Ex: data extraction and permission changes), and malicious content of uploaded objects. When anomalies are detected, security alerts are triggered automatically in Azure Security Centre.

***Note:**

POSIX (Portable Operating System Interface) access control is a security mechanism used by many Unix-based operating systems to restrict access to files and directories. The permissions are divided into owner permissions, group permissions, and others permissions, and can be represented by numeric values or symbolic representations.

7. Have you ever participated in designing a Data Lake architecture? If so, could you please elaborate on the steps involved in designing a Data Lake architecture?

Ans:

Yes! I experienced in designing an Enterprise Data Lake Architecture for various Bigdata Projects. It involves a lot of factors, and careful considerations especially when we need to deal with strict regulatory compliance. However, I'll try to explain the steps in simple terms:

- **Identify the data sources and type of data:** Identify the various sources from where the data will be ingested into the data lake. **Ex:** RDBMS, NoSQL, File System, Object stores, Network shares, organization internal and external sources, web and mobile apps, social media, sensors, devices, and other applications. Also, assess the data format requirements such as structured, semi/quasi-structured, unstructured, etc.
- **Determine the data processing requirements:** Determine the types of data processing and analytics required. **Ex:** Batch, streaming, real-time, or near real-time processing. This will help determine the technologies required for processing.
- **Choose a storage platform:** Choose a storage platform that can scale to store large volumes of data, such as a distributed file system like Hadoop Distributed File System (HDFS) or cloud object storage like ADLS Gen 2.

- **Design Data Storage Layers:** Considering the security and performance aspects, we need to design our storage using a layered approach based on the data use case. **Ex:** Bronze, Silver, Gold layers. Also, define the directory structure, suitable file format (Parquet, ORC, Avro, CSV, Text etc.) based on data format requirements.
- **Define data organization and storage format:** Define the data organization and storage format to ensure easy access, management, and querying of the data. **Ex:** Use schema-on-read approach, where the schema is applied at the time of querying the data, rather than at the time of ingestion.
- **Define the business intelligence and reporting tools:** Choose the right technology for reporting, visualizing purpose. While choosing the reporting tools, we must consider the business case, data volume, feasibility, and integration between data storage, processing & Analytics tools and services.
- **Implement data governance and security:** Implement data governance policies to ensure the data is secure, consistent, and compliant with industry regulations. This includes data access control, data masking, data encryption, and other security measures.
- **Plan and implement data ingestion process:** Plan for data ingestion to ensure data is ingested efficiently and accurately, with appropriate validation and cleansing. This includes data validation, data transformation, data enrichment, and data quality checks. **Ex:** Determine the right technology such as Azure Data Factory, Synapse pipelines, Databricks, etc. and create the Data Pipeline jobs with an execution schedule.
- **Implement data processing and analytics:** Implement data processing and analytics to generate insights and value from the data. This includes implementing machine learning models, predictive analytics, and other advanced analytics techniques.
- **Monitor and maintain the data lake:** Monitor the data lake to ensure it is running smoothly, and perform regular maintenance activities, such as data backups, software upgrades, and performance tuning.

By following these steps, we can design a data lake architecture that is scalable, secure, and supports the requirements of an enterprise big data project.

8. What is the Medallion Architecture?

Ans:

The Medallion Architecture is a data design pattern used to logically organize data within a data Lakehouse. In an Enterprise Data Analytics world, "Bronze," "Silver," and "Gold" layers are used in data lake architectures to describe the different levels of data refinement and quality. This data design pattern is referred as the "Medallion Architecture." The Medallion Architecture, initiated by Databricks and subsequently adopted by Microsoft in their Fabric platform.

Medallion Architecture:

- **Bronze layer (Raw, unprocessed data):** This is the initial data layer where data is ingested into the data lake in its original form. It may include data from various sources and in different formats. We typically grant read-only access to the Bronze layer to enable data reproduction or regeneration, as we maintain the raw, original dataset in its entirety on this layer.
- **Silver layer (Cleansed, transformed, and structured data):** Data is cleaned, transformed, and structured on this layer for efficient processing and analysis. Metadata is often included to enhance data discoverability and understanding.
- **Gold layer (Enriched data):** Representing the highest level of refinement, this layer contains data further enriched with contextual information and advanced analytics. It is primarily used to derive high-value business insights and inform decision-making.
- **Optional layers:**
    - **Masked:** Stores masked or faked data generated by applying specific algorithms. This layer is primarily used for testing purposes.
    - **Sensitive:** Houses all Personally Identifiable Information (PII) and highly classified data. Access is restricted to specific users on a need-to-know basis.
    - **Laboratory or Sandbox:** Intended for advanced analysts and data scientists to conduct experiments, identify patterns, and correlations.

9. Consider the following use case and provide answers:

- **Imagine we are working with a health insurance customer.**
- **We receive both batch and streaming data from various data sources on a daily basis.**
- **Some data pipelines run on a scheduled basis, while others run continuously.**
- **We may receive member, policy, and claims data from various data sources.**
- **We need to build a data lake with bronze, silver, and gold layer architecture.**

Could you explain what kind of data is stored on each layer and possible use cases?

Ans:

High level Medallion Architecture in a Health Insurance Company:

Bronze Layer:

- **Data Source:** Raw data from various enterprise systems such as Electronic Health Records (EHR), claims processing systems, customer relationship management (CRM) systems, and external data providers (Ex: third-party healthcare data, government datasets).
- **Data Ingestion:** Data is ingested in its raw format, without any transformations or filtering. This might include batch processing for large datasets or real-time streaming for continuously generated data, using tools like Azure Data Factory, Azure Event Hubs, Kafka etc.

- **Expected Output/Storage:**
  - **Storage**: ADLS Gen 2 Bronze Layer Directory.
  - **Output:** The raw, unstructured or semi-structured data is stored in its original format, which can include CSV files, JSON files, XML files, log files, or even raw binary formats.
- **Sample Data:**
  - Claims data files with all fields, including potentially erroneous or redundant data.
  - EHR data in JSON format with patient details, diagnosis codes, and treatment records.
  - CRM data with customer interactions, including incomplete or duplicate records.

Silver Layer:

- **Data Source:** Data from the Bronze layer
- **Data Ingestion:** Data is processed, cleaned, and enriched. This might involve removing duplicates, correcting errors, joining related datasets, and applying business rules to create a more refined and structured dataset. Tools like Azure Data Factory, Azure Databricks, can be used for this purpose.
- **Expected Output/Storage:**
  - **Storage**: ADLS Gen 2 Silver Layer Directory, Data Warehouse like Azure Synapse Analytics.
  - **File Format:** When dealing with structured or semi-structured data, it's typically preferred to maintain a consistent format for all datasets stored on the Silver layer. This often involves converting file formats from Bronze (CSV, JSON, XML, Parquet, etc.) to a Parquet format on the Silver Layer. However, depending on the type of data and access needs, we may need to choose between Parquet, ORC, and AVRO file formats.
  - **Schema:** Similar datasets should be transformed to a central or unified schema. For example, member identification might be referred to as 'memid' in Salesforce, 'mid' in an operational system, and 'cust_id' at a vendor. Since data originates from diverse sources, these columns remain same (original format) on the Bronze Layer. However, on the Silver Layer, they are mapped to a central schema structure, such as (memid, cust_id, mid) >> MemberId. By establishing enterprise-level data dictionaries, this transformation can be automated through dynamic column mapping using programming languages.
  - **Common Data Layer:** Typically, the Silver Layer is referred to as the enterprise common data layer because it houses cleaned and standardized data, often involving schema mapping and unifying file formats. This approach facilitates data consumption by various stakeholders, including data engineers, data scientists, and data analysts, who can readily utilize this common data layer for subsequent processing.
  - **Output:** Structured and semi-structured data that is ready for deeper analysis but may still require further refinement for specific use cases.

- **Sample Data:**
    - Claims data with validated and cleaned fields, such as member ID, provider details, claim amounts, and service dates.
    - EHR data where patient records have been standardized and enriched with additional attributes (Ex: patient demographics).
    - CRM data where duplicate records have been resolved, and customer interactions are linked to unique customer IDs.

Gold Layer:

- **Data Source:** Data from the Silver Layer.
- **Data Ingestion:**
    - Data is further aggregated, transformed, and optimized for specific business intelligence and analytics use cases. This includes creating business-specific datasets, applying advanced analytics, and generating key performance indicators (KPIs) for reporting. Tools like Power BI, AWS QuickSight, or Google Data Studio are typically used.
    - Transformations depend on the business case. Stakeholders who utilize the Gold layer data for decision-making dictate the necessary operations or transformations to be applied to the data. Examples of these transformations include aggregations, normalization, data validation, creating new data from existing data, and applying mathematical or statistical functions to derive additional insights.
- **Expected Output/Storage:**
    - **Storage**: Data Warehouse (Azure Synapse Analytics, Azure Databricks Delta Lake), or ADLS Gen 2 Gold Layer.
    - **Reasons for Gold Layer on ADLS Gen 2:** Typically, gold layer or consumption-ready datasets are stored in a data warehouse. However, there are scenarios such as Data Virtualization, On-demand querying, or dealing semi-structured data, where storing gold layer data directly in ADLS Gen2 is necessary. **Ex:** ADLS allows the use of data virtualization techniques, where external tables (Ex: Synapse Serverless SQL Pool) can be created to query data directly from the data lake.
    - **Output:** Highly curated, business-ready data that is optimized for querying and analysis by business users, data scientists, and decision-makers.
- **Sample Data:**
    - Aggregated claims data by provider, member demographics, and service types, ready for analysis in claims dashboard.
    - Summarized EHR data, such as the number of patient visits by clinic and diagnosis type over a specific period.

- Customer lifetime value (CLV) metrics derived from CRM data, segmented by customer type, region, and product line.
- Other sample reports and dashboards may include member health risk scores, insurance provider performance metrics, claims volume dashboard, claim approval rate, network provider utilization report, cost analysis dashboard, claims fraud analysis dashboard, and financial performance report.

Connect Gold Layer to a Reporting Tool/Service:

- Configure connectivity (authentication, authorization, network, firewall, bandwidth, etc.) between a reporting, visualization, or self-service analytics tool (Power BI, Tableau, SAS, Google Looker, ThoughtSpot, etc.) and the Gold Layer (database, data warehouse, data lake, etc.).
- The BI team can develop the data model, apply additional calculations, create reports or dashboards, and finally review and publish the reports.
- This empowers end users (business analysts, leadership, customers, etc.) to make informed decisions.

This structured approach using the bronze, silver, and gold layers helps ensure that the data in your health insurance company is efficiently processed, stored, and made accessible in a way that meets the diverse needs of your business stakeholders.

10. What is your recommendation for designing a file/directory structure in an Enterprise Data Lake?

Ans:

It's essential to organize data in a way that makes it easy to locate and access. Below are some general recommendations:

- **Use a Hierarchical Structure:** Organize the directory structure by Domain > Sub-Domain > Project > Application, etc.
- **Apply Clear and Consistent Naming Conventions:** Ensure that names are intuitive and standardized across the Data Lake.
- **Organize Data by Subject Area or Data Type:** Group similar datasets at the same level, such as Sales, Customer, Year, Raw, Parquet, etc.
- **Consider Key Aspects:** Partitioning, file formats, security and access control, and environments (Ex: DEV, QA, PROD).
- **Document the File/Directory Structure:** Create documentation, such as a data dictionary, that describes the contents of each directory and provides instructions for accessing and using the data. This ensures that others can easily understand and utilize the data.

Explore:

In practice, enterprise data architects are influenced by various factors when designing a file/directory hierarchy in a Data Lake. For example, files might be stored in a YEAR > MONTH > DATE hierarchy. Other influencing factors include:

- **Data Ingestion Patterns:** Full, Incremental, Batch, Streaming, etc.
- **Security Scope:** Confidential, Restricted, Internal, Private, Public, Partners, etc.
- **Application-Specific Structure:** For example, App_ABC, App_XYZ.
- **Data Source:** SQL Server, MongoDB, MySQL, Teradata, etc.
- **File Format:** Parquet, CSV, Excel, Text, Avro, Orc, etc.
- **Subject Area:** Customer, Sales, Claims, etc.
- **Date and Time:** Year > Month > Date.
- **Region:** North America, Europe, Asia, etc.
- **Ownership:** Data Engineer, Business Analyst, Data Scientist, etc.
- **Retention Policies:** Temporary, Permanent, Time-Fixed, Archived, etc.
- **Data Impact:** Critical, High, Medium, Low.

A sample Directory Structure:

- ADLS Gen 2 Root
- >>ABC_Product
- >>>>Bronze
- >>>>>>Confidential
- >>>>>>>>SQL_DataSource
- >>>>>>>>>>Sales
- >>>>>>>>>>>>USA
- >>>>>>>>>>>>>>Year_2025
- >>>>>>>>>>>>>>>>Month_01
- >>>>>>>>>>>>>>>>>>Date_01
- >>>>>>>>>>>>>>>>>>>>Parquet
- >>>>>>>>>>>>>>>>>>>>>>01012025_1.parquet
- >>>>>>>>>>>>>>>>>>>>>>01012025_N.parquet

11. How do you create a Data Lake in Azure?

Ans:

If you're familiar with creating an Azure Storage Account, setting up a Data Lake is just an additional configuration step. To enable Data Lake Storage capabilities, simply select the "**Enable hierarchical namespace**" option under the Advanced tab on the Create Storage Account page.

Explore:

Here are the steps:

- Go to Azure Portal > Storage Accounts > Create > Fill all mandatory details. "Create Storage Account" page contains various tabs:
- **Basics:** Subscription, resource group, region, performance (Standard, Premium – Choose it for low latency / ADLS Gen 2), Premium type: Block blobs; redundancy (LRS, ZRS, GRS etc.) etc.
- **Advanced:** Security related (public access, storage account key, Require secure transfer (HTTPS) for REST API operations etc.); **Enable hierarchical namespace** – Enable it to use this storage account for ADLS Gen 2; SFTP; Cross tenant replication; Access Tier (Hot, Cool, Archive) etc.
- **Networking:** Network Access – Enable / Disable Public Access, Enable Public Access through a specific Virtual Networks and Ips etc.; End point type and routing preferences etc.
- **Data Protection:** Configure point-in-time restore for containers; Configure soft delete for blobs/ containers / file shares; Enable versioning for blobs; Enable blob change feed etc.
- **Encryption:** Encryption type (Microsoft managed Keys or Customer Managed Keys), Configure Infrastructure Encryption (when enabled, encrypts data at both service and infrastructure levels).
- **Tags:** Give some resource manager tabs based on our project, application and resource type.
- **Review + Create:** Review all configurations and create the storage account.

12. What are the options available for copying, moving, or uploading data into Azure Data Lake Storage?

Ans:

There are various options available for transferring data to Azure Storage and ADLS Gen 2. The right choice depends on factors such as business case, feasibility, performance, security, and cost.

Here are some common options:

- **Azure Storage Explorer (UI):** Drag and drop files.
- **Azure Portal (UI):** Upload/download using a browser.
- **Azure Data Factory (UI + Program):** ETL as a Service.
- **Azure CLI (Program):** A native command-line interface for interacting with Azure services.
- **Azure Storage SDKs (Program):** Program storage communication using SDKs like .NET, Java, or Python.
- **AzCopy (Tool/Program):** Migrate object data from on-premises to Azure.
- **SFTP (Secure File Transfer Protocol):** Securely transfer files from an SFTP client to Azure Storage.
- **DistCp (Utility/Program):** Migrate data from HDInsight/Hadoop cluster to Azure Storage.
- **BlobFuse2 (Open-source library/Program):** Mount an Azure Blob Storage Container or ADLS Gen 2 file system to a Linux VM.

- **Mount Storage using NFS:** Enable NFS 3.0 to mount an Azure Blob Storage container to a Linux VM.

Each option has its advantages and disadvantages. Based on my experience, Azure Storage Explorer, ADF, AzCopy, and Azure Storage SDKs are commonly used in many scenarios

Explore:

Know more about these options:

- **Azure Storage Explorer:** A free, cross-platform (Windows, macOS, and Linux), and open-source tool for managing Azure Storage accounts, including ADLS Gen2. Drag and drop files to upload them to ADLS Gen2. Work offline, customize with extensions, and handle multiple storage accounts with different subscriptions.
- **Azure Portal:** A web-based interface for managing Azure resources, including ADLS Gen2. Upload files and folders to ADLS Gen2 using the Azure Portal.
- **Azure Data Factory:** A cloud-based data integration service for copying data from various sources to ADLS Gen2 by creating a Data Pipeline.
- **Azure CLI:** A command-line interface for managing Azure resources, including ADLS Gen2, using commands. Use the "az storage blob upload-batch" command to upload files and folders to ADLS Gen2.
- **Azure Storage SDKs:** Interact with Azure Storage services, including ADLS Gen2, programmatically. Use the Azure Storage SDKs to write code that copies data to ADLS Gen2. Choose from .NET, Java, Python, JavaScript, or REST SDKs.
- **AzCopy:**
  - A cross-platform (Windows, Linux, macOS) command-line utility for copying blobs or files to or from an Azure storage account.
  - Download the AzCopy executable, authorize it to access Azure Storage using Microsoft Entra or a SAS token, and start transferring data.
  - Supports Azure Storage, AWS S3, and Google Cloud Storage. Typically used for migrating object data from on-premises to Azure.
- **SFTP:**
  - Securely connect to the Blob Storage endpoint of an Azure Storage account using an SFTP client and upload/download files.
  - Install an SFTP Client on your local machine, connect to the Azure Storage account using the Power Shell sftp command (Storage_Account_Name.Local_User_Name@ storageaccountpath), and start downloading/uploading files.
- **DistCp (Distributed Copy):**
  - A Hadoop tool for efficiently copying data between Azure HDInsight/Hadoop clusters or from a Hadoop cluster to other file systems.

- Use cases of **DistCp** in Azure Storage include:
  - Migrating data between HDInsight clusters.
  - Migrating data from HDInsight cluster to Azure Storage.
  - Migrating data from on-premises Hadoop Clusters to Azure Storage using Data Factory DistCp mode.
  - Moving data between different stages (Ex: Raw - Cleansed) of a big data processing pipeline.
  - Copying/moving data from Azure Blob Storage to ADLS Gen2.
  - Creating backups of data stored in HDInsight clusters in Azure Storage archive layer.

- **Data Factory DistCp mode:**
  - It is a recommended approach for migrating data from an on-premises Hadoop cluster or Azure HDInsight Cluster to Azure storage (Blob Storage or ADLS Gen 2).
  - It maximizes the capacity of your existing Hadoop cluster. You can use DistCp for large inter-cluster or intra-cluster copying. DistCp uses MapReduce to affect its distribution, error handling and recovery, and reporting.
  - Each task copies a file partition that's specified in the source list. You can use Data Factory integrated with DistCp to build pipelines to fully utilize your network bandwidth, storage IOPS, and bandwidth to maximize data movement throughput for your environment.

- **BlobFuse2:**
  - A virtual file system driver for Azure Blob Storage. Access existing Azure block blob data through the Linux file system.
  - An open-source project that uses the libfuse opensource library (fuse3) to communicate with the Linux FUSE kernel module.
  - Mount Azure Blob Storage Container or ADLS Gen2 file system on Linux and start reading/ writing data between the Linux system and Azure Storage account.

- **Mount Storage by NFS:**
  - Mount a container in Azure Blob Storage from a Linux-based Azure virtual machine (VM) or an on-premises Linux system using the Network File System (NFS) 3.0 protocol.
  - The NFS 3.0 protocol is best suited for high throughput, high scale, read-heavy workloads like media processing, risk simulations, and genomics sequencing.
  - To mount a Blob container using NFS, create an Azure Virtual Network (VNet), configure network security, create and configure a storage account that accepts traffic only from the VNet, create a container in the storage account, mount the container in the Linux VM, and start uploading/downloading data.
  - NFS 3.0 protocol uses ports 111 and 2048. Ensure your client allows outgoing communication through these ports if connecting from an on-premises network.

- **Other Ways through Integrations:** Integrate ADLS Gen2 with Synapse or Databricks to communicate (read/write) with ADLS.

13. What is the query acceleration feature in Azure Data Lake Storage?

Ans:

- It is an optimization feature of Azure Storage.
- It is a powerful capability that allows users to perform efficient, server-side filtering and transformation of data. This feature helps to reduce the amount of data that needs to be transferred over the network, improving performance and reducing costs associated with data processing.
- While the query acceleration feature incurs additional costs, it can significantly reduce overall costs when dealing with large datasets.

Explore:

As you know, data from ADLS Gen 2 can be processed and analysed in various ways. You can directly mount ADLS Gen 2 and perform data processing and analysis using Synapse Analytics and Databricks. Alternatively, you can run queries directly on ADLS Gen 2 using Azure Data Explorer, Azure CLI, or Azure Storage SDKs. You can install Visual Studio Code on your local machine, connect to ADLS Gen 2, and run your .NET/Python programs to analyze data.

Here's how the Query Acceleration feature works:

- **Enable this feature using the Azure CLI command:** az storage account blob-service-properties update --account-name <your-storage-account-name> --enable-query-acceleration true
- **Without Query Acceleration**: When running a query on a CSV file, the entire file is read from the ADLS Gen 2 container, regardless of query predicates. This unnecessarily incurs additional network and compute costs.
- **With Query Acceleration enabled**: Rows and columns are filtered (Server-side data processing) at the time data is read from disk. Only the relevant data is transferred over the network to the application, reducing network latency and compute costs.
- **File-Format Support:** Query Acceleration supports CSV and JSON formatted data as input to each request.
- **Cost:**
  - It's important to note that the Query Acceleration feature incurs additional costs and requires proper planning and optimization to achieve desired performance improvements.
  - Before deciding to use this feature, compare the Query Acceleration feature cost impact with the network and compute costs to choose the right option.
  - If you're dealing with large datasets and frequently reading subsets (row and column filters) of data, enabling query acceleration can save costs.

- This feature is not limited to ADLS Gen 2 and also works for data stored on Blob Storage.

14. What do you know about Azure Data Lake Analytics (ADLA)?

Ans:

Azure Data Lake Analytics (ADLA) is a scalable, on-demand big data analytics service built on Apache Hadoop YARN. ADLA can process big data (terabytes to petabytes of data) jobs in seconds. It offers USQL as a native programming language, which is a combination of "Schema-on-read + SQL + C#".

Retirement:

- Azure Data Lake Analytics service was retired in February 2024.
- Due to ADLA's retirement, customers must migrate their workloads to other services like Azure Synapse Analytics or Azure Databricks.
- Existing U-SQL scripts can be rewritten using T-SQL, PySpark, or Scala, depending on the specific use case.

15. What are the key factors that affect the pricing of Azure Data Lake Storage?

Ans:

Azure Data Lake Storage (ADLS) Gen 2 pricing is influenced by several factors:

- **Service Level:**
    - **Standard:** Suitable for general-purpose workloads.
    - **Premium:** Optimized for low-latency big data analytics.
- **Storage Capacity:** Ex: 50 TB per month, 500 TB per month etc.
    - **Data Storage:** Charged based on the amount of data stored.
    - **Capacity Reservations:** Discounted pricing for long-term storage commitments.
- **Data Access and Transactions:** Charges apply based on the amount of data processed and accessed. This includes costs for read/write operations, iterative read/write operations, data transfers, indexing, etc. For example, pricing might be quoted for 10,000 transactions, assuming each transaction deals with at least 4 MB of data.
- **File Structure (Hierarchical vs. Flat):** Storage costs are the same, but hierarchical namespaces incur additional metadata management fees.
- **Data Redundancy**: Costs increase (LRS, ZRS, GRS, RA-GRS, GZRS) with the level of redundancy, as maintaining multiple copies across zones and regions requires more resources.
- **Data Retention**: Charges are based on how long data is retained. Longer retention periods will result in higher monthly bills.
- **Data Access Tiers:** Pricing varies by access tier (Hot, Cool, Cold and Archive).

- **Cool, Cold and Archive Early Deletion**: Data moved to the Archive tier must remain there for at least 180 days, data in the Cool tier must stay for at least 30 days, and data in the Cold tier must stay for at least 90 days. Moving data back to the Hot tier or deleting it early may incur additional prorated charges.

Explore:

Let's suppose the following ADLS Gen 2 configurations:

- Storage: 50 TB
- File Structure: Hierarchical
- Data Redundancy: GRS

Below is the rate card for monthly charges:

- Hot Tier: $0.043 per GB
- Cool: $0.034 per GB
- Cold: $0.0081 per GB
- Archive: $0.003 per GB

Additionally, there will be separate charges for read/write operations, iterative read/write operations, query acceleration features (data scanned/data returned), metadata storage like index storage, etc.

16. How do you monitor Azure Data Lake Gen 2 storage?

Ans:

Azure Monitor is the native centralized monitoring and alerting service in Azure. It is fully integrated with Azure services, including Azure Storage. To monitor Azure Data Lake Storage Gen 2, follow these steps:

- **Enable Diagnostic Settings**: Configure diagnostic settings to collect the required metrics and logs, and store them in a chosen destination (such as a storage account, Log Analytics workspace, or Event Hub).
- **Analyze Metrics**: Use Azure Monitor or the ADLS Gen 2 Monitor tab to start analyzing the collected metrics.
- **Analyze Logs**: Use Azure Log Analytics with Kusto Query Language (KQL) to analyze logs. Navigate to the ADLS Gen 2 > Logs tab > Query Editor, and run KQL queries to analyze the logs.
- **Set Alerts**: Configure alerts to monitor specific conditions and send notifications when those conditions are met, ensuring proactive monitoring of the storage environment.

17. Can you describe step-by-step process to enable and analyze metrics and logs for ADLS Gen 2?

Ans.

Monitoring ADLS Gen 2:

Platform Metrics and Activity Logs:

- These are collected and stored automatically by default.
- Can be routed to other locations using a diagnostic setting.
    - **Platform Metrics:**
        - Measure performance, availability, and utilization.
        - **Ex:** request rates, success rates, error rates, data transfer rates.
        - Useful for monitoring performance and optimizing ADLS Gen 2 storage.
    - **Activity Log:**
        - Records activities performed on the storage account.
        - **Ex:** resource creation, updates, deletions, access control changes.
        - Useful for monitoring security, compliance, auditing, and troubleshooting.

Resource Logs:

- Resource logs are not collected and stored until you create a diagnostic setting and route them to one or more locations.
- Contain information about operations performed on resources within the data lake. They include:
    - **Storage analytics logs**: Information on data ingress and egress, read and write operations, and storage capacity.
    - **Blob storage logs**: Details on blob creations, modifications, and deletions.
    - **Audit logs**: Information on file accesses and modifications, folder creations and deletions, and permission changes, among others.

Enabling Diagnostic Settings:

- Navigate to the Azure portal > Data Lake Storage Gen2 account > Monitoring section > Diagnostic settings.
- Click "Add diagnostic setting" and provide a name.
- Under "Logs," select the types of logs to collect (Ex: storage logs, file system logs, audit logs).
- Under "Metrics," select the metrics to collect.
- Choose a destination for logs and metrics (Log Analytics workspace, Event Hub, Azure Storage account).

- Configure additional settings (retention period, filter rules).
- Save the settings to enable the diagnostic setting.
- Once diagnostic settings are enabled, if there is enough activity on ADLS Gen 2, you should start seeing logs and metrics in the destination you selected.
- Use this information to monitor and troubleshoot your ADLS Gen 2 account.

Alerts:

- Under the Azure Monitor section, in the alerts tab, on the "New alert rule" page, you can configure alert conditions and actions.
    - **Ex:** You can set an alert to trigger when the total number of requests exceeds a certain threshold or when a storage account failover is initiated.
- Azure Monitor alerts proactively notify you when important conditions are found in your monitoring data. They allow you to identify and address issues in your system before your customers notice them. You can set alerts on metrics, logs, and the activity log.

Analyzing Metrics:

Once diagnostic settings are configured and ADLS Gen 2 metrics are being collected, you can monitor the metrics from the specific Azure resource (in this case, the ADLS Gen 2 account) or from a central location using Azure Monitor.

- In the ADLS Gen 2 storage account page, under the monitor section, you can view various insights, metrics, alerts, and recommendations.
- **Metrics and insights** are categorized into failures, performance, availability, capacity, etc., and you can view various KPIs and metrics, including availability percentage, transaction count, server latency, total requests, bytes read, bytes written, and more.
- You can filter by specified metrics and use the **time range picker** to select the time period for which you want to view the metrics data.
- Use the "**Chart options**" to customize the chart by selecting the chart type, aggregation, and other options.
- You can save the customized chart and **pin it to the dashboard**.

Analyzing Logs:

You can access resource logs as blobs in a storage account, as event data, or through Log Analytics queries. Here are the steps to analyze ADLS Gen 2 logs:

- Open the Azure portal > ADLS Gen 2 storage account > "Logs" tab.
- In the "Logs" blade, view the list of available logs for your storage account.
- Select the log that you want to analyze, such as "**StorageLogs**."
- After selecting the log, click on "**Query editor**" to open the Log Analytics Query Editor.

- Run **KQL** (Kusto Query Language) queries to filter, group, and aggregate the log data to gain insights into the performance, usage, and security of your storage account.
- You can also use the "**pre-built queries**" available in the "**Logs**" blade to quickly analyze common scenarios, such as identifying failed requests or suspicious activity.

Some common KQL queries:

- **Query 1: To list the top 10 operations that caused the most errors over the last seven days.**
    - StorageBlobLogs
    - | where TimeGenerated > ago(7d) and StatusText !contains "Success"
    - | summarize Count = count() by OperationName
    - | top 10 by Count desc
- **Query 2: To list the top 10 operations with the longest end-to-end latency (Long running) over the last 7 days.**
    - StorageBlobLogs
    - | where TimeGenerated > ago(7d)
    - | top 10 by DurationMs desc
    - | project TimeGenerated, OperationName, DurationMs, ServerLatencyMs, ClientLatencyMs = DurationMs - ServerLatencyMs
- **Query 3: To create a pie chart of operations used over the last seven days.**
    - StorageBlobLogs
    - | where TimeGenerated > ago(7d)
    - | summarize Count = count() by OperationName
    - | sort by Count desc
    - | render piechart

18. Can you tell me a few significant metrics to consider when monitoring health and performance of ADLS Gen 2?

Ans:

Some important metrics include total requests, bytes read/written, ingress/egress, and average response time etc.

Explore:

Below are the Common and significant Metrics of ADLS Gen 2:

- **Total requests:** Total number of requests made to the storage account. It includes both successful and failed requests.

- **Bytes read:** Total number of bytes read from the storage account.
- **Bytes written:** Total number of bytes written to the storage account.
- **Ingress:** The amount of data that is being ingressed into the storage account.
- **Egress:** The amount of data that is being egressed from the storage account.
- **Success rate:** Percentage of successful requests made to the storage account.
- **Availability:** Percentage of time that the storage account is available.
- **Average response time:** Average response time for requests made to the storage account.
- **Throttling errors:** Number of requests that are being throttled due to exceeding the account limits.
- **Server errors:** Number of requests that are resulting in server errors.
- **BlobCount:** The number of blob objects stored in the storage account.
- **ContainerCount:** The number of containers in the storage account.
- **SuccessE2ELatency:** The average end-to-end latency of successful requests made to a storage service or the specified API operation. This value includes the required processing time within Azure Storage to read the request, send the response, and receive acknowledgment of the response.

19. What are the most common challenges we may need to tackle with Data Lakes?

Ans:

Data Lakes are a popular way to store and manage Big Data, but they come with their own set of challenges. Here are the top challenges:

- **Data Reprocessing:** Broken pipelines cause data issues.
- **Data Quality:** Inconsistent data delays analysis.
- **Batch and Streaming:** Unifying batch and stream datasets is challenging.
- **Operations:** Data lakes are not optimized for updates/deletes.
- **Data Governance:** Consistent policies are difficult to establish.
- **Data Security:** Protecting sensitive data is crucial.
- **Performance:** Large datasets and inefficient queries can impact performance.

Explore:

- **Data Reprocessing:** Reprocessing missing or corrupted data due to a broken pipeline is a major issue. It requires significant time and effort to identify, delete, and reprocess the corrupted or missing data.
- **Data Quality:** Data lakes often store data from various sources, which may vary in quality. Ensuring data accuracy, completeness, and consistency can be difficult. For example, the same dataset might be pulled and stored in a data lake by different teams for different purposes, leading to duplicate datasets. Compared to structured data warehouses, updating data in a data lake can be more costly and complex.

- **Dealing with Batch and Streaming Data:** It is crucial to integrate and update both batch and streaming data consistently to ensure data reliability.
- **Bulk Updates, Merges, and Deletes:** Data lakes are optimized for inserting data but are not inherently designed for bulk update, merge, and delete operations. Specialized optimization techniques are required to handle Update/Merge/Delete operations efficiently.
- **Data Governance:** Data lakes pose a risk of creating data silos, where different teams or departments manage data in different ways. This can make establishing and enforcing proper data governance policies and procedures challenging.
- **Data Lineage and Metadata Management:** Tracking data origins, transformations, and usage is essential but challenging at scale.
- **Data Swamp:** Without proper organization and metadata management, a data lake can quickly turn into a "data swamp," where the data becomes difficult to find, understand, or use.
- **Data Security:** Data lakes can store sensitive information, making security a critical concern. Compared to data warehouses, data lakes may offer fewer built-in security features. Any breaches or unauthorized access can result in significant harm to the organization.
- **Data Lake Performance:** Data lakes can hold data ranging from kilobytes to petabytes, so optimizing the Data Lake query engine for performance at scale is essential. Common performance bottlenecks include:
    - **Data Ingestion Speed:** Loading large volumes of data quickly and efficiently can be difficult, especially when dealing with real-time data streams.
    - **Large Number of Small Files:** It's generally better to have a smaller number of large files rather than a large number of small files. A high number of small files can significantly impact data lake performance due to I/O throughput limitations. Merging and compacting smaller files into larger ones can improve performance.
    - **Query Performance:** Optimizing queries for efficient data retrieval can be challenging, particularly with unstructured data.
- **Cost Management:** Storing vast amounts of data can be expensive, necessitating cost-effective storage solutions and data lifecycle management. Without proper cost management strategies, organizations might face unexpectedly high operational costs, making the data lake solution less sustainable in the long term.

While data lakes offer many benefits, they also present significant challenges that organizations must address to get the most value out of their data.

Note: Many of these challenges can be mitigated by using a Data Lakehouse Architecture, which provide transactional capabilities (ACID properties) on data lakes.

20. Can you describe problems you've experienced using Azure Data Lake Gen 2?

Ans:

Common Issues:

- Unable to access the data lake.
- Timeout errors.
- Network, server, or forbidden errors.
- Service or tool-level issues.
- Performance issues.
- Soft-deleted folders and blobs not displaying correctly in the Azure Portal.
- Ability to access containers, folders, and blobs, but unable to copy files from ADLS Gen 2.

Possible Causes:

- **Transient failures**, such as network glitches or temporary connectivity loss.
- **Internal server errors** in ADLS Gen 2.
- **Network access is blocked**, either at the Azure Storage Account level or on the user side.
- **Insufficient user permissions**, Ex: read access is granted, but write access is denied.
- **High traffic** on the Azure Data Lake Gen 2 storage account.
- **Issues with reserved names:** Even with proper permissions, files with reserved names, such as Parquet files starting with a "." (dot) or containing "_metadata," may not be accessible because these names are used for internal purposes.
- **Using outdated versions** of tools or services, leading to support and compatibility issues.
- **Issues with rename:** Soft-deleted items not displaying correctly in the Azure Portal when the parent directory is renamed.

Resolutions:

- **Error Analysis:** Understand the error message, perform root cause analysis, and provide possible solutions. Based on the type of error, consider the following resolutions:
- **Retry:** In many cases, simply retrying the operation solves the problem. Ensure the client tool or service has retry functionality configured.
- **Network Access:** Check and enable network access. Add firewall rules at the Azure Storage Account level. Consider options like Private Endpoint and ExpressRoute while verifying access.
- **Permissions:** Grant the required permissions if insufficient permissions are the issue.
- **Access Keys:** Regenerate the access key if it has expired.
- **User-Side issues:** Validate and resolve issues on the end-user side, such as local/on-premises firewall blocks, proxies, or network interruptions.
- **Increase network bandwidth** to handle large datasets over the network efficiently.

- **Reduce Concurrency:** If increasing network bandwidth isn't an option, reduce concurrency. For example, in Azure Data Factory (ADF) Self-hosted Integration Runtime (IR), configure the number of concurrent jobs.
- **Update timeout configurations** on the client side. For example, in ADF Linked Service for ADLS Gen 2, adjust the "Connection timeout (seconds)" setting to handle large datasets. Similar adjustments may be needed in other client applications.
- **Regional consistency:** Ensure that both the source and target (ADLS Gen 2) are hosted in the same region. For instance, when creating an ADF Self-Hosted IR, make sure it's in the same region as ADLS Gen 2. Cross-region data transfers can lead to high latency and timeouts.
- **Avoid reserved names:** If facing issues due to reserved file names (such as "." or "_metadata"), change the file names to avoid reserved names.
- **Tool/service updates:** Check if you are using the latest versions of tools and services, such as AzCopy and Azure Storage Explorer. Always download and install the latest version of the software from the relevant Microsoft website.
- **soft-deleted items visibility issues:** If soft-deleted items are not visible in the Azure Portal due to renaming the parent directory, use PowerShell or Azure CLI to list and restore soft-deleted items properly.
- **Support:**
    - Contact your organizations internal cloud support teams for assistance.
    - If all else fails, raise a support case with Microsoft Azure Support for further help.

21. Have you ever worked with Azure Storage Explorer?

Ans:

Yes! Azure Storage Explorer is a standalone application from Microsoft that provides a graphical user interface (GUI) to manage and interact with Azure storage accounts. It allows users to easily access, view, upload, download, and manage data in various Azure storage services, including Azure Blob Storage, Azure Data Lake Storage Gen 2, Azure Files, Azure Queues and Azure Table storage.

22. What are some common scenarios for using Azure Storage Explorer?

Ans:

Azure Storage Explorer is like a file explorer for your cloud storage.

When to Use Azure Storage Explorer:

- **File Management:** Use it to upload, download, and manage files (blobs) in your Azure storage accounts. This includes copying, moving, renaming, and deleting files.
- **Data Access:** Access and explore the data stored in Azure Blob Storage or Azure Data Lake Storage in a user-friendly way without writing complex scripts or using the Azure portal.

- **Token Management:** Easily generate and manage Shared Access Signatures (SAS) tokens for secure, temporary access to storage resources.
- **Data Transfer and Migration:** Transfer data between your local machine and Azure storage or between different Azure storage accounts.
- **Debugging and Troubleshooting:** View and manage logs and diagnostic data stored in Azure storage, which can be helpful for debugging and troubleshooting applications.

Explore:

Azure Storage Explorer is one of the most frequently used tools because it allows us to easily access and manage our Azure Storage accounts from our local machines. Key features:

- **Easy access:** Connect to Azure storage accounts from your local machine. You can simply download the latest version (v1.35.0 as of October 2024), install it on your local machine, connect to an Azure Storage account, and start accessing and managing the storage account locally.
- **Platform support:** Works on Windows, macOS, Ubuntu, and other platforms.
- **Multiple connection methods:**
  - **Sign into Azure to access subscriptions and resources:** This allows us to see all storage accounts with their associated tree structures.
  - **Attach an individual Azure Storage resource to Storage Explorer:** For example, if you don't need access to the entire account but only to a specific container, this is the right approach. You can connect to a storage account, Blob container, Gen 2 container, Gen 2 directory, file share, storage queue, or table.
- **Access Types:**
  - **Shared Access Signature (SAS):** Connection string/URL that supports all types of Azure Storage resources, including Storage Accounts, Blobs, ADLS Gen 2, Files, Queues, and Tables.
  - **Microsoft Entra ID:** Supports all Azure Storage resources except Azure Files.
  - **Storage Account Key:** Used to access Storage Accounts.
  - **Public Access:** Supports Blob Storage and Data Lake Gen 2.
- **Diverse tasks:** Access and view data, edit data, upload/download files, set access policies, create/delete containers/directories, search/filter data, manage multiple accounts, generate SAS tokens, and more.
- **User friendly interface:** It is a popular tool among Azure cloud administrators, data engineers, and developers, as it makes managing and organizing Azure Storage resources easy.

23. What is the difference between Azure Blob Storage and Azure Data Lake Gen 2 Storage?

Ans:

Azure Blob Storage and Azure Data Lake Storage Gen 2 (ADLS Gen2) are both Azure services designed to store large amounts of unstructured data. However, they are optimized for different use cases and have distinct features:

Feature	**Azure Blob Storage**	**ADLS Gen 2**
Purpose	General purpose object store for storing unstructured data. Ex: Text, Binary, Images, Videos etc.	Optimized storage for Bigdata analytics and Machine Learning workloads.
Account Size limits	For standard storage account, per account max 5 PiB. We can create 250 storage accounts per region.	No limitations imposed and it is highly scalable.
Performance	Good	Better
Storage features	Scalability, durability, availability, redundancy, high security, cost-effectiveness, storage tiers (Hot, Cool, Cold, Archive), etc.	ADLS Gen 2 is built on top of Blob storage. Hence it supports Blob storage features + hierarchical namespace, fine-grained access controls, large file sizes, HDFS API's etc.
Structure	Flat namespace.	Hierarchical namespace (like file system).
***Cost**	Cheaper – Depends on various factors.	Slightly Higher - Depends on various factors.
***Use Cases**	Images, videos, backups, static content.	Big Data, advanced Data analytics, Data lakes, data warehousing, and machine learning workloads.

Table 8.2

Explore:

***Cost:** It depends on lots of factors includes, Storage capacity, storage tier (Hot, Cool, Cold, Archive), data transfer (ingress, egress), data access pattern etc. For example:

- **Blob Storage**: Costs are lower for long-term storage but higher for frequent access in certain tiers.
- **ADLS Gen 2:** While pricing is based on Azure Blob Storage, additional costs might be incurred due to the advanced features like hierarchical namespace and enhanced security options.

***Use Cases:**

- **Blob Storage:**
  - **Storing Unstructured Data:** Ideal for storing images and documents that need to be directly served to the browser via HTTPS.
  - **Content Distribution:** A great option for businesses that need to store and share data with clients or partners.
  - **Streaming:** Suitable for businesses with audio or video streaming requirements.
  - **Backups, Disaster Recovery, and Archiving:** Stores backups, logs, and other data for disaster recovery and archival purposes.
- **ADLS Gen 2:**
  - **Big Data Processing:** Optimized for quickly processing large amounts of data.
  - **Central Data Lake:** Enables the creation of a centralized enterprise data lake for storing large to very large datasets (structured and unstructured).
  - **Hadoop Compatibility:** ADLS Gen 2 is compatible with all major big data processing platforms, such as Azure HDInsight, Synapse Analytics, and Databricks.
  - **ML Workloads:** Supports building batch, interactive, streaming analytics, modern data warehouse, and machine learning solutions.

24. Can you tell me some of the features that work in Azure Blob Storage but don't work in ADLS Gen2?

Ans:

Since ADLS Gen2 is built on top of Blob Storage, it supports the majority of Blob Storage features. However, there are certain features that are not currently supported in ADLS Gen2. For example, Azure storage accounts with a hierarchical namespace enabled do not currently support blob versioning or the Blob Change Feed.

Note:

- Microsoft is actively working on adding new features and improving existing ones in ADLS Gen2. It's always recommended to check the latest Microsoft documentation for the most up-to-date information on feature support.
- For information on high availability, disaster recovery, security, and other general storage account features, please refer to the Azure Storage chapter.

25. How can we secure data in ADLS using access control lists (ACLs)? Or Can you explain how ACLs works in ADLS Gen 2?

Ans:

Azure Data Lake Storage Gen2 (ADLS Gen2) provides granular control over data access using Access Control Lists (ACLs). By assigning specific permissions to users, groups, or service principals, you can effectively safeguard your data.

Key Points:

- **POSIX-style Permissions:** ADLS Gen2 employs a POSIX-style permission model, granting read, write, and execute (a program or an executable file) privileges to the owner, group, and others.
- **Inheritance:** Permissions can be inherited from parent directories, simplifying management for large hierarchies.
- **Setting ACLs:** Use the Azure portal, Azure CLI, or PowerShell to set ACLs for files and folders.

Explore:

Let's suppose, you have an ADLS Gen2 file system with a directory structure for storing project files. You want to ensure that different users have the appropriate level of access to these files:

- **Data Engineering Managers** should have read and write access to all files and directories.
- **Data Engineers** should have read access to all files and directories.
- **Junior Developers** should only have read access to certain directories.

ADLS Gen 2 Directory Structure:

- /DEProjects
  - /projectABC
    - reportA.docx
    - dataA.csv
    - ETL_ScriptA.sql
    - DataPrepA.py
    - Sales_Data_2024
  - /projectDEF
    - reportB.docx
    - dataB.csv
    - ETL_ScriptB.sql
    - DataPrepB.py
    - Deploy_SQL.ps1
    - Promotional_Data_2024

ACL Step-by-Step Process:

- **Create Users and Groups in Microsoft Entra ID**:
  - **Data Engineering Managers** group: DEMGroup
  - **Data Engineers** group: DevDEGroup
  - **Junior Developers** group: JDGroup
  - **Specific users:**
    - Ram: A member of DEMGroup

- Alison: A member of DevDEGroup
- Charlie: A member of JDGroup

- **Set ACLs on the /DEprojects Directory**:
  - Navigate to the Data Lake Storage Gen2 account, and access the file system.
  - Use the Data Explorer to locate the /DEProjects directory.
  - Right-click on the /projects directory and select **Manage ACLs**.
- **Set the following ACLs:**
  - **Owner**: full access (rwx)
  - **DEMGroup**: read, write, and execute (rwx)
  - **DevDEGroup**: read and execute (r-x)
  - **JDGroup**: no access (---)
  - **Other**: no access (---)
- **Sample command using Azure CLI to set these ACLs:**
  - az storage fs access set --acl "user::rwx,group::r-x,other::---,default:user:DEMGroup:rwx, default:group:DevDEGroup:r-x,default:group:JDGroup:---" --path "/DEprojects" --account-name "<storage_account_name>" --auth-mode login
  - The default: keyword ensures that any new files or directories created under /DEprojects inherit these permissions automatically.
- **Set ACLs on Individual Directories or Files (if needed):**
  - For /DEProjects/projectABC, or /DEProjects/projectABC/DataPrepA.py, you might want to apply different ACLs if this file should have more restricted access. However, if inheritance from the directory level is sufficient, no additional settings are required.
- **Verify the ACLs**:
  - You can check the ACLs applied to a directory or file using the Azure CLI. Following command will display the current ACLs for the specified directory.
  - az storage fs access show --path "/DEProjects/projectABC" --account-name "<storage_account_name>" --auth-mode login

By setting the appropriate ACLs, you can ensure that users and groups have only the necessary permissions, following the principle of least privilege.

26. Can we use Role Based access Control (RBAC) and Access Control Lists (ACLs) together to control access in ADLS Gen2?

Ans:

Yes! By combining RBAC with ACLs, you can achieve a robust, scalable, and flexible access control strategy that meets the security and compliance needs of your organization.

- **RBAC (High level):** Grants permissions based on user roles.
- **ACLs (Granular level):** Granular control over permissions for individual files or folders.

Explore:

- **RBAC**: It provides a way to control access at a high level (Ex: storage account or container level) based on user roles (Ex: Storage Blob Data Contributor, Storage Blob Data Reader etc.), which is useful for managing broad access permissions and quickly assigning or revoking access.
- **ACLs:** It offers more granular control, allowing you to specify permissions at the file and directory level. They are essential for scenarios where you need to restrict access to specific files or directories beyond what RBAC roles allow.
    - After setting up RBAC, you can use ACLs to further refine access at the directory and file level. For example, within a directory, you might use ACLs to restrict access to sensitive files, allowing only specific users from a data engineers Entra group to modify certain documents, while others in the group have only read access.
    - ACLs can override the permissions granted by RBAC, adding another layer of control. Even if a user has broad access via RBAC, ACLs can limit access to specific files or directories.

27. What is the Blob Storage API, and why is it relevant for ADLS Gen2?

Ans:

- Azure offers various REST APIs that enables users to interact programmatically with Azure Storage. **Ex:** Azure Blob Service API, Azure Data Lake Gen 2 API, Queue Service API, Table Service API and File Service API.
- Blob Storage API and ADLS Gen 2 REST APIs have similar capabilities as ADLS Gen2 is built on top of Azure Blob storage.
- These APIs allows developers to perform various operations programmatically. **Ex:** creating, reading, updating, deleting containers, blobs, directories, files, and setting permissions etc.
- ADLS Gen2 API supports multiple authorization methods. **Ex:** Microsoft Entra ID, Shared Key, and shared access signature (SAS) authorization.

28. What are the top 5 best practices for optimizing Azure Data Lake Storage performance, cost, security and efficiency?

Ans:

Here are some best practices for Azure Data Lake Gen2:

- For critical workloads, consider using the premium tier of ADLS Gen 2.
- Select appropriate file formats and sizes based on business requirements.
- Optimize storage efficiency by leveraging data compression and partitioning.
- Enhance data security by utilizing Azure-provided features like RBAC, ABAC, ACL, and data encryption.
- Choose data redundancy options carefully.
- Leverage the hierarchical namespace of ADLS Gen 2 and adopt consistent naming conventions.
- Utilize query acceleration feature to speed up data processing while reducing compute costs.

Explore:

Optimize ADLS Scalability and Performance:

- **Consider Premium Tier for ADLS Gen 2:** It make sure that data is available through high performance hardware (SSD) which is optimized for low latency. The storage costs of premium performance are higher, but transaction costs are lower. ADLS Gen 2 Premium tier is ideal for big data analytics workloads that require low consistent latency and have a high number of transactions. **Ex:** Interactive workloads, IoT, streaming analytics, AI and ML etc.
- **Use Hierarchical Namespace**: Leverage the hierarchical namespace for organizing data into directories and subdirectories. This allows for faster access and better management of data.
- **Use the right File Formats:** Use optimized file formats like Parquet, AVRO and ORC. For feature engineering use Azure Data Factory and Synapse Analytics whereas for Data Science workloads use Azure Databricks.
  - **Choose Avro (Write Optimized):** Where your I/O patterns are more write heavy, or the query patterns favour retrieving multiple rows of records in their entirety. **Ex:** Avro works well with Event Hubs or Kafka that write multiple events/messages in succession.
  - **Choose Parquet & ORC (Read Optimized):** Parquet works well with "write-once, read-many" analytics workloads. ORC is suitable for read-heavy operations. ORC is optimized for Hive data, while Parquet is considerably more efficient for querying. With both ORC and Parquet, read transactions can be optimized to retrieve specific columns instead of reading the entire record.

- **Optimize File Size:**
  - Having too many small files can negatively affect the performance.
  - Organize your data into larger sized files for better performance Ex: Minimum file size is from 256 MB to 1 GB. Also, it influences the cost factor, as read write operations are billed in 4 Megabyte increments. Which means we are charged for operation whether or not the file contains 4 megabytes or only a few kilobytes.
  - Tools like Azure Data Factory or Apache Spark can be used to merge smaller files into larger ones, optimizing read and write performance.
- **Data Partitioning**: Organize data by partitioning it based on common query patterns, such as date ranges or geographic regions, to speed up query performance.
  - **Logical Partitioning**: You can partition data into directories based on various factors such as time (Ex: /year=2024/month=12/day=28), geography (Ex: /region=us-east), or other business-specific attributes. This logical partitioning allows for more efficient data retrieval, as processing engines (like Apache Spark, HDInsight, Synapse Analytics, or Databricks) can easily filter and read only the relevant partitions.
- **Data Compression:** Compress data when appropriate to save storage space and improve transfer speeds. By using compression (such as Gzip, Snappy, or LZO), you can reduce the size of data files. Compression can be applied when writing data to ADLS Gen2, and many big data processing frameworks natively support reading compressed data.
- **Query Acceleration:** A feature in ADLS Gen 2 significantly speeds up data retrieval by allowing applications to filter and project data at the storage level. This means that only the necessary data is transferred from the storage account to the processing environment, reducing network latency and compute costs

Cost Optimization:

- **Leverage Lifecycle Management Policies**: Use lifecycle management policies to automatically transition data to different tiers (hot, cool, archive) based on the frequency of access, thereby optimizing storage costs.
- **Avoid over-redundancy**: Choose the appropriate redundancy option (LRS, GRS, ZRS) based on your needs for data durability and availability.
- **Monitor and Analyze Usage**: Regularly monitor your storage usage and access patterns using Azure Monitor and Azure Storage Analytics to identify opportunities for cost savings. Also, configure alerts for capacity thresholds.

Security Best Practices:

- **Control Data Access:** Implement Role-Based Access Control (RBAC), Attribute-Based Access Control (ABAC) and Access Control Lists (ACLs) to control access to the data. Assign permissions at the container, directory, or file level depending on your security needs.

- **Use Managed Identities**: For secure and streamlined authentication, use managed identities for applications accessing data in the Data Lake.
- **Enable Azure Private Link**: Use Private Link to access Azure Data Lake Storage Gen2 over a private endpoint in your virtual network, preventing data exposure on the public internet.
- **Encrypt Data**: Ensure all data at rest is encrypted. Azure Data Lake Storage Gen2 supports automatic encryption with Microsoft-managed keys, or you can use your own keys (customer-managed keys).

Data Governance and Compliance:

- **Tag Resources**: Use resource tagging for easier management, billing, and cost allocation of data lake resources.
- **Implement Data Classification**: Classify data within the data lake based on sensitivity and regulatory requirements, and apply appropriate security measures.
- **Audit and Monitor Access**: Use Azure Monitor and Azure Policy to track and audit access to your data, ensuring compliance with internal and external regulations.

Other best practices:

- **Consistent Naming Conventions**: Establish and enforce consistent naming conventions for files, directories, and resources. This helps in managing, searching, and accessing data efficiently.
- **HADR - Use Geo-Redundant Storage**: For critical data, consider using geo-redundant storage (GRS) to ensure that data is replicated across different geographic regions.
- **Adopt an Azure-First approach:** Given your use of Azure Data Lake, prioritize Azure services over open-source or third-party tools whenever possible. This ensures seamless integration and reduces complexity.
- **Automate data management tasks:** Leverage ADLS Gen2 REST APIs or Azure PowerShell to streamline common operations like creating directories, uploading files, and managing permissions.

29. Imagine we are a large insurance company with a global customer base. If I request you to develop a Data Lake strategy for our organization, what key factors would you take into account, and how would you implement the strategy using Azure Data Lake Storage Gen2?

Ans:

To design a multi-region, globally distributed data lake using Azure Data Lake Storage Gen2 (ADLS Gen2) for a global insurance company, we must consider various aspects, including design patterns, data considerations, deployment strategies, data lake layers, and other key factors. Below, I'll outline a comprehensive approach to the given scenario:

Step 1. Data Lake Design Patterns:

- **Unified Data Lake (Single Storage Account):**
    - **Use Case:** Suitable for scenarios where data residency and compliance requirements are not strict, and the organization prefers centralized management.
    - **Pros:** Easier to manage and govern, lower complexity, and potentially lower costs.
    - **Cons:** May face latency issues and compliance challenges with data residency laws.
    - **Ex:** A centralized data lake stored in a single region, such as adls-central-globalinsurancelake. All data, regardless of the region, would be ingested, processed, and accessed from this central location.

- **Federated Data Lake (A Storage Account for Each Region):**
    - **Use Case:** Ideal for a global insurance company needing to comply with data residency laws and reduce data access latency. Data specific to a region is stored in that region's storage account.
    - **Pros:** Enhanced compliance with data jurisdiction/sovereignty laws, reduced latency for local data access, better disaster recovery, and region-specific optimizations.
    - **Cons:** Increased complexity in management, potential data silos, and higher costs.
    - **Ex:** Multiple regional storage accounts like adls-us-east-globalinsurancelake, adls-europe-north-globalinsurancelake, adls-asia-southeast-globalinsurancelake, where each storage account hosts data specific to that region.

Step 2. Data Consideration:

- **Data that can be shared globally across all regions:**
    - **Ex:** Global reference data, product definitions, standard pricing models, and risk assessment algorithms.
    - **Strategy:** Store this data in a central storage account and replicate it to regional storage accounts as needed using tools like Azure Data Factory (ADF) or Azure Synapse Pipelines.

- **Data that needs to be isolated to a region:**
    - **Ex:** Customer personal information (PII), local claims data, regional regulatory data.
    - **Strategy:** Store this data exclusively in regional storage accounts to comply with local data residency regulations. For example, US customer data would be stored in the adls-us-east-globalinsurancelake storage account.

Step 3. Deployment Strategies:

- **Active-Active:**
    - Both primary and secondary regions are active and capable of handling requests.

    - **Use Case:** Useful for achieving low-latency access and high availability. For example, critical global services such as fraud detection could operate from multiple regions.
    - **Ex:** Data replicated between adls-us-east-globalinsurancelake and adls-europe-north-globalinsurancelake, with both actively serving requests.

- **Active-Passive:**
    - One region is active, and another is on standby to take over in case of failure.
    - **Use Case:** Suitable for disaster recovery scenarios where cost savings are prioritized over low-latency access.
    - **Ex:** adls-us-east-globalinsurancelake as the primary active storage, with adls-us-west-globalinsurancelake as the passive backup.

- **Multi-Homed:**
    - Different data sets are actively served from different regions, with no real-time replication.
    - **Use Case:** When different regions manage distinct data sets, and there's minimal inter-region data access requirement.
    - **Ex:** North American data served from adls-us-east-globalinsurancelake, European data from adls-europe-north-globalinsurancelake, without constant replication between them.

Step 4. Data Lake Layers:

- **Bronze (Raw) Layer:** Stores raw, unprocessed data.
    - **Ex:** /bronze/us/east/customers/raw, where raw customer data ingested from the US East region is stored.

- **Silver (Curated) Layer:** Stores data that has been cleaned and conformed.
    - **Ex:** /silver/us/east/customers/curated, where customer data from the Bronze layer has been cleansed and transformed.

- **Gold (Enriched) Layer:** Contains data that has been enriched, aggregated, or combined with other data sources.
    - **Ex:** /gold/us/east/customers/enriched, storing enriched datasets ready for analytics and reporting. Alternatively, Gold data can be stored in Data Warehouse tables like Synapse dedicated SQL Pool.

- **Archive Layer:** For long-term storage of infrequently accessed data, typically to comply with regulatory retention requirements.
    - **Ex:** /archive/us/east/claims, where historical claims data is archived for compliance. We can leverage Azure storage access tiers (Hot, Cool, Cold and Archive) tiers.

- **Workspace/Sandbox/Lab:** Areas for data scientists and analysts to experiment with and develop models.
    - **Ex:** /workspace/us/east/experiments, where data scientists can perform their experiments.

Step 5. Design Data Lake Structure:

- **Hierarchical Namespace:**
    - ADLS Gen2 provides a hierarchical namespace that allows files to be organized into a folder and subfolder structure, similar to a traditional file system. This structure enables fine-grained access control, efficient file management, and faster performance for specific operations.
    - In the context of a global insurance company, the hierarchical namespace can organize data into logical partitions based on key attributes such as region, business domain, and data lifecycle stage (Bronze, Silver, Gold).

- **Directory Structure:**
    - The directory structure defines how data is organized within the data lake, influencing data management, accessibility, and analytics. It should reflect the logical organization of business operations and data use cases. Consider the following recommendations.
    - **Root Directory:** /insurance/ - Root folder containing all data for the insurance company.
    - **Subdirectories by Global or Regional Scope:** /global/, /region/, /archive/
    - **Global Data Directory:** /insurance/global/ - For storing globally relevant data such as corporate policies, standardized pricing models, or fraud detection algorithms.
    - **Regional Directories:** /insurance/region/us-east/, /insurance/region/europe-north/, /insurance/region/asia-southeast/ - For region-specific data such as local customer information, regional claims, and regulatory data.
    - **Data Lifecycle Stages:** Each region or global directory can further include subdirectories for different data lifecycle stages including /bronze/, /silver/, /gold/ etc.
    - **Ex:** /insurance/region/us-east/gold/policies/enriched_data_2024.parquet.

- **File Formats:**
    - Choosing the right file formats is crucial for optimizing storage, data processing, and compatibility with analytics tools. The choice should be driven by the nature of the data, use cases, and processing requirements. Ex:
        - **CSV** for raw data ingestion.
        - **Parquet** for optimized querying and storage efficiency.
        - **Avro** for schema evolution and streaming data.
        - **JSON** for semi-structured, flexible data handling.
        - **ORC** for performance-critical large datasets.

Step 6. Other Key Considerations:

- **Data Ingestion Strategy:**
  - Use Azure Data Factory, Azure Event Hubs, Spark Structure Streaming, or Azure IoT Hub for real-time data ingestion. Batch data can be ingested using scheduled ADF pipelines.
  - Regional ingestion endpoints ensure data enters the data lake closest to its source, minimizing latency.
- **Data Replication Strategy:**
  - Choose a replication strategy based on performance, availability, and cost requirements.
  - Leverage Azure Storage Data Redundancy features (LRS, ZRS, GRS etc.)
  - Use Azure Blob Storage Lifecycle Management for automated replication policies. Tools like ADF or custom scripts can replicate data across regions for active-active setups.
- **Distributed Data Processing:**
  - Utilize Azure Synapse Analytics, or Azure Databricks configured to run in each region for localized processing, minimizing data movement and latency.
- **Data Access Requirements:**
  - Define how users will access data, including tools, permissions, and security measures.
  - Implement Azure RBAC, ABAC and ACLs to control access. Sensitive data is isolated and accessible only by authorized personnel, enforcing the principle of least privilege.
- **Query Patterns:**
  - Analyze query patterns to optimize data storage and processing.
  - Consider partitioning and indexing for improved query performance.
  - Use Azure Databricks and Synapse Analytics for distributed querying, data virtualization, and ad-hoc analysis, ensuring queries are routed to the appropriate region to minimize latency.
- **Data Lake Management:**
  - Implement governance policies, data quality standards, and metadata management.
  - Implement Azure Data Lake management practices using Azure Purview for data cataloging, lineage tracking, and classification.
- **Data Lake Cost Management:**
  - Use Azure Cost Management and Azure Storage Lifecycle policies to manage storage costs. Implementing a tiered storage approach with Hot, Cool, Cold and Archive tiers can optimize costs.

- **Data Lake Monitoring:**
  - Use Azure Monitor, Azure Log Analytics, and Azure Security Center to monitor the health, performance, and security of the data lake. Set up alerts for anomalies or potential breaches.
- **Data Governance and Security:**
  - Implement data classification, encryption, access controls, and auditing.
  - Implement robust data governance practices using Azure Purview. Leverage platform native capabilities to ensure all data is encrypted at rest and in transit.
  - Use Azure Key Vault for managing encryption keys.
  - Regular audits and compliance checks should be performed.

By following this structured approach, a global insurance company can effectively design and manage a multi-region, globally distributed data lake using ADLS Gen2, ensuring compliance, performance, and scalability.

30. What is the role of ADLS Gen 2 in Synapse Analytics and Azure Databricks?

Ans:

Azure Data Lake Storage Gen2 (ADLS Gen2) is a scalable and secure storage service designed for handling large amounts of structured and unstructured data. It is commonly used as the underlying storage for big data analytics solutions across Azure services including Azure Synapse analytics, Azure Databricks, Azure HDInsight etc.

Explore:

Azure Synapse Analytics and ADLS Gen2:

- **Primary Data Store:** ADLS Gen 2 serves as the primary data storage layer for Synapse Analytics. You can store all your data, including structured, semi-structured, and unstructured data, in ADLS Gen 2.
- **Integration:** Synapse Analytics seamlessly integrates with ADLS Gen 2, providing a unified experience for managing and querying data across both platforms.

Azure Databricks and ADLS Gen2:

- **Primary Data Lake:** In Azure Databricks, ADLS Gen2 acts as the central repository for large-scale data. It is frequently used for storing raw data for ingestion, staging, and processing via Databricks' Apache Spark clusters.
- **Delta Lake Support:** ADLS Gen2 is often used with Delta Lake, a storage layer that brings ACID transactions to big data workloads, allowing Databricks to perform efficient reads/writes, updates, and data versioning.

- **Integration:** Databricks can mount ADLS Gen2 as a file system, allowing you to interact with the data directly in the Databricks workspace. Integration typically requires using OAuth 2.0 with a Service Principal to securely access ADLS Gen2.

Azure HDInsight and ADLS Gen2:

- **Data Storage:** ADLS Gen2 can be used as a Hadoop-compatible file system (HDFS) in HDInsight. It serves as the storage layer for big data clusters in HDInsight, such as Spark, Hadoop, or Hive clusters.
- **Integration:** HDInsight clusters can be configured to use ADLS Gen2 as their storage by specifying the ADLS Gen2 account in the cluster setup. The integration enables HDInsight to store and process data in ADLS Gen2 directly.

Note: Similarly, we can easily integrate ADLS Gen 2 with **most** data analytics tools and suites such as Azure Data Factory, Azure Machine Learning, Microsoft Fabric, Snowflake, Power BI, Tableau, Dremio, etc.

31. What are the different types of data that enterprises deal with?

Ans:

Based on their structure and characteristics, data can be primarily categorized into, Structured, Semi-Structured and Unstructured data.

Explore:

- **Structured data (Fully structured – Analysis is very easy):** RDBMS tables with rows and columns. Ex: Customer records, sales transactions etc.
- **Semi-structured data (Data has some structure – Analysis is easy):** CSV, Excel, Logs, XML, JSON, Parquet, Avro, ORC etc.
- **Quasi Structured (Data has some structure – Analysis is not easy):** Complex XML, JSON, Clickstream (user interactions with a website/app) data, Google search results, HTML documents, web server logs, etc.
- **Unstructured data (No pre-defined structure - Analysis is difficult):** emails, documents (word, pdf, ppt, plain text, html etc.), media (images, audio, video), social media posts, sensor data etc.
- **Binary data (Machine readable language):** Images, audio, and video files in their raw format, executable files (.dll, .exe), database files, Archive files (.ZIP .TAR), disk images (ISO, IMG), etc.

Note:

Differentiating between semi-structured and quasi-structured data can be challenging due to their overlapping characteristics.

    - **Semi-structured data** often has a basic schema or metadata, making it easier to parse and process.
    - **Quasi-structured data** has more irregular patterns and requires more complex analysis techniques.

- Binary data can be structured, semi-structured, or unstructured depending on how it's organized and interpreted. For instance, a structured database can be stored in a binary format, but the data within it is structured.

32. What are the most widely used file formats for data storage and processing in the field of data analytics?

Ans:

In the world of data and analytics, various file formats are used including csv, xml, Json, Parquet, AVRO, ORC, Delta Lake, Iceberg etc.

The choice of file format depends on factors such as the nature of the data, the desired level of efficiency, performance, and compatibility with analysis tools.

Explore:

Structured and Semi-Structured Data Formats:

- **CSV (Comma-Separated Values)**: A plain text format where data is separated by commas. Widely used for tabular data.
- **TSV (Tab-Separated Values):** Similar to CSV but uses tabs as separators, which can be more readable in certain cases.
- **XLS/XLSX**: Excel file formats used for spreadsheets. Supports both structured data and formulas.
- **XML (Extensible Markup Language)**: A more complex format that allows for hierarchical data structures and metadata.
- **JSON (JavaScript Object Notation)**: Lightweight, human-readable format used primarily for transmitting data between web services.
- **Avro**: A row-based binary serialization format, used in Hadoop ecosystems for big data.
- **Parquet**: A columnar storage format designed for efficient data analytics on large datasets (optimized for reading).
- **ORC (Optimized Row Columnar)**: Similar to Parquet, designed for optimized performance in Hadoop and Spark ecosystems.
- **YAML (YAML Ain't Markup Language)**: A human-readable data format often used for configuration files.
- **NDJSON (Newline-Delimited JSON)**: Each line is a separate JSON object, useful for streaming data.

Unstructured Data Formats:

- **Text (TXT)**: Plain text format, often used for unstructured data.
- **Log Files**: Unstructured records of system or application activity, often stored in plain text.
- **HTML (Hypertext Markup Language)**: A markup language used for web pages, containing both text and tags.

Big Data/Analytics Specific Formats:

These are used for optimized analytics and big data processing:

- **HDFS (Hadoop Distributed File System)**: Used in big data frameworks for distributed storage.
- **Delta Lake Format**: Used for managing large-scale data lakes with support for ACID transactions and time travel.
- **Iceberg**: An open table format optimized for analytic datasets, providing support for schema evolution and efficient querying.
- **Hudi (Hadoop Upserts, Deletes, and Inserts)**: A transactional data lake framework that provides ACID guarantees on large datasets. It allows efficient upserts, incremental data processing, and data versioning.

Image/Media Data Formats:

- **PNG, JPEG, GIF**: Image formats used for data such as graphs or visualizations.
- **MP4, AVI**: Common video formats.

33. Can you describe the file formats Parquet, ORC, and Avro?

Ans:

Parquet, ORC, and Avro are three popular file formats for storing and processing large datasets, especially in big data environments. Each format has distinct features and internal mechanisms for efficiently storing data.

- **Parquet (Columnar Storage):** Parquet was created to meet the needs of efficient storage and querying of large datasets in a columnar format. Traditional row-based storage formats (like CSV or JSON) were inefficient for analytic workloads where only specific columns of data were frequently queried.

    - **Origin:** Developed by Twitter and Cloudera in collaboration (in 2013), with contributions from the Apache Hadoop ecosystem.
    - **Suits:** Well-suited for analytics and scenarios where querying specific columns from large datasets is frequent (Ex: reporting or OLAP workloads).

- **ORC (Columnar Storage):** ORC (Optimized Row Columnar) was specifically designed for Apache Hive to address the inefficiencies in the RCFile (Record Columnar File) format, which was previously used by Hive for data storage.

- **Origin:** ORC was developed by Facebook (in 2013) and was later contributed to the Apache Hive project.
- **Suits:** Excellent for Hadoop-based workloads, optimized for heavy data processing, and provides strong compression and indexing for large datasets.

- **Avro (Row-based storage):** Avro was designed to solve issues with data serialization in Big Data applications, particularly within Hadoop. It was created to efficiently serialize data for transmission over the network or for storage.
    - **Origin:** Developed by Doug Cutting (creator of Apache Hadoop and Lucene – in 2009) and the Apache Software Foundation as part of the Apache Hadoop project.
    - **Suits:** Ideal for use cases involving data streaming, serialization, and schema evolution (Ex: Kafka pipelines or real-time data transport).

34. Can you explain how Parquet, ORC, and Avro file formats store data, their internal workings for optimal data storage, and their common use cases?

Ans:

Parquet: Parquet is a columnar storage format, designed for efficient querying and processing of large datasets. Here's how it works:

- **Columnar Storage**: Parquet stores data in a columnar format, meaning that data for each column is stored together rather than row-by-row. This allows for efficient compression and faster query performance, especially for analytic queries that only need to read certain columns.
- **Encoding**: Parquet uses various encoding techniques like dictionary encoding, run-length encoding (RLE), and delta encoding to reduce storage size and improve performance. These techniques optimize how data is stored within each column.
- **File Structure**:
    - **Row Groups**: Parquet files are divided into row groups, which consist of column chunks. Each row group contains data for a set of rows.
    - **Column Chunks**: Data for each column is stored in separate column chunks within a row group, allowing for efficient reads and writes.
    - **Page Structure**: Each column chunk is further divided into pages (data pages, dictionary pages, etc.), making data processing more granular.
- **Optimizations**:
    - **Efficient Compression**: Since data in each column typically shares similar values or types, Parquet can compress it more efficiently.
    - **Selective Reading**: Because of its columnar structure, Parquet enables "predicate pushdown," allowing queries to read only the required columns, reducing I/O and speeding up query execution.

- **Suits:** Parquet is ideal when you need efficient querying of specific columns in large datasets. It's well-suited for analytical workloads and big data environments where data is read often but not written frequently.
- **Ex:** A global insurance company stores policyholder claims data (Ex: claim ID, claim amount, customer ID, claim status) in Parquet format to analyze historical claim trends. Since analysts frequently run queries on specific columns (Ex: total claim amount by region), Parquet's columnar storage speeds up these operations by reading only the necessary columns.

ORC: Optimized Row Columnar (ORC) is another columnar storage format, specifically optimized for Hadoop workloads. Here's how it works:

- **Columnar Storage**: Like Parquet, ORC stores data in columns, which makes it efficient for analytical queries where only a few columns are accessed at a time.
- **Compression**: ORC supports advanced compression algorithms (like Zlib, Snappy, and LZO) and encodes data efficiently, using dictionary encoding, run-length encoding (RLE), and bit packing to reduce storage footprint.
- **File Structure**:
    - **Stripes**: ORC files are divided into large stripes (typically 64 MB or more). Each stripe contains rows of data stored as column chunks.
    - **Indexing**: ORC files contain built-in indexes for stripes, allowing for faster reads by skipping irrelevant data.
    - **Footer**: Each ORC file has a footer that contains metadata about the columns and indexes for easy access and faster data reading.
- **Optimizations**:
    - **Indexing**: ORC files have lightweight indexes at multiple levels (file, stripe, row) that allow queries to skip over irrelevant parts of the data, improving query performance.
    - **Predicate Pushdown**: Similar to Parquet, ORC allows for predicate pushdown, enabling queries to read only the necessary columns and data ranges.
    - **Efficient Compression**: ORC files are heavily compressed, often outperforming other formats in terms of compression ratios.
- **Suits:** ORC is like an advanced version of Parquet and it is highly optimized for read-heavy data warehousing environments where you need advanced compression, metadata, and indexing for fast query performance.
- **Ex:** A large insurance company stores underwriting data (Ex: risk factors, premium amounts, underwriting decision) in ORC format in their data warehouse. Since the company runs complex queries that involve aggregating and filtering data across multiple dimensions (Ex: premium calculation based on risk categories), ORC's compression and indexing features optimize query performance. Note: Underwriting - Assessing an individual or business's risk before issuing an insurance policy.

Avro: Avro is a row-based storage format that is commonly used for data serialization, especially for streaming applications and data transport. Here's how it works:

- **Row-Based Storage**: Avro stores data in row format, meaning that entire records (rows) are stored together. This format is efficient for use cases where all the fields of a record need to be read together, such as streaming or transactional workloads.
- **Schema Evolution**: Avro files are self-describing, meaning that each file includes a schema, allowing for schema evolution. This is especially useful when the structure of the data changes over time (e.g., adding or removing fields).
- **File Structure**:
    - **Header**: Avro files start with a header that contains the schema and metadata.
    - **Data Blocks**: After the header, data is stored in blocks, where each block contains multiple rows of data serialized according to the schema. These blocks are encoded using the same schema for all rows.
- **Optimizations**:
    - **Compact Storage**: Avro uses JSON or binary encoding for efficient data serialization, making it ideal for fast data serialization/deserialization.
    - **Schema-Based Compression**: Avro supports codec-based compression (e.g., Snappy, Deflate), which compresses blocks of data.
    - **Schema-Driven Parsing**: When reading Avro data, the schema helps parse and validate the data, ensuring compatibility between old and new data versions.
- **Suits:** Avro is best for data serialization, transport, and when there is a need for schema evolution. It's widely used in streaming applications and systems that require cross-platform data interchange.
- **Ex:** An insurance company uses Avro to stream customer policy updates (Ex: changes in coverage, adding new policies) from their customer management system to a central data processing platform. Since Avro efficiently serializes data and allows seamless schema evolution (Ex: adding new fields to the customer data), it's suitable for real-time data transmission.

35. Can you illustrate how data is stored in Parquet, ORC, and Avro formats using a sample dataset?

Ans:

Let's take a simple customer dataset with the following columns as an example:

CustomerID	**Name**	**Age**	**Country**
1001	Jaji	28	UK
1002	Alison	35	USA
1003	Hamsa	25	IND

Table 8.3

We'll now examine how this data would be stored in Parquet, Avro, and ORC.

Parquet: Data is stored column by column, optimizing for analytics. Compression is efficient, and queries for specific columns are fast.

- The data is split and stored column by column. Each column is stored in a separate contiguous block. Ex:
    - CustomerID: [1001, 1002, 1003]
    - Name: [Jaji, Alison, Hamsa]
    - Age: [28, 35, 25]
    - Country: [UK, USA, IND]
- **Benefits**:
    - Efficient for analytic queries that only need a subset of columns.
    - Great compression because similar data types are stored together.
    - Supports predicate pushdown: If you're querying customers only from the "USA," Parquet can skip scanning irrelevant columns (like Name or Age) at the file level itself.

ORC: Similar to Parquet in storing data by column, but with extra optimizations for query performance (such as metadata, statistics, and indexing). Great for large data warehouses with complex queries.

- Data is split into columns, but with additional compression and metadata to improve efficiency.
- ORC files contain built-in lightweight indexes for each column, so query performance is enhanced even further.
- For the given dataset, it stores data like this:
    - CustomerID: [1001, 1002, 1003]
    - Name: [Jaji, Alison, Hamsa]
    - Age: [28, 35, 25]
    - Country: [UK, USA, IND]
- **Benefits**:
    - ORC also stores statistics (like min/max values for numeric columns) and metadata for each column to improve query performance further.
    - Excellent compression and optimized for read-heavy workloads.
    - Supports predicate pushdown and stores indexing and statistics for each column, making it highly efficient for querying large datasets.
    - ORC often provides better compression than Parquet because it stores metadata and indexes that further reduce the amount of data read during queries.

Avro: Data is stored row by row, with schema evolution and serialization as key features. It is good for data streaming and transport but not optimized for columnar queries.

- Each record (row) is stored as a block, and each block contains multiple rows. It also stores the schema with the data. For the given dataset, it stores the entire row of each customer sequentially, like this:
    - Row 1: {CustomerID: 1001, Name: Jaji, Age: 28, Country: UK}
    - Row 2: {CustomerID: 1002, Name: Alison, Age: 35, Country: USA}
    - Row 3: {CustomerID: 1003, Name: Hamsa, Age: 25, Country: IND}
- **Benefits**:
    - Excellent for data serialization and schema evolution.
    - Cross-platform compatibility: Avro's schema is stored with the data, making it easy to read and write in different programming languages.
    - Fast for write operations because the entire row is written at once.

Note: Please note that the data storage structure explained above is a basic representation. The real storage architecture could be more complex, incorporating more information about data and metadata.

36. What are Apache Hudi, Delta Lake, and Apache Iceberg?

Ans:

Apache Hudi, Delta Lake, and Apache Iceberg are all open-source Data Lakehouse frameworks designed to address the challenges of managing large-scale, evolving datasets in modern data lakes. They provide efficient and reliable mechanisms for ingesting, updating, and querying data, making them suitable for various data-driven applications.

- **Apache Hudi:** Focuses on incremental data processing, supporting upserts and real-time processing, making it suitable for transactional data lakes.
- **Delta Lake:** Emphasizes ACID transactions, data reliability, and schema enforcement, making it a robust solution for managing both streaming and batch processes in Spark ecosystems.
- **Apache Iceberg:** Provides table-level management, optimized for cloud environments, with hidden partitioning and support for multiple query engines, making it highly versatile for multi-engine data lakes.

37. Could you elaborate on the capabilities and real-world scenarios where Apache Hudi, Delta Lake, and Apache Iceberg are commonly used?

Ans:

Apache Hudi:

- Apache Hudi (Hadoop Upserts Deletes and Incrementals) is a data management framework that supports incremental data processing. It enables streaming and batch workloads, focusing on managing data changes (insert, update, delete) in HDFS or cloud-based storage systems like Amazon S3.

- **Key Features**:
  - **Upserts and Delete Support**: Hudi supports upserts and deletes on large datasets, enabling efficient change-data-capture (CDC).
  - **Incremental Processing**: Allows reading data that has changed, enabling efficient incremental queries.
  - **Support for Transactions**: It brings ACID compliance to data lakes.
  - **Multiple Storage Modes**:
    - **Copy on Write (CoW)**: When data is updated, Hudi creates a new version of the file instead of modifying the existing one. This ensures data integrity and avoids concurrent write conflicts.
      - **Suits**: CoW is ideal for scenarios with low update frequency and read-heavy workloads, as it optimizes for fast query performance but incurs higher write costs.
    - **Merge on Read (MoR)**: In the Merge-On-Read storage type, updates and deletes are written to delta files (log files), and the base files are not immediately rewritten. During read operations, these delta files are merged with the base files on-the-fly to provide the latest view of the data.
      - **Suits**: MoR is suited for write-heavy and real-time processing scenarios where update frequency is high, as it allows faster writes and compacts data during reads.
  - **Data Versioning**: Hudi supports time travel, allowing users to query historical data versions.
- **History/Origin**:
  - Created by Uber in 2016 to handle real-time updates and efficient large-scale data management for analytical pipelines. It became an Apache top-level project in 2020.
- **Use Cases**:
  - Real-time data lakes, where data freshness and efficient data management (upserts, deletes) are critical.
  - Financial services and e-commerce, where changes to data (Ex: transactions) must be tracked efficiently.
- **Ex:** An e-commerce platform needs to track and analyze fraudulent transactions in real-time. Using Hudi in Merge-on-Read (MoR) mode, the platform ingests transaction data continuously from various sources. Updates and corrections to existing transactions (like chargebacks) are managed efficiently with upserts. Hudi enables real-time analytics to detect and flag suspicious activities while keeping the data lake updated incrementally.

Delta Lake:

- Delta Lake is an open-source storage layer that adds ACID transactions, data versioning, and schema enforcement to Apache Spark and big data workloads. It enables building reliable data lakes with structured and unstructured data.
- **Key Features**:
    - **ACID Transactions**: Ensures consistency across multiple write and read operations.
    - **Schema Enforcement and Evolution**: Allows schema changes while enforcing consistency in data structure.
    - **Time Travel**: Supports querying historical data versions.
    - **Scalable Metadata Handling**: Optimizes performance for big data applications.
    - **Data Compaction**: Merges small files into larger ones to optimize performance.
- **History/Origin**:
    - Developed by Databricks in 2019 to address challenges with data lakes, such as data corruption, lack of consistency, and difficulty in handling updates and deletes. It extends Parquet data files with a transaction log, enabling scalable metadata handling and reliable data processing.
    - It is closely integrated with the Apache Spark ecosystem and has become a popular choice for building reliable data pipelines.
    - Open-sourced in 2019, Delta Lake was initially tied to Databricks but is now widely adopted in Spark-based environments.
- **Use Cases**:
    - Building reliable and scalable data lakes with features like versioning and transactions.
    - Streaming and batch processing in large-scale data engineering pipelines.
- **Ex:** A retail chain is building a “Customer 360” platform to gain insights from both streaming and historical data on customer behavior. Delta Lake ensures that all data from different sources (Ex: purchase history, web activity) can be stored in a central data lake with ACID compliance. Delta Lake’s schema enforcement ensures data integrity as the system evolves, while time travel allows analysts to look at historical customer snapshots to understand behavior changes over time.

Apache Iceberg:

- Apache Iceberg is an open-source table format built to enable large-scale analytics on cloud object stores like Amazon S3. It is designed to handle petabyte-scale tables with high performance and reliability. It supports big data storage and works across multiple query engines like Apache Spark, Presto, Hive, and Trino.

- **Key Features**:
  - **Hidden Partitioning**: Automatically manages partitions and optimizes query performance without exposing partition logic to the user.
  - **ACID Compliance**: Supports atomic writes, isolation, and consistency across concurrent operations.
  - **Schema Evolution and Versioning**: Provides advanced schema management with schema evolution and data versioning capabilities.
  - **Time Travel**: Allows querying historical versions of data with efficient rollback.
  - **Support for Multiple Engines**: Works with a wide array of processing engines, including Spark, Flink, and Hive.
  - **Data Optimization**: Manages and compacts data files for optimized read and write performance.
- **History/Origin**:
  - Originally developed by Netflix in 2018 to solve issues with Hive table formats, Iceberg became an Apache Incubator project in 2019 and a top-level project in 2020. Netflix needed a format that could handle massive datasets with performance optimizations for cloud-native storage systems. Iceberg was adopted by Snowflake as an interchange format.
- **Use Cases**:
  - Large-scale data lakes in cloud environments, particularly where multiple engines (like Presto and Spark) need to access the same data.
  - Complex data versioning and schema evolution in high-volume analytics.
- **Ex:** A streaming service needs to store and manage large-scale video usage data for its data warehouse, with different teams querying data using multiple engines (Ex: Spark, Presto). Iceberg allows the service to manage partitioning transparently and enables time travel to analyze past usage patterns (Ex: most-watched shows in a specific week/season). Iceberg's multi-engine support ensures compatibility with different query tools, while its hidden partitioning simplifies data management and improves performance.

Choosing the Right Framework:

- The choice between Hudi, Delta Lake, and Iceberg depends on specific requirements and use cases. Hudi is well-suited for large-scale data ingestion and updates, while Delta Lake offers strong ACID guarantees and integration with the Spark ecosystem. Iceberg provides a flexible and compatible data lake table format. Consider factors like data volume, update frequency, performance requirements, and integration needs when making a decision.

38. Do all cloud data lake and data warehouse solutions, such as Azure Synapse Analytics, Google BigQuery, AWS Redshift, Databricks, and Snowflake, support Hudi, Delta Lake, and Iceberg?

Ans:

Here is the support matrix:

	Hudi	**Delta Lake**	**Iceberg**
Products/Services			
Azure Synapse	Read-Write	Read-Write	NA
Azure HDInsight	Read-Write	Read-Write	NA
AWS Redshift	Read	Read	NA
AWS EMR	Read-Write	Read-Write	Read-Write
Google BigQuery	Read	NA	Read
Google Dataproc	Read-Write	Read-Write	Read-Write
Databricks	Read-Write	Read-Write	Read-Write
Snowflake	NA	Read	Read-Write
Apache Spark	Read-Write	Read-Write	Read-Write
Apache Flink	Read-Write	Read-Write	Read-Write
Apache Impala	Read-Write	NA	Read-Write
Hive	Read	Read	Read-Write
Kafka	Write	Write	NA
Key Feature Support			
ACID Properties	Yes	Yes	Yes
Time Travel	Yes	Yes	Yes
Schema Evolution	Limited	Yes	Yes
Index Management	Yes	No	No
Primary Keys	Yes	No	No

Table 8.4

Note: The support matrix may change. Please check the official product documentation for the latest version.

Explore:

Analytics Offerings:

- **Azure Synapse:** Unified analytics platform combining data warehousing and data lake capabilities.
- **Azure HDInsight:** Managed Hadoop, Spark, and other open-source clusters on Azure.
- **AWS Redshift:** Fully managed, petabyte-scale data warehouse in the cloud.
- **AWS EMR:** Managed Hadoop and Spark clusters on AWS.
- **Google BigQuery:** Serverless data warehouse with automatic scaling and optimization.
- **Google Dataproc:** Fully managed Hadoop and Spark clusters on Google Cloud Platform.
- **Databricks:** Unified analytics platform for data engineering, machine learning, and data science.
- **Snowflake:** Cloud-based data warehouse with elastic scalability and performance.
- **Apache Spark:** Fast and general-purpose distributed data processing engine.
- **Apache Flink:** Distributed streaming engine for real-time data processing.
- **Apache Impala:** High-performance SQL query engine for Apache Hadoop.
- **Hive:** Data warehouse infrastructure built on top of Hadoop.
- **Kafka:** Distributed streaming platform for building real-time data pipelines.

Features:

- **ACID transactions** provide a way to implement transactions on top of data lakes, which was not possible in traditional analytics systems. This means that data lake operations can now be guaranteed to be atomic, consistent, isolated, and durable, ensuring data integrity and reliability.
- **Time Travel:** Time travel allows users to query historical versions of data, enabling them to access data as it was at a specific point in the past. It allows users to query and restore data to previous states, enabling data auditing, versioning, and recovery.
- **Schema Evolution:** Schema evolution allows a data schema to evolve (change) over time without breaking existing data. This means adding, removing, or updating columns while ensuring compatibility with existing datasets.
- **Index Management:** Provides mechanisms for creating, managing, and optimizing indexes to improve query performance.
- **Primary Keys:** Uniquely identifies rows within a table, ensuring data integrity and facilitating efficient data retrieval.

CHAPTER 09

Azure Cosmos DB

1. Can you describe what Azure Cosmos DB is?

Ans:

Azure Cosmos DB is a highly versatile, fully managed database service that supports NoSQL, relational, and vector data models. It offers exceptional performance with single-digit millisecond response times, automatic and instant scalability, and guaranteed speed at any scale.

Explore:

Cosmos DB organizes data hierarchically:

- **Databases:** Similar to RDBMS databases, top-level containers for your data. **Ex:** “eCommerce_DB”.
- **Containers/Collections:** Similar to tables in RDBMS, they hold your data. **Ex:** Suppliers, Products, Customers, Orders etc.
- **Items/Documents/JSON:** Similar to rows in a table in RDBMS, individual data entries within a collection, typically stored in JSON format. **Ex:** Microsoft Surface, DELL Inspiron, Apple 13 MacBook within the “Products” collection.
- **Properties/JSON Properties:** Similar to columns in a table in RDBMS, these are attributes within an item document. **Ex:** product_name, price, weight, availability etc.

2. Can you describe 2 or 3 key features of Cosmos DB?

Ans:

Here are the key features of Cosmos DB:

- **Fully Managed:** Cosmos DB is a Platform as a Service (PaaS) offering from Microsoft Azure. This means Microsoft handles all infrastructure management and maintenance, allowing you to focus on your applications.
- **Multi-Model Database:** Cosmos DB offers a unique advantage – it supports multiple data models through different APIs:
    - **NoSQL:**
        - Azure Cosmos DB for NoSQL (native document database)
        - MongoDB API (for document data)
        - Cassandra API (for columnar data)

        - Gremlin API (for graph data)
        - Azure Table API (for key-value store)

    - **Relational:** Azure Cosmos DB for PostgreSQL – a managed service for running PostgreSQL at any scale, leveraging distributed tables from the Citus open-source project. It can store data on a single node or distribute it across multiple nodes.
    - **AI Integration:** Cosmos DB caters to AI needs with functionalities like integrated vector database and seamless integration with Azure AI Services to support Retrieval Augmented Generation (RAG) techniques. **Ex:** OpenAI uses Cosmos DB for dynamic scaling of their ChatGPT service.

- **Elastic Scalability:** Cosmos DB offers virtually "unlimited" capacity. Databases and containers can automatically scale provisioned throughput based on your needs, without disrupting client connections, applications, or impacting Cosmos DB SLAs (Service Level Agreements).
- **Globally Distributed:** Cosmos DB offers multi-master functionality. Reads and writes can be scaled elastically across any number of Azure regions worldwide. This ensures data availability in multiple data centers for both read and write operations.
- **High Availability:** Cosmos DB maintains strong data consistency by keeping 4 replicas within a region. Additionally, you can configure read-only replicas across different regions for geographically distributed access.
- **High Performance:** Cosmos DB guarantees exceptional performance with latency below 10 milliseconds (for 1 KiB documents) at the 99th percentile for both reads and writes across all consistency levels.
- **Automatic Indexing:** Cosmos DB simplifies data management by automatically indexing all fields in all documents by default, eliminating the need for manual configuration of secondary indexes. This automatic indexing applies to all supported data models.
- **Multi-Language Support:** Cosmos DB provides SDKs and tools for various programming languages, including Java, .NET, Python, Node.js, JavaScript, and more.
- **Default Encryption:** As an Azure data storage solution, Cosmos DB encrypts data at rest by default and also encrypts data in transit, ensuring robust data security.

These features make Cosmos DB a versatile and powerful database solution for various use cases.

3. What are the Cosmos DB APIs and how to choose the right one for our business workloads?

Ans:

Cosmos DB offers a variety of APIs that allow your applications to interact with it as if it were different database technologies. This flexibility often translates to easier migration. In many cases, you can switch from an on-premises NoSQL database like MongoDB or Cassandra to the corresponding Cosmos DB API by simply modifying the connection string in your client application.

Azure Cosmos DB offers below API's:

- **NoSQL API:** Flexible schema document database for various data types with built-in features like automatic indexing and global distribution.
- **MongoDB API:** Familiar interface for existing MongoDB users offering schema flexibility and compatibility with MongoDB tools.
- **Cassandra API:** High-performance columnar store for massive datasets with frequent writes and reads of specific data columns.
- **Gremlin API:** Works with graph data models using Gremlin query language for complex relationships and advanced graph analytics.
- **Table API:** Simple and fast key-value store for frequently accessed data with a focus on inserts, updates, and deletes.
- **PostgreSQL API (Azure Cosmos DB for PostgreSQL):** Managed service to run PostgreSQL databases at scale with a familiar SQL interface for querying relational data.

Explore:

NoSQL API:

- Combines features of both SQL and NoSQL databases.
- Stores data in JSON documents and allows querying using SQL syntax as a JSON query language.
- **Choose when:** Migrating from other databases (Ex: Oracle, DynamoDB, HBase) or looking to modernize your application development process with NoSQL features.
- **Business Case:** Hosting applications requiring a semi-structured data model. **Ex:** An e-commerce application with product categories. Adding a new category with new parameters in a relational database (RDBMS) might require schema changes and downtime. With NoSQL API's JSON documents, you can simply add a new document without impacting production. Similar functionality is available in MongoDB, but NoSQL API offers additional features like modernized development and SQL querying.

MongoDB API (RU/vCore):

- Stores data in documents using the BSON (Binary JSON) format.
- Compatible with the MongoDB wire protocol, allowing existing MongoDB client applications to work with Azure Cosmos DB seamlessly.
- **Choose when:** Migrating existing MongoDB applications to Azure Cosmos DB with minimal code changes.
- **Business Case:** Merchandising categorization, metadata storage, purchasing order processing. **Ex:** An online photo sharing service uses MongoDB to manage over 6 billion+ images. One of the world's largest countries has been using MongoDB to manage its citizens' demographic and biometric data (over 1.4 billion records).

Cassandra API:

- Stores data in a column-oriented schema.
- Wire protocol compatible with Apache Cassandra, enabling existing Apache drivers (CQLv4 compliant) to work with Azure Cosmos DB as if it were an actual Cassandra database.
- **Choose when:** Migrating an existing Cassandra instance to Azure.
- **Business Case:** Transaction logging (test scores, movies watched, movie locations), time series data, health tracker data, weather service history, IoT data, etc.

Gremlin API:

- Enables users to make graph queries using Gremlin query language. Data is stored as edges and vertices.
- Based on the Apache TinkerPop graph computing framework and supports the Gremlin query language.
- Wire protocol compatibility with open-source Gremlin allows using open-source Gremlin SDKs for application development.
- Azure Cosmos DB Gremlin API also works with Apache Spark and GraphFrames for complex analytical graph scenarios.
- **Choose when:** Migrating existing Gremlin systems to Azure.
- **Business Case:** Ideal for scenarios with dynamic data, complex data relationships, or data too complex for relational databases. **Ex:** Predicting customer behavior (people who bought product A also bought product B), managing social networks, geospatial use cases (finding optimal routes), modelling networks and connections between IoT devices.

Table API:

- Stores data in key-value format and offers premium features for applications designed for Azure Table storage.
- If you're using Azure Table storage, you might face limitations in latency, scaling, throughput, global distribution, and query performance.
- Table API overcomes these limitations and is recommended for migrating apps from Azure Table storage to Cosmos DB Table API.
- **Choose when:** Migrating from Azure Table Storage to Azure Cosmos DB Table API.
- **Business Case:** Cosmos DB Table API is a premium version of Azure Table Storage. Both offer schema-less NoSQL data storage. However, Cosmos DB offers low latency and high throughput compared to Azure Table Storage. **Ex:** Storing user session data or application configuration settings for fast retrieval and updates.

PostgreSQL API (vCore):

- A managed service for running PostgreSQL at any scale, leveraging the Citus open-source technology for distributed tables.
- Ideal for starting with a single-node database with rich indexing, geospatial capabilities, and JSON support. Nodes can be added later for increased performance without downtime.
- **Choose when:** Building highly scalable relational applications.
- **Business Case:** Applications requiring the power of PostgreSQL's relational model, such as SaaS applications, real-time operational analytics applications, or complex transactional applications with high throughput requirements. These applications can span various industries like sales and marketing automation, healthcare, IoT data, finance, logistics, and search.

4. What are the data models supported by Azure Cosmos DB?

Ans:

Azure Cosmos DB's multi-model capabilities provide the flexibility to choose the best data model and API for your specific application needs, making it a versatile solution for modern, scalable applications. Here are the models supported by Cosmos DB:

- **Document:** Flexible and hierarchical data structures (NoSQL API, MongoDB API, Cassandra API).
- **Key-Value:** Simple key-value pairs for rapid read/write operations (Table API).
- **Column-Family:** Row and column organization for large-scale, sparse datasets, time series and IoT data (Cassandra API).
- **Graph:** Vertices and edges for navigating complex relationships (Gremlin API).
- **Relational:** It also supports largescale distributed relational database model. (PostgreSQL API).
- **Vector:** Azure Cosmos DB supports vector data models for AI (Vector Store in MongoDB vCore).

5. Can you describe the pricing model for Azure Cosmos DB?

Ans:

Azure Cosmos DB bills for three different types of usage: compute, storage and bandwidth.

- **Compute:** You are billed based on the compute resources used by your database. Depending on the chosen Cosmos DB API, there are two flavours available Request Units (RU) or vCores.
- **Storage:** There are again two options depending on the chosen API:
    - **Consumed Storage:** You are billed for the actual space your data uses.
    - **Disk Storage:** This refers to the total disk space allocated to your database, regardless of actual data usage.
- **Bandwidth:** You are charged for data egress when your data leaves the Azure network boundary.

Explore:

Compute Pricing:

- **Request Unit (throughput):** Azure Cosmos DB bills using Request Units (RU) measured per second (RU/s). Think of Request Units (RUs) as tokens that represent the computational resources needed to perform operations like reading or writing data in Azure Cosmos DB. Each operation consumes a certain number of RUs, which serves as a measure of the compute, memory, and input/output (I/O) resources utilized by that operation. So, the more complex or intensive an operation is, the more RUs it will require. Options for throughput include:
- **Provisioned Throughput:** You choose a fixed amount of RU/s (Request Units per second) upfront to meet your workload's needs. You are billed for all the RU/s you provision, even if you don't use them all.
- **Auto-scale:** You set minimum and maximum RU/s limits. So that it automatically scales between min and max RU/s based on the demand. You are billed only for the RU/s used. However, if your usage falls below the minimum, you will still be billed for the minimum RU/s.
- **Serverless:** You do not provision any RU/s upfront. You are billed only for the RU/s your operations consume. There are some limitations. Ex: Geo-distribution is not available, compared to other modes, it may have slightly higher latency for write operations (under 30 milliseconds).
- **Applicable APIs:** RUs are applicable for NoSQL, MongoDB (RU), Cassandra, Gremlin, and Table.
- **vCore:** Azure Cosmos DB bills for vCores (compute and memory) per node to process database operations and are billed on the size and number of nodes provisioned.
- **Applicable APIs:** MongoDB (vCore) and PostgreSQL.

Storage Pricing:

- **Consumed Storage:** Azure Cosmos DB bills for consumed storage rounded up to the next GB per container/collection/table/graph per region. Consumed storage includes all transactional and analytical data and indexes, and backups.
- **Applicable APIs:** NoSQL, MongoDB (RU), Cassandra, Gremlin, and Table.
- **Disk Storage:** Azure Cosmos DB bills for disks provisioned for each node by storage size.
- **Applicable APIs:** MongoDB (vCore) and PostgreSQL.

Bandwidth Pricing:

- **Data Egress:** Azure charges a fee when your data leaves the Azure cloud or travels between different Azure regions or availability zones.
- **Applicable APIs:** All APIs.

6. In Azure Cosmos DB, is it possible allocating resources at the database level or container level?

Ans:

Yes. In Azure Cosmos DB, resource allocation (RU/s) can be done at two levels:

- **Database Level:** Resources are shared across all the containers in the database.
- **Container level:** Resources are exclusively reserved for the container.

Explore:

Database Level: You can allocate RU/s to the entire database. This means all containers within that database will share the allocated resources. This is a good option for workloads where all containers have similar performance needs. **Ex:** You have a social media application with a single database containing containers for user profiles, posts, and comments. All containers have moderate and predictable read/write workloads.

Container Level: You can allocate RU/s to individual containers within the database. This is useful if you have containers with significantly different access patterns or data sizes. **Ex:** You have an e-commerce application with a database containing containers for product information (frequently accessed) and order history (less frequent access).

7. How does Cosmos DB work, and how does it benefit globally distributed applications?

Ans:

Cosmos DB is a highly scalable NoSQL and RDBMS (PostgreSQL) database from Microsoft. With Cosmos DB, we can deploy multiple read-only and read-write replicas worldwide. It distributes local workloads using logical partitions and global workloads using physical partitions. The key aspect of Cosmos DB lies in its speed and flexibility in creating and moving data across different zones and regions globally. The performance of your Cosmos DB primarily depends on factors such as the partition key, throughput mode, and data consistency level.

Explore:

Here are the Cosmos DB internals:

- **Global Distribution and Replication:**
    - **Global Replication:** With a single click, Cosmos DB allows placing secondary replicas of your database in multiple regions. You can have read-only or read-write replicas across regions. Azure takes care of data synchronization. Ex:
        - **Scenario:** Assume you have a website hosted on Azure used by users from various regions. If the database is in the USA, US users will experience faster data access compared to users in India due to network latency. **Solution:** Unlike a single database

location, Cosmos DB replicates your data across multiple Azure regions closest to your users. This ensures low latency access for users worldwide.

  - **Multi-Master Feature:** Having multiple read-write replicas is known as the "Multi-Master" feature. When enabled, data is written concurrently to all selected regions simultaneously.

- **Automatic and Configurable Failover:**
  - **Failover:** Cosmos DB offers automatic and configurable failover to ensure business continuity during regional outages.
    - **Automatic Failover:** This service-managed ensures your application remains functional by seamlessly switching to a healthy replica in another region when the primary region experiences an outage.
    - **Configurable Failover:** It allows you to perform controlled failover scenarios as part of your disaster recovery drills.
  - **Region Priority Configuration:** You can control the sequence of regional failovers during outages using "Region Priority" configuration. Ex: You can direct your application to failover to region 4 if region 1 is down, and then to region 6 if region 4 is also unavailable.
- **Data Consistency:** Data consistency is crucial for globally distributed databases. All replicas should be in sync and maintain the same state of a data object at any given time. Otherwise, users from different regions might see different versions of the same data.
  - **Consistency Levels:** Cosmos DB offers various consistency levels, allowing you to choose between strong, bounded staleness, session consistency, consistent prefix and eventual consistency. This flexibility enables you to optimize your application's performance and consistency trade-offs based on your specific needs.
- **Optimistic Concurrency:** Cosmos DB implements optimistic concurrency, avoiding locks or blocks. If two transactions collide on the same data, one will fail and be retried.
- **Cosmos DB Backups:** Cosmos DB automatically backs up your data every four hours, and two backups are always retained. Additionally, backups are kept for 30 days after database deletion before permanent discard.
- **Data Expiry (TTL):** Cosmos DB allows setting a Time-To-Live (TTL) for each item (or all items) in a container. Expired data is automatically deleted, improving storage management.
- **Container Partition Management:** In Cosmos DB, containers are horizontally partitioned and replicated across regions. Based on the partition key, data is automatically distributed across logical partitions for efficient management. It's recommended to choose a granular key with highly distinct values. Cosmos DB will split or merge partitions to maintain proper data distribution.

- **Partition/Shared Key:** Partitioning divides container items into distinct subsets called logical partitions based on a partition key value. Each item has a unique ID within its logical partition. Combining the partition key and item ID creates the item's unique index. For example, if "UserID" is the partition key, item ID + UserID uniquely identifies each item.
- **Logical Partitions:** A logical partition consists of items with the same partition key. For example, if you create a container for employee payroll information and choose "Department" (sales, marketing, IT, etc.) as the partition key, and there are 10 unique departments, 10 logical partitions are created. All employee data from the "sales" department would reside in a single logical partition. There's no limit to the number of logical partitions in a container.
- **Physical Partitions:** A container is scaled by distributing data and throughput across physical partitions. Internally, one or more logical partitions are mapped to a single physical partition. Smaller containers might have many logical partitions but require only one physical partition. If your container has over 100 GB of data or 30,000 RU/s provisioned, you might need more than one physical partition.
- **Choosing a partition key** significantly impacts Cosmos DB performance. Here are two key points to consider:
  - Choose a property that doesn't require frequent updates.
  - Choose a property with high cardinality (many unique values).
- **Controlling Logical and Physical Partitions:** Your responsibility is to choose the right partition key. Cosmos DB manages everything else internally.

- **Automatic Scaling:** Cosmos DB automatically scales both throughput and storage based on your application's requirements. It can handle varying workloads without manual intervention, ensuring high performance and availability.
- **SLAs and Guarantees:** Cosmos DB provides comprehensive SLAs for throughput, consistency, availability, and latency. It guarantees high availability with multi-region replication and financially-backed SLAs for uptime.
- **Throughput Mode:** Throughput mode refers to how you pay for the processing power of your database. In the RU/s compute model, it offers three types of throughput modes, including provisioned, auto-scale, and serverless. We need to choose the right mode based on our business needs.

By leveraging these features, Cosmos DB delivers a globally available, scalable, and consistent database solution for modern applications.

8. When utilizing Request Unit (RU/s) compute model, how do you choose the right throughput mode for Azure Cosmos DB, and how does it impact billing?

Ans:

The best throughput mode depends on your workload's predictability and traffic patterns. Here's a breakdown:

- **Provisioned Throughput:** Ideal for **predictable workloads** with sustained traffic. You set a fixed RU/s limit upfront (like reserving capacity). Billing is based on the provisioned RU/s, regardless of usage. Manually scale up/down as needed.
- **Auto-scale Throughput:** Good for **variable traffic**. Sets minimum and maximum RU/s limits. Cosmos DB automatically scales within those limits based on usage. Billed for the **maximum** RU/s used per hour, not total consumed.
- **Serverless Throughput:** Best for **unpredictable or bursty workloads**. No upfront provisioning, pay per consumed RU/s. Ideal for new applications or low average traffic. Billing based on monthly consumed RU/s.

Explore:

Understanding Billing with 4000 RU/s Provisioning:

Let's consider a scenario where you've provisioned 4000 RU/s to understand how billing works in three different modes:

Provisioned Mode:

- **Billing:** You are charged for the full provisioned capacity (4000 RU/s) regardless of actual usage.
- **Ex:**
  - **Hour 1:** 0 Requests / 0 RU/s (Charged for 4000 RU/s).
  - **Hour 2:** 30 RU/s (Charged for 4000 RU/s).
  - **Hour 3:** 1000 RU/s (Charged for 4000 RU/s).
  - **Hour 4:** 5000 RU/s (Only 4000 RU/s served, remaining 1000 RU/s rate-limited) - Still charged for 4000 RU/s.
- **Billing Rate:** Standard manual rate (Ex: $0.008 per 100 RU/s per hour).

Auto Scaling Mode:

- **Configuration:** You set a maximum limit of 4000 RU/s. The service automatically scales between a minimum of 10% (400 RU/s) and your maximum limit.
- **Billing:** You are charged based on the actual utilized capacity, with a minimum charge of 400 RU/s per hour.

- **Ex:**
  - **Hour 1:** 0 Requests / 0 RU/s (Charged for 400 RU/s - minimum).
  - **Hour 2:** 30 RU/s (Charged for 400 RU/s - minimum).
  - **Hour 3:** 1000 RU/s (Charged for 1000 RU/s).
  - **Hour 4:** 5000 RU/s (Only 4000 RU/s served, remaining requests are terminated) - Charged for 4000 RU/s.
- **Billing Rate:** 1.5 times the standard manual rate (Ex: $0.012 per 100 RU/s per hour).

Serverless Mode:

- **Billing:** You are only charged for the resources you use.
- **Ex:**
  - **Hour 1:** 0 Requests / 0 RU/s (No Charge).
  - **Hour 2:** 30 RU/s (Charged for 30 RU/s).
  - **Hour 3:** 1000 RU/s (Charged for 1000 RU/s).
  - **Hour 4:** 5000 RU/s (Charged for 5000 RU/s).
  - **Billing Rate:** Per-use rate (Ex: $0.25 per 1 million RU/s).

Note:

- **Billing Rate:** This is an example for a hypothetical billing rate for a single-region write account. The actual rate may vary depending on your specific provider and plan.
- For vCore models (like PostgreSQL and MongoDB vCore), billing depends on factors like allocated memory, single/multi-node configuration, and vCores per node.

9. How does Cosmos DB handle data consistency and latency for users in different regions when using cross-region read/write replicas?

Ans:

Cosmos DB offers different consistency levels to balance data consistency and latency across regions. Choose the level that best suits your needs:

- **Strong Consistency:** Ensures all users see the latest data (highest consistency, but slowest).
- **Eventual Consistency:** Users might see slightly outdated data (fastest, but least consistent).
- **Other Levels (Bounded Staleness, Session, Consistent Prefix):** Offer a balance between consistency and performance.

Explore:

Globally distributed systems can face consistency challenges due to replication time. Users in different regions might see different versions of the same data after an update. To address this, Cosmos DB offers various consistency levels:

- **Strong:** Provides the highest consistency but offers lower performance. Users always see the latest committed data, ideal for mission-critical applications like trading platforms. However, it's typically scoped to a single region.
- **Bounded Staleness:** Defines an acceptable delay (staleness period) for data updates to propagate across replicas. For example, with a 10-minute staleness period, users might see slightly outdated data for a short duration. Setting staleness to 0 behaves like strong consistency.
- **Session:** Ensures users within the same session or those sharing a session token see the latest committed data. However, users in other regions might see an older version until replication completes.
- **Consistent Prefix:** Ensures data is read in the same order it was committed. Suppose data writes are performed in the order A, B, C, users see the data in a consistent sequence (Ex: A, AB, or ABC), never out-of-order (Ex: C, AC, BCA etc.).
- **Eventual:** Offers the weakest consistency but provides the highest performance. Data is eventually replicated across regions, but users might see stale data for a brief period, and the data order might not be guaranteed. Suitable for non-critical applications like social media counters (retweets, likes) or non-threaded comments.

Recommendation:

- For applications requiring strict data consistency, strong or bounded staleness might be suitable.
- For applications where data freshness is less critical but high performance is desired, session consistency or eventual consistency could be options.

10. What is the difference between MongoDB API (RU) and MongoDB API (vCore) models in Azure Cosmos DB?

Ans:

- **RU (Request Unit) Model:** Paying for operations (reads, writes, queries) performed on your data. Ideal for unpredictable workloads.
- **vCore (Virtual Core) Model:** Paying for dedicated instances with a set amount of CPU, memory, and storage resources. Ideal for consistent workloads with predictable performance requirements.

Explore:

Ideal cases for RU/s:

- You're building new cloud-native MongoDB apps or refactoring existing apps for cloud-native benefits.
- Your workload has more point reads and few long-running queries and complex aggregation pipeline operations.

- You want limitless horizontal scalability, instantaneous scale up, and granular throughput control.

Ideal cases for vCore-based:

- You're migrating (lift & shift) an existing MongoDB workload to Azure Cosmos DB.
- Your workload has more long-running queries, complex aggregation pipelines, distributed transactions, joins, etc.
- You prefer high-capacity vertical and horizontal scaling with familiar vCore-based cluster tiers.

11. What is the difference between MongoDB Atlas and Azure Cosmos DB MongoDB API?

Ans:

- **MongoDB Atlas:** Pure MongoDB experience, potential vendor lock-in.
- **Azure Cosmos DB MongoDB API:** More flexible, wide range of options and seamless integration with other Azure services.

Explore:

MongoDB Atlas and Cosmos DB for Mongo API are cloud solutions for running MongoDB.

MongoDB Atlas: MongoDB Atlas is the fully-managed cloud database version of MongoDB. It takes care of all the complexities of deploying and managing databases on a cloud service provider (Azure, AWS, Google Cloud) of our organization's choice. Choose it when:

- You prioritize a pure MongoDB experience with MQL.
- You have existing MongoDB deployments and want a familiar cloud solution.

Azure Cosmos DB MongoDB API:

Microsoft Azure solution for running mission critical NoSQL database workloads. Along with the MongoDB capabilities Azure provides additional benefits including multi-API support, millisecond response time, global distribution, and automatic scaling. Choose it when:

- You need flexibility for potentially using other data models in the future.
- Cost-effectiveness for fluctuating workloads (RU model) is important.
- You have existing Azure infrastructure and prefer a unified cloud platform.

12. Does Azure Cosmos DB have any limits on storage and throughput?

Ans:

No. Azure Cosmos DB offers scalable storage and throughput, meaning there's no practical limit on how much data you can store or how many operations you can perform per second. The service uses horizontal scaling to automatically adjust capacity based on your needs.

However, there might be soft limits depending on the specific Cosmos DB API you're using. These limits can typically be increased by contacting Azure Support.

13. What is the primary difference between Azure Database for PostgreSQL and Azure Cosmos DB for PostgreSQL?

Ans:

Azure Database for PostgreSQL: Managed relational database service built on PostgreSQL. Offers a familiar experience for existing PostgreSQL users.

- **Scalability:** Vertical scaling of compute and storage.
- **Ideal for:**
    - Migrating or modernizing existing PostgreSQL apps.
    - Migrating Oracle apps to Azure.

Azure Cosmos DB for PostgreSQL: Globally distributed database service with a PostgreSQL API. Designed for high availability, scalability, and performance across geographically distributed regions.

- **Scalability:** Fast, high-performance horizontal scaling and multi-node distributed SQL capabilities.
- **Ideal for:**
    - Building new cloud-native and highly scalable apps.
    - Optimized for building multi-tenant SaaS apps, high throughput transactional apps and large-scale enterprise apps.

14. Does Azure Cosmos DB support referential integrity or foreign keys?

Ans:

Currently there is no concept of foreign key in Cosmos DB. Referential integrity and data dependencies (Ex: create order only when the product is available) must be done either using server-side triggers, custom program at application layer, or stored procedures on Azure Cosmos DB. **Ex:** Utilize Azure Functions or stored procedures to enforce data consistency when changes occur.

Explore:

- **Unique Key (NoSQL API):** With unique keys, you make sure that one or more values within a logical partition is unique. The partition key combined with the unique key guarantees the uniqueness of an item within the scope of the container.
- **Primary Key and Foreign Key (PostgreSQL API):** PostgreSQL API supports primary key and foreign keys with some limitations.

15. Similar to how transactions work in relational databases, I need all modifications in the batch to succeed or fail together. Does Cosmos DB support ACID transactions for batch updates within a container?

Ans:

Yes, Cosmos DB offers functionalities similar to transactions in RDBMS, but with some key differences. These transactions are ACID (Atomicity, Consistency, Isolation, Durability) compliant. We can implement transactions within a single logical partition using Multi-item transactions, and transactional batch operations features.

Explore:

- **Multi-item transactions:**
  - Azure Cosmos DB allows you to write stored procedures, pre/post triggers, user-defined-functions (UDFs) and merge procedures in JavaScript. You can register these on a container and later execute them transactionally within the Azure Cosmos DB database engine.
  - The JavaScript-based stored procedures, triggers, UDFs, and merge procedures are wrapped within an ambient ACID transaction with snapshot isolation across all items within the logical partition. During the course of its execution, if the JavaScript program throws an exception, the entire transaction is aborted and rolled-back.
- **Transactional Batch Operations:** Cosmos DB supports Transactional Batch operations using the SDKs (.NET, Java and Python). This allows you to group document operations (creates, reads, updates, deletes) within a batch and execute them as a single unit. If any operation fails, the entire batch is rolled back, ensuring atomicity.
- **Limitations:** Cosmos DB transactions work differently than they do in relational database systems. Transactions are scoped to a single partition within a collection. You cannot perform transactions across different partitions or collections.
- **Alternative for wider consistency:** If you need eventual consistency across partitions or collections, consider optimistic concurrency control (OCC) mechanisms. OCC protects your data from accidentally overwriting changes that were made by others. It also prevents others from accidentally overwriting your own changes.

16. Can we perform a transaction with two collections in Azure Cosmos DB?

Ans:

No, Cosmos DB transactions are currently limited to operations within a single partition of a collection. This means you cannot perform transactions across different collections or between documents with different partition key values.

Ex: In an e-commerce Cosmos DB, if you have a collection named "Orders" and another named "Inventory", you cannot perform a transaction that simultaneously updates an order in the Orders collection and adjusts the stock level in the Inventory collection. Additionally, if you want to update multiple documents within the Orders collection, they must all have the same partition key value to be part of a single transaction. If an Orders collection is partitioned by CustomerId, you can update multiple documents related to a single customer in one transaction but not documents belonging to different customers.

17. In Azure Cosmos DB, is it possible changing/updating a partition key once a container and collection is created?

Ans:

Unfortunately, Cosmos DB doesn't directly support changing the partition key of an existing container. The partition key you define during creation forms the foundation for data distribution across partitions. Modifying it would require restructuring the entire dataset. However, you can achieve a similar effect by either manually migrating your data to a new container or using the "**Change Partition Key**" feature.

Explore:

Migrate to new container - Manual: Changing the partition key in Azure Cosmos DB involves creating a new container with the desired partition key and migrating the data from the old container to the new one.

Azure Portal – Change Partition Key (New feature - Preview): Azure Cosmos DB NoSQL API offers the ability to seamlessly change the partition key using the Azure portal.

- **Partition Key Setting:** Navigate to > Azure Cosmos DB > Data Explorer > Scale & Settings > Partition Keys > Change > Select "New Container" or specify the ID of container, if it is already created within the same database.
- **Data Copy:** Data is copied from the source container to the destination container in an offline manner utilizing the Intra-account container copy job.
- **Freeze data modifications at the source.** It is recommended to stop all updates on the source container before proceeding to change the partition key of the container for entire duration of copy process to maintain data integrity.
- **Start using new container:** Once the copy is complete, you can start using the new container with desired partition key and optionally delete the old container.
- **Limitations:** For containers with over 1,000,000 provisioned throughput or more than 4 TB of data, please contact Microsoft support for assistance with changing the partition key.

18. What is the difference between Point Reads and Queries in Azure Cosmos DB?

Ans:

There are two ways to read data in Azure Cosmos DB: point reads and queries.

- **Point Reads (Cost effective):** A point read retrieves a single document from the database using its unique identifier (ID) and partition key.
    - **Ex:** You want to retrieve the details of a specific customer with ID "UNC12345" who lives in "Chicago".
- **Queries:** Queries retrieve one or more documents based on specified conditions. They use the SQL API to filter and return documents that match the criteria.
    - **Ex:** You want to find all customers who live in "California" and have placed orders above $500.

19. In Azure Cosmos DB, what are the different types of indexes available?

Ans:

Azure Cosmos DB supports three types of indexes:

- Range Indexes (Default)
- Spatial Indexes
- Composite Indexes

Explore:

Range Indexes:

- Cosmos DB automatically creates range indexes on all properties (strings, numbers) by default.
- They are used for equality queries (Ex: category = 'Electronics'), range queries (Ex: **>, <, >=, <=**), ORDER BY queries (Ex: ORDER BY abc.property), system string functions (Ex: STRINGEQUALS, CONTAINS), JOIN queries and for checking the presence of a property (Ex: IS_DEFINED).
- **Ex:** Range indexes are used for queries like
- SELECT * FROM container c WHERE c.property = 'value'
- SELECT * FROM container c WHERE c.property > 'value'
- SELECT child FROM container c JOIN child IN c.properties WHERE child = 'value' ORDER BY c.property.

Spatial Indexes:

- Designed for geospatial queries involving points, linestrings, polygons, and other geographic data types.
- They are useful when you need to perform proximity searches.

- **Ex:** You might have a mobile app that needs to find all coffee shops within a 1-mile radius of the user's current location.
- SELECT * FROM c WHERE ST_DISTANCE(c.location, {'type': 'Point', 'coordinates': [longitude, latitude]}) < 1000

Composite Indexes:

- Composite indexes are used when you want to sort or filter on multiple properties.
- **Ex:** A composite index on properties property1, property2, and property3 can help the below query.
- SELECT * FROM container c WHERE c.property1 = 'value' ORDER BY c.property1, c.property2

Indexing mode: Azure Cosmos DB supports two indexing modes:

- **Consistent:** The index is updated synchronously as you create, update or delete items.
- **None:** Indexing is disabled on the container. This mode is commonly used when a container is used as a pure key-value store without the need for secondary indexes. It can also be used to improve the performance of bulk operations.

20. What is a synthetic partition key in Azure Cosmos DB?

Ans:

A synthetic partition key is a custom partition key that is constructed by combining multiple properties of a document to create a composite key. It's particularly useful when your data doesn't have a natural candidate for a partition key that offers a high cardinality (many distinct values).

Explore:

- **Natural Partition Key:** Ideally, your data model should have a property that serves as a natural partition key. This property should have a high number of unique values to ensure even distribution of data across partitions. Examples include UserID or OrderID.
- **Synthetic Partition Key:** When a natural candidate for the partition key doesn't exist, you create a synthetic one. This involves combining multiple properties from your data model to create a new property with high cardinality.
- **Ex:** Imagine you have a collection storing sensor data with properties like deviceId, sensorType, SensorProperty, value and timestamp. While deviceId could be a candidate, it might not have enough unique values for optimal distribution. You could create a synthetic partition key by combining deviceId and sensorType to ensure a higher cardinality and better performance.

21. What is the purpose of the "_etag" property in Azure Cosmos DB?

Ans:

The _etag (entity tag) in Azure Cosmos DB is a system-defined property that every item stored in an Azure Cosmos DB container has. The value of the _etag is automatically generated and updated by the server every time the item is updated. In other words, it acts like a version number and changes whenever the document is modified.

The _etag property is used for optimistic concurrency control (OCC). This means if you have an operation that needs to be broken into separate steps, you can use the eTag property to avoid data loss in concurrent writes.

Explore:

Imagine two users trying to update the same document simultaneously. OCC helps prevent conflicts:

- You retrieve a document and get its current _etag value.
- You modify the document data locally.
- When you try to update the document in Cosmos DB, you include the original _etag value.
- Cosmos DB compares the provided _etag with the current server-side version.
- If they match, the update succeeds (your version is still valid).
- If they don't match (another user modified the document in the meantime), the update fails, indicating a conflict.

Note:

- You don't need to use _etag explicitly in most scenarios. Cosmos DB handles OCC internally. However, if your application requires strict data consistency, you can leverage the _etag value in your update operations to implement custom conflict resolution logic.

22. What is the Azure Cosmos DB change feed feature?

Ans:

The Change Feed feature in Azure Cosmos DB is a mechanism that records and provides changes to a container in the order they occur. It acts like an audit log, recording inserts, updates, and deletes as they happen in your Cosmos DB container. Advantages:

- **Real-time updates:** Enables applications to react to data modifications almost instantly.
- **Data synchronization:** Allows you to keep other systems or databases synchronized with the latest changes in Cosmos DB.
- **Offline processing:** Change feed data can be captured and processed asynchronously for tasks like analytics or building materialized views.

Explore:

Sample Use Cases of Change Feed feature:

- **Real-time Dashboards:** Integrate the change feed with a dashboarding tool to display real-time data updates, such as stock price fluctuations or social media activity.

- **Event-driven Architectures:** Leverage the change feed to trigger actions in response to specific data changes. Ex: Update a search index whenever a document is modified or send notifications when a new order is placed.
- **Data Warehousing and Analytics:** Capture changes and store them in a data warehouse for historical analysis or to populate analytical dashboards.
- **Data Pipelines:** Integrate the change feed with data pipelines to move modified data to other systems for further processing or integration.
- **Auditing:** Track and log changes to data for compliance, auditing, or monitoring purposes.

23. We have a premium customer with a large number of enterprise NoSQL (MongoDB, Cassandra etc.) workloads running on-premises. As a lead consultant, considering factors like security, cost, and performance, which Azure options do you recommend for migrating their on-premises NoSQL workloads?

Ans:

There's no one-size-fits-all solution. To provide the most suitable Azure solution, a more in-depth analysis of their on-premises workloads is recommended. However, here are some general recommendations:

- **Migrating MongoDB and Cassandra Workloads:** If the customer uses Cassandra or MongoDB with compatible wire protocols, migrating to the respective Azure Cosmos DB API (Cassandra API or MongoDB API) offers the easiest path. This allows them to switch the connection and leverage Cosmos DB features without major application-level code changes.
- **Migrating Gremlin Workloads:** For existing Gremlin workloads, Azure Cosmos DB Gremlin API is a suitable choice. It also works well for new applications requiring complex data relationships.
- **Upgrading from Azure Table Storage:** For existing Azure Table Storage users, migrating to Azure Cosmos DB Table API is highly recommended due to its superior performance and scalability.
- **Modern Cloud-Based NoSQL:** If the customer uses a generic on-premises NoSQL database and seeks a modernized, versatile cloud solution, Azure Cosmos DB NoSQL API is ideal. However, this might require refactoring their application's data access layer.
- **Highly Scalable Relational Database:** If a highly scalable distributed relational database is needed, Azure Cosmos DB PostgreSQL is a good option.
- **Highly customized and complex systems:** For NoSQL database systems that are highly customized using a specific product and cannot leverage Cosmos DB APIs, and where the customer is unwilling to invest in refactoring their existing applications, we may need to host these workloads using an IaaS approach on Azure VMs.

24. What are the different methods and tools available to migrate databases from on-premises to Azure Cosmos DB?

Ans.

Azure Cosmos DB supports multiple APIs, allowing you to migrate data from various on-premises NoSQL and SQL sources to any of these APIs.

Cosmos DB API	Migration Solution	Migration Type	Data Volume Support
NoSQL API	Azure Cosmos DB Data Migration Tool	Offline	Small – Medium
	Cosmos DB bulk executor library	Offline	Large - VLDB (10 TB+)
	Cosmos DB Functions + ChangeFeed API	Online	Small – Medium
	Custom Migration Service using ChangeFeed	Online	Medium – Large
	Striim	Online	Medium – Large
Mongo API	Azure Cosmos DB Data Migration Tool	Offline	Small – Medium
	Mongo native backup, restore tools – mongodump, mongorestore, mongoexport, mongoimport, Studio3T	Offline	Small – Large
	Cosmos DB bulk executor library	Offline	Large - VLDB (10 TB+)
	Azure DMS	Offline/Online	Small – Large
	MongoDB migration extension for Azure Data Studio	Offline	Small – Medium
Cassandra API	cqlsh COPY command	Offline	Small – Medium
	Apache Kafka Connect	Online	Small - Medium
	Striim, Blitzzm, Arcion	Online	Medium – VLDB
Gremlin API	Graph bulk executor library	Offline	Medium – VLDB
	Gremlin Spark	Offline	Medium – VLDB
Table API	Azure Cosmos DB Data Migration Tool	Offline	Small - Medium
	AzCopy	Offline	Medium – VLDB
PostgreSQL API	Azure DMS	Online	Medium – Large
	pg_azure_storage Extension	Offline	Medium – Large

Table 9.1

Explore:

Azure Cosmos DB Migration Tools:

- **Azure Database Migration Service (DMS):** Leverage this native service for migrations when supported by the desired Cosmos DB API.
- **Azure Cosmos DB Data Migration Tool**: This is an open-source command-line application for importing or exporting data from Azure Cosmos DB. The tool can migrate data to and from many sources and targets, including Azure Cosmos DB NoSQL API, MongoDB API, Table API, Azure Table storage, MongoDB, SQL Server, etc.
- **Cosmos DB Bulk Executor Library**: Azure Cosmos DB provides the Bulk Executor Library, which can be easily scaled out across multiple instances (Ex: scaling out threads on a single node to consume about 500K RUs) and is resilient to transient failures. Additionally, the custom tool can pause and resume migration at various checkpoints. The Bulk Executor Library also partitions the source dataset into micro-batches that operate independently, providing a form of checkpointing.
- **Azure Data Studio**: The MongoDB migration extension for Azure Data Studio is the preferred tool for migrating your MongoDB workloads to the API for MongoDB vCore.
- **Apache Kafka (Cassandra API):** Data from source database will be pushed to Apache Kafka using the Debezium PostgreSQL connector, which is a “Kafka Connect” source connector. Inserts, updates, or deletion to records in the source table will be captured as change data events and sent to Kafka topic(s). The DataStax Apache Kafka connector (Kafka Connect sink connector), forms the second part of the pipeline. It will synchronize the change data events from Kafka topic to Azure Cosmos DB for Apache Cassandra tables.

Migrating from Specific Sources:

- **HBase to Cosmos DB (NoSQL API):** Use Azure Data Factory, Spark, or a custom tool with the bulk executor library.
- **DynamoDB/Couchbase to Cosmos DB (NoSQL API):** Leverage ADF for these migrations.
- **PostgreSQL to Cosmos DB (PostgreSQL API):** Utilize the pg_azure_storage extension for direct data manipulation and loading from Azure Blob Storage.

Universal Migration Tools (for most APIs):

- **Azure Data Factory:** This cloud-based ETL/ELT service supports data movement and transformation for migrating data to most Cosmos DB APIs.
- **Azure Cosmos DB Spark Connector/Azure Databricks**: This is the official connector for Azure Cosmos DB and Apache Spark. The connector allows us to easily read from and write to Azure Cosmos DB via Apache Spark Dataframes in Python and Scala.

Third-Party Tools and Scripts: Consider marketplace tools or explore custom scripts and third-party services beyond the Azure marketplace.

- **Striim, Blitzz**: These are widely used third-party tools for migrating data from data warehouses and databases (Ex: Oracle) to Azure Cosmos DB. These tools need to be purchased from the Azure Marketplace and installed in the user's environment.
- **Arcion (Acquired by Databricks)**: Arcion is a tool that offers a secure and reliable way to perform zero downtime migration from other databases to Azure Cosmos DB. This tool offers automatic migration of business logic (tables, indexes, views) from Apache Cassandra to Azure Cosmos DB.

Recommendation:

- **Small & Medium Data Volume:** Native database tools or migration tools such as Azure Cosmos DB Data Migration Tool is ideal for smaller datasets, especially for initial testing or proof-of-concept migrations.
- **Medium & Large Data Volume:** Both ADF and the Azure Data Migration Tool can handle these data transfers.
- **Large & Very Large Data Volume:** When dealing with massive datasets, consider ADF, Spark Connector or Azure Databricks. ADF excels in orchestration and data transformation for large-scale migrations. Spark Connector and Azure Databricks are powerful for leveraging existing Spark infrastructure to handle VLDB scenarios.

25. Can you describe ways to migrate MongoDB to Azure Cosmos DB Mongo API?"

Ans:

There are several methods to migrate your MongoDB data to Azure Cosmos DB for MongoDB API, depending on the size and complexity of your data:

- **Smaller Datasets:** Cosmos DB Data Migration Tool is a good choice for migrating smaller datasets due to its ease of use.
- **Specific Documents:** Utilize the familiar MongoDB Native export/import (mongoexport and mongoimport) commands for selective migration of specific documents or collections.
- **Multiple Sources or Large Datasets:**
    - **Azure Data Factory (ADF):** This cloud-based ETL/ELT service excels at handling complex migrations, especially when dealing with data from multiple sources.
    - **MongoDB Spark + Azure Databricks:** Leverage Apache Spark's capabilities for efficient migration of very large datasets (VLDB, exceeding 10 TB) using Azure Databricks.
- **Full Database Migration:**
    - **Offline Migration (DUMP & RESTORE):** Use the familiar mongodump and mongorestore commands for offline migrations of entire databases.

  - **Online Migration (DMS):** For enterprise-scale online migrations with minimal downtime, consider the Azure Database Migration Service (DMS).

- **Mongo DB API vCore:** "Azure Cosmos DB for MongoDB vCore migration extension for Azure Data Studio" can help us in assessing and migrating selected MongoDB databases and collections to Azure Cosmos DB for MongoDB vCore.

Note: Azure Explorer allows launching a browser-based Mongo Shell instance for interacting with your Cosmos DB for MongoDB API using Mongo commands.

26. Could you explain the step-by-step process for migrating MongoDB from on-premises to Azure Cosmos DB Mongo API?

Ans:

Here's a high-level overview of the migration process:

- **Assess and Prepare Source MongoDB:** Use MongoDB Shell or Compass to gather information about your source MongoDB deployment, including databases, collections, size, version, and resource utilization statistics. **Note:** Currently supported MongoDB binary protocol versions in Cosmos DB are 3.2, 3.6, 4.0, 4.2, 5.0, and 6.0.
- **Map Source Resources to Cosmos DB:** Based on the source assessment, define corresponding Cosmos DB resources. This includes:
  - Data model (JSON document structure)
  - Sharding key (partition key)
  - Compute model (RU/s, vCore)
  - Throughput (RU/sec) - choose between shared (database level) or dedicated (container level), provisioned, auto-scale, or serverless modes.
  - Consistency level (session, eventual, etc.)
  - Other settings like region priority
  - Estimate throughput using the Azure Cosmos DB calculator with factors like database size, document size, and read/write operations per second.

- **Choose the Migration Approach:** Select the most suitable migration approach considering, source database type (single/multiple sources, native MongoDB or files), data volume, online or offline migration requirement.
- **Perform and Validate Migration:** Start with a pre-production migration to gather statistics for capacity planning in production. Validate the migration by ensuring all databases, collections, and documents are transferred correctly.
- **Cutover and Post-Migration Activities:** Switch your application to use Azure Cosmos DB. Carefully plan indexing, global distribution, consistency, and other Cosmos DB properties for optimal performance.

Explore:

While the overall migration process using Azure DMS for MongoDB is similar to other database migrations (network configuration, service registration, DMS instance creation, migration project creation and configuration etc.), there are some additional settings to consider for optimal efficiency:

Server-Side Retry:

- During migration, Azure Cosmos DB might throttle requests exceeding the container's provisioned RU/s. These throttled requests need to be retried.
- While DMS can handle retries, the network latency between DMS and Cosmos DB can impact response times. Enabling Cosmos DB's Server-Side Retry feature allows the service to identify and retry throttled requests with a lower round-trip time, improving overall performance.
- You can enable this from the Azure portal by navigating to your Cosmos DB account > Features > Server-Side Retry > Enable.

On-premises MongoDB Connectivity: When configuring the source details in your migration project, you have three options for connecting to your on-premises MongoDB instance:

- **Standard:** Provide the source MongoDB server's IP address or FQDN.
- **Connection String:** Specify a URI containing source database server details, access control information, and replica details.
- **Data from Azure Storage:** If migrating from MongoDB dumps (BSON or JSON) stored in Azure Storage, use the Blob container's SAS URL.

27. What are the options for securing data stored in Azure Cosmos DB?

Ans:

Azure Cosmos DB offers multiple layers of security to control access to your data:

- **Network IP firewall:** This feature allows you to restrict access to your Cosmos DB account to specific IP addresses or ranges. The IP-based access controls are similar to the firewall rules used by traditional database systems.
- **Authentication and Authorization:**
  - **Microsoft Entra Integration**: Use Entra to authenticate and authorize access to Azure Cosmos DB resources. This allows you to manage access through RBAC and leverage the security features of Entra.
  - **Role-Based Access Control (RBAC)**: Define roles and permissions to restrict access to data. You can assign built-in roles (Cosmos DB Account Reader Role, DocumentDB Account Contributor, CosmosBackupOperator, CosmosRestoreOperator) or create custom roles to grant the necessary permissions to users or applications.

- Hash-based message authentication code (HMAC): Azure Cosmos DB uses HMAC for authorization. Each request is hashed by using the secret account key, and the subsequent base-64 encoded hash is sent with each call to Azure Cosmos DB. To validate the request, Azure Cosmos DB uses the correct secret key and properties to generate a hash, and then it compares the value with the one in the request. If the two values match, the operation is authorized successfully and the request is processed. If they don't match, there's an authorization failure and the request is rejected.
- **Tokens:**
  - **Master key (Primary/Secondary Keys) tokens** are the all-access key tokens that allow users to have full control of Cosmos DB resources in a particular account.
  - **Resource Tokens:** Resource tokens are used to provide fine-grained access control to specific resources within a Cosmos DB account, such as individual databases, collections, or documents.

- **Data Encryption:**
  - **Encryption at Rest**: Azure Cosmos DB automatically encrypts all data at rest using Microsoft-managed keys. You can also opt for customer-managed keys stored in Azure Key Vault for additional control over encryption keys.
  - **Encryption in Transit**: All connections to Azure Cosmos DB support HTTPS. Data in transit is secured using TLS (Transport Layer Security) to ensure that data is encrypted while being transferred over the network.

- **Monitoring and Auditing**:
  - **Azure Monitor**: Use Azure Monitor to track and log activities on your Azure Cosmos DB account. This includes monitoring query execution, request and response times, and overall performance.
  - **Azure Cosmos DB Diagnostic Logging**: Enable diagnostic logging to capture detailed information about operations performed on your database. Logs can be sent to Azure Monitor logs, Event Hubs, or Azure Storage for analysis and auditing.

28. What are the differences between Master (Primary Key/ Secondary Key) Tokens and Resource Tokens in Azure Cosmos DB?

Ans:

Master Key (Primary and Secondary Key) Tokens: Provide full access to the entire Cosmos DB account; used for administrative purposes.

Resource Tokens: Provide limited, specific access to individual resources within the Cosmos DB account; used for granting secure, temporary permissions to clients or applications.

Authorization header: All REST operations, whether you're using a master key token or resource token, must include the authorization header with the authorization string in order to interact with a resource. The authorization string has the following format:

- type={typeoftoken}&ver={tokenversion}&sig={hashsignature}
- **{typeoftoken}:** Master, resource, or aad(if you are using Azure Cosmos DB RBAC).
- **{tokenversion}:** Version of the token, currently 1.0.
- **{hashsignature}:** Hashed token signature or the oauth token (if you are using Azure Cosmos DB RBAC)

Explore:

- **Master Key Token**: Grants access to all resources in the Cosmos DB account, enabling full administrative capabilities. The master key (primary key and the secondary key) is created during the creation of an account. The purpose of dual keys is to let you regenerate, or roll, keys, providing continuous access to your account and data.
    - **Security**: Because they grant extensive permissions, master key tokens should be securely stored and managed. They are typically used for administrative tasks and initial setup.
- **Resource Token**: Grants access to specific resources within the Cosmos DB account, allowing for fine-grained and limited access control. Resource tokens are created when users in a database are set up with access permissions for precise access control on a resource. Resource tokens are time bound (default expiration is 1 hour) with a customizable validity period (up to 24 hours).
    - **Security**: Resource tokens offer a more secure way to grant access as they can specify precise permissions and have an expiration time, reducing the risk associated with long-term or overly broad access.
    - **Resource:** In the context of Azure Cosmos DB, "resource" refers to any object or entity that can be created, managed, or accessed within a Cosmos DB account, but the scope and granularity of access differ based on the type of token used.
    - **Ex:** Resources may refer to Databases, collections/containers, documents/items, users, permissions, stored procedures, triggers, and user defined functions.

29. Have you heard of the CAP theorem?

Ans:

The CAP theorem, also known as Brewer's theorem, is a fundamental principle in the design of distributed systems. It states that it is impossible for a distributed data store to simultaneously provide more than two out of the following three guarantees:

- **Consistency (C):** Every read receives the "most recent write" or "an error".
  - **Ex:** If a customer updates their shipping address (with success), when the customer views their profile, they should see the updated address instantly, no matter which server responds to the request.
- **Availability (A):** Every request receives a (non-error) response, with no guarantee that it contains the most recent write.
  - **Ex:** If one server is down, the customer's request to view their profile or make a purchase should still be processed by another server without returning an error.
- **Partition Tolerance (P):** The system continues to operate even if the network partitions the system, meaning some nodes become disconnected from others.
  - **Ex:** If there's a network issue and the servers in Europe cannot communicate with the servers in North America, both sets of servers should still handle requests independently.

Explore:

According to the CAP theorem, a distributed system can satisfy any two of these guarantees at the same time, but not all three. **Ex:** CA, CP, or AP.

- **CP (Consistent and Partition Tolerant):** This system prioritizes consistency over availability. In case of a failure, reads might be unavailable, but all nodes will eventually have the same consistent data once the partition heals. This is often used in financial transactions or other scenarios where data integrity is critical.
- **AP (Available and Partition Tolerant):** This system prioritizes availability over consistency. Reads will always be successful, but during a failure, different nodes might have different versions of the data. This is often used in social media platforms or e-commerce websites where immediate availability is more important than perfect consistency.
- **CA (Consistent and Available):** This scenario violates the CAP theorem. It's theoretically impossible to guarantee both perfect consistency and availability in the presence of network failures.

30. What are the use cases of the CAP theorem

Ans:

The CAP theorem is a guiding principle for architects and engineers designing distributed systems. The choice of which two properties to prioritize (Consistency, Availability, Partition Tolerance) depends on the specific requirements and constraints of the application, the nature of the data, and the business goals. By understanding and applying the CAP theorem, organizations can design more robust, scalable, and efficient distributed systems.

CAP theorem is utilized by various industries and organizations (cloud service providers, social media platforms, e-commerce, financial services, healthcare, telecommunications etc.) that rely on distributed systems to ensure data availability, consistency, and reliability.

Explore:

- **Distributed Database Systems:** The CAP theorem helps in understanding the limitations and making informed decisions about the trade-offs between consistency, availability, and partition tolerance. As a result, distributed database systems prioritize only two properties at a time.
- **Cloud Applications:** All cloud applications are distributed systems, so it's essential to understand the CAP theorem when designing a cloud app. This helps in choosing a data management system that delivers the characteristics your application needs most.
    - **Ex:** Google Spanner balances between consistency and availability. AWS DynamoDB is designed around eventual consistency to ensure high availability and partition tolerance. Azure Cosmos DB offers multiple consistency models, allowing users to choose their desired balance between consistency, availability, and latency.
- **NoSQL Databases:** NoSQL databases are often classified based on the CAP theorem. The CAP theorem helps in understanding the trade-offs made by different NoSQL databases and their suitability for various use cases.
    - **Consistency and Partition Tolerance (CP):** These databases ensure that the data is consistent across the distributed system and can handle network partitions, but they might sacrifice availability in the event of a network partition. Ex: HBase.
    - **Availability and Partition Tolerance (AP):** These databases ensure that the system remains available and can tolerate network partitions, but they might provide eventual consistency, meaning that the data may not be immediately consistent across all nodes. **Ex:** Cassandra, MongoDB, Redis (Cluster Mode), Couchbase.
    - **Consistency and Availability (CA):** These databases ensure that every read receives the most recent write (strong consistency) and the system is always available, but they do not provide partition tolerance.
        - **Ex:** This model is not suitable for distributed systems where network partitions are a concern. Traditional relational databases often fall into this category. Most NoSQL databases are designed to handle partition tolerance.

CHAPTER 10

Azure Cloud Migration 1 – Fundamentals

1. What are the phases of Cloud Migration?

Ans:

Cloud migration involves moving IT infrastructure, applications, and data from on-premises systems to a cloud environment. Here are the typical phases of cloud migration:

- **Business Case:** This phase involves outlining the reasons for migrating to the cloud and the expected benefits. You'll want to quantify the potential cost savings, increased agility, improved scalability, or other improvements your business will achieve.
- **Prepare:** This phase involves assessing your current IT environment, identifying what needs to be migrated, and determining the best migration strategy for your needs. This includes tasks like understanding your existing applications and data dependencies.
- **Plan:** Here, you develop a detailed plan for your migration, including the timeline, resources, and tools required. You'll also choose a cloud provider and service model (IaaS, PaaS, SaaS) that aligns with your goals.
- **Migrate:** During this phase, you actually move your data and applications to the cloud environment. This can involve using various tools and techniques depending on your chosen strategy.
- **Operate:** Once migrated, you need to manage and monitor your applications and data in the cloud. This includes ensuring security, performance, and ongoing maintenance.
- **Optimize:** This final phase is about getting the most out of your cloud investment. You can continually optimize your cloud resources to improve cost-efficiency, performance, and scalability.

Explore:

More detailed cloud migration phases and sub-phases:

Business Case:

- **Sub-phases:**
  - **Identify Business Goals:** Define your organization's objectives for migrating to the cloud. Is it cost reduction, improved scalability, disaster recovery, or something else?
  - **Evaluate Current State:** Assess your existing IT infrastructure, applications, and data to understand their cloud readiness and potential migration challenges.

  - **Cost-Benefit Analysis:** Quantify the expected financial benefits of cloud migration, including potential cost savings, increased revenue, or improved efficiency.
- **Expected Output:** A compelling document outlining the reasons for migration, projected benefits, and a preliminary cost analysis.

Prepare (This Phase May Be Iterative):

- **Sub-phases:**
  - **Prioritization:** Based on business criticality, technical feasibility, and migration complexity, prioritize applications for migration. Start with a smaller, less critical subset for a pilot migration.
  - **Detailed Inventory and Discovery:** Conduct a deep dive into the prioritized applications. This includes:
    - Application functionality and dependencies.
    - Data types, sizes, and access requirements.
    - Underlying infrastructure (servers, storage, network).
    - Operational processes (monitoring, patching, etc.).
  - **Application Assessment:** Evaluate each prioritized application's cloud readiness using tools and frameworks. Consider factors like:
    - Architecture (monolithic, microservices, etc.).
    - Programming languages and frameworks.
    - Security requirements and compliance needs.
  - **Data Classification:** Classify data associated with prioritized applications based on:
    - Sensitivity (public, internal, confidential).
    - Regulatory compliance requirements.
    - Access control needs (hot, warm, cool data).
  - **Cloud Migration Strategy Selection:** Choose an appropriate migration strategy for each application and data set (lift-and-shift, refactoring, re-platforming, etc.). Consider cloud-native options where feasible.
- **Expected Output:** A detailed understanding of the prioritized applications and their cloud readiness. Migration strategy recommendations with justifications.

Plan (This Phase Can Be Done Iteratively for Each Prioritized Set):

- **Sub-phases:**
  - **Define Migration Timeline (per batch):** Create a detailed timeline for each prioritized migration batch, outlining milestones and deliverables.

- **Resource Allocation (per batch):** Allocate resources for each migration batch, including personnel, budget, and cloud migration tools.
- **Cloud Provider Selection:** Select a cloud provider considering:
  - Service offerings (IaaS, PaaS, SaaS) to match application needs.
  - Cost structure based on anticipated resource usage.
  - Security and compliance capabilities.
- **Security and Compliance Planning:** Develop a cloud security and compliance strategy for each migration batch. This includes data encryption, access control, and meeting regulatory requirements.

- **Expected Output:** Well-defined migration plans for prioritized applications with timelines, resources, chosen cloud provider, and documented security and compliance strategies.

Migrate (This Phase Can Be Done Iteratively in Batches):

- **Sub-phases:**
  - **Pilot Migration:** Perform a pilot migration with a small, less critical application to test migration processes, tools, and validate the chosen strategy.
  - **Production Migration (per batch):** Based on pilot learnings, execute the migration of prioritized applications and data sets in batches according to the plan.
  - **Testing and Validation:** Thoroughly test migrated applications and data to ensure functionality, performance, and security meet expectations.
- **Expected Output:** Successful migration of prioritized applications and data sets to the cloud environment.

Operate (Ongoing for All Migrated Applications):

Sub-phases:

- **Cloud Management:** Establish processes for ongoing management of cloud resources for migrated applications, including:
  - Performance monitoring and optimization.
  - Security monitoring and threat detection.
  - Cost optimization and resource utilization tracking.
- **User Adoption and Training:** Provide user training and support for migrated applications to ensure smooth user experience.
- **Incident Management:** Implement procedures for handling incidents, outages, and security threats in the cloud environment.

- **Expected Output:** Efficiently managed cloud environment for migrated applications with ongoing monitoring, trained users, and well-defined incident management protocols.

Optimize (Ongoing for All Migrated Applications):

- **Sub-phases:**
  - **Cost Optimization:** Continuously analyze and optimize cloud resource usage for all migrated applications to minimize costs and improve efficiency.
  - **Performance Optimization:** Monitor and fine-tune cloud resources to ensure optimal application performance. This may involve:
    - Scaling cloud resources up or down based on demand.
    - Identifying and eliminating performance bottlenecks.
    - Leveraging cloud-native features like auto-scaling and serverless options.
  - **Scalability Management:** Implement strategies to easily scale your cloud resources up or down to meet changing business demands. This may involve:
    - Using elastic cloud services that can automatically provision resources.
    - Implementing horizontal scaling for stateless applications.
    - Implementing vertical scaling for applications requiring more processing power.
- **Expected Output:** Cost-effective and high-performing cloud environment that can adapt to your business needs for all migrated applications.

Additional Considerations for Large Scale Migration:

- **SWOT Analysis:** Analyze the application's Strengths, Weaknesses, Opportunities, and Threats. This will help determine if migration is beneficial and identify areas for potential modernization.
- **Environment Assessment:** Evaluate the application's dependencies on hardware, software, and network infrastructure. This will help plan for replicating the environment in Cloud.
- **Phased Migration Approach:** Given the large number of applications, a phased migration with smaller batches is recommended. This allows for better risk management and facilitates course correction if needed.
- **Center of Excellence (CoE):** Establish a dedicated CoE team to oversee the migration process. This team can provide expertise, manage resources, and ensure consistency across migration batches.
- **Automation:** Leverage cloud migration tools, Infrastructure-as-Code pipelines, and automation scripts to streamline repetitive tasks and improve migration efficiency.
- **Change Management:** Develop a comprehensive change management plan to address user concerns and ensure smooth adoption of cloud-based applications.

2. How does a large organization perform a detailed inventory and discovery during the cloud migration preparation phase? Specifically, how is all the necessary information collected from the source environment across the organization?

Ans:

Performing a detailed inventory and discovery process in preparation for cloud migration in a large organization involves gathering comprehensive information about the existing IT infrastructure, applications, data, and dependencies across various departments and business units. Here's how you can approach it:

- Automated Discovery Tools.
- Agent-based Discovery.
- Asset Management Systems.
- Manual Collection.
- Data Validation and Reconciliation.

Explore:

Automated Discovery Tools: Use it to scan the entire network and collect data about hardware, software, virtual machines, servers, applications, databases, storage, network configurations, and dependencies.

- **Servers:** Hardware configuration (CPU, memory, storage), operating system details, installed software, running processes.
- **Applications:** Identify applications, their dependencies, and communication patterns.
- **Database:** Discover relational, NoSQL, hierarchical, timeseries, graph databases, operational data stores, data warehouses, data lakes etc.
- **Storage:** Discover storage types (SAN, NAS), capacity utilization, data types stored.
- **Network Configuration:** Map network topology, identify network devices and security configurations.
- **Ex:** Azure Migrate, AWS Application Discovery Service, Google Cloud Migrate, VMware vRealize Network Insight, Microsoft Assessment and Planning (MAP) Toolkit, ServiceNow Discovery, BMC Discovery etc.

Agent-based Discovery: Deploy lightweight agents on servers or virtual machines to collect deeper insights:

- **Detailed application profiling:** Analyze application behavior, resource utilization, and dependencies.
- **Configuration management data:** Gather configuration details for operating systems and applications.
- **Ex:** Azure Migrate, AWS CloudEndure Migrate, Dynatrace, AppDynamics by Cisco etc.

Asset Management Systems: Leverage existing asset management systems, such as Configuration Management Databases (CMDBs) or IT Service Management (ITSM) platforms, to gather information about servers, storage devices, network devices, and software applications. Ensure that these systems are up-to-date and accurately reflect the organization's IT landscape.

Manual Collection: Utilize manual methods to capture information not readily available (Ex: Legacy applications) through automated tools:

- **Documentation Review**: Review existing documentation, including network diagrams, system configurations, application inventories, and architectural diagrams. Update and supplement this documentation as needed to ensure it reflects the current state of the environment.
- **Surveys and questionnaires:** Distribute surveys (data collection templates) to IT teams and application owners to gather details on application functionality, usage patterns, and criticality.
- **Collaboration with IT Teams**: Collaborate closely with IT teams responsible for different areas of the infrastructure, such as network, storage, databases, and applications. Conduct interviews and workshops with system administrators, database administrators, network engineers, and other relevant stakeholders to gather detailed information about their respective domains.

Data Validation and Reconciliation: Cleanse and validate the collected data to ensure accuracy and consistency. This might involve:

- **Centralized repository**: Consolidate the collected data from various sources into a centralized repository or database for analysis. Use data analysis tools or scripts to identify patterns, dependencies, redundancies, and potential migration challenges.
- **Deduplication:** Remove duplicate entries identified from different sources.
- **Normalization:** Standardize data formats to facilitate analysis and reporting.
- **Verification:** Cross-check information with IT teams and application owners for accuracy.

Risk and Complexity Assessment: Assess the risk and complexity of migrating each application or workload based on factors such as business criticality, technical dependencies, data sensitivity, compliance requirements, and interdependencies with other systems. It helps use prioritizing migration candidates accordingly.

3. In cloud migration, which phase is possibly the most important: business case, prepare, plan, migrate, operate, or optimize? Why?

Ans:

It's difficult to say conclusively which phase is the most important in cloud migration. Because, all phases of cloud migration are important as they each serve a unique purpose in ensuring a successful migration. However, three phases hold significant weight for different reasons:

- **Business Case (Sets direction and secure resources):** Provides a clear vision for the migration and convinces stakeholders of its value.

- **Prepare (Reduces risks and ensures smooth migration):** Mitigates potential roadblocks by identifying dependencies and choosing the right strategies.
- **Plan (Focuses on developing a detailed roadmap for the migration):** A well-defined plan helps manage expectations, keeps the project on track, and minimizes disruptions during migration.

While all phases are essential, the Business Case, Prepare & Plan phases hold significant weight in setting the stage for a successful cloud migration. They ensure you're migrating for the right reasons and with a clear understanding of your existing environment, ultimately leading to a more efficient and cost-effective cloud journey.

Explore:

Introduction: As the saying goes, "If you fail to plan, you are planning to fail." This applies not just to finances, but to every choice we make, including cloud migration. Let's explore this concept with an analogy.

Travel Analogy:

- Imagine Mr. A, excited for a week-long Swiss vacation. He secures visas for his family, then searches for flights, prioritizing departure time, cost, and convenience. He quickly booked tickets from New York to Zurich Airport.
- **Extra Fees:** On travel day, at boarding, they discover the baggage allowance is much lower than expected, leading to extra fees.
- **Layover:** Their itinerary, New York (US) > Boston (US) > Lisbon (Portugal) > Zurich (Switzerland), reveals long layovers: 4 hours in Boston and an exhausting 10.5 hours in Lisbon. With a total travel time of 28 hours, they finally arrive in Zurich, exhausted.
- **Immigration throws another surprise**: Mr. A's name is partially missing on his covid-19 vaccination certificate. After a tense two-hour wait, officials grant them entry. However, at 2:30 AM with heavy snowfall, their troubles continue.
- **A rule is a rule:** Additionally, the hotel required a negative COVID-19 test certificate within the last 48 hours, forcing Mr. A to find accommodation on the outskirts of the city. Eventually, they secured a room by 6:30 AM.
- **Nightmare:** To top it off, Switzerland was experiencing extreme weather conditions that persisted for the next five days, resulting in an unpleasant holiday trip due to poor planning.

Lesson learned:

Mr. A failed to properly check airline limitations, layover times, immigration rules, hotel policies, arrival times, and weather conditions. He made a flawed plan and blindly followed it. This example can be compared to a cloud migration project.

Similarly, for cloud migration, don't choose resources only on price.

- For example, while serverless options may be cheaper, they may not meet all your requirements.

- Opting for 'Standard SSD' for a database workload VM in Azure for production workloads only because it's cheaper may not be the best choice. The right choice can only be determined after considering IOPS and throughput requirements. However, premium SSD is the minimum requirement for all production workloads.
- Failure to consider migration timelines could lead to critical release planning conflicts or overlap with maintenance activities in the target environment.

Conclusion:

A successful cloud migration requires a well-defined plan based on thorough analysis. Only with meticulous planning and execution can your migration project be a success story, not a travel nightmare.

The primary principle to consider for a successful cloud migration is to "**strike a balance between cost and performance, ensuring that security remains a non-negotiable aspect.**"

4. A C-level business executive recently asked a critical question: "Why should we migrate to the cloud?" How would you respond, considering their focus on business rather than technology?

Ans:

Well, that's a valid question, and we refer to it as a Business Case. This is what we address in the first phase of cloud migration. Before initiating the migration project, we need to establish a Business Case for migration and set expectations for cost, return, and the timing of those costs and returns. Money is everything in business, so the migration business case showcases the TCO (Total Cost of Ownership) and ROI (Return on Investment) calculations, demonstrating the cost benefits of migrating to the cloud.

While the business case focuses on the financial aspects, cloud migration offers a wider range of benefits (enhanced scalability, improved agility & Innovation) that contribute to overall business success.

5. I understand that business cases drive cloud migration projects. As a senior data professional, what are the most common or general benefits you highlight to clients when building a cloud migration business case?

Ans:

From a data ecosystem perspective, the top benefits of cloud migration are:

- Enhanced Scalability, Flexibility and customizations.
- Improved Data Accessibility and Sharing.
- Advanced Analytics Solutions.
- Advanced Security Features.

Explore:

- **Enhanced Scalability and Flexibility:**
    - **Wide Range of Services**: Choose from a broad range of cloud services tailored to specific needs, from basic storage to advanced computing and analytics.
    - **Elastic resources:** Easily scale computing power, storage, and networking resources up or down based on workload demands.
    - **Rapid provisioning:** Spin up new environments or clusters quickly to meet project timelines.
- **Improved Data Accessibility and Sharing:**
    - **Centralized data storage:** Consolidate data into a single, accessible location.
    - **Data sharing capabilities:** Facilitate collaboration and data-driven decision making across teams.
- **Advanced Analytics and Machine Learning:**
    - **Cloud-based platforms:** Leverage powerful tools and services for data processing, analysis, and modelling.
    - **Accelerated innovation:** Experiment with new technologies and algorithms more rapidly.
- **Disaster Recovery and Business Continuity:**
    - **Data backup and recovery:** Implement robust data protection strategies with built-in redundancy.
    - **Business continuity:** Ensure uninterrupted operations through cloud-based disaster recovery solutions.
- **Focus on Core Competencies:**
    - **Outsourcing infrastructure management:** Free up time to focus on data analysis, modelling, and insights.
    - **Increased agility:** Respond to business needs more quickly by leveraging cloud-based services.
- **Security:**
    - **Advanced Security Features**: Cloud providers offer robust security features, including encryption, identity and access management, and threat detection.
    - **Compliance**: Many cloud services are compliant with industry standards and regulations, aiding in meeting regulatory requirements.
- **Cost Efficiency:**
    - **Pay-per-use model:** Optimize costs by paying only for the resources used.

- **Reduced infrastructure overhead:** Eliminate expenses related to hardware, software, and maintenance.

Ex: For example, let's suppose your proposal for a new software project is approved, and you need to initiate the development phase.

- **On-premises:** Traditionally, on-premises, provisioning the necessary infrastructure—including servers, VMs for development, testing and production environments, CI/CD server capacity, Active Directory setup, user onboarding, and software installations—could take weeks or even months.
- **Cloud:** With cloud computing, this infrastructure can often be provisioned within minutes or hours, and the process can be automated.

This accelerated provisioning allows us to concentrate on core development activities and rapid business response rather than investing significant time in infrastructure setup and maintenance.

6. Can you describe TCO and ROI in the context of cloud migration?

Ans:

Absolutely! TCO (Total Cost of Ownership) and ROI (Return on Investment) are key metrics used to build a strong business case for cloud migration. Both focus on the financial impact, helping you understand the costs involved and the potential gains.

- **TCO (Total Cost of Ownership):** A complete financial metric including all direct and indirect costs associated with IT infrastructure. This includes hardware, software licenses, maintenance, electricity, and potential hidden costs like downtime or security breaches.
- **ROI (Return on Investment):** A key performance indicator used to assess the financial viability of cloud migration. It measures the net gain achieved by comparing the initial investment (migration costs) with the projected long-term benefits.

Explore:

TCO (Total Cost of Ownership): This represents the sum of expenses associated with purchasing, deploying, using, and retiring a product, equipment, or asset. Essentially, it includes the purchase and operating costs over the asset's lifetime. There are two categories of costs involved: direct and indirect.

- **Ex:** When we buy a car, direct costs include the retail price, registration tax, road tax, insurance premium, etc., while indirect costs include parking tickets, toll charges, and maintenance expenses. Similarly, for our organization's technology infrastructure, TCO includes hardware, software, and operational costs.

On-premises TCO calculation: Conducting an infrastructure audit helps identify direct and indirect costs.

- **Direct costs:** These remain on our organization's balance sheet and include hardware, software, management, support, and implementation expenses.
- **Indirect costs:** These are challenging to calculate but equally significant, including expenses like unscheduled maintenance, business impact due to downtime, power consumption, asset depreciation, etc.

Cloud TCO calculation: Most cloud providers offer advanced TCO calculators. Based on our on-premises analysis, we input infrastructure details, and the tool estimates the cloud TCO. Additionally, we consider one-time investments in migration activities.

- **Direct costs:** These include cloud subscriptions, cloud services, integration, testing, consulting, training, and migration expenses.
- **Indirect costs:** Include excess compute and storage reservations, premium service packages without proper SLAs, surrendered software licenses (loosing or giving up in the transition), required on-premises infrastructure after migration, etc.

ROI (Return on Investment): ROI indicates the profit or loss earned from an investment and is expressed as a percentage.

- **General ROI formula:** (Net Profit / Cost of Investment) x 100
  - **ROI** = (Net Profit / Cost of Investment) x 100
    - **Net Profit** = Gain from investment - Cost of Investment
      - **Gain from investment** = On-premise Cost – Cloud Cost
      - **Cost of Investment** = Migration Cost

7. Let's consider a scenario where a large organization migrated its IT infrastructure from on-premises to Azure Cloud. Could you explain how to calculate the ROI with some sample values?

Ans:

Generic ROI formula:

- **ROI** = (Net Profit / Cost of Investment) x 100
  - **Net Profit** = Gain from investment - Cost of Investment
    - **Gain from investment** = On-premise Cost – Cloud Cost
    - **Cost of Investment** = Migration Cost

- **On-premise Cost:** This represents the total cost associated with your IT infrastructure before migrating to the cloud. It includes hardware Costs, software licenses, IT staff costs, electricity & maintenance costs, downtime costs.
- **Cloud Cost:** This represents the projected total cost associated with your IT infrastructure after migrating to the cloud. It includes Cloud Services Subscription, migration costs, reduced On-Premises Costs, reduced electricity & maintenance.

- **Cost of Investment:** This specifically refers to the one-time costs associated with the cloud migration project itself. This typically includes consulting fees, data transfer costs and training costs.

Scenario: A medium sized retail company (let's call it "TheOneRetail") is considering migrating its IT infrastructure to the cloud.

A) Current (On-Premises) Costs:

- **Hardware:** $5 million (servers, storage)
- **Software licenses:** $2 million (annual)
- **IT Staff:** $8 million (annual salaries and benefits)
- **Electricity & Maintenance:** $2 million (annual)
- **Downtime Costs (estimated):** $1 million (annual)
    - **Total On-premise Cost:** $18 million

B) After Cloud Migration:

- **Cloud Services Subscription:** $8 million (annual) - This is an estimated cost based on resource usage with a cloud provider.
- **On-Premises Costs (reduced):** $6 million (annual) - TheOneRetail will retain a portion of on-premises for specific application that includes hardware, software, IT-Staff, electricity, downtime costs etc.
    - **Total (Cloud + On-premise reduced) Cost after Cloud Migration:** $14 million (annual)

C) Cost of Investment (Migration Cost): $3 million (One time)

D) ROI Calculation:

- Net Profit = Cost Before Migration – Cost After Migration
- Net Profit = $18 Million – $14 Million = $4 Million
- Migration Cost: $3 Million
- ROI = (Net Profit / Cost of Investment) x 100
- ROI = ($4 Million / $3 Million) X 100 = 133.33%

The ROI for "TheOneRetail" in the first year after cloud migration is 1.33 or 133.33%.

Explore:

- The above scenario is a simplified calculation. Actual ROI may vary due to factors like unforeseen costs, changes in cloud service pricing, and the effectiveness of the migration process.
- The ROI calculation for subsequent years will be based on the ongoing savings from cloud migration.

- In most scenarios, the first-year ROI would be negative, as it is not practically possible to reduce on-premise costs immediately after the migration. Additionally, after the cloud migration, we will need time to tune and optimize the cloud environments, which can be done in the coming years.
    - **Here are some factors that could influence the actual ROI:**
    - **Hidden Costs:** There might be additional costs associated with cloud migration, such as data transfer fees, training, and potential consulting fees.
    - **Underestimations:** Cloud service subscription costs are often underestimated due to unaccounted variable costs (Ex: network bandwidth, scaling, advanced features etc.).
    - **Long-Term Savings:** The ROI calculation is based on the first year. Long-term savings might be affected by changes in cloud pricing, increased usage, or unforeseen factors.
    - **Performance and Reliability:** Cloud migration might impact application performance or reliability. If there are performance issues or downtime, it could affect the overall cost-benefit analysis.
    - **Return on Investment in Other Areas:** The ROI calculation only considers financial benefits. It's essential to evaluate the impact of cloud migration on other factors, such as agility, innovation, and risk reduction.

8. During this TCO and ROI process, have you heard about CapEx and OpEx?

Ans:

Absolutely! CapEx (Capital Expenditures) and OpEx (Operational Expenditures) are standard accounting terms that categorize costs.

- **CapEx:** Upfront costs for long-term assets (Ex: servers, data centers).
- **OpEx:** Ongoing costs for using services (Ex: cloud storage, SaaS subscriptions).

Explore:

- **CapEx (Upfront Costs):** CapEx refers to the upfront investment in physical assets or infrastructure that are expected to provide long-term benefits to the organization. In simpler terms, CapEx is about predicting future usage and investing in advance.
    - **On-Premise:** Purchasing servers, storage devices, network equipment, and the physical location (like a data center) to house these assets, software licences (that are bought as a one-time purchase.) etc.
    - **Cloud:** Upfront costs for reserved instances (reserving a SQL Database or a VM usage for 3 years etc.) or committed use contracts where you commit to use certain services for a period of time in exchange for a discount.

- **OpEx (Pay-as-You-Go Costs):** OpEx refers to ongoing operational expenses incurred by the organization to maintain and run its business operations.
    - **On-Premise:** Ongoing costs such as electricity for power and cooling, maintenance and upgrades of hardware and software, and salaries of IT staff managing the infrastructure.
    - **Cloud:** Monthly or usage-based fees for cloud services (like charges for compute instances, storage, and data transfer), as well as costs (salaries, training etc.) for managing and maintaining these services, including security and software updates.

9. What is the best approach for cloud migration: lift-and-shift or phased migration?

Ans:

There's no single "best" approach between lift-and-shift and phased cloud migration. The optimal choice depends on several factors such as the organization's goals, priorities, constraints, existing infrastructure, resources, and timeline.

A lift-and-shift migration might be best if you need to move quickly, while a phased migration could be a better choice if you're able to invest more time and resources to optimize and modernize your applications for the cloud.

Explore:

Lift-and-shift / Rehosting / Forklift: This approach involves migrating applications or systems to the cloud without making any significant changes to their architecture. It's typically faster and simpler but may not fully leverage the benefits of cloud-native features. It's suitable for situations where the primary goal is to quickly move existing workloads to the cloud, such as minimizing on-premises infrastructure costs or addressing end-of-life hardware.

- **Pros:**
    - Faster and simpler to implement.
    - Lower upfront costs as it involves minimal code changes.
    - Well-suited for applications with low complexity.
- **Cons:**
    - May not leverage all the benefits of the cloud (modernization, scalability, agility).
    - Might not optimize performance or cost in the long run.
    - Potential security vulnerabilities if legacy security practices are migrated.

Phased: This approach involves migrating to the cloud in stages, typically starting with a pilot project or less critical workloads before gradually moving more complex or critical applications. It allows for more careful planning, optimization, and testing, potentially resulting in better cost savings, performance improvements, and reduced risks.

- **Pros:**
  - Allows for gradual transition and risk mitigation.
  - Enables application modernization and optimization for the cloud.
  - Can lead to better cost efficiency and security posture in the long run.
- **Cons:**
  - More complex and time-consuming to implement.
  - Requires more planning and resources compared to lift-and-shift.
  - May involve some downtime during migration phases.

Hybrid Approach: This strategy is your go-to approach, especially for large-scale migrations. You can combine both methods. Migrate less critical applications with lift-and-shift, while taking a phased approach for complex ones.

10. I understand that phased migration is often the preferred approach. However, are there scenarios where lift-and-shift might be a better fit?

Ans:

Absolutely! Lift-and-shift can be a good choice in certain situations:

- **Limited Connectivity:** If restrictions at the source environment make it difficult to establish a reliable connection between on-premises and cloud infrastructure.
- **Faster Migration Time:** When speed is a top priority, especially for large-scale migrations.
- **"Hands-Off" Applications:** For legacy applications with tight coupling or where business stakeholders prefer not to modify the application architecture, lift-and-shift avoids the need for refactoring.
- **Post-Migration Optimization:** If an application has the flexibility to be optimized after migration, you can lift-and-shift it initially and then gradually leverage cloud features.

11. In your experience, have you ever done a lift-and-shift migration? If so, what were the top challenges you faced with this approach?

Ans:

I successfully migrated 95 applications and 300 TB of data for a client to Azure using lift-and-shift. However, there were challenges:

Specific Challenges Faced:

In our lift-and-shift project, we encountered four main issues:

- **Technical Difficulties and Integration:** We had to deal with technical challenges and integration issues with the public cloud platform and services.

- We had difficulties integrating our on-premise authentication system with the cloud provider's identity and access management service.
- We couldn't use managed database services, resulting in additional management overhead for database administration tasks.

- **Unexpected Costs:** Costs were slightly higher than anticipated due to factors like overprovisioning.
  - We initially overprovisioned virtual machine instances (VM) in the cloud to ensure smooth migration and avoid performance bottlenecks. However, this resulted in higher compute costs than anticipated. We optimized the VM sizes after monitoring usage patterns for a few weeks.
- **Performance Degradation:** Few applications performance got suffered after migration.
  - A particular application reliant on custom network configurations experienced performance issues after migrating to the cloud. We identified inefficiencies in the way network traffic was routed within the cloud environment. Optimizing network security groups and implementing a cloud-based content delivery network (CDN) improved application responsiveness.
- **Limited PaaS Usage:** Unable to leverage Platform-as-a-Service (PaaS) features that could offer benefits.
  - We couldn't take advantage of the cloud provider's managed database service because our applications were tightly coupled with a specific database software version that wasn't supported.

Explore:

Another use case (collected from a whitepaper):

- A well-known healthcare organization (name withheld due to confidentiality) migrated their workloads using lift-and-shift. Unfortunately, they experienced significant performance degradation. Attempts to improve performance resulted in a 38% increase in cloud costs compared to their on-premise environment. Ultimately, they had to rollback and return to their local data center.

12. Suppose we have 50 applications running on-premises. In a phased cloud migration, which application would you choose first and why?

Ans:

We prioritize applications for cloud migration based on a scoring system that considers three key factors:

- **Business Impact:** This includes the number of users or transactions affected by downtime, and potential revenue impact if the application is unavailable.
- **Application Complexity:** We consider the number of dependencies, integrations involved, and overall architecture complexity.
- **Data Sensitivity and volume:** Applications handling non-sensitive and low-volume data are prioritized initially.

Selection Process:

- **Complexity Rating:** We assign a numerical score (1 being easiest, 50 being most complex) based on the factors mentioned above.
- **Cloud Suitability:** We evaluate how readily an application can utilize cloud features and benefits.

Ideal First Candidate:

The application with the **lowest complexity score and highest cloud suitability** becomes the ideal first candidate for migration. This approach minimizes risks, allows your team to gain experience, and paves the way for a successful transition.

Explore:

Possible first candidate scenarios:

- **Internal Applications:** Start with applications used internally by IT or for non-critical functions. This provides a safe space to test the migration process.
- **Standardized Applications:** Applications built on common platforms are easier to migrate due to existing resources and procedures.
- **Simple Web Apps:** Identify standalone web applications with minimal dependencies for easier migration.
- **Low-Traffic Applications:** Select applications with low user traffic or transactions to minimize impact during migration.

13. What is the "R Strategy" in cloud migration?

Ans:

The "R Strategy" in cloud migration refers to a set of approaches represent different ways to migrate applications and data to the cloud. There are typically 6 or 7 Rs included in the R Strategy framework. The number of R's you use in your cloud migration strategy depends on your specific needs and goals.

- Rehost (Lift-and-Shift).
- Re-platform (Lift-Reshape-and-Shift).

- Refactor/Re-architect.
- Repurchase (SaaS Adoption).
- Retire (Decommission).
- Retain or Re-visit.

Explore:

- **Rehost (Lift-and-Shift):** This involves migrating applications "as-is" to the cloud environment with minimal to no code modifications. It's a fast and easy approach but may not leverage all the cloud's benefits.
  - **Ex:** Creating Azure VMs and simply migrating on-premise applications and databases to the cloud without any changes.
- **Re-platform (Lift-Reshape/Optimize-and-Shift):** This involves making minor configuration changes to applications to better suit the cloud environment, without altering the core architecture.
  - **Ex:** Migrating web applications to VMs (IaaS) as-is and database instances to a database-as-a-service platform like Azure SQL Database. This approach allows you to leverage some cloud benefits without refactoring the application.
- **Refactor/Re-architect:** This involves significant code changes to optimize the application for the cloud environment. This can be expensive and time-consuming, but offers long-term benefits like improved performance and scalability.
  - **Ex:** Rewriting applications using cloud-native technologies like microservices architecture, serverless functions, containers, and load balancers. This approach is ideal for situations with strong business needs for scalability, speed, and performance, or when migrating legacy applications with long-term cloud benefits in mind.
- **Repurchase (Drop & Shop - SaaS Adoption):** This involves replacing your on-premise application with a cloud-native software-as-a-service (SaaS) offering.
  - **Ex:** Switching from an on-premise CRM system to Salesforce.com, from an on-premise HR system to Workday or migrating data analytics Jupyter notebooks environment to Azure Databricks etc.
- **Retire (Decommission - Sunsetting):** This involves identifying and removing applications that are no longer needed.
  - **Ex:** After an assessment and discovery phase, you can identify unnecessary applications within your IT portfolio. Statistics suggest that 10-20% of enterprise IT infrastructure might not be relevant anymore and can be retired during cloud migration, leading to cost savings.

- **Retain or Re-visit:** This acknowledges that not everything needs to be migrated to the cloud. Some applications or data might be better suited to remain on-premises due to security, compliance, or other factors.
  - **Ex:** Legacy application with high security compliance needs, applications with no business case for investment, applications nearing retirement, or situations where you decide to revisit the migration decision later.

Choosing the right R strategy depends on your specific needs and goals for cloud migration.

14. I understand we previously discussed cloud migration phases. This time, I'd like to focus specifically on the data migration process itself. From your expertise in data, can you detail the steps involved in migrating databases and data from an on-premises environment to the cloud?

Ans:

I'm giving you a detailed answer intentionally. In case you face a similar question in an interview, you can describe some high-level steps and respond by saying, "These are the high-level steps. If you'd like me to walk you through the details, I can certainly do that."

Here is the Database migration process:

Migration Planning:

Assess and Discover: Gather all relevant information about data (file shares, network shares, etc.) and database systems (SQL, NoSQL, etc.) in the source environment. Document this information in a data inventory or data sheet. Include details like:

- Database instances (Type (RDBMS, NoSQL), version, edition, license etc.).
- Instance type (database engine, SSRS, SSAS, etc.).
- Configurations (trace flags, collation, etc.).
- Features (FileStream, PolyBase, etc.).
- Host details (virtualization, physical servers, OS type, license, etc.).
- Computing power (memory, disk, CPU, throughput, etc.).
- Storage (data volume, growth rate, etc.).
- Partition information (keys, distribution rate).
- Data type (transactional, warehouse, archive, etc.).
- Environment (Dev, QA, Staging, Pre-Prod, Prod).
- Tools (Development, deployment, monitoring).
- Networking & Security (NSG, firewalls, SSL, encryption, login credentials, service accounts, permissions, enterprise vault services etc.).
- Backup, HA and DR strategy.
- Database IT operations (change, incident, problem request management, etc.).
- Key Performance Indicators (IO, CPU, Memory usage, query timeouts, errors).

- **Integration Matrix:** A data entity can be a data provider, consumer, or both. Create a matrix that maps all dependencies of your data entities and databases. Identify applications, services, and programs that use your databases, including:
    - Application priority (based on revenue impact).
    - Complexity (number of components involved).
    - Route information (source, destination, IP, port, port type, inbound/outbound, access credentials, etc.).
- **Define the Migration Scope:** Based on the assessment details, classify your data entities for:
    - Migration to the cloud.
    - Retention on-premises.
    - Retirement/decommissioning.
- **Define the Cloud Solution:** Identify:
    - **Cloud model:** Public, private, hybrid, or multi-cloud.
    - **Cloud service provider:** Azure, AWS, Google Cloud, Oracle Cloud Infrastructure, etc.
    - **Cloud service model:** PaaS, IaaS, or SaaS. For databases, we typically deal with PaaS and IaaS.
- **Resource Mapping:** Map on-premises resources to their cloud equivalents. If you plan to re-platform or refactor, check compatibility and conduct a Proof of Concept (POC) in the cloud. Consider expected performance and allocated budget when sizing cloud resources. It's generally recommended to allocate slightly more compute resources than initially required to facilitate faster migrations. Once migrated, you can downgrade the service tier to match your exact needs.
    - **Examples:**
    - SQL Server Standalone Instance to Azure SQL Database, Database Pool, SQL Managed Instance, AWS RDS, Serverless Database, Google Cloud SQL, Azure VM, AWS EC2, Google Compute Engine (GCE) etc.
    - If you're running SQL Server 2008R2 on-premises, plan for a version upgrade alongside the migration.
    - Windows Servers to Azure VM, AWS EC2, GCP Google Compute Engine (GCE).
    - Network drives and shared folders to Azure Files, AWS Elastic File System (EFS), Google Cloud FileStore.
    - Virtual server disks to Azure Managed Disks, AWS Elastic Block Storage (EBS), Google Cloud Persistent Disk.
    - Storage solutions to Azure Blob Storage, Azure Data Lake, AWS S3, Google Cloud Storage.
    - Serverless RDBMS to Azure SQL Database Serverless, AWS Aurora Serverless.

- NoSQL to Azure Cosmos DB API, AWS DynamoDB, SimpleDB, Amazon DocumentDB, Google Cloud Firestore and Google Cloud Bigtable.

- **Define the Cloud Migration Approach and Tools:** For each component marked for migration, assign a cloud migration strategy (rehost, refactor, re-architect, etc.). For databases, this is typically rehosting (IaaS) or refactoring (PaaS). Choose the right migration tool based on your needs (online or offline migration). Examples include Database Migration Service, Data Migration Assistant, backup & restore, replication, Always-On, export/import, third-party tools, etc.
- **Define the Rollback Plan:** Create a plan for reverting back to the on-premises environment in case of issues after migration. The plan should include steps for identifying changes, potentially reversing those changes, and verifying functionality after rollback. The plan should cover four scenarios:
  - Application testing fails after migration (simple rollback by updating connection strings).
  - Issues arise after using the cloud system for a while (requires data and schema change reversal).
  - Rolling back from a cloud Platform-as-a-Service (PaaS) deployment (may require more efforts).
  - Rolling back from a cloud Infrastructure-as-a-Service (IaaS) deployment (generally easiest).

Pre-Migration Activities:

- **Define the Target Architecture:** Considering the migration scope and resource mapping, clearly define the target state architecture and establish a clear roadmap for your cloud journey.
- **Identify and Document Solutions:** Based on compatibility validations and proof-of-concept (POC) results, identify potential challenges, errors, and solutions (both short-term and long-term). Document all test cases for future reference.
- **Establish KPIs:** After migration, you need to measure the performance of your applications and databases. Define key performance indicators (KPIs) to compare with on-premises workloads and assess cloud migration success from a performance perspective. Tools like Azure Event Hubs and Functions can simulate production load on Azure SQL Database to measure resource utilization. Additionally, load testing can be done using Visual Studio or third-party tools. Common KPIs include:
  - **Databases:** Compute usage (CPU, IO, Memory, Wait Statistics, Throughput), average query/stored procedure response time, blockings, deadlocks, and error rates etc.
  - **Applications:** Page loading time, response time, lag, session length, error rates etc.

- **Establish Performance Baselines:** Baselining involves measuring the current (pre-migration) performance of your application or database to determine if its future (post-migration) performance meets expectations. Set baseline metrics for each chosen KPI. Choosing the baseline period (data collection duration) is crucial. Typically, metrics captured during business peak hours are considered.

- **Data-Quality Check:**
  - **Data Profiling:** Analyze your on-premises data to understand its characteristics. Look for missing values, inconsistencies, invalid formats, duplicates, and outliers. Profiling tools can identify data quality issues and help establish cleaning priorities.
  - **Data Validation:** Define data quality rules based on business requirements. These rules could specify valid data ranges, formats, and relationships between different data points. Validate your data against these rules to identify and fix errors before migration.
  - **Data Cleansing:** Cleanse your on-premises data to address identified issues. This may involve removing duplicates, correcting invalid formats, populating missing values, and ensuring data consistency. For example, historical data where modifications are not allowed can be archived and migrated separately. Remove or clean unnecessary objects, including duplicate, incomplete, or corrupted data, backup tables created during change requests, and staging tables. If specific data from code objects (stored procedures, agent jobs) is collected into tables (**Ex:** error logs, audit logs, monitoring logs), seek business approval to delete/archive older data (**Ex:** less than 2 years old). This step reduces migration pressure and improves speed and performance.
- **Prioritize Data Entities:** Based on factors like revenue impact, number of dependencies, and data size, prioritize databases and data stores for migration. Generally, the easiest entities are migrated first. Additionally, migrate non-production workloads before production environments.
- **Develop a Migration Timeline:** Carefully evaluate details from POCs and migration assessments to define realistic timelines. Consider development release cycles, business hours (peak and low), maximum allowed downtime, downtime impact, estimated migration times, and cloud maintenance windows.
- **Obtain Business Approval:** Present the migration plan to business owners and secure all necessary approvals. Address and update the plan if any concerns arise.
- **Freeze:** Perform a health check on the source database and freeze schema changes (meaning no change requests or new releases) until migration is complete.
  - **For offline migrations**, freeze both schema and data changes.
  - **For online migrations**, restrict schema changes but allow database operations. Data changes will be replicated automatically to the target database using tools like DMS, replication, or AlwaysOn.
- **Prepare Scripts and Backups:** Back up encryption certificates and create scripts for logins, users, roles, permissions, system database objects (if applicable), agent jobs, drop and recreate scripts for constraints, triggers, foreign keys, etc. This varies based on the target instance type

(Single Database, managed instance) and migration type (backup & restore, export/import, DMS, etc.).

- **Prepare a Backup Copy:** Before initiating the migration, ensure a latest backup is available at a remote location for recovery in case of migration surprises.
- **Create the Target Environment:** Provision cloud resources in your chosen platform (**Ex:** Azure SQL Database, VM, VPN, ExpressRoute, or VPN Gateway for on-premises network connection, DMS service, Blob storage). We typically automate this process using IaC (Infrastructure-as-code) pipelines.

Cloud Preparation (Can Be Done in Parallel with Pre-Migration Activities):

- **Data Modelling and Architecture:** Design your cloud data storage structure. This might involve optimizing schemas for cloud databases and leveraging cloud-specific data warehousing solutions.
- **Security and Compliance:** Ensure your cloud environment meets security best practices and regulatory compliance requirements. Define access controls, encryption strategies, and data backup procedures.
- **Migration Preparation:** Set up your cloud environment, configure database instances, and establish secure communication channels between your on-premises and cloud infrastructure.

Execute Migration Project:

- **Refactoring at On-Premises (if applicable):** Legacy applications might not support direct upgrades to the latest versions. In such cases, upgrade them on-premises before migration (**Ex:** SQL Server 2000 to 2022). No upgrade is necessary if you're not using backup-restore or HA/DR features. Simply migrate schema and data using import/export, BACPAC, etc.
- **Schema and Data Migration:** The process varies based on the migration approach (online, offline, lift-and-shift, refactor) but here are the general steps:

    - **Backup and Restore (Simple Approach):** If using backup and restore, schema and data migration are combined. No separate steps are needed.
    - **Schema Migration:** Migrate all database objects like tables, views, stored procedures, functions, user-defined types, constraints, triggers, etc.
    - **Encryption Certificates (if applicable):** If using Transparent Data Encryption (TDE) on-premises and migrating with backup and restore to Azure SQL Managed Instance or SQL on Azure VM, manually transfer the encryption certificate to the cloud instance. DMS takes care of this if using Azure DMS service.
    - **Disable Constraints and Indexes at Target (Best Practice):** As a best practice, temporarily disable constraints (foreign key, check, triggers) and indexes at the target environment to bypass validations during data transfer. This also aids in parallel data processing. Scripts to drop and recreate constraints and indexes can be generated at the source database and executed at the target for simplicity.

- **Data Migration:** Upon successful schema migration, initiate data transfer for databases. Similarly, transfer data from shared folders/network drives to cloud storage solutions (Azure Storage, AWS S3) using tools like Azure AzCopy, Azure Storage Explorer, AWS DataSync, or AWS S3 Browser Premium Service.
- **Data Migration Methods, Tools and Services:** This is the core data transfer phase. Here are the common methods:
    - **Full Cutover:** Transfer all data at once during a scheduled downtime. Ex: Backup/Restore, BACPAC etc.
    - **Continuous Replication:** Continuously synchronize data changes between on-premises and cloud databases. **Ex:** Transactional replication, always-on availability etc.
    - **Batch Migration:** Migrate data in smaller batches to minimize downtime. Ex: BCP, Azure Data Factory, SSIS, AWS Glue, Google Cloud Data Flow, Google Cloud Data Fusion etc.
    - **Cloud Provider Tools:** Many cloud providers offer built-in data migration services to simplify the process. **Ex:** Azure Data Migration Assistant (DMA), Database Migration Service (DMS), Azure SQL Data Sync, Azure SQL migration extension for Azure Data Studio, AWS DMS, AWS DataSync, GCP DMS etc.
- **Data Quality during the migration activity:**
    - **Data Monitoring:** Monitor the data transfer process to ensure data integrity is maintained. Tools can track data volume, identify errors during transfer, and alert you of potential issues.
    - **Data Transformation (if applicable):** If your cloud database schema differs from your on-premises schema, data transformation may be needed during migration. Validate the transformed data to ensure it adheres to the new schema and maintains accuracy.
- **Enable Constraints and Indexes:** Since you already have the script, execute it to create constraints and indexes, and validate the output log.
- **Create Logins, Users, and Permissions:** Existing scripts can be used to quickly create SQL Server logins, users, roles, and permissions. For Windows Authentication, manual effort might be required to map them to Microsoft Entra accounts.
- **Data Migration Cutover (Internal):** Review migration logs to ensure complete data transfer. Then, initiate the cutover process.

Migration Validation:

We should thoroughly review and validate various aspects of the migration, including:

- **Detailed Log Review:** Review all audit and error logs generated throughout the process. This includes logs related to migration execution, data extraction from the source, transformation steps, data loading to the destination, migration tools, database engine, Cloud platforms, and logs generated by custom scripts.

- **Data Quality:**
    - **Data Comparison:** Compare schema and data between source and target environments. This can involve comparing, row counts and Metadata (Ex: tables, columns, constraints).
    - **Ex:** In SQL migration, compare row counts, metadata (sys.objects, sys.all_columns, sys.key_constraints, sys.check_constraints, sys.default_constraints, sys.check_constraints, sys.tables, sys.foreign_keys, sys.foreign_key_columns, sys.indexes, sys.index_columns, sys.triggers, etc.) using tools like SQL Server Data Tools (SSDT) schema and data compare option, or third-party solutions like Redgate SQL Compare.
    - **Checksum Validation:** In SQL Server migration, you can run the below TSQL to get checksum both at source and destination databases and validate the source and restore data being identical. This query calculates a single hash value representing the entire content of a table.
    - SELECT CHECKSUM_AGG(CHECKSUM(*)) FROM <table_name>;
    - **Data Validation:** Re-run your data validation rules against the cloud database to verify data quality hasn't degraded during migration.
    - **Sampling:** Take random samples of the migrated data and compare them against the original source to identify any discrepancies or errors.
    - **Functional Testing:** Ensure application functional tests return the same data (type, count) as in the on-premises environment.
    - **Data Lineage:** Document the origin and flow of your data throughout the migration process. This helps trace the source of data quality issues.
    - **Data Quality Governance:** Establish a data quality governance framework to define data quality standards, ownership, and processes throughout the migration lifecycle. This includes defining rules and guidelines for data access, usage, and retention.
    - **Data Monitoring (Ongoing):** Continuously monitor your cloud database for data quality issues. Schedule regular checks and establish alerts for data anomalies.

- **Connectivity:** Validate database and file share accessibility and permissions from all integrated components (applications, services, interfaces, programs) to ensure they function as expected in the cloud environment.
- **Security:** Identify and address any potential security vulnerabilities in the cloud architecture. This includes:
    - Restricting access by default and granting access only to authorized users and applications.
    - Updating firewalls and network security groups accordingly.
    - Using strong passwords and storing secrets (keys, passwords, certificates) in a key vault.
    - Enabling multi-factor authentication wherever possible.
    - Validating access to sensitive data and ensuring compliance with relevant requirements.

- **Performance:** Test scalability and performance by comparing baselines and KPIs. You can monitor database performance manually using predefined scripts with DMVs and system objects, or leverage advanced analytics tools like Azure Monitor SQL insights. Compare the performance for the top 5 most costly queries identified in the on-premises environment.

- **HA&DR:** Validate that backups and high availability/disaster recovery (HA/DR) are configured and functioning as per the service level agreement (SLA).

Final Cutover and Go-Live: Switch workload traffic to the cloud environment. This might involve updating DNS entries to point to the cloud resources.

Post-Migration Activities:

- **Monitor & Optimize:** We monitor resource utilization and adjust sizing and configurations as needed. We also identify opportunities for automation and integration with cloud features.
- **Documentation:** This is a mandatory step that helps us improve future migration activities. We document all essential details, such as timelines, common challenges faced, failures, applied resolutions, logs, and so on.
- **Learn, Improve, Repeat:** We learn from proof-of-concepts and pre-production workload migrations. Based on the predictive analysis, we adjust estimations for production workloads. This iterative process continues until the last database/data store within scope is migrated to the cloud.
- **Report to the Business:** We process and analyse the complete migration activity (logs, documents, etc.) and prepare comprehensive reports with key performance indicators (KPIs). Examples of KPIs include estimated and actual total cost of ownership (TCO) and return on investment (ROI), migration time per database, total instance count, application level, business vertical level, success rates (meeting time and cost targets), failure cases, average number of errors, and data volume. These reports are presented to business owners to gain migration approval.
- **Handover and Training:** We handover the cloud environment to the customer's chosen support team. This includes documentation, explanations of SLAs (service level agreements), configurations, special functions, integrations, monitoring items, and maintenance activities.
- **Final Sign-off & Release:** After presenting the migration activity report, we seek official customer approval. Upon receiving final sign-off, the migration project is considered complete.

Overall Migration Process:

This is the general migration process I followed in successfully migrating major enterprise data workloads: 5 workloads to Azure, 2 to AWS and 1 to GCP. Remember, specific steps may vary depending on your unique data and chosen approach.

15. What are the most common challenges in cloud data/database migration?

Ans:

Sure! With a proper migration plan and execution, we can prevent 90-95% of problems. However, some common challenges can still arise:

- **Poor planning:** This is the leading cause of migration failures. Dedicate quality time to clearly define, research, and map your source and target environments.
- **Skipping the "R" strategy:** Not every application or infrastructure component is cloud-ready. Consider refactor, re-architect, or retire if necessary. For example, regulations may require sensitive data to reside in a specific region without a cloud data centre. Similarly, legacy applications with highly customized infrastructure might not be suitable for the cloud.
- **All at Once:** Don't rush to migrate everything at once without proper testing, proof of concept (POC), or addressing potential issues. A phased approach may require more time and investment upfront, but it minimizes risk.
- **Unrealistic cost and timeline estimates:** Unrealistic timelines and cost estimations lead to cloud migration disasters. Improper sizing and resource allocation increase migration timelines. Overspending on resources leads to higher costs. Also, most people overlook hidden costs (data transfer, extra backup, cross-region replication, etc.) during the planning phase.
- **Lack of having a Plan B:** We must anticipate challenges and prepare a risk mitigation plan. This involves checking compatibility issues, providing resolutions, performing POCs if required, learning from non-production workloads, etc. We should have answers and solutions ready for the most anticipated issues.
  - **Ex:** data corruption during migration (requiring a proper backup), unexpected downtime (having a DR secondary on-prem), network failures (automatic retries from the point of failure), partial or complete data migration failure (having a rollback plan), etc.
- **Cloud adoption and skill shortage:** This is a major threat. Migrating from a legacy IT model to the cloud requires modernization. IT operations become decentralized, and roles will change. Beyond applications and databases, consider processes, operations, HR, automation, technical support, training, and education.
- **Insufficient testing:** Testing is not a one-time event. Integrate it throughout your migration plan to identify potential issues early. The more you test and address problems proactively, the smoother your migration will be.
- **Common Issues in Data Migration:** Data migration relies on three critical components: Source system (On-premise), Target system (Cloud), Communication Channel (Network). If one component fails, migration comes to a halt. Common challenges include:
  - **Validation Failures:** Running parallel data import processes while constraints (Ex: foreign keys) are still enabled can lead to validation errors.

- **Network Failures:** Misconfiguration of the communication channel can significantly impact data transfer speed. The absence of a direct channel (Ex: Azure ExpressRoute, AWS Direct Connect, Google Cloud Interconnect) between source and target can lead to inconsistent bandwidth.
- **Unexpected Outages:** Power failures, regional outages in the cloud, or other unforeseen events can disrupt the migration process.
- **Resource Capacity Limitations:** Data migration services may have a maximum capacity for concurrent tasks. New tasks might be queued until resources become available if the limit is reached.
- **Large Datasets:** Selecting more databases than the allowed limit per migration instance can lead to errors. It's recommended to migrate larger databases separately.
- **Data Loss:** Data loss can occur due to various reasons, including:
    - Missing encryption certificates.
    - Manually restarting failed transfers without proper precautions.
    - Data type mismatches.
    - Collation issues.
    - Selecting the wrong migration solution for incremental updates (data changes after initial migration).
    - Applying incorrect data filters.
- **Compatibility Issues:** We are supposed to resolve all compatibility issues and showstoppers before initiating the migration process; missing this step can impact our entire migration activity.
- **Security and Compliance:** Inadequate security measures can lead to data leaks and put your organization at risk. Missing data classification, security policies, or non-compliance with relevant standards can result in audit failures.

Overall, careful planning, a phased approach, and addressing potential challenges upfront will significantly increase your chances of a successful cloud migration.

16. You mentioned successfully migrating databases/datastores to Azure, AWS, and GCP. Did you encounter any issues or errors during these migrations? How do you define a "successful migration" in this context?

Ans:

It is almost impossible to execute a migration without encountering errors or issues.

For me, a "successful migration" means "completing the data migration on time within budget, and with minimal disruption while maintaining data integrity".

We encountered challenges during migration, but we addressed them effectively. We learned from those issues, documented the solutions, and leveraged this knowledge to predict and prevent similar problems for subsequent workloads.

Explore:

- **Here's why I believe data migration is a critical and potentially high-risk activity:** A well-known global survey suggests that 80% of data migrations exceed budgets, timelines, or fail entirely. Poor planning is often mentioned as a major factor in these failures.
- That's why I prioritize systematic analysis and planning during the initial phase. This helps us identify and resolve compatibility issues early on. Additionally, addressing challenges encountered during proof-of-concept (POC) and non-production migrations allows us to anticipate and mitigate risks associated with production workloads.

17. Could you please walk me through the recent cloud migration project you handled? I'm seeking a brief explanation of the business case, the cloud migration journey, the migration outcome, and the improvements achieved.

Ans:

We successfully migrated a large Engineering and Construction Firm to Azure.

Business Case: We recently migrated the workloads for a major European engineering and construction firm with a global presence. They operate from 85 offices worldwide, have a staff of 13,000 (including 4,300 IT staff), and achieve revenues exceeding $6.5 billion. The firm serves over 400,000 customers.

Key Challenges: We identified two key challenges that informed our cloud migration proposal:

- **Data Management on Expensive Storage:** The firm was struggling to manage and maintain a rapidly growing volume of data at their on-premises data centers. Additionally, disaster recovery solutions were becoming increasingly complex and costly.
- **Scalability Limitations:** Existing systems lacked the scalability to handle the firm's ever-increasing workload demands.

Cloud Solution with Azure:

- Given their existing Microsoft environment (.NET, Windows OS, SQL Server, Office suite including Email, SharePoint, etc.), Azure was identified as the optimal cloud solution. We projected significant benefits in terms of Total Cost of Ownership (TCO), Return on Investment (ROI), and compatibility.

Migration Challenges:

The migration presented several complexities, including:

- **Legacy Systems:** Migrating from older systems like SQL Server 2000 and Windows 2003.
- **Large Data Sets:** Moving massive volumes of data.

- **Database Migration:** Transitioning Oracle databases to Azure SQL Database (as per the client's requirement).
- **Tailored Strategies:** Developing different migration approaches for various applications (refactoring, re-platforming, lift-and-shift, phased migration).
- **Critical Application Migration:** Ensuring near-zero downtime during the migration of critical applications.
- **Hybrid Cloud Integration:** Creating a hybrid cloud environment for five applications, with some components remaining on-premises and others moving to Azure.
- **Heterogeneous Database Systems:** Migrating databases across various platforms (SQL Server, Oracle, MySQL, PostgreSQL, MongoDB, HDFS, Teradata, Spark based workloads etc.).
- **Service Selection:** Optimizing service selection across PaaS (Platform as a Service), SaaS (Software as a Service), IaaS (Infrastructure as a Service), and Serverless options.

Migration Tools and Services:

We employed a comprehensive suite of tools and Azure services to facilitate the migration:

- **Azure Migrate:** Discovery, assessment, and migration of VMs and SQL Servers (using Server Migration Services).
- **Azure Data Box:** Secure physical transfer of over 40 TB of data.
- **DMA & DMS (Data Migration Assistant & Database Migration Service):** Streamlined database migration.
- **Azure Data Factory:** Efficient migration of large datasets using ETL pipelines.
- **AzCopy:** Storage and unstructured data migration from on-premise to Azure Storage.
- **Virtual Machine Converter (MVMC) / Virtual Machine Manager (VMM):** Conversion of VMs on VMware or physical machines to Microsoft Hyper-V VMs.
- **Azure Site Recovery (ASR) / Azure DRaaS (Disaster Recovery as a Service):** VM migration and disaster recovery.
- **Recovery Services Vault:** Secure storage of VM backups in Azure.
- **VPN Gateway/ExpressRoute:** Establishment of secure communication channels between on-premises and Azure environments.
- **Azure Synapse Pathway:** Conversion of DDL and DML statements for compatibility with Azure Synapse Analytics (during data warehouse migration).
- **SQL Server Migration Assistant (SSMA):** Migration from other RDBMS platforms (MySQL, Oracle, etc.) to SQL Server and Azure Synapse Analytics.
- **Microsoft Entra (AD) Connect:** Synchronization of on-premises Active Directory with Microsoft Entra.

Migration Outcomes:

The migration yielded significant benefits:

- **Application Rationalization:** We identified and retired 180 unused/unnecessary on-premises VMs.
- **Successful Migration:** We successfully migrated 260 applications, 1400+ servers and VMs (1100 Windows, 300+ Linux), 650+ database instances (across SQL Server, Oracle, MySQL, MongoDB), Big Data workloads, data warehouses (SQL Server, Teradata), reporting and ETL solutions (SSAS, SSIS, Informatica, SSRS, Power BI), project environments (DEV, TEST, STAGE, PRE-PROD, PROD), 38 file shares, 12,000+ active users, 29+ domains, 30+ messaging services, and migrated 1.5 petabytes (1500+ TiB) of data.
- **Datacenter Consolidation:** We decommissioned a significant portion (92%) of on-premises legacy data center resources.
- **Improved Scalability and Performance:** Auto-scaling cloud infrastructure eliminated peak load issues and ensured smooth operations.
- **Enhanced Reliability:** During the first-year post-cloud migration, we encountered challenges optimizing and streamlining workloads. However, the second year marked a significant improvement over our previous on-premises experience, with no major outages in the first six months and only one in the latter half.
- **Optimized Storage Costs:** By leveraging storage tiers based on utilization frequency (Hot, Cool & Archive), we achieved substantial cost savings for the client.
- **Streamlined Development and Management:** The migration facilitated faster, more efficient application development, management, and support.

Business Impact: Key Performance Indicators (KPIs):

Following the successful cloud migration, we monitored critical parameters for a period ranging from weeks to months, depending on their importance. This monitoring allowed us to predict future trends and compare them with on-premises performance. A detailed KPI report was then presented to the business stakeholders. Here's a breakdown of the key improvements we observed:

- **Reduced Unplanned Downtime:** 85% reduction in unplanned downtime.
- **Faster New Equipment Deployment:** New equipment deployment time was reduced by 98%.
- **Improved Software Deployment:** Software application deployment time improved by 35%.
- **Increased Application Deployments:** The number of applications deployed per year increased by 110%.
- **Reduced Total Cost of Ownership (TCO):** The 3-year TCO was decreased by 25%
- **Increased Return on Investment (ROI):** The 3-year ROI increased by 10%.

Timelines:

Since this is a large-scale migration, various business, architecture, engineering, product, and operational teams are involved in the process. From the cloud migration kick-off to the final handover, it took 24 to 32 months. These are general timelines, and some phases and tasks got executed in parallel.

- **Preparation and Planning Phase:** 3-4 months.
- **Pilot and Proof of Concept:** 2-3 months.
- **Migration (Phased) Execution Phase:** 14-18 months.
- **Post-Migration Optimization and Stabilization:** 3-6 months.
- **Closure and Handover:** 2-3 months.

18. You mentioned migrating some legacy systems from on-premises to Azure. Can you describe a typical use case and how you handled it?

Ans:

Legacy systems can be a major challenge. We had a client using a simple application based on SQL Server 2000 and a web application running on Windows Server 2003 OS. They weren't ready to retire the application or invest in refactoring, so they insisted on a "lift-and-shift" migration to a cloud VM.

We prepared a detailed analysis report outlining potential problems and issues, presented it to the business team. For example, SQL Server 2000 being a 32-bit application faced compatibility issues with the OS (No support for latest Intel processors), memory limitations, and lacked product support (support was ended in 2013 hence no longer receives security updates). This made it unsuitable for the modern data world.

To offer a simpler solution, we suggested re-platforming SQL Server 2000 to Azure SQL Database. This avoided additional investment, requiring only migration of schema and data to Azure SQL Database. After considering the feasibility, cost-benefit analysis, performance improvements, and potential risks, they approved the re-platforming approach, which we successfully completed.

Explore:

In another scenario, we had to migrate Windows Server 2003 to Azure. We followed the below steps:

- Converting the Windows 2003 Server to a VMware VM using the VMware converter tool.
- Migrating the VMware VM to a Microsoft Hyper-V VM.
- Finally, migrating the Hyper-V VM to an Azure VM.

19. Have you ever experienced or seen any failures or disasters in your cloud journey?

Ans:

Before addressing this question, I'd like to provide a definition for the term "failure." Failures can be categorized into two types:

- A) **Failing to meet expectations** based on the initial plan. This could include exceeding cost estimates, missing migration deadlines, or encountering performance issues in the cloud.
- B) A **complete failure** of the migration plan, necessitating a rollback.

Fortunately, due to the substantial time and effort invested in the analysis and planning phases, I have not experienced scenario "B." However, when dealing with large enterprises, despite careful planning, unforeseen variables can significantly impact our estimations.

Explore:

Given my active involvement in various tech community gatherings and interactions with professionals from diverse domains, I frequently assist consultants seeking guidance and support, both internally and externally. Throughout this journey, I have provided assistance to numerous organizations. Allow me to briefly outline a few case studies:

Case 1: Public Data Exposure

Problem:

- A small vendor (300 employees) was assisting a UK customer with their cloud migration to AWS. During the migration, they accidentally left an S3 storage bucket publicly accessible. This bucket contained scanned copies of sensitive employee documents (passports, tax documents, offer letters, etc.).
- The public exposure went unnoticed for eight days after the production launch. This meant anyone with the S3 bucket URL could potentially access, read, and download the sensitive data.

Cause:

- The vendor mistakenly left the S3 bucket public while performing a proof of concept (POC) in a development environment. Unfortunately, this configuration was accidentally carried over to the production environment.

Resolution:

- A senior engineer from the vendor sought my assistance in handling the situation. I recommended four immediate actions to mitigate the damage:
    - **Make S3 bucket access private:** Restrict access to the S3 bucket to authorized users only.

  - **Raise an incident:** Flag the issue internally for further investigation and resolution.
  - **Inform the customer:** Disclose the incident to the customer, explain the cause, and reassure them of the corrective actions taken.
  - **Track S3 bucket access:** Utilize S3 Server Access Logs and AWS CloudTrail to track access attempts to the bucket. This data can reveal the date and time of access, accessed objects, actions performed, source IP addresses, and access types (browser, API, etc.).

- **Dealing with the Customer:**

  - Fortunately, the access logs revealed no unauthorized access during the public exposure period. The vendor informed the customer, acknowledged the human error, assured them that no data breach occurred, and promised to:

    - Re-perform security testing for the entire infrastructure.
    - Implement preventative measures to avoid similar incidents in the future.

- After two months of communication and reassurance, the vendor resolved the issue without penalty or legal action from the customer.
- However, this incident highlights the potential severity of such mistakes, especially in industries like finance or healthcare where data breaches can have serious consequences.

Case 2: Unexpected Azure Bill

Problem:

A customer experienced a surprise with their monthly cloud bill. The amount was nearly three times higher than the previous month's charges. Upon investigation, they discovered a significant number of Azure virtual machines (VMs) with premium features had been created without notifying application owners.

Investigation:

- The investigation revealed an automated, scheduled job that was creating a new VM every 6 hours. This job functioned as intended; however, it was discovered that an unhappy employee, on his way out of the organization, had intentionally created and scheduled this program.
- Adding to the complexity, the Azure support team attempted to notify the customer about the suspicious activity, but their notification email was bypassed due to an expired email distribution list (DL).

Root Causes:

- **Excessive Administrative Privileges:** A large number of administrators with full access privileges allowed anyone to create resources unchecked.
- **Lack of Resource Creation Policies:** The absence of policies limiting VM creation facilitated the unexpected resource surge.

- **Inadequate Monitoring and Notifications:** Insufficient monitoring and notification processes prevented timely detection and response to the abnormal activity.

Resolution:

- **HR Intervention:** Human Resources took appropriate action to address the situation with the departing employee.
- **Collaboration with Cloud Support Team:** I recommended that the customer contact the Cloud Service Provider support team, explain the situation, and seek their assistance. The customer provided a detailed root cause analysis to the support team.
- **Negotiated Resolution:** Fortunately, due to the accidental nature of the incident and the customer's recent cloud migration, they were able to negotiate a significant discount on the additional charges incurred from the unnecessary VMs.
- **Security Enhancements:** I further suggested implementing security best practices such as Azure policies to restrict resource creation, reducing the number of administrative accounts with full privileges, regular monitoring and alerting, implement separation of duties to prevent a single person from having complete control over the cloud environment, establish clear offboarding procedures (disabling access to cloud resources) for departing employees etc.

Case 3: Configuration Error Leads to Data Inconsistency

Problem:

A team successfully migrated an application and its database to the cloud. After 15 days in production, an application engineer discovered a critical error. The application itself and the database were migrated correctly, but the application configuration file on the cloud platform remained pointed to the on-premises database.

- **Configuration change:** Fearing consequences, the engineer opted to quietly update the configuration file to point to the cloud database instead of informing their supervisor. Unfortunately, this decision had unintended consequences.
- **Incident:** Exactly one month later (45 days after go-live | 30 days after this configuration change), the customer reported data inconsistencies and missing data within the application. The investigation revealed the configuration error, and the application engineer ultimately had to confess their mistake. For example:
  - **Go-live date (01-Apr-2024):** App is pointing to on-premise database.
  - **Configuration change (01-May-2024):** App is repointed to cloud database.
  - **Issue identified (15-May-2024):** Customer reported the missing data or inconsistencies.

Root Causes:

- **Inadequate Post-Migration Testing:** The team failed to conduct thorough testing after the migration to ensure the application functioned correctly with the cloud database.

- **Missing Migration Checklist:** The absence of a defined migration checklist likely contributed to overlooking the configuration update step.
- **Human Error and Delayed Communication:** The engineer's decision to avoid informing their supervisor resulted in a one-month delay in addressing the configuration issue. This significantly extended the period of data inconsistency.
- **Unnecessary On-Premises Database Exposure:** Leaving the on-premises database online after a successful migration to the cloud created an unnecessary security risk.

Resolution:

The most challenging aspect of resolving the issue was identifying the missing data for the 15-day period between the initial go-live and the configuration update. The team performed a table-by-table comparison between:

- The initial go-live database copy.
- The on-premises database copy 15 days after go-live
- The cloud database copy 45 days after go-live

Through this comparison, they identified INSERT, DELETE, and UPDATE operations that occurred during the 15-day window. This information allowed them to perform the necessary data load to restore consistency between the cloud database and the actual user activity.

Case 4: Ransomware Attack on Cloud VMs

Problem:

- A medium-sized organization experienced a critical incident when a customer application stopped working. Upon investigation, they discovered that the SQL Server database service within a virtual machine (VM) was down. Restarting the service failed, and the logs revealed a critical issue: the SQL Server system database files were missing.
- Alarmingly, all database files (MDF, NDF, and LDF) had their extensions changed from their standard formats (Ex: .MDF, .NDF, .LDF) to an unknown string (Ex: .xto). This indicated a ransomware attack. A ransom notes demanding $300,000 was found on the VM.

Reasons:

- **Root Cause:** The investigation identified a single point of failure: a user with administrative privileges on the VM used their personal email and unknowingly clicked a phishing email. This email downloaded a malware program directly onto the VM. The malware then stopped the SQL Server service, encrypted all data and log files, including the backup folder. Unfortunately, no secondary replica of the database instance existed.
- **Unnecessary Public Internet Exposure:** The affected VM was likely exposed to the public internet, increasing its attack surface.

- **Excessive Administrative Privileges:** Granting unnecessary administrative rights to users increased the potential damage caused by a single compromised account.
- **Lack of Security Awareness Training:** Insufficient security awareness training for developers and other users left them vulnerable to phishing attacks.
- **Inadequate Malware Protection:** The absence of proper malware protection software on the VM allowed the malware to execute freely.
- **Insufficient Monitoring:** A lack of robust monitoring practices may have prevented early detection of the suspicious activity.

Resolution:

- **Recovery Efforts:** While a secondary replica wasn't available, the organization did have recent database backups stored in Azure storage and VM backups on Azure Backup. This allowed them to quickly create a new VM with the same IP address, minimizing business disruption.
- **Isolation and Scanning:** All access to the infected VM was restricted, except for a single administrator. A thorough scan of the VM and the entire network was conducted to ensure the malware hadn't spread to other resources within the virtual network (VNet).
- **Laptop Security:** As a precaution, all developer and database administrator (DBA) laptops that may have accessed the affected VM were disconnected from the corporate network. The security team then scanned these individual laptops for potential malware infection.

Conclusion: The Human Factor in Cloud Failures

- These case studies illustrate a common thread: Human error is a major contributor to cloud failures. From misconfigurations and security oversights to a lack of proper planning and procedures, human actions can significantly impact cloud deployments.
- By implementing best practices like stronger access controls, improved monitoring, and regular security awareness training, organizations can minimize human error and ensure a more secure and reliable cloud environment.

20. You might have heard that many organizations face performance degradation issues after migrating their workloads to the cloud. In your opinion, what are the top reasons for performance degradation after cloud migration?

Ans:

Migrating workloads to the cloud can be a great way to improve efficiency and scalability, but it's not without its challenges. Here are some of the most common reasons why performance might suffer after migrating to the cloud:

- Inadequate Resource Allocation.
- Network Latency.

- Storage Access Latency.
- Poor Cloud Configuration.
- Lifting and Shifting Inefficient Workloads.
- Lack of Cloud Monitoring and Optimization.

Explore:

- **Inadequate Resource Allocation:** Allocating insufficient or incorrectly sized cloud resources (CPU, memory, IOPS, storage) can lead to performance issues. **Ex:**
  - **Problem:** An online retail company migrated its e-commerce platform to Azure. They selected smaller VM sizes that lacked sufficient CPU and memory to handle peak traffic. During peak traffic hours, the website becomes sluggish and unresponsive because the VMs don't have enough processing power to handle the surge in customers.
  - **Solution:** Upgrading to larger VM sizes provided the necessary resources to meet demand, improving performance.
- **Network Latency:** High network latency occurs when there is a significant delay in data transmission between the cloud and end-users, often due to geographical distance or poor network configuration. **Ex:**
  - **Problem:** A global SaaS provider moved its application to Azure, hosted in the East US region. Users in Europe and Asia experienced slow response times due to the distance.
  - **Solution:** Deploying additional instances in Azure's Europe and Asia regions and using Azure Front Door to direct traffic, reduced latency and improved performance.
- **Storage Access Latency:** Slow access times to cloud storage can impact application performance, especially if the storage type or configuration is not optimized for the workload. **Ex:**
  - **Problem:** A media company migrated its video content storage to Azure Blob Storage. They initially used the Cool tier, which was not optimized for frequent access, leading to slow video loading times.
  - **Solution:** Moving frequently accessed content to the Hot tier and using Azure Content Delivery Network (CDN) for caching improved access speed.
- **Poor Cloud Configuration:** Incorrect VM types, suboptimal network settings, or misaligned service tiers, can lead to performance degradation. **Ex:**
  - **Problem:** An e-commerce platform moved its entire data warehouse to Azure Synapse Analytics. They used the same schema and indexing strategy from their on-premises system, which wasn't optimized for Synapse.
  - **Solution:** Redesigning the schema wherever required, updating indexing strategies, and partitioning large tables optimized their data queries and improved performance.

- **Lifting and Shifting Inefficient Workloads:** Directly moving on-premises applications to the cloud without optimization can carry over inefficiencies, leading to poor performance. **Ex:**
    - **Problem:** A logistics company migrated its route optimization software to Azure VMs. The monolithic application wasn't designed to scale efficiently in a cloud environment, causing slow processing times.
    - **Solution:** Refactoring the application to use Azure Functions and microservices architecture improved scalability and performance.
- **Lack of Cloud Monitoring and Optimization:** It can result in degraded performance over time as workloads and usage patterns change. **Ex:**
    - **Problem:** An e-commerce company migrated its data analytics platform to Azure Synapse Analytics but did not set up adequate monitoring. Therefore, performance issues went undetected, leading to delayed insights and reporting.
    - **Solution:** Implementing Azure Monitor and Azure Advisor provided insights and recommendations for optimizing query performance and resource utilization, leading to improved system performance.

21. When selecting a cloud solution, tool, or service, how should one prioritize factors such as compatibility, cost, security, and performance?

Ans:

There's no single "one size fits all" answer to this question as the priority between compatibility, cost, security, and performance depends on the specific needs of your project and the type of cloud service you're choosing. However, a general prioritization order can be outlined as follows:

- **Security:** Mitigates data breaches, protects user information, and ensures regulatory compliance.
- **Compatibility:** Minimizes development effort and ensures existing infrastructure can integrate with the cloud service.
- **Performance:** Optimizes user experience, responsiveness, and application functionality.
- **Cost:** Reduces operational expenses, but shouldn't compromise on the above factors.

22. I am a large enterprise considering migrating the majority of my workloads to Azure. What cost optimization techniques should I follow?

Ans:

When migrating workloads to Azure, here are some cost optimization techniques you can follow:

- Right-sizing Resources.
- Leverage Azure Hybrid Benefit for existing Windows and SQL licenses.

- Consider using reserved instances for predictable workloads.
- Utilize Autoscaling and Auto-shutdown capabilities.
- Leverage Microsoft Cost Management and Billing features to continuously monitor, track, and optimize cloud resource costs.

Explore:

Efficient Resource Utilization:

- **Assess Workloads**: Analyze your workloads to ensure you're using appropriately sized resources. Avoid over-provisioning.
- **Rightsizing resources:** Ensure your databases, storage, networking, virtual machines, and other resources are appropriately sized to match workloads.
- **Leverage Managed Services**: Utilize PaaS and SaaS offerings to reduce management overhead and infrastructure costs.
- **Azure Automation**: Use Azure Automation to automate routine tasks and optimize resource usage.
    - **Auto-scaling:** Leverage Azure's auto-scaling capabilities to adjust resources based on demand.
    - **Auto-Shutdown**: Schedule auto-shutdown of non-critical VMs during off-hours to save costs.

Azure Savings Options:

- **Reserved instances:** Purchase reserved capacity for workloads with predictable usage to save up to 70% compared to pay-as-you-go pricing.
- **Spot VMs**: Use Azure Spot VMs for workloads that are flexible and can handle interruptions, benefiting from significantly reduced costs.
- **Azure Hybrid Benefit**: Leverage AHB to save on licensing costs by reusing your on-premises Windows Server and SQL Server licenses on Azure.
- **Azure Dev/Test Pricing:** Azure offers a special lower price for non-production workloads.
- **Azure Price Matching:** In certain cases, this option allows us to match the price of a competitor's cloud offering for Azure services.

Optimize Storage Costs:

- **Tiered Storage**: Utilize Azure Storage tiering (Hot, Cool, and Archive) based on access patterns. Store frequently accessed data in Hot tier and infrequently accessed data in Cool or Archive tiers.
- **Blob Storage Lifecycle Management**: Implement lifecycle policies to automatically transition data to lower-cost storage tiers.

Optimize Database Cost:

- **SQL Elastic Pools**: Use SQL Elastic Pools to manage and scale multiple databases that have varying and unpredictable usage patterns.
- **Automatic Scaling and Performance Tuning**: Enable automatic scaling and performance tuning for databases to optimize performance and costs.
- **Free DR replica in Azure:** If you have Software Assurance, you can implement hybrid disaster recovery (DR) plans with SQL Server without incurring additional licensing costs for the passive disaster recovery instance. You also qualify for license-free DR replicas with pay-as-you-go licensing if all replicas are hosted in Azure.

Optimize Networking Costs:

- **Data Transfer**: Minimize data transfer costs by keeping data transfer within the same region and using Azure ExpressRoute for high-bandwidth, low-latency connections.
- **Traffic Manager**: Use Azure Traffic Manager to route traffic efficiently and reduce costs.

Use Serverless Architectures:

- **Azure Functions:** Leverage Azure Functions for event-driven workloads to eliminate the need for always-on resources, paying only for execution time.
- **Logic Apps:** Use Logic Apps for orchestrating workflows without provisioning underlying infrastructure.

Cost Management and Governance:

- **Microsoft Cost Management:** Utilize this built-in service to track, analyze, and optimize costs.
    - **Cost Analysis**: Regularly monitor your spending and usage patterns using Microsoft Cost Management and Billing.
    - **Predictive cost insights:** Use Cost Analysis forecasting capabilities to anticipate future costs.
    - **Budgets and alerts:** Set spending limits and configure alerts to prevent unexpected costs.
    - **Cost optimization recommendations:** Leverage Azure Advisor and Cost Management features to identify potential cost-saving recommendations and implement them.
- **Cost allocation tags:** Implement a tagging strategy to allocate costs accurately across departments or projects.
- **Azure Monitor:** Continuously monitor resource utilization and identify optimization opportunities.

By following these cost optimization techniques, an enterprise can effectively manage and reduce expenses while taking full advantage of Azure's powerful features and capabilities.

***Note:** Azure Cost Management and Billing has been rebranded as Microsoft Cost Management.

23. We have various relational databases, NoSQL databases, and data warehouses on-premises. I understand that I can host these databases on Azure using either PaaS (Azure-provided services) or IaaS (by setting up a VM and installing my database software). Can you explain the Platform-as-a-Service options available for hosting databases in Azure?

Ans:

Here are the primary Azure native Platform-as-a-Service options for hosting relational and NoSQL databases on Azure.

RDBMS (Relational Database Management Systems):

- **Azure SQL Database**: A fully managed service for SQL databases.
    - **Single Database**: A standalone, isolated database with its own resources.
    - **Elastic Pool**: A set of databases sharing resources to optimize costs.
- **Azure SQL Managed Instance**: A fully managed SQL Server with more control, supporting most of the standalone SQL Server features.
- **Azure Database for MySQL**: A managed service for hosting MySQL databases.
- **Azure Database for PostgreSQL**: A managed service for PostgreSQL databases.
- **Azure Database for MariaDB**: A managed service for MariaDB databases.
- **Oracle Database@Azure:** A service that lets you run Oracle databases on Oracle hardware in Azure data centers. It combines Oracle's performance with Azure's scalability and security, enabling seamless integration between the two cloud platforms.

NoSQL:

- **Azure Table Storage**: A simple, scalable NoSQL service for semi-structured data.
- **Azure Managed Instance for Apache Cassandra**: A managed version of the open-source Apache Cassandra NoSQL database.
- **Azure Cosmos DB**: A globally distributed, multi-model NoSQL database.
    - **NoSQL API**: General NoSQL support.
    - **MongoDB API**: For MongoDB-compatible applications.
    - **PostgreSQL API**: PostgreSQL-compatible (large-scale workloads) API in Cosmos DB.
    - **Cassandra API**: Supports Cassandra-like operations.
    - **Gremlin API**: For graph databases.
    - **Table API**: For key-value and document-based data.

Data Warehouse:

- **Azure Synapse Analytics – Dedicated SQL Pool**: A fully managed Data Warehouse.
- **Microsoft Fabric – Synapse Data Warehouse:** Microsoft Fabric is a unified platform for data analytics that integrates data engineering, data warehousing, real-time analytics, and business intelligence in one ecosystem. It offers Synapse as a native Data Warehouse.

Note: You can explore more about the Azure SQL Family in "Azure The One – Part 2."

CHAPTER 11

Azure Cloud Migration 2 – Tools and Services

1. What are the various data and database migration tools, services, and features available to migrate on-premises workloads to Azure?

Ans.

The choice of migration tools, services, and features depends on several factors, including deployment model, migration strategy (phased or lift-and-shift), feasibility, compatibility, cost, and performance. Here are the available options for migrating database workloads from on-premises to Azure:

- **Database native features:** For example, SQL Server Backup, restore, detach-attach, Always-On AGs, etc.
- **Azure offerings:** Azure Data Migration Assistant (DMA), Database Migration Service (DMS), etc.
- **Open-source and third-party tools:** Smart BCP Tool, MSSQL-Scripter Tool, Cloud Atlas, etc.

Explore:

SQL Server Native:

- **Backup and Restore:** Transfer backup files to Azure storage and restore them to a SQL Managed Instance (MI) or SQL Database on a VM.
- **Detach and Attach:** Move or copy MDF and LDF files directly to an Azure VM and attach them to a SQL Server instance there.
- **Always-On Availability Groups:** Configure Always-On AG for your on-premises SQL Server and add a SQL Server on Azure VM as a secondary replica. Once data synchronization is complete, perform a failover to the secondary. This method requires site-to-site connectivity between source and target.
- **Log Shipping:** Configure log shipping between your on-premises SQL Server database and a database residing on SQL Server on an Azure VM. Similar to Always-On AG, this approach also requires site-to-site connectivity.
- **Transactional Replication:** Configure transactional replication by adding the on-premise database as a publisher and the target database (on Azure) as a subscriber. The distribution database can reside on-premises. Replication works for all three deployment options (SQL Database, SQL Managed Instance, and SQL on VM). Once all incremental data changes are propagated to the subscriber, perform a cutover and start using the target database.

- **SSMS/Azure Data Studio Options:**
  - **Deploy Database to Azure SQL Database:** This wizard-based GUI allows you to export an on-premises database to a BACPAC file and import it into Azure SQL Database. It reports any compatibility issues and is only applicable to Azure SQL Database.
  - **Export Data-Tier Application (DACPAC/BACPAC):** This method involves manually exporting and importing DACPAC/BACPAC files. It also reports compatibility issues.
  - **Export/Import Wizard:** You can directly export tables with data from on-premises to Azure. This is a suitable option for small tables in non-production environments.
  - **Generate Scripts:** Generate T-SQL scripts for both schema and data, which can then be applied to the target database.
- **Azure Data Studio Extensions:** It offers an easy way to add more functionality to the base Azure Data Studio installation. Here are the sample extensions:
  - **Azure SQL migration extension:** It enables you to assess, get right-sized Azure recommendations and migrate your SQL Server databases to Azure SQL Database, Managed Instance and Azure VM. It leverages Azure Database Migration Service.
  - **Database Migration Assessment for Oracle:** This extension helps you assess an Oracle workload for migrating to Azure SQL and Azure Database for PostgreSQL.
  - **Database Schema Conversion Toolkit (DSCT):** This extension is designed to help database schema conversion from Oracle and SQL Server.
  - **Schema compare extension:** It provides an easy-to-use way to compare two database definitions and apply the differences from the source to the target.
  - **Other:** Azure Cosmos DB for MongoDB RU extension, Azure PostgreSQL migration etc.
- **SQL Server Data Tools for Visual Studio (SSDT):**
  - Use this option to migrate source database and schema to target.
  - Also, SSDT is helpful for assessing and identifying compatibility issues between on-premises and Azure SQL Database.
  - Import the source database schema into Visual Studio database project for analysis, specify the target platform as Azure SQL Managed Instance or Azure SQL Database, build the project. It analyzes and reports all incompatibility issues, fix and rebuild the project. After successful build, publish the schema to Azure SQL Database.
- **SQLPackage.exe:** This command-line utility allows you to export an on-premises database to a BACPAC file and import it to the target database. It's useful for automating database lifecycle management and works for all deployment options. It can also identify compatibility issues and is included in SSDT.
- **Bulk Copy (BCP):** Use the Bulk Copy Program (BCP) tool to migrate data. It utilizes a data file for export and import. For better performance, consider the Smart BCP tool, which supports parallel copy tasks.

- **SSIS:** Create ETL packages to migrate data from on-premises to Azure. You can directly connect to Azure SQL Database from your on-premises SQL Server package using either ADO.NET or OLEDB connections. Simply specify the full name of the Azure SQL logical server, database, and the correct credentials.

Azure Provided Tools and Services:

Microsoft Azure offers various options to migrate on-premises workloads to the Azure platform.

- **Azure Migrate:** Provides a centralized hub for assessing and migrating on-premises servers, infrastructure, applications, and data to Azure.
    - **Discovery and assessment:** Evaluates on-premises VMware VMs, Hyper-V VMs, physical servers, and SQL Servers for migration readiness.
    - **Server Migration:** Migrates various server types, including VMware VMs, Hyper-V VMs, physical servers, other virtualized servers, and public cloud VMs, to Azure.
    - **Azure App Service Migration Assistant:** Analyses on-premises websites built with .NET and PHP for migration to Azure App Service.
    - **Data Migration Assistant (DMA):** Assesses SQL Server databases, identifying potential migration blockers, unsupported features, and recommended new features. It supports all three deployment options (Azure SQL Database, Azure SQL Managed Instance, and SQL on VM).
    - **Azure Database Migration Service (DMS):** This fully managed service facilitates near zero-downtime migration of on-premises workloads to Azure databases. It supports migrations from various data sources (SQL Server, MySQL, PostgreSQL, MongoDB, Oracle, AWS SQL Server RDS) to Azure databases, with both online and offline migration options. Be mindful of costs associated with this service.
        - We can use Azure DMS via "**Azure SQL Migration Extension in Azure Data Studio**", or via Azure Portal, or through Azure PowerShell and Azure CLI.
- **Azure Synapse Pathway**: It is a tool designed to simplify and accelerate the migration of your existing data warehouse scripts (tables, procedures, functions, etc.) to Azure Synapse Analytics. It essentially translates your code written for other data warehouse platforms (like SQL Server, Snowflake, etc.) into T-SQL code compatible with Azure Synapse SQL.
- **Azure Site Recovery (ASR):** Primarily designed for disaster recovery, ASR can also be used to migrate VMs (on VMware, AWS, Hyper-V, and physical servers) to Azure.
- **Azure Data Factory (ADF):** Leverage the Copy Activity in ADF to migrate data from various sources to Azure databases. ADF natively supports over 90+ data sources (including RDBMS, NoSQL, Big Data, file systems, services, and applications). Cost is a factor to consider here as well.

- **SQL Data Sync (for Azure SQL Database):** This built-in Azure SQL Database solution offers an alternative for replicating data bidirectionally across multiple databases, both in Azure SQL Database and on-premises SQL Server.
- **Azure Log Replay Service (LRS) (for Azure SQL Managed Instance):** DMS and LRS utilize similar underlying technology (similar to log shipping) to migrate databases from on-premises to Azure. If DMS cannot be used due to network port restrictions or for complex migrations with little tolerance for downtime, LRS serves as an alternative.
- **Azure File Sync (for migrating file shares):** Migrate file servers from on-premises to Azure with near zero downtime using Azure File Sync.
- **AzCopy:** This command-line tool facilitates uploading and downloading blobs/files to and from Azure Blob Storage. Use AzCopy to copy data between file systems and storage accounts, or between storage accounts themselves. It can also be used to copy data from on-premises locations to an Azure storage account.
- **Physical hardware transfer:** This method involves directly transferring hardware from on-premises to Azure, followed by data loading into Azure storage.
    - **Azure Import/Export Service:** This service allows you to ship internal SATA HDDs or SSDs from your on-premises datacentre to an Azure datacentre for data transfer.
    - **Azure Data Box:** Similar to the Import/Export service, the Data Box provides a physical appliance from Microsoft. This eliminates the need to purchase hard drives and manage logistics yourself.

Other Microsoft Tools:

- **Microsoft Assessment and Planning Toolkit (MAP Toolkit):** The MAP Toolkit is a free tool that helps you automatically check your computer systems (desktops, servers, software, hardware details, Microsoft Volume Licensing compliance, etc.) to see if they're ready to be moved to the cloud (Azure).
- **SQL Server Migration Assistant (SSMA):** Designed to automate database migrations to SQL Server from various sources like Microsoft Access, DB2, MySQL, Oracle, and SAP ASE. Specific SSMA versions exist for each source RDBMS. It helps assess, migrate schema, data, and objects across database platforms to SQL Server, Azure SQL Database, and Azure SQL Managed Instance.

Open-Source Tools:

- **Smart BCP Tool:** An open-source tool for bulk data loading between various destinations: Azure SQL Databases, SQL Server instances (on-premises or Azure), and even cross-cloud environments (Ex: AWS to Azure). It leverages the BCP API with parallel task processing for efficiency.
- **MSSQL-Scripter Tool:** A Python-based, open-source command-line tool similar to the SSMS Generate Scripts Wizard but with a wider range of options and cross-platform compatibility. Use “mssql-scripter” on Linux, macOS, or Windows to generate DDL/DML T-SQL scripts as .sql

files. It supports SQL Server running anywhere (on-premises or Azure). These scripts can be version-controlled and integrated with DevOps deployments.

Third-Party Tools:

- **Cloudamize, Cloud Atlas, Flexera Cloud Migrator etc.:** These suites of migration tools assist with migrating on-premises workloads to Azure. They offer comprehensive support for complex cloud migrations, including infrastructure and cloud readiness assessments, target SKU recommendations, migration strategy identification, TCO calculations, effort estimations, migration automation, cloud optimization, and security & compliance.
- **Cloud Volumes ONTAP:** A cloud-based storage solution designed for compatibility with your existing on-premises storage managed by NetApp's ONTAP software. This compatibility allows you to leverage SnapMirror data replication for seamless "lift and shift" migration of your data from on-premises ONTAP systems to Azure.

2. Can we use Log Shipping to migrate on-premises SQL Databases to Azure SQL Managed Instance?

Ans:

No, Log shipping cannot be used to migrate on-premises SQL databases directly to Azure SQL Database or SQL Managed Instance. However, there are alternative solutions available, such as Azure Database Migration Service (DMS) or Azure Log Replay Service.

Note: If you have a proper site-to-site connection between your on-premises network and Azure, you may leverage Log Shipping to migrate small to medium databases to SQL Server on Azure VMs.

3. In Azure Database Migration Service (DMS), what are the differences between online and offline migrations?

Ans:

- **Offline Migration:** Database is not available to users during the migration process.
- **Online Migration:** Database remains available to users during the migration process, and only experiences downtime during the final stages of the migration.

Explore:

Azure DMS allows you to migrate your databases in two ways: online and offline.

Online Migration:

- **Downtime:** Minimal downtime, limited to the final cutover to the target database.
- **Database Availability:**
  - **Reads:** Available throughout the migration process.
  - **Writes:** Generally available, but performance might be impacted. Minimize writes during migration for a smoother process.

- **Ideal for:** Applications requiring maximum uptime. **Ex:** Production environments.

Offline Migration:

- **Downtime:** Applications become unavailable during the entire migration process.
- **Database Availability:** Not available for reads or writes during migration.
- **Ideal for:** Applications that can tolerate planned downtime windows. **Ex:** Development and testing environments, or production environments with acceptable downtime.

Choosing Between Online and Offline:

- Test an offline migration first to assess the acceptable downtime for your application.
- If downtime is critical, opt for online migration.

4. What are the supported scenarios for online migration using Azure Database Migration Service (DMS)?

Ans:

Here's a breakdown of currently supported offline and online migration scenarios with DMS:

Offline Migration:

- **Azure SQL Database, SQL Managed Instance & Azure SQL VM:** DMS supports offline migration from standalone SQL Server and Amazon RDS SQL Server.
- **Azure Database for MySQL (Single Server, Flexible Server):** DMS supports offline migration from a standalone MySQL server and Amazon RDS MySQL.
- **Azure Cosmos DB:** DMS supports offline migration from MongoDB.

Online (Continuous Sync) Migration:

- **Azure SQL Database:** Currently, DMS **doesn't support** online migration to Azure SQL Database.
- **Azure SQL Managed Instance & Azure SQL VM:** DMS supports online migration from standalone SQL Server and Amazon RDS SQL Server.
- **Azure Database for MySQL Flexible Server:** DMS supports online migration from a standalone MySQL server, Amazon RDS MySQL, and Azure Database for MySQL - Single Server.
- **Azure Database for PostgreSQL (Single Server, Flexible Server):** DMS supports online migration from a standalone PostgreSQL server, Amazon RDS PostgreSQL, and Azure Database for PostgreSQL - Single Server.
- **Azure Cosmos DB:** DMS supports online migration from MongoDB.

Note: Just to give clarity, the side headings in this answer represent the targeted database deployment models that support migrations. Each model (**Ex:** Azure SQL Database, SQL Managed Instance, Azure Cosmos DB) indicates where the respective migration methods (offline or online) can be applied using DMS (Database Migration Service).

5. Can we migrate master, model, and msdb databases from a SQL Server Standalone instance to Azure SQL Database Logical Server or Azure SQL Managed Instance?

Ans:

Since Azure SQL Database and Azure SQL Managed Instance are PaaS services, we have limited control over system databases. Restoring system databases is not supported. Direct migration of system databases from on-premises to Azure PaaS SQL deployment options is not possible. However, some objects (stored in system databases) can be migrated to Azure SQL Database or Managed Instance using T-SQL scripts, though there are some limitations.

Explore:

- **Applicable System Databases:**
  - **Azure SQL Database:** The only applicable system databases are master and tempdb.
  - **Azure SQL Managed Instance:** All system databases (master, tempdb, model, msdb) are applicable.
- **System Database Migration:**
  - **Azure SQL Database/SQL MI:** Objects from system databases can be migrated using T-SQL scripts.

6. It seems like we have a lot of options available for migrating on-premises database workloads to Azure. Suppose I am your customer and I am seeking your help to assist with the database migration activity. What is your recommendation for the best migration tool, feature, or service?

Ans:

As we always emphasize, the choice depends entirely on business requirements, feasibility (target deployment type, online/offline, database size, tool/feature performance, and cost), and the customer-defined budget. From my experience, in most cases, we have utilized the following tools and services for Azure database migrations:

To identify compatibility issues:

- **DMA:** Data Migration Assistant.
- **SSDT:** SQL Server Data Tools for Visual Studio.
- **Azure Data Studio:** Azure SQL migration extension.

To migrate databases:

- **DMS:** Azure Database Migration Service.
- **Other options:** Backup/Restore, Always-On, Log-Replay Service (LRS), BACPAC, Azure Data Factory - Copy activity etc.

Explore:

These are the recommended tools/services to assess and migrate database workloads to Azure.

To assess and identify the source database compatibility with the target:

- DMA
- SSDT
- Azure SQL migration extension

To migrate Database:

- **Azure VM:**
    - **Online:** DMS, Always-On Availability Groups.
    - **Offline:** DMS, Backup & Restore.
- **Azure SQL Managed Instance:**
    - **Online:** DMS, LRS.
    - **Offline:** DMS, Backup & Restore.
- **Azure SQL Database**
    - **Online:** Transactional Replication, SQL Data Sync.
    - **Offline:** DMS, DMA, SSDT, SQLPackage.exe etc.

Note:

- **Offline:** Planned downtime window.
- **Online:** Minimal or Near-Zero Downtime.

7. Have you ever migrated an on-premises database to Azure SQL Database using the Data Migration Assistant (DMA) tool? If yes, can you explain the procedure?

Ans:

Here are the steps to migrate a complete database from on-premises to Azure SQL Database using DMA:

- Install the latest DMA on the source (on-premise) Windows server.
- **Assess the Source Database:**
    - Create a new project to assess the source database.
    - Analyze the assessment reports, and fix any breaking issues or feature limitations.
- **Migrate Schema and Data:**
    - Create a new project for migrating the source database to Azure SQL Database with the migration scope set to "Schema and Data."

- Specify the source server, source database, target server, and target database.
- Select the specific schema objects from the source that you want to migrate to Azure SQL Database.
- **Migrate Schema:** Generate a SQL script and deploy it to the target database.
- **Migrate Data:** Select all the required tables and start the data migration process.
- Finally, DMA will report the migration status with detailed KPIs, including the number of successfully migrated objects, failed objects, warnings, and other relevant metrics.

- **Redirect Applications to Azure SQL Database:**
  - Connect to Azure SQL Database, validate the data migration, and then redirect your applications to use the migrated database.

Explore:

DMA is a tool used to assess the compatibility of your on-premises SQL Server database for migration to various targets, including other on-premises SQL Servers, Azure SQL Database, Azure SQL Managed Instance (MI), or SQL Server running on an Azure VM. DMA can be used for source database assessment, upgrading, and migration within on-premises environments, or for migrating databases from Azure VMs to Azure SQL Database. However, for cloud migrations from on-premises to Azure, the recommended tool is Azure Database Migration Service (DMS).

Using DMA for On-Premises to Azure SQL Database Migration

Here's a step-by-step guide:

- **Download and Install DMA:**
  - Download and install the latest version of DMA (currently v5.8) from the official Microsoft website on your source Windows server.
- **Assess Source Database Compatibility:**
  - Launch DMA and create a new project for assessment.
    - Project Type: Assessment
    - Source Server Type: SQL Server
    - Target Server Type: Azure SQL Database
  - Specify the source server, connection details, and select the source database(s) for assessment.
  - DMA will analyze the database and provide a report on compatibility issues, supported and unsupported features, and recommendations for improvement after migration.
  - Review the report and address any compatibility issues to ensure a smooth migration.

- **Migrate Database Schema and Data:**
    - Create a new project in DMA for migration.
        - Project Type: Migration
        - Source Server Type: SQL Server
        - Target Server Type: Azure SQL Database
        - Migration Scope: Schema and Data
    - Specify the source and target database connection details with appropriate authentication.
    - If migrating Windows users, provide the target external user domain name (Ex: "microsoft.com").
    - Always choose "Encrypt Connection" when connecting to both databases.
    - Select the specific schema objects (tables, triggers, views, etc.) you want to migrate.
    - DMA will generate a T-SQL script to migrate the schema to the target database.
    - Deploy the script and review the deployment results in DMA for any errors. Fix any issues before proceeding.
    - Select the tables you want to migrate data for and initiate the data migration process.

Verify Migration and Redirect Applications:

- After migration, DMA will display an overall status report. Verify that all objects were successfully migrated.
- Connect to Azure SQL Database and validate the migrated data.
- Finally, redirect your applications to use the migrated database in Azure SQL Database.

8. Can you explain how to migrate a database from an on-premises SQL Server instance to an Azure SQL Managed Instance using Azure Database Migration Service (DMS)?

Ans:

You can use Azure Database Migration Service (DMS) through several methods, including the Azure SQL Migration Extension in Azure Data Studio, the Azure portal, Azure PowerShell, or Azure CLI. However, we recommend using the Azure Data Studio extension for its user-friendly interface.

Here are the high-level steps:

- Launch the "Migrate to Azure SQL" wizard in Azure Data Studio.
- Assess the source SQL Server database(s) and collect performance data.
- Get recommendations (Azure SQL migration feature includes this) for configuring the target SQL Managed Instance.
- Specify the details of your source SQL Server, backup location, and target Azure SQL Managed Instance.
- Create a new or utilize existing Azure Database Migration Service.

- Install the self-hosted integration runtime if your database backups are in a network share.
- Start and monitor the progress of your migration.
- Perform the final cutover.

Explore:

Prerequisites:

- Install Azure Data Studio and Azure SQL migration extension.
- Create a target Azure SQL Managed Instance.
- **Configure permissions:**
    - **Source SQL Server logins:** sysadmin server role or CONTROL SERVER permission.
    - **Azure account:** Contributor for target instance/storage account, Reader for resource groups, Owner/Contributor for subscription.
- **Prepare backups:**
    - **Storage options:** SMB share, Azure storage file share, or blob container.
    - **Permissions:** Service account running source SQL Server needs read/write access to the SMB share.
- **Transparent Data Encryption (TDE):** Migrate the source server certificate to the target instance before migration.
- **Always Encrypted:** Azure Data Studio automatically migrates Always Encrypted keys during migration.
- **Self-hosted integration runtime (a VM):**
- Azure DMS will retrieve backups from the Azure Storage account and restore them to the target SQL Managed Instance. If your backups are located on an on-premise network share, then it is your responsibility to provide a runtime (compute using a VM) capable of migrating database backups from the on-premise network share to the Azure Storage account. We can set up a self-hosted integration runtime on-premises or on an Azure VM.
- If your database backups are already on an Azure storage blob container, you don't need to set up a self-hosted integration runtime.
- If your database backups are in a network file share, provide a machine to install self-hosted integration runtime to access and migrate database backups. The migration wizard provides the download link and authentication keys to download and install your self-hosted integration runtime on a machine (server/VM).
    - **Permissions:**
        - Ensure the machine with self-hosted integration runtime can connect to the source SQL Server instance (Enable outbound 1433) and the network file share (enable outbound 445) where backup files are located.

  - Ensure that the machine where you install the self-hosted integration runtime has the following outbound firewall rules and domain names enabled:
    - {datafactory}.{region}.datafactory.azure.net, 443
    - download.microsoft.com, 443
    - *.core.windows.net, 443
- **Register DMS:** Ensure that Microsoft.DataMigration resource provider is registered in your subscription.

Run Assessment on Source Database and Get Azure Recommendations:

- In Azure Data Studio, launch "Migrate to Azure SQL" wizard.
- Select the source database(s) (on-premise) and the Azure SQL Target (Azure SQL Managed Instance or SQL Server on Azure VM).
- **Source Assessment:** Based on the target selection, it will perform a compatibility assessment and give us the results. If any issues are reported in the assessment results, they need to be fixed before initiating the migration.
- **Target Recommendations:**
  - Select the "Get Azure recommendation" and "collect performance data now" options, and provide a path for performance logs to be collected.
  - Azure Data Studio will now collect performance data from your source database until you stop the collection.
  - After 10 minutes (minimum), you will see a recommended configuration for your Azure SQL Managed Instance. Following this recommendation is optional (which means we can edit those parameters). Along with the recommendations, it will also give us the detailed justification.
  - After analyzing the collected data, it will recommend the target SQL Managed Instance or Azure SQL VM configurations. **Ex:** Gen 5, General Purpose, 4 vCore, 32 GB.

Configure Migration Settings:

- Specify your target Azure SQL Managed Instance by selecting your Azure account, Tenant, subscription, location, resource group and Azure SQL Managed Instance etc.
- Choose the migration mode (Online/Offline).
- Indicate the location of your database backups. Your database backups can be located either on an on-premises network share or in an Azure storage blob container.
  - For backups located on a network share, provide the details of your source SQL Server, source backup location, target database name, Azure storage account for the backup files to be uploaded, and login credentials, etc.
  - For backups stored in an Azure storage blob container, specify the details of the Target database name, Resource group, Azure storage account, Blob container, and login credentials, etc.

- **Network Access Configurations:**
  - Enable access from the self-hosted integration runtime machine to the Azure storage account. For example, you need to add your client IP address of the hosting machine to your Azure Storage account. This step is applicable only when backups are placed in an SMB Network share. If backups are directly placed on Azure Storage account, we can skip this step.
  - Enable access from the target SQL Managed Instance to the Azure Storage account. We need to ensure that the target SQL Server instance can communicate with the Azure Storage account to restore the backups from the container.

Create Azure Database Migration Service:

- **Choose DMS Service:**
  - Within the Migration Wizard, after configuring migration settings, you'll be prompted to choose the Azure Database Migration Service (DMS).
  - You can either create a new DMS or reuse an existing one.
- **Resource Group:**
  - Select the resource group where you have an existing DMS or want to create a new one. The DMS dropdown will list any existing services in the chosen group.
  - If your backups reside directly in Azure Storage, you can skip the SHIR step and proceed to "Initiate Migration."
- **Self-Hosted Integration Runtime (SHIR) (Optional):**
  - If your backups are on an on-premises network file share, you'll need to install and configure SHIR. Skip this step for backups directly in Azure Storage.
  - After creating/selecting a DMS, you'll receive details to set up SHIR.
  - **Download and Install SHIR:** Click "Download and install integration runtime" to open the download link in a web browser. Complete the download and install SHIR on a machine that can connect to the source SQL Server and access the backup location.
  - **SHIR Registration:**
    - After installation, the Microsoft Integration Runtime Configuration Manager will launch automatically.
    - Copy and paste one of the authentication keys provided in the Azure Data Studio wizard. A green checkmark will appear in the manager if the key is valid, indicating you can proceed with registration.
    - Once registration is complete, close the manager and return to the migration wizard in Azure Data Studio.

- **Test Connection:** Click "Test connection" in the Create Azure Database Migration Service screen to validate the connection between the newly created DMS and the registered SHIR.

Initiate Migration:

- Upon successful DMS and SHIR (if applicable) configuration, you'll be directed to the Summary page.
- Review the migration details and click "Done" to begin database migration.

Monitor your migration:

- On the Database Migration Status, you can track the migrations in progress, migrations completed, and migrations failed (if any).
- The migration details page displays the backup files and the corresponding status. Ex: Arrived, uploading, restoring, restored, cancelled, ignored etc.

Complete migration cutover:

The final step is the migration cutover, which briefly switches users to the new database. Careful planning is needed as this will cause downtime for connected applications. To complete the cutover:

- **Stop incoming transactions:** Block writes to the source database.
- **Update application configs:** Point applications to the target database in Azure SQL Managed Instance.
- **Final log backup:** Take a final log backup of the source database in the backup location specified.
- **Read-only mode:** Switch the source database to read-only mode (users can only read data).
- **Verify restore status:** Confirm all backups are in "Restored" status on the monitoring page.
- **Initiate cutover:** Click "Complete cutover" on the monitoring page.

Final Status Check:

- During the cutover process, the migration status changes from **in progress** to **completing**.
- When the cutover process is completed, the migration status changes to **succeeded** to indicate that the database migration is successful and that the migrated database is ready for use.

Note: After the cutover, availability of SQL Managed Instance with Business-Critical service tier can take significantly longer than General Purpose as three secondary replicas have to be seeded for Auto-Failover groups.

9. Can I create Azure Database Migration Service (DMS) directly in the Azure portal instead of using Azure Data Studio?

Ans:

Yes, you can. The recommended method depends on the database you're migrating:

- **SQL Server migration:** Use Azure Data Studio with the Migrate to Azure SQL extension.
- **MySQL, MongoDB, PostgreSQL migration:** Use DMS via the Azure portal.

10. What are some best practices for optimizing Azure Database Migration Service (DMS) for database workload migrations?

Ans:

Here are the top points to improve the performance of Azure Database Migration Service (DMS):

- **Optimize Source Database Performance**: Indexing, cleaning up unnecessary data, and optimizing queries.
- **Indexing Strategy:**
    - **Source Database:** Ensure the source database has appropriate indexes in place, as read performance at source is critical during the migration.
    - **Target Database:** To optimize write performance during the migration process, consider dropping indexes on the target database before migration and recreating them afterwards.
- **Hardware Limitations:** The hardware of the source server will also play a role in the migration's performance. To achieve optimal migration performance, it is highly recommended that you dedicate a machine exclusively to running the Self-hosted integration runtime (SHIR). This machine should have a fast and reliable connection to your source and target database.
- **Network Configuration**: Ensuring sufficient bandwidth, minimizing latency, and using private network connectivity.
- **Resource Allocation**: Choosing a Premium service tier will give you the lowest time for migration. Even if you are planning to run this database in a Standard Tier, you are better off migrating into a higher Premium Series SQL DB and then lower the Service Tier once the migration has completed.
- **Offline vs Online Migration:** You can use Azure DMS to perform offline and online migrations. It is suggested that you test an offline migration to determine whether the downtime is acceptable; if not, do an online migration.
- **Parallelism and Batch Processing**: Enabling parallel processing and configuring optimal batch sizes.
    - DMS allows you to configure the batch size for data transfer. Experiment with different batch sizes to find the optimal balance between throughput and resource utilization.

  - Adjust the allocated bandwidth for data migration within DMS settings. This can be especially helpful if you have dedicated network resources available.

11. A premium customer has requested a cloud database migration. We plan to use Azure Database Migration Service (DMS) to migrate their on-premises SQL Server databases to Azure. However, due to restrictions at the source datacenter, a site-to-site connection (VPN or ExpressRoute) cannot be established between their on-premises network and Azure. Given this limitation, are there any alternative approaches to perform the migration using DMS without a direct connection?

Ans:

Azure DMS offers a Hybrid mode specifically designed for situations with limited network bandwidth between on-premises environments and Azure. This is ideal for migrating large databases without a site-to-site connection (ExpressRoute or VPN).

How DMS Hybrid Mode Works:

The DMS hybrid mode employs a combination of on-premises and cloud resources to facilitate database migration. It consists of two components:

- **On-premises migration worker:** This software is installed on a server within your on-premises network.
- **Cloud service instance:** This is the standard Azure DMS running in the cloud (Azure).

Here are the additional steps to configure when using DMS in Hybrid Mode:

DMS with Hybrid Mode.

  - **Azure Mode:** Choose when direct site-to-site connectivity is available. Migration activity runs in Azure.
  - **Hybrid Mode:** Choose when there is no site-to-site connectivity or connectivity with limited bandwidth. Migration activity runs with a combination of on-premise and cloud resources.

- **On-premises Worker Communication:** Three elements enable the on-premise hybrid worker to communicate with the Azure DMS instance:
  - DMS Resource ID.
  - Azure App registration ID.
  - Public certificate.

- **Worker Installation and Configuration:**
  - Install Azure Database Migration Service Hybrid Worker on the on-premises server.
  - Create a communication channel between the on-premises Hybrid Worker and Azure DMS by mapping Resource-ID, Application (Client)-ID, and a public security certificate.

Note: Hybrid mode can seem a bit complex. However, don't worry about explaining it step-by-step in an interview if asked about this approach. Just ensure you understand the overall process.

Explore:

Here is the detailed process: We need to create a communication channel between on-premises Hybrid Worker and Azure DMS for securely migrate data from source to cloud:

Get DMS Resource-ID:

- It tells on-premises Hybrid Worker about the DMS resource details (Subscription, resource name etc.) in Azure. So that Hybrid Worker can reach the DMS instance for communication.
- In Azure, once DMS instance is created, you can get the Resource Id from the DMS properties. You need to copy and save resource id that can be used while installing Hybrid Worker at on-premises.

Get Azure App registration ID:

Using Resource-ID Hybrid Worker can find the DMS instance. But it needs a proper authentication and authorization to utilize the DMS instance. Hence, you follow the Azure standard procedure to authenticate and authorize the source connection to the DMS instance using App Registration ID.

- **Authentication:** Create an Azure App Registration ID
    - Azure Portal > Entra/Azure Active Directory > App registrations > New registration > Give a Name and select Account type > Register
    - Once App ID is registered copy the Application Client ID that can be used while installing Hybrid Worker at on-premises.
- **Authorization:** Give App ID permissions to use DMS Instance
    - In the Azure portal > Azure Database Migration Service > Access control (IAM) > Add> Add role assignment > Assign contributor access to the App ID.

Configure & Install Hybrid Worker at On-Premises:

- **Download the installer:** We can download the installer from DMS properties page in Azure portal. Azure Portal > DMS Instance > Settings > Hybrid > Installer Download.
- **Configure Hybrid Worker:** Copy the downloaded installer folder to the on-premises server and extract the installer folder. From the Install folder, locate the configuration file dmsSettings.json, update Application Id, Resource Id and save the file.
- **Generate a public certificate:** Azure Database Migration Service can use this certificate to authenticate the communication from the hybrid worker. We can generate the certificate using the command:

- D:\Temp\HybridDMS\Install>DMSWorkerBootstrap.exe -a GenerateCert
- It generates a security certificate in the same Install folder.
- **Upload certificate to Azure Portal:** In the Azure portal, navigate to the App ID, under Manage, select Certificated & secrets, and then select Upload certificate to select the public certificate we generated at on-premises.
- **Install the Azure DMS hybrid worker:** On our on-premises server by running the following command:
- D:\Temp\HybridDMS\Install>DMSWorkerBootstrap.exe -a Install -IAcceptDMSLicenseTerms -d

Check the DMS Readiness & Start the Migration: In Azure portal, go to Azure DMS instance and from overview page check the status. If it is "Online" we are all set to start the Database Migration using DMS Hybrid mode.

12. When assessing an on-premise SQL Server database for migration to Azure SQL Database, what types of compatibility issues have you typically encountered?

Ans:

Compatibility issues are organized in the following categories:

- **Breaking changes:** Changes that cause existing code or functionality to fail completely when migrating to Azure.
  - **Ex:** Certain SQL Server features such as SQL CLR assemblies, FILESTREAM, linked servers, database mail, cross-database queries, Non-ANSI Join Syntax are not supported in Azure SQL Database.
- **Behavior changes:** These are changes that don't necessarily break the system but alter the way it behaves.
  - **Ex:** Azure SQL Database doesn't support compatibility levels below 100. Similarly, while Azure SQL Database supports transactional replication, it can only act as a subscriber, not as a publisher.
- **Deprecated features:** These are features or functionalities that are still available in the system but are not recommended for use because they will be removed in future versions.
  - **Ex:** While creating external data sources to Azure storage, we should use new connectors:
  - Azure Blob Storage: Old (wasb), New (abs).
  - ADLS Gen 2: Old (abfs), New(adls).

Explore:

Let's say we're planning to migrate a SQL Server database to Azure SQL Database. During the source assessment using the Data Migration Assistant, it can identify compatibility issues. Here are some common compatibility issues you might encounter:

Issue: BULK INSERT and OPENROWSET with non-Azure blob data source isn't supported in Azure SQL Database.

- **Solution:** You need to convert BULK INSERT and OPENROWSET T-SQL statements that use local windows files or file shares to use files from Azure Blob Storage instead.

Issue: The COMPUTE clause generates totals that appear as additional summary columns at the end of the result set. However, this clause is no longer supported in Azure SQL Database.

- **Solution:** The T-SQL module needs to be rewritten using the ROLLUP operator instead.

Issue: FASTFIRSTROW query hint is no longer supported and has been removed.

- **Solution:** Instead of FASTFIRSTROW query hint use OPTION (FAST n).

Issue: FILESTREAM isn't supported in Azure SQL Database

- **Solution:** Upload the unstructured files to Azure Blob storage and store metadata related to these files (name, type, URL location, storage key etc.) in Azure SQL Database. For this, you need to re-engineer your application and database code. Alternatively, for a fully functional filestream feature, migrate to SQL Server on Azure VM.

Issue: Non-ANSI left/right outer join is no longer supported and has been removed.

- **Solution:** Use ANSI join syntax.
    - **Old Style:** *= (Left-Outer), =* (Right Outer)
        - SELECT * FROM table1, table2 WHERE table1.id *= table2.id;
    - **ANSI standard:**
        - SELECT * FROM table1 LEFT OUTER JOIN table2 ON table1.id = table2.id;

Other common Issues and Solutions: Other commonly used features in SQL Server that are not supported by Azure SQL Database.

- **Cross database queries:** Use Elastic Database Query.
- **Linked server:** Use Elastic Database Query.
- **Server Audits:** Consider Azure SQL Database audit feature to replace SQL Server "Server Audits".
- **Server-scoped credentials:** Use Database scoped credentials. A credential is a record that contains the authentication information (credentials) required to connect to a resource outside SQL Server.
- **Server-scoped triggers:** Use database-scoped trigger instead.
- **Database Mail:** Consider using Azure functions and SendGrid to accomplish mail functionality.

- **SQL Agent Jobs:** Use elastic jobs.
- **Windows Authentication:** Federate the on-premise Active Directory with Microsoft Entra ID. The Windows identity can then be replaced with the equivalent Microsoft Entra identities.
- **CLR assemblies, MS DTC, Service Broker, Trace flags:** Migrate it to Azure SQL Managed Instance or SQL on Azure VM.

Note: If a compatibility issue arises and there's no suitable alternative solution available within Azure SQL Database, consider migrating to Azure SQL Managed Instance or SQL on Azure VM.

13. When migrating different types of database workloads (Ex: SQL Server, MySQL) to Azure, what challenges or issues have you typically encountered?

Ans:

Here are some of the top common problems you might encounter when migrating databases using Azure Database Migration Service (DMS):

Network Connectivity:

- **Limited bandwidth:** If on-premises network connection to Azure has limited bandwidth, large database migrations can take a significantly longer time.
- **No site-to-site connectivity:** DMS typically relies on a site-to-site connection (VPN or ExpressRoute) for communication between your on-premises databases and Azure. If such a connection isn't available, alternative approaches with DMS might be required (Ex: DMS hybrid mode, Azure Data Box Disk etc.).

Source Database Issues:

- **Compatibility issues:** Not all SQL Server/MySQL/PostgreSQL features are directly supported in Azure SQL Family. The DMA can help identify potential compatibility issues during the assessment phase. However, resolving these issues might involve schema or code modifications to adapt to Azure SQL Database functionalities.
- **Large transactions:** DMS might struggle with exceptionally large transactions within the source database (Ex: A long running transaction blocking DMS read operation). Breaking down large transactions into smaller chunks before migration can improve performance.

Migration Process Challenges:

- **Downtime:** While DMS strives for minimal downtime, some downtime during the cutover phase (switching from source to target database) might be unavoidable. Careful planning and minimizing application dependency on the database during this window can help reduce its impact.
- **Complex schema migrations:** Databases with very complex schemas or multi-layered relationships between tables can pose challenges for DMS during the migration process.

Dependencies between database objects (Ex: tables, views, stored procedures) can complicate the migration process. Ensuring that all dependencies are resolved correctly in the target environment is crucial for a successful migration.

- **Large database migration:** Migrating large databases can pose challenges related to data transfer speeds, storage limitations, and performance optimizations in the target environment.
- **Data integrity and consistency:** Maintaining data integrity and consistency throughout the migration process is essential. Issues such as data loss, corruption, or inconsistency can occur if not managed properly.

Other challenges:

- **Monitoring and troubleshooting:** Monitoring the migration process and troubleshooting any errors or performance issues that arise are essential for a successful migration. Having effective monitoring tools and processes in place can help identify and address problems promptly.
- **Security and compliance requirements:** Ensuring that security configurations and compliance standards are met in the target environment is critical. This includes user permissions, encryption settings, and data protection measures.
- **Post-migration optimizations:** After the migration is complete, optimizing the database and application performance in the new environment is necessary. This includes compatibility check, index maintenance, tuning queries, and configurations to ensure optimal performance and scalability.

Explore:

Some of the sample issues:

- **Error connecting to source SQL Server when using dynamic port or named instance:** This issue happens when the source SQL Server instance is using a dynamic port or a named instance. Verify that Azure Database Migration Service can connect to the source SQL Server Browser service on UDP port 1434 and the SQL Server instance through the dynamically assigned TCP port as applicable.
- **Connection error when using ExpressRoute:**
    - **Root Cause:** When using ExpressRoute, Azure Database Migration Service requires provisioning three service endpoints on the Virtual Network subnet associated with the service:
        - Service Bus endpoint.
        - Storage endpoint.
        - Target database endpoint (Ex: SQL endpoint, Azure Cosmos DB endpoint).
    - **Solution:** Enable the required service endpoints for ExpressRoute connectivity between source and Azure DMS.

- **Migration activity in queued state:** This issue occurs when the Azure Database Migration Service instance has reached maximum capacity for ongoing tasks that concurrently run. Any new activity is queued until the capacity becomes available.
- **Max number of databases selected for migration:** This error occurs when you've selected more than four databases for a single migration activity. At present, each migration activity is limited to four databases.
- **Error when attempting to stop Azure Database Migration Service:** This error occurs when the service instance you're attempting to stop includes activities that are still running or present in migration projects.
- **DMS Online migration cutover fails with the 'AuthorizationFailed' error:**
    - **Root Cause:** This error indicates the application principal being used for online migration from SQL Server to SQL Managed Instance doesn't have contribute permission on the subscription.
    - **Solution:**
        - Use the Get-AzureADServicePrincipal PowerShell cmdlet with -ObjectId available from the error message to list the display name of the application ID being used.
        - Validate the permissions to this application and ensure it has the contributor role at the subscription level.
- **Faulty backup media:** Azure DMS doesn't support backups that are appended to a single backup file. Take full, differential and log backups to separate backup files.
- **Issue with multiple log files:** Azure DMS doesn't support databases with multiple log files. If you have multiple LDFs, shrink and reorganize them into a single transaction log file.
- **Size limitations of PostgreSQL:** You can migrate up to 1 TB of data from PostgreSQL to Azure Database for PostgreSQL, using a single DMS service.
- **Primary key is missing on source database:** While performing online migration for a PostgreSQL using DMS, if there's no primary key on tables, changes might not be synced to the target database. Temporarily set a primary key for the table for migration to continue. Remove the primary key after data migration is finished.
- **Schema mismatch:** To avoid unnecessary migration issues, we must make sure that schema (data types, default values, object names etc.) matches between on-premise and Azure database.
- **Failed to generate invisible primary key. Auto-increment column already exists:**
    - **Root Cause:** This error might occur when we are migrating MySQL database to Azure Database for MySQL. Migration to MySQL Flexible Server instance where sql_generate_invisible_primary_key is enabled is not supported by DMS.

  - **Solution:** To resolve this issue, set the server parameter sql_generate_invisible_primary_key for target MySQL Flexible Server to OFF.

- **Foreign key validation errors:** To resolve these issues, we recommend dropping the foreign key at target database and re-creating it after the migration process is completed.
- **TLS/SSL certificate issues during MongoDB to Cosmos DB migration with DMS:**
  - **Root Cause:** Migration fails due to an invalid TLS/SSL certificate. This might happen even with open firewall ports if a self-signed certificate is used. (Self-signed certs are for internal testing only.)
  - **Solution:** Use a trusted certificate from a Certificate Authority (CA) to enable TLS securely in Azure DMS.

14. How can I monitor the progress of my database migrations using Azure Database Migration Service?

Ans:

- **Azure Portal:** Provides a quick visual overview of migration status at database and table levels.
- **Azure Monitor:** Offers in-depth analysis with detailed metrics and customizable visualizations for proactive monitoring.

Explore:

Azure DMS offers several ways to monitor the progress and status of your database migrations:

Azure Portal (A quick visual overview of migration):

- **Database-level monitoring:** The DMS blade in the Azure portal provides a high-level overview of the migration activity for each database. It displays the current status (Running, Succeeded, Faulted), estimated duration, and migration details like full data load and ongoing synchronization progress.
  - **Error Tracking:** When migration failed with Activity status = Faulted, select the 'See error details' link under migration details for the complete error message.
- **Table-level monitoring:** You can drill down further into individual tables within the database view. This view shows the completion status for full data load and incremental updates for each table, providing a more granular level of detail.
  - **Error Tracking:**
    - **Column "Tables in error state":** Represents the number of tables that are in 'error' state during migration. **Ex:** Duplicates identified in the target or data isn't compatible loading in the target table due to schema issues.
    - **Column "Data Errors":** Number of data errors happened in this table. **Ex:**

- **511:** Cannot create a row of size %d which is greater than the allowable maximum row size of %d.
- **8114:** Error converting data type %ls to %ls.
- Customer should query from dms_apply_exceptions table in Azure target to see the error details.

Azure Monitor integration (In-depth analysis with detailed metrics):

- DMS integrates with Azure Monitor, allowing you to collect and analyze detailed metrics about the migration process.
- These metrics include data transfer rates, latency, errors encountered, and overall migration progress. You can set up custom visualizations and alerts based on these metrics for proactive monitoring.

15. We're migrating our production databases to Azure using Azure DMS. From a security standpoint, it's important to understand if DMS stores any of our customer data during the migration process. Can you answer this question?

Ans:

Data Storage:

- **Customer Data:** Azure DMS does not store customer data. Data is copied directly from the source environment to the target database in Azure. DMS acts as a facilitator for data movement, not a storage medium.
- **Metadata:** DMS does maintain a metadata store internally that includes information about mapping details between source and target, network locations, credentials, backup files, and migration progress logs.

Explore:

Azure DMS employs various security measures to safeguard customer data during migration:

- **Data Encryption:** Data transferred between the source database, DMS service, and the target database in Azure is encrypted using industry-standard protocols like TLS 1.2. This encryption helps protect data confidentiality during transit.
- **Metadata Security:** DMS maintains a metadata store internally. Credentials and selected fields, like account keys, are encrypted. Data, like table names that may be included in telemetry, is hashed. Telemetry is siloed by region, governed by retention policies and available only to authorized personnel within Microsoft for valid troubleshooting purposes.

- **Authentication and Authorization:** DMS leverages Microsoft Entra for user authentication and authorization. Only users with assigned roles and permissions can access and manage migration jobs.
- **Auditing:** DMS provides audit logs that track user activities and migration job execution details. These logs can be used for monitoring and compliance purposes.

16. What do you know about SMART BULK COPY? Do you know how it works?

Ans:

- Smart Bulk Copy (An advanced version of Bulk Copy) is a high-speed tool designed to move data between two instances of SQL Server.
- This tool can also be used to efficiently and quickly move data between two instances of SQL Server running in two different cloud providers, or to move data from on-premises to the cloud.
- It smartly uses logical or physical partitions to maximize transfer speed using parallel copy tasks.
- It's a popular open-source project on GitHub by Microsoft and leverages the SQL Server Bulk Copy API for efficient data transfer.

Explore:

Smart Bulk Copy and Partitioning:

- **Partitioned Source Tables:** When the source table is already partitioned, Smart Bulk Copy leverages the existing physical partitions. It then executes multiple queries in parallel to efficiently move these partitions to the destination table.
- **Non-Partitioned Source Tables:** For non-partitioned tables, Smart Bulk Copy employs a logical partitioning strategy by using SQL Server Virtual Columns. It utilizes the physical location of each row/record to create non-overlapping partitions that can be safely read concurrently.
- **SQL Server Virtual Columns:**
    - SQL Server tables can have virtual columns that define row metadata used by the database engine.
    - One example is the %%PhysLoc%% virtual column, which reveals the physical address of a row.
    - You can use a query like SELECT Sale_ID, %%PhysLoc%% FROM Sales to retrieve data from the Sales table along with each row's physical location.
    - Smart Bulk Copy leverages this same virtual column to logically partition non-partitioned tables for parallel processing.

Using Smart Bulk Copy:

Here's a step-by-step guide on using Smart Bulk Copy:

- **Download or Clone:** Download the code or clone the Smart Bulk Copy repository from GitHub onto your source server.
- **Create Configuration File:** Create a configuration file named smartbulkcopy.config based on the provided template file smartbulkcopy.config.template.
- **Configure Settings:** Update the configuration file with specific details about your migration, including source and destination information, tables to be copied, batch size, and the desired number of parallel tasks.
- **Execute:** Once configured, execute the Smart Bulk Copy tool to initiate the data migration process.

Note:

- Smart Bulk Copy only copies data between existing databases and existing objects. It will not create databases or tables for you.
- Smart Bulk Copy is also available as a Docker Image. You can run Smart Bulk Copy via Docker, or using Azure Container Instances. It provides a script azure-deploy.sh to create an Azure Container Instance and execute Smart Bulk Copy.

17. Have you ever used Smart Bulk Copy? Do you recommend it for copying data between SQL Servers?

Ans:

Yes, I've used Smart Bulk Copy (SBC) successfully to move a large table between SQL Server instances hosted on Azure VMs. While I haven't used it for cloud migrations from on-premises yet, it's a valuable tool for such scenarios.

In my experience, I configured SBC with 7 parallel tasks and a batch size of 100,000 rows. This approach allowed me to copy a 25 GB partitioned ROWSTORE clustered index table from one Azure VM to another (both in the same region) in approximately 12 minutes. It's important to remember that other factors like VM type, server load, and network bandwidth can also impact the copy time.

I would definitely recommend using Smart Bulk Copy for copying large tables between SQL Servers.

Explore:

Ensure that source and destination tables meet the following preconditions:

Source Table:

- **Partitioned Table:** If the table is already partitioned, you can use the existing partitions for efficient parallel copying with SBC.
- **Non-Partitioned Table:** For non-partitioned tables, it's recommended to use a database snapshot or a read-only database as the source.

- **Reason:** During the copy process, SBC uses the physical location of rows to logically partition the table. Any DML (insert, update, or delete) operations on the source table can change row locations, potentially leading to inconsistencies. Using a snapshot or read-only database ensures a stable source for reliable copying.

Destination Table:

- **No Foreign Key Constraints:** The destination table ideally shouldn't have foreign key constraints. Alternatively, you can temporarily drop these constraints on the destination table until the copy is complete.

18. What is Azure Log Replay Service (LRS) and how does it work?

Ans:

LRS: Log Replay Service (LRS) is PowerShell/Azure Command Line based database migration feature enabled for Azure SQL Managed Instance. Azure Database Migration Service (DMS), the Azure SQL migration extension for Azure Data Studio, and LRS all use the same underlying migration technology and APIs. LRS is based on SQL Server Log Shipping technology.

Choose it: When Azure DMS is not fulfilling your migration requirement, you can use LRS as an alternative solution to migrate databases to Azure SQL Managed Instance.

LRS Migration approach:

- **Backup Source Database:** Take database backups (Full, Diff and Tran) on-premises SQL Server with CHECKSUM enabled.
- **Copy backups to Blob Storage:** Upload the backup files to Azure Blob Storage using AzCopy or if possible, we can directly take "Backup to URL".
- **Start Log Replay Service**: Start LRS command (Start-AzSqlInstanceDatabaseLogReplay) and it starts restoring files from Blob Storage to SQL Managed Instance.
    - **Autocomplete mode**: Migration will be finished automatically when the last of the specified backup files has been restored.
    - **Continuous mode:** LRS service will continuously restore any new backup files (Diff and Tran) that are added. The migration will finish on the manual cutover only.
- **Cutover:**
    - **Autocomplete mode:** We need to start the command by specifying the last backup file name (Ex: -LastBackupName "AdventureWorks2022_diff.bak") to be restored.
    - **Continues mode:** We can control the cutover time based on the log backup size. Once we see the least possible sized log backup, we can take the tail log at source, upload it to blob

storage, and do a cutover (complete-azsqlinstancedatabaselogreplay)) by restoring the last file to Azure SQL MI.

- **Redirect your applications** to use database from Azure SQL Managed Instance

Explore:

LRS Restore Procedure (More details):

- **Backup File Scanning:** LRS scans all files placed on Azure Blob Storage for the restore process. No specific naming convention is required for these files. LRS constructs the backup chain by analyzing the backup file headers, identifying the order and relationships between the backups.
- **Destination Database State:** During the LRS restore process on Azure SQL MI, the target databases are restored in "WITH NORECOVERY" mode. This means the databases are not immediately usable for reads or writes until the final cutover step.
- **Migrating multiple databases in parallel:**
  - Place backup files for each database in a separate folder on the Blob Storage account in a flat-file structure. Ex: Use separate database folders:
    - blobcontainer/AdvWorks2019/files
    - blobcontainer/ AdvWorks2022/files
  - Don't use nested folders inside database folders, because nested-folder structure isn't supported.
  - Start LRS separately for each database.
- **Cutover:** The final step involves the cutover process. This brings the restored database online, making it accessible for read-write operations on the SQL MI.
- **Supporting sources:** LRS supports migration from SQL Server hosted on-premises, Azure VM, AWS EC2, AWS RDS for SQL Server, SQL on Google Compute Engine, GCP- Cloud SQL for SQL Server.

19. I'm using Log Replay Service (LRS) to migrate on-premises databases to Azure SQL MI. One database migration is complete, and the database is now online in SQL MI. However, I need to restore one additional transaction log file from my on-premises environment to SQL MI. Since no changes have been made to the destination database, can I resume the LRS service and restore just the missing log file?

Ans:

Unfortunately, no. Once the cutover process is complete (either in automatic or manual mode), you cannot resume the restore process to add just a single log file. The only way to restore additional backups is to delete the database from SQL MI and then restart the LRS to restore the full backup chain from scratch.

20. When to use LRS (Log Replay Service) instead of DMS (Database Migration Service) for migrating to Azure SQL Managed Instance?

Ans:

DMS and LRS use the same underlying migration technology and the same APIs. Consider using LRS when DMS is not fully supporting your migration requirements.

Explore:

DMS is a fully managed migration service and it supports migrating various database systems to Azure. LRS is specifically designed for handling custom and complex migrations to Azure SQL MI. I always recommend using Azure SQL migration extension for Azure Data Studio or DMS when migrating workloads to Azure SQL MI.

Here are the most common scenarios where LRS is a suitable choice:

- **Limited Source Server Access:** If you lack administrative access to the source database server's operating system, you cannot install the DMS executable. LRS doesn't require any agent installation on the source server, making it a viable alternative.
- **Network Constraints:**
    - Restricted firewall rules that prevent opening all ports necessary for DMS to access Azure from your on-premises environment.
    - Network throttling or limitations imposed by multiple corporate firewalls.
- **Cutover Downtime Control:** When your business has minimal downtime tolerance and requires control over the migration cutover process, LRS offers a manual cutover approach. This allows you to schedule the cutover window for minimal disruption, unlike DMS which might have a longer automated cutover process.

21. I have a business case to migrate our on-premise SQL Server instance to Azure SQL MI. I have a database sized greater than 8 TB. However, we learned that Azure SQL Managed Instance has a maximum limit of 8 TB for reserved storage. How can I handle this scenario?

Ans:

In this given use case, you don't need to worry about the database size. Azure SQL MI imposes overall instance, database, or individual data file size limitations based on the selected service tier and hardware configurations. For example, it supports up to 32 TB in size. Below are the detailed limitations from the storage point of view:

Managed Instance Size: For Azure SQL MI, the maximum storage size depends on the service tier and hardware configuration. **Ex:** The maximum instance storage for

- General Purpose is 16 TB
- Next Gen General Purpose is 32 TB
- Business Critical – Premium Series is 5.5 TB, and
- Business Critical - Memory optimized premium-series is 16 TB

Single Database Size: Up to the currently available maximum managed instance size.

Single Data File (Ex: MDF or NDF) Size:

- For the General-Purpose service tier, based on the chosen vCores, it can support a maximum individual data file size of 8 TB. If your data file size is larger than 8 TB and you are migrating it to the General-Purpose service tier, then we would recommend splitting the data file into multiple data files.
- This limitation is applicable only to the General-Purpose service tier. For Next Gen General Purpose and Business Critical service tiers, just like Database Size, there is no limit on the individual data file size, and they support the maximum allowed instance size (depending on the vCores).

Alternatives: If your on-premise workload does not fit into an Azure SQL Managed instance due to any of the above specified limitations, we could consider other options such as Azure SQL Database – Hyperscale, or running SQL Server on an Azure VM.

22. We have a business case: Currently running a SQL Server 2016 workload on-premises with the following architecture:

- **Database size:** 200 GB
- **Always-On Availability Group configured:**
    - Primary database
    - 1 synchronous read-only replica
    - 3 asynchronous read-only replicas
- **Applications:**
    - **App-1:** Read-write activity on the primary database (uses an availability group listener).
    - **App-2, App-3, App-4:** Read-only workloads on read-only replica databases (uses a load balancer for round-robin access).

Migration Requirement: After compatibility testing and budget considerations, the client decided to migrate to **Azure SQL Database**. However, the business has strict downtime constraints:

- **Read-only workload:** Migrate with **minimal** downtime (ideally near zero)
- **Read-write workload:** Migrate with minimal downtime (maximum allowed: 120 minutes)
- **Any extended downtime beyond 120 minutes is considered a failure.**

Can you describe your approach to fulfil these requirements?

Ans:

Always-On Availability Groups cannot be directly configured between an on-premises SQL Server instance and Azure SQL Database or SQL Managed Instance. However, Azure SQL Database and SQL Managed Instance (Azure SQL PaaS options) offer high availability and disaster recovery (HA/DR) solutions like Geo-replication and Auto Failover Groups, which internally leverage Always-On technology.

In this scenario, we can achieve near-zero downtime migration to Azure SQL Database using transactional replication. To minimize risk, a phased approach is recommended:

- **Configure Transactional Replication:**
    - Set up transactional replication for the on-premises SQL Server database, with Azure SQL Database as a push subscriber.
    - Since the source database uses Always-On Availability Groups, consider the necessary steps for configuring replication for a database participating in an Always-On AG.
    - Create a "distribution" database on all secondary replicas with identical configurations.
    - Establish publications for the primary replica and all secondary replicas.
    - Redirect the original publisher to the Always-On AG listener name. This ensures the secondary replica can take over after a failover.
        - By default, transactional replication points to a specific SQL Server instance (the original publisher) as the data source. However, in an Always-On AG environment, the primary replica holding the active database can change during a failover.
        - The sp_redirect_publisher stored procedure in SQL Server allows you to redirect the replication connection from the original publisher server name to the AlwaysOn AG listener name. This guarantees the subscriber (Azure SQL Database in this case) always connects to the current primary replica, regardless of its location after a failover.
- **Configure Active Geo-replication:** To accommodate read-only traffic scaling needs in Azure, create four readable secondary databases for Azure SQL Database using active geo-replication.
- **Redirect App-2 Traffic to Azure:** Once the replication topology is stable for a period, use a load balancer to redirect App-2's read-only traffic from on-premises to the Azure SQL Database geo-replication readable secondaries.

- **Monitor and Adjust Azure Resources:** Monitor Azure SQL Database resource utilization. Based on statistics and performance, adjust the Azure SQL Database service tier and performance levels as needed.
- **Phased Application Traffic Redirection (Apps 3, and 4):** Repeat steps 3 (Redirect App-3&4 Traffic to Azure) and 4 (Monitor and Adjust Azure Resources).
- **Hybrid Architecture:** At this stage, your application operates in a hybrid architecture, with read-only traffic directed to Azure SQL Database and read-write traffic still using the on-premises database.
- **Test Rollback Plan:** Before migrating the read-write workload, we need to test the rollback plan. If migration encounters issues, you should be able to identify data changes in Azure after cutover and apply them back to the on-premises database.
    - To test rollback, use a week-old on-premises backup:
        - Restore it as a test database in a separate SQL Server instance.
        - Compare it with the Azure SQL Database to identify data changes (delta).
        - Apply these data changes to the test database using SQL Server Data Tools (SSDT) data comparison features.
- **Final Cutover:**
    - Freeze read-write access to the primary database for App-1 (on-premises) – downtime begins for App-1.
    - Wait for remaining transactions to replicate to Azure SQL Database.
    - Remove the replication topology from the on-premises SQL Server database.
    - Redirect App-1 read-write traffic from on-premises to Azure SQL Database (downtime ends; App-1 becomes available).
    - **Finally redirected:**
        - App-1 read-write traffic to the Azure SQL Database primary database.
        - App-2, App-3, and App-4 read-only traffic to the Azure SQL Database geo-replication read-only replicas.
- **Cleanup On-Premises:**
    - After a full business cycle of monitoring, decommission the on-premises SQL Server environment.

Note: More details about the features '**Active-Geo Replication**' and '**Auto-Failover Groups**' will be covered in '**Azure The One - Part 2: Azure SQL Family.**'

23. How can I configure transactional replication from an on-premises SQL Server database to Azure SQL Database? Are there any special considerations?

Ans:

Configuring transactional replication to Azure SQL Database follows the same general steps as setting up a normal replication, but with some key points to remember:

- **Push subscriptions only:** Only push subscriptions are supported for Azure SQL Database subscribers.
- **SQL Server version requirement:** The publisher and distributor (on-premises SQL Server instance) must be running SQL Server 2012 SP2 CU8 or later.
- **Authentication:** Only SQL Server authentication works for replication with Azure SQL Database.
- **Azure SQL Database firewall:** Configure the Azure SQL Database firewall to allow connections from your distributor SQL Server.
- **Snapshot folder size:** Ensure the snapshot folder has enough space to hold the BCP (Bulk Copy Program) output for every table you want to replicate.
- **Snapshot locking:** Tables involved in snapshot creation are locked until the process finishes. Schedule snapshots accordingly to minimize impact.
- **Monitoring and troubleshooting:** Replication monitoring and troubleshooting can only be done from the source (on-premises) server.

Configuring Transactional Replication from On-Premises to Azure SQL Database:

- **On-premises Configuration:**
    - **Connect to your SQL Server instance** using SSMS.
    - **Configure Distributor:** Similar to normal replication setup, define the snapshot folder location and distributer database files (.mdf and .ldf).
    - **Configure Publisher:**
        - Specify the source database and the specific articles to replicate (tables, stored procedures, views, functions).
        - Schedule the snapshot agent to run periodically and configure security for the Snapshot Agent and Log Reader Agent (using a domain account is recommended).
- **Azure SQL Database Configuration:**
    - **Choose the appropriate service tier/performance level** for your Azure SQL Database based on your needs.
    - **Create an empty database** within your Azure SQL Database.
- **Subscriber Configuration:**
    - **Navigate to the publication** you created in your on-premises SQL Server instance.
    - **Create a new subscription:**

        - Select the publication database and choose "Run all Agents at Distributor" as Azure SQL Database only supports push subscriptions.
        - In the subscription wizard, select "Add SQL Server Subscriber" and connect to your Azure SQL Database using the following details:
            - **Server Name:** Enter the full Azure SQL Database logical server name (Ex: demorepladv2024.database.windows.net).
            - **Authentication:** Use SQL Server authentication.
            - **Login:** Specify the login with appropriate permissions (Ex: advadmin).
            - **Password:** Enter the password for the login.
            - **Database:** Select the empty database you created earlier.
    - **Configure Distribution Agent Security:** Use a SQL Server login with "Database Owner" permissions on the Azure SQL Database.
- **Start Replication:**
    - **Create an initial snapshot:** This will replicate all objects and data to the Azure SQL Database.
        - Open the Snapshot Agent by clicking "View Snapshot Agent Status" on the publication and then "Start" the agent.
- **Monitor Replication:**
    - Once the initial snapshot completes, replication will begin automatically (if configured for continuous replication). You can monitor the replication status using the replication monitor in SSMS.

24. Can we configure Snapshot Replication from on-premises to Azure SQL Database?

Ans:

Yes, we can configure both transactional and snapshot replication from a SQL Server standalone instance to Azure SQL Database.

Explore:

For a better understanding, check the below matrix:

Replication Type	Azure SQL Database	Azure SQL Managed Instance
Snapshot	Yes (Only as subscriber)	Yes
Transactional	Yes (Only as subscriber)	Yes
Bidirectional	No	Yes
Merge	No	No

Replication Type	Azure SQL Database	Azure SQL Managed Instance
Peer-to-Peer	No	No
Updatable Subscriptions	No	No

Table 11.1

25. Have you migrated any large databases (VLDBs) to Azure VMs? If so, what were the biggest challenges you faced in running them on Azure VMs?

Ans:

Yes, we successfully migrated a large SQL Server database to Azure VMs. We utilized different approaches depending on whether the database was online or offline during migration.

Offline Database Migration:

- **Full Backup and Restore (Source Database is online):** We performed a full backup on-premises, transferred it to Azure, and restored it with "no recovery" mode.
- **Differential Backups (Source Database is online):** We took differential backups on-premises, transferred them to Azure, and restored them with "no recovery" mode.
- **Transaction Log Backups (Source Database is online):** We transferred transactional log backups to Azure and restored them with "no recovery" mode.
- **Tail Log Backup and Restore (Source Database is offline):** During off-business hours, we took a tail (last) log backup, locked database access (causing downtime), transferred the backup to Azure, and restored it with "recovery" mode.
- **Application and DNS Cutover (Cloud Database is Online):** Finally, we redirected all applications and DNS entries to point to the cloud database.

Online Database Migration (With near zero downtime):

- **Always-On Availability Groups:** We configured Always-On Availability Groups between the on-premises and SQL Instances on Azure VM to ensure data synchronization.
- **Manual Failover to Cloud:** Once data was synchronized, we manually initiated a failover to the cloud instance, making it the primary database.
- **Application Validation and Removal of On-premises Instance:** After verifying successful application operation on the cloud instance, we removed the on-premises instance from the Always-On Availability Group.

Challenges:

For very large databases (VLDBs), once data migration is completed, three major operations require attention: **A)** Backup, **B)** Consistency check, and **C)** Index maintenance.

The duration of these operations can vary from hours to days depending on the database size and available resources. In a scenario where the database size is 8.5 TB, with a VM configuration of

32 Cores, 448 GB RAM, and 20000 MBPS network bandwidth, it took 12.3 hours to complete the full backup.

Best practices for dealing with VLDBs include:

- **Cleansing:** Before migration, perform data cleansing and remove/archive all unnecessary, unused, and historical data.
- **Index maintenance:** Instead of running index rebuild or reorganization for all indexes simultaneously, divide them into three categories based on fragmentation level statistics: daily, weekly, and monthly. Schedule index maintenance accordingly.
- **Consistency checks:** Run filegroup or table-level checks with the Physical_Only option.
- **Backup:** Utilize compression feature, employ differential backups, explore the feasibility of file snapshot backup, and always take split backups.
- **Datafiles, File Groups & Partitions:** Considering disk-wise IOPS and throughput limitations, partition tables based on data distribution, map partitions to separate filegroups, add separate datafiles for each file group, and place those data files on separate managed disks (Azure VM Disks).
    - To simplify: Table > Partitions > Separate File Group > Separate NDF > Separate VM Disk.

26. While migrating SQL Server workloads to Azure VMs, did you consider using the File Snapshot backup feature for your SQL Server instances?

Ans:

In a recent migration project, we moved an 8.5 TB database to an Azure VM. As discussed previously, challenges like lengthy backup times, index maintenance, and consistency checks remained.

- **Problem:** Full backups were taking half a day, and differential backups (four days after the full backup) still required eight hours. Additionally, the maximum Blob size limitation of 195 GB necessitated split backups to avoid exceeding this limit.
- **Solution:** When I consulted an expert engineer from the Azure team, they recommended the file snapshot approach. We conducted a proof-of-concept (POC) and then implemented it for our production database.

Explore:

Benefits of SQL Server Data Files on Azure Storage:

Placing SQL Server database files as Page Blobs in Azure Blob Storage offers advantages that are not available with traditional storage systems.

- **Instant File Initialization (IFI):** In traditional storage, without IFI enabled, allocating new space involves a “zeroing” process to clear the disk (security measure). This only applies to data files, not log files. Azure Blob Storage automatically handles zeroing, and IFI applies to both data and log files. When using the Put Page API, it simply clears the requested range, guaranteeing zeroes upon read requests. This allows for incredibly fast log file allocation (1 second for sizes between 50 MiB and 1 TiB).

- **File Snapshot Backup:** Unlike traditional streaming backups, File Snapshot creates a storage snapshot for each database file. This approach is remarkably faster. For our 8.5 TB production database under normal operation (72% CPU utilization), a full backup using File Snapshot completed in just 2 minutes and 30 seconds! This speed improvement is because File Snapshot doesn't move data; it simply stores pointers to snapshots and other backup metadata, maintaining backup consistency.
- **Running Data Consistency Checks (DBCC):** We can quickly restore (5 to 10 seconds) the latest file snapshot backup to another SQL instance and then run DBCC commands. This offers two benefits:
    - **Full Consistency Checks:** We can perform complete consistency checks (no limitations like "Physical Only" or partial checks).
    - **Checking on the Latest Copy:** We can check the latest copy without impacting production workloads.

Limitations:

Every feature has limitations, and File Snapshot is no exception. It's best suited for specific scenarios:

- **Unsupported Features:** FileStream data, geo-replication for storage accounts, In-Memory OLTP, and Always-On Failover Cluster instances are not currently supported.
- **Storage Account Considerations:** Standard storage (with a 500 TB limit) is not recommended due to potential performance issues. Premium storage offers a 35 TB limit.

27. How can I migrate logins, users, roles, and permissions from an on-premises SQL Server instance to Azure SQL Database, Azure SQL Managed Instance, and SQL Server on Azure VM?

Ans:

Before migrating security objects, it's crucial to understand the structural differences and limitations of Azure PaaS solutions, particularly Azure SQL Database. For example, Azure SQL Database doesn't support migrating logins that rely on Windows Authentication. Instead, you can map them to Microsoft Entra identities.

Here are the recommended options for migrating logins based on your destination environment:

Migrating Logins to Azure PaaS (SQL Database, SQL Managed Instance, Azure Synapse Analytics): Use either DMS, Migrate to Azure SQL wizard in Azure Data Studio or a T-SQL or PowerShell script created by the Microsoft Azure Migration team.

- **Azure SQL Managed Instance:** T-SQL, PowerShell standard scripts, DBATools work well.
- **Azure SQL Database:** Customized T-SQL scripts or manual creation.

Migrating Logins to Azure IaaS (SQL Server on Azure VM):

- For a simple security model migration, use DMA (Data Migration Assistant).
- For a complex security model migration, consider using a PowerShell script or a combination of DBATools (PS Module), sp_help_revlogin and custom T-SQL scripts to capture object-level permissions.

Explore:

Understanding Azure Security Model:

Here are some limitations:

- **Windows Authentication:** Azure SQL Database and Managed Instance don't support logins using Windows Authentication. You can map these users to Microsoft Entra identities instead.
- **Security Identifiers (SIDs):** SIDs from on-premises environments cannot be directly transferred to Azure SQL Database.
- **Role Mapping:** There might not be direct equivalents for all on-premises server and database roles in Azure SQL Database. However, you can map them to functionally similar roles based on scope and permissions. Ex:
    - On-premises SQL Server securityadmin server role can be mapped to the Azure SQL Database loginmanager/##MS_LoginManager## role. Similarly, the on-premises dbcreator fixed database role is mapped to Azure SQL Database dbmanager/##MS_DatabaseManager## role.

Login Migration Tools:

Here are tools you can use to migrate logins depending on your destination environment and complexity:

- **Azure Data Migration Assistant (DMA):** This tool is suitable for transferring logins between SQL Server instances (on-premises or Azure) for simple security models.
- **Azure Database Migration Service (DMS):** For offline migration of logins from on-premises to Azure SQL Managed Instance, use DMS or Azure SQL Migration extension in Azure Data Studio. You can select specific logins in the Migration Wizard for migration. Additionally, to migrate Windows user/group logins to Azure SQL Managed Instance, enable the "Enable Windows user/group login migration to Azure SQL Managed Instance" setting within DMS.
    - Currently, only Azure SQL MI and SQL on Azure VM targets are supported for login migration.
- **PowerShell Script (MoveLogins.ps1):** This script, created by the Microsoft Azure Migration Team, offers a more comprehensive way to migrate logins, server roles, database users, database roles, role memberships, and selected object-level permissions.

  - It currently doesn't support Application Roles or contained database users.
  - This script automatically maps Windows Server Active Directory accounts to Microsoft Entra accounts.
  - It connects to the source SQL Server and generates a T-SQL script for login migration. You'll need to review and execute this script on the target database server.

- **sp_help_revlogin T-SQL Stored Procedure:** This standard procedure allows migrating logins, users, and passwords between SQL Server instances. However, it requires creating two additional stored procedures (sp_hexadecimal and sp_help_revlogin) to handle logins, users, passwords, and script generation.
- **DBATools:** It is a powerful and comprehensive PowerShell based toolset that can handle various migration scenarios, including migrating logins, jobs, linked servers, and other objects between SQL Server instances, whether they are on-premises or in Azure. This makes it a valuable resource for database administrators looking to streamline their migration processes.
  - **Note:** While DBATools can migrate many aspects of a SQL Server instance, there are some limitations when it comes to Azure SQL Database. This process may involve extracting login information from your on-premises server and then manually creating contained users in Azure SQL Database.
- **Custom Scripts:** You can develop custom T-SQL or PowerShell scripts leveraging "MoveLogins.ps1" and "sp_help_revlogin" as a foundation to script users, logins, passwords, roles, and object-level permissions, allowing customization for specific source environments.

28. When restoring/migrating an Azure SQL Database from one logical server to another Azure logical server, how can I migrate logins and users between the databases?

Ans:

- **Contained Users:** When a database is restored, users are also restored automatically.
- **Traditional Logins and Users:** We need to script the logins at the source database and recreate them in the target database.

Explore:

Restoring an Azure SQL Database using the COPY (CREATE DATABASE .. AS COPY OF) option or geo-restore is a straightforward process. This process can migrate both SQL Server logins and Microsoft Entra identities to the target database.

Security Model Considerations:

The approach for migrating logins and users depends on the security model used by your source database:

- **Contained Users:** If your source database uses contained users, these are managed entirely within the database itself. When restoring the database, contained users are automatically transferred to the target database.
- **Traditional Users and Logins (Master Database Logins):** If your source database employs the traditional model with logins stored in the master database and users in the individual database, additional steps are required (T-SQL script works):
  - **Identify Logins at the Source Database:** List the logins and their corresponding Security Identifiers (SIDs) in the source database. Prepare a script to create these logins.
  - **Create Logins at the Target Master Database:** Execute the script on the target logical server to create the logins in the target master database. Since you're transferring logins with the same SIDs, they will automatically map to the corresponding database users in the restored database.
- **Firewall and Network Security:** Depending on the location of the target database, you might need to configure Network Security Groups (NSGs) and firewall rules to match the access restrictions of the source database.

29. We're migrating on-premises workloads to Azure SQL Database. Can we also migrate SQL Server Agent jobs and Windows Scheduler jobs? If not, what alternative options are available?

Ans:

Azure SQL Database doesn't directly support SQL Server Agent and windows scheduler Jobs. However, you can achieve similar automation functionalities using Azure services like Azure SQL Database elastic jobs, Azure Functions, or Azure Logic Apps etc.

Explore:

- **Azure SQL Database Elastic Jobs:** This is the recommended option for scheduling tasks directly within Azure SQL Database. You can create jobs to execute periodically against one or more databases.
- **Azure Data Factory (ADF):** As an orchestration service, ADF pipelines with recurring triggers can execute stored procedures and SQL code based on schedules or blob events.
- **Azure Automation / Runbooks:** This cloud-based service allows you to create and schedule workflows (runbooks) to automate repetitive tasks for Azure resources.
- **Azure Functions:** This serverless compute service lets you run code on-demand, triggered by events, without managing infrastructure.
- **Azure Logic Apps:** This platform helps you build automated workflows integrating apps, data, services, and systems. (Ex: sending emails upon file uploads).
- **Power Automate (Formerly Microsoft Flow):** Similar to Logic Apps, Power Automate allows you to create workflows automating processes and integrating with various services.

- **Azure WebJobs (a feature within Azure App Service):** This feature enables running programs or scripts (Windows commands, PowerShell, Python, etc.) in the same instance as your web app for broader automation needs.
- **Calling SP in Azure SQL Database from SQL Server Instance:** If your SQL Agent job simply calls stored procedures, consider this approach:
  - Create a linked server from a SQL Server instance (on-premises SQL Server, SQL MI, or SQL on VM) to the Azure SQL Database.

Schedule a job on the SQL Server instance to use the linked server, reference the Azure SQL Database stored procedure, and execute it.

30. What is the recommended approach to migrate SQL Server Agent Jobs to the Azure SQL PaaS platform?

Ans:

- **Azure SQL Database:** SQL Agent is not supported. Use Elastic Jobs as an alternative.
- **Azure SQL Managed Instance:** Supports SQL Agent with some limitations (Ex: notifications are partially supported, proxies are not supported, etc.).
- **Azure Synapse Analytics:** SQL Agent is not supported. Use ADF pipelines with recurring triggers.
- **SQL on Azure VM (IaaS):** Supports SQL Agent full functionality.

CHAPTER 12

Azure Cloud Migration 3 – Storage and MSBI

1. What are AzCopy and Azure Storage Explorer, and how are they used?

Ans:

AzCopy and Azure Storage Explorer are data transfer tools used to migrate or transfer data to and from Azure Storage accounts. While both leverage the same underlying technology, they are designed for different business needs.

- **AzCopy:** This is a command-line utility that offers a lightweight approach for data transfer. It's compatible with Windows, Linux, and Mac machines, making it versatile for scripting and automation.
- **Azure Storage Explorer:** This graphical user interface (GUI) tool provides a user-friendly experience for interacting with Azure Storage. It allows you to upload, download, and manage various Azure Storage resources like blobs, files, queues, tables and Data Lake. Additionally, it supports managing Azure Cosmos DB and Azure Data Lake Storage entities. Notably, Azure Storage Explorer utilizes AzCopy internally to handle the actual data transfer processes.

Explore:

Use Cases for Data Transfer:

Here are some common scenarios where these tools can be used for data transfer:

- Between different Azure storage accounts.
- From your on-premises environment to Azure Storage.
- From Azure Storage back to your on-premises environment.
- Between cloud storage providers, such as migrating data from AWS S3 or Google Cloud Storage to Azure Storage.

2. How can I migrate data from on-premises to Azure Blob Storage using AzCopy?

Ans:

Here's a step-by-step guide for migrating data with AzCopy:

Download AzCopy:

- Visit the Microsoft download page and download the latest version of AzCopy (v10 as of Nov, 2024).

- Since it's an executable file, there's no separate installation required. Unzip the downloaded file and store it in a convenient location on your local machine.

- **Authorize AzCopy:** You'll need to provide AzCopy with authorization credentials to access your Azure Storage account. There are two common methods:
    - **Microsoft Entra:** Use your Entra credentials with sufficient permissions to access the target Azure Storage account.
    - **Shared Access Signature (SAS) token:** Alternatively, you can obtain a SAS token for your Azure Storage account and append it to each AzCopy command you execute.

- **Transfer Data:** Once authorized, you can leverage AzCopy commands to initiate the data transfer process. The specific commands will vary depending on your desired behavior (Ex: uploading individual files, transferring entire directories with wildcards).

Explore:

Transferring/Copying Files to Azure Blob Storage

Prerequisites:

- An Azure storage account with a container created.
- A Microsoft Entra user account with the "Storage Blob Data Owner/Contributor" role assigned for the storage account.
- AzCopy downloaded and unzipped on your on-premises server.

Using Microsoft Entra Credentials:

- **Login and Authentication:**
    - Open a command prompt on your on-premises server and navigate to the AzCopy directory.
    - Run "azcopy login" command to initiate Entra authentication.
    - This command will display an authentication code and automatically open a web page (https://microsoft.com/devicelogin).
    - Enter the displayed code on the web page and then log in using your Azure credentials.
    - Upon successful login, the command prompt will show a "login succeeded" message.

- **Create Container (Optional):**
    - If you haven't already created a container in your storage account, use the following command:
    - azcopy make "https://absOrg.blob.core.windows.net/abcSales2024"
    - Replace absOrg with your storage account name and abcSales2024 with your desired container name.
    - Similarly, we can transfer data to an Azure Data Lake Gen 2.

- **Upload a Single File:**
    - To upload a single file from your local machine to the Azure Blob Storage container, use the following command:
    - azcopy copy "E:\USASales\productZ.csv" "https://absOrg.blob.core.windows.net/abcSales24"
    - Replace E:\USASales\productZ.csv with the path to your local file.
- **Upload an Entire Folder:**
    - To upload all files from a local folder to the Azure Blob Storage container, use the following command with the **--recursive** flag:
    - azcopy copy "E:\USASales" "https://absOrg.blob.core.windows.net/abcSales24" --recursive
    - Replace E:\USASales with the path to your local folder.

Using a Shared Access Signature (SAS) Token:

- **Generate SAS Token:**
    - In the Azure portal, navigate to your storage account > Shared access signatures > Generate SAS and connection string.
    - Specify the allowed IP addresses (consider including your on-premises server IP), start/end date/time, and desired permissions for the SAS token.
    - Download the generated SAS token.
- **Transfer File from on-premise to Azure using SAS Token:**
    - Open a command prompt on your on-premises server.
    - Use the following command to copy a file, appending the SAS token to the Azure storage container URL:
        - azcopy copy "E:\USASales\productZ.csv" "https://absOrg.blob.core.windows.net/abcSales24/?sv=2018-03-28&ss=bjqt&srt=sco&sp=rwddgcup&se=2024-05-31T05:01:17Z&st=2024-05-27T05:01:17Z&spr=https&sig=MGCXiyEzbtttkr3ewJIh2AR8KrghSy1DGM9ovN734bQF4%3D"
    - Replace E:\USASales\productZ.csv with the path to your local file.
    - Note that the long string after the question mark (?) is the SAS token you generated.

Key Points:

- Microsoft Entra credentials provide a more secure way to authenticate with Azure Blob Storage.
- SAS tokens offer more granular control over access permissions but require careful management due to their time-bound nature.

3. Can I copy a large number of application files from on-premises to Azure Storage using AzCopy in parallel?

Ans:

Absolutely! AzCopy supports concurrent requests by default, allowing you to optimize the copy process for faster transfers. We can control the parallel tasks using the variable "AZCOPY_CONCURRENCY_VALUE".

Explore:

Here's how to configure AzCopy for parallel copying:

- **Setting the Concurrency Value:**
    - AzCopy uses an environment variable named AZCOPY_CONCURRENCY_VALUE to specify the number of concurrent requests it can handle.
    - If on-premises server has fewer than 5 CPUs, it's recommended to set this value to 32.
    - Otherwise, the default value is equal to 16 multiplied by the number of CPUs. The maximum default value of this variable is 3000, but you can manually set this value higher or lower.
- **Optimizing Concurrency:**
    - It's recommended to run benchmark tests to identify the ideal number of concurrent processes for your specific environment. This helps ensure optimal performance.
    - If your network bandwidth is inconsistent, you can set AZCOPY_CONCURRENCY_VALUE to "Auto". This allows AzCopy to automatically determine the most suitable number of concurrent requests based on your network conditions.
    - Here's the command to run an AzCopy performance benchmark:
    - Azcopy benchmark <Azure Storage Account><SAS Token>
- **High Concurrency for Storage Account Transfers:**
    - If you're transferring blobs between Azure Storage accounts while running AzCopy from your local machine, consider setting AZCOPY_CONCURRENCY_VALUE to a higher value (greater than 1000).
    - This is because, during transfers between Azure storage accounts, AzCopy leverages storage server-to-server APIs and doesn't rely heavily on your local machine's processing power.

4. What are the most common issues encountered when using AzCopy, and how can we troubleshoot them?

Ans:

Common issues include network failures, resource utilization issues, access and permission issues, and so on. AzCopy generates a detailed log. By reviewing the log, you can identify the issue, resolve it, and then resume the copy operation.

Explore:

Here's a breakdown of common AzCopy issues and troubleshooting tips:

Common Issues:

- **Network Errors:** Network connectivity issues between the source and destination can interrupt transfers.
- **Timeouts:** Operations might time out due to slow connections or large file sizes.
- **Server Busy Errors:** The source or destination storage system might be overloaded, causing temporary transfer failures.
- **Access Issues:** You might encounter access errors if your credentials or permissions are insufficient.
- **Permission Issues:** Lack of appropriate permissions on the source or destination storage can prevent file transfers.
- **Resource Utilization Issues:** High memory usage or insufficient disk space can hinder AzCopy operations.

Identifying Failures and Errors:

- **Logs:**
    - Each AzCopy transfer creates a job with an associated log file located in the \.azcopy directory.
    - These log files record transfer statistics and error details, including status codes like UPLOADFAILED, COPYFAILED, and DOWNLOADFAILED, along with file paths and failure reasons.
- **Auto Retry:** AzCopy automatically retries transfers for issues like network errors or server busy states (usually up to 20 retries).
- **Log Analysis:** If in case the operation failed, we can get the log details using PS command:
    - **Syntax:** >Select-String <search string>.\<logfile name>.log
    - **Ex:** The following commands will get all errors with COPYFAILED and UPLOADFAILED status from the specified log file.

- >Select-String COPYFAILED .\09ac9ca9-158f-7945-4833-564021086a99.log
- >Select-String UPLOADFAILED .\09ac9ca9-158f-7945-4833-564021086a99.log

Troubleshooting Tips:

- **Log Files:** Log files are your primary troubleshooting resource. They provide information to pinpoint the problem.
- **Resolving Network/Authorization Issues:** Ensure a stable connection between source and destination. Verify your credentials and authorization (Ex: check SAS token validity).
- **Generate logs only for errors** and suppress informational messages by setting the log-level parameter from INFO to ERROR. This ensures logging focuses on errors instead of every operation.
- **Disable file length checking:** After copying the file, AzCopy validates the file size between source and destination, which can impact performance. To improve performance, you can disable this check by setting --check-length false (use with caution).
- **Skip modified date comparison:** If you are sure, you can overwrite existing files at the destination, use the --overwrite flag. This eliminates the need for AzCopy to check the source and destination file modified dates.
- **Limiting Data Rate:** Control the data transfer rate based on your network bandwidth using the --cap-mbps parameter (Ex: --cap-mbps 25 for 25 Mbps).
- **Memory Buffer Management:** You can adjust AzCopy's memory usage using the AZCOPY_BUFFER_GB environment variable.
- **Optimizing Concurrent Requests:** Utilize realistic concurrency values obtained from AzCopy benchmarks using the AZCOPY_CONCURRENCY_VALUE variable.

Resuming AzCopy Operations:

Once you've identified and addressed the issue using the log files, you can resume the AzCopy operation:

- **List Jobs:** Use "azcopy jobs list" to view all running or completed jobs.
- **View Specific Job:** Use "azcopy jobs show <job-id>" to get details about a particular job.
- **Filter by Status:** Use "azcopy jobs show <job-id> --with-status=Failed" to filter jobs by failed status.
- **Resume Job:** Resume a failed job using "azcopy jobs resume <job-id>" optionally specifying source or destination SAS tokens and data rate limits.

5. A client is planning for cloud migration to Azure. They've been operating for over two decades and have a significant amount of on-premises data (approximately 3 PB) including databases, application files, documents, and media. Can you recommend data migration strategies for this large-scale transfer?

Ans:

Data migration is a crucial factor in a successful cloud journey. Azure offers various native and third-party tools and services to facilitate data transfer. The optimal migration approach depends on several factors, including:

- Migration Timelines
- Online/Offline Migration
- Migration Strategy (Upgrade and Migration Needs)
- Data Characteristics (data type, volume, and environment).
- Network Bandwidth

Database Migration Strategies: For database systems, we typically recommend native backup and restore approaches, high availability solutions, or the Azure Database Migration Service.

Large Data and Application Data Migration:

For large volumes of media files, documents, and other application or business-critical data, a careful evaluation is necessary to choose the most suitable solution. Here are some possible methods:

- **Physical Hardware Transfer:** This involves directly transferring physical storage hardware from the on-premises datacenter to Azure and loading data into Azure storage.
  - **Azure Import/Export Service:** This service allows you to ship your existing internal SATA HDDs or SSDs from your on-premises datacenter to an Azure datacenter. You would:
    - Obtain the required number of hard drives.
    - Copy all your on-premises data to the drives.
    - Ship the drives to the Azure datacenter.
    - Azure will then upload the data to Azure Storage.
  - **Azure Data Box:** Similar to Azure Import/Export, but with Microsoft providing the physical appliance. This eliminates the need for purchasing hard drives and managing logistics. Microsoft ships you a secure, tamper-resistant transfer appliance and handles the entire process.
- **Network Transfer Methods:** These methods involve transferring data over the network to Azure storage. Popular options include:
  - **AzCopy:** This command-line utility offers efficient data transfer from various sources to Azure storage.

- **Azure Storage Explorer:** This GUI tool simplifies data management tasks and leverages AzCopy under the hood.
- **Azure Data Factory (Data Pipelines):** This service allows creating and scheduling data-driven workflows (pipelines) for data ingestion from diverse data stores. It can also process and transform the data using services like Azure HDInsight (Hadoop, Spark), Azure Data Lake Analytics, Azure Synapse Analytics Azure Databricks and Azure Machine Learning,

6. What is Azure Databox and how does it facilitate data transfer to Azure?

Ans:

Azure Databox:

- Azure Data Box is a physical appliance provided by Microsoft that offers a straightforward way for customers to move large data sets to and from the Azure cloud. It's particularly beneficial for scenarios where traditional network transfers might be slow or infeasible due to limited bandwidth constraints.

Data Encryption: Microsoft provides Databox with 256-bit (Data Box & Data box heavy)/128-bit (Data Box Disk) encryption.

Flavors: Azure Data Box comes in 3 different flavours plus 1 virtual device option for continues data ingestion:

- **Data Box Disk (8 TB):** It comes in packs of up to 5 disks per order (5 X 8 = 40 TB). We can transfer 40 TB (35 TB is useful) data per order. Copy data from our servers to Data Box Disk using Robocopy or similar tools.
- **Data Box:** 100 TB (80 TB is useful) capacity per order. Copy data using standard NAS protocols (SMB/NFS).
- **Data Box Heavy:** 1 PB (800 TB is useful) capacity per order. Copy data using standard NAS protocols (SMB/NFS).
- **Data Box Gateway:** is a virtual device provisioned in your on-premises server (Hyper-V or VMWare). This is for continues data ingestion from on-premises to Azure. We copy data from on-prem server to gateway and it uploads the data to Azure storage.

Explore:

Here's the Azure Databox transfer process:

- **Order the Databox:** You order the Databox device through the Azure portal. Each unit comes with a 10-day rental period. There's a service fee of $250 and a shipping charge of $95 per unit.
- **Databox Delivery:** Microsoft ships the physical Databox device to your specified address (typically your datacenter location).
- **Connect Databox:** Once received, connect the Databox device to your on-premises server.

- **Data Copy:** You can copy data to the Databox using standard NAS protocols (SMB/NFS) and tools like Robocopy.
- **Databox Return:** After completing the data copy, return the Databox back to Azure following Microsoft's return instructions.
- **Data Upload:** The Azure team will upload the data from the Databox to your designated Azure storage container(s).
- **Data Box Erasure:** Once the data upload is complete, Microsoft will securely erase the data from the Databox device.

7. In your experience, have you helped any customers migrate their data to Azure using Azure Databox?

Ans:

In my experience, yes, I have helped a customer migrate their workloads to Azure using Azure Databox.

- **Business Case:** The customer had a production data (structured and unstructured) located in a Canadian datacenter with a segmented network zone (DMZ) known for stricter bandwidth limitations and security measures. A DMZ (Demilitarized Zone) network sits between our customer organization's internal network ("trusted") and an external network (such as the internet). This 300 TB on-premises dataset was too large for efficient transfer via their regular network.
- **Challenge:** Transferring such a large dataset through the limited DMZ bandwidth would not meet the migration timeline.
- **Solution:** We leveraged Azure Databox for a secure and streamlined data transfer.
- **Planning and Execution:**
  - We chose a low-traffic period for the migration.
  - Non-critical applications were taken offline and migrated entirely using Databox.
  - Critical applications used a combination of Databox and online network transfer with a jump box and AzCopy.
  - We ordered four Azure Databoxes, which offer 80 TB of usable storage each (with a total capacity of 4 X 80 = 320 TB)
  - Data (database full backups, text documents, multi-media files, website content etc.) was copied to Databoxes. Leveraged split backups and data compression when necessary.
  - Databoxes were shipped back to Azure for data upload to Azure storage.
  - **Unstructured Data:** We loaded unstructured data to various Azure storage options based on business and application requirements. These options include Azure Blob storage, Azure Data Lake Storage Gen2, and managed disks attached to Azure VMs.
  - **Structured Data:**
    - **Full Database Backups:** Full database backups shipped through Azure Databox were restored to the corresponding Azure SQL Managed Instances and Azure VMs.

  - **Differential and Log Backups:** After restoring the full backups, differential and log backups were copied from the production machines to a JumpBox located in our organization's internal network zone. These backups were then transferred from the JumpBox to Azure Storage using AzCopy. Finally, the differential and log backups were restored to the destination SQL instances.
  - **Tail Log Backups and Application Redirection:** Finally, tail log backups were performed. Offshore databases were set to read-only, transferred using AzCopy, restored to the destination SQL instances, and applications were redirected to use the cloud databases.

- **Benefit:** By utilizing Azure Databox, we significantly reduced the time required to copy large datasets to Azure, overcoming the limitations of the on-premises network.

8. One of our customers' needs to migrate their on-premises file server (currently storing 30 TB of data that contains around 15 million files) to Azure. While 70% of the applications using the file server will be migrated to Azure, the remaining 30% will continue to operate on-premises. They require a solution where the same file share remains accessible from both (on-premise and Azure) environments. Can you suggest a solution?

Ans:

There are two main deployment approaches for migrating on-premises file servers to Azure Files:

- **Cloud-only deployment:** This involves migrating all data and applications to a fully managed SMB Azure file share.
- **Hybrid deployment (Recommended):** This approach utilizes Azure File Sync to synchronize an existing on-premises Windows file server with an SMB Azure file share.

Explore:

In the given scenario, hybrid deployment using Azure File Sync is the most suitable solution. Here's how it works:

- **Azure Files Setup:** Create an Azure storage account with the appropriate performance tier and provision an Azure file share to accommodate the required data volume.
- **Azure Files Sync Agent Deployment:** Deploy the Azure Files Sync agent on a dedicated server in the customer's on-premises environment. This server will act as a cloud endpoint for synchronization. Configure the agent to connect to the Azure storage account and the on-premises file server.
- **Data Seeding (Optional for near-zero downtime):** To minimize downtime during cutover, consider copying all data from the on-premises file server to the Azure file share beforehand using AzCopy or Azure storage explorer.

- **File Share Permissions:** Configure appropriate NTFS permissions on the on-premises file server for the applications that remain on-premises. Set Share-level ACLs (Access Control Lists) within Azure Files to control access for applications potentially running in the Azure environment.
- **Synchronization Configuration:** Establish a one-way or two-way continuous synchronization between the on-premises file server and the Azure file share using the Azure Files Sync agent.
- **Caching Configuration (Key for Performance):** Configure caching settings to determine which files or folders are prioritized for local availability on the on-premises server. This allows frequently accessed data to be cached locally, improving performance for on-premises applications.
- **Accessing Data:** Post migration, your applications in Azure can directly access the file share in Azure Files. For on-premises applications, they will continue to access the local file share which is now backed by Azure Files.

9. How can you move/migrate an Azure storage account from one region to another?

Ans:

There are two approaches:

- **Failover (for geo-redundant storage accounts):** Initiate a failover for the Azure storage account from the primary region to the destination region. **Suits for:**
    - Larger datasets.
    - Situations demanding minimal downtime.
    - Environments with sufficient budget.
- **Manual Migration:** Manually create a storage account with similar configurations in the destination region and move data from the source to the destination account using tools like AzCopy or Azure Data Factory. **Suits for:**
    - Smaller datasets.
    - Scenarios requiring more control over the migration process.
    - Situations with an acceptable amount of downtime.
    - Limited budgets.

10. Can you explain the steps involved in migrating or moving Azure Storage Accounts across regions?

Ans:

Here are the options for storage account cross region migrations:

- **Storage Account Failover:** A seamless process for automatically switching to a secondary storage location in a different region if the primary location becomes unavailable. This ensures minimal data loss and service continuity.

- **Manual Migration:** A more hands-on approach involving manually creating a new storage account in the desired region, copying data from the old account to the new one, and updating applications to use the new account. This provides more flexibility but requires more effort and potential downtime.

Explore:

Azure Storage Account Failover:

For this process to work, your storage account needs to be configured with geo-redundant storage (GRS/GRS-RA or GZRS/GZRS-RA). GRS replicates your data to a secondary region in real-time, maintaining a mirror copy. If the primary endpoint becomes unavailable, you can initiate an account failover, updating the secondary endpoint to become the primary. Once completed, clients can write to the new primary region. Here are the steps to initiate a forced failover:

- Go to Azure Portal > Storage Account > Settings > Geo-replication > Prepare for failover.
- Review the Last Sync Time, indicating the extent of potential data loss.
- To minimize data loss, freeze write operations at the source storage or wait until the Last Sync Time matches the current time.
- Confirm the failover by selecting Yes.
- After a successful failover, ensure that your applications are pointing to the target storage account, and clean up the source storage account.
- **Limitations:** Storage account failover has some limitations, such as lack of support for Azure File Sync, storage accounts with hierarchical namespace enabled, premium block blobs, and accounts with WORM immutability policy enabled. ***Note:** Customer managed failover feature for ADLS Gen 2 is currently in preview.

Manual Migration:

- **Deployment and Configuration:**
    - Export a template from the source storage account.
    - Modify the template JSON file by adding the target region and storage account name.
    - Deploy the template to create the new storage account, duplicating the original in the targeted region.
    - Configure the new storage account, as some features don't export to a template (Ex: Event Subscriptions, lifecycle management policies, alerts, etc.).
- **Move Data:** Transfer data to the new storage account using either AzCopy or Azure Data Factory.
- **Update Applications:** Modify any applications or services that reference the old storage account's URL to point to the new account in the target region.

- **Cleanup:** Once the data transfer is complete and applications are updated, delete the original storage account in the source region.

11. What are the various deployment options available to migrate SSIS packages from on-premises to Azure?

Ans:

- **SSIS migration mainly depends on 4 factors:**
- **SSIS Runtime:** The environment where SSIS packages are executed.
- **SSIS Package Store:** A storage location where SSIS packages are stored.
- **SSIS Package Execution Scheduled Jobs:** Jobs created in SQL Server Agent to schedule the execution of SSIS packages at specified times or intervals.
- **Target Deployment model:** Azure SQL Database, SQL MI or SQL On Azure VM.

Below are the possible SSIS deployment options in Azure:

- **IaaS (Lift-and-Shift - Rehost):** This approach is similar to migrating SSIS between on-premises servers. No significant changes are required.
- **PaaS (Lift-and-Shift – Rehost with modernization):** Migrate SSIS Runtime and scheduled jobs to ADF (Azure Data Factory - SSIS IR), and SSIS Catalog database to Azure SQL Database or Azure SQL Managed Instance.
- **PaaS (Refactor or Re-architect with full modernization):** This approach involves completely revamping your SSIS packages to leverage the capabilities of Azure Data Factory (ADF). You'll rewrite your existing SSIS logic using ADF pipelines. It allows you to leverage the full potential of Azure for data integration.

Explore:

Let's see the detailed migration options:

Deployment	SSIS Runtime	SSIS Package Store	SSIS Scheduled Jobs
On-premises	Standalone SSIS Service	File System, MSDB, SSIS Package Store, SSIS Catalog (SSISDB).	SQL Agent
SQL on Azure VM	Standalone SSIS Service	All of the above options work in Azure VM	Migrate to SQL Agent
Azure SQL Database	ADF (SSIS IR)	**SSISDB:** Redeploy all packages using SSDT/ SSMS to SSISDB hosted on Azure SQL Database. **File System, MSDB & SSIS Package Store**: Redeploy all packages to Azure Files via dtinstall /dtutil /manual copy.	Schedule using ADF Triggers

Deployment	SSIS Runtime	SSIS Package Store	SSIS Scheduled Jobs
Azure SQL MI	ADF (SSIS IR)	**SSISDB:** Migrate the database to Azure SQL MI using Azure DMS or redeploy all packages to SSISDB hosted on SQL MI. **File System, MSDB, SSIS Package Store:** Export and redeploy them to file shares/ Azure Files via dtinstall /dtutil /manual copy.	Migrate to SQL MI SQL Agent Or use ADF Triggers

Table 12.1

***Note:**

- **Azure Files:** Enterprise cloud-based File Share storage solution.
- **ADF-SSIS IR:** Azure Data Factory SSIS Integration Runtime is a fully managed cluster dedicated to running your SSIS packages. It supports running packages deployed into the SSIS catalog (SSISDB) hosted on Azure SQL Database/SQL Managed Instance, and packages deployed into the Azure Files. ADF SSIS IR allows:
    - **Lift and shift for SSIS:** Migrate on-premises SSIS packages to Azure with minimal code changes.
    - **Execute packages:** Run SSIS packages on-demand or schedule them for automated execution in Azure.
- **SSIS Package Storage Supported Locations:** There are several options to store SQL Server Integration Services (SSIS) packages in SQL Server:
- **File System:** Packages can be saved in the windows file system. The location of these files is specified in the configuration file for the SSIS.
- **MSDB Database:** SSIS packages can be stored in the sysssispackages table in the SQL Server msdb database.
- **SSIS Package Store:** A package management layer on top of two subtypes:
    - MSDB, which is a system database in SQL Server used to store SSIS packages.
    - Managed file system (Windows filesystem/Azure Files), which is a specific folder in SQL Server installation path used to store SSIS packages.
- **SSIS Catalog (SSISDB):** Starting from SSIS 2012, there is a new place for packages - SSIS Catalog, stored in SSISDB database. It is created by SSMS wizard (not created during installation of SQL Server) and accessible both as User's database and Integration Services branch in SSMS Database connection.

12. Can you describe the process to migrate SSIS packages from on-premises to Azure?

Ans:

Migrating SSIS packages to Azure involves several steps:

- **Assessment:**
  - Use the Data Migration Assistant (DMA) or SSDT (SQL Server Data Tools) to assess your SSIS packages in batches.
  - Create a DMA project of type "Integration Services" to identify compatibility issues, including blockers and informative messages.
  - DMA supports assessing packages stored in File System, Package Store, and SSIS Catalog.
- **Resolve Blockers:**
  - Fix all issues and blockers identified during the assessment.
  - Ensure source and destination connections in your SSIS packages point to the correct Azure resources and have proper access permissions.
- **Prepare Azure Environment:**
  - Depending on your deployment target, provision either:
    - An Azure SQL Managed Instance (MI).
    - An Azure SQL Logical Server.
  - These will serve as the host for your SSISDB.
- **Provision SSIS Integration Runtime:**
  - Create an Azure Data Factory (ADF) and provision an Azure SSIS Integration Runtime within it.
  - Configure the runtime to connect to the SSISDB hosted in your Azure SQL Database or SQL Managed Instance.
- **Migration:** Choose the migration approach based on your target database workloads:
  - **Azure SQL Database:**
    - Use SSMS or SSDT to "lift-and-shift" your SSIS ETL workloads from on-premises to Azure. Redeploy packages using either the SSMS Integration Services Deployment Wizard or the SSDT project deployment option.
  - **Azure SQL Managed Instance:**
    - Use the Azure Database Migration Service (**DMS**) to migrate SSIS packages to Azure SQL MI. When creating a DMS project, select "SSIS Package Migration" as the activity type.

- You can also redeploy packages to Azure SQL Managed Instance using SSMS or SSDT.

- **SSIS Catalog Environment:**
    - The SSIS Catalog allows running the same package in multiple environments (DEV/QA/PROD).
    - To migrate these environments, use a custom stored procedure or T-SQL code to generate creation scripts from the system tables. This script will capture project references, environment variable mappings, etc.

- **Migrate SSIS Jobs:** You have two options:
    - **Migrate to Azure Data Factory (ADF):**
        - Convert SQL Agent jobs to ADF pipelines.
        - Convert SSIS Job steps to "Execute SSIS package" activities within ADF pipelines.
        - Convert SQL Agent schedules to ADF "Schedule triggers."
        - Use the SSMS (SQL Agent) "**Migrate SSIS Jobs to ADF**" wizard for automated conversion, or manually create ADF pipelines.
    - **Migrate to Azure SQL Managed Instance - SQL Agent:**
        - At your on-premises SQL instance, generate create scripts for all required jobs.
        - Run these scripts on your Azure SQL Managed Instance.
        - Ensure you use the correct logins and grant necessary permissions on the SQL Managed Instance.

13. How can I assess SSIS packages for readiness to migrate to Azure? Additionally, what are some common compatibility issues you've encountered during SSIS migrations?

Ans:

We can assess SSIS packages either using DMA or SSDT. Common compatibility issues include Windows authentication, resolving dependencies with custom components, custom scripts, file paths, and hostnames.

Explore:

There are two main tools you can use to assess SSIS packages for Azure migration:

- **Data Migration Assistant (DMA):** This free tool from Microsoft allows you to assess SSIS packages in batches. When creating a DMA project, select "**Integration Services**" as the assessment type instead of "Database Engine." DMA will identify both blockers and informative issues related to Azure compatibility.
- **SQL Server Data Tools (SSDT):** While not a dedicated assessment tool, SSDT can help identify potential issues during development and deployment. You can enable Azure for

your project using the "Azure-Enabled Project" feature. This involves updating the project configuration manager through Visual Studio or using the Azure-Enabled Project Wizard (where you'll provide Azure subscription, Data Factory account, and Integration Runtime details). Once enabled, you can assess individual packages using the "Assess Package for Execution in Azure" option.

Common Compatibility and blocking issues with SSIS:

Hostnames in Connection Managers: SSIS packages often use server hostnames instead of IP addresses when defining source and destination connections. Since you're migrating to Azure Data Factory SSIS IR, these hostnames might not be resolvable if the source or destination remains on-premises.

- **Resolution:**
  - If both source and destination databases are migrating to Azure, simply update the connection strings (including connection string, initial Catalog, credentials, etc.) within the SSIS package.
  - If the source or destination (or both) remains on-premises:
    - Create a Self-Hosted Integration Runtime (IR) to act as a proxy for the Azure SSIS IR.
    - Configure a Domain Name System (DNS) server for the Azure SSIS IR and connect it to a virtual network (VNet) that's further connected to your on-premises network.

Windows Authentication: Some SSIS packages might rely on Windows Authentication for connecting to source or destination databases.

- **Resolution:**
  - If the source or destination (or both) are moving to Azure PaaS services (like Azure SQL Database or Managed Instance), modify the connection string to use SQL authentication or Microsoft Entra authentication.
  - If the source or destination (or both) remain on-premises, you can enable the Windows Authentication feature within the Azure SSIS IR.

Deprecated Drivers: Outdated drivers like the SQL Server Native Client (SQLNCLI) driver might be used in connection managers.

- **Resolution:** Avoid using deprecated drivers. Instead, switch to the newer Microsoft OLE DB Driver for SQL Server (MSOLEDBSQL), which receives regular updates with the latest server features.

File System Access: There are high chances that your SSIS packages read or write data from the file system.

- **Resolution:** You need to modify them to use Azure Storage (like Azure Blob Storage, Azure Files, or Azure Data Lake Storage) as Azure-SSIS IR does not have access to a local file system.

Custom Scripts: Some custom components or scripts used in your packages might not be available or compatible with Azure SSIS IR.

- **Resolution:** Investigate if alternatives exist within the Azure ecosystem. Consider refactoring packages to remove dependencies on incompatible components.

Proxy Accounts: Packages might use features like impersonation or proxy accounts, which are not fully supported in Azure SSIS IR.

- **Resolution:** Evaluate if these features are crucial for functionality. If not, consider removing them. Explore alternative approaches achievable within Azure.

Data Movement Considerations: SSIS packages may involve large data movements that could incur additional costs or performance issues in Azure.

- **Resolution:** Optimize data movement strategies by leveraging Azure Data Factory features such as Data Flows, Mapping Data Flows, Azure Databricks Notebooks, or Azure Data Factory Integration Runtime for efficient data processing and movement in the Azure environment.

Environment Variables: SSIS packages may use environment variables configured for on-premises environments, which may not be applicable in Azure.

- **Resolution:** Review and update environment variables to reflect Azure-specific configurations and settings.

14. What is the need for SSIS scale out, and what options are available in Azure?

Ans:

SSIS Scale Out in SQL Server: Prior to SQL Server 2017, SSIS package execution was limited to a single machine. With SQL Server 2017, Microsoft introduced SSIS Scale Out, which allows you to run SSIS packages on multiple machines in parallel to improve performance. This feature has two components:

- **Scale Out Master:** This manages the scale-out process and receives package execution requests from users.
- **Scale Out Workers:** These workers pull execution tasks from the Scale Out Master and run the packages.

SSIS Scale Out in Azure Data Factory (ADF) with SSIS Integration Runtime (IR):

The SSIS IR in ADF is a fully managed cluster of Azure VMs dedicated to running your SSIS packages. When you create an SSIS IR in ADF, it automatically provisions a cluster with the specified node size (compute power - CPU and memory) and the desired number of nodes. This offers a highly scalable and highly available solution for your SSIS workloads.

- **Scalability:** You can scale up the processing power of the cluster by specifying node sizes and scale out by increasing the number of nodes.
- **Cost Management:** A key benefit is the ability to manage costs by stopping and starting the Azure SSIS Integration Runtime as needed.

15. How can we execute SSIS packages stored in Azure?

Ans:

There are several ways to run SSIS packages stored in various Azure locations, including SSISDB in Azure SQL Database, SQL Managed Instance, Azure File Share, and Network Shares from on-premises. Here are the ways:

From On-Premises or Azure VM:

- **SQL Server Management Studio (SSMS):** Connect to the SSISDB that hosts your package, navigate to the desired package, and execute it directly.
- **SQL Server Data Tools (SSDT):** Create Azure-enabled SSIS projects using the "Integration Services Project (Azure-Enabled)" template. This allows you to connect to the Azure Data Factory SSIS Integration Runtime (IR) for package management and execution.

Using Azure Data Factory Pipelines:

- **Execute SSIS Package Activity:** Create an ADF pipeline with the "Execute SSIS Package" activity. You can then add triggers to schedule package execution. To draw a comparison with the traditional SQL Agent, we can view the pipeline as a JOB, the activity as a job step, and the trigger as a schedule.
- **Stored Procedure Activity:** Similar to the "Execute SSIS Package" activity, ADF also provides a "Stored Procedure" activity. This allows you to execute SSIS packages using stored procedures within the SSIS Catalog.

Using Scripts:

- **SSIS Catalog Stored Procedures:** Connect to your SSISDB (hosted in Azure SQL Database, Azure SQL Managed Instance, or a standalone SQL Server instance) and execute packages using the catalog stored procedures:
    - [catalog].[create_execution],
    - [catalog].[set_execution_parameter_value], and
    - [catalog].[start_execution].
- **Other Scripting Options:** You can also leverage PowerShell (Get-ChildItem <SSIS Package Path>. Execute) or C# (Microsoft.SqlServer.Management.IntegrationServices namespace) code to execute SSIS packages.

Recommendation:

The recommended option depends on your specific needs and preferences:

- For simplicity and integration with ADF workflows, the ADF SSIS Package Execution activity is a strong choice.
- If you require more control and native compatibility for your SSIS Catalog, consider migrating to a Managed Instance/SQL On VM and using native execution methods such as SQL Agent Jobs.

16. We've migrated our SSIS workloads to Azure using ADF SSIS IR as the runtime and Azure SQL Database to host SSISDB. Can I schedule an SSIS package execution (stored in Azure SQL Database) from on-premises?

Ans:

Absolutely! You can schedule SSIS package execution using the latest version of SSMS.

- **Connect from On-Premises:** Connect to the SSIS Catalog hosted in Azure SQL Database using SSMS.
- **Locate and Schedule:** Navigate to the desired package and right-click on it. Select "Schedule" from the context menu.
- **Configure Schedule:** A new window will open, like a SQL Agent Job window. Here, you can configure execution settings like logging level and retry attempts etc. Additionally, you can define the schedule for package execution.
- **Behind the Scenes:** When you configure the schedule, SSMS creates an Azure Data Factory (ADF) pipeline in the background. This pipeline includes an "Execute SSIS Package" activity to run your package. It also sets up a trigger within the pipeline that corresponds to the schedule you defined in SSMS.

17. We're planning to migrate a large on-premises SSIS environment to Azure, but only 40% of the source and destination SQL Server workloads will move to the cloud. The remaining 60% will stay on-premises. Additionally, our current environment relies on Windows Authentication for source and destination connectivity. We want SSIS packages running in Azure Data Factory (ADF) with SSIS Integration Runtime (IR) to access these on-premises resources using Windows Authentication. Can you suggest a solution?

Ans:

There are two main approaches to enable SSIS packages in Azure to connect to on-premises SQL Servers and network shares using Windows Authentication:

- **Connect Azure SSIS IR and On-Premises Networks:**
    - **Create an Azure VNet:** This virtual network will host your Azure SSIS IR.

  - **Establish a Connection to Your On-Premises Network:** Configure a site-to-site VPN gateway connection or ExpressRoute connection from the SSIS IR VNet to your on-premises network. This allows direct communication between Azure and your on-premises resources.

- **Configure Self-Hosted IR as a Proxy:**
  - **Use a Self-Hosted IR:** If corporate policies or restrictions prevent connecting the Azure SSIS IR directly to your on-premises network, you can configure a self-hosted IR to act as a proxy.
  - **Enable Windows Authentication on Azure SSIS IR:** This is required for the self-hosted IR to connect to on-premises resources using Windows Authentication.
  - **Deploy Self-Hosted IR On-Premises or Azure VM:** Download and install the latest version of the self-hosted IR on a machine either on-premises or in an Azure VM.

Note: Currently, Windows Authentication with self-hosted IR is only supported for specific SSIS tasks, such as Data Flow and Execute SQL/Process tasks.

Explore:

There are four primary approaches to enable Windows Authentication for SSIS packages running in ADF SSIS IR:

- **Enable Windows Authentication for Execute SSIS Package Activity (Per Activity):** Within your ADF pipeline, configure the "Windows Authentication" property for the "Execute SSIS Package" activity. This sets up an "Execution/Run as" context specifically for that activity.
- **Enable Windows Authentication at SSISDB (Per Azure-SSIS IR):** Execute the catalog.set_execution_credential stored procedure within the SSISDB Catalog. This procedure allows you to define an "Execution/Run as" context by providing domain, username, and password. These credentials will be used by the SSIS package data sources to connect to on-premises systems.
- **Enable Windows Authentication at Azure SSIS IR using "cmdkey" (Per Azure-SSIS IR):** If your packages access file shares (Azure Files, on-premises file shares, or SQL Server), you can include a custom setup script (main.cmd) during Azure SSIS IR provisioning. Within this script, use the "cmdkey" command to store credentials for on-premises resources:
- cmdkey /add:On-Premises SQL Server –FQDN or IP:SQLServerPort /user: DomainName\Username /pass: Password
- **Enable Windows Authentication at Package Level (Per Package):** This approach is suitable only for accessing on-premises file shares, and Azure Files. It involves mounting the network share as a drive during package execution. Add an "Execute Process Task" at the beginning of your package control flow and use the net use command:
- net use D:\\FileShareServerName\FolderName

Note:

- The most common options are SSISDB level (option 2) or using cmdkey (option 3).
- On-premises tasks executed by a self-hosted IR are billed separately.
- We do not recommend "self-hosted IR as a proxy", due to its complexity of configurations, limitations, potential billing confusion, and troubleshooting challenges.

18. Our customer currently uses SSRS reports on-premises. We're planning to migrate all on-premises workloads to Azure. Can you explain the different ways to host SSRS workloads in Azure?

Ans:

There are three main approaches to migrate SSRS to Microsoft Azure:

- **Lift-and-Shift (IaaS):** Deploy SQL Server with Reporting Services (both Report Server and Report Server databases) on an Azure Virtual Machine (VM).
- **Lift-and-Shift with Managed Database (IaaS + PaaS):** Deploy the Report Server on an Azure VM, but leverage Azure SQL Managed Instance for hosting the report server databases.
- **Migration and Modernization (PaaS):** Migrate your SSRS paginated reports (developed in Report Definition Language - RDL) to the Power BI Premium service. While this offers a cloud-native solution, it's important to note that only paginated reports are compatible, and some reports might require redevelopment during the migration.

Explore:

Lift-and-Shift (IaaS):

- A perfect fit for the lift-and-shift strategy. This approach allows you to create an identical environment to your on-premises setup within an Azure VM, including installing SSRS with a SQL Server instance.
- We can easily migrate (backup/restore) SSRS databases from on-premise to SQL installed on Azure VM.
- While Azure VMs offer flexibility, you can leverage cloud-provided features like Azure Backup and Azure Storage for enhanced functionality.
- However, setting up HA/DR requires additional configuration. You might need to deploy one or more VMs for Always-On Availability Groups.

SSRS Service on Azure VM & SSRS Databases on Azure SQL Managed Instance:

- This approach involves installing the Report Server on an Azure VM. However, the SSRS databases (ReportServer and ReportServerTempDB) reside on an Azure SQL Managed Instance service.
- We can easily migrate (backup/restore) SSRS databases from on-premise to Azure SQL MI.

- This option is ideal for a lift-and-shift with a fully managed database service. Azure handles HA/DR, scalability, and database administration tasks (Ex: Failover groups, point-in-time restore etc.).

Convert SSRS Reports to Power BI:

- This approach involves modernizing your reporting applications by migrating from on-premises SSRS to Power BI in the Azure cloud. It offers an opportunity to upgrade your reporting capabilities while migrating.
- However, careful consideration is needed.
    - Compare SSRS reports with Power BI functionalities to identify unsupported or deprecated features in Power BI that might require alternative solutions.
    - Depending on the complexity of your data sources and reporting logic, development effort might be necessary, potentially impacting cost and timeline.

Note:

- Paginated reports (also known as pixel-perfect reports) are designed for printing, exporting to PDF, or sharing. They are formatted to fit on a single page or multiple pages, displaying all data in tables even if they span across pages. Examples include sales invoices and profit and loss statements.

19. Do you know the process for migrating reports from SSRS to Power BI?

Ans:

Absolutely! Here's a breakdown of the migration process after setting up your Power BI Premium environment:

- **Assess the Source Environment:** Use the Microsoft Assessment and Planning (MAP) Toolkit to analyse your SSRS reports. This tool simplifies the migration by identifying features unsupported or deprecated in Power BI. **Ex:** In Power BI, we need to seek alternative ways to implement some of the SSRS features, such as Linked Reports, Custom Assemblies, Custom Fonts, etc.
- **Map Features to Power BI Equivalents:** Translate SSRS features to their Power BI counterparts. For example:
    - SSRS shared data sources and datasets become Power BI embedded data sources and datasets.
    - SSRS drill-through reports can be converted to Power BI paginated reports with URL parameters.
    - Custom assemblies might be handled using DAX or embedded code functionalities in Power BI.

- **Migrate SSRS Reports to Power BI:** Choose the migration method based on your needs:
    - **Manual Migration (Small Reports):** Download the .rdl file, open it in Power BI Report Builder, validate elements, and publish to your Power BI workspace.
    - **Built-in "Publish .rdl files to Power BI" Feature:** If using Power BI Report Server or a compatible SSRS version (SSRS 2017 and above), leverage the built-in tool to directly publish reports to Power BI.
    - **Automated Migration (RDL Migration Tool - Enterprise Environments):** For large-scale migrations, consider the Microsoft RDL Migration Tool. It automates report migration, validates features and data sources, converts resources, and publishes reports to your Power BI workspace.

- **Review Functionality and Performance:**
    - Ensure the migrated reports function correctly, including special cases like email subscriptions.
    - Monitor report execution time and resource utilization (memory, CPU) to meet business expectations. If needed, adjust resources within your Power BI Premium capacity.

20. What are the different deployment options available for migrating SQL Server Analysis Services (SSAS) from on-premises to Azure?

Ans:

Azure offers several options for migrating on-premises SSAS models:

- **Azure Analysis Services (AAS - PaaS):** AAS is a fully managed service nearly identical to on-premises SSAS for tabular models. Migration to AAS is straightforward due to its similar functionality. However, AAS doesn't support multidimensional models or PowerPivot for SharePoint.
- **SSAS on Azure VM (IaaS):** This option involves provisioning an Azure VM, installing the SSAS service, and configuring it to access required data sources (Azure SQL Database, Azure SQL Managed Instance, Azure Synapse Analytics, or SQL Server on a VM).
- **Power BI Premium (PaaS + Modernization):** For tabular models, migrating to Power BI Premium is a feasible option. Microsoft prioritizes Power BI development, adding features continuously.

21. What are the approaches for migrating SQL Server Analysis Services (SSAS) workloads to Azure?

Ans:

Here are the migration options:

Migrate from SSAS to AAS:

This option is ideal if you're currently using tabular models in SSAS. Here's how you can migrate:

- **Rebuild Models:** You can rebuild your tabular models directly in AAS. While this offers the most control, it requires the most effort.
- **Manual:** At on-premises server we just need to point our Visual Studio SSAS project to AAS and deploy all tabular models from on-prem to Azure Analysis Service.
- **Migrate using SSIS (Automation):** SSIS packages can be used to automate the migration process between SSAS and AAS.

Lift and Shift to Azure VMs:

This option involves migrating your entire SSAS instance, including multidimensional models, to an Azure VM. Here's what's involved:

- **Deploy SQL Server with SSAS:** Install SQL Server with the Analysis Services component on an Azure VM.
- **Migrate databases and configurations:** Transfer your SSAS databases and configurations to the Azure VM instance.
- **Manage the VM yourself:** You'll be responsible for managing the VM itself, including patching, backups, and high availability configurations.

Migrate to Power BI Premium:

You can migrate SSAS models to Power BI Premium. The process involves migrating your SSAS models to AAS and then to Power BI Premium.

- **Background:** SSAS and AAS are built on mature BI data modeling technology. This same technology also forms the foundation of Power BI semantic models. Microsoft has been actively integrating AAS capabilities into Power BI Premium, allowing you to consolidate your data models alongside reports within Power BI. While not all AAS features may be currently available in Power BI Premium, Microsoft is continuously adding functionalities. Azure offers an "Azure Analysis Services to Power BI Premium" migration feature, simplifying the process of moving from AAS to Power BI Premium.
- **Migration process:**
- **Prerequisites**: Ensure that the AAS server and the Power BI workspace are in the same tenant. You should have the necessary permissions and roles.
- **Power BI Requirements**: Verify that you have the necessary Power BI license and Workspace administrator permission.
- **Storage and Backup**: Configure an Azure Storage account with a container and enable backup for the AAS server. Connect the Power BI workspace to an Azure Data Lake Storage Gen 2 (ADLS Gen 2) storage account in the same tenant.
- **XMLA Endpoint**: Enable the XMLA endpoint for read-write for the capacity.
- **Data Gateway**: If a Microsoft on-premises data gateway is configured for the AAS server to connect to on-premises data sources, install and configure a gateway in Power BI.

- **Migration**: Use the backup and restore functionality to migrate the models from AAS to Power BI Premium.
- **Post-Migration**: After the migration, make any necessary modifications to the server properties in Analysis Services.

Migrating Multidimensional Models: There are two main approaches for migrating multidimensional models to Azure:

- **Convert Multidimensional to Tabular Model:**
    - SSAS Multidimensional and Tabular are fundamentally different technologies, and there is no easy method for converting from multidimensional to tabular. In most cases, rebuilding the model from scratch may be necessary.
    - In a legacy multidimensional model, each dimension corresponds to one XML file, with separate XML files for cubes, roles, data sources, and relationships between physical tables. In tabular mode, the model consists of a single JSON file containing metadata for the OLAP cube (dimensions (tables), measures, roles, hierarchies, relationships, etc.).
    - To convert all XML files into a single JSON file, XSLT (Extensible Stylesheet Language Transformations) is needed.
    - Once migrated to tabular models, it can be easily migrated to Azure (AAS).
- **Lift-and-Shift to Azure VM:** Create an SSAS instance on an Azure VM and deploy the workloads from on-premises to Azure.

Enabling Access to On-premises Data:

- **On-premises Data Gateway (Hybrid Scenario):** If your Azure-hosted Analysis Services models need to access data sources still residing on-premises, you'll need to configure an on-premises data gateway. This gateway acts as a secure bridge between your on-premises data and various Azure services, including Power BI, Power Apps, Power Automate, Azure Analysis Services, and Azure Logic Apps.

Note:

- **SSAS:** SQL Server Analysis Services.
- **AAS:** Azure Analysis Services.

CHAPTER 13

Azure Cloud Migration 4 - Heterogeneous Databases

1. Does Azure offer PaaS service similar to Azure SQL Database for hosing IBM DB2?

Ans:

Azure does not offer a Platform as a Service (PaaS) specifically for IBM DB2 like it does for SQL Server/ MySQL/PostgreSQL Databases. For migrating IBM DB2 to Azure, there are a couple of options:

- Hosting DB2 cluster using Azure Kubernetes Service (AKS).
- Hosting DB2 cluster on ARO (Azure Red Hat OpenShift).
- Migrating DB2 to Azure SQL Database/SQL Managed Instance.

Explore:

- **Hosting DB2 cluster using Azure Kubernetes Service (AKS):** This option involves deploying a DB2 database on Azure's managed Kubernetes service, AKS. The process includes setting up an Azure account, creating an AKS cluster based on specific requirements, and setting up file and block storage classes. The DB2 Operator is then run to deploy the database instance to the AKS cluster. Once deployed, users can connect to the database in the same way they connect to an on-premises data source.
- **Hosting DB2 cluster on ARO (Azure Red Hat OpenShift)**: This option involves deploying a DB2 database on Azure's managed OpenShift service, ARO. The process is similar to the AKS option but uses Red Hat OpenShift Data Foundation (ODF) for storage. After setting up an Azure account and creating an ARO cluster based on specific requirements, ODF is installed on the cluster for storage. The DB2 Operator is then run to deploy the database instance to the ARO cluster. Once deployed, users can connect to the database in the same way they connect to an on-premises data source.
- **Migrate to Azure SQL Database/SQL Managed Instance:** Microsoft provides a detailed guide on how to migrate your IBM DB2 databases to Azure SQL Database using SQL Server Migration Assistant (SSMA) for DB2. The process involves pre-migration steps, assessing and converting the database schema, and finally publishing the schema and migrating the data.

Note: When DB2 is hosted on AKS or ARO, you can leverage other Azure services like Azure VNet, Azure Managed Disks, File Share, Load Balancer, and Monitor etc.

2. What are the high-level steps for migrating an IBM DB2 database to Azure SQL Database?

Ans:

Here are the steps to migrate your IBM DB2 databases to Azure SQL Database using SQL Server Migration Assistant (SSMA) for Db2:

Prerequisites:

- Verify that your source environment is supported. Ex: .NET Framework version 4.7.2 or a later version, Microsoft OLE DB Provider for DB2 version 5 or a later version, DB2 supported versions ("DB2 on z/OS" version 9.0, 10.0, and later, "DB2 on LUW" version 9.8, 10.1, and later, "DB2 for I" version 7.1 and later) etc.
- Download SQL Server Migration Assistant (SSMA) for Db2.
- Ensure you have a target database in Azure SQL Database is created and configured.
- Ensure connectivity and sufficient permissions to access both source and target.

Pre-migration:

- Discover the topology of your environment and assess the feasibility of your Azure cloud migration.
- **Assessment:** Use SSMA for DB2 to review database objects and data, and assess databases for migration. Schema assessment will generate an HTML report. Review the HTML report to understand conversion statistics and any errors or warnings.
- **Validate data types:** Validate the default data type mappings, and change them based on requirements if necessary.

Schema Migration:

- **Convert schema:**
  - Connect to both on-premise DB2 and Azure SQL Database.
  - Perform Convert Schema operation on source (DB2) database.
  - After the conversion completes, compare and review the structure of the schema to identify potential problems. Address the problems based on the recommendations.
  - Converting the table schema from DB2 to SQL Server might be straightforward. However, converting other database objects like SQL queries, stored procedures, views, and functions may require manual intervention and a thorough development and testing phase.
- **Resolve Schema Issues:** After identifying any conversion problems in SSMA for DB2, address them to ensure a smooth schema migration.
- **Publish the Schema:** Once issues are resolved, use the "Synchronize with Database" option in SSMA for DB2 to publish the converted schema to your Azure SQL Database.

Data Migration:

- **Select Migration Options:** In SSMA for DB2, choose the "Migrate Data" option. You can then select whether to migrate the entire database or specific tables.
- **Start Data Migration:** Once you've chosen the data to migrate, initiate the migration process.
- **Review Data Migration Report:** After migration is complete, review the Data Migration Report for any errors or warnings.

Post-Migration:

- **Connect and Validate:** Connect to your target Azure SQL Database and verify the data and schema by reviewing them directly.
- **Redirect Applications:** After successful data migration, update your applications to connect to the new Azure SQL Database.
- **Perform Comprehensive Testing:** Conduct thorough testing after migration, including migration testing, functional testing, performance testing, and security testing.

Note: We can also leverage migration tools like "**Database Compare Utility** (Developed by Azure Engineering team)" that allows comparison of Oracle, Db2, MySQL, PostgreSQL, Teradata or Netezza databases to SQL Server.

3. Does Azure offer a PaaS service similar to Azure SQL Database for hosting Oracle databases?

Ans:

No. Azure offers different ways to run Oracle databases, but it doesn't directly provide Oracle hosting in PaaS model for now.

While technically both "**Oracle Database Service for Azure**" and "**Oracle Database@Azure**" could be categorized as a form of managed PaaS (Platform as a Service), Azure itself doesn't directly offer Oracle database hosting as a core service. It provides the infrastructure (IaaS) and tools to deploy and manage Oracle databases.

4. What are the possible deployment options available for Oracle databases in Microsoft Azure?

Ans:

Here are the options you can consider for migrating your Oracle workloads to Azure:

- **Lift & Shift (IaaS):** Move existing Oracle environment "as-is"
    - **Oracle VM images:** Pre-configured VMs with Oracle for easy setup.
    - **Custom VM Images:** Create your own VMs with specific Oracle configurations.
    - **Azure VM + NetApp Files:** Combine Azure VMs with NetApp storage for better performance.

- **Hybrid Approach (PaaS - Supports Lift-and-Shift):**
    - **OracleDB for Azure (Cross Cloud):** Run Oracle databases on Oracle Cloud Infrastructure (OCI), apps on Azure, connect both the clouds using a high-speed private network connection, and manage through Azure.
    - **Oracle Database@Azure:** Deploy & manage Oracle databases directly within Azure (uses OCI infrastructure).
- **Refactor/Rearchitect (PaaS):** Completely migrate databases to another platform like SQL Server or PostgreSQL.

Note: Oracle Database@Azure offers the best of both worlds, combining Oracle's capabilities with Azure's simplicity.

Explore:

Lift and Shift to Azure: This involves moving your existing Oracle environment, including databases and applications, "as-is" to Azure. This is the fastest approach but might not be the most cost-effective or performant in the long run.

- **Oracle VM images on Microsoft Azure:**
    - Leverage pre-configured virtual machine images containing Oracle Database and Linux OS provided by Oracle in the Azure Marketplace.
    - Minimizes setup time but limits customization options.
- **Custom VM Images:**
    - Create your own VM images (create from scratch in Azure) with your specific Oracle version and configurations. Or upload a custom image from your on-premises environment.
    - Offers greater control but requires more effort to manage.
- **Azure VM + NetApp Files:**
    - Combine Azure VMs with NetApp storage solution for Oracle databases.
    - Oracle Database Service runs on an Azure VM and the database files are placed on Azure NetApp File storage.
    - Offers potential performance benefits and scalability for storage needs.

Hybrid Deployment Options: Collaborative offering between Microsoft and Oracle.

Oracle Database Service for Azure (Multi-Cloud):

- Run Oracle databases on Oracle Cloud Infrastructure (OCI) while accessing them from your Azure environment. This approach keeps your data on OCI but allows management through Azure. That means:

- Your business applications are migrated to Azure.
- Oracle databases are migrated to Oracle Cloud Infrastructure (OCI).
- Both Azure and OCI are connected using Oracle Interconnect for Azure, delivers a private, low-latency connection between the two cloud environments. This service will enable a private high-speed connection between these clouds by using Azure ExpressRoute and OCI FastConnect.
- There are no charges for Oracle Interconnect for Microsoft Azure or data ingress/egress over the Interconnect. You will be billed normally for consumption of Oracle Database service.

Oracle Database@Azure (Oracle Infra at Azure Datacenter):

- It allows you to procure, deploy, and manage Oracle databases directly within Azure datacenters.
- You can leverage the familiar Azure portal and APIs for managing these databases.
- However, it's important to note that the underlying infrastructure for Oracle Database@ Azure resides on Oracle Cloud Infrastructure (OCI) hosted in Azure Datacenter. That means,
  - We migrate both our applications and Oracle databases to Azure.
  - App infra will be managed by Azure.
  - Database infra will be managed by OCI.

Refactor or Rearchitect:

- This involves completely rethinking your application and potentially migrating your data to a different database platform like Azure SQL Database or PostgreSQL.
- This can be a complex process but may offer long-term benefits in terms of cost, performance, and manageability, especially if you're not heavily reliant on Oracle-specific features.

5. If we host Oracle on an Azure VM, can we purchase the Oracle license directly from Microsoft Azure?

Ans:

No. When deploying a product on an Azure VM, you're responsible for obtaining the proper license from the product owner.

Oracle VM images are considered "Bring Your Own License" (BYOL). This means you'll only be charged for the compute, storage, and networking resources used by your VM. Microsoft assumes you have the necessary Oracle licenses and a valid support agreement in place. However, Oracle does offer guaranteed license mobility from on-premises environments to Azure.

Explore:

Oracle on Azure VMs: Hosting Oracle databases on Azure VMs is a popular approach for many users. This is because:

- **Official Support:** Oracle and Microsoft have partnered to ensure certified compatibility for running Oracle Database systems on Azure.

Key Considerations for Oracle VMs on Azure:

- **Pre-built Images:** Oracle offers various pre-configured VM images in the Azure Marketplace. These images include Oracle Database 12.1 and higher (Standard and Enterprise editions) pre-installed on Oracle Linux. Additionally, they support Oracle WebLogic Server.
- **Storage Optimization:** For production workloads, use premium-SSD or ultra-SSD managed disks for optimal performance. When using multiple disks, consider spreading database data across them for improved IOPS (Input/Output Operations Per Second). Oracle Automatic Storage Management (ASM) can further enhance performance in such configurations.
- **Licensing:** Oracle offers license mobility when migrating software and workloads from on-premises environments to Azure. This allows you to transfer your existing licenses by mapping them to the compute resources used in Azure. If your VMs have hyper-threading enabled, remember that two vCPUs (virtual CPUs) count as one Oracle Processor license.
- **Backup Strategy:** A recommended approach is to leverage Oracle Recovery Manager (RMAN) along with Azure Backup for application-consistent backups. For added resiliency, consider using Azure BlobFuse2 to mount a highly redundant Azure Blob Storage account and store your RMAN backups there.
    - **BlobFuse:** BlobFuse is a virtual file system driver that allows you to access your existing Azure block blob data through the Linux file system.
- **HA/DR:** Implementing HA/DR solutions is your responsibility when using Oracle on Azure. Here are some options to consider:
    - **Oracle Data Guard:** This provides high availability by setting up a primary database in one VM and a secondary (standby) database in another VM, with one-way replication between them.
    - **Oracle Active Data Guard:** This extends Data Guard functionality, enhancing performance for critical transactions and enabling read-only access to the standby database.
    - **Oracle GoldenGate:** This allows bi-directional replication between primary and secondary databases, making it suitable for multi-primary or Active-Active workloads.
    - **Leveraging Azure Features:** While configuring HA/DR, you can benefit from built-in Azure platform features like Availability Sets, Availability Zones, geo-redundancy, and storage redundancy. **Ex:** Configure your primary and standby databases in separate regions and connect them using a VPN Gateway. Combining Azure Availability Zones with Oracle Active

Data Guard with Fast Start Sync (FSFO) can achieve an uptime availability of 99.99% for your database tier.

Monitoring: Utilize Oracle Enterprise Manager for comprehensive management, monitoring, and logging of your Oracle databases on Azure VMs.

By considering these factors, you can effectively deploy and manage Oracle databases on Azure VMs.

6. What tools and services I can use to migrate an Oracle database to either PostgreSQL or SQL Database in Azure?

Ans:

Here are the tools/service available to migrate an Oracle database to either a PostgreSQL or a SQL database in Azure:

Target	Oracle Assessment	Schema Conversion	Data Migration
PostgreSQL	Oracle scripts artifacts Migration Extension in ADS	Ora2pg	Azure DMS (Online)
SQL Server	Oracle scripts artifacts Migration Extension in ADS	SSMA for Oracle	SSMA for Oracle

Table 13.1

***ADS:** Azure Data Studio

***SSMA:** SQL Server Migration Assistant

***DMS:** Database Migration Service

Explore:

- **Microsoft Oracle Inventory Script Artifacts:** The Microsoft data migration engineering team offers a collection of Oracle scripts. You can connect to your on-premises Oracle database and run these scripts (using SQL Developer, other tools, or the command shell) to analyze various aspects of your source database. These scripts can provide information such as total number of objects, object types, size of objects, compatibility, target sizing information etc.
- **Migration Extension in ADS:** The "Database Migration Assessment for Oracle extension in Azure Data Studio (ADS)" helps you assess an Oracle workload for migrating to Azure SQL and Azure Database for PostgreSQL. The extension identifies an appropriate Azure SQL or PostgreSQL target with right-sizing recommendations, and how complex the migration can be.
- **Ora2pg:** This is a free, open-source tool specifically designed to migrate Oracle databases to PostgreSQL databases. It can be used to migrate both on-premises and cloud-based databases.

The tool connects to your Oracle database, scans it automatically, and extracts its structure or data. Then, Ora2Pg generates SQL scripts that you can load into your PostgreSQL database.

- **SSMA for Oracle:** This is a free, on-premises tool offered by Microsoft that helps migrate schema, and data from Oracle database to SQL Server, Azure SQL Database, or Azure Synapse Analytics.
- **Azure Database Migration Service:** Azure DMS enables online (minimal downtime) migrations of Oracle databases hosted on-premises or on a virtual machine to Azure Database for PostgreSQL.
- **Other Options:** Depending on your specific business needs, you can also consider using other Oracle-specific tools, third-party solutions, or open-source tools for migrating Oracle workloads to SQL Server or PostgreSQL. **Ex:** Oracle Data Integrator (ODI), SQLLoader etc.

7. Why do some customers choose Azure over Oracle Cloud Infrastructure (OCI) to host their Oracle workloads?

Ans:

Here are some common reasons why customers might choose Azure for Oracle deployments:

- **Existing Azure environment:** Customers with a significant investment in Azure infrastructure may prefer to keep their Oracle workloads within the same cloud platform for simplified management and integration.
- **Perceived maturity of Azure:** Some customers might perceive Azure as a more mature cloud platform overall, offering better performance, feature support, services, and technical support compared to OCI.
- **Cost Optimization:** For customers whose business needs don't require the full range of Oracle features, migrating Oracle workloads to Azure SQL Database or PostgreSQL can potentially save up to 70% on licensing fees.

8. How can I migrate an Oracle database from on-premises to an Azure VM?

Ans:

There are several approaches to consider, depending on your specific needs:

- **Backup and Restore (Standard Approach):** This method involves creating a backup of your on-premises Oracle database and then restoring it to a newly provisioned Azure VM. This is a straightforward approach suitable for offline migration scenarios.
- **HA/DR with Oracle Data Guard:** You can set up an HA/DR solution using Oracle Data Guard. This creates a synchronized standby database on your Azure VM, allowing you to failover to the cloud in case of an outage on-premises.
- **Oracle Data Guard with RMAN (Large Databases):** For databases exceeding 3 TB, consider combining Oracle Data Guard with Oracle Recovery Manager (RMAN). This approach allows

for efficient data transfer and synchronization between your on-premises database and the Azure VM standby.

- **Data Pump for Very Large Databases (VLDB):** For databases larger than 10 TB, migrating the initial bulk data transfer with another method (Ex: storage area network copy) followed by ongoing data replication using Data Pump is a recommended strategy. Data Pump offers advantages like parallelism, flexible extraction options, and scalability, enabling efficient data movement with minimal downtime.

Explore:

Here's the high-level steps for migrating an Oracle database to Azure VM using Oracle Data Guard:

- **Prepare Azure Target Environment:** Provision a VM in Azure using a pre-configured Oracle VM image from the Azure Marketplace. Ensure the VM meets your requirements for compute resources, operating system version, and Oracle version compatibility.
- **Establish Network Connectivity:** Create a secure connection between your on-premises environment and Azure. You can achieve this using either a site-to-site VPN or Azure ExpressRoute.
- **Restore Database to Azure VM:** Utilize Oracle Recovery Manager (RMAN) to restore a full backup of your on-premises database to the target standby database on the Azure VM. This can be done using either the traditional backup/restore method or the duplicate database method.
- **Configure Oracle Data Guard:** Configure the restored database on the Azure VM as a physical standby database using Oracle Data Guard. This enables continuous synchronization of transaction/redo data changes from the primary on-premises database to the standby database in Azure.
- **Perform Failover to Azure:** Once the primary and standby databases are synchronized, you can initiate a failover to switch operations to the standby database on the Azure VM. This process converts the standby database into a read-write primary database.
- **Update Application Connections:** After failover, redirect your application connections to the new primary database residing on the Azure VM.
- **Optional: Configure Secondary Database (HA/DR):** For enhanced High Availability/Disaster Recovery, you can set up a secondary database in a different Azure Availability Zone (or even a different region) to provide additional redundancy.
- **Decommission On-Premises Environment:** As a final step, you can decommission your on-premises environment once you've confirmed successful migration and application functionality on Azure.

9. Do you know the deployment options for migrating MySQL workloads to Azure?

Ans:

Azure offers two main options for hosting MySQL:

- **IaaS:** MySQL on Azure VM.
- **PaaS:** Azure Database for MySQL (Single Server / Flexible Server).

Explore:

- **IaaS:** Your MySQL Server runs on a hosted Azure VM,
    - **MySQL VM Images:** Azure Marketplace offers pre-configured VM images with MySQL Community Edition installed. You can deploy these images on Azure VMs to quickly set up a MySQL environment without manual installation and configuration.
    - **Custom:** You can deploy MySQL on Azure VMs just like you would on-premises or any other cloud provider. This option gives you full control over the MySQL environment, including the choice of MySQL version, operating system, and configuration settings.
- **PaaS:** Azure is offering a fully managed solution for MySQL called **Azure Database for MySQL**. It comes in two flavours:
    - **MySQL Single Server (Retiring):** A fully managed MySQL Server. It is on the retirement path.
    - **MySQL Flexible Server:** Provides more granular control over configuration and management settings. Offers high availability within a single zone or across multiple zones for redundancy. Ideal for workloads with varying compute needs due to options like Burstable compute tier and server stop/start functionality. We can assume it functions more like Azure SQL Managed Instance.
- **MySQL on AKS:** For containerized MySQL workloads, you can deploy MySQL on Azure Kubernetes Service (AKS).

10. What is the difference between MySQL Single Server and Flexible Server deployments in Azure PaaS?

Ans:

Flexible Server offers more control, high availability, and cost-optimization options compared to Single Server for Azure Database for MySQL.

Explore:

Single Server (Retiring):

- It's a fully managed MySQL database engine based on the stable version of the MySQL community edition.

- It provides built-in features like automated patching, high availability, automated backups, elastic scaling, enterprise-grade security, compliance and governance, monitoring and alerting.
- However, Azure Database for MySQL single server is on the **retirement path**.

Flexible Server:

- It's a fully managed, production-ready database service and offers greater control over MySQL server and database configuration compared to Single Server.
- **More control over configuration parameters:** Azure exposes 30% more settings compared to Single Server. **Ex:** "host_case_size" and "innodb_adaptive_flushing".
- **Custom Maintenance Windows:** Manage automatic patching and updates by defining custom maintenance windows. This allows you to schedule patching for underlying hardware, OS, and the database engine at your convenience.
- **Cost Optimization:**
    - **Reserved instances:** Allows you to save up to 63% cost, which is ideal for production workloads with predictable compute capacity requirements.
    - **Start & Stop on Demand:** Stop and start the server on-demand to optimize costs. The compute tier billing stops immediately when the server is halted, leading to significant cost savings.
    - **Burstable SKU (Stock Keeping Unit)**:
        - Burstable SKU is one of the compute tiers (other: General Purpose & Business Critical) in Azure Database for MySQL Flexible Server.
        - It's designed for workloads that don't need full CPU capacity continuously. If your MySQL database experiences periods of low activity followed by bursts of high activity, a Burstable SKU can be a good fit.
        - You only pay for the compute resources you use. During low activity periods, you primarily use the baseline resources. When bursts occur, you consume burstable credits.
- **Read Replicas for Scalability:**
    - The read replica feature enables replicating data from a Flexible Server to a read-only server. Up to 10 replicas can be created from the source server.
    - Replication is asynchronous, using the MySQL engine's native binary log (binlog) file position-based technology.
    - You can leverage a load balancer proxy solution like ProxySQL to seamlessly scale-out your application workload to read replicas without modifying your applications.
- **High Availability (HA) Configuration:** Configure HA across a single zone or across multiple availability zones for disaster recovery.
- **MySQL Version Support:** It supports the community version of MySQL 5.7, 8.0 and later.

11. What are the different options for migrating MySQL databases from on-premises to Azure Database for MySQL? Which approach is recommended for most scenarios?

Ans:

Offline migration options:

- DMS – Offline.
- Export and Import.
- Dump and restore.
- mydumper/myloader.
- MySQL Workbench Migration Wizard.
- ETL tools Ex: Azure Data Factory.

Online Migration:

- DMS – Online.
- Data-in replication feature.

Recommended Approach:

It depends on your existing environment and business needs. A general guideline:

- **For large and complex databases:** Consider using Azure Database Migration Service (DMS) or tools like mydumper/myloader.
- **For small and medium workloads:** The Workbench Migration Wizard can be a good option due to its user-friendly interface and suitability for smaller database sizes.

Explore:

Offline Migration with Downtime

Here are some common methods for migrating MySQL databases to Azure Database for MySQL with downtime:

- **Azure Database Migration Service (DMS) - Offline:**
    - This service performs a one-time full database migration by taking a snapshot of your source database at a specific point in time. The captured data is then copied to the target database in Azure.
    - **Use Case:** Ideal for large databases where you need to migrate everything and have downtime scheduled for the migration process.
- **Export and Import:**
    - You can export a database from your on-premises MySQL server and import it into Azure Database for MySQL using tools like MySQL Workbench. This method offers flexibility as you can choose specific objects (tables, views, procedures, etc.) to migrate.

- **Use Case:** Suitable for small to medium-sized databases where you only need a subset of data and objects migrated, and downtime is acceptable.

- **Dump and Restore:**
  - Similar to a traditional backup and restore, you can use the mysqldump utility to create a dump of your entire source database and restore it into Azure Database for MySQL. This method provides granular control over the restore process, allowing you to disable triggers, foreign key checks, or index creation until the restore is complete.
  - **Use Case:** Well-suited for small to medium-sized databases when migrating the entire database and downtime is available.

- **mydumper/myloader:**
  - Migrating databases to Azure Database for MySQL using mydumper/myloader involves creating a backup of your existing database using mydumper, and then restoring that backup to Azure Database for MySQL using myloader.
  - **Process:** You'll need to install these packages on a virtual machine (either an Azure VM or an on-premises VM) that can access both your source and target MySQL instnace. if your source is on-premises and has a high bandwidth connection to Azure (using ExpressRoute), consider installing the tool on an Azure VM. If you have a challenge in the bandwidth between the source and target, consider installing mydumper near the source and myloader near the target server. mydumper creates a logical backup of your source database, which is then transferred securely and imported into the target server using myloader.
  - **Use case:** This method is particularly useful when you need to migrate large databases (larger than 1 TB) as it allows for parallel exporting and importing, resulting in faster migration times.

- **MySQL Workbench Migration Wizard:**
  - MySQL Workbench, similar to SQL Server Management Studio (SSMS), is a popular GUI tool for managing MySQL databases. It offers a Migration Wizard that allows you to configure the source schema, select objects for migration, and specify the target Azure Database for MySQL server. The wizard first creates the schema in the target database and lets you validate the results before triggering the data migration using bulk data transfer techniques.
  - **Use Case:** Applicable for small to large databases where you need to migrate everything and have downtime window for the migration.

Note: Export/Import and Dump/Restore functionalities can be achieved using various MySQL tools including command-line tools, MySQL Workbench, phpMyAdmin, dbForge Studio for MySQL, and others.

Online Migration with Minimal Downtime:

- **Azure Database Migration Service (DMS) - Online:**
    - DMS performs an initial full data copy from your on-premises database to Azure. It then continuously synchronizes any new transactions occurring on the source database to the target database in Azure.
    - Once synchronization is complete, you can switch your client applications to use the Azure database and then stop the synchronization process.
    - **Use Case:** Ideal for large and critical databases where downtime is not an option.
- **Data-in replication feature:**
    - This feature functions similarly to DMS-Online, but here we need to configure the replication process.
    - You can set up the source as the primary server and the target Azure database as a replica, enabling continuous synchronization of new transactions while your application remains operational.
    - Once data is synchronized on the Azure side, you can stop the application briefly (minimizing downtime) to allow any remaining data to be copied. You then update your connection string to point to the Azure database. After the application is live in Azure, replication with the on-premises server can be removed.
    - **Use Case:** Well-suited for medium to large databases where only minimal downtime is acceptable.

Note:

- All tables on the source server must use the "InnoDB" storage engine. If you have "MyISAM" tables, convert them before migration.
- When creating the MySQL database in Azure, it's recommended to choose the same version as your on-premises database.

12. What are the steps involved in migrating an on-premises MySQL database to Azure Database for MySQL Flexible Server using Azure DMS (Online)?

Ans:

Here are the high-level steps to migrate MySQL databases to Azure Database for MySQL:

- In Azure portal, create a DMS instance.
- Create a MySQL migration project in DMS.
- Migrate a MySQL schema using DMS.
- Run the data migration.
- Monitor the migration, do the final cutover and perform the post migration activities.

Explore:

While the general migration process using DMS is similar for various databases (SQL Server, MongoDB, MySQL, PostgreSQL), here's a breakdown of the steps specifically for MySQL:

- **Prerequisites:** Ensure you have an Azure account with an active subscription, an on-premises MySQL database (version 5.7, 8.0 or above), and a Microsoft Azure Virtual Network for Azure DMS set up.
  - **Preparing the On-Premises MySQL Server:**
  - **InnoDB Storage Engine:** Ensure all tables on your source server use the InnoDB storage engine. If you have MyISAM tables, convert them before migration.
  - **Enable Binary Logging:** Binary logging is mandatory for online migration. This involves editing your my.ini (Windows) or my.cnf (Unix) configuration file to enable binary logging parameters (Ex: binlog_format = row) and restarting the MySQL server.
  - **Network and Firewall Access:** Configure your network and firewall rules to allow the DMS service to access your source MySQL database. Typically, this involves enabling MySQL's TCP port 3306.
- **Create a DMS instance:** In the Azure portal, create an instance of Azure DMS.
- **Create a MySQL migration project in DMS:** In the DMS instance, create a new migration project.
- **Configure the migration project:** Specify the source (your on-premises MySQL server) and target (Azure Database for MySQL Flexible Server) details.
  - **Basic Details:** Input a name for the project, specify source type as MySQL, target type as "Azure Database for MySQL". Choose Online data migration as the type of activity.
  - **Specify Source Details:** Enter the details of your on-premises MySQL server, including the server's name, port, and admin credentials.
  - **Specify Target Details:** Enter the details of your Azure Database for MySQL Flexible Server, including the server's name, port, and admin credentials.
  - **Select Databases to Migrate**: Select the databases on your source MySQL server that you want to migrate. You can choose to migrate all databases or select specific databases.
    - **Non-Table Objects:** You can also select the non-table objects such as views, triggers, events, routines etc. Non-table objects that you marked will be migrated, while the items you didn't select will be skipped.
  - **Select Tables to Migrate:** Select the tables that you want to migrate. If the selected source table doesn't exist on the target server, the online migration process will ensure that the table schema and data is migrated to the target server.
  - **Configure Advanced Settings:** If needed, configure advanced settings such as enabling SSL for the source database connection, choosing the type of data consistency check to perform, and setting the maximum allowed downtime during cutover.

- **Start the Migration:** Review the migration summary and start the migration. Azure DMS will validate the migration before it starts. If the validation passes, the migration will start, and you can monitor its progress in the Azure portal.
- **Monitor the migration:** DMS provides a monitoring dashboard within the Azure portal to track the migration progress. You can monitor data transfer rates, errors encountered (if any), and estimated completion time.
- **Cutover to Azure Database for MySQL:**
  - On migration monitoring window, monitor the Seconds behind source and as soon as it nears 0, proceed to start cutover by navigating to the Start Cutover menu tab at the top of the migration activity screen.
  - Select Confirm, and then select Apply to perform the final cutover.
- **Post-Migration Activities:**
  - **Security Configuration:** Create/migrate logins, roles, and permissions within Azure Database for MySQL according to your application's security requirements.
  - **Application Update:** Update your applications and DNS mapping to connect to the migrated database in Azure.
  - **Testing and Validation:** Perform thorough testing of your application against the target database to ensure successful migration.
- **Resource Cleanup:**
  - **Azure Resources:** After successful migration, you can clean up Azure resources used specifically for the migration process, such as the Database Migration Service instance or any temporary ExpressRoute connections.
  - **On-Premises Resources:** Once you've verified the migration and no longer require the on-premises database, you can decommission the source server and related resources (Ex: database, VM).

13. Azure Database for MySQL vs. MySQL on Azure VM: Which is the best option and why?

Ans:

The best option depends on your existing workloads, business needs, and budget.

Azure Database for MySQL:

- **Benefits:**
  - **Fully Managed:** Azure handles backups, patching, auto-scaling, encryption, and other management tasks.
  - **Cost-Effective:** Can be cost-effective for small to medium sized database workloads.

- **Limitations:**
  - **Storage Limit:** Supports a maximum of 16 TB overall storage, with a single data file limited to 4 TB on general purpose storage v2 (partitioning can help with larger tables).
  - **MySQL Version Support:** Currently supports MySQL versions 5.7 and 8.0 only (older versions require upgrade).
  - **Storage Engine Support:** Does not support MyISAM, BLACKHOLE, ARCHIVE, and FEDERATED storage engines. (migration to InnoDB or MEMORY storage engine is required).
- **Choose it:** for a fully managed, cost-effective solution for small to medium databases with compatible versions and storage engines.

MySQL on Azure VM:

- **Benefits:**
  - **Fine-Grained Control:** Offers full control over the database environment and MySQL configuration.
  - **Flexibility:** Supports all MySQL versions and storage engines.
  - **No Storage Limitations:** Offers greater storage scalability compared to Azure Database for MySQL.
- **Limitations:**
  - **Self-Managed:** Requires managing backups, high availability, patching, and other maintenance tasks.
  - **Auto-Scaling:** Requires manual configuration of auto-scaling features provided by Azure VMs.
  - **Storage Management:** Managing large deployments with multiple disks and RAID configurations can be complex.
- **Choose it:** for greater control, flexibility, and scalability for larger databases or those requiring specific versions or storage engines.

14. Do you know the deployment options for hosting PostgreSQL in Azure?

Ans:

Absolutely! Here are the two primary options for deploying PostgreSQL in Azure:

- **IaaS:** PostgreSQL on Azure VM.
- **PaaS:** Azure Database for PostgreSQL (Single Server/Flexible Server).

Explore:

- **IaaS:** Your PostgreSQL Server runs on a hosted VM

- **PostgreSQL VM Images:** Azure Marketplace offers pre-configured VM images with PostgreSQL installed. You can deploy these images on Azure VMs to quickly set up a PostgreSQL environment without manual installation and configuration.
- **Custom:** You can deploy PostgreSQL on Azure VMs from scratch just like you would on-premises or any other cloud provider. This option gives you full control over the PostgreSQL environment. However, you'll be responsible for managing the database itself, including backups, HA/DR and patching.

- **PaaS:** Azure offers a fully managed PostgreSQL database service called Azure Database for PostgreSQL. It comes in two flavours:

  - **Azure Database for PostgreSQL Single Server (Retiring):** This option offers a fully managed PostgreSQL server with 99.99% availability. Since it's on the retirement path, consider using PostgreSQL Flexible Server instead. Supported versions PostgreSQL v10, v11.
  - **Azure Database for PostgreSQL Flexible Server (Recommended):** This service extends the functionality of Single Server by providing more control over configuration and PostgreSQL database setup. You can assume it functions more like Azure SQL Managed Instance. Supported versions PostgreSQL v11, v12, v13, v14, v15, v16.

- **Other Options:**

  - **PostgreSQL on AKS:** For containerized PostgreSQL workloads, you can deploy PostgreSQL on Azure Kubernetes Service (AKS).
  - **Azure Arc-enabled PostgreSQL server:** It lets you deploy and manage the open-source PostgreSQL database in a variety of environments alongside built-in Azure integration. Deploy PostgreSQL on any Kubernetes infrastructure, including on-premises environments, other cloud providers like AWS and GCP, or even edge deployments using lightweight Kubernetes like K3s.

15. What are the various options/tools/services available for migrating PostgreSQL databases from on-premises to Azure? And which is the recommended migration approach?

Ans:

There are several methods to migrate your PostgreSQL databases to Azure, each with its advantages:

Offline Migrations:

- **pg_dump and pg_restore:** These built-in utilities allow you to create a local backup (dump) of your database and then restore it into Azure Database for PostgreSQL. This approach is ideal for smaller databases or those requiring specific control over the migration process.
- **Export and Import:** This method involves exporting data from your PostgreSQL database using tools like pgAdmin and then importing it into Azure. While suitable for selective schema and data migrations, pg_dump and psql are generally preferred for their efficiency.

  - **ETL Tools (Azure Data Factory):** For very large data migrations, ETL tools offer a flexible approach for data extraction, transformation, and loading into Azure Database for PostgreSQL.

Online Migration:

- **Azure Database Migration Service (DMS):** This managed service simplifies online migrations by continuously replicating data from your on-premises database to Azure. DMS is a user-friendly option that minimizes downtime for your applications.
- **PostgreSQL Logical Replication (for Azure VMs):** This approach utilizes PostgreSQL's built-in replication functionality to establish a publish-subscribe relationship between your on-premises database and a PostgreSQL server on an Azure VM. While offering granular control, it requires more technical expertise to manage.

Recommended Approach:

The best migration approach depends on your specific needs. Here's a general recommendation:

- For **most scenarios**, Azure DMS is the recommended choice for online migrations.
- For **smaller databases** or offline migrations, consider pg_dump and pg_restore.
- For **complex migrations** involving data transformations or integrations with other sources, explore Azure Data Factory (ADF).
- For **very large-scale migrations** with specific needs, PostgreSQL logical replication on Azure VMs can be an option, but only with sufficient technical expertise.

16. Do we have DTU and vCore purchasing models available for PostgreSQL and MySQL?

Ans:

No, the DTU purchasing model is specific to Azure SQL Database and is not available for Azure SQL Managed Instance, Azure Database for PostgreSQL or MySQL. For Azure SQL MI, PostgreSQL and MySQL, compute resources are provisioned using the vCore model with different service tiers offering varying vCore options.

Explore:

Here is the service tier information:

MySQL Flexible Server:

- **Burstable (B Series):** Best for workloads that don't need the full CPU continuously. Ex: Standard_B20ms.
- **General Purpose (D Series):** Best for workloads that require balanced compute and memory with scalable I/O throughput. Ex: Standard_D64ds_v4.

- **Business Critical (E Series):** Suits for high-performance database workloads. Ex: Standard_E96ds_v5.

PostgreSQL Flexible Server:

- **Burstable (B Series):** Best for workloads that don't need the full CPU continuously. Ex: B20ms
- **General Purpose (D Series):** Best for workloads that require balanced compute and memory with scalable I/O throughput. Ex: D96ads_v5
- **Memory Optimized (E Series):** Suits for high-performance database workloads. Ex: E96ads_v5

***Note:** Focusing only on the Flexible Server model as the Single Server option is being retired.

17. What are the various options to host Teradata workloads on Azure?

Ans:

Below are the main options for hosting Teradata on Microsoft Azure Cloud:

- **Teradata VantageCloud Enterprise on Azure (SaaS):** This is a fully managed Software as a Service offering that provides a secure and scalable environment for enterprise analytics. With VantageCloud Enterprise, you don't need to manage the underlying infrastructure as Teradata handles that for you. This option offers predictable pricing and simplifies budgeting.
- **Teradata Software on Azure VM (IaaS):** This option involves deploying Teradata software on Azure Virtual Machines (VMs). Users have full control over the configuration, management, and maintenance of the Teradata environment. This option is suitable for specific compliance or security requirements. It requires expertise in managing Teradata and Azure infrastructure.
- **Migrate to Azure Synapse Analytics (Re-platforming - PaaS):** Migrating Teradata workloads to Azure Synapse Analytics involves transferring your existing data, processes, and applications from Teradata, an on-premises data warehousing solution, to Azure Synapse Analytics, a cloud-based data warehousing and analytics service offered by Microsoft.

Explore:

Teradata VantageCloud: Teradata Vantage is a connected multi-cloud data platform designed for enterprise analytics. It essentially helps businesses analyze large and complex datasets across various cloud environments. Think of it as a cloud-based Teradata Solution. It offers a unified platform for various data workloads including data warehouse, data lake, Lakehouse, data engineering etc.

18. What tools and services are available to migrate schema and data from Teradata to Azure Synapse Analytics?

Ans:

Below are the options to migrate Teradata to Azure Synapse analytics:

- Azure Data Factory.
- Physical Data Transfer (Data Box).
- Third Party Tools or Custom Scripts.

Explore:

- **Microsoft Data Migration Tools:** Microsoft offers several tools to help you migrate your existing data warehouse to Azure Synapse. Some of these tools include:
    - **Azure Data Factory:** This cloud-based ETL (Extract, Transform, Load) service allows you to orchestrate and automate the data movement between Teradata and Azure Synapse Analytics. It provides a visual interface to design data pipelines, schema mapping and supports various data transfer activities.
    - **Physical Data Transfer:** Microsoft services for physical data transfer including Ex: AzCopy, Azure Data Box etc.
    - **Azure Synapse Pathway (Going forward):** It supports conversion of database, schema, and tables from IBM Netezza, SQL Server, and Snowflake. Microsoft has been working on to provide support for Teradata, followed by Redshift, BigQuery and Hive based Hadoop solutions.
    - **Azure VMs with Teradata Instance:** You can leverage Azure Virtual Machines to deploy a Teradata instance within the Azure cloud environment. This allows you to use familiar Teradata utilities like Teradata Parallel Data Transporter (TPT) to migrate data to the VM instance. Once the data is on the VM, you can then transfer it to Azure Synapse Analytics using other methods.

- **Third-Party Data Warehouse Migration Tools:** There are several third-party tools that can help you migrate your existing data warehouse to Azure Synapse. These tools often provide features like schema conversion, data transformation, and progress monitoring. Some popular options include Datometry, Ispirer Asgard and Attunity Replicate.

    - **Datometry:** Datometry Hyper-Q makes existing applications written for Teradata run natively on Azure Synapse. Datometry emulates commonly used Teradata SQL, including analytical SQL, and advanced operational concepts like stored procedures, macros, SET tables, and more.

- **Custom ETL Scripts:** For experienced users, writing custom scripts using languages like Python (Apache Sqoop, Pandas) or SQL with ODBC/JDBC connections can be an option for migrating data. This approach offers flexibility but requires significant development effort and expertise in both Teradata and Azure Synapse Analytics.

Recommendation:

- **For simple migrations:** Consider using Azure Data Factory.
- **For complex and large-scale migrations:** Explore custom or third-party migration tools.

19. We have on-premises SAP systems and are planning to migrate them to the Azure cloud. Does Azure offer any solutions specifically designed for SAP workloads?

Ans:

While I haven't personally migrated SAP workloads to the cloud, I recently participated in a customer case study where they discussed migrating a large SAP system to Azure. Based on that experience, I can share some theoretical knowledge.

SAP systems, especially those with large databases, require two key resources:

- **Large Storage:** Azure offers solutions to address this need.
- **Elastic Compute Capacity:** Azure can provide the necessary scalability for processing power.

Azure Offerings for SAP:

Azure supports deployment of various SAP systems, including SAP NetWeaver, SAP S/4HANA, BW/4HANA, BI, and HANA in both scale-up and scale-out configurations. Following are two optimized solutions from Azure. Both options are certified to run SAP workloads, and as our client mentioned, they offer a "best of both worlds" scenario by combining SAP with the benefits of Azure cloud services.

- **SAP on Azure Virtual Machines:** This option utilizes on-demand VMs suitable for small to medium SAP workloads. They offer up to 4 TB RAM and 128 vCPUs.
- **SAP HANA on Azure Large Instances:** This offering is specifically designed for very large SAP workloads. Azure runs your workloads on dedicated, non-shared bare-metal hardware. This means your virtual machine has its own dedicated compute, server, networking, and storage infrastructure. Large Instances provide up to 24 TB RAM and 480 Intel CPU cores.

Microsoft offering for Sybase DB:

- **SSMA for SAP ASE for Migrating Sybase to Azure SQL:** Microsoft SQL Server Migration Assistant (SSMA) for SAP ASE (Adaptive Server Enterprise). SSMA for SAP ASE is a tool to automate migration from SAP ASE database(s) to SQL Server, Azure SQL Database and Azure SQL Database Managed Instance.
- **SAP ASE:** originally known as Sybase SQL Server / Sybase DB / Sybase ASE, is a relational model database server developed by Sybase Corporation, which later became part of SAP SE.

SAP Migration to Azure (High level):

During SAP migrations involving large databases, several tools are commonly used: AzCopy, R3load, and Migmon (Migration Monitor).

For R3load, which exports data in a platform-independent format and enables parallel processing, on-premises infrastructure is often provisioned. In your example, four physical servers were set up with accelerated networking to handle the R3load tasks:

- **Server 1:** Dedicated to loading the top 5 tables.
- **Servers 2 & 3:** Used for loading tables that have been split for parallel processing.
- **Server 4:** Assigned to migrate all remaining tables.

Since R3load performs parallel exports, a signal file (SGN) automatically generated upon completion of all export packages controls the import sequence. This ensures data is imported in the correct order.

20. In your experience, have you ever used or built custom data migration tools for moving workloads from on-premises environments to Azure? If so, could you elaborate on the tool and its capabilities?

Ans:

Absolutely. There are situations where building a custom migration tool becomes necessary. These situations include, but are not limited to:

- Strict security and compliance requirements.
- Cost-effectiveness for large-scale migrations.
- Complex data migrations requiring granular Control over the underlying ETL tasks.
- Legacy system integrations where out-of-the-box cloud-native tools lack the necessary functionality.

I've actually worked with custom tools on several occasions, specifically designed for unique customer environments. For instance, we built a custom migration tool called "TheOneMig" for one of our healthcare clients. This tool facilitated the migration of terabytes of data from their on-premises Teradata data warehouse to an Azure Synapse Analytics dedicated SQL pool. Here is some background on the tool and its capabilities:

Environments:

- **Source:** This is our on-premise Teradata data warehouse.
- **Staging (Transit Hub/Buffer Zone):** This is an Azure Blob Storage where the data will be temporarily stored after extraction from the source.

- **Target:** This is the Azure Synapse Analytics where the data will be finally loaded.

Technology Stack:

- **SQL:** For writing Teradata queries to extract data and potentially for creating target table schemas in Synapse Analytics.
- **Python:** Used for scripting data extraction logic, interacting with Teradata APIs using libraries like Teradata-Python, teradatasql, and potentially data transformation tasks using libraries like pandas.
- **Azure Blob Storage:** For staging the data.
- **Azure Synapse Analytics:** As the target data warehouse.
- **ADLS Gen 2 (Azure Data Lake Storage):** Serves as the target data lake for hosting semi-structured or unstructured data, as well as storing archived datasets.
- **PolyBase:** Massively parallel processing technology within Synapse Analytics for efficient data loading from Azure Blob Storage.
- **Azure Data Factory:** For orchestrating and automating the data movement and transformation from Azure Blob Storage to synapse.

File Formats:

- **Parquet:** This columnar format is used for efficient data loading into Synapse Analytics using PolyBase. It offers compression and schema flexibility.

Migration Paths:

- **Source Controlled Pipeline:** Extract data from Teradata using SQL queries, transform the data using Python, and load the data into Azure Blob Storage in Parquet format.
- **Azure Controlled Pipeline:** Used Azure Data Factory to move data from Azure Blob Storage to Azure Synapse Analytics.
- **Differentiated Export:** This approach focuses on separating the data export, transfer, and import steps. Each step involves distinct operations with data being read from or written to intermediate files. Additionally, TheOneMig can support extracting only the delta changes (new or updated data) from the Teradata source for incremental loads.
- **Integrated Export:** This tool also supports, combining data export, transfer and import directly from the source data system to Azure Synapse with no intermediate files created. We used it for loading small datasets.

Data Quality Management:

- TheOneMig incorporated basic to advanced data quality checks during the extraction and loading process.
- Implemented Python code to validate data types, identify missing values and duplicate values, checksum validations, sample dataset comparisons, and potentially carry out data cleansing tasks before writing data to the Blob Storage.

Migration Execution:

Schema Migration:

- **Tables:** TheOneMig can use Teradata system catalogs to extract table schema definitions. Python code can then translate these definitions into T-SQL CREATE TABLE statements compatible with Synapse Analytics. These T-SQL are deployed to Synapse Analytics for table creation.
- **Other Objects (Mostly manual):** Extracted SQL scripts for stored procedures, views and other objects from Teradata. Used automated scripts or manual processes to translate Teradata SQL to Synapse SQL. Validated and deployed the translated code in Synapse.

Data Migration:

- **On-premise to Azure Blob Storage:**
  - TheOneMig leverages its Python capabilities to establish secure connections to the Teradata database.
  - Data is extracted from Teradata tables using Teradata APIs or SQL queries and written to Azure Blob Storage in Parquet format. The tool has built-in basic orchestration capabilities to schedule and automate the data transfer from Teradata to Blob Storage.
- **Azure Blob Storage to Synapse Analytics:**
  - Azure Data Factory (ADF) and PolyBase is used to orchestrate the data loading process from Blob Storage to Synapse Analytics.
  - In certain cases, we also used certain ADF activities to perform data transformations before loading into Synapse.

Additional Features: TheOneMig further enhances its capabilities by leveraging cloud-native features like security (data encryption, access control), detailed auditing and logging, UI-based monitoring, version control (Git) support etc.

Note: This is a high-level overview of "TheOneMig" functionalities. The actual development process will involve detailed technical design, coding, testing, and deployment of the tool.

21. We are a large enterprise with a lot of diversified datasets on-premises. These datasets include structured data (RDBMS, Excel data, etc.), semi-structured data (XML, JSON, etc.), unstructured data (text documents, images, audio, video, logs, etc.), and streaming data (IoT data, social media posts, etc.). We are planning to migrate our workload to Azure. What are the various services, features, and solutions offered by Azure to store, analyze, manage, and utilize our data?

Ans:

Azure provides a technically rich and modern data platform for storing, managing, utilizing, and analyzing data. Here's a subset of the Azure Data Platform solutions that can address your needs:

- **Storage:** Blob Storage, Azure Files, Data Lake, Managed Disks etc.
- **RDBMS:** Azure SQL Database, Azure Database for PostgreSQL/MySQL etc.
- **NoSQL:** Cosmos DB etc.
- **Data Warehouse:** Synapse, Databricks.
- **Time Series:** Azure Time Series Insights (Retired). Azure Data Explorer, Cosmos DB, Microsoft Fabric – Realtime Intelligence.
- **BI Data & Data Analytics:** Microsoft Fabric, Azure Data Factory, Synapse analytics, Azure Databricks, Power BI, Stream Analytics etc.

Explore:

Here is a detailed list of features and services offered by Azure that help you build more reliable, scalable, and modernized data workloads on the Azure platform.

Data Storage:

- **Azure Blob Storage:** Ideal for storing large amounts of unstructured data like text files, images, videos, and backups. **Ex:** Storing medical images for a hospital or large video archives for a media company
- **Queue Storage:** Used for managing a queue of messages for asynchronous processing. **Ex:** Sending notifications to users in a queue to avoid overwhelming the system
- **Table Storage:** Stores simple, schema-less data with a key-value pair structure. **Ex:** Storing sensor data from IoT devices with device ID as the key and temperature as the value.
- **Managed Disks:** High-performance block storage for deploying VMs and applications.
- **Azure Data Lake Storage:** Designed for storing massive amounts of unstructured and semi-structured data for big data analytics. **Ex:** Storing clickstream data for a website or social media feeds for analysis.
- **Azure Files:** Cloud-based file shares accessible from Windows, Linux, and macOS machines. **Ex:** Sharing documents and folders between teams across locations.
- **Azure NetApp Files:** High-performance, scalable file storage for demanding workloads like enterprise applications. **Ex:** Storing financial data for a large financial organization.
- **Azure Elastic SAN:** Block storage optimized for mission-critical applications requiring low latency and high availability. **Ex:** Storing data for real-time stock trading platforms, ERP systems etc.

RDBMS (Relational Database Management System):

- **Azure SQL Database:** Managed relational database service in the cloud based on the Microsoft SQL Server engine. **Ex:** Storing customer information for an e-commerce website.
- **Azure SQL Managed Instance:** Provides a fully managed instance of SQL Server with native VNet support. **Ex:** Lift and shift migration of on-premises SQL Server applications to the cloud.

- **SQL Server Stretch Database (Deprecated in SQL Server 2022 and Azure SQL Database.):** Allows transparently migrating cold data from SQL Server to Azure for cost-effective storage. **Ex:** Moving old but occasionally accessed data to a cheaper tier in Azure.
- **Azure Database for MySQL/PostgreSQL/MariaDB:** Managed database services for popular open-source relational databases. **Ex:** Running web applications built with these technologies)
- **SQL Server Enabled by Azure Arc:** Extends Azure data services to hybrid and multi-cloud environments using Azure Arc. **Ex:** Managing SQL Server instances running on-premises, at the edge, or in other clouds.

NoSQL (Non-relational Database):

- **Azure Cosmos DB:** Globally distributed NoSQL database with high availability and scalability for various data models (document, key-value, graph). Azure Cosmos DB offers multiple database APIs, which include NoSQL, MongoDB, PostgreSQL, Cassandra, Gremlin, Table. **Ex:** Storing user data for a globally distributed mobile application).
- **Azure Managed Instance for Apache Cassandra:** Fully managed Apache Cassandra service with open-source compatibility. **Ex:** Building real-time analytics, recommendation engines, or event logging platforms.

Data Warehouse:

- **Azure Synapse Analytics (Dedicated SQL Pool):** Unified analytics service for large-scale data processing and warehousing. **Ex:** Running complex analytical queries, predictive modelling, or business intelligence reporting.
- **Azure Databricks (Databricks SQL and Delta Lake):** Unified data analytics platform for big data, ML and AI workloads. It is an Apache Spark-based data analytics platform with SQL capabilities and Delta Lake for reliable data storage. **Ex:** Performing data preparation, machine learning, or streaming analytics on large datasets.

Cache:

- **Azure Cache for Redis:** Fully managed, highly available, and scalable Redis cache service. Ideal for caching frequently accessed data, session management, or real-time analytics. **Ex:** Caching product information for a faster e-commerce website experience.
- **Azure HPC Cache:** High-performance cache for HPC workloads with low-latency access to storage. **Ex:** Accelerating data access for high-performance computing simulations, rendering, or genomics research.

Data Integration (ETL/ELT):

- **Azure Data Factory (ADF):** Fully managed data integration service for orchestrating and automating ETL/ELT workflows or Data Pipelines. **Ex:** Extracting data from multiple sources, transforming it, and loading it into a data warehouse or data lake.

- **Azure Synapse Pipelines:** ADF capabilities are offered as a part of Synapse Analytics in the form of Synapse Pipelines.
- **Azure Databricks Pipelines:** Unified data engineering platform for building and deploying ETL/ELT pipelines at scale. Data pipelines built within the Databricks environment for complex data transformations. **Ex:** Extracting data from diverse sources, performing data transformations, and loading it into a data warehouse or lake. Building machine learning pipelines for data preparation and model training.

Analytical Modelling:

- **Azure Analysis Services**: Fully managed service for enterprise-grade data modeling and analysis. Ex: Lift-and-shift on-premise SQL Server Analysis Services to Azure AS for Building tabular models, and performing ad-hoc data analysis.
- **Power BI Data Modelling**: Built-in capability for creating data models within Power BI. You can connect to various data sources, define relationships between them, and transform data for creating insightful reports and visualizations.

Reporting & Analysis:

- **Power BI**: A business analytics tool for creating interactive visualizations and reports from various data sources. **Ex:** Generating sales dashboards, financial reports, or operational analytics for decision-making.
- **Jupyter Notebooks**: It provides a browser-based shell that lets data scientists create notebook files. Its an open-source web application for creating and sharing documents containing live code, equations, visualizations, and narrative text. Most varieties of Azure HDInsight clusters, such as Spark or Hadoop, come preconfigured with Jupyter notebooks for interacting with data and submitting jobs for processing. **Ex:** Data exploration, machine learning model development, or collaborative research analysis.
- **Jupyter Notebooks in VS Code**: An extension that allows you to use Jupyter Notebooks within the popular code editor Visual Studio Code for seamless development and collaboration. **Ex**: Data science projects, debugging code, or sharing insights within a development team.
- **Zeppelin Notebooks**: It is another option for a browser-based shell, similar to Jupyter in functionality. Some HDInsight clusters come preconfigured with Zeppelin notebooks.

Log Management and Monitoring:

- **Log Analytics, Application Insights, Azure Monitor**: Azure services for collecting, analyzing, and visualizing telemetry data from applications and infrastructure. **Ex:** Monitoring application performance, database performance, detecting anomalies, or troubleshooting issues in real-time.
- **Azure Managed Grafana**: A fully managed instance of Grafana for creating dashboards and visualizing data from various sources. **Ex:** Monitoring system metrics, visualizing logs, or building custom dashboards for operational insights.

Big Data Analytics:

- **Microsoft Fabric**: It is an all-in-one analytics solution for enterprises. It covers everything from data movement to data science, Real-Time Analytics, and business intelligence. It offers a comprehensive suite of services, including Data Factory, Synapse Data Engineering, Synapse Data Warehousing, Synapse Data Science, Synapse Real Time Analytics, Power BI and OneLake, all in one place.
- **Azure Data Lake Storage Gen 2**: Scalable and secure data lake storage for big data analytics workloads. **Ex:** Storing raw, unstructured data for data exploration, transformation, or archival purposes.
- **Azure Data Lake Analytics (Retired)**: A distributed analytics service for processing big data stored in Azure Data Lake Storage. **Ex:** Analyzing, running parallelized queries and data transformations, on large datasets for patterns, trends, and insights.
- **Azure Data Explorer (Kusto Explorer)**: A fast and highly scalable data exploration service for analyzing large volumes of data in real-time. **Ex:** Analyzing logs, telemetry data, or time-series data for operational insights or trend analysis.
- **Azure Synapse Analytics**: A unified data warehousing and analytics service offering data warehousing, data pipelines, and analytics capabilities. **Ex:** Building a data warehouse for historical sales data analysis, integrating data from various sources, running complex analytics and integrating it with Power BI service.
- **Azure Databricks**: An Apache Spark-based analytics platform offering data warehousing, processing, and machine learning capabilities. **Ex:** Running complex data pipelines, building machine learning models on big data, performing large-scale data processing and running interactive data analysis using Apache Spark.
- **Azure HDInsight**: Managed Hadoop clusters for running big data analytics workloads using frameworks like Apache Spark, HDFS, and Hive. Traditionally used for big data analytics on-premises, now offered as a managed service in Azure. **Ex**: Running Apache Hadoop or Spark clusters for processing large datasets, executing batch or stream processing jobs.
- **Azure Stream Analytics**: Real-time stream processing service for analyzing and reacting to data streams from IoT devices, sensors, or applications. **Ex:** Detecting anomalies in sensor data, triggering alerts, or aggregating data for real-time dashboards.
- **Microsoft Graph Data Connect**: Service for extracting and exporting Microsoft 365 data for analytics and reporting purposes. **Ex:** Analyzing employee productivity, collaboration patterns, or usage trends within Microsoft 365 applications.

AI & ML:

- **Azure Machine Learning (AML):** This is a cloud service that helps data scientists and developers build, train, and deploy machine learning models. It provides a workspace/workbench that includes machine learning tools for data preparation and feature engineering, and it supports both code-first and low-code experiences. **Ex:** Developing predictive maintenance models for equipment, fraud detection algorithms for financial transactions, recommendation systems for e-commerce platforms, predict future sales based on historical data for a retail company etc.

- **Azure AI Services:** These are a collection of services that allow developers to embed AI and machine learning capabilities into their applications. This includes services for vision, speech, language, decision, and web search. **Ex:** A customer service platform can use Azure AI Services to create a chatbot that can understand and respond to customer queries in natural language.
- **Azure Open Datasets:** These are curated public datasets that you can use to add scenario-specific features to machine learning solutions for more accurate models. They are readily available to Azure Machine Learning and other Azure services. **Ex:** A healthcare research institute can use Azure Open Datasets to access publicly available health data for research purposes.
- **Azure OpenAI Service:** This service provides REST API access to OpenAI's powerful language models including GPT-4, GPT-3.5-Turbo, and others. It allows developers to integrate these models into their applications for tasks like content generation, summarization, and natural language to code translation. **Ex:** A software development company can use Azure OpenAI Service to create a code generation tool that takes natural language descriptions of a program and generates the corresponding code.

IoT (Internet of Things):

- **Azure Time Series Insights (TSI - Retired):** A specialized service for storing and analyzing time-series data from IoT devices. It's optimized for fast ingestion, efficient storage, and real-time queries of sensor data. **Ex:** Analyzing temperature data from factory sensors to identify machinery malfunctions or monitoring energy usage from smart meters in real-time.
- **Azure SQL Edge:** A lightweight database engine designed for processing data at the edge, closer to IoT devices. It enables local analytics and filtering before sending data to the cloud. **Ex:** Pre-processing sensor data on wind turbines to identify anomalies before sending it to the cloud for further analysis or performing local control actions based on edge analytics.

Data Governance:

- **Azure Data Catalog (Retired):** A service for registering, searching, and understanding your data assets across various locations. It helps organizations discover, understand, and manage their data effectively. **Ex:** Creating a Catalog of all your customer data stored in various databases, data lakes, and applications to improve data discoverability for data analysts.
- **Microsoft Purview:** A unified data governance solution that builds upon Azure Data Catalog. It offers additional features like data lineage tracking, classification, and access control for comprehensive data governance. **Ex:** Defining data usage policies, tracing the origin and movement of data through your systems, and ensuring only authorized users can access sensitive data.

Secure Data Sharing:

- **Azure Data Share:** A service for securely sharing your data with external organizations in a controlled manner. You can define access levels and permissions for the shared data. **Ex:** Sharing sales data with a marketing partner while restricting access to specific customer information.

Workflow & Automation:

- **Azure Functions:** Serverless compute platform for running small pieces of code triggered by events. Ideal for building lightweight APIs or automating tasks. **Ex:** Triggering a function whenever a new sensor reading arrives in Azure Time Series Insights and performing real-time data analysis.
- **Azure Logic Apps:** Cloud-based workflow automation service for orchestrating tasks across various Azure services and SaaS applications. **Ex:** Building a workflow that automatically sends an alert email and creates a maintenance ticket when an anomaly is detected in sensor data.
- **Azure Automation:** Service for automating management tasks on Azure resources like VMs, databases, and storage accounts. **Ex:** Automating the patching process for all your virtual machines in Azure on a weekly basis.
- **Microsoft Power Automate:** This is a powerful cloud-based service created by Microsoft that provides a solution for automating repetitive and time-consuming tasks, streamlining workflows, improving productivity and freeing up time for more important activities. **Ex:** Automating the process of generating sales reports by pulling data from different sources and sending them to email recipients)

Messaging and Event-Driven Solutions in Azure: These services facilitate communication and data exchange between different parts of your application or across various services.

- **Azure Event Hubs:** High-throughput data ingestion service for streaming large volumes of telemetry and event data from various sources. Alternative solutions for Azure Event Hubs are Apache Kafka, Amazon kinesis, Google Pub/Sub. **Ex:** Capturing real-time data from millions of connected devices like sensors or user interactions in an application.
- **Azure IoT Hub:** Managed service specifically designed for communication with IoT devices. It provides secure two-way messaging, device management, and message routing capabilities. We can receive data from devices (capture sensor information – pressure, temperature etc.), also we can send commands and policies back to the devices (update sensor software etc.). **Ex:** Connecting millions of sensors in a smart factory to the cloud, receiving sensor readings, and sending commands to control devices remotely.
- **Azure Notification Hubs:** Service for sending push notifications to various mobile platforms (iOS, Android, etc.) at scale. **Ex:** Sending real-time notifications to users about breaking news, order updates, or promotional offers from a mobile application.
- **Azure Event Grid:** Serverless event routing service that reacts to events happening across various Azure services or on-premises applications. **Ex:** Triggering a workflow in Azure Functions

whenever a new file is uploaded to Azure Blob Storage. Reacting to changes coming from IoT devices, responding to user clicks on mobile apps, or initiating business processes from customer requests etc.

- **Azure Service Bus:** Messaging service for reliable and secure message exchange between applications. It offers different message queuing options (point-to-point, publish-subscribe) depending on your needs. **Ex:** Decoupling different parts of a microservices application by allowing them to communicate asynchronously through message queues.
- **Azure Storage Queues:** Simple message queuing service for asynchronous message processing. Messages are delivered in a first-in-first-out (FIFO) order. **Ex:** Queuing up tasks like image/order processing or sending email notifications for later execution by a worker process.

Industry-Specific Data Management Services:

- **Azure Data Manager for Agriculture:** A specialized solution for collecting and managing agricultural data, including crop monitoring, soil analysis, weather forecasting, and farm management. **Ex:** Collecting and analyzing sensor data from agricultural equipment and farm machinery, monitoring soil and crop health, and optimizing irrigation schedules and predict crop yields.
- **Azure Data Manager for Energy:** A specialized solution for managing energy-related data, including smart grid monitoring, asset management, predictive maintenance, and energy optimization. **Ex:** Integrating data from drilling operations, pipelines, and refineries to optimize energy production, ensure efficient resource utilization, and improve operational safety.

Other Services: for Managing and Administering Data Workloads in Azure.

- **Microsoft Entra ID (formerly Azure AD):** Cloud-based identity and access management service for securing access to Azure resources, on-premises applications, and other SaaS applications. **Ex:** Enforcing multi-factor authentication for accessing sensitive data in Azure Data Lake Storage and Azure SQL Database using Microsoft Entra Identity.
- **Azure ExpressRoute:** Dedicated private connection between your on-premises network and Azure datacenters for private, low-latency access to Azure resources. **Ex:** Establishing a secure and reliable connection for transferring large amounts of data between your on-premises data center and Azure.
- **Azure DevOps:** Set of cloud services for managing the entire application lifecycle, from development and testing to deployment and monitoring. **Ex:** Managing building testing and deployment of data pipelines, automating CI/CD pipelines, tracking work items, and collaborating on code changes in a team environment.
- **Azure Kubernetes Service (AKS):** Managed Kubernetes service for deploying and managing containerized applications in Azure. **Ex:** Running microservices-based applications, deploying containerized workloads, or building scalable and resilient cloud-native applications.

- **Network Watcher:** Service for monitoring network traffic, diagnosing network connectivity issues, and getting insights into your virtual network health. **Ex:** Troubleshooting network connectivity problems between your Azure Virtual Machines and on-premises resources.
- **Azure Backup:** Service for backing up your data in Azure VMs, databases, and storage accounts to protect against accidental deletion or outages. **Ex:** Backing up VMs, databases, and files to Azure for data protection, disaster recovery, and long-term retention.
- **Azure Site Recovery:** A disaster recovery service for replicating and orchestrating the failover of virtual machines and applications between Azure regions or from on-premises to Azure. **Ex:** Failing over your on-premises database server to a pre-provisioned VM in Azure in case of a disaster.
- **Azure Databox:** Service for securely transferring large datasets between your on-premises environment and Azure datacenters. **Ex:** Migrating a large on-premises data warehouse to Azure Data Lake Storage using Databox for offline data transfer.
- **Azure Policy:** Service for defining and enforcing rules to govern the creation and management of resources within your Azure subscription. **Ex:** Creating a policy to enforce encryption at rest for all data storage accounts to ensure data security.
- **Azure Monitor:** Service for collecting, analyzing, and visualizing logs and telemetry data from various Azure resources. **Ex:** Monitoring the performance of your Azure Data Factory pipelines to identify bottlenecks and optimize data processing workflows.
- **Azure Cost Management and Billing:** Tools for monitoring, optimizing, and managing your Azure resource spending. **Ex:** Analyzing cost trends, setting budgets, identifying underutilized resources in your Azure environment to reduce costs or setting up spending alerts to avoid unexpected charges.
- **Azure Migrate:** A service that provides the advice and tools needed to migrate on-premises workloads to Azure. **Ex:** A company could use Azure Migrate to assess their on-premises workloads for migration to Azure, test migrations, and to perform the migration itself.

***Note:** Service retirements.

- **Azure Data Lake Analytics** was retired in February 2024, and its workloads need to be migrated to **Azure Synapse Analytics**.
- **Azure Data Catalog** was retired in May 2024, and its workloads should be transitioned to **Microsoft Purview**.
- **Azure Time Series Insights** was retired in July 2024, and all associated workloads can be migrated to **Azure Data Explorer.**

CHAPTER 14

Bonus - Azure Functions and Logic Apps

1. Can you define "Azure Functions"?

Ans:

- Azure Functions (Functions-as-a-Service) is a serverless computing service provided by Microsoft Azure. It allows us to build and deploy small, event-driven applications or functions in the cloud without worrying about the underlying infrastructure.
- In another way, Azure Functions is a cloud-based solution to quickly execute your code with zero administration or maintenance of underlaying infrastructure (Servers, networking etc.).
- **Ex:** You need to send promotional emails to your customers during specific events such as Thanks Giving Day sales. Instead of developing your own system using resources like VMs, storage, network, web servers, SMTP, and monitoring solutions, you can simply write the necessary code to send notifications/emails to customers and place that code in an Azure Function with an appropriate event trigger. This eliminates the need to worry about infrastructure creation and maintenance. Azure Functions work on a pay-as-you-go consumption model and provide auto-scaling functionality for peak workloads.

2. What are the key features and advantages of Azure Functions?

Ans:

Azure Functions offer significant benefits in many scenarios. For example, they eliminate the need for server management, scale automatically to meet demand, support a variety of programming languages, and provide built-in security features.

Explore:

- **Serverless Architecture:** With serverless, we can simply create and upload the code and execute it based on an event. This will reduce the overall development lifecycle as we don't need to worry about the underlaying infrastructure.
- **Highly Scalable:** Azure Functions automatically scales (up and down) the execution of functions based on demand with the zero administration and maintenance of underlaying infrastructure.
- **Convenient Pricing Model:** Pay-as-you-use pricing model helps us saving a lot of costs. We just need to pay for the code execution time.
- **Multi Language Support:** It supports several programming languages, including C#, Java, JavaScript, Python, PowerShell, TypeScript, PHP, Node.js, etc.

- **Event-driven triggers:** Azure Functions can be triggered by a variety of events, such as HTTP requests, timers, queues, event hubs, or storage blobs. This makes it easy to integrate with other Azure services or external systems.
- **Easy Integration with Azure services:** Azure Functions seamlessly integrates with other Azure services, such as Azure Storage, Azure Cosmos DB, Azure Event Hubs, Azure DevOps services, GitHub, Azure Event Grid, Azure Service Bus, Data Factory, Synapse Pipelines, and more. This enables us to build complex workflows and process data from multiple sources.
- **DevOps and CI/CD support:** Azure Functions can be easily integrated into your DevOps pipelines and CI/CD workflows. You can automate the deployment and management of your functions using Azure DevOps, GitHub Actions, or other CI/CD tools.
- **Integrated Security:** Azure Functions offers a strong integrated security framework through various security features. Ex: Vulnerability scanning, Microsoft Entra authentication, automatic threat protection, data encryption, network security etc.
- **Monitoring and diagnostics:** Azure Functions provides built-in monitoring and logging capabilities. We can view execution logs, track performance metrics, and set up alerts to monitor the health and performance of our Azure Functions.

3. Could you explain the security features of Azure Functions?

Ans:

Azure Functions offers robust security features, including Microsoft Entra ID authentication, RBAC, Managed Identity, network security, data encryption, and threat protection. It also integrates with tools like Azure Key Vault and Microsoft Defender for additional security measures.

Explore:

Azure Functions provides a number of security features to help you protect your applications. These features include:

Authentication and Authorization:

- **Authentication and authorization:** Supports built-in authentication with Microsoft Entra ID, OAuth providers, and custom identity solutions.
- **Managed Identity**: Automatically manage identities for Azure resources, allowing Functions to securely access other Azure services without storing credentials.
- **Role-Based Access Control (RBAC)**: Controls who can manage and deploy Azure Functions using Azure RBAC.
- **Access Keys & API Keys**: Uses function-level access keys and API keys to restrict access to function endpoints.

Network Security:

- **Private Endpoints:** Create private endpoints to access Azure Functions from within a virtual network without exposing them to the public internet.
- **Azure Firewall:** Use Azure Firewall to set IP restrictions, and configure firewall rules to filter network traffic and protect your Azure Functions from threats.

Data Security:

- **Data Encryption at Rest:** When you create an Azure function app, you must create or link to a general-purpose Azure Storage account. Data stored in Azure Storage is encrypted at rest by default. You can also use customer-managed keys for additional control. When connecting a storage account to your Function App, you can choose one that's in a private network (service endpoint or private endpoint enabled storage), making it more secure.
- **Data Encryption in Transit:** Data transmitted between Azure Functions and other services is encrypted using HTTPS.
    - **Enforce HTTPS:** By default, clients can connect to function endpoints by using either HTTP or HTTPS. You should redirect HTTP to HTTPS because HTTPS uses the SSL/TLS protocol to provide a secure connection.
- **Azure Key Vault:** When building cloud applications, credentials should never appear in application code, developer workstations, or source control. Instead, use a key vault to store and retrieve keys and credentials. Azure Key Vault provides a way to securely store credentials, secrets, and other keys.
    - Ex: When connecting to an Azure SQL Database from an Azure Function, instead of hardcoding the SQL credentials in the code, you can store them securely in Azure Key Vault as secrets. In the function, you reference the Key Vault rather than embedding credentials directly. When the function runs, it uses a Managed Identity (a service-level identity in Azure) to authenticate itself with the Key Vault—no credentials are required in the code. The function retrieves the SQL credentials from the Key Vault, connects to the database, and completes the task. This approach enhances security by eliminating hardcoded sensitive information while ensuring the function can securely access the database.

Other Security Features:

- **Vulnerability scanning:** Azure Functions integrates with Microsoft Defender for Cloud to provide vulnerability scanning for your Azure functions.
- **Threat protection:** Azure Functions integrates with Microsoft Defender which helps us protect our functions from attacks, such as DDoS and malware.

- **Monitoring:** Azure Functions provides in-built monitoring and logging capability. We can leverage Azure Monitor to monitor your Azure Functions for suspicious activity and anomalies. Enable detailed logging to track function execution, errors, and security events.
- **Custom Code Analysis Tools:** You can use custom code analysis tools to identify potential security issues in your programming code.

4. What are the components of an Azure Function?

Ans:

Here are the components of an Azure Function:

- **Function App:** A container to host a group of functions
- **Function:** Actual Code where logic is implemented)
- **Durable Functions:** Stateful functions which we can use it to build workflows
- **Triggers:** An event that initiate the function execution
- **Runtime:** Compute environment
- **Hosting:** Options available to host a function
- **Scaling:** Auto-scaling capability
- **Bindings:** Input and output variable capabilities
- Configurations and settings
- Development Tools

Explore:

- **Function App:** A Function App is the container for our functions. Which means we can deploy a collection of functions in a container that provides the environment to host and execute our functions. It includes settings, configurations, and resources that are shared by all functions within the app.
- **Function:** A Function is the smallest unit of code which is triggered by an event. It supports various programming languages.
- **Durable Functions:** Azure Durable Functions is an extension of Azure Function that is used to write Stateful Functions. It consists of Orchestrator and entity functions that can be defined as a workflow. As a state-based services, it enables checkpoint and restarts from it.
- **Trigger:** A Trigger is an event that initiates the execution of a function. Triggers can be HTTP requests, timers, file uploads, data changes in Azure services, etc. Each function can have one or more triggers.
- **Runtime:** It is responsible for loading our code, providing the necessary runtime environment, and executing our code when it is triggered. It is based on the .NET Framework, and it supports a variety of languages, C#, F#, JavaScript, and Python etc.

- **Hosting:** It refers to the process of deploying and running functions. Azure Functions can be hosted in a variety of environments, including Azure App Service, Kubernetes, and Azure Functions Consumption Plan.
- **Scaling:** Azure Functions automatically scales based on the load and demand of our functions. We can configure scaling options based on factors like the number of concurrent requests, the number of instances, etc.
- **Bindings:** Bindings define the input and output connections between your functions and other Azure services or external resources. They allow us to easily integrate your functions with data sources, storage, queues, databases, etc. Azure Functions support various binding types, such as HTTP, Azure Storage, Azure Cosmos DB, Service Bus, Event Hubs, etc.
- **Configuration and Settings:** You can control the behaviour and settings of your functions such as environment variables, connection strings, host configurations, and other application-specific settings.
- **Development Tools:** Azure Functions can be developed using various tools like Visual Studio, Visual Studio Code, or command-line interfaces.

5. How is the cost calculated for Azure Functions, and what are the different pricing models or hosting options available?

Ans:

Azure Functions offers two main pricing models based on the usage and type of workload.

- Consumption Plan (pay-as-you-go)
- Premium Plan (High performance and dedicated resources)

Cost calculation depends on multiple factors such as hosting options (consumption/premium), execution time, number of executions, vCPU, memory usage, triggers and bindings, outbound data transfer (additional cost for data transfers out of Azure backbone) etc.

Explore:

Azure Functions offers several pricing models allow flexibility for different workloads and scaling requirements depending on the nature of the functions you're running.

Consumption Plan: You are charged based on the number of executions, memory consumption, and execution time.

- **Free Grant:** 1 million executions and 400,000 GB-s of resource consumption free per month.
- **Scale:** Scales automatically based on demand, handling thousands of executions.
- **Billing:**
    - **Executions:** Number of function executions.
    - **GB-seconds:** Memory consumed in GB multiplied by the execution time in seconds.

- **Cold Starts:** Initial request to the function may experience a slight delay due to cold starts.
- **When to use:**
    - Ideal for unpredictable or low-traffic applications.
    - Best for lightweight functions that don't run for long durations.
    - **Ex:** Event-driven, occasional, or bursty workloads, such as processing queue messages or responding to HTTP triggers.

Flexible (Flex) Consumption Plan (In Preview): Similar to the traditional Consumption Plan but provides more granular scaling options.

- **Granular Scaling:** Unlike the standard Consumption Plan, which scales by one instance at a time, on the Flex Consumption Plan, instances of the Functions host are dynamically added and removed based on the configured per instance concurrency and the number of incoming events.
- **Dedicated Resources:** You have more control over how your resources scale, avoiding cold start issues by keeping specific resources "warm."
- **Networking Integration:** VNET integration and access to more advanced networking features compared to the basic Consumption Plan.
- **Billing:** Charges are based on memory consumption (GB-s) and execution time but with more predictable cost structures and scaling controls.
    - **When to use:**
    - Ideal if you want more control over scaling and to avoid cold starts without the higher costs of a Premium Plan.
    - **Ex:** Applications with variable traffic that need more precise control over scaling thresholds or performance.

Premium Plan: Pre-warmed instances are (nearly) always running to avoid cold starts and ensure low latency.

- **Auto-scaling:** Scales based on demand but allows pre-warmed instances to reduce startup time.
- **VNET Integration:** You can connect to virtual networks (VNET).
- **Unlimited Execution Duration:** Functions can run indefinitely (as opposed to 10-minute max execution in Consumption Plan).
- **Custom VM Sizes:** Choose from different compute sizes (memory and CPU).
- **Billing:** You pay for the number of instances running and the memory/CPU allocated to those instances.
- **When to Use:**
    - When you need better performance with no cold starts, longer execution times, and VNET integration requirements, especially for high-traffic or latency-sensitive applications.

- **Ex:** Real-time processing, APIs with consistent traffic, or workloads needing advanced network integration.

Dedicated (App Service) Plan: Runs on dedicated VMs, billed like Azure App Service.

- **Underutilized resources:** Suitable for scenarios where functions need to run on specific dedicated VMs or where you already have reserved compute capacity.
- **Scaling:** Full control over scaling.
- **VNET integration** and no cold start concerns.
- **Billing:** Regular App Service plan rates are applicable.
- **When to use:**
  - You already have existing App Service resources or need dedicated compute instances for functions.
  - **Ex:** High-control environments where functions need to run on dedicated VMs or integrate with other App Service workloads.

Container Apps Plan (Azure Functions in Container Apps): Pay for the underlying resources used by the Azure Container Apps infrastructure.

- **Kubernetes-like Environment:** Azure Functions are deployed within Azure Container Apps, providing a more managed Kubernetes-like experience.
- **Longer Execution Time:** Unlike the Consumption Plan, the Container Apps Plan allows functions to run indefinitely.
- **Custom Scaling:** You can scale your apps based on custom scaling rules using Kubernetes-based autoscaling (KEDA).
- **Billing:** You are billed for the vCPU, memory, and execution time used by the underlying Container Apps infrastructure.
- **When to use:**
  - Best for containerized workloads or when using a microservices architecture.
  - **Ex:** Microservices-based applications, event-driven architecture, or complex apps requiring Docker container deployment.

Additional Costs:

- **Storage:** Azure Functions require a storage account for logging and state persistence, which incurs additional costs.
- **Networking:** Using Premium or Dedicated plans with VNET integration may result in additional networking charges.

6. What are the various ways where we can work and execute with Azure Functions?

Ans:

We can create, manage and execute Azure Functions in various ways and below are the few:

- **Triggers:** It supports various types of triggers such as HTTP, Event, Timer/Scheduler, etc.
- **Azure Portal:** We can use the Azure portal to execute a function individually or in bulk.
- **Visual Studio Code:** We can use VS Code IDE to develop, debug and execute Azure Functions from local machine.
- **Command-Line Tools and SDKs:** We can execute Azure Functions using Azure CLI, PowerShell, and SDKs like .Net, Java, Python etc.
- **Data Binding:** Azure Functions support data binding, which allows us to bind input and output data directly to our function code. **Ex:** Our function can automatically receive input data from a source, such as Azure Storage, Azure Cosmos DB, etc. and we can bind output data to send the function's response to a specified destination.
- **Other Azure Services:** We can call an Azure function from an Azure Logic Apps, ADF, Synapse Pipeline, Azure SQL Database etc.

7. What are the different types of Triggers offered by Azure Functions?

Ans:

Azure Functions offers various triggers, including HTTP, Timer, Blob, Queue, Table, Azure SQL trigger etc.

Explore:

- **HTTP triggers:** These triggers are invoked when an HTTP request is received.
    - **Use Case:** We can use it to create serverless APIs. **Ex:** Create an HTTP trigger that is invoked when a user submits a form on our website. The Azure Function then process the form data and save it to a database.
- **Timer triggers:** These triggers are invoked at a specified interval.
    - **Use Case:** We can use it for scheduled tasks that needs to be executed on a regular interval. **Ex:** For every 1-hour check for new data and process it.
- **Blob triggers:** These triggers are invoked when a blob is created or updated in Azure Blob storage.
    - **Use Case:** They can be used to process images or videos as they are uploaded to storage. **Ex:** Create a blob trigger that is invoked when a new image is uploaded to our website. The function could then resize the image and optimize it for the web.

- **Queue triggers:** These triggers are invoked when a message is added to an Azure Queue storage queue.
    - **Use Case:** It can be used to process messages from a messaging system, such as Azure Service Bus. **Ex:** Create a queue trigger that is invoked when a new message is received from our customer support system. The function then read the message and send out a response to the customer.
- **Table triggers:** These triggers are invoked when a row is inserted, updated, or deleted in an Azure Table storage table.
    - **Use Case:** It is used to process data from a database. **Ex:** We could create a table trigger that is invoked when a new row is inserted into our customer database. The function then sends out an email to the customer welcoming them to our service.
- **Event Hub triggers:** These triggers are invoked when an event is received in an Azure Event Hub.
    - **Use Case:** It is used to process streaming data, such as data from IoT devices. **Ex:** Create an event hub trigger that is invoked when a new sensor reading is received from our factory floor production line. The function then sends out an alert if the reading is outside of a safe range.
- **Cosmos DB Trigger:** It can be used to monitor changes in an Azure Cosmos DB.
    - **Use Case:** We can create a Cosmos DB Triger so that it would trigger the Azure function when new data is inserted or modified in Cosmos DB collection.
- **Azure SQL Triggers for Functions**: It allows you to create serverless functions that are triggered by changes in an Azure SQL Database. This means that when data in a specific SQL table changes (through insert, update, or delete operations), the Azure Function is automatically triggered to execute certain logic in response to that event. This trigger uses SQL change tracking feature to monitor a table for changes and triggers an Azure Function.
    - **Use Case:** We can leverage this feature for Real-Time Data Processing, Database Automation etc. **Ex:** In E-commerce database, when a new order is inserted into the Orders table, trigger a function to calculate inventory, update shipping statuses, or send notifications.

Additionally, there are other triggers also available, such as Service Bus (Queue, Topic) triggers, Webhook, and Event Grid Triggers etc.

8. What is a Durable/Stateful function in Azure Functions?

Ans:

A durable and stateful function is a function that can maintain state between executions. This means that the function can remember what it was doing the last time it ran, and it can pick up where it left off. Durable functions are often used to implement workflows or long-running processes.

Explore:

Azure Durable Functions is an extension of Azure Functions which helps us creating stateful and durable functions with serverless architecture. It manages state, checkpoints, and restarts for us, so we can focus on our business logic.

Here are some common examples of stateful and durable functions:

- **Monitor a website for errors:** The function would need to remember the last time it checked the website, so it can know when to check it again.
- **Send Emails:** The function would need to remember which emails it has already sent, so it can avoid sending the same email twice.
- **Running Workflows:** If we need to implement a workflow or a long-running process, then a stateful function is a good option. If we need to implement an application that needs to be highly available, then a durable function is a good option.

Note: If you have large number of workflows then Azure Logic Apps would be a better choice.

9. What are the most suitable use cases for Azure Functions?

Ans:

There are a lot of use cases where you can use Azure Functions as a solution. **Ex:** Event-driven processing, scheduled jobs, running backups at backend, form or image processing, to build serverless applications and microservice architecture etc.

Explore:

Giving a scenario followed by a simple example.

- **Event-driven processing:** Create a function to receive incoming messages from an IoT device, process it, update a database and send notification. More examples include, process data when a file is uploaded into a storage account, process a form when it is submitted in an app etc.
- **Data processing and integration:** Create a function to capture Metadata that we are receiving from various data sources like Azure Event Hubs or Azure Service Bus, apply some business rules, aggregate it and push it to Azure Purview.

- **Serverless web applications:** Azure Functions can power serverless web applications, where functions act as the backend logic for handling requests and performing computations. We can use Azure Functions to build APIs, handle authentication and authorization, process user inputs, and integrate with databases. Ex: Chat applications, notification and alert systems etc.
- **Scheduled tasks and batch processing:** For example, data backups, generating reports, image processing, or performing batch processing on a regular basis without the need for a dedicated server.
- **Microservices architecture:** Azure Functions are well-suited for building microservices-based architectures. We can develop individual functions for specific tasks, such as authentication, data validation, or image processing. These functions can be independently scaled and deployed, allowing for a highly scalable and flexible architecture.
- **File processing:** Azure Functions can be used to process files, such as converting documents to PDF or uploading photos to a cloud storage service.
- **Build lightweight Web APIs:** Using Azure Functions we can create Web APIs for a mobile app.
- **R&D or Proof of Concept (POC):** Azure Functions helps us in quickly creating POCs for new feature implementations.

Sample Business Cases:

- In a manufacturing company we are using Azure Functions to copy backups and logs from staging to archive layer.
- In an insurance company, we used it as a solution to process the member submitted forms.
- In a supply chain management application, we are using Azure Functions to calculate the distance and delivery time between two shipping points.

10. What is the difference between an Azure Function and Azure Function App?

Ans:

Both refers to Azure Functions but with different capabilities.

- **Azure Function:** A single unit of code that perform a specific task or action.
- **Azure Function App:** A container (a logical group) for hosting Azure Functions. When you need to develop multiple functions for completing a task, you can host all those functions using Azure Function App. So that it makes your job easier to develop, deploy, scale, monitor and manage the group of functions using a single Function App.

Note: Even for creating an individual / single function, first you need to create a Function App and then create a function inside of it.

11. Can you explain how to create and execute an Azure Function?

Ans:

You can create an Azure Function using various ways like Visual Studio, VS Code, Azure Portal, Azure CLI, etc. Let's see how to create a function using Azure Portal:

Create An Azure Function App:

- Azure Portal > Create Resource > Compute > Function App > Create
- You need to specify the basic details such as subscription, resource group, function app name, region, OS (Windows / Linux), runtime stack (Node.js, C#, Python, etc.), hosting plan (consumption plan or app service plan), storage account etc.
- Also, you can play with the advanced options like Application Insights, networking etc.
- Review and create the Function App

Create an Azure function:

- Go to the Function App (that we just created) > Functions > Create > Select the Template.
- You can select a trigger template such as Timer trigger, HTTP Trigger, Blob Storage, Queue Storage trigger etc. Based on the template selection, it offers the features and asks for more required details.
- For example, if you select the timer trigger it will ask for the schedule. You need to give the schedule information. Remember, it follows the NCRONTAB (similar to CRON) expression.
- Once a function is created, then you can add/write/develop the required function code at Function > Developer > Code + Test;
- Once code is ready, you can test/run and see the logs from the same window.
- Similarly, you can deal with function keys, monitor the execution and integrations from the function developer tab.

Explore:

Specifying schedules with NCRONTAB expressions. If you are new to CRON expressions here is the way how you need to specify the function schedules.

Syntax: {second} {minute} {hour} {day} {month} {day-of-week}

Week Days: Represented with 0 (Sunday) to 6 (Saturday).

Ex:

Now, let's see the sample expressions for scheduling an Azure Function using timer trigger.

Schedule	Second	Minute	Hour	Day	Month	Day-of-week
Once every four hours	0	0	*/4	*	*	*
Once every 15 minutes	0	*/15	*	*	*	*
Once every hour from 10 AM to 3 PM	0	0	10-14	*	*	*
11:30 AM Every day	0	30	11	*	*	*
8:30 PM Every weekday	0	30	20	*	*	1-5

Table 14.1

Note:

- "/": Interval
- "*": All values
- "-": A range operator
- Day-of-week (1-5): Every week day (0-Sun, 6-Sat)

12. How long an Azure Function can execute?

Ans:

- Maximum execution time depends on the hosting (Consumption, Premium, etc.) plan we choose. However, by default, the maximum execution timeout for a function is:
  - **Consumption Plan:** 5 Min.
  - **Other Plans:** 30 Min.

Explore:

- Maximum timeout is a soft limit, which means if function is actively running, then it allows the execution beyond the timeout limit. If it is in idle state after 5 min, then it will end the execution and release the resources.
- We can control the timeout limit through the Function App ARM templates by configuring a setting in JSON file. Ex: Set it to 15 min: {"functionTimeout": "00:15:00"}

Note: Considering the cost model long running functions will have an intense impact on cost.

13. Can you write a simple Azure Function Code for below scenario:

- **Write a simple Azure Function code using Python**
- **Make sure that your script accepts a parameter**
- **Execute the Azure Function using Azure CLI**

Ans:

I am not going into creating function app, adding function stuff. Instead, here is the sample code that accepts a numeric parameter to determine if the number is even or odd. Here is the Azure Function Code:

#Python Code

- import azure.functions
- def main(req: azure.functions.HttpRequest) -> str:
- inputNum = req.params.get('inputNum')
- if number % 2 == 0:
    - return f'The number {inputNum} is even.'
- else:
    - return f'The number {inputNum} is odd.'

Execute Azure Function using Azure CLI:

Here is the sample execution command:

- Az functionapp invoke

```
--resource-group my-resource-group
--function-name my-function
--parameter inputNum ="20"
```

This will call the Azure Function, if it executes successfully, it returns the following output:

- "The number 20 is even."

14. I understand you have a data background, but do you have any knowledge of what Azure App Service is?

Ans:

Yes! Although hands-on experience with App Service may not be necessary, a typical database admin, database developer or data engineer should be familiar with it.

- We can compare it with Azure SQL Database. If you have a SQL Server, PostgreSQL, or MySQL instance on-premises, you can migrate it to Azure PaaS using Database-as-a-Service (DBaaS) options like Azure SQL Database, Azure Database for PostgreSQL, or Azure Database for MySQL.
- Similarly, if you have web applications running on-premises and need to migrate them to the Azure cloud, Azure offers a Platform-as-a-Service (PaaS) option called Azure App Service.

Explore:

More details:

- Azure App Service provides a platform for developers to build, deploy, and manage web applications, REST APIs, and mobile backends without worrying about the underlying infrastructure.
- With Azure App Service, you can develop applications in your preferred language, such as .NET, .NET Core, Java, Ruby, Node.js, PHP, or Python, in both Windows and Linux environments.
- Since it is a PaaS for hosting your web applications, it offers many benefits such as integrated security, load balancing, autoscaling, custom domains, TLS/SSL certificates, containerization with Docker, connections to SaaS platforms, serverless code, and high availability for apps.
- Additionally, it offers seamless integration with Azure DevOps, GitHub, Bitbucket, Docker Hub, Azure Container Registry, and other Azure services.

15. What is the "WebJobs" feature in Azure?

Ans:

- "WebJobs" is a feature of Azure App Service that enables you to run a program or script in the same instance as a web app, API app, or mobile app.
- Like Azure Functions, WebJobs provides a serverless environment to run scripts and executables. But WebJobs is specifically designed and integrated as part of Azure App Service.
- We can run a WebJob in continues mode or triggered (manual or scheduled) mode.
- It supports wide range of files and scripts such as cmd, bat, exe, PowerShell, Python, Node.js, Java, Bash etc.

16. What is the relationship between Azure Functions and Azure App Service?

Ans:

"**Azure Functions**" is built on top of the "**Azure App Service**" infrastructure. This means it leverages the same underlying resources and benefits from the same features like scaling and integration capabilities.

While Azure App Service is great for hosting full-fledged web applications, Azure Functions excels in handling discrete, event-driven tasks.

Explore:

Azure App Service and Azure Functions are both platform-as-a-service (PaaS) offerings in Azure, but they serve different purposes while sharing some underlying infrastructure.

- **Azure App Service:** A fully managed platform for building, deploying, and scaling web apps, mobile app backends, and RESTful APIs.
  - **Use Case**: Ideal for hosting web applications and APIs that require a robust, scalable, and managed environment.
- **Azure Functions:** A serverless compute service that allows you to run event-driven code without having to explicitly provision or manage infrastructure.
  - **Use Case**: Best for executing small pieces of code (functions) in response to events such as HTTP requests, database changes, or messages from a queue.

17. Any idea about Microsoft Power Automate?

Ans:

Microsoft Power Automate is a cloud-based (low code/no code) service that helps you automate workflows and business processes. It's like having a personal assistant that can handle repetitive tasks for you, saving you time and effort. **Ex:** You want to automatically send an email notification whenever a new file is added to a specific folder in your OneDrive.

Explore:

More details:

- Power Automate (formerly known as Microsoft Flow) is a part of the Microsoft Power Platform which also includes Power Apps and Power BI.
- It is easy to use, we can simply create automated workflows using a drag-and-drop interface. No coding experience is required. It also offers a lot of pre-built template library which we can use to create our own automated workflows.
- With Power Automate, we can create automated workflows that connect different apps and services, such as Microsoft Office 365, Dynamics 365, Google Workspace, Salesforce, etc.
- **Primary benefits:** Saves time, improves business productivity, increases efficiency, reduces errors and Improves compliance.
- **Primary beneficiaries**: Business people, and IT professionals. Ex: Sales representative, marketing managers, HR managers, IT leads etc.

18. Can you tell me one or two business use cases of Microsoft Power Automate?

Ans:

There are a wide range of tasks that we can automate using Power Automate. For example:

- Automatically save Office 365 email attachments to OneDrive for Business.
- Convert emails into PDF documents and copy it to a specified folder on OneDrive.
- Send a customized email whenever a new file is added to a specified SharePoint document library.
- Schedule a reminder to follow up on a message.
- Track Microsoft Forms responses in an Excel Online spreadsheet.
- Automatically create tickets in a help desk system when a customer sends an email.
- Automatically onboard new employees by creating accounts in various systems across the enterprise.
- Sending automatic welcome emails and notifications to new employees.

19. What do you know about "Azure Logic App" service?

Ans:

- Azure Logic Apps is a leading integration platform as a service (iPaaS) built on a containerized runtime.
- It helps in creating and designing automated tasks and workflows that are capable of integrating wide range of services, systems, and applications.
- In a majority of enterprises Azure Logic Apps are using in B2B scenarios for developing highly scalable integration solutions.

Note: Azure Functions provides workflow experience through Durable Functions but Logic App is primarily designed for workflow automations.

20. What are the business use cases of Azure Logic Apps?

Ans:

Azure Logic Apps provides a workflow automation platform to integrate various services and applications. Common use cases include workflow automation, business process automation, event-driven workflows, data integration, social media and marketing automation, file and data processing etc.

Explore:

Here are the sample use cases:

- **Workflow Automation:** We can create a Logic App that triggers when a new item is added to a SharePoint list, then sends an approval request to a resource, wait for the response, and updates the list based on the response received. Similarly, when a file is uploaded to SFTP or FTP, use Logic App to move it to Azure Data Lake.

- **e-Commerce:** We can create a Logic App that triggers when a new order is received, updates inventory, sends an order confirmation email to the customer, and notifies the shipping department.
- **Healthcare:** When a health insurance claim is received, Azure Logic App will be triggered and sends a notification to the concerned teams for approval / authorization.
- **Logistics Company:** Create a Logic App that monitor and automatically track the location of a shipment and send shipment notifications to the customers.
- **Social Media Integration:** We can use Logic Apps to automatically post a message on all social media handles when a new notification or message is published on our organization website. In another scenario, monitor tweets with specific tags, analyze the sentiment, and create alerts or tasks for items that need review.

21. What are the components of Azure Logic App service?

Ans:

Here are the key components and terms associated with Azure Logic Apps:

- **Logic app:** An Azure resource you create when you want to build a workflow.
- **Workflow:** A series of steps that are performed in order to complete a task, or process. Each workflow starts with a single trigger, after which you must add one or more actions.
- **Triggers:** Triggers are events that initiate the execution of a Logic App workflow. **Ex:** Time-based or event-based triggers.
- **Actions:** Actions are the steps performed within a Logic App workflow. **Ex:** Actions can include activities like sending an email, creating a file, making an HTTP request, transforming data, executing custom code, etc.
- **Connectors:** Connectors are integration components that provide connectivity to various services and systems. There are two types of connectors in logic apps:
    - **Built-in connectors:** A set of pre-built connectors that are provided by Microsoft. Built-in connectors are faster and more reliable than managed connectors. **Ex:** Office 365, Azure Blob Storage, Salesforce, Twitter etc.
    - **Managed connectors:** These are created and managed by third-party developers. Managed connectors can be slower and less reliable than built-in connectors. **Ex:** Google Drive connector for uploading, downloading and managing files on google drive.
- **Conditions:** Conditions allows us to define logical branching within a Logic App workflow. It helps us building conditional (True/False) workflows where different actions are executed based on specified criteria. **Ex:** If condition is true, process data, if false send a notification etc.

- **Variables:** Variables are used to store and manipulate data within a Logic App workflow. We can assign values to variables, update their values, and use them in expressions or conditions throughout the workflow.
- **Iterations:** Iterations/loops allow us to repeat a set of actions for each item in a collection or array. This is useful for scenarios where we need to process multiple items or perform a specific action multiple time.
- **Expressions (To control flow):** It allows you to dynamically assign values to parameters, variables, and properties of actions based on logic and conditions. Ex: if(equals(1, 1), 'Yes', 'No'). They can be used to:
  - **Manipulate data:** Perform operations like concatenation, arithmetic calculations, and data conversions.
  - **Evaluate conditions:** Make decisions within your workflow based on specific criteria.
  - **Access runtime values:** Retrieve values from actions that might not yet exist when your workflow starts running.
- **Expression Functions (To manipulate data):** "Expressions" and "Expression Functions" are used to dynamically manipulate data or control the flow of actions within a workflow. Expression Functions are predefined functions that you can use within expressions to perform specific operations. These functions cover a wide range of tasks, including:
  - **String operations:** concat(), substring() etc.
  - **Mathematical operations:** add(), subtract() etc.
  - **Date and time operations:** addDays(), utcNow(), etc.)
  - **Logical operations:** and(), or(), and not().
- **Integration Accounts:** Create this Azure resource when you want to define and store B2B artifacts. When you are running workflows for B2B scenarios, integration account will act as a secure container to store B2B artifacts like Trading Partners, agreements, Maps, Schemas, Certificates etc. So that you can securely manage those artifacts, your workflows can communicate between stakeholders as per the regulations.

22. What are the different types of triggers in Azure Logic App?

Ans:

Triggers are categorised into two types:

- **Polling Triggers:** Periodically checks a service or system for new data or changes at regular intervals. **Ex:** Poll an email inbox every 5 minutes to check for new emails.
- **Push Triggers:** Reacts immediately when an event occurs, as the service pushes the event to the Logic App. **Ex:** Immediately triggered when a new email arrives.

Explore:

Polling triggers:

- It checks a service endpoint at regular intervals for data or an event that meets the trigger condition. Recurrence / schedule trigger, HTTP trigger, Email Trigger, Azure Service Bus Trigger etc. are the examples of pooling triggers.
- **Ex:** It can be used to check a social media feed for new posts. The trigger would be configured to check the feed every 5 minutes. When a new post is published, the trigger would fire, creating a new workflow instance that would then process the post.

Push triggers:

- It listens and wait at a service endpoint for data or an event that meets the trigger condition. Request Trigger, HTTP Webhook trigger, Azure Event Grid Trigger etc. are the examples of Push triggers.
- **Ex:** It can be used to send an email notification when a new order is placed in an online store. The trigger would be configured to listen for new orders from the store's API. When a new order is placed, the trigger would fire immediately, creating a new workflow instance that would then send an email notification to the customer.

23. What are the different types of actions that we can perform using Azure Logic App?

Ans:

Azure Logic App supports a wide range of actions for creating powerful and scalable workflows. Below are the sample actions:

- Send an email
- Parse JSON
- IF/ELSE
- Create/List/Read/Update/Delete files and folders from object storage such as SharePoint, Azure Storage etc.
- Create Blob, Create VM etc.

Explore:

Azure Logic Apps supports a rich set of actions and we can categorise those actions into:

- **Control Actions:** These actions help you control the flow and behaviour of your logic app. **Ex:** "If/Else" and "Switch" actions that allows us to make decisions based on conditions.
- **Data Operations Actions:** Using these we can perform various operations on data **Ex:** "Compose" to create complex data structures, "Join" to combine multiple strings, or "Parse JSON" to extract data from a JSON payload etc.

- **Data Conversion Actions:** We can use it for data conversions **Ex:** "JSON to XML" or "XML to JSON" etc.
- **File System Actions:** It helps us interacting with files and folders. **Ex:** We can perform operations such as creating, reading, updating, or deleting files and folders in storage systems like Azure Blob Storage, SharePoint, or OneDrive.
- **Integration Actions:** These actions are used to integrate with external systems and services. **Ex:** We can use "HTTP" to make HTTP requests, "SQL" to interact with a SQL database, or "Send Email" to send emails through SMTP etc.
- **Notification Actions:** We can use it to send notifications or alerts. **Ex:** "Send Email" or "Send Push Notification" to notify users or administrators about specific events or conditions.
- **Azure Service Actions:** These actions provide integration with various Azure services. **Ex:** We can use actions like "Create Blob" to create a new blob in Azure Blob Storage, "Create VM" to provision a virtual machine in Azure, or "Create Cosmos DB document" to insert data into a Cosmos DB collection.
- **Custom Connector Actions:** Azure Logic Apps support custom connectors, which allows us to integrate with our own APIs or third-party services.

24. Could you provide the high-level steps required to fulfil the business use case below?

- **We are working with an insurance company, and the customer and policy data are stored in an Azure SQL Database.**
- **The customer has asked us to automate the "Policy Expiration" reminder notifications to their clients.**
- **This means we need to monitor the policy expiration details and send an email reminder to the customer 30 days before the policy expiration date.**
- **Additionally, the reminder email should include a link to a webpage where the customer can renew their policy.**

Can you provide a solution for the above scenario using Azure Logic App?

Ans:

Sure! Well, we need to leverage the below Azure Resources:

- **Azure SQL Database:** Where we have customers and policy data available.
- **Azure Logic App:** We define a workflow to fulfil the requirement
- **Azure Function:** To generate and add a web page link to the email.
- **Other:** Resources like Azure AD, Firewall, NSG, Azure Monitor etc.

Here are the high-level steps:

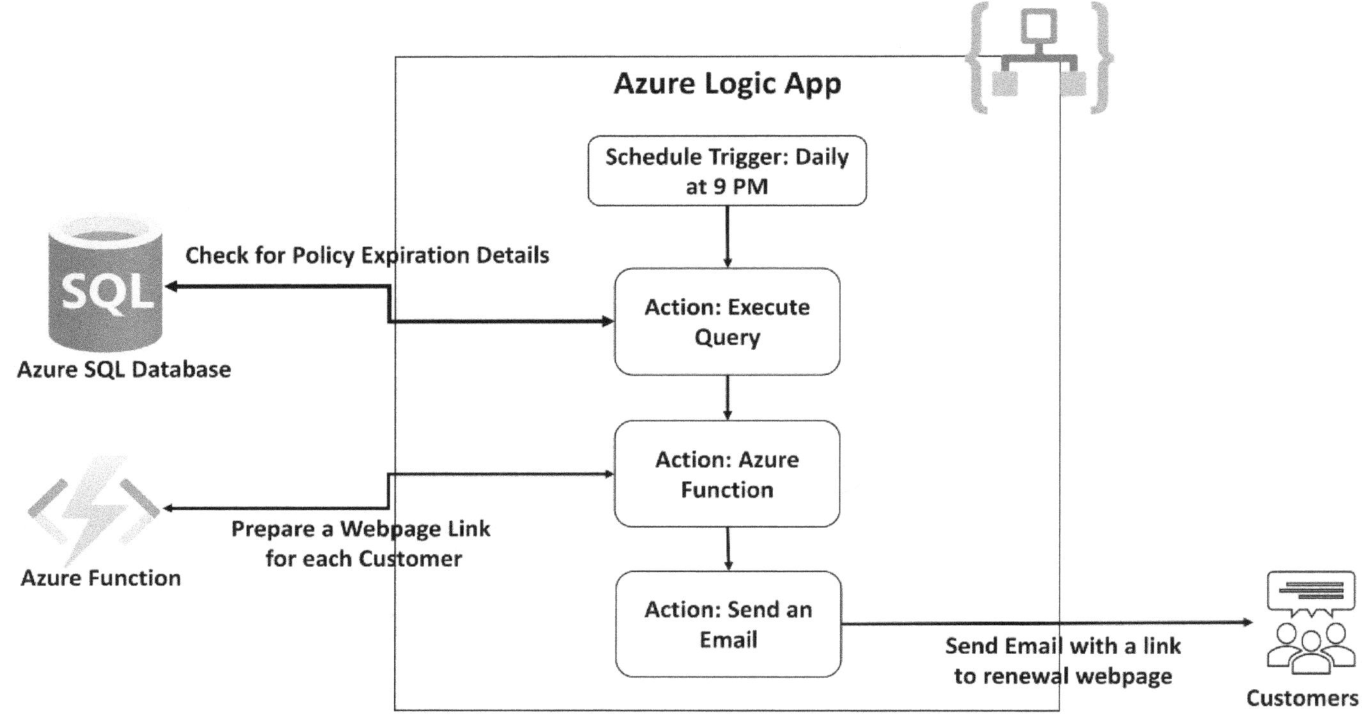

Image 14.1

Assumptions and Prerequisites:

- **Azure SQL Database:** Assuming that we already have an Azure SQL Database with the customers and policy details loaded.
- **Azure Function:** Created and published an Azure Function with C# code. It accepts the customer and policy details as input parameters, generates a web page link and returns it back to the Azure Logic App.

Here is the Azure Logic App workflow for the given scenario:

- **Create an Azure Logic App:** We can create a Logic App resource by specifying the basic details such as name, subscription, resource group, location etc. and select a blank Logic App template.
- **Create a Schedule Trigger:** Workflow has to start with creating a trigger. In this case we will use schedule trigger with the recurrence of every day at 9 PM.
- **Create an Action - Execute Query:**
    - This action is used to query the SQL Database table and get the customer details with the policies expiring in next 30 days.
    - In connectors and actions, search for the Built-in connector “SQL Server”, then it will show a lot of actions such as get/insert/update/delete rows, get tables, execute query

and execute stored procedure etc. Select "Execute a SQL Query (V2)" Action, provide the database authentication type, connection string and specify the query to be executed.

- **Create an Action – Azure Function:**
    - We need to call an Azure Function to generate a web link which can be attached to the email body so that customers can easily renew their policy.
    - Search for "Azure Function" and select the action named Choose an Azure function.
    - It will show the all-available Azure Function Apps list. When you select your Function App, it shows the functions with-in that function app, select the right one and you can send the input in a JSON format. We can dynamically pass the customer and policy details that we captured from the previous action (from SQL Database).
- **Create an Action - Send an email:**
    - We can use the "Send an email" action from the Office 365 connector.
    - Configure the email action to send a reminder email to the customer. We can use dynamic content from "Execute Query" and "Azure Function" actions. That includes customer email address, policy details, expiration date, premium information, and web link.
    - Finally save, test and deploy the Logic App.

By following these steps, we'll have a solution that monitors policy expiration details in the Azure SQL Database, sends reminder emails to customers 30 days prior to the expiration date, and includes a web page link for policy renewal.

***Note:**

- A Logic App can be created and managed using Azure Portal, Azure Logic App Visual Workflow Designer, Visual Studio, VS Code, Azure CLI, PowerShell, Azure ARM Templates etc.
- In Azure Logic Apps, we can handle dynamic content using system variables, user defined variables, parameters, output, expressions and expression functions. **Ex:** A variable can be referred across the logic app using @ symbol Ex: @CustomerEmail

25. Can you explain how to create a Logic App for the requirement below?

"When a new file is created in SharePoint, we should automatically trigger an Azure Logic App to load data from the file into an Azure SQL Database."

Ans:

- **Step 1 -** Create a new Azure Logic App
- **Step 2 -** Create a Trigger:
    - Create a SharePoint trigger. In the "When a file is created in a specific location" section, select the SharePoint site where you want to listen for new files.

    - In the File name pattern section, enter a pattern for the file names that you want to listen for.

- **Step 3 -** Create an action to read data from SharePoint: Create "Get file content" action and in the File path section, select the file that you want to read the contents of.
- **Step 4 -** Create an action to load data into Azure SQL Database:
    - Though SQL Server connector, you can create "Insert row" action.
    - In the Table name section, select the table that you want to insert the file contents into.
    - In the Column names and values section, map the columns in the table to the properties of the file object.
- **Save** and publish the Azure Logic App.

Now, your Azure Logic App is ready to automatically trigger when a new file is created in SharePoint and load the file contents into the Azure SQL Database.

26. What are the various monitoring options available to monitor Azure Logic Apps?

Ans:

There are multiple ways to monitor Azure Logic Apps.

- Azure Portal
- Logic App Designer
- Azure Monitor
- Azure Log Analytics - KQL
- Azure Application Insights
- Programmatically Ex: PowerShell, Azure CLI, SDKs, REST API etc.

By leveraging these monitoring options, you can effectively track and analyze the performance, execution, and health of your Azure Logic Apps, ensuring smooth operation and timely detection of any issues.

Explore:

Azure Logic App offers several options to track the execution, performance, and health of your logic app workflows.

- **Azure Portal:** Azure portal provides a number of tools that can be used to monitor Logic Apps. For example, you can use the overview and logs pages to view the status of our Logic Apps. Also, you can create a custom Azure Dashboard to display key metrics and visualizations related to your logic apps.
- **Logic App Designer:**
    - **Run history:** The Logic App Designer provides a run history that displays the details of each execution run, including trigger events, inputs, outputs, and status of each action. You can use this to monitor the execution flow and investigate any issues.

- **Azure Monitor:**
  - **Metrics:** Azure Monitor provides various metrics such as the number of executions, successful runs, failed runs, throttled runs, execution duration, average execution time, number of errors etc.
  - **Logs:** Azure Logic Apps can be configured to send diagnostic logs to Azure Monitor that includes input, output data and error information for each execution. You can analyze these logs using Azure Log Analytics or query them using KQL (Kusto Query Language) to gain insights into the execution details.
  - **Alerts:** Azure Monitor can be used to create alerts that will be sent when certain conditions are met, such as when a Logic App fails to execute or when metric specific thresholds are exceeded etc.
- **Azure Application Insights:** To track custom metrics and for advanced analytics support, you can enable integration with Azure Application Insights to gain deeper visibility into the performance and behaviour of our logic apps.
- **PowerShell and Azure CLI:** It provides a command-line interfaces to manage and monitor Azure resources, including Logic Apps. You can use these tools to query and retrieve information about the execution status, triggers, runs, etc.
- **Azure Logic Apps REST API:** You can use the Logic Apps REST API to programmatically retrieve information about runs, trigger events, inputs, outputs, and errors. This allows us to build custom monitoring solutions or integrate with external systems.
- **Azure SDKs:** Azure provides SDKs for various programming languages. You can use it to programmatically interact and monitor various Azure resources, including Logic Apps.

27. Can you describe how do you debug an Azure Logic App?

Ans:

We can debug an Azure logic App by setting breakpoints to pause the execution at the required point, using step through code option to check through the line-by-line code execution and by monitoring the variable values. VS Code or Logic App Designer provides the built-in debugger feature.

Explore:

Debugging is a must feature for developers / engineers. Azure Logic App offers various ways to debug the logic app workflows. Here are the most common methods:

- **Breakpoints:** Breakpoints allow us to pause the execution of our Logic App at a specific point. This is helpful for inspecting variable values and examining the execution of our code.
- **Step through code:** Once breakpoint is setup, we can use the "Step Into" button to step through the execution of our code line by line. So that we can track the exact error in our code if any.

- **View Variable Values:** By observing the variable values, we can understand how these values are getting changed throughout the workflow execution and track down the issues or missing things which are not happening as per the requirement.

Below are the various tools or services to debug an Azure Logic App:

- **Visual Studio Code:** VS Code IDE can be used to develop and debug Logic Apps. The Logic Apps extension for Visual Studio Code provides a number of debugging features, such as the ability to set breakpoints, step through code, and view variable values.
- **Logic Apps Debugger:** It allows us to step through code, view variable values, and even modify the execution of our Logic App.
- **Azure Portal:** We can use the Trace feature to view the execution history of our Logic App, and the Logs feature to view any errors that occurred during execution.

28. How can you implement "Error Handling" mechanism in Azure Logic Apps?

Ans:

Azure Logic Apps offers below error handling features:

- **Error retries:** We can configure Logic Apps to retry failed actions a specified number of times.
- **Error scopes:** We can define error scopes to group related actions together and handle errors that occur within the scope.
- **Run after:** We can configure Logic Apps to run a specified action after an error occurs. This can be used to perform clean-up tasks (Ex: Clean the stage) or to retry the action.
- **Custom:** We can use the try-catch statement to handle errors that occur in your Logic App code.

29. Can you provide a solution for the scenario below?

- **We are using an Azure Logic App with an HTTP trigger.**
- **Hundreds of client calls are triggering our Logic App via HTTP triggers.**
- **The Logic App then performs specific actions according to the business requirements.**
- **Occasionally, we need to analyze the Logic App logs for various purposes.**
- **It is difficult to track which run instance is associated with which client.**
- **Can you suggest a solution that would help us clearly track Logic App calls by client?**

Ans:

Background: In a typical Logic Apps Production environment, we configure Azure Monitor-log analytics for Azure Logic Apps. Logic Apps will ingest log data into the log-analytics workspace repository. We can then go to the Log Analytics workspace, and query the logs using KQL (Kusto Query Language) to see and analyse the logic app execution details.

Solution:

- Here in the given scenario, if you can log a custom detail something like unique ID called Client_ID into Log Analytics, then it would be easy to track and analyse the Logic App Execution statistics and details.

Explanation: This solution (Logging Custom Properties) can be implemented using Tracked Properties.

- **Tracked Properties:**
    - Tracked properties are key-value pairs that can be used to store information about a Logic App run in Azure Log Analytics.
    - It can be used to track the progress of a Logic App run, troubleshoot problems, and analyze performance.
    - You can view tracked properties by going to the "Run History" tab in your Logic App.
- **Configuring Tracked Properties:**
    - In Azure Logic App, you can find the Tracked Properties" section under the properties of a trigger or an action. There we can configure the number of custom properties that you want to log. In our case we will just need to log the client ID.
    - The HTTP action is used to receive an HTTP request and the output of the HTTP action is a JSON object.
    - The header object in JSON contains the headers of the HTTP request.
    - The clientId property in the JSON headers object contains the client ID of the HTTP request.
    - We can capture clientId and configure Tracked Properties with the below expression:
        - Key: clientId
        - Value: @{outputs('HTTP')?['body']['headers']['clientId']}
    - Once we configure it, every time when the logic app is executed/triggered along with the other details it will log the tracked properties (clientId) to the log analytics workspace.
- **Query the Log Analytics using KQL:**
    - Since you are logging clientId, it is easy to query and track the Logic App execution statistics for a specific client. Below KQL query get all logic app execution details for the client 1123
        - AzureDiagnostics
        - | where trackedProperties_clientId_s contains "1123"

***Note:** Azure Monitor, Log Analytics, log and alert management are covered in "Azure The One – Part 2 – SQL Family".

30. What are the pricing models in Azure Logic Apps?

Ans:

Azure Logic Apps offers two flavours of pricing models:

- **Consumption Plan (Multi-tenant):** Pay-as-you-go – Suits small or unpredictable workloads.
- **Standard Plan (Single-tenant):** Fixed Monthly Cost - Dedicated resources – Suits for predictable enterprise workloads.

Explore:

Consumption Plan: You pay based on the number of actions your Logic App executes and the connectors you use. This model is serverless, meaning you only pay for what you use.

- **Cost factors**:
    - **Actions and Triggers**: You are billed for each action (including retries) and trigger execution.
    - **Connectors**: Costs may vary depending on whether you use standard or enterprise connectors.
    - **Integration accounts and Data Retention**: There may be additional charges if you store runtime history or diagnostic logs for extended periods. Also, separate cost applies based on the integration account type that you create and use with your logic app.
- **Suits**: Scenarios with unpredictable workloads, low to medium usage, or projects where you want to minimize infrastructure costs.

Standard Plan: You pay for a fixed amount of infrastructure to run your Logic App. It provides more control over the environment and predictable pricing.

- **Cost Factors**:
    - **Pricing Tiers:** It offers various pricing tiers, each allocating different resources (vCPUs and memory). For example, WS1, WS2, and WS3.
    - **Dedicated resources**: You pay for the dedicated resources (CPU, Memory) allocated to run the Logic App, even if it's not actively running. This plan includes an unlimited number of free built-in operations that your workflow can run.
    - **High Throughput**: Suitable for workloads with higher performance requirements or the need to run workflows on a virtual network (VNet).
    - **Single-Tenant Environment**: This offers isolation and more advanced capabilities compared to the multi-tenant environment in the Consumption Plan.
    - **Integration accounts and Data Retention**: Costs are applicable same like Consumption plan.

- **Suits**: High-volume workloads, scenarios requiring dedicated performance, or workflows that need to be integrated into a virtual network (VNet) using Private Endpoint.

31. What is the difference between Azure Logic App and Azure Function?

Ans:

Azure Functions is a serverless compute service, whereas Azure Logic Apps is a serverless workflow integration platform. Azure Functions provides workflow (running a sequence of actions to perform a task/process) capability using Durable Functions. Here are the basic differences:

Feature	Azure Durable Functions	Azure Logic Apps
Define	Code being triggered by an event	Workflow being triggered by an event
Type of Service	Compute Service	Workflow orchestration service
Development IDE	Visual Studio, VS Code	Visual Studio, VS Code, Logic App Workflow Designer
Connectivity	Limited built-in binding types. We can code and build custom bindings.	Wide range of built-in connectors. Supports custom connectors.
Actions	Each individual action is an Azure Function	Large-number of readymade actions available.
Security	Both supports AAD, Authorization Keys, Shared Access Signature, RBAC, Auditing, Data Encryption at rest and transit.	
Advanced Security	Both supports Web Application Firewall (WAF), DDoS protection, and Vulnerability Scanning.	
Error Handling	Try-Catch. Retry only works with Azure Queue and Blob Storage.	Built-in features: retries, scopes, and run after. Also support Try-Catch
Monitoring	Execution history, we can configure Azure Monitor integration, Azure Application Insights, supports custom monitoring tools	Run-history, built-in integration with Azure Monitor, Azure portal, Azure Monitor Logs, Microsoft Defender for Cloud, supports custom monitoring tools.
Billing Models	Consumption, flexible consumption, premium, dedicated, container apps	Consumption, Standard
Primary Use Case	Event-driven Microservice	Complex Workflows

Table 14.2

32. How to choose the right option between Azure Logic Apps and Azure Functions?

Ans:

Both offers serverless platform to run our code and workflows. The best choice depends on your business requirement.

Azure Logic App: If you need to create complex workflows that integrate different services, then Azure Logic Apps is a right choice. **Ex:**

- For building complex workflows and orchestrating multiple steps and services together.
- Azure Logic App offers a wide range of built-in connectors hence it is the right choice if your workflow solution includes integrating with various services and systems such as SaaS applications, APIs, databases, etc.
- Azure Logic App can respond to events, but it also provides strong capabilities for scheduled and recurring workflows.

Azure Functions: If you need to run code in response to events, then Azure Functions is a good choice. **Ex:**

- For building small, focused, and event-driven microservices.
- Azure Functions offers a lot of flexibility and customizations through code. Hence it is the right choice if your solution involves complex business logic, data transformations, or decision-making processes.
- Azure Functions flexible and customizable nature helps us building high performance and scalable solutions.

Reality:

- In real-time business cases, we often combine Azure Functions and Azure Logic Apps. This hybrid approach allows for seamless interaction, enabling functions to be called from Logic Apps and vice versa. I've personally designed numerous real-time solutions where an Azure Function is triggered from within an Azure Logic App workflow.

33. It seems that Azure Logic Apps can also perform ETL tasks, similar to SSIS, Talend, or Azure Data Factory. What are the differences, and how do you choose the right option between an ETL tool and Azure Logic Apps?

Ans:

Choose:

- **Azure Logic Apps:** Building general-purpose workflows with orchestration capabilities.
    - **Ex:** Create an automated workflow that sends an email notification when a new file is uploaded to Azure Blob Storage container.

- **ETL Tool:** Building complex and large-scale Data Integration Pipelines with orchestration capabilities.
    - **Ex:** Use Azure Data Factory and build a Data Pipeline to perform an incremental data load from various data sources into a central data lake storage, apply cleansing operations, capture aggregated values and push it into a central data warehouse like Synapse Dedicated SQL Pool.

34. Azure offers a variety of compute and workflow options for running code, programs, executable files, workflows, or processes. These services include Azure Batch, Azure Functions, Azure Web Jobs, Power Automate, and Azure Logic Apps. When and how should you choose the right option?

Ans:

For decision-making questions like this, the typical starting point is the standard answer: "It depends on your business requirements." However, here are some general recommendations:

- **Azure Batch:** For large-scale parallel or HPC (High Performance Computing) workloads.
- **Azure Functions:** For event-driven execution of small (code blocks) functions.
- **Azure Web Jobs:** For continuous or scheduled background tasks alongside web applications.
- **Power Automate:** For automation of recurring tasks and business processes.
- **Logic Apps:** For automating workflows across applications and services.

Explore:

Below are the primary capabilities of each service. Also, adding simple insurance-related scenarios for each of the Azure services.

Azure Batch: It is a cloud-based job scheduling service for running large-scale parallel and HPC workloads. **Use Cases:**

- Involves large-scale parallel or HPC workloads that require distributed processing.
- Need full control over resource allocation and scaling.
- Need to automate the management of job scheduling, resource provisioning, and task execution.
- **Ex:** For processing large volumes of insurance claims data in parallel, such as running simulations for claims risk assessment or premium calculations.

Azure Functions: It is a serverless compute service that lets us run individual functions based on event triggers. **Use Cases:**

- We have specific events/triggers that should execute independent code blocks or functions.
- Our solution should respond to events quickly and efficiently with zero administration of underlaying infrastructure.

- We are looking to build microservice based architecture.
- **Ex:** For automatically updating a customer's policy status after a claim is approved, based on event triggers from the claims system.

Azure Web Jobs: It is a part of Azure App Service and is designed for running continuous or long-running background tasks alongside web applications. **Use Cases:**

- We need to execute long-running background tasks continuously or on a schedule. Ex: file processing, message queue processing, or scheduled batch jobs etc.
- Our tasks are tightly coupled with our web application and share the same resources.
- **Ex:** For generating and sending daily or scheduled reports on policy renewals or claims status, running in the background alongside an insurance company's web portal.

Microsoft Power Automate: It helps us automate business processes. **Use Cases:**

- Automating repetitive tasks, such as sending emails or updating spreadsheets etc.
- We want to automate workflows and business processes across multiple applications and services.
- We prefer a visual and low-code or no-code approach to build workflows. Ex: Business Analysts with no programming experience.
- **Ex:** For automating the process of collecting and compiling documents (proof of loss, medical reports) required for claims approval, by automatically sending reminders to customers and agents, and updating the claims system when all documents are received.

Azure Logic Apps: It is a cloud-based service for building and orchestrating workflows and integrations. **Use Cases:**

- We need to create advanced and complex automated workflow and integration solutions with conditional logic, loops, error handling, and transformation capabilities.
- We want to leverage pre-built connectors for seamless integration with different services.
- **Ex:** For integrating and automating workflows between different insurance systems, such as connecting customer support, claims, and policy management platforms to streamline claims processing. Logic Apps can be used to create a workflow that triggers the fraud detection service when a new claim is submitted and updates the claim status based on the results.

Note:

- It is important to evaluate each service's capabilities and match them with your business requirements to make the right choice.
- While selecting a tool or service, there are factors plays a vital role. **Ex:** Compatibility, security, cost, performance, ease of use, and support etc.

35. What CI/CD options are available for Azure Functions and Azure Logic Apps?

Ans:

To deploy Azure Functions and Azure Logic Apps, Azure Ecosystem offers several options:

- Azure DevOps Pipelines
- GitHub Actions
- Azure App Service
- Jenkins
- Azure Resource Manager (ARM)/Bicep Templates

Explore:

- **Azure DevOps:** It offers a wide range of features, including support for multiple languages, automating continuous integration, continuous delivery, and release management. It offers end-to-end DevOps tools such as Azure Repos, Azure Pipelines, Azure Boards, Azure Test Plans, etc.
- **Azure Pipelines:** Azure Pipelines is a specific tool in Azure DevOps that helps teams automate the build, test, and deploy process.
- **ARM/Bicep Templates**: ARM/Bicep templates, allowing for infrastructure as code (IaC) deployments. These templates can be included in CI/CD pipelines to automate the deployment process.
- **GitHub Actions:** GitHub Actions is a CI/CD platform that is integrated with GitHub. GitHub Actions makes it easy to automate the build, test, and deploy of Azure Functions and Azure Logic Apps from within GitHub. We can also integrate with other GitHub features, such as GitHub Packages, GitHub Pages, etc.
- **Azure App Service:** This is a web app hosting service that supports various languages and frameworks. We can use it to enable continuous deployment for our Azure Functions and Azure Logic Apps projects from various sources, such as GitHub, Bitbucket, Dropbox, etc.
- **Jenkins:** It is a popular open-source CI/CD platform that can be used to automate the build, test, and deploy of Azure Functions and Azure Logic Apps.

***Note:** In most enterprise environments, organizations use either Azure DevOps or Jenkins as their CI/CD solution for Azure Functions and Azure Logic Apps.

www.ingramcontent.com/pod-product-compliance
Ingram Content Group UK Ltd.
Pitfield, Milton Keynes, MK11 3LW, UK
UKHW061959290726
14090UKWH00021B/1293